NEGOTIATED AUTHORITIES

Essays in Colonial Political and Constitutional History

NEGOTIATED AUTHORITIES

Essays in Colonial Political and Constitutional History

Jack P. Greene

UNIVERSITY PRESS OF VIRGINIA
Charlottesville and London

THE UNIVERSITY PRESS OF VIRGINIA

Copyright © 1994 by the Rector and Visitors
of the University of Virginia

First published 1994

Library of Congress Cataloging-in-Publication Data
Greene, Jack P.
   Negotiated authorities : essays in colonial political and
constitutional history / Jack P. Greene.
      p.   cm.
Includes bibliographical references and index.
   ISBN 0-8139-1516-3 (cloth). — ISBN 0-8139-1517-1 (paper)
   1. United States—Politics and government—To 1775.   2.
United States—Constitutional history.   I. Title.
JK54.G74   1994
973.2—dc20   93-42238
                                                      CIP

Printed in the United States of America

For
W. W. ABBOT

Contents

Tables

Figures

Preface

Two men, Hugh T. Lefler, a professor of early American and North Carolina history, and Samuel T. Emory, a professor of cultural and historical geography, first excited my interest in colonial British-American history while I was an undergraduate at the University of North Carolina between 1948 and 1951. Among the few undergraduates who majored in history, Lefler's caustic wit, a characteristic I very much admired, was legendary, and his skepticism and cynicism ran as deep even as my own. In contrast to Lefler, whose teaching style was to provide a running commentary on a detailed outline he supplied to his students, Emory, whose course I had originally taken because my fraternity brothers assured me that he was an easy grader, was a compelling narrative lecturer who could weave a vivid story out of a complex assortment of geographical and historical data.

By making it such mischievous good fun, such an exciting arena for the doubt that I seemed to have in abundance, Lefler was certainly responsible for drawing me into historical study, but Emory was the person who first made me sufficiently interested in any subject to think of doing research in it. When I decided to postpone my intended entry into law school to experiment with graduate work in history, my choices of both a research subject and a graduate school came directly out of his course on geographical influences in American history. My fascination with the riverine communications networks between the Great Lakes and the Ohio and Mississippi valleys discovered by Amerindians, followed by early French traders and explorers, and developed by early American canal builders seemed to suggest that I pick a graduate school in the

Midwest, and I went to Indiana University in the fall of 1951 intending to pursue this subject. This move had the double advantage of getting me into an area of history involving my native Midwest and out of the South, to which my family had taken me during my last years in secondary school.

Although I managed to pursue my interest in a research paper on portage routes for a course on American historical geography, my M.A. thesis adviser, A. L. Kohlmeier, found the topic uninteresting and esoteric and, in any case, discovered in less than a five-minute interview that my French, which was limited to a few words picked up from returning World War II veterans, was insufficient to do research in French materials. He advised me to pick instead a subject in the mainstream of colonial history and suggested that I study controversies between governors and colonial assemblies in some colony for which the principal records were published and available in the Indiana University library. He specifically recommended that I work on the place whence I had just come, North Carolina. Controversies sounded like fun, the subject was one about which I had already heard a lot from Lefler, and I had no good reason not to follow Kohlmeier's advice. Accordingly, during the nine months I spent in Bloomington, I practically lived with the *Colonial Records of North Carolina*, developed considerable admiration for its bumptious legislators, and wrote a rip-roaring, partisan, and highly whiggish account of the North Carolina assembly's triumphs over one governor after another from William Drummond in the early 1660s to Josiah Martin in the early 1770s.

Why Kohlmeier accepted this thesis has always puzzled me. Within a year after I had written it I began to think of ways to spirit it out of the Indiana University Library and destroy it, and I count myself fortunate that so few people have ever read it. I recall that when my doctoral adviser, John R. Alden, examined it in the fall of 1952, he considerately made no comments about the interpretation or the point of view and merely complimented me on the extensiveness of the research and the unbridled vigor of the prose. However great its deficiencies, this thesis was the project that introduced me to colonial political and constitutional history, the subject of this book of essays and an area of inquiry from which I have often strayed but which I have never entirely left during my forty years as an early American historian.

By the time I began research in London in the fall of 1953 on my doctoral dissertation, a study of the development of the legislatures of all the southern colonies between 1730 and 1763, I had read enough serious history to be able to perceive the pitfalls of whiggery but not enough to break out of existing paradigms of early American political history. At the time I was conceiving my study, available models for doing colonial political history were limited. What passed for political history among historians like Charles M. Andrews, Herbert Levi Osgood, and their students was really the history of political institutions, and I proceeded to design my research and to construct my study in the style of Andrews, Evarts B. Greene, and Leonard W. Labaree. Indeed, I thought of my study as a considerable amplification of Labaree's *Royal Government in America*[1] and a counterpart to Greene's *Provincial Governor.*[2] Only during the course of that year did I discover the works of Sir Lewis Namier on eighteenth-century British politics and begin to glimpse the possibilities for a history of colonial politics that would focus on the history of the groups, processes, and patterns of interaction that held center stage in his work and that had sometime before come to be the subjects of political histories of the American Revolution and subsequent periods of American history. Slowly, I began to sense that what I was doing was less political than constitutional history.

Published in 1963, the book that grew out of my dissertation, *The Quest for Power: The Lower Houses of Assembly in the Southern Royal Colonies, 1689–1776*, remained primarily an institutional study with important implications for colonial political and constitutional history, but even before the completion of that book I had already begun in several essays, some of which are republished in this volume, to go beyond the framework employed in the book to study problems of political leadership, constitutional conflict, political culture, political ideology, and political development. But my research interests beginning in the early 1960s shifted into a later period and eventually in other directions altogether, moving from the politics of Revolutionary Virginia and the origins of the American Revolution to the social and economic history of the colonies during the early eighteenth century and, starting in the mid-1970s, to problems of identity formation in the plantation societies of colonial British America.

In the meantime, however, superb studies published in the 1960s by Gary B. Nash, Robert Zemsky, Richard L. Bushman, Patricia U. Bonomi, Jere Daniell, and others[3] redefined the study of colonial political

---

[1] Leonard W. Labaree, *Royal Government in America: A Study of the British Colonial System before 1783* (New Haven, 1930).

[2] Evarts B. Greene, *The Provincial Governor in the English Colonies* (New York, 1898).

[3] John M. Murrin, "Political Development," in Jack P. Greene and J. R. Pole, eds., *Colonial British America: Essays in the New History of the Early Modern Era* (Baltimore,

life and raised it to new levels of sophistication. Stimulated by their examples, many of my early doctoral students at Johns Hopkins, including
Edward M. Cook, Jr.,[4] Richard A. Ryerson,[5] Alan Tully,[6] Richard Waterhouse,[7] Roger Ekirch,[8] and Thomas L. Purvis,[9] wrote dissertations
that they subsequently turned into books representative of this new style
of colonial political history.

But the late 1960s and early 1970s was the high-water mark for colonial political history. As first social and then cultural history became the
vogue, political history came to be seen as the study of elite white men,
about whom we already knew enough, and proportionately fewer published works in early American history focused on colonial politics. Not
even the craze for studying political ideology during the Revolutionary
era translated into much interest in that subject for the colonial period,
T. H. Breen's 1970 study of colonial New England political thought being the only sophisticated modern book-length study of colonial political
thought beyond the early years of Puritan New England.[10]

Except for a few legal historians, most of whom concentrated on the
era just before the Revolution,[11] interest in the constitutional history of
the colonial era has been practically nonexistent. During my first
twenty-five years at Johns Hopkins only one of my doctoral students,
Peter S. Onuf, did a dissertation which might be classified as constitutional history, and that one dealt principally with the Revolutionary

---

1984), 408–56, provides an excellent discussion of this literature as well as of that that
preceded and followed it.

[4] Edward M. Cook, Jr., *The Fathers of the Towns: Leadership and Community Structure
in Eighteenth-Century New England* (Baltimore, 1976).

[5] Richard Alan Ryerson, *The Revolution Is Now Begun: The Radical Committees of Philadelphia, 1765–1776* (Philadelphia, 1978).

[6] Alan Tully, *William Penn's Legacy: Politics and Social Structure in Provincial Pennsylvania, 1726–1755* (Baltimore, 1977).

[7] Richard Waterhouse, *A New World Gentry: The Making of a Merchant and Planter Class
in South Carolina, 1670–1770* (New York, 1989).

[8] A. Roger Ekirch, *"Poor Carolina": Politics and Society in Colonial North Carolina, 1729–
1776* (Chapel Hill, N.C., 1981).

[9] Thomas L. Purvis, *Proprietors, Patronage, and Paper Money: Legislative Politics in New
Jersey, 1703–1776* (New Brunswick, N.J., 1986).

[10] T. H. Breen, *The Character of the Good Ruler: A Study of Puritan Political Ideas in New
England, 1630–1730* (New Haven, 1970).

[11] This literature is discussed in Jack P. Greene, "From the Perspective of Law: Context
and Legitimacy in the Origins of the American Revolution. A Review Essay," *South Atlantic Quarterly* 65 (1986): 56–77.

era.[12] My 1986 book, *Peripheries and Center: Constitutional Development in the Extended Polities of the British Empire and the United States, 1607–1788,* and several related essays written about that time represented a preliminary attempt to address the absence of systematic study in colonial constitutional history and to open that subject up for serious study.

The movement to social and cultural history has, of course, been extraordinarily salutary, and I have actively and strongly encouraged doctoral students to participate in it. But there is still a lot to be learned about colonial political life and the constitutional arrangements under which it operated. One hopes that the recent renewal of interest in problems of state formation and political history in early modern Europe will soon result in a revival of attention to those subjects in colonial America.

The sixteen essays collected in this volume represent my own early and continuing interest in the history of colonial public life. Fourteen of them have been published previously, four as chapters in books, ten as journal articles, and one as the introduction to a collection of documents. Six of them first appeared between 1959 and 1963, two in 1969–70, two in 1975–76, one in 1981, two in 1992, and one in 1994. Of the two previously unpublished essays, one was written in 1969–70 for a book that I never finished, and the other during the past year.

Written over four decades, these essays address three broad themes in colonial political and constitutional history. First is the nature of authority in the broad extended polity of the British Empire and within the new colonial entities that formed parts of that empire. Second is the political and constitutional development of those new entities and the role of metropolitan ideological and cultural imperatives in shaping that development. Third is the nature and changing character of constitutional tensions within the empire and the conflicts that developed out of those tensions.

The volume begins with a new general essay, "Negotiated Authorities: The Problem of Governance in the Extended Polities of the Early Modern Atlantic World," which is intended to be thematic for the volume as a whole. Examining patterns of governance in early modern overseas empires in the light of the new literature on European state formation, this chapter suggests that coercive models of empire are as inappropriate for the analysis of those entities as models of the modern centralized states are for early modern European states. It proposes instead a con-

---

[12] Peter S. Onuf, *The Origins of the Federal Republic: Jurisdictional Controversies in the United States, 1775–1787* (Philadelphia, 1983).

sensual model that emphasizes the importance of negotiation in imperial governance and the significant role of peripheral entities in constructing authority in the extended polities represented by the new transatlantic empires.

The next three chapters offer general interpretive analyses of colonial constitutional development. Chapter two, "The Colonial Origins of American Constitutionalism," describes the emergence of a tradition of constitutionalism during the colonial era and stresses the centrality of custom in that tradition. Chapter three, "Metropolis and Colonies: Changing Patterns of Constitutional Conflict in the Early Modern British Empire, 1607–1763," provides a broad overview of metropolitan-colonial interactions over questions involving constitutional authority during the century and a half following the establishment of the first English-American colony. Chapter four, "The Glorious Revolution and the British Empire, 1688–1783," considers the impact of the Revolutionary Settlement of 1688–89 on the colonies and the ways colonial leaders used that settlement to define their own constitutional situation.

Chapters five through eight treat at a general level selected aspects of colonial political history between the Restoration and the conclusion of the Seven Years' War. Chapter five, "The Gifts of Peace: Social and Economic Expansion and Development in the Periodization of the Early American Past, 1713–63," argues for the primacy of the expansive socioeconomic and demographic conditions in defining colonial life and providing the context for politics between 1713 and 1763. Chapter six, "The Growth of Political Stability: An Interpretation of Political Development in the Anglo-American Colonies, 1660–1760," describes the emergence of sophisticated polities in the colonies during the century before the American Revolution and argues that by the middle decades of the eighteenth century the major colonies had developed impressive political resources and achieved considerable political stability. Chapter seven, "The Role of the Lower Houses of Assembly in Eighteenth-Century Politics," provides a general account of the emergence of representative institutions during the eighteenth century and assesses their changing place in colonial politics, while chapter eight, "Political Mimesis: A Consideration of the Historical and Cultural Roots of Legislative Behavior in the British Colonies in the Eighteenth Century," discusses the origin and nature of the ideological imperatives that underlay and drove that development.

Chapters nine and ten are quantitative studies of aspects of colonial political life. Chapter nine, "Legislative Turnover in British Colonial America, 1696–1775: A Quantitative Analysis," analyzes changing patterns of electoral turnover in all the British colonies from Barbados north to Nova Scotia. Based on a prosopographical analysis of the 110 most prominent committee members, chapter ten, "Foundations of Political Power in the Virginia House of Burgesses, 1720–76," provides a case study of the social attributes of leadership in the oldest colonial representative body.

Chapter eleven, "Society, Ideology, and Politics: An Analysis of the Political Culture of Mid-Eighteenth-Century Virginia," provides a detailed case study of the context and culture of political life in Britain's oldest and largest colony during the twenty-five to forty years preceding the Declaration of Independence.

Chapters twelve through fifteen examine specific conflicts that grew out of imperial constitutional tensions during the years from 1759 to 1775. Chapter twelve, "The Attempt to Separate the Offices of Speaker and Treasurer in Virginia, 1758–66: An Incident in Imperial Conflict," shows how one skillful governor was able to maneuver between the competing demands of metropolis and colony to avoid a potentially grave political and constitutional conflict. Chapter thirteen, "The Gadsden Election Controversy and the Revolutionary Movement in South Carolina"; chapter fourteen, "The Jamaica Privilege Controversy, 1764–66: An Episode in the Process of Constitutional Definition in the Early Modern British Empire"; and chapter fifteen, "Bridge to Revolution: The Wilkes Fund Controversy in South Carolina, 1769–75," provide narrative treatments of three major local political controversies during the 1760s and 1770s and assess their significance in the political and constitutional histories of the colonies in which they occurred.

Coauthored with my friend Richard M. Jellison, who put his knowledge of the intricacies of currency finance at my disposal and helped me interpret my research, a final chapter, "The Currency Act of 1764 in Metropolitan-Colonial Relations, 1764–76," examines one of the principal issues separating metropolis and colonies during the crucial years before independence and shows how, almost alone among many such issues, it was resolved.

In readying this volume for publication, I have been careful to make no substantive changes in the fourteen republished pieces. For that reason, the volume contains some minor repetitions of general themes. I have, however, made a few minor editorial changes; standardized form, spelling, and citations; and added at the end of each chapter a short paragraph providing its history and giving the details of original publication.

Many people helped me to put this volume together. Don Higginbotham, Alan Tully, and Peter S. Onuf sorted through a large number of pieces and offered useful advice about selection and organization. Amy Turner Bushnell provided valuable editorial help. Sarah Springer re-typed older essays that were not already on computer disks and began the process of standardizing citations. Kim Klein, James Baird, and Nuran Çinlar read proofs, and Kim did the index. The Johns Hopkins University provided financial assistance.

This volume is affectionately dedicated to W. W. Abbot. He had taken his doctorate at Duke University a few years before me, but I did not know him when, as book review editor of the *William and Mary Quarterly*, he asked me to do a review essay on the publication of the official records of the southern colonies. The first person to show much interest in my dissertation, Bill encouraged me to move beyond conventional categories of analysis, arranged the session at which I presented my first scholarly paper (chapter ten in this volume), and published two of the pieces in this volume (chapters seven and fifteen) while he was editor of the *Journal of Southern History*. After publishing the second, he told me that I had learned well enough how to do that style of history and counseled me to move on to another genre. Over the years he has remained a generous and supportive friend.

One

Negotiated Authorities:
The Problem of Governance in the Extended Polities of the Early Modern Atlantic World

T HIS ESSAY SEEKS TO REOPEN a very old question: What was the nature of the vast new transatlantic political entities that came into existence during the early modern era? Implicit in that general question are several more specific ones. How were those entities created? What were the relationships between the initiating and, to one degree or another, established Old World polities that claimed jurisdiction over these entities and the new polities established in the American (or even more distant) peripheries that comprised their outermost units? How— by what processes and by whom—was authority established in and over these peripheral polities?

Among the earliest problems addressed by historians of all parts of early America, these traditional questions have not been central to historical inquiry since the 1920s and 1930s and have received little scholarly attention since the early 1960s. Over the last decade, however, wholesale changes in contemporary patterns of state organization in Europe, especially the movement toward European federation, the demand for regional autonomy by disaffected regions or groups in many states, and the breakup of the Soviet empire, have stimulated a new interest in the general process of state formation and organization and an exciting new literature on that process as it was experienced in medieval, early modern, and modern Europe. In turn, this new literature strongly suggests the desirability of looking once again and in some detail at this process as it operated in the creation and functioning of European overseas empires during both the early modern and modern eras. These brief remarks use the new literature on European state formation as a point of departure for a preliminary consideration of this complex problem.

Professional history took shape and acquired personality during an era in which European colonialism was at its zenith. Although much of the previously colonized world had been decolonized during the late eighteenth and earlier nineteenth centuries, and although some of the larger settler segments of the British colonial world were beginning to move toward an autonomous status during the late nineteenth and early twentieth centuries, the competition among national European industrial states for markets, raw materials, and international preeminence led after 1850 to the systematic European subjugation of a large portion of the globe. In the Americas, only the vestiges of older empires remained— in Canada and the West Indies and at a few points along the coasts of Central and northern South America. In Africa, by contrast, few independent political entities any longer existed, the British, French, Germans, Portuguese, Belgians, and Spanish having, mostly during the six decades before World War I, divided the continent among them. In Asia only Siam and China had nominally escaped a similar fate, albeit the latter had had to yield strategic places or spheres to Europeans. Britain controlled the Indian subcontinent, Ceylon, Burma, and the Malay states; France had hegemony over Indochina; and the British, Dutch, and Portuguese had divided the East Indies among them. Japan, the one Asian state to have wholly resisted the encroachments of this renewed European imperialism, controlled Korea and Formosa. Elsewhere, in the oceans of the world, every island had been claimed, occupied, or drawn into some sort of political relationship either with a European state or with the United States or one of the other new American states.

The agglomerated national empires that emerged out of this new wave of modern imperialism all had at their center a powerful modern national state with authoritative—that is, sovereign—central governing institutions; responsibility for an expanding number of political functions including defense, adjudication, and even production and distribution; and a monopoly of force. Authority in these states flowed outward from central governmental institutions through various bureaucratic and coercive agencies into the usually contiguous areas that composed the core state and to the far-flung system of colonies that comprised its overseas empire. Colonies "belonged to" or were "possessed by" the national states that exercised sovereign, that is, absolute and full, authority over them.

In these outlying colonies, only a few of which had populations with more than a small percentage of people of European descent, individuals, corporations, and government-licensed monopolies often wielded enormous informal influence and power by virtue of their organization of and control over labor, land, minerals, and other economic resources, but European core states exerted and maintained effective authority over colonies through well-developed and elaborate systems of formal imperial institutions, including viceroys, bureaucracies, armies, and navies: institutions that supplied the administrative expertise and the force necessary to maintain effective authority of the center over distant colonies.

The model of imperial organization that these modern empires presented to historians after 1880 was thus one in which colonies were presided over by powerful national states with vast administrative and coercive resources to enforce their claims to sovereignty. In these coherent entities, authority, even in colonies with substantial numbers of settlers, flowed not upward from colonial populations, most of whom were, in any case, disenfranchised subject populations, but downward from distant centers. The very concepts of *colony* and *colonial* were freighted with powerful overtones of subjection, subordination, dependence, domination, inferiority, incapacity, alterity. Colonies were places and colonials were peoples over whom national states exercised hegemonic control. Scarcely surprisingly, early professional historians tended to apply, largely uncritically, this coercive and centralized model of imperial organization derived from modern empires to the early modern empires that preceded them.

Contemporary trends in the social sciences both reinforced and perpetuated this tendency. Although historians have long complained about the preference of political and social scientists and theorists both in and out of the academy for explanatory models that shoehorn the messy, irregular, and sometimes seemingly incomprehensible details of the past into coherent, regular, and comprehensible systems, they have at the same time been both attracted to and enormously influenced by those models. Perhaps even more importantly, most historical analysts, no doubt influenced by the centralizing tendencies and growing coercive power of practically all national states over the past century, seem, whether they were critics or defenders of existing social, economic, and political arrangements, to have preferred models of social and political organization that were essentially coercive in their operation.

Especially as a result of recent findings in social history, however, the explanatory power of such models, including especially their comprehensiveness, has been called into question. Wherever historians have looked, at the level of gender and family relations, at the organization and operation of plantations and communities or at the dynamics of broader structures of economic, social, and political relations, they have found that authority structures have been created not strictly by imposition from the top down or from the center out but through an elaborate process of negotiation among the parties involved. The power of the contending parties in this process may rarely, if ever, have been equal. Through a combination of resistance and acquiescence, however, even the most disadvantaged, most apparently powerless parties have had some significant input. However disproportionately *power*, defined as strength, force, and might, may have been distributed in any given relationship or set of relationships, *authority*, a term that implies legitimacy, justice, and right, is thus, we have learned, almost always the product of negotiation among and sanction by all the parties involved.

Recent literature on state formation strongly suggests that this insight may be as relevant to the analysis of large entities such as states and empires as it is to smaller social groupings. Objecting to the deeply ingrained tendency for historians "to reduce the political history of Europe to the creation of nation states" and to interpret that history from the point of view of the successful actors in that process, the contributors to this literature have shown that the organization of Europe into "a small number of unitary and integrated nation states" is both a relatively recent phenomenon and a highly contingent and by no means inevitable one.[1] "It took a long time," wrote Charles Tilly, one of the principal contributors to this literature, "for national States—relatively centralized, differentiated, and autonomous organizations successfully claiming priority in the use of force within large, contiguous, and clearly defined territories—to dominate the European map. In 1490," at the beginning of the early modern era, Tilly has contended, "the future remained open; despite the frequent use of the word 'kingdom,' empires of one sort or another claimed most of the European landscape, and federations remained viable in some parts of the continent."[2]

---

[1] Mark Greengrass, ed., *Conquest and Coalescence: The Shaping of the State in Early Modern Europe* (London, 1991), vii.

[2] Charles Tilly, *Coercion, Capital, and European States, AD 990–1990* (Cambridge, Mass., 1990), 43–44, 224.

Indeed, at that date, "Europe's political structure," as Mark Greengrass has noted, "was dominated by a multiplicity of regional political entities" that "were remarkably durable and robust." With just under 500 independent polities in 1500, Europe was a complex mosaic of different types of states with "a rich variety of [political] traditions." These included "large old-established states, new principalities, dynastic empires, city states, confederations," and "a continuing widespread acceptance of the ideal of universal world monarchy in the Holy Roman Empire and the spiritual and temporal jurisdiction of the Papacy." Even the largest states were usually divided into a wide assortment of lordships presided over by "regional magnates who enjoyed great autonomy within their own terrains." "Only gradually" did many of these polities surrender "their independence" and accept "a destiny of coalescence within a larger entity." As late as 1789 Europe still had nearly 350 independent polities, and "the last major zones of fragmented sovereignty [were] only consolidated into national states" during the modern era. By 1900 Europe contained just 25 independent political units.[3]

In this effort to escape "reading history backwards," contributors to the new literature on state formation have sought to reexamine European political development from the perspective not of El Escorial, Versailles, or Whitehall but of the periphery, from the experience of not just "those states which succeeded in imposing their identity upon others" but also those that were absorbed in the process. By concentrating on the emergence of those "elements of state power" that lay at the heart of the success of the nation-state, "its officialdom, its fiscal base, and its military power," older approaches, as Greengrass has pointed out, "inevitably" saw "state-building . . . as a process" that began "from the centre" and that required that "peripheral regions, independent or autonomous territories[,] . . . be militarily 'conquered,' juridically rendered subservient, institutionally 'integrated' or culturally 'assimilated.'" Mistakenly assuming that monarchs and their ministers during the early modern era were engaged in "a deliberate effort to construct the sort of substantial centralized states that came to dominate European life during the nineteenth and twentieth centuries," exponents of this approach stressed "the centralizing activities of the state" and the coercive elements involved in the process of state building.[4]

---

[3]Greengrass, *Conquest and Coalescence*, vii, 1–2, 3; Tilly, *Coercion, Capital, and European States*, 23, 41–42.

[4]Greengrass, *Conquest and Coalescence*, viii, 3, 6, 15; Tilly, *Coercion, Capital, and European States*, 11.

In contrast, by examining the same process from the point of view of the periphery, more recent analysts, as Greengrass has written, have made it clear that "local society could be a motive force in the formation and consolidation of the European state, that local notables were capable of both opposing and exploiting the state for their own ends, and that successful integration was not just the conquest and absorption of the small by the large but also the coalescence and continuity of local and wider interests within a larger political framework." From this new perspective, it is possible to comprehend just "how aware rulers were of the importance of sustaining local identities and accepting regional differences," how they had to take into account "the will and determination of local elites in the process of forging new loyalties," and how a "sense of wider national belonging did not simply, or quickly, supplant local identities, but co-existed alongside them." Almost always, successful "integration involved the active engagement of the localities, and particularly their elites," who, more often than not, seem to have associated their incorporation into a larger state not with "the loss of their [local] privileges but rather" with the protection of those privileges "within a wider unit."[5]

Coercion was not unimportant, but most states lacked the necessary military, administrative, and financial resources necessary to impose their will upon neighboring polities. With the notable exception of Ireland, "conquest was what happened to non-Christian infidels." As a consequence, in all but a few instances amalgation involved negotiation, or what Tilly called "bargaining." As long as "local potentates . . . contained the monarch's enemies and kept the revenues flowing to the national capital," Tilly observed, monarchs were willing to enter into all sorts of arrangements that "left considerable power and discretion in" local hands. "All along the continuum[,] bargaining over the state's extractive claims" thus "created or confirmed individual or collective claims on the state, individual and collective rights vis-à-vis the state, and obligations of the state to its citizens. It also created rights—recognized enforceable claims—of states with respect to their citizens."[6]

At the same time that rulers were "consolidating and extending their domains," they were thus also producing "rights, privileges, and protective institutions," including representative institutions, "that had not

---

[5] Greengrass, *Conquest and Coalescence,* 6–7, 19–20.

[6] Ibid., 10; Tilly, *Coercion, Capital, and European States,* 25, 102–3. See also Ciaran Brady, "The Decline of the Irish Kingdom," in Greengrass, *Conquest and Coalescence,* 94–105.

previously existed." Such bargains meant that, at least in the early phases, the emergence of national states would be characterized not by direct but by indirect rule. "On a national scale, in fact, no European state (except, perhaps, Sweden) made a serious attempt to institute direct rule from top to bottom until the era of the French Revolution," Tilly has written. "Before then all but the smallest states relied on some version of indirect rule, and thus ran serious risks of disloyalty, dissimulation, corruption, and rebellion. But indirect rule made it possible to govern without erecting, financing, and feeding a bulky administrative [and coercive] apparatus."[7]

The "composite monarchies" of early modern Europe were thus most often "built on a mutual compact between the crown and the ruling class[es] of their different provinces." Ensuring that "the constituent kingdoms continued after their union to be treated as distinct entities" with "their own laws, *fueros* and privileges," such compacts, as J. H. Elliott has noted, provided for a "looseness of . . . association" which "allowed for a high degree of continuing local self-government at a time when monarchs were simply in no position to bring outlying kingdoms and provinces under tight royal control." Simultaneously, Elliott added, such arrangements "guaranteed to provincial elites continued enjoyment of their existing privileges combined with the potential benefits to be derived from participation in a wider association."[8]

The ubiquity of this bargaining or negotiating process dramatically testifies to the "practical limits to political integration through" either coercive or "administrative means" during the early modern era.[9] Increasingly, larger states with access to capital through taxation, tribute, or commerce acquired impressive coercive and administrative resources in the form of armies and navies and fiscal, administrative, and judicial organizations. As Daniel Szechi has pointed out, however, the deployment of such resources "was prohibitively costly. No [early modern] regime," he observed, "could [possibly have] afford[ed] the expense of relying solely on its armed forces to control and administer its population," while the cost of any very sizable bureaucracy would have quickly eaten up all the gains of acquisition. As a result, the early modern state, a state which served a society that "was still overwhelmingly hierarchical, with bonds of paternalism and deference running vertically up and down

---

[7] Tilly, *Coercion, Capital, and European States*, 25, 41, 103.

[8] J. H. Elliott, "A Europe of Composite Monarchies," *Past and Present*, no. 137 (1992): 52–53, 57, 69.

[9] Greengrass, *Conquest and Coalescence*, 11.

the social ladder," had "to have the cooperation of at least some of the area's 'nobility'" if it "wished to control an area without directly using its armed forces."[10]

The price for such collaboration was not cheap. In return for their support, "the state had [both] to allow . . . local elites a substantial degree of autonomy" and to permit them "to distribute the state's patronage and interpret its requirements in accord with local circumstances as they saw them. *De facto* the burgeoning ability of the early modern state to coerce its subjects was thereby limited to more socially acceptable proportions. In the round," Szechi added, central "power was held in check by exigency."[11] "Every form of rule" during the early modern era, Tilly agreed, "faced significant limits to its range of effectiveness within a particular kind of environment. Efforts to exceed that range produced defeats or fragmentation of control, with the result that most rulers settled for" much less than an integrated system of centralized control.[12]

The structure of the earliest national states displayed all of these characteristics. During the late fifteenth and sixteenth centuries, Spain was neither a consolidated nor a very well integrated state. Rather, in J. H. Elliott's words, it "consisted of a variety of kingdoms and provinces," Castile, Aragon, Leon, Navarre, Catalonia, "almost all of which owed allegiance to the same ruler as a result either of dynastic accident or dynastic design." These several political units "were nominally subject to the king on an equal footing. Legally they retained their traditional institutions, rights and privileges, and each succeeding monarch was under oath to preserve their laws and liberties intact. Since these" polities "differed widely among themselves, the Spanish monarchy of Philip II and his successors was an extraordinary patchwork of variegated subject territories, with a wide diversity of laws and institutions" that the monarch was "sworn to protect." To govern each of these territories, Spanish monarchs appointed a separate council composed of native councillors to oversee government business. Although bullion from the New World eventually enabled Spanish monarchs to dispense with representative institutions, these kingdoms and provinces remained politically distinct and retained other local rights and privileges.[13]

---

[10] Daniel Szechi, "The Hanoverians and Scotland," ibid., 131. See also Tilly, *Coercion, Capital, and European States*, 35, 125, 190.

[11] Szechi, "Hanoverians and Scotland," 131.

[12] Tilly, *Coercion, Capital, and European States*, 15.

[13] J. H. Elliott, "The Spanish Monarchy and the Kingdom of Portugal, 1580–1640," in Greengrass, *Conquest and Coalescence*, 50, 54.

By contrast, Portugal had long been a unified kingdom. At the end of the fifteenth and beginning of the sixteenth centuries, centralizing monarchs, specifically John II and Manuel I, had made a considerable effort to strengthen the power of the state at the expense of towns and the nobility, both of which had long enjoyed special liberties and privileges of the kind that appertained to their counterparts throughout the rest of western Europe. Resources derived from Portugal's early successes in overseas expansion made Portuguese monarchs less dependent on "subsidies voted by municipal representatives in cortes" and gave them the wherewithal to put paid royal officials into most political jurisdictions.[14] Commercial expansion also provided rulers with lucrative sources of patronage in the form of licenses to engage in overseas trade that could be used to purchase the loyalty of noble families. These developments enabled the crown to achieve a "degree of consolidation" that, in comparison with other European monarchs, was "striking." Ultimately, however, the crown's substantial trading profits turned out to be insufficient to meet the costs of the enlarged bureaucracy and other state expenses. As a result, both the towns and the nobility, the latter gaining new power as a consequence of its eager participation in commercial activities, "retained many of their ancient rights" and enjoyed considerable authority over their respective areas.[15]

Like Spain, England included "a wide diversity of ethnic, linguistic and cultural groups." Like Portugal, however, it early built "a durable central structure," including a royal treasury and a national court system. By the early sixteenth century it was already relatively "highly integrated," Wales and Cornwall having been incorporated into the national government and the Tudors having had considerable success in their efforts to curb "the great aristocrats, with their private armies and claims to autonomous power." Despite the upheavals of the mid-seventeenth century, by 1700 England "was one of the most unified countries in Europe." Nevertheless, it continued in many respects to be what some social scientists have called a "model of under-statization," its authority relying far less on an extensive state apparatus than on local elites, particularly its nobility and gentry, who, as Greengrass noted, "played a far greater role in making state power more effective in England than [similar groups did] elsewhere in Europe." Moreover, in

---

[14] Lyle N. McAlister, *Spain and Portugal in the New World 1492–1700* (Minneapolis, 1984), 66–68; James Lang, *Portuguese Brazil: The King's Plantation* (New York, 1979), 4–7.

[15] Lang, *Portuguese Brazil*, 4–6.

containing the "latent fissiparousness" of English or, after the Anglo-Scottish union of 1707, British society, a powerful sense of national identity which was shared by Welsh and Scots as well as English people seems to have been considerably more significant than state power.[16]

Like that of England, the French national state was built upon the principle of incorporation. Having long followed "a tradition of piecemeal annexation and integration," the French monarchy throughout the late Middle Ages "had incorporated feudal principalities which had never formed part of its domain" and were "fundamentally different in linguistic background, legal tradition, customs and history." It "united and [then] absorbed into the French kingdom" first Toulouse and Champagne, and then Brittany, Gascony, Burgundy, and Flanders, "not as separate entities but as integral parts of it." To forward this process, French, in contrast to English, monarchs created a large "standing officialdom" composed of intendants and other officers that by the mid-seventeenth century had made France "uniquely the office-holding state of early modern Europe." Yet, even in company with a large standing army, this massive administrative structure did not make France an integrated and highly centralized state in the modern sense. As was revealed by the mid-seventeenth-century Fronde, the monarchs' solemn obligations to respect local traditions involved them in constant negotiations with local notables acting as agents of cooperation or obstruction through local parliaments.[17]

Among other emerging national states during the early modern era, the Dutch republic, which "remained one of Europe's dominant states for more than a century," pursued a wholly different path and took a different form from any of the others. Far more of a federation "of largely autonomous city-states" than a unified polity, it developed little "permanent state structure" and often seemed to be on the verge of dissolving "into the governments of its major constituencies." Less powerful than the state-licensed trading companies that presided over an extensive international trade, its formal rulers had little authority, and that "was severely curbed by well-entrenched constitutional liberties" and by the necessity for "constant negotiation . . . over state policy" with the republic's many constituent parts.[18]

---

[16] Szechi, "Hanoverians and Scotland," 116–17; Tilly, *Coercion, Capital, and European States*, 7, 154, 156; Greengrass, *Conquest and Coalescence*, 15–16.

[17] Greengrass, *Conquest and Coalescence*, 13–14.

[18] Tilly, *Coercion, Capital, and European States*, 30, 53–54, 62, 150; Elliott, "Spanish Monarchy and the Kingdom of Portugal," 51.

In view of these specific experiences and the general conditions they expressed, it is scarcely surprising that the modern concept of sovereignty was slow to develop in early modern Europe. "Throughout the sixteenth and seventeenth centuries," Greengrass noted, "sovereignty was still the exercise of authority within different domains (seigneurial, ecclesiastical, juridical, etc.)." "Impatient with archaic rights and corporate privileges when they stood in the way of modernizing change," a new generation of statesmen during the seventeenth century, including Richelieu in France and Olivares in Spain, came, in Elliott's words, "to see order, discipline and a greater concentration of authority in the hands of the crown as the only means of enhancing the power and efficiency of their states in a ruthlessly competitive world," and French "jurists were the first in Europe [both] to articulate the concept of sovereignty" and to develop the political theory of absolutism.[19] Yet, by continuing in many instances to follow the ancient practice of "co-opting local powerholders" by "confirming their privileges," even the France of Louis XIV did not move decisively and completely away from traditional forms of indirect rule toward a system of direct governance which, like those employed by the national states of the nineteenth and twentieth centuries, "reduced the role of local or regional patrons and placed representatives of the national state in every community."[20]

The early modern national state was thus not the highly centralized, tightly integrated, and highly coercive entity that emerged in the wake of the French Revolution. With an only recently articulated conception of national sovereignty and as yet quite limited fiscal, administrative, and coercive resources, it was rather characterized by systems of indirect governance and fragmented sovereignties. The products of a process of state building in which authority had not flowed from the center outward to the periphery but had been constructed out of an ongoing series of negotiations, of reciprocal bargaining, among the center and the peripheries, these systems involved some concentration of power in agencies of the central state but also left considerable authority in the hands of the principal holders of power in the peripheries.

[19] Greengrass, *Conquest and Coalescence,* 3, 13; Elliott, "Spanish Monarchy and the Kingdom of Portugal," 58–59.

[20] Tilly, *Coercion, Capital, and European States,* 63, 103–4.

At the very time that early modern European national states were first coalescing, each in its own particular way tentatively groping for ways to hold itself together, several of them, principally the five states briefly mentioned above, also began the equally slow process of establishing overseas empires. In the following remarks, this essay proposes two principal contentions about this process. The first is that the extended polities or imperial structures that evolved within each of these empires, every one of which reflected the specific experiences of the initiating state with which it was associated, had far more in common with the early modern state than with the centralized and highly coercive empires that characterized the imperial systems that developed after 1850. The second is that a comprehension of the extent to which overseas peripheries, like those closer to the new seats of national power in Europe, were active participants in the construction of early modern arrangements of imperial governance considerably alters our understanding of the nature of both early modern imperialism and the character of the extended polities that resulted from it.

Traditionally, historians have seen the establishment of early modern European empires in America as the result of an extraordinary devolution of authority outward from European centers to new American peripheries. But even a casual inspection of the subject reveals that this conception seriously distorts the process by which authority was created in these new entities. Far from having been carried by would-be colonizers from Europe to America, authority in these empires seems rather to have been constructed in a process characterized by two phases. The first involved the creation in America, through the activities of the participants in the colonizing process, of new arenas of individual and local power. The second involved the actual creation of authority through negotiation or bargaining between those new arenas and the European centers that aspired to bring them under their jurisdiction and to which those arenas desired to be attached.

At the beginning of the era of early modern colonization, none of the emerging nation-states of Europe had either the coercive resources necessary to establish its hegemony over portions of the New World nor the financial wherewithal to pay the high costs involved in mobilizing those resources. As a consequence, during the early stages of colonization, all the nation-states farmed out that task to private groups organized into chartered trading companies or to individuals known, in the case of the Spanish, as adelantados and, respectively, in the case of the Portuguese, English, Dutch, and French, as *donatarios*, proprietors, patroons, and seigneurs. In return for authorization from the ruler and in the hope of realizing extensive economic or social advantages for themselves, such people agreed to assume the heavy financial burdens of founding, defending, and succoring beachheads of European occupation in America. In effect, European rulers gave these private agents licenses with wide discretion to undertake activities in domains that were often extensive and contained aboriginal populations of varying numbers, domains to which those rulers had only a highly tenuous claim and over which they had no effective control, much less authority. In this way European rulers sought to secure at least nominal jurisdiction over American territories and peoples at minimal cost to royal treasuries.

Some of these early private agents of European imperialism, especially the trading companies operating under the aegis of the Portuguese and Dutch, enjoyed considerable success in establishing trading footholds to tap some of the economic potential of the new worlds they encountered not just in America but in Africa and Asia as well. However, unless they encountered wealthy native empires to plunder, rich mineral deposits to exploit, or vast pools of native labor that relatively quickly could be turned to profit, something that during the early modern era in America happened on a large scale only in Mexico and Peru, few private adventurers had sufficient resources by themselves to sustain for more than a short period the high costs of settlement, administration, and development of colonies. Lack of resources to finance such activities early forced those who presided over them to seek cooperation and contributions from settlers, traders, and other individual participants in the colonizing process.

These efforts to enlist such cooperation acknowledged the fact that the actual process of establishing effective centers of European power in America was often less the result of the activities of colonial organizers or licensees than of the many groups and individuals who took actual possession of land, built estates and businesses, turned what had previously been wholly aboriginal social landscapes into ones that were at least partly European, constructed and presided over a viable system of economic arrangements, created towns or other political units, and subjugated, reduced to profitable labor, killed off, or expelled the original inhabitants. Making up for their scarcity of economic resources, thousands of Europeans, including large numbers of Spaniards and Englishmen, substantial numbers of Portugese and French, and significant numbers of Dutch and other Europeans, had by dint of their industry and initiative created social spaces for themselves and their families in America and thereby acquired or, one might better say, manufactured for themselves status, capital, and power.

Throughout the new European Americas during the early modern era, independent individual participants in the colonizing process were thus engaged in what can only be described as a deep and widespread process of individual self-empowerment. In contemporary Europe only a tiny fraction of the male population ever managed to rise out of a state of socioeconomic dependency to achieve the civic competence, the full right to have a voice in political decisions, that was the preserve of independent property holders. By contrast, as a consequence of the easy availability of land or other resources, a very large proportion of the adult male white colonists acquired land or other resources, built estates, and achieved individual independence.

This development gave rise to strong demands on the part of the large empowered settler populations for the extension to the colonies of the same rights to security of property and civic participation that appertained to the empowered, high-status, and independent property holders in the polities from which they came. In their view colonial government, like metropolitan government, should guarantee that men of their standing would not be governed without consultation or in ways that were patently against their interests. Along with the vast distance of the colonies from Europe, these circumstances powerfully nudged those who were nominally in charge of the colonies toward the establishment and toleration of political structures that involved active consultation with, if not the formal consent of, local settlers. Consultation meant that local populations would more willingly both acknowledge the legitimacy of the authority of private agencies of colonization and contribute to local costs. The earliest stages of colonization thus resulted in the emergence in new colonial peripheries of many new and relatively autonomous centers of European power effectively under local control.

Once these centers of local power had been established, agents of metropolitan centralization found it exceedingly difficult to bring them under regulation. The discovery of precious metals and other riches in Hispanic America during the first half of the sixteenth century provided the Spanish monarchy with the resources slowly to reduce the several enclaves of private power earlier established by its agents in America to some semblance of effective control. Thenceforth, Spain's rulers could purchase and man the ships needed to defend its colonies and shipping against foreign interlopers, pay for troops and missionaries to bring new areas under its hegemony, and support a growing bureaucracy of royal officials to oversee the colonies from Spain and to provide a powerful royal presence in the colonies. Although private initiatives continued to characterize the first stages of Spanish activity in any new area of occupation, the crown rarely delayed long in extending its authority over such enterprises.

By contrast, in the case of the English or, after 1707, British American Empire, the failure to find similar sources of wealth meant that the system of colonization through private agents persisted for well over a century after the first successful establishment of a colony in Virginia during the early decades of the seventeenth century. Before the 1730s all twelve of the English colonies established on the North American mainland and seven of the eight English colonies founded in the West Indies were the result of private initiatives by chartered companies or individuals or groups of landed proprietors. Only Jamaica, conquered by an English force from the Spaniards in 1655, was the result of a government effort. Although the British state spent considerable and slowly increasing sums to defend the colonies after 1689, it did not assume any substantial portions of the direct costs of American settlement until the founding of Georgia in 1732 and the expansion of Nova Scotia in 1748.[21]

The limitation of funds that perpetuated this continuing reliance on privately sponsored colonization by the English also had a profound effect upon the structure of governance within the British Empire. Until the last years of the colonial era the British state itself demonstrated a notable reluctance to pay for large military and civil establishments for the colonies. Simultaneously, the large population of independent property holders (who, as a consequence of the relatively easy availability of land, consisted of a large majority, up to 80 to 90 percent in some colonies, of free white adult males) insisted upon living under political arrangements that provided them with the fundamental guarantees of Englishmen, including especially the principles of government by consent, rule by law, and the sanctity of private property, defined as property in individual legal and civil rights as well as property in land and other forms of wealth.

Combined with the reluctance of the metropolitan government to spend money for imperial purposes, these expectations on the part of empowered colonials inevitably meant that authority in the British Empire would not be concentrated at the center but distributed between the center and the peripheries. More specifically, these conditions meant that the metropolitan government would lack the means unilaterally to enforce its will and authority in distant overseas polities, that central direction in the British Empire would be minimal, that metropolitan

---

[21] See Kurt William Nagel, "Empire and Interest: British Colonial Defense Policy, 1689–1748," Ph.D. diss., The Johns Hopkins University, 1992.

authority in the colonies would be consensual and heavily dependent upon provincial opinion, and that effective power in distant colonial polities would be firmly situated in provincial and local governments that were widely participatory and solidly under the control of large, broadly based, and resident land- and property-owning classes.

To the extent and under the conditions that they did, these self-produced possessing classes acknowledged metropolitan authority not because it was imposed upon them from the center or primarily even because, as some contemporaries wrote, it afforded them at least some minimal degree of protection in a frequently war-torn world. Rather, they accepted that authority because it brought with it incorporation into a larger system of national identity which carried with it guarantees of their Englishness, their continuing ability to enjoy the protections embedded in English legal and political traditions, and a high degree of autonomy over the internal affairs of the polities that they and their ancestors had helped to create and to which they had committed the destinies of themselves and their progeny. For the most part and at most times reflecting a respect for the extensive empowerment and high degree of individual liberty of colonial landowning classes, British imperial governance functioned primarily to preserve that empowerment and liberty and the property on which it was founded.[22]

Contemporary commentators had no doubt that Britain had "dealt more liberally with her colonies than [had] any other nation." No other European state seemed to have extended its colonies so much "liberty to manage their own affairs their own way." "In every thing, except their foreign trade," Adam Smith noted, "the liberty of the English colonists" was "complete. It is in every respect equal to that of their fellow-citizens at home, and is secured in the same manner, by an assembly of the representatives of the people." "The government of the English colonies," he observed, "is perhaps the only one which, since the world began, could give perfect security to the inhabitants of so very distant a province."[23]

Yet, if the system of negotiated authority that characterized imperial

---

[22] The argument made here is an extension of those presented in Jack P. Greene, *Peripheries and Center: Constitutional Development in the Extended Polities of the British Empire and the United States, 1607–1788* (Athens, Ga., 1986), and "The Glorious Revolution and the British Empire, 1688–1763," in Lois G. Schwoerer, ed., *The Revolution of 1688–89: Changing Perspectives* (Cambridge, Eng., 1992), 260–71 [chap. 4 below].

[23] Adam Smith, *An Inquiry into the Nature and Causes of the Wealth of Nations* (1776), in *The Glasgow Edition of the Works and Correspondence of Adam Smith*, ed. R. H. Campbell and A. S. Skinner, 6 vols. (Oxford, 1976–83), 2:572, 583–85.

governance in the early modern British Empire was distinctively British, it was by no means peculiar among early modern empires. Even in the Hispanic Empire, which was under the aegis of monarchs who had the greatest financial resources at their disposal and, next to the French, were most determined to abolish local privileges, the structure of authority was negotiated in a perpetual tug-of-war between the center and the peripheries.

Spanish New World settlements displayed many centrifugal tendencies. Attempting to re-create their European inheritance, conquerors and settlers quickly organized themselves into towns, whose governing cabildos or councils were elected annually by resident landowners, merchants, and townsmen. To distinguish themselves from the large indigenous populations among whom most of them lived, these settlers "claimed the status of gentry *(hidalgos)* and insisted upon their right to exemption from degrading forms of punishment, to imprisonment only in the form of house arrest, and to freedom from *pechos*—direct taxes which might be collected only from the lowest classes." Although "royal officials resisted the colonists' claims," Woodrow Borah has written, "they never dared to try to levy *pechos* in the New World, and because of lack of a standing army, they were forced to use colonists as militia in exactly the capacity the latter claimed should be their principal contribution to the Crown." In its dealings with its American subjects, in other words, the Spanish crown "was forced to use the [same] wariness and care it employed with its nobles in Spain."[24]

Indeed, whereas "royal intervention had destroyed most local autonomy" among towns in Spain, in the "New World, where white settlement began far in advance of the reach of royal authorities and beyond their power to meet emergencies, there was necessarily a revival of the earlier vigorous, medieval Spanish town life," some early towns in America exercising "almost sovereign attributes." Periodically, the crown sought to reduce local autonomy, and particularly during the sixteenth century its efforts were relatively successful in seats of viceregal authority such as Mexico City and Lima. By the seventeenth century, however, declining fiscal resources considerably diminished the forces of centralization in the American peripheries. Needing the assistance of the settlers "to protect the exposed outposts of empire," the crown, as Elliott has observed, "found itself at a serious disadvantage" in its attempts to augment its authority at the expense of the towns. As a consequence, even viceregal

---

[24] Woodrow Borah, "Representative Institutions in the Spanish Empire in the Sixteenth Century: The New World," *The Americas* 12 (1956): 249–50.

towns managed, in Borah's words, to preserve "a great deal of their original vitality," while towns farther away "retained virtually undiminished autonomy and popular control." Throughout the Spanish Empire, town councils continued to serve "as centers for the formulation of demands upon the Crown and resistance to increases of taxes and extensions of royal authority."[25]

Two further developments contributed to ensure that the peripheries would have a significant voice in the governance of the Spanish Empire. First was the principle of consultation in legislation. If lawmaking power resided solely in the hands of the crown, royal officials in Spain often consulted with their representatives in the colonies before finalizing royal cedulas, while the early development of the principle that "presiding magistrates" in America could "postpone the execution of royal orders whose implementation might create injustice or undesirable social conflicts" provided colonial bureaucrats with the flexibility necessary for them "to strike a delicate balance between the orders of" their "superiors and the dictates of local pressures." As John Leddy Phelan has pointed out, this rule effectively served as "an institutional device" for taking into account local opinion on local conditions and for "decentralizing decision making."[26]

A second development which led in the same direction was the slow creolization or naturalization of the royal bureaucracy in America. Especially during the seventeenth and first half of the eighteenth century, emerging creole oligarchies throughout the empire "exploited the weakness of the crown . . . to establish a general domination of colonial life." By purchasing a large proportion of judgeships in the territorial audiencias and, beginning in the late seventeenth century, higher administrative offices as well, these oligarchies further enhanced local power at the expense of the crown.[27]

At least down to the Bourbon reforms in the mid-eighteenth century, the peripheries of the Spanish-American Empire thus managed to retain wide control over the operation of local polities. Through local town councils, through the operation of the principle of consultation in legislation, and through the creolization of the royal bureaucracy, the peripheries, in Elliott's words, "effectively achieved a substantial degree of local

---

[25] Ibid., 251–56; John H. Elliott, "The Role of the State in British and Spanish Colonial America," unpublished paper, Apr. 27, 1990, 28.

[26] John Leddy Phelan, "Authority and Flexibility in the Spanish Imperial Bureaucracy," *Administrative Science Quarterly* 5 (1960): 59–60.

[27] Elliott, "Role of the State in British and Spanish Colonial America," 28.

self-rule, even if it remained self-rule at the king's command." Nominally, the crown always retained wide authority to take all sorts of measures in reference to the empire. In implementing those measures, however, the crown's colonial representatives often adapted them to local circumstances as defined by local notables. As in the case of the British Empire, bargaining between metropolis and colonists had thus produced an arrangement of divided and negotiated authority which seems to have been characteristic of early modern empires.[28]

Conditions in the Portuguese Empire in Brazil operated to produce similar results. Planters, farmers, ranchers, and other settlers took possession of the land, reorganized the landscape, built estates, and created pockets of independent power well before the Portugese crown made much effort to establish its authority over the donatary captaincies into which Brazil was divided. As in the Spanish case, the theory behind this effort was that all authority emanated from the throne in Lisbon. But the Portuguese monarchy never had adequate resources to pay for a colonial bureaucracy of sufficient size and scope to enforce the wide lawmaking powers it claimed over Brazil. In fact, Bahia was the "only . . . captaincy" in which the crown managed to establish a well-developed bureaucracy, and even there, few royal officials penetrated much beyond the immediate bounds of the capital at Salvador. In the adjacent sugar captaincies of Pernambuco and Rio de Janeiro, the royal presence was much less in evidence, and wealthy local families "controlled political patronage" well into the eighteenth century, while few of the king's officials ever ventured across the mountains to the settlements around São Paulo, much less into the ranching areas of the interior, where "powerful families managed local affairs" without substantial royal interference. Through the extensive purchase of offices, moreover, representatives of wealthy local families managed to infiltrate even the rudimentary royal bureaucracy that did exist. So extensive was this practice that by the eighteenth century the "lower echelons" of the bureaucracy, as James Lang has observed, had become "essentially the property of the colonial elite."[29]

From early on, those elites had exerted political influence through the institution of the *câmara,* or muncipal council, that was responsible for local government. Although these bodies did not have authority to initiate laws, they enjoyed extensive jurisdiction over municipal affairs. They awarded citizenship, collected taxes, administered laws, and, unlike the

---

[28] Ibid.

[29] Lang, *Portuguese Brazil,* 37–38, 50–51, 57.

Portuguese institutions on which they were modeled, appointed judges. Drawn from panels selected by local citizens, these bodies faithfully reflected "the dominant interests of the community" and served as instruments for the expression of local opinion. By "appeal[ing] decisions and delay[ing] enforcement of legislation" emanating from Lisbon, they could sometimes modify or reverse royal decisions. Indeed, any royal measure that encountered substantial local resistance—the 1639 prohibitions against slave raiding among Indians provide a dramatic example— "simply could not be enforced."[30] As in the case of the British and Spanish empires, authority in Portuguese Brazil was thus necessarily also the product of a process of negotiation among royal demands emanating from the center and local power and opinion deriving out of the peripheries.

When the French crown took over the scattered trading posts and agricultural settlements in Acadia, New France, and the West Indies in the early 1660s, the societies and economies of those places were small and relatively undeveloped. In contrast to the situation in the British, Spanish, and Portuguese colonies when they were taken over by the crown, none of these colonies had as yet developed a powerful local elite with sturdy claims to local governing privileges. Both for that reason and because the crown also offered heavy subsidies and demanded little in the way of taxes from the colonies, the French crown quickly succeeded in establishing an effective system of imperial governance with comparatively little resistance from the colonies.

Devised at the very moment when the absolutist state of old regime France was at its zenith, this system represented a conscious effort by Louis XIV's ministers to extend the absolutist principles of political centralization, royal paternalism, religious orthodoxy, and state control over economic life and the social order to the New World. In theory, all authority flowed outward from the crown through the Ministry of Marine in France to the crown's appointed officials in the colonies, including the governor general and intendant at the colonial capital, and from them through local governors in subordinate provinces to parish militia captains *(capitaines de milice)*, the chief agents of the provincial government in the localities, and thence to the wider population of traders, settlers, and planters. All colonial officials, judicial as well as administrative, were appointive, those at the provincial level by the crown and the *capitaines de milice* by the governors general. In this system local property owners had no formal institutions through which they could imple-

---

[30] Ibid., 52–53.

ment their wishes. Unlike the British colonists, they did not have representative assemblies; unlike the Spanish and Portuguese colonists, they did not have powerful town councils of elected notables. An earlier arrangement whereby "elected syndics" from each district of New France "made known the views of the people" of their jurisdictions failed to survive the implementation of the new royal system.[31]

But French colonial property holders had two informal avenues through which they enjoyed at least "an indirect say" in the regulations and decisions that affected them. First, various forms of consultation at every level ensured that few political actions would be undertaken without the colonists' support. The Ministry of Marine rarely issued decrees without first seeking advice from the governors general and intendants. Before issuing ordinances and edicts, those officials in turn consulted with local notables through either the Superior Council, the members of which all were drawn from the local elite, or occasional advisory assemblies called by governors or intendants to seek the views of prominent local people on issues of moment or by intendants to reach a consensus over the best way to resolve some local problem. Second, all colonial offices were open to colonists, and many were actually filled by them, conditions that also helped to make the French colonial regime sensitive to local opinion. Indeed, as in the Spanish and Portuguese colonies, even when they were not themselves creoles, royal officials, army officers, and merchants were frequently closely allied, sometimes through marriage, with prosperous colonials.[32]

Along with the small size of the overseas bureaucracy, which was never large enough to be highly intrusive in colonial affairs, such informal mechanisms helped to mitigate the authoritarian and centralizing tendencies of the early modern French system of imperial governance. Most significantly, they enabled French central officials to adjust to the same central underlying condition that so powerfully determined the character of contemporary structures of governance in the British, Spanish, and Portuguese empires: the extreme difficulty for representatives of the center to implement in distant peripheries any measure to which there was significant local opposition. Only continuous negotiations between agents of the center and strategic segments of the population of the peripheries could keep authority secure and government running smoothly in such extended polities.

---

[31] W. J. Eccles, *France in America* (New York, 1972), 67–70.

[32] Ibid., 70–71, 153; Allana G. Reid, "Representative Assemblies in New France," *Canadian Historical Review* 27 (1946): 19–26.

During the early modern era, the Netherlands never became a centralized state and never sought to assert political control over the territories
acquired by the two great trading companies, the Dutch East India
Company and the Dutch West India Company, established to oversee
Dutch overseas ventures at the beginning of the seventeenth century. In
the words of Charles Boxer, each company, and especially the East India
Company, effectively functioned as "a state within a state." Before the
Dutch East India Company was dissolved in 1799, Dutch imperial governance remained company governance. For much of the seventeenth
and eighteenth centuries, most Dutch colonies were primarily trading
settlements with only small populations of Dutch people, almost all of
whom were company agents or employees. Only gradually during the
eighteenth century did areas of principal focus, such as Java and Suri-
nam, cease to be primarily commercial enclaves and become territorial
entities. More concerned with pursuing the interests of shareholders
than with constructing a polity, company directors in Amsterdam endeavored to keep a monopoly of power in their own hands. Authority
devolved outward from the directors to a small group of appointed officials in each colony, the most important of whom was a director general,
who presumably exercised all power in the name of the company.[33]

Notwithstanding the autocratic nature of this system, colonial directors general or governors never had the resources required to make it
work the way it had been designed. They had neither the bureaucratic
personnel to prevent company employees from trading on the side nor,
in colonies with large settler populations such as New Netherland and
the Cape of Good Hope, the coercive power to prevent those populations
from scattering across the landscape and engaging in economic enterprises that sometimes competed with those of the company. Moreover,
to meet exigencies in settler colonies, governors often found themselves
forced to call together "groups of men elected by the populace" to solicit
advice and negotiate the terms for their support. Such ad hoc assemblies
were part of a broader pattern of consultation through which governors
and other company officials negotiated the support of prominent locals.
Indeed, in such settler colonies, local independent traders, burghers, and
farmers early demanded the basic rights and privileges associated with

---

[33]C. R. Boxer, *The Dutch Seaborne Empire, 1600–1800* (New York, 1970), 24, 103–4;
Oliver A. Rink, *Holland on the Hudson: An Economic and Social History of Dutch New
York* (Ithaca, N.Y., 1986), 96–98, 226–27; Langdon G. Wright, "Local Government and
Central Authority in New Netherland," *New-York Historical Society Quarterly* 57
(1973): 7–29.

traditional Dutch municipal government. Although governors invariably resisted such demands, they eventually, at least in New Netherland, had to give way and to grant charters that permitted communities "some measure of autonomy" with the "right to levy taxes and to apply the revenues to local purposes." By such concessions, even the authoritarian colonial regimes of the Dutch trading companies showed their recognition that imperial governance in the early modern era required the establishment of some sort of "balance between central authority and local autonomy."[34]

These brief remarks point to the need for a reconception of the nature of the extended imperial polities of the early modern era. They strongly suggest the utility of abandoning existing coercive models derived out of the experiences of later, modern empires and of developing new, less anachronistic models, perhaps compact models or even consensual models, that stress the peripheral as well as the central contributions to the negotiated authorities by which those polities seem to have been governed.

Any new model must be based on an awareness of the composite nature of the European states involved in the formation of those polities and of the systems of indirect rule that characterized those states. It must proceed from recognition that the establishment of private enclaves of settler authority often preceded metropolitan efforts to impose central control and that the process of colonization invariably involved the proliferation of such enclaves, even in those polities, such as the French, in which imperial centralization was most successful. A new model must acknowledge that fiscal resources were never sufficient, not even in the case of the Spanish, to support the bureaucratic, military, and naval machinery necessary to impose central authority from above without the consent or acquiescence of the dominant, self-empowered possessing classes in the peripheries. To obtain the consent or cooperation of those classes, metropolitan officials had little choice but to negotiate systems of authority with them. This bargaining process, so similar to that which characterized state formation within early modern Europe, produced varieties of indirect rule that at once set clear boundaries on central power, recognized the rights of localities to varying degrees of

---

[34] Boxer, *Dutch Seaborne Empire*, 242–67; Wright, "Local Government and Central Authority," 17, 27, 29.

self-government, and ensured that in normal circumstances metropolitan decisions affecting the peripheries would consult or respect local interests.

Infiltration of the agencies of colonial administration by members of colonial elites and the "naturalization" of officials sent from the center further enhanced the influence of the peripheries in imperial governance during the early modern era. So long as metropolitan officials abided by established systems of negotiated authority and respected the delicate balance between the central and peripheral interests and influences on which those systems were based, these processes of infiltration and naturalization could function to help hold extended polities together and even to bolster central authority within them. When, however, metropolitan officials violated those established systems of authority, as did both the British and the Spanish during the last half of the eighteenth century, they encountered the powerful resistance that between 1775 and 1825 tore those polities asunder and led to the creation of new independent states in the Americas.

This chapter is a revised version of a paper presented to the State Studies Focused Research Program, University of California, Irvine, May 15, 1992, and at a session on "Political Ideology" at the symposium "Lois Green Carr: The Chesapeake and Beyond—A Celebration," University of Maryland at College Park, May 22, 1992. Portions of it have since formed the basis for lectures at Kenyon College, Gambier, Ohio, on September 30, 1992, and the Hebrew University of Jerusalem, Israel, on January 25, 1993.

Two

The Colonial Origins of American Constitutionalism

W ITHIN THE ENGLISH-SPEAKING WORLD, the idea that English political society had a constitution seems to have only gradually
taken shape during the late Middle Ages and the early modern era. Even
as late as the American Revolution, English political and legal thinkers
had difficulty in defining precisely what the English constitution was,
and they used the term in an inclusive way to refer to several analytically
separable, if related, phenomena. The phrase *British constitution*, declared the political writer Robert Robinson in the early 1780s, was "expressive first of a natural constitution of rights native and inherent in all
the inhabitants of this kingdom and in all mankind—next a body of laws,
peculiar to this kingdom, declaratory of these natural rights—and lastly,
of a form of making and executing these laws."[1]

Of course, many of the most fundamental principles associated with
the idea of the English constitution were incorporated within various
great state papers, including especially Magna Charta (1215), the Petition of Right (1625), and the Declaration of Rights (1689). But the constitution, according to emerging English conceptions, was never thought
of in modern, that is, *later* American, terms as a single inclusive written
document. Rather, it was conceived of as an accumulation of customary
practices, long-standing legal procedures and principles, and basic individual rights that had slowly taken shape over the centuries not just in
the courts and legislative chambers in the capital but also in the various

---

[1] Robert Robinson, *A Political Catechism* (London, 1784), 38, as quoted by John Phillip
Reid, *Constitutional History of the American Revolution* (Madison, Wis., 1986), 6.

administrative and judicial institutions in the local communities, an accumulation of concepts and practices, moreover, that expressed the fundamental rules by which the polity was "constituted" and on which it operated. These concepts and practices in turn depended for their authority upon their prescriptive character and their widespread acceptance by local populations as appropriate and just.

Basic to the emerging English idea of a constitution was the concept of *limitation.* In unlimited governments the will of the sovereign was absolute. By contrast, constitutional government was government in which the will of the sovereign as well as the scope of authority exercised by the basic political institutions responsible for carrying out the sovereign's commands were limited by the constitution. The most important constitutional limitations upon the power of the sovereign were the two principles of the rule of law and consent. According to the principle of the rule of law, all people, including the monarch, were equally subject to and protected by the laws of the realm and the basic processes and procedures those laws expressed. In turn, laws consisted of not merely legislative enactments but also the myriad judicial decisions and practices, again both national and local, that made up the English common law.

The principle of consent involved the idea that citizens could not be subjected to any laws or taxes not first approved by themselves through either long-standing acquiescence or the medium of their elected representatives in the House of Commons. Although it had long been claimed by the House of Commons as part of the "ancient constitution" of the realm, this principle, along with most of the other important constitutional rights of English citizens, was only finally secured after a long series of bitter constitutional struggles during the seventeenth century.

During the sixteenth century English monarchs had exercised extraordinary power, one historian having characterized the government of Henry VIII as a "royal dictatorship." During the first eight decades of the seventeenth century, Parliament had sought, with modest success, to diminish the relative authority of the crown by appeals to fundamental law and customary restraints on arbitrary power. From the early 1640s on, as Corinne C. Weston has shown, radical advocates of the expansion of parliamentary power had invoked the coordination principle in lawmaking in an effort to redefine "relationships between the king and the two houses of Parliament by elevating the two houses at the expense of the king." A "theory of shared legal sovereignty by which the two houses became the predominant partners in lawmaking," this doctrine held that sovereignty rested not in the king alone but in the king-in-Parliament.[2]

But the diminution of the king's power within England during the seventeenth century was relatively minor compared to that which took place in the wake of the Glorious Revolution of 1688. As a result of that revolution, the principle of coordination was enshrined as the new constitutional orthodoxy. As Jennifer Carter has observed, England now "had a monarch depending on a parliamentary title, and a constitution based on [parliamentary] law." The "two salient features of the post-Revolution constitution were, first, that however much it was disguised a parliamentary monarchy had replaced a divine right monarchy; and, secondly, that since 1689 the monarch had learned somehow to live with Parliament."

As Carter has emphasized, however, these developments were by no means a "foregone conclusion" at the time of the Glorious Revolution. Only gradually over the next half century did Parliament grow from what Edmund Burke called "a mere representative of the people, and a guardian of popular privileges for its own constituents . . . into a mighty sovereign," from a body which was not simply "a control on the crown on its own behalf" to one that, as Burke put it, "communicated a sort of strength to the royal authority." As several historians recently have pointed out, however, the "concept of a sovereign parliament" had not been "reasonably foreseeable in 1689," was largely "a development of the mid-eighteenth century," and was only just "hardening into an orthodoxy" during the 1760s on the eve of the American Revolution.[3]

Before the Glorious Revolution the English constitution had been very largely a customary constitution. That is, it was based mostly not

---

[2] A. F. M. Madden, "1066, 1776, and All That: The Relevance of English Medievel Experience of 'Empire' to Later Imperial Constitutional Issues," in J. E. Flint and G. Williams, eds., *Perspectives of Empire* (London, 1973), 24; Corinne C. Weston, "Coordination—A Radicalising Principle in Stuart Politics," in Margaret Jacob and James Jacob, eds., *The Origins of Anglo-American Radicalism* (London, 1984), 85–104.

[3] Jennifer Carter, "The Revolution and the Constitution," in Geoffrey Holmes, ed., *Britain after the Glorious Revolution, 1689–1715* (New York, 1969), 39–40, 47, 55; Edmund Burke, "Letter to the Sheriffs of Bristol," *The Works of Edmund Burke*, 16 vols. (London, 1826), 3:188; H. T. Dickinson, "The Eighteenth-Century Debate on the Sovereignty of Parliament," Royal Historical Society, *Transactions*, 5th ser., 26 (1976): 189; Barbara A. Black, "The Constitution of Empire: The Case for the Colonists," *University of Pennsylvania Law Review* 124 (1976): 1210–11; H. T. Dickinson, "The Eighteenth-Century Debate on the 'Glorious Revolution,'" *History* 61 (1976): 33, 39.

upon codified statutes or other written documents but upon custom—unwritten but widely accepted law—and the slow accretion of precedents favorable to the rights of the citizenry. During the half century following the Glorious Revolution, however, people began to think of Parliament's role within the English polity as omnipotent, and the British constitution came to be seen—within Britain—as virtually identical with Parliament itself. As a result, parliamentary statutes gradually thereafter came to be thought of as taking precedence over custom and precedent, and the constitution became in essence whatever Parliament said it was. This was the prevailing conception of the British constitution within Great Britain at the time of the American Revolution.

How these great constitutional changes within Britain affected Britain's overseas possessions in Ireland and America was never explicitly worked out before the American Revolution. Indeed, from the beginnings of English colonization in the early seventeenth century, there was considerable confusion over precisely what the constitutional status of the colonies was. By the early seventeenth century, the English had had extensive experience in dealing with areas that, though parts of the monarch's dominions, did not come within the realm of England. These included several French possessions, which by 1600 had long since passed out of the monarch's control, the Channel Islands of Guernsey and Jersey, Wales, Ireland, and the Isle of Man.

Most of the dominions of this medieval empire had come to the monarchy through inheritance, but two—Wales and Ireland—had been acquired by conquest. Each was adjacent to or reasonably close to England, well-peopled with non-English inhabitants, and possessed of its own peculiar socioeconomic, legal, and political traditions that differed from and were to varying extents independent of those of England. Of them all, only Wales had been fully incorporated into the realm of England and then not until 1536. The rest were a series of small satellite states bound together by their mutual connection with the monarchy and its advisers either in the conciliar Parliaments of the Middle Ages or in the Privy Council under the Tudors. With the accession of James I in 1603, Scotland came into this loose association of political entities, although before the Act of Union in 1707 it was explicitly and formally independent of the realm—as opposed to the monarchy—of England.[4]

The American colonies differed from these old dominions in many re-

---

[4] The best discussion of England's medieval empire and the relationship among its various parts is Madden, "1066, 1776, and All That," 9–16. On the Welsh experience, see B. E. Howells, "Society in Early Modern Wales," in Stale Dyrvik, Knut Mykland, and

spects. First, they were three thousand miles away. Second, although all but one or two island colonies had significant native populations at the time of initial settlement, population density was low relative to the most fully occupied areas of Europe; much of the land was uncultivated and therefore according to contemporary European theory "waste" and available for colonization; and the natives were both pagan and, the English thought, culturally less advanced than most Europeans. Showing very little interest in absorbing the natives, the English preferred to displace them through physical expulsion, purchase of their land, or both. Thus, unlike the monarch's dominions on the eastern side of the Atlantic, those in America to an important degree were composed of emigrants from the British Isles and their descendants, new settler populations in places from which the old populations had been or soon would be almost entirely removed. The very newness of these new societies—the absence of long-settled traditions, institutions, and patterns of social relations—constituted still a third important distinction between them and the various components of the English monarchy's medieval empire.

The new plantations of English and Scots established in Ireland under the first two Stuarts were in several respects similar to the American colonies. But they differed in two important ways. First, they were established on territories conquered from a people that was numerous, Christian, and, by European standards, civilized. Second, the English and Scottish immigrants and their increase became a majority only in a few localities and thus had to live in the midst of a numerically superior and often hostile native population.[5] To be sure, a few of the American colonies had, like Ireland, also been conquered. Previously settled by colonists from rival European societies, Jamaica had been wrested from the Spanish in 1655, New York from the Dutch in 1664, and Nova Scotia and half of St. Christopher from the French in 1713. Except in Jamaica, from which all of the Spanish settlers fled following the English conquest, many of the old inhabitants of these colonies chose to remain un-

---

Jan Oldervoll, eds., *The Satellite State in the 17th and 18th Centuries* (Bergen, Norway, 1979), 80–98.

[5] On the Elizabethan and Jacobean plantations in Ireland, see a series of articles by Nicholas Canny: "The Ideology of English Colonization: From Ireland to America," *William and Mary Quarterly*, 3d ser., 30 (1973): 575–98; "Dominant Minorities: English Settlers in Ireland and Virginia, 1550–1650," in A. C. Hepburn, ed., *Minorities in History* (London, 1978), 51–69; and "The Permissive Frontier: The Problem of Social Control in English Settlements in Ireland and Virginia, 1550–1650," in K. R. Andrews, N. P. Canny, and P. E. H. Hair, eds., *The Westward Enterprise: English Activities in Ireland, the Atlantic, and America, 1480–1650* (Detroit, 1979), 17–44.

der English governance. In contrast to the situation in Ireland, however, incoming immigrants from the British Isles quickly became a majority and eventually established their political and cultural predominance over the earlier inhabitants.

If the American colonies differed in many ways from the monarch's more ancient dominions in the British Isles and Europe, they were also somewhat different from most other colonies with which contemporaries were familiar. Colonization had, of course, been a familiar phenomenon in antiquity. As early modern Europeans understood these early colonies, those of Greece had been autonomous settlements in previously unoccupied lands by surplus population from Greece itself, and those of the Roman, as an eighteenth-century commentator remarked, had been "planted among vanquished nations to over-awe, and hold them in subjection."[6] The plantation in Ireland bore some strong resemblance to the Roman prototype, as, many English people believed, did the contemporary Spanish colonies in Mexico and Peru. Similarly, some of the Anglo-American colonies were initially conceived and at least to some extent actually functioned for a time much like the garrison settlements on the English frontiers and in Ireland.[7]

But observers early recognized that the colonies in America were unlike either of these ancient models. Unlike the Greeks, they did not have de jure autonomy; unlike the Romans, they were not primarily concerned with "keep[ing] conquered Countries in Subjection." Rather, like most of the early modern European colonies in America, they were groups of people who, with the authorization of the monarch, settled in vacant or lightly occupied places for the specific purposes of cultivating the land and promoting trade "for the good of themselves and that [of the] state they belong[ed] to." Thus "intended to increase the Wealth and

---

[6] See among many similar characterizations of Greek and Roman colonization, Samuel Estwick, *A Letter to the Reverend Josiah Tucker, D.D. . . .* (London, 1776), 92–93. The most extensive contemporary analysis of the bearing of the colonial experience in antiquity upon that of the early modern British is by James Abercromby, a Scottish lawyer and member of Parliament. See Jack P. Greene, Charles F. Mullett, and Edward C. Papenfuse, Jr., eds., *"Magna Carta for America": James Abercromby's "An Examination of the Acts of Parliament Relative to the Trade and the Government of Our American Colonies" (1752) and "De Jure et Gubernatione Coloniarum, or An Inquiry into the Nature, and the Rights of Colonies, Ancient and Modern" (1774)* (Philadelphia, 1986).

[7] See Stephen Saunders Webb, *The Governors-General: The English Army and the Definition of Empire, 1569–1681* (Chapel Hill, N.C., 1979), which provides an extended discussion of the ways metropolitan experience with garrison government affected English official thought about the colonies.

Power of the[ir] native Kingdom," these "Colonies of Commerce," people gradually came to perceive, were an entirely "new species of colonizing, of modern date, and differing essentially from every other species of colonizing that is known."[8]

There is some evidence that in the early days of colonization metropolitan officials hoped that the colonies eventually might be incorporated into the realm of England in the manner of Wales.[9] But they soon recognized that distance made such a goal unfeasible with the result that the American colonies, like the monarchy's older non-English territories, soon came to be thought of not as "Part of the Realm of England" but as "Separate and Distinct Dominions." In this conception each colony was thus a separate corporate entity, a body politic authorized by the crown, with jurisdiction over a well-defined territory and its own distinctive institutions, laws, customs, and, eventually, history and identity — all of which reflected its peculiar "Circumstances . . . in respect of its Soil, Situation, Inhabitants, and Commerce."[10]

Separateness did not, of course, mean independence. The colonies might indeed be "distinct . . . dominions" and not actually part of the English realm. Nevertheless, virtually all English officials agreed that they were also "dependent . . . dominions." They were much less certain about the further constitutional questions of in what ways and to what extent the colonies were dependent and how much autonomy or independence such dependent institutions might enjoy.[11]

The basic objectives of the English in establishing colonies dictated

---

[8] John Trenchard and Thomas Gordon, *Cato's Letters,* 4 vols. (London, 1724), 3:282–84; William Douglass, *Summary, Historical and Political, of the First Planting, Progressive Improvements, and Present State of the British Settlements in North-America,* 2 vols. (Boston, 1749–51), 1:205–7; Malachy Postlethwayt, *The Universal Dictionary of Trade and Commerce,* 2 vols. (London, 1757), 2:471; Estwick, *Letter to Josiah Tucker,* 92–93; and Anthony Stokes, *A View of the Constitution of the British Colonies* (London, 1783), 1–3, all contain contemporary discussion of the nature of colonies. An interesting short modern analysis is M. I. Finley, "Colonies—An Attempt at a Typology," Royal Historical Society, *Transactions,* 5th ser., 26 (1976): 167–88.

[9] W. L. Grant and J. Munro, eds., *Acts of the Privy Council of England, Colonial Series,* 6 vols. (London, 1908–12), 1:49. For the confusion over whether the colonies were "foreign" or "home," see the description of the House of Commons debate over whether Sir George Somers, admiral of the fleet that sailed for Virginia in May 1609, should lose his seat in Parliament for having left the realm in Wilcomb E. Washburn, "Law and Authority in Colonial Virginia," in George A. Billias, ed., *Law and Authority in Colonial America* (Barre, Mass., 1965), 121.

[10] William Smith, *Mr. Smith's Opinion Humbly Offered to the General Assembly of the Colony of New-York* [New York, 1734], 17; James Knight, "The Natural, Moral, and Politi-

that these questions would not be easily resolved. The American colonies were "first planted on *Commercial Views*" with trade and profit as "their first principle." To obtain these goals at minimal costs to itself and the nation, the monarchy encouraged private adventurers—either organized into chartered companies or acting as lords proprietors—to sponsor colonies by granting them exclusive title to vast areas of land and "sundrie verie large immunities and privledges," including extensive self-governing powers and, in many cases, special economic concessions. Such arrangements were similar to those earlier used in the expansion of England into the Celtic fringe, where the monarchy had granted local magnates in places such as Chester and Durham a large measure of autonomy in return for their continuing fealty. Lacking the fiscal resources to enable them to undertake such territorial expansion on their own, English monarchs had no other means by which to establish the legitimacy of their claims to both new territories and the allegiance of the inhabitants of those territories.[12]

But the colonies differed from English border areas in three important respects. First, they were far more distant. Second, they did not have settled native populations that could be easily mobilized to achieve the objectives of the colonizers. Third, the new, predominantly English settlers brought with them English traditions of law and governance, which put a high premium upon individual and local corporate liberties and autonomy, especially upon the traditional English constitutional principles of limited government and consent. Tudor England, as Kenneth R. Andrews has remarked, was "a largely self-governing society—under the crown," and the "increase in governance" through the establishment of many "new local institutions that tied the counties [more closely] to the center" during the century following the accession of Elizabeth I does not seem to have seriously dampened "the fierce, full-hearted localism" that both supported and encouraged those local self-governing tendencies.

One important consequence of this deeply etched "characteristic of

---

cal History of Jamaica, and the Territories Thereon Depending," 2:112, in Long Papers, Additional Manuscripts 12419, British Library, London; Jeremiah Dummer, *A Defence of the New-England Charters* (London, 1726), 56; John Vaughan, *The Reports and Arguments of the Learned Judge Sir John Vaughan* (London, 1677), 401–2; Opinion of Henley and Yorke, May 18, 1757, in George Chalmers, ed., *Opinions of Eminent Lawyers* (Burlington, Vt., 1858), 209.

[11] Stokes, *View of the Constitution*, 12.

[12] *Acts of the Privy Council, Colonial* 1:48–49; "The Watchman, Letter IV," *Pennsylvania Journal and Weekly Advertiser* (Philadelphia), Apr. 27, 1758; Michael Hechter, *Internal*

early modern English society" was what Andrews refers to as a powerful "tendency towards self-government in the emergent empire." At the same time that the sponsors of the several colonial enterprises invariably proved to be both "particularly jealous of" their "autonomy and resistant to royal interference," they found that they could not recruit settlers for such distant and unfamiliar areas in numbers sufficient to meet their objectives without generous guarantees of self-governing rights and concessions in the form of access to land and, occasionally, temporary exemption from taxation and other public obligations.[13]

Mostly settled contemporaneously with the great constitutional struggles of the seventeenth century, England's colonies in Ireland and America thus inherited the seventeenth-century English constitutional traditions of limited government, consent, and local control. Accordingly, long before John Locke's elegant formulation of the theory of emigration in his *Two Treatises on Government,* colonial leaders had developed the view that English people had a right to migrate to a new country, to take their constitutional rights as Englishmen with them into the new political entities they founded overseas, and to establish local institutions and adopt local customs to secure those rights to themselves and their posterity.

From the colonists' point of view, the crown seemed to have recognized the legitimacy of this theory by granting them royal charters that not only empowered them to establish governments over a specific territory but also confirmed their entitlement to all the traditional rights, privileges, and immunities of Englishmen. In the few cases in which groups of people settled without such a charter—the Plymouth colony being the earliest example—the settlers themselves often adopted written "plantation covenants" in which they pledged their mutual cooperation in establishing a government modeled along the lines of the one they had left behind in old England.

American constitutional historians have emphasized the centrality of these charters and covenants in early American constitutional development and have traced the beginnings of the subsequent American attachment to written constitutions to them. But the early settlers seem never

---

Colonialism: The Celtic Fringe in British National Development, 1536–1936 (Berkeley and Los Angeles, 1975), 62–63.

[13] Kenneth R. Andrews, *Trade, Plunder, and Settlement: Maritime Enterprise and the Genesis of the British Empire, 1480–1630* (Cambridge, Eng., 1984), 16–17; Mark A. Kishlansky, "Community and Continuity: A Review of Selected Works on English Local History," *William and Mary Quarterly*, 3d ser., 37 (1980): 140, 146.

to have thought of their colonial constitutions as being wholly or even principally contained within these documents. Rather, they regarded the charters not as the principal component of their several constitutions but, as in the case of Magna Charta itself, as mere legal confirmations by the English crown of their entitlement to rights they already possessed by virtue of their birthright as English people. In any case, the crown subsequently revoked, withdrew, purchased, or amended the charters of most of the colonies. By 1750 the only colonies that still had charters were Maryland, Connecticut, Rhode Island, Pennsylvania, and Massachusetts. Indeed, like the English constitution before the Glorious Revolution, the several colonial constitutions were, from the start, primarily unwritten customary constitutions that developed slowly over time through a series of precedents that functioned to protect and extend the colonists' inherited rights as Englishmen.

Notwithstanding the provisions in the early charters, English officials were never willing to admit in their fullest extent the colonists' claims to enjoy all the rights of the English constitution. For that reason, the exact nature of those constitutions rapidly became the main point of contention between crown and colonies in much the same way that the nature of the English constitution had been at the heart of the struggles between crown and Parliament in seventeenth-century England. The many contests that everywhere developed over this issue revolved around two principal questions: whether the colonists were entitled to all the benefits of the laws of England, and whether the representative assemblies that were established early in the history of every colony to make laws for the local populations enjoyed the same status in the colonial constitutions as the House of Commons did in the English constitution.

Crown officials never accepted the colonists' demands for explicit statutory guarantees of their rights to the benefits of English laws. Nevertheless, through the extensive use of English legal precedents and statutes by colonial judges, the colonists seem eventually to have managed to secure those benefits through custom, usage, and practice. Most of the empirical research necessary to nail down this point and to show fully the precise extent and character of the transfer of English law to the colonies remains to be done. Nevertheless, the diminution of demands for explicit guarantees of English laws in the colonies during the first three decades of the eighteenth century strongly suggests that provincial and local courts had by that time effectively established the customary rights of the colonists in this broad area.

In much the same way, the colonial assemblies succeeded in establishing their strident and often reiterated claims to constitutional authority within their respective jurisdictions equivalent to that of the House of Commons in Britain. Although crown officials consistently recognized the assemblies' authority to pass laws, they always insisted that they were subordinate institutions much like the governing bodies of English corporations and without the full rights and privileges of the English Parliament. Because they controlled the power of the purse, however, and because the crown's colonial governors found it impossible to govern effectively without their consent, the colonial assemblies slowly managed to obtain in practice the authority that crown officials denied them in theory.

Like the English House of Commons had itself done during the seventeenth century, the colonial assemblies by the middle of the eighteenth century had thus managed through precedent and custom to establish their authority and status as local parliaments, as the most important institutions in the colonial constitutions and the primary guardians of the colonists' inherited rights as Englishmen, including especially the right not to be subjected to any taxes or laws relating to their internal affairs without the consent of their representatives in assembly.

Custom carried enormous authority within the British constitutional tradition. The British constitution was itself based as much upon custom as upon statutes. Both the common law and Parliament itself derived their authority from the force of custom. As J. G. A. Pocock has noted, however, with the rise of the doctrine of parliamentary supremacy during the seven or eight decades after the Glorious Revolution, "the concept of custom, and of English institutions as founded on custom," received less and less emphasis until it was revived by Edmund Burke during the last quarter of the eighteenth century. Yet, even in Britain, custom continued to be accorded considerable weight in the courts, in local legal and social relations, and in the works of some political and legal writers, including especially the Cambridge legal theorist Thomas Rutherforth. That the colonies had been settled long enough to claim their liberties and privileges by custom was denied by most British authorities. Yet from very early on, colonists had defended their rights to government by consent on the basis not just of English custom but of their own.[14]

---

[14] J. G. A. Pocock, *The Ancient Constitution and the Feudal Law: English Historical Thought in the Seventeenth Century* (New York, 1967), 30–38, 50–51, 170–78, 233–43; Thomas Rutherforth, *Institutes of Natural Law; Being the Substance of a Course of Lectures on Grotius' De Jure Belli ac Pacis*, 2 vols. (Cambridge, Eng., 1754–56).

At least at the provincial level, then, constitutional development within the colonies was thoroughly within the mainstream and largely merely an extension of English constitutional traditions of the seventeenth century. No less than their English counterparts, colonial legislators, lawyers, judges, and citizens displayed an obsessive concern with constitutional rights, including especially those associated with the principles of consent and due process, and their constitutions, like the seventeenth-century English constitution, were largely customary. Indeed, the broad similarities arising out of the common Englishness of their emerging constitutional traditions alone make it possible even to talk about a colonial—but not without anachronism an American colonial—constitutional tradition as well as specific Virginia, South Carolina, New York, or Jamaican constitutional traditions. Yet, specific provincial circumstances, experiences, and traditions made possible manifold and important variations among the several constitutions of individual provinces in the early modern colonial world. Indeed, the very range of these variations has made it very difficult for constitutional historians to discover a general colonial constitutional tradition which can be easily related to later American national constitutional history.

In recent years there has been a growing trend for scholars to suggest that in resisting parliamentary authority during the 1760s and 1770s, the American colonists were "reject[ing] the results of" the Glorious Revolution and placing themselves outside of the British constitutional tradition. But there are major difficulties with this argument. The ascendancy of Parliament within Britain and the eventual triumph of the doctrine of parliamentary omnipotence during the mid-eighteenth century may have been the most important results of the revolution, but they were by no means the only ones. Within Britain, as Jennifer Carter has pointed out, another consequence of the revolution was "a distinct, though not complete, withdrawal of central authority from local affairs."

Earlier in the seventeenth century Charles I had undertaken an extensive effort to exert the authority of the central government over county and local affairs in both the civil and the religious realms, and although this effort was interrupted during the Civil War, the later Stuarts resumed it after the Restoration. "Perhaps nothing done in the 1680s by Charles II and James II," Carter has noted, "caused so much reaction against them as their interference with local privilege and the accustomed pattern of existing hierarchies—in counties, in corporations, or in university colleges." At least in the short run, the revolution effectively put an end to this effort and thereby created the conditions necessary for "the typical eighteenth-century situation of gentry and aristocratic independence in the localities." Within Britain the localities, along with the people who dominated them, enjoyed much less interference from the central government than they had at any time under the Stuart monarchy. During the eighty years following the Glorious Revolution, Britain seems to have experienced a significant redistribution of power to the localities, as English, Welsh, and (after 1707) Scottish counties became what Edward Shils has referred to as "pockets of approximate independence."[15]

The preoccupation of historians with the rise of Parliament and the establishment of a constitution of parliamentary supremacy in the wake of the Glorious Revolution has thus drawn attention away from the important extent to which the Glorious Revolution also represented a reassertion of the authority of local magistracies, whose pervasive jurisdiction over many of the constitutive elements of the English polity had never been stronger than it was during the eighteenth century. Notwithstanding the alleged supremacy of Parliament in the eighteenth-century British constitution, these local magistracies, historians are coming increasingly to realize, continued to exert widespread authority over a large range of constitutional matters, including especially issues concerning due process of law, while the foundations of that authority continued, like the basis of the authority of Parliament itself before the Glorious Revolution, to be to a significant degree based upon custom, usage, and prescription as sanctioned by local consent and enforced by a broad group of citizens who, serving as jurors and administrative and judicial officials, gave English local government a participatory character which often astonished foreign observers.

The same development was evident in Britain's more distant peripheries in Ireland and America. As each of these overseas entities developed its own peculiarly local constitutional tradition, the localities in each of them played a significant role in the creation and perpetuation of those

---

[15] Alison Gilbert Olson, "Parliament, Empire, and Parliamentary Law, 1776," in J. G. A. Pocock, ed., *Three British Revolutions: 1641, 1688, 1776* (Princeton, N.J., 1980), 289; Carter, "Revolution and the Constitution," 53, 56; T. H. Breen, *Puritans and Adventurers: Change and Persistence in Early America* (New York, 1980), 4–24; Edward Shils, *Center and Periphery: Essays in Microsociology* (Chicago, 1975), 10. See also Norma Landau, *Justices of the Peace, 1679–1760* (Berkeley and Los Angeles, 1984), on the continuing independence of county elites in regard to the internal affairs of the counties, and E. P. Thompson, "The Grid of Inheritance: A Comment," in Jack Goody, Joan Thirsk, and E. P. Thompson, eds., *Family and Inheritance: Rural Society in Western Europe, 1200–1800* (Cambridge, Eng., 1976), 328–60, on the "tenacity and force of local custom" in determining patterns of social and legal relations in English local society.

traditions. Perhaps even to a greater extent than in contemporary Britain, the constitutional order in the several colonies was throughout the colonial period at once local, consensual, participatory, lay-directed, and customary. This diffusion and localization of authority ensured that, in contrast to contemporary Continental monarchies, Britain's expanding nation-state and overseas empire would not be founded on methods of centralization and absolutism.

In both Ireland and the American colonies, the growth of parliamentary power during the eighteenth century epitomized this development. Before the Glorious Revolution the Irish Parliament had convened only rarely. Beginning in 1692, it both met regularly and developed a vigorous "spirit of independence."[16] The same happened in the American colonies. Hence, in terms of the constitutional development of the British Empire as a whole, perhaps the most important results of the Glorious Revolution over the following eighty years were the localization of authority and the growth of parliamentary institutions, not just within Britain itself but throughout the overseas British Empire. Just as the growth of parliamentary power after 1689 had changed the constitution of Britain in fundamental ways, so also had similar developments in Ireland and the colonies altered the constitutions there.

Throughout the British Empire, constitutions were basically customary. That is, they were all the products of evolving usage. By the early 1760s the unformulated and unasked question was whether in the process of changing the constitutions of their respective political jurisdictions, the several legislatures and judicial systems of the empire were also changing the constitution of the whole to which they all belonged. Without as yet having formulated a coherent and fully articulated sense of empire, the British political nation had not, before the 1760s, developed any explicit sense of an imperial constitution. Indeed, the tendency within Britain was to conflate the British constitution with the imperial constitution. Yet the absence of the concept did not mean that an imperial constitution did not exist or was not being slowly formed through the same evolutionary process that was shaping and reshaping the constitutions of the several entities that composed the British Empire.

As Burke would subsequently remark, during the eighteenth century an imperial constitution had gradually emerged out of "mere neglect; possibly from the natural operation of things, which, left to themselves, generally fall into their proper order." In this constitution, as Andrew C.

---

[16] J. C. Beckett, "The Irish Parliament in the Eighteenth Century," Belfast National History and Philosophical Society, *Proceedings*, 2d ser., 4 (1955): 18–20.

McLaughlin, the doyen of American constitutional historians, pointed out half a century ago, the metropolitan government exercised general powers and the Irish and American colonial governments exerted de facto and virtually exclusive jurisdiction over all matters of purely local concern.[17]

According to the practice of the extended polity of the British Empire as it had developed during the three-quarters of a century following the Glorious Revolution, there were thus three separate kinds of constitutions. First, there was a British constitution for the central state and its immediate dependencies, including Cornwall, Wales, and, after 1707, Scotland. Second, there were separate provincial constitutions for Ireland and for each of the colonies in America. Third, there was an as yet undefined, even unacknowledged, imperial constitution—the constitution of the British Empire—according to the practice of which authority was distributed in an as yet uncodified and not very clearly understood way between the center and the peripheries, with Parliament exercising power over general concerns and the local legislatures handling local affairs within their respective jurisdictions.

That the American colonists would not readily subscribe to the emerging British doctrine of parliamentary omnipotence could easily be surmised from the thrust of their own constitutional development between 1660 and 1760. Their view of the constitution was developmental in the sense that they saw their own constitutions and, by implication, the constitution of the empire as moving in the same direction as had the British constitution in the wake of the Glorious Revolution: that is, toward increasing limitations upon prerogative power and greater security for individual and corporate rights under the protection of a strong legislature. According to this view, further gains in the direction of still greater limitations and security could still be achieved, but those already made could not—constitutionally—be lost. From this perpective, any effort to impose the principle of unlimited parliamentary authority upon the colonies was bound to appear to the colonists as retrogressive and unacceptable. Because they had for so long exercised exclusive jurisdiction over their own internal affairs, while the British Parliament had limited its interference in colonial matters to regulating trade and other aspects

---

[17] John Phillip Reid, "In Accordance with Usage: The Authority of Custom, the Stamp Act Debate, and the Coming of the American Revolution," *Fordham Law Review* 45 (1976): 341; Richard Koebner, *Empire* (Cambridge, 1961), 61–193; Burke, "Letter to the Sheriffs of Bristol," *Works* 3:190; Andrew C. McLaughlin, *The Foundations of American Constitutionalism* (New York, 1932), 138.

of the external economic life of the colonies and the general welfare of the empire, the colonial legislatures thus protested vigorously that Parliament's effort to tax them for revenue by the Stamp Act in 1765 was a violation of their inherited and customary constitutional right not to be taxed except by their own local representatives.

For the next ten years the colonists engaged in a prolonged effort to wrest from British authorities explicit guarantees of these constitutional rights. They repeatedly pointed out that over the previous 150 years the British Empire had developed an unwritten customary constitution which was quite distinct from either the British constitution or the specific constitutions of the several colonies. According to this developing imperial constitution, they contended, the empire was organized in a federal way with legislative authority distributed among many local legislatures, with the British Parliament retaining unlimited jurisdiction only over matters of specific concern to Great Britain itself and general concern to the empire as a whole. They argued that these customary constitutional developments limited the authority of the British Parliament in the colonial sphere. In the colonists' view, Parliament was subordinate—and could not act contrary—to this unwritten imperial constitution.

But the widespread commitment in Britain to the emerging doctrine of parliamentary supremacy meant that few people there could consider the possibility that there might be any limitations upon parliamentary authority. The impasse over this question eventually in 1776 drove thirteen of the continental colonies to seek independence. Throughout the colonial period their constitutions had been composed almost entirely of uncodified and unratified custom and inheritance. Enormously frustrated between 1765 and 1775 by their inability to obtain any recognition from the British government of the validity and scope of these unwritten constitutions, they quickly moved beginning in 1776 to give their constitutions explicit and concrete form by writing them down. Two colonies, Connecticut and Rhode Island, simply adapted their colonial charters to this purpose. Between 1776 and 1781 each of the other eleven revolting colonies adopted new written constitutions. By the end of the War for Independence the tradition of written constitutions, a marked departure from both their English inheritance and their own earlier colonial experience, had been firmly established in American political life.

Contrary to the work of many recent historians, this analysis of constitutional development in Britain and America before the establishment of the American nation assumes that, far from being authoritative, pronouncements from the centers of early modern extended polities like the

British Empire acquired constitutional legitimacy for the whole only through implicit or explicit ratifications by the peripheries. Had Britain had the requisite coercive resources, which it did not, it presumably could have enforced the views of the center in all the peripheral areas of the empire. To have secured obedience through force, however, would have constituted an admission of the absence or breakdown of authority, which, as most contemporary political thinkers in the British-American world were acutely aware, was always a function of opinion.

In practice, then, political and constitutional arrangements within the extended polity of the early modern British Empire were founded upon the consent of its many constituent components. That is, local sanction from the peripheries was essential to endow any position of the center with constitutional authority—and vice versa. Constitutional customs and doctrines could emanate from either the center or the peripheries, but they could not attain full constitutional authority outside the area of emanation—or for the empire as a whole—until they had been accepted by all parties to which they might apply.

Both in its origins and in its results, the American Revolution provides a classic illustration of the truth of these observations. Between 1765 and 1775 the metropolis simply could not secure colonial consent to its emerging view of the constitutional structure of the empire without resorting to force, and when, after nearly eight years of war, its will and resources proved inadequate to that task, it had no alternative but to permit the former colonies to go their own independent ways. With this experience behind them, political leaders of the United States in the 1770s and 1780s automatically understood that no new center for the American Union could be constituted without the formal and explicit consent of the several entities that composed that union.

In conclusion, it might be said that the fixation of modern historians upon the concept of the nation as the most significant unit of historical discourse and their focus almost exclusively upon the national stage and the development and functioning of national institutions has not been entirely salutary, and one of the important results of the new appreciation of the local dimensions of constitutional development in eighteenth-century Britain has been to facilitate the emergence of a broader and richer conception of the nature and content of not just colonial but later American constitutional history. For there is no reason to suppose that the vigorous flow of these local streams of constitutional development was immediately stemmed in the United States by the superimposition of a national constitutional system during the final decades of the eighteenth century or that the local customary foundations of that development were immediately overthrown by the establishment of explicit written constitutions. What may be suspected is that more attention to the local context of constitutional development after the establishment of the American nation—with *local* being conceived of as applying both to states and to localities within states—will reveal significant continuities between prenational and postnational constitutional history that will greatly enrich our appreciation of the dimensions of that subject and thereby help us to identify more fully the relevance of colonial to national history.

The earliest version of this chapter was presented as a comment at a session on "The Origins of Southern Constitutionalism," at a conference on "The South and the American Constitutional Tradition," held at the College of Law, University of Florida, Gainesville, March 16, 1987. A revised version was given at a symposium on "Constitutional Roots, Rights and Responsibilities," at the Smithsonian Institution, Washington, D.C., May 20, 1987; at a seminar in the Department of Law, Hokkaido University, Sapporo, Japan, July 24, 1987; as a lecture at the University of Rhode Island, Kingston, September 16, 1987; as the Annual Harriett Elliott Lecture, University of North Carolina at Greensboro, February 3, 1988; at the Whig-Cliosophic Society, Princeton University, Princeton, New Jersey, February 15, 1988; at the American Legal History Seminar at the Law School, New York University, October 30, 1990; and at a session on "The American Revolution of the Eighteenth Century," at a conference on "New Approaches to the Study of American History," Institute of General History, USSR Academy of Sciences, Moscow, March 20, 1991. Under the title "The Customary Foundations of American Rights," a shortened version was presented at a "Public Policy Forum Celebrating the Bicentennial of the Bill of Rights," University of Tennessee-Chattanooga, February 25, 1991. It is here reprinted with permission of the publisher from A. E. Dick Howard, ed., *The United States Constitution: Roots, Rights, and Responsibilities* (Washington, D.C.: Smithsonian Institution, 1992), 23–42. Copyright Smithsonian Institution, 1992.

—THREE—

Metropolis and Colonies: *Changing Patterns of Constitutional Conflict in the Early Modern British Empire, 1607–1763*

"THE SETTLEMENT OF *our* COLONIES," Edmund Burke wrote in 1757, 150 years after the establishment of Jamestown, "was never pursued upon any regular plan; but they were formed, grew, and flourished, as accidents, the nature of the climate, or the dispositions of private men happened to operate." "Nothing of an enlarged and legislative spirit," he added, "appears in the planning of *our* colonies."[1] Burke's remarks accurately describe the process by which the English planted their colonies in America during the first three quarters of the seventeenth century. Undertaken almost entirely at their own expense by adventurers either singly or in proprietary or corporate groups, the colonies were not established according to any comprehensive design and during the early years received little direction and still less protection from the metropolitan government. Insofar as the colonies impinged upon metropolitan consciousness at all, English officials thought of them not as subordinate political communities, not as colonies of Englishmen organized into separate or auxiliary societies overseas, but rather as a series of economic units intended to contribute to the prosperity of England and to provide it with a solid claim to a portion of the vast riches of the New World.

Within the plantations, however, these broader purposes of colonization were submerged beneath a welter of personal and highly individual goals. To induce them to undertake so troublesome and expensive a work as the establishment of plantations, the crown gave the sponsors of the several colonial enterprises exclusive title to vast areas of land, extensive

---

[1] *An Account of the European Settlements in America,* 2 vols. (London, 1757), 2:288.

governing powers, and, in many cases, special economic privileges. The sponsors in turn found it necessary to make generous concessions in the form of access to land, guarantees of self-governing rights, and, occasionally, temporary exemption from taxation to recruit settlers. Thus, on both levels—between the crown and the sponsors on one hand and between the sponsors and individual colonists on the other—the English colonizing process depended initially upon contractual arrangements. These assured the sponsors and the individual colonists a generous amount of political freedom and the widest possible latitude to pursue their own personal objectives, with a minimum of reciprocal obligations either to the various governing agencies within the colonies or to the metropolitan government at home.

The result was the accentuation and acceleration of certain tendencies already present in English social and economic life. Already well on its way to becoming what C. B. MacPherson has recently and appropriately termed a "possessive market society," English society in the early seventeenth century was organized around and operated on a series of assumptions that MacPherson has called "possessive individualism." Among these assumptions, three were so extraordinarily congenial to conditions of settlement in the English colonies that they quickly came to govern in practice, if not in theory, most social relationships within the colonies and to determine the attitudes of the colonists toward the role of the home government in their affairs. The first of these assumptions was that all men are free from dependence upon the wills of others; the second, that freedom from dependence on others meant freedom from any relationships with others not entered into voluntarily by an individual with a view to his own interest; and the third, that the function of government was to protect the individual's property in his person and goods and to maintain orderly relations of exchange between the various individuals in society so that each could pursue his own interest.[2] Everywhere, even in colonies like Massachusetts Bay, where it was ostensibly subordinated to broader social and religious goals, individual enterprise was the dominant note. The beliefs that every individual should be free to seek his own interest and that both the crown and the governments of the individual plantations were obligated by contract to protect him in that search were integral to English colonial life.

Before 1660 the metropolitan government made no sustained attempt to subordinate this individual enterprise to its own broader purposes, to

---

[2]C. B. MacPherson, *The Political Theory of Possessive Individualism* (Oxford, 1962), esp. 263–71.

counteract the centrifugal forces inherent in the conditions of settlement. When the crown assumed control over Virginia in 1625 after the courts had vacated the charter of the Virginia Company, it asserted its jurisdiction over all the English plantations in America and declared its intention to provide "one uniforme Course of Government" for them all.[3] In developing an effective administration for Virginia, metropolitan officials did indeed work out an institutional framework for the internal administration of the colonies. They also articulated a series of policy objectives that explicitly asserted the right of the home government to regulate in its own interests all aspects of the internal government of the colonies. But the failure to develop any central agency in England for colonial administration, the distractions of the Civil War, the refusal of the colonists to abide by regulations they opposed, and the lack of adequate enforcement machinery prevented either crown or Parliament from establishing effective controls over the colonies, despite sporadic attempts by one or the other to do so.

As the colonies increased in extent and population through the middle decades of the seventeenth century, however, and as their value both as sources of raw materials and as markets for English manufactures became more apparent, English commercial and political leaders alike began to fear lest the benefits of such valuable possessions be lost in the colonists' reckless pursuit of their several corporate and individual interests, lest they enter into destructive economic competition with each other or with England. They feared that the colonists might even take advantage of their extensive political privileges to set themselves up as autonomous polities or semi-independent allies of the Dutch, who had already successfully engrossed a large part of their carrying trade during the early years of the English Civil War. In response to these several fears Parliament enacted the system of commercial regulations known as the Navigation Acts between 1650 and 1673. The first comprehensive attempt to define the economic relationship between England and the colonies, these measures gave expression to the mercantilist assumption that the economic interests of the colonies should be subordinated to those of the mother country. They also theoretically established a na-

---

[3] "A Proclamation for Settlinge the Plantations of Virginia," May 13, 1625, in Thomas Rymer, ed., *Foedera, Conventiones, Literal, Acta Publica, Regis Anglicae*, 2d ed., 20 vols. (London, 1726), 18:72–73.

tional monopoly of colonial trade and served as the basis for metropolitan economic policy toward the colonies for the remainder of the colonial period.

Although the Navigation Acts contained significant concessions to colonial interests, they proved exceedingly difficult to enforce, especially in the private colonies. The extensive powers conferred by the royal charters on the proprietors and governing corporations of those colonies made it possible for them to disregard and, in many cases, openly to flout the acts. When Edward Randolph, sent by metropolitan authorities in 1676 to investigate conditions in Massachusetts Bay, insisted that its leaders enforce the Navigation Acts, he was told that "laws made by your Majesty and your Parliament obligeth" Massachusetts residents "in nothing but what consists with the interests of that colony; that the legislative power is and abides in them solely to act and make laws by virtue" of their royal charter.[4] A simultaneous effort to persuade the colonies to remodel their political systems in such a way as to make them correspond as closely as possible to the English system was only somewhat more successful, encountering especially strenuous opposition in Massachusetts Bay.[5]

Reinforced by the pronounced tendency of both Charles II and James II to regard the colonies not simply as units for economic production but also, in the words of A. P. Thornton, as "adjuncts of the royal power, jewels in His Majesty's Crown,"[6] the realization grew among metropolitan authorities that the movement for strict economic control and political uniformity would have to be accompanied by closer supervision in England if the Navigation Acts and the royal authority were ever to be fully obeyed in the private colonies. During the half century after 1675, this realization resulted in a sporadic attempt to reconstruct the political relationship between England and the colonies by substituting for the traditional contractual arrangement in which both colonists and crown had been bound by certain mutual obligations set down in the charters a

---

[4] As quoted by A. Berriedale Keith, *Constitutional History of the First British Empire* (Oxford, 1930), 104–5.

[5] The most important attempt was by the Royal Commission of 1664–66 charged with capturing New Netherlands from the Dutch and regulating the affairs of the New England colonies. Its success in both conquering and pacifying the New Netherlands and securing considerable cooperation from Connecticut and Rhode Island contrasted markedly with its failure in Massachusetts, where colonial leaders obstructed the commission in every way possible.

[6] A. P. Thornton, *West-India Policy under the Restoration* (Oxford, 1956), 18.

new relationship in which the authority of the crown would be unlimited and preeminent, if also benign and just. This movement proceeded in two phases, the first phase lasting from the mid-1670s until the Glorious Revolution of 1688, and the second from the establishment of new commercial regulations and new agencies of administration in 1696 until the early 1720s, when, under the long ministry of Sir Robert Walpole, metropolitan officials adopted a more casual attitude toward the colonies.

The first phase began with the creation in 1675 of the Lords of Trade, a permanent committee of the Privy Council responsible for overseeing the colonies. For ten years, until it lost its power to the Privy Council under James II, this body, assisted by a permanent staff and a flock of new crown officers in the colonies, provided, for the first time since the beginning of English colonization nearly three quarters of a century earlier, vigorous and systematic supervision. In a concerted effort to secure colonial obedience to royal authority and the Navigation Acts, the Lords developed a comprehensive program which may be divided into three parts. The first part was simply to strengthen the crown's hand in the four existing royal colonies: Virginia; Jamaica, which had been captured from the Spanish during the Interregnum; and Barbados and the Leeward Islands, which had passed from proprietary to royal control in 1663. In pursuit of this objective, the Lords sought to bring the royal governors themselves under closer supervision. Not only did it insist upon more frequent and fuller reports from all governors, but it also placed the governors under much more detailed and rigid regulations than ever before by greatly expanding both in scope and specificity the royal instructions given to governors to direct them in the conduct of their administrations.

Equally important in trying to establish effective metropolitan control over the royal colonies were the Lords' efforts to curtail the extensive powers of the elected legislative assemblies, the bastions of colonial opposition to metropolitan policy. Derived in large part from the dependence of the governors upon the assemblies for money, both for their own personal support and for all normal expenses of government, the power of the assemblies extended over virtually every aspect of colonial government. The assumption of such full and complete legislative authority had already led colonial legislators to the heady conclusion that each assembly was the "epitome of the [English] House of Commons."[7] To render royal governors less dependent upon the assemblies, the Lords of

---

[7]The quotation is from Agnes M. Whitson, *The Constitutional Development of Jamaica, 1660 to 1729* (Manchester, Eng., 1929), 162.

Trade sought to persuade the assemblies of Virginia and Jamaica to follow the example of the legislatures of Barbados and Leeward Islands.
These, in 1663 and 1664, respectively, had voted a permanent revenue
from which the salaries of the governor and other royal officials as well
as many other ordinary expenses of government were drawn. The campaign, which was successful in Virginia and unsuccessful in Jamaica, was
accompanied by a direct assault upon the legislative powers of the assemblies, in which the Lords not only attempted unsuccessfully to apply
Poynings' Law—which required the crown's prior approval of all laws
passed by the Irish Parliament—to Jamaica and Virginia but also ruled
that the assemblies existed only by the favor of the crown and not as a
matter of right, as the assemblies claimed.

The second part of the Lords' program was to prevent the creation of
any more private colonies and to convert those already in existence into
royal colonies. Upon its recommendation, the New Hampshire towns
were separated from Massachusetts Bay in 1679 and made a royal colony. Although the Lords was unable to block the grant of Pennsylvania
to William Penn in 1681, it did secure the insertion in the Pennsylvania
charter of a series of limitations and restrictions that subjected Penn to
much stricter controls than any of his predecessors. Beginning in 1684,
the Lords also engineered the general assault upon the charters of the
private colonies in the courts that resulted in the forfeiture of the charter
of Massachusetts Bay.

The third part of the program, a logical extension of the previous two,
was the consolidation of the colonies into three general governments,
presided over by vice-regal representatives and unhampered by representative assemblies. This objective—evidently inspired at least in part
by Colbert's reforms in the French colonial system—was in the air as
early as 1678. In 1686, after the accession of James II, who shared with
the Lords of Trade an antipathy to private colonies and colonial representative institutions, it led to the establishment of the Dominion of
New England, intended to include all of the colonies from Maine south
to Pennsylvania.

The second phase in the metropolitan attempt to reconstruct the political relationship between England and the colonies and to strengthen
the navigation system was inaugurated in 1696 with two related developments. First was the passage of a new navigation act to provide for
stricter enforcement of the old measures and to declare null and void all
colonial laws violating any of the Navigation Acts. Second was the creation of the Board of Trade to take over the chores formerly handled
by the then defunct Lords of Trade. For some time after the Glorious

Revolution of 1688–89 metropolitan officials acted as if they might adopt a more permissive policy toward the colonies. Neither the new king, William III, nor his advisers showed any disposition to revive the Dominion of New England, which had been overthrown by the New Englanders in the wake of the revolution, or to govern without representative assemblies. In 1691 they granted a new charter to Massachusetts Bay, albeit one embodying severe limitations upon the colony's self-governing powers. In 1694 they restored Pennsylvania, which had been taken over by the crown in 1692, to William Penn.

But it soon became clear after 1696 that the new Board of Trade would pursue policies that bore a remarkable resemblance to those of its predecessor. Established in the midst of the first of the four major intercolonial wars between England and the Latin powers between 1689 and 1763, it was beseiged during its first months with complaints from royal officials and private individuals in the continental colonies about the failure of the colonies to unite in common defense against the French and Indians. The cause of the difficulty, the complainants agreed, was "the number and independency of so many small governments" which by "reason of their several interests" regarded each other "in a manner . . . as foreigners, so that, whatsoever mischiefs happen in one part the rest . . . remain unconcerned."[8]

Reprehensible enough in peacetime, such patent parochialism could be disastrous in the face of a unified enemy. Because experience seemed to indicate, as the board declared in one of its first major reports, that the colonies "in their present state" would "always . . . refuse each other mutual assistance, minding more their present profit than the common defence,"[9] the board, like the Lords of Trade a decade earlier, quickly concluded that the only remedy was consolidation of the colonies adjacent to the French. The board was careful, however, not to repeat the mistakes of its predecessor. It deliberately sought to avoid offending local interests and raising a political storm by establishing only a military, rather than a civil, union, securing the appointment in early 1697 of the earl of Bellomont as governor of the three northern royal colonies— Massachusetts, New Hampshire, and New York—and commander-in-chief of the forces of all of the colonies north of Pennsylvania.

Resistance to Bellomont in the charter colonies of Rhode Island and

---

[8] The quotation is from John Nelson, Memorial to Board of Trade, [Sept. 23, 1696], in William Noel Sainsbury et al., eds., *Calendar of State Papers, Colonial,* 43 vols. (London, 1860–), *1696–97,* 134–38.

[9] Board of Trade to Lords Justices, Sept. 30, 1696, ibid., 165–67.

Connecticut and continued reports of their violation of the laws of trade convinced the Board of Trade that the old Lords of Trade had been right in another of its objectives: the private colonies had to be brought under direct crown supervision if they were ever to be properly subordinated to the metropolitan government. Nor did the board expect to have to use the costly and time-consuming process of going through the courts to accomplish this objective. It had a weapon unavailable to its predecessor: the authority of Parliament. Parliament's competence in this area would have been denied by Charles II or James II, but after 1688 metropolitan administrators counted on the assistance of Parliament in handling difficult colonial situations.

When the board began to consider recalling the colonial charters, it automatically assumed that the recall would be handled by parliamentary statute. In a stinging indictment of the private colonies, presented to the king in March 1701, the board declared that these colonies had in no way answered the design "for which such large tracts of land, and such privileges and immunities were granted"; charged them with disobeying the Navigation Acts, failing to defend themselves, and passing laws repugnant to those of the mother country; and recommended that they be "put into the same state and dependency as those of your Majestie's other Plantations . . . *by the Legislative power of this Kingdom.*"[10] Parliament entertained bills for this end in 1701, 1702, and 1706. But a combination of factors—the opposition of the proprietors, a genuine reluctance by many members of Parliament to tamper with private property, the vagaries of party politics, and, after the beginning of Queen Anne's War in 1702, an uncertain international situation which made any measure likely to produce discontent in the colonies seem highly imprudent—prevented any of these bills from receiving a full hearing. As a consequence, all failed to pass, and the board temporarily abandoned the project.

But the private colonies were not the only source of difficulties for the Board of Trade. Governors of the royal colonies complained of continued violations of the Navigation Acts and of their inability to enforce their instructions from the crown or to cope with the representative assemblies, whose devotion to the protection of local interests and pretensions to the status of colonial Houses of Commons seemed to have increased dramatically since the Glorious Revolution. From Jamaica, Governor Sir

---

[10] Board of Trade to Queen, Mar. 26, 1701, ibid., *1701*, 141–43; italics added. The board first suggested the possibility of calling on Parliament in a report of Feb. 26, 1698, ibid., *1697–98*, 121–22.

William Beeston wrote in 1701 that the members of the lower house believed "that what a House of Commons could do in England, they could do here, and that during their sitting all power and authority was only in their hands."[11] Similar reports came from Lord Cornbury and Robert Hunter in New York and New Jersey and from Robert Lowther in Barbados, Cornbury remarking that "as the Country increases they grow saucy, and noe doubt but if they were allowed to goe on, they will improve upon it."[12] Such behavior, so obviously patterned after the "various and dissonant models in the Charter and Propriet[ar]y Governments," could only be interpreted, the governors universally agreed, as nothing less than a design among the colonists "to make themselves an independent people, and to that end . . . to divest the administration . . . [in the colonies] of all the Queen's power and authority and to lodge it in the Assembly." "This project hath been a long time on foot and a great progress hath been made in it," Lowther wrote in 1712, "for they have extorted so many powers from my predecessors, that there is now hardly enough left to keep the peace, much less to maintain the decent respect and regard that is due to the Queen's servant."[13]

Resolved to prevent them from ever obtaining "the independency they thirst after," the Board of Trade rigidly adhered to the position laid down by the Lords of Trade a quarter of a century earlier, insisting that the lower houses existed not as a matter of right but only by the favor of the crown and would never be permitted to assume "all the priviledges of the House of Commons in England."[14] No matter how strong its resolution, however, the board, as a body with only advisory authority, was powerless either to check the growing pretensions of the lower houses or to provide effective support for the governors in carrying out their instructions against the opposition of local colonial interests.

Such obvious impotence, combined with the colonists' frequent defiance even of executive orders direct from the king and Privy Council, caused metropolitan officials to think more and more in terms of parliamentary intervention. How far they were willing to go in involving Parliament in the administration of the colonies was revealed in 1711–13 by

---

[11] Beeston to Board of Trade, Aug. 19, 1701, ibid., *1701*, 424–25.

[12] Cornbury to Board of Trade, Nov. 6, 1704, Feb. 19, 1705, ibid., *1704–5*, 386.

[13] Hunter to St. John, Jan. 1, 1712, ibid., *1711–12*, 189–90; Lowther to Board of Trade, Aug. 16, 1712, ibid., *1712–14*, 29.

[14] Board of Trade to Bellomont, Apr. 29, 1701, ibid., *1701*, 180; to Cornbury, Feb. 4, 1706, ibid., *1706–8*, 45; to St. John, Apr. 23, 1712, ibid., *1711–12*, 267–68; to Hunter, June 12, 1712, ibid., 298–99; and to Lowther, July 20, 1713, ibid., *1712–14*, 207–9.

their attempts to force the New York lower house to settle a salary upon Robert Hunter, who became governor of the colony in 1710. When the assembly failed to vote as large a salary as stipulated by Hunter's instructions or to provide for other executive officials, the Privy Council, upon the recommendation of the board, took the unprecedented step in March 1711 of threatening to bring before Parliament a bill "for Enacting a Standing Revenue . . . within the Province of New York for the Support of the Governor there, and the necessary Expences of the Government," if the assembly did not itself provide the "Necessary Support."[15] Although the board repeated this threat on several occasions and the Privy Council twice ordered bills to be brought before the House of Commons, the assembly stood firm for over two years. Finally, Hunter, despairing of getting any effective backing from London, agreed to a compromise solution in the summer of 1713 which led ultimately to the resolution of the conflict and the abandonment by metropolitan authorities of any plans to turn to Parliament.

That no bill was actually brought into Parliament during this long controversy casts considerable doubt upon the sincerity of metropolitan threats and upon the ultimate willingness of crown officials to take such a radical departure from traditional practice by admitting Parliament into the actual administration of the internal political affairs of the colonies. But both the statements and the behavior of the Board of Trade strongly indicate that its members did indeed want Parliament to intervene, hoping thereby to establish a precedent which would serve as a standing example to the "other Governments in America" of what might happen to them if they persisted in assuming "pretended rights tending to an independency on the Crown of Great Britain."[16] Whatever the real motives and intentions of either the members of the board or higher crown officials, this incident illustrates the extent to which they had come both to realize that executive power alone was insufficient to force the colonies to comply with royal commmands and to expect that Parliament could and would be called upon whenever its assistance seemed necessary to handle any unusual emergency within the colonies.

Although the Board of Trade was unsuccessful in its efforts to enlist

[15] Board of Trade to Privy Council, Mar. 1, 1711, and Order in Council, Mar. 1, 1711, in W. L. Grant and J. Munro, eds., *Acts of the Privy Council of England, Colonial Series*, 6 vols. (London, 1908–12), 2:641–42.

[16] Board of Trade to Dartmouth, Apr. 1, 1713, to Lowther, July 20, 1713, and to Lord Archibald Hamilton, Mar. 22, June 21, 1714, *Cal. St. Papers, Col., 1712–14*, 168, 207–9, 322, 359–60.

Parliament's aid in its campaigns to recall the charters of the private colonies and to enforce the royal instructions, it had no trouble in securing parliamentary legislation on the internal economic life of the colonies. In the decades following the Restoration, the initial enthusiasm for colonies among English commercial groups had waned somewhat. Many of them even began to argue that the colonies, by drawing people out of England and thereby reducing the size of the labor pool, retarded the development of manufacturing and slowed economic growth. After the Glorious Revolution, economic writers such as Sir Josiah Child and Charles Davenant tried to counter these arguments. They pointed out that the colonies at once supplied England with commodities that would otherwise have had to be purchased from foreign competitors, created additional "domestic" markets for English manufactured goods, encouraged the growth of English shipping and overseas trade, and otherwise stimulated the English economy.

This counterargument was convincing enough when applied to the sugar colonies in the West Indies and the tobacco colonies of the Chesapeake, colonies whose economies obviously supplemented that of England, whose exports to England yielded large customs revenues, and whose labor requirements had been responsible for the development of the lucrative traffic in African slaves. But it was not so persuasive in regard to the northern continental colonies, whose economies were so similar to that of England as to be potentially competitive. In canvassing this question, economic thinkers and metropolitan officials gradually came to the conclusion that the northern colonies must be discouraged from embarking upon competitive manufactures and that, if possible, their economies should be reshaped so that they might complement the parent economy.

This fear of future competition was behind the extension to the colonies of the Woolen Act of 1699, which, though primarily aimed at Ireland, limited the sale of finished woolens produced in the colonies to strictly local markets. The desire to divert the northern colonies from trade and encourage them to produce naval stores, for which England was otherwise dependent upon the Baltic, was an important consideration in Parliament's decision to establish bounties for colonial naval stores by an act in 1705. Although it did indeed stimulate the development of a thriving naval stores industry in the Carolinas, this last statute failed to achieve the desired results in the northern colonies, and in New England the colonists openly violated a provision reserving all pine trees suitable for the production of masts for the Royal Navy. During Queen Anne's War it became apparent that at least in wartime the northern colonies performed a vital function by supplying the West Indian colonies with provisions, lumber, work animals, and other necessaries that they could not then obtain directly from England. But there was still considerable sentiment among metropolitan officials for a legislative program which would, by operating directly upon the internal economic life of the northern colonies, make them fit more closely the prevailing concept of what an ideal colony should be.

This sentiment, plus the obvious difficulties encountered in trying to enforce metropolitan policies in both private and royal colonies, made it extremely likely that as soon as Queen Anne's War was over, the Board of Trade would seek some major revisions in the existing colonial system. No sooner had the board been created than it began to receive reform proposals from individuals concerned about the diversities and anomalies in the system and anxious to play the role of imperial statesmen. In the years following the Treaty of Utrecht in 1713, the number of such proposals increased sharply. The details of these proposals varied greatly. Some wanted to take colonial administration out of politics entirely and place it in the hands of a board of experts with full power to make and enforce decisions. Others wanted a more elaborate structure of government in the colonies. Still others wanted to reorganize the colonies on the continent into one or more general governments. Whatever the differences in means, however, the basic objective of these proposals was the same: establishment of closer metropolitan controls. Yet few advocated any drastic curtailment of colonial liberties. Most agreed with Charles Davenant that "nothing but such an arbitrary power as shall make them desparate, can bring them to rebel."[17]

Although the Board of Trade was obviously sympathetic with the central aim of these proposals, the uncertainty of the internal domestic situation arising out of the Hanoverian accession in 1714 and the Jacobite uprising in 1715 prevented the adoption of the comprehensive reforms it had long hoped for. In 1715 the board's campaign to convert the private colonies into royal colonies received a major setback when Parliament failed for the fourth time to pass a bill for that purpose and the Privy Council decided to return Maryland, which had been taken over by the crown in the wake of the Glorious Revolution, to the Calvert family. The board did manage to make a few piecemeal changes, disallowing a number of laws that encroached upon the royal prerogative, inserting in the royal instructions several clauses intended to clamp down on the power

---

[17] Charles Davenant, "On the Plantation Trade," in *Political and Commercial Works*, 5 vols. (London, 1771), 2:10–11.

of the colonial assemblies, and securing the appointment of its own special legal counsel to facilitate the review of colonial legislation. But continued reports of the lower houses' refusal to abide by the royal instructions and the opposition of the charter governments to royal customs officials charged with enforcement of the Navigation Acts seemed to indicate that major alterations were required.

The board got its chance in August 1720, when the advisers of the crown, uncertain how to respond to the recent uprising against the proprietors in South Carolina, asked it to submit a report on the "state and condition" of the colonies, with recommendations for their "better government and security." The board's response—"the most complete and illuminating of all the reports prepared by the office"[18]—took over a year to complete and was of massive proportions. Finally submitted on September 8, 1721, the report, not surprisingly, called for a major renovation of colonial administration. Basically, it recommended establishment of a more rational system which would permit the achievement of most of the specific objectives of British colonial policy as they had emerged since the Restoration. To remove the many ambiguities from the metropolitan-colonial relationship, achieve greater administrative unity, and secure more effective enforcement of the laws of trade were major priorities. The report also wished to divert the colonies from manufacturing, find some way to make the northern colonies fit more snugly into the mercantile system, give the crown tighter control over the disposition of its lands and woods in the colonies, improve royal revenues through more systematic collection of quitrents, convert the proprietary and corporate colonies into royal colonies, check the extensive authority of colonial lower houses and the rampant particularism of the colonies, and render royal officials financially independent of the lower houses. All of these ancient goals of the board and, in many cases, the Lords of Trade before it, were important elements in the recommended program.

Although the board's general objectives were not new, some of its proposals for achieving them were. Having by this date abandoned hope of securing parliamentary action on the recall of the charters of the private colonies, it now urged that the crown resume the charters "by purchase, agreement or otherwise"—a procedure suggested by the recent offer from the proprietor of Pennsylvania to sell that colony to the crown and by the petition of the insurgents in South Carolina for royal government. Acting on proposals frequently made by colonial officials and other inter-

---

[18]Charles M. Andrews, *The Colonial Period of American History*, 4 vols. (New Haven, 1935–38), 4:389–90.

ested observers, the board sought to secure more efficient administration in both London and the colonies by recommending that authority over the colonies be concentrated in one agency whose head would have direct access to the king; that all colonial officeholders be required to discharge their duties "in person"; and that a general government be set up for the continental colonies, to be presided over by a lord lieutenant with absolute control over military affairs, supervisory power over governors of individual colonies, and, in conjunction with an advisory council of deputies from each colony, authority to set quotas of men and money in time of war.[19]

The fate of this report is instructive. A few of its specific proposals were eventually carried out. Although there was no intensive effort to redirect the economies of the northern colonies, Parliament did enact additional naval stores acts in 1722 and 1729, and while there was no comprehensive program to purchase the private colonies, the metropolitan government did buy both Carolinas in 1729. Additional recommendations were implemented, at least in part, in the 1750s and 1760s. But the immediate failure of the metropolitan government to adopt a significant number of the proposals underlined the long-term failure of the Board of Trade. In twenty-five years it had been unable to gain sufficient support to enable it fully to carry out any of its projects for the political reconstruction of the empire. The result was that the colonists still refused to obey any trade laws that seemed, as one official in the colonies complained, to hinder "the growth and prosperity of their little commonwealths."[20] Metropolitan political authority within most colonies remained infinitely weaker and more uncertain than the members of the board and officers in the colonies would have preferred.

Despite its failure to achieve many of its general policy objectives, the board had, in the process of formulating them, articulated a cluster of working assumptions about the nature of the relationship between Britain and the colonies that had, at least within metropolitan circles, come to be so widely accepted that they had been elevated to the status of unchallengeable ideals. Two of the most important of these assumptions had been inherited from the Lords of Trade. The first and most fundamental was implied in the familiar parent-child metaphor employed increasingly to describe the metropolitan-colonial connection. If England was the mother country and the colonies were her offspring, it clearly

---

[19] This report is in *Cal. St. Papers, Col., 1720–21*, 408–49.

[20] Caleb Heathcote to Board of Trade, Sept. 7, 1719, as quoted by Dixon Ryan Fox, *Caleb Heathcote, Gentleman Colonist* (New York, 1926), 186–89.

followed that the colonies were dependents, who needed the protection of and who were obligated to yield obedience to their parent state. In any conflict of wills or judgment, the colonies had to defer to the superior strength and wisdom of the metropolitan government.

The second assumption held that the welfare of the whole empire had to take precedence over the good of any of the individual parts. It was "an unalterable Maxim," one writer declared, "that a lesser publick Good must give place to a greater; and that it is of more Moment to maintain a greater, than a lesser Number of Subjects, well employed to the Advantage of any State."[21] A hallowed political convention, this idea was a potentially useful counterbalance to the particularist and individualist inclinations of the colonists. As in most similar political associations, however, there was a strong tendency among governing officials to define the corporate welfare in terms of the interests of the dominant member. To metropolitan officials in London, the good of the whole empire meant the supremacy of the royal prerogative and the commercial interests of Great Britain. The worth of a colony, Sir Josiah Child wrote in 1693, was to be measured according to how it contributed to "the gain or loss of *this* Kingdom."[22] As economist Charles Davenant declared in 1698 in a passage copied into a number of later treatises on the colonies, it was an accepted principle that "colonies are a strength to their mother kingdom, while they are under good discipline, while they are strictly made to observe the fundamental laws of their original country, and while they are kept dependent on it."[23]

This feeling that the colonies should be dependent gave rise to still a third assumption about the metropolitan-colonial relationship: that the colonial governments had to be and were subordinate to the metropolitan government; that, however similar they might be in appearance, structure, and function to the government of Britain, they were in the final analysis no more than "so many Incorporations at a Distance, invested with an Ability of making temporary By-Laws for themselves agreeable to their respective Situations and Climates, but no ways interfering with the legal Prerogative of the Crown, or the true legislative Power of the Mother State." Thus, although the Board of Trade, in contrast to the Lords of Trade, accepted the representative assemblies as

---

[21] Sir William Keith, "A Short Discourse on the Present State of the Colonies in America with Respect to the Interest of Great Britain," Nov. 1728, *Collection of Papers and Other Tracts* (London, 1740), 174.

[22] Sir Josiah Child, *A New Discourse of Trade* (London, 1693), 204–8.

[23] Davenant, *Political and Commercial Works* 2:10.

necessary and desirable elements in the constitutions of the colonies, it could never admit that those bodies, no matter what the aspirations and pretensions of their members, were in any way equal to the British House of Commons. To emphasize their subordinate status, metropolitan authorities always insisted that the assemblies existed not as a matter of right, not because they were necessary to provide for colonials their just rights as Englishmen, but only through the favor of the crown.

Finally, if the primary reason for the existence of colonies was to contribute to the well-being of the parent state, and if colonial governments were necessarily "dependent" and "provincial," it followed that the colonies should be and were, in the phrase of Sir William Keith, onetime governor of Pennsylvania, "justly bound" by the laws of the mother country. Thus Parliament, as the supreme lawmaking power in Britain, obviously had jurisdiction over every aspect of colonial life, political and internal, as well as commercial and external. Ordinarily, colonial administration would be handled by the crown and its officers, acting in their executive and judicial capacities; but as the Board of Trade's proposals for parliamentary intervention to settle a permanent revenue in New York made clear, metropolitan authorities assumed after the Glorious Revolution that the authority of Parliament over the colonies was unlimited.[24]

Because there was no articulate opposition within metropolitan circles to any of these assumptions, and because all of the specific policy objectives of the Board of Trade were logical expressions of one or more of them, the board's inability to achieve more of those objectives would seem, at least on the surface, almost incomprehensible. In some measure, the board's failure may be traced to the vagaries of British politics and the preoccupation of men in power with other more immediate problems. The domestic political readjustments required by the Glorious Revolution, two major wars, the need to ensure the security of the Protestant and Hanoverian succession, and the constant and bitter churn of factional politics—all combined between 1689 and 1721 to push all but the most pressing colonial questions well into the background of British public life. Yet the difficulties encountered by colonial officials at all levels in enforcing measures they could implement on their own, or that did have ministerial or parliamentary support, strongly suggest that, in a larger sense, the failures of British colonial policy between 1660 and 1721

---

[24] Keith, "A Short Discourse," *Collection of Papers*, 167–70, 175.

derived ultimately from a deeper source, from the very nature of the empire itself.

For both that policy and the assumptions behind it were essentially foreign to the commercial traditions on which the empire had originally been based and to the spirit of individual enterprise in which the colonies had been founded. The colonists did not dispute the notion that their behavior should contribute to the welfare of the whole empire, but they saw that welfare from a very different perspective than did metropolitan officials. To them, the common good seemed to require that they be able to pursue their own interests, while any restraints by the metropolitan government appeared to be a breach of the original contract, by which the colonists had been granted the right to pursue those goals in return for risking their lives to plant colonies in the wilderness and tropics of America. "In former daies," declared Edward Littleton, a planter of Barbados, in *The Groans of the Plantations,* a remarkable pamphlet published in London in 1689 in objection to certain features of the Navigation Acts he considered injurious to the sugar islands, "we were under the pleasing sound of Priviledges and Immunities, of which a free Trade was one, though we counted That, a Right and not a Priviledge[;] . . . without such Encouragements, the Plantations had been still wild Woods. Now those things are vanisht and forgotten. . . . All the Care now is, to pare us close, and keep us low. We dread to be mention'd in an Act of Parliament; because it is alwaies to do us Mischief."

What Littleton found most objectionable was that measures injurious to the colonies had been passed under "fair Pretences" that they were "for the common Good and Benefit of the *English* Nation." He did not go so far as Sir Dalby Thomas, another West Indian, who argued in 1690 that the "Colonies themselves are proper Judges of what they suffer, want, and would have," that "their minds must best appear in [their several] generall Assemblies," and that no *"Laws or Designs"* affecting the colonies should be undertaken "untill the Colonies by their Assembly[s] were consulted." But Littleton did insist that it was unfair always to improve one part of the empire to the disadvantage of the rest, unjust for the colonists to be *"commanded as Subjects, and . . . crusht as Aliens. Which Condition is the most dismal and horrid, that people can be under."* Did not the colonists "have as good *English* Bloud in our Veins, as some of those that we left behind us?" he inquired. "How came we to lose our Countrey, and the Priviledges of it? Why will you cast us out?" "No Society of Men," he wrote, "can stand without equal Justice, which is the Lady and Queen of all the Vertues. If the equal dividing the common Booties, be necessary to Pirates and *Buccaneers;* the equal distribution of publique Burdens, is much more to a State."[25]

The thrust of Littleton's argument was that the colonists ought to enjoy the same rights as those Englishmen who stayed at home, and that the interests of the colonies were entitled to equal consideration with those of England. This demand that the colonists be placed upon an equal footing with other Englishmen was implicit in such documents as the Bill of Privileges drawn up by the Jamaica assembly in 1677, the Charter of Liberties enacted by the first New York assembly in 1683, and the rash of attempts by the legislatures of Virginia, New York, Massachusetts, South Carolina, and Maryland—inspired by Parliament's example in passing the Declaration of Rights in 1689—to secure formal legal guarantees of their rights to English liberties between 1691 and 1696.[26] Such attempts revealed a markedly different conception of the metropolitan-colonial relationship from that held by English officials, a conception which involved a considerably greater measure of colonial equality than metropolitan theory allowed.

The tension between these two opposing views was intensified in the older settlements as early as the closing decades of the seventeenth century by the ambitions of emergent political elites within the colonies. However much they may have fought among themselves for wealth, status, and power, members of these elites all manifested a common desire to reproduce in the colonies a society and a political system which resembled as closely as possible that of Britain itself. Because the primary outlet for the political ambitions of the vast majority of them was through the elected lower houses, they were especially intent upon making those bodies the equivalents on the provincial level of the English House of Commons. They wanted full legislative powers over their respective jurisdictions, by virtue of their constituents' inherited English right not to be subject to any laws passed without the consent of their representatives. Although they were remarkably successful in their efforts, the persistent refusal of metropolitan authorities to admit in theory what had been achieved in fact made the status of the lower house extremely uncertain.

---

[25] Edward Littleton, *The Groans of the Plantations* (London, 1689), 16, 20, 22–24; Sir Dalby Thomas, *An Historical Account of the Rise and Growth of the West-India Colonies* (London, 1690), iii, 32.

[26] Thornton, *West-India Policy,* 171–172; David S. Lovejoy, "Equality and Empire: The New York Charter of Libertyes, 1683," *William and Mary Quarterly,* 3d ser., 21 (1964): 493–515; Keith, *Constitutional History,* 141–42.

The ambiguous status of the lower houses was a matter of continual concern to colonial legislators and other political leaders. To have removed the ambiguity would have required, as Charles Davenant once suggested, that the "bounds between the chief power and the people" be somehow clearly delineated. What he proposed was passage of a declaratory law guaranteeing to all Englishmen the "right to all the laws of England, while they remain in countries subject to the dominion of the kingdom."[27] But colonials wanted something more. In the words of Jeremiah Dummer, agent for the New England colonies and author of the celebrated *Defence of the New-England Charters,* they wanted "a free Government, where the Laws are sacred, Property secure, and Justice not only impartially, but expeditiously distributed." Assuming that "the Benefit which *Great-Britain* receives from the Plantations, arises from their Commerce" and that "Oppression is the most opposite Thing in the World to Commerce," they wanted, as Dummer inferred, freedom to pursue their own individual and corporate interests under conditions such as those agreed to by all parties in the original charters, and freedom from the oppression, the "direct plundering [of the] . . . People, and [the many] . . . other Acts of Misrule and lawless Power" that had sometimes marked the behavior of governors in the plantations and that rendered both the property of the colonists and their liberty to pursue it extremely precarious. But the full achievement of these goals required something far more than simply a jealous guarding of the original "Liberties of the People" by the lower houses in the colonies and additional curbs on potentially imperious or corrupt governors by metropolitan authorities in Britain.[28] It demanded, as an anonymous Virginian perceived in 1701, no less than "a Just and Equal Government" based on a "free Constitution," which would remove all ambiguity from the metropolitan-colonial relationship by defining "what is law, and what is not" in the colonies and specifying "how far the Legislative Authority is in the Assemblies."[29] In the absence of such an arrangement, the lower houses and the people and interests they represented could never be entirely secure, could never enjoy the same degree of protection of their liberties and properties as their fellow Englishmen did at home, and could never fully satisfy their mimetic impulses to reproduce in the colonies a complete English society.

---

[27] Davenant, *Political and Commercial Works* 2:35–36, 55.

[28] Jeremiah Dummer, *Defence of the New-England Charters* (London, 1721), 68–69, 73.

[29] Louis B. Wright, ed., *An Essay upon the Government of the Plantations on the Continent of America* (San Marino, Calif., 1945), 15–17, 23.

Ironically, the very ambiguity that had been responsible for much of the tension between the home government and the colonies between 1689 and 1721 provided the basis for the development over the next thirty years of a remarkably stable political relationship. This development coincided and was closely associated with the rise to political hegemony of Sir Robert Walpole, who was first minister from 1721 until 1742, and derived largely from the application to colonial matters of many of the underlying principles and techniques he had employed with such brilliant success in managing domestic affairs. To avoid any issues involving fundamentals and all debates over basic principles, to restrict the active role of government as much as possible and act only when it was expedient or necessary to do so, to attempt to bind potentially disruptive groups to the administration by catering to their interests, to seek to adjust all disputes by compromise and manipulation, and, if a choice had to be made between competing interests, always to align the government with the strongest—each of these characteristically Walpolean modes of procedure inevitably spilled over into and affected the handling of the colonies.

Based on a clear recognition that the continued prosperity of the colonies—which had been such an important "Cause of enriching this Nation"—depended to some considerable degree upon their having, as one writer put it, "a Government . . . as Easy & Mild as possible to invite people to Settle under it" and to keep them happy once they were there, the new metropolitan posture toward the colonies was succinctly characterized by Charles Delafaye, one of Walpole's subordinates. "One would not Strain any Point," Delafaye warned Governor Francis Nicholson of South Carolina early in Walpole's administration, "where it can be of no Service to our King and Country, and will Create Enemys to one[']s Self."[30] To promote the economic well-being of the empire in general and, not incidentally, to avoid political difficulties for the administration at home, the traditional goals of British colonial policy as they had been worked out since the Restoration were, whenever expedient, thus to give way to immediate political advantage. In practice, if not in theory, there was to be a partial return to something resembling the old contractual

---

[30]The quotations are from Joshua Gee, *The Trade and Navigation of Great-Britain* (London, 1729), 98, and Charles Delafaye to Francis Nicholson, Jan. 26, 1722, in Jack P. Greene, ed., *Settlements to Society, 1584–1763* (New York, 1966), 231–32.

relationship between mother country and colonies as it had existed during the first half century of English colonization.

But this more relaxed attitude toward the colonies was not immediately copied by those most directly concerned with colonial administration. The Board of Trade at home and governors and other members of the official bureaucracy in the colonies still evaluated the colonial situation in terms of the old imperatives. Governors continued to complain that the colonists paid "little or no defference to any opinion or orders . . . from the Ministry at Home" and to rail at the lower houses for "making attempts upon the few Prerogatives" still "reserv'd to ye Crown."[31] Customs officials and others in the colonies bitterly denounced the colonists for flagrantly violating the Navigation Acts, wantonly turning the timber reserved for the Royal Navy to their own uses, and openly attempting to frustrate attempts to enforce the acts of trade through the vice-admiralty courts. For its part, the Board of Trade persisted in its attempts to hold royal governors to a rigid enforcement of their instructions, to achieve a more centralized and regular system of colonial control in London, to consolidate the colonies for more effective administration and defense, to try to bring the charter colonies under closer supervision, to secure permanent revenues from the colonies for the support of crown officials, and, on occasion, to threaten parliamentary intervention if its recommendations were not complied with.

But the board regularly failed to get full ministerial support for its recommendations after 1721. Two cases, both involving the board's efforts to deal with the refractory Massachusetts House of Representatives, may be cited as examples. The first grew out of a long series of charges levied against the house in August 1723 by Governor Samuel Shute, who, after several years of bitter wrangling with that body, had come to England to seek direct help from his superiors. The board reported favorably on Shute's complaints and urged the "interposition of the British Legislature" to restrain the house "within the due bounds of obedience to the Crown." But the administration would not go that far. Although it agreed that each of the charges was valid, and strongly censured the house for having "unlawfully assumed . . . Powers which [did] not belong to [it]," it would do no more than issue an explanatory charter confirming the governor's position on only two of seven original charges

---

[31] Samuel Shute to Board of Trade, Oct. 29, 1722, and Shute to Crown, [Aug. 16, 1723], *Cal. St. Papers, Col., 1722–23*, 157–58, 324–30.

and threaten that any resistance to the new charter might result in refer-
ral of the whole matter to Parliament.[32]

The board's inability to obtain administration support for its directives in the colonies was even more dramatically revealed over the following decade by its failure to force the Massachusetts House of Representatives to establish a permanent revenue to provide salaries for crown
officers. After repeated instructions and entreaties had failed to move
the house, the board, in desperation, threatened in early 1729 to turn to
Parliament. But the administration, as the duke of Newcastle (who as
secretary of state for the southern department from 1724 until 1746 had
primary responsibility for colonial decisions) admitted to Governor William Burnet, was not eager to bring "things to that extremity." The result was that the Massachusetts house stood firm, and the board, unable
to carry through on its threats, had first to give in temporarily, while
disclaiming that its concession could be "construed to enervate the Validity of . . . [the] former Instructions," and finally in 1736 to abandon the
cause altogether and permit the governor (by then, Jonathan Belcher) to
accept annual grants from the house.[33]

The board's gradual retreat on this issue coincided with and symbolized a general decline in its activity and effectiveness, a decline which
began in the early years of Walpole's administration and accelerated during the presidency of Lord Monson between 1737 and 1748. The board
never explicitly abandoned the program for which it had pressed so hard
before 1721, but it was repeatedly forced, by a combination of the reluctance of the ministry to support it and the intransigence of the colonists,
to bow before the practical necessity of getting on with day-to-day government within the colonies. Apparently because of "neglect and distraction," Newcastle was during much of his tenure as secretary similarly
ineffective.[34] Royal officials in the colonies thus had to resign themselves

[32] Shute to Crown, [Aug. 16, 1723], and Board of Trade to Lords Justices, Sept. 23, 1723,
ibid., 324–30, 339–40; Shute to Dartmouth, Mar. 5, 1724, and Newcastle to William
Dummer, Sept. 30, 1725, ibid., *1724–25*, 50–52, 442; *Acts of the Privy Council, Colonial*
3:92–204.

[33] Leonard Woods Labaree, ed., *Royal Instructions to British Colonial Governors, 1670–
1776*, 2 vols. (New York, 1935), 1:257–65; Mass. House of Representatives to Crown,
Nov. 22, 1728, Board of Trade to Newcastle, Mar. 27, 1729, and Newcastle to Burnett,
June 26, 1729 (two letters), *Cal. St. Papers, Col., 1728–29*, 311–13, 339–40, 412–14;
Belcher to Newcastle, June 11, 1734, and Board of Trade to King, Aug. 29, 1734, ibid.,
1734–35, 130–31, 194–95; *Acts of the Privy Council, Colonial* 3:259–64.

[34] Philip Haffenden, "Colonial Appointments and Patronage under the Duke of Newcastle, 1724–1739," *English Historical Review* 108 (1963): 417–35.

to the fact that it was difficult to get anyone in Britain "to think of Plantation affairs," that the ministers were simply "too busily employ'd another way to mind Such Trifles."[35] With such "small countenance" from their "superiors in England,"[36] governors and other crown officers were thus forced to rely largely upon their own resources in handling the domestic political affairs of the colonies.

The reluctance of the administration to give close attention to the governance of the colonies did not carry over into the economic realm. Extraordinarily sensitive to the demands of powerful interest groups within Britain, both the administration and Parliament regularly responded to their requests for new economic regulations concerning the colonies. Whenever colonial interests coincided with those of some influential group in Britain, the colonies could count on a favorable response to their requests. Thus, the rice growers of Carolina combined with rice traders in Britain in 1730 to persuade Parliament to permit the direct exportation of rice from Carolina to southern Europe, and South Carolina indigo planters joined with woolen manufacturers in 1748 to secure a bounty to encourage the production of Carolina indigo. The prevailing ideal, in fact, was still, as James Oglethorpe declared in the House of Commons in 1732, that "in all cases that come before this House, where there seems to be a clashing of interests between one part of the country and another[,] . . . we ought to have no regard to the particular interest of any country or set of people; the good of the whole is what we ought only to have under our consideration: our colonies are all a part of our own dominions; the people in every one of them are our own people, and we ought to shew an equal respect to all."[37]

Yet, whenever there actually was "a clashing of interests" between British and colonial groups, the British group invariably came out best

---

[35] The quotations are from Cadwallader Colden to George Clinton, Dec. 8, 1748, Clinton Papers, box 8, William L. Clements Library, Ann Arbor, Mich., and James Logan to William Logan, Dec. 1733, as quoted in Joseph E. Johnson, "A Quaker Imperialist's View of the British Colonies in America, 1732," *Pennsylvania Magazine of History and Biography* 60 (1936): 100.

[36] Governor Gabriel Johnston to Lord Wilmington, Feb. 10, 1737, in Historical Manuscripts Commission, *The Manuscripts of the Marquess of Townshend* (London, 1887), 262–64.

[37] Jan. 28, 1732, in Leo Francis Stock, ed., *Proceedings and Debates of the British Parliaments respecting North America*, 5 vols. (Washington, D.C., 1924–41), 4:125.

in Parliament. In 1732 British hatmakers had no difficulty in obtaining legislation designed to cramp a budding colonial hat industry and British merchants a law to make it easier for them to secure payment of colonial debts. Because the subjects were more complicated and rival British groups disagreed about what should be done, it required a long campaign by British iron producers and British merchants to secure regulation, respectively, of colonial iron manufacturing and colonial paper currency. Eventually both succeeded, but each had to accept some concessions to colonial interests. Even when they had the backing of the administration, no colonial interest group could hope for success in any proposal opposed by a major British lobby. To their great disappointment, the Virginia tobacco planters discovered this stark political fact in 1733, when they unsuccessfully joined with Walpole in his excise scheme in the hope of remedying some aspects of the tobacco trade they found objectionable.

Moreover, whenever there was a collision of interests among colonials, the North American colonists had to reconcile themselves to the existence of a strong preference within Britain for the West Indies. The metropolitan valuation of the continental colonies increased enormously through the middle decades of the eighteenth century as their importance as markets for British manufactures became more and more obvious. The most dramatic measure of this development was Parliament's willingness—for the first time in the history of English colonization—to vote funds for the establishment of a new colony. Largely for strategic considerations, to strengthen the defenses of the southern colonies on the continent, Parliament began in 1732 to contribute an annual grant to defray the costs of the entire civil establishment and other expenses of Georgia. In the first twenty years alone, Parliament appropriated £136,608 for that colony.

But if metropolitan authorities were ever more disposed to believe that it was "the true Interest of *Great Britain* to . . . encourage and nourish its Northern as well as Southern Colonies,"[38] they could not, when the choice was thrust upon them, yet overcome their traditional partiality for the sugar colonies. This preference was clearly revealed between 1731 and 1733, when the West Indian and mainland colonies clashed over West Indian demands for protection from competition by the foreign islands. During the first decades of the eighteenth century, the foreign islands, especially the French, began to produce sugar more

[38] John Ashley, *Memoirs and Considerations concerning the Trade and Revenues of the British Colonies in America* (London, 1740).

cheaply than the British and to undersell them on the world market, with the result that New England merchants developed a thriving trade with the foreign islands after the Treaty of Utrecht in 1713. The economic fortunes of the British islands began to decline, and West Indian interests in London pressed Parliament to exclude the New Englanders from trading with the foreign islands. After a long and vigorous debate, Parliament responded in 1733 by passing the Molasses Act, which sought to discourage the trade with the foreign islands by placing prohibitive duties on their sugar products. The edge of this potentially grievous regulation for the northern continental colonies was only blunted by the failure of customs officials to enforce it strictly.

Parliament's willingness to act upon such a wide range of economic problems pointedly contrasted with its refusal on three occasions during the 1730s and 1740s to intervene to strengthen royal political authority in the colonies. Thus, in 1734 a House of Lords committee proposed a bill to prevent any colonial laws from taking effect until they had been approved by the crown, but the Lords never formulated the proposal into a bill.[39] Similarly, two bills to regulate colonial paper currencies considered by the Commons in 1744 and 1749 contained clauses that would have given royal instructions the force of law in the colonies. But the Commons did not pass either, and the currency law finally enacted in 1751 included no such provision. The net effect of this inaction was to create the impression among the colonists that Parliament's undefined colonial authority did not include the right to intervene in the internal political life of the colonies.

Along with Walpole's tendency to let the colonies proceed on their own without interference by the administration except in such matters as were of serious and pressing concern to powerful interest groups in Britain, Parliament's inaction in the colonial domestic sphere gave the local governors more room for political maneuver than they had had at any time since the Restoration. For those governors operating from an actual or potential position of political strength, this relaxation of pressure meant that they could pursue the "real Advantage" of the parent state without having to be constantly on guard against reprimands from home for failing to enforce the "long established Maxims" of the Board of Trade.[40] Thus, in Massachusetts, the abandonment in 1736 of the at-

---

[39] Laws relating to emergencies and defense were to be excepted.

[40] The quotations are from Sir William Gooch, "Some Remarks on a Paper Transmitted into America, Entitled a Short Discourse on the Present State of the Colonies in America

tempt to force the House of Representatives to vote a permanent revenue provided the basis for an extraordinary extension of the influence of the royal governor over the next twenty years. William Shirley, who became Massachusetts governor in 1741, combined a remarkable talent for political management, powerful connections in Britain, and adroit use of a growing system of patronage in order to command the loyalty and secure the cooperation of the colony's elite, to make himself "the dominant figure" in Massachusetts politics, and to put an end to the battles between governors and legislatures that had characterized the political life of the colony for almost all of its first half century under the crown.[41] In Virginia, Lieutenant Governor William Gooch, who administered the colony from 1727 to 1749, was similarly successful, though for somewhat different reasons. With almost no patronage at his disposal, he could not employ Shirley's techniques of management. But by joining with local political leaders to stress the baneful effects of factionalism in politics, the desirability of disinterested behavior by magistrates and legislators, and, in the manner of Walpole, the necessity of institutional cooperation, Gooch managed to extirpate old factions and achieve a remarkable amount of political harmony and tranquillity.

Elsewhere, however, governors were neither so fortunate nor so successful in promoting the interests of the crown. The kind of well-integrated society and polity that made possible Gooch's success in Virginia existed in no other royal colony, and no other governor had at his command the extensive patronage available to Shirley. Had governors been able to give each of the growing number of royal offices in the colonies to influential members of local elites, they could, like Shirley, have gone a long way toward parrying the opposition to British policy and securing the support of a critical segment of colonial society. Instead, authorities in Britain weakened the governors by taking most of the patronage out of their hands and appointing needy place seekers from England to many of the offices, without pausing to consider "how despicable the Governor of a Province must be when stript of the Power of disposing of the few places that fall within his Government, and how little serviceable to the Crown, when deprived of the only means of re-

---

[41] The quotation is from John M. Murrin, "From Corporate Empire to Revolutionary Republic: The Transformation of the Structure of the Concept of Federalism," paper delivered at the Annual Meeting of the American Historical Association, Dec. 1966.

warding Merit and creating [and exerting] Influence."[42] Indeed, for those colonies whose governors had little influence at home, there was a marked tendency through the middle decades of the eighteenth century for crown officials to do the same with colonial council seats, which had formerly been reserved for wealthy and well-affected colonials.

In this situation many governors chose simply not to "consider any Thing further than how to sit easy," and to be careful "to do nothing, which upon a fair hearing . . . can be blamed."[43] Because the surest way to "sit easy" was to reach a political accommodation with local interests, they very frequently aligned themselves with dominant political factions in the colonies. Such governors sought to avoid disputes with the lower houses by taking especial care not to challenge their customary privileges and, if necessary, even quietly giving way before their demands. As a consequence, the royal governors in many colonies were fully integrated into the local political community and came to identify and be identified as much with the interests of the colonies as with those of the metropolitan government.

This domestication of the governors eased tensions significantly as their personal prestige and sometimes even their political influence actually increased, while the lower houses contented themselves with the rather large amount of de facto power they could wield whenever it became necessary to do so. In this situation, the lower houses virtually ceased to demand the kind of explicit recognition of colonial rights they had so often sought during the years from 1660 to 1721. The effort of the Jamaica house in 1723 to obtain the crown's specific acknowledgment that Jamaicans were entitled to all the rights of Englishmen in return for voting a perpetual revenue to the crown was notable because it was the last such attempt by any assembly before the disturbances that immediately preceded the American Revolution.

The primary difficulty with this informal and pragmatic political arrangement was its extraordinary fragility. A loss of political influence in Britain or a volatile economic or social situation within a colony could suddenly bring a governor to total ruin. Similarly, a governor who refused to abide by the conditions of the arrangement—who, for whatever

---

[42]Gooch, "Some Remarks," 2:243–44. On the general point about the crown's assumption of patronage, see Haffenden, "Colonial Appointments," 417–35, and Bernard Bailyn, *The Origins of American Politics* (New York, 1968), 72–80.

[43]Johnson, "A Quaker Imperialist's View," 114; Johnston to Wilmington, Feb. 10, 1737, *Manuscripts of Townshend,* 262–64.

reason, was either intent upon making "a mighty change in the face of affairs" or reluctant to accept a status of equal or subordinate partner with the assembly—could easily revive old fears among legislators and powerful local interests and throw a colony into political deadlock or even chaos.

The insecurity that derived from the possibility of getting a governor who was determined either to "suck up the Treasure of the Land, and to devour the Fruit of their honest Labours" or to turn "Topsy Turvy long established Constitutions in [the] Colonies" was intensifed by the uncertain relationship of Parliament to the colonies.[44] That Parliament, whether or not it had the right, might exert its awesome power was ever a potentially disturbing possibility. Although there was some hope that "so great" a body would do nothing that by "preparing Slavery to us would give a presedent and hand it against themselves," there was always the unsettling prospect that it might act to augment prerogative power in the colonies and thereby strike "Emediately at the Liberty, of the Subject and Establish arbetrary pour to all the Contenant and Islands in American and Else where under the Kings Dominions."[45]

Notwithstanding these uncertainties, the relationship between the mother country and most of the colonies was, for the time being at least, a viable one. Reinforced by the mutual prosperity of most parts of the empire, and reflecting the phenomenal economic and social growth of the colonies in the decades following the end of Queen Anne's War, there was a growing pride among the colonists in their connection with Britain and a conscious cultivation of traditional English social and political values. The largely unarticulated and unacknowledged quid pro quo between metropolitan and colonial leaders that emerged in the decades after 1721 permitted the colonists a considerable amount of self-government and economic freedom, without requiring metropolitan officials explicitly to abandon any of the traditional ideals and assumptions of British colonial policy. The many ambiguities in this arrangement were thus not only its central weakness—the source of its latent insecurities and its extreme fragility—but also its primary strength. As long as British officials could believe in the old ideals without feeling compelled to try to achieve them, as long as they could assume that Parliament had the power and author-

[44] The questions are from Johnston to Wilmington, Feb. 10, 1737, *Manuscripts of Townshend*, 262–64; [Henry St. John, 1st Viscount Bolingbroke], *The Craftsman* 9 (London, 1727): 267; and Gooch, "Some Remarks," 2:231.

[45] Henry Beekman to Henry Livingston, Jan. 7, 1745, as quoted by Philip L. White, *The Beekmans of New York in Politics and Commerce, 1674–1877* (New York, 1956), 190.

ity to set things right in the colonies without ever becoming convinced that it was necessary for it to do so, as long as the lower houses in the colonies did not demand positive metropolitan recognition of all the privileges and powers they actually exercised and believed were rightfully theirs, as long as potentially grievous features of the navigation system were only loosely enforced—as long, in sum, as all parties were content to leave the wide divergence between metropolitan ideals and colonial practice implicit, this arrangement was functional.

What finally undermined the system and prepared the way for its total collapse after 1763 was the simultaneous outbreak of severe political disturbances in most of the colonies in the late 1740s and early 1750s. During the last stages of King George's War, which lasted from 1744 to 1748, there were so many problems in so many colonies that the empire seemed to people in London to be on the verge of distintegration. Violent factional disputes had thrown New Jersey into civil war, put an end to all legislative activity in New Hampshire and North Carolina, and seriously undermined the position of the royal governors in Jamaica and New York. From New York, South Carolina, New Jersey, Bermuda, Jamaica, North Carolina, and New Hampshire—from all of the royal colonies except Massachusetts, Virginia, Barbados, and some of the smaller islands—governors complained that they were impotent to carry out either metropolitan directions or their own projects against the exorbitant power of the lower houses. The ultimate message in this rising chorus of laments came through with resounding clarity: governors needed help from the metropolitan government. "The too great and unwarrantable encroachments of the Assemblies," declared Governor Lewis Morris of New Jersey, "make it necessary that a stop some way or other should be put to them, and they reduced to such propper and legall bounds as is consistent with his majestie's Prerogative and their dependence."[46] Drastic measures were required, echoed George Clinton from New York, "to put a stop to these perpetually growing Incroachments of the Assemblies . . . on the executive Powers."[47] What was the more alarming was that

---

[46] To Board of Trade, Jan. 28, 1744, in New Jersey Historical Society, *Collections* (1852) 4:225.

[47] To the Board of Trade, Oct. 20, 1748, in Edmund B. O'Callaghan and Berthold Fernow, eds., *Documents Relative to the Colonial History of the State of New-York,* 15 vols. (Albany, 1853–87), 6:456–57.

the decay of executive authority seemed to be matched by a decline in public respect for governors, the chief symbol of metropolitan authority in the colonies. From Bermuda came reports that the status of the governor had sunk so low that one member of the assembly had even offered a reward for his assassination. So desperate was the situation all over the colonies that nothing less than a complete remodeling of their constitutions seemed necessary.

The urgency of these appeals could scarcely be ignored by the metropolitan government. The Board of Trade had responded by showing some signs of its earlier vigor during the last three years of the presidency of Lord Monson. But it was not until 1748, when Monson died and the war was concluded, that an opportunity presented itself for the major overhaul in the colonial system that governors had been calling for. When the duke of Newcastle proposed to replace the casual Monson with Newcastle's brother-in-law, the duke of Leeds, who wanted "some office which required little attendence and less application,"[48] the duke of Bedford, then secretary of state for the southern department, reminded Newcastle in a classic piece of understatement that it would have been "Highly improper, considering the present Situation of things, to have a nonefficient Man at the head of that Board."[49] What was needed, obviously, was an energetic man with a turn for business, and such a man was found in the person of the ambitious and indefatigable George Dunk, earl of Halifax, who was president of the Board of Trade from 1748 to 1761 during what were to be its most active years.

Halifax performed as expected. Under his guidance, the board presided over a major enterprise to strengthen the defenses of the British colonies against French Canada by turning Nova Scotia, hitherto only a nominal British colony inhabited almost entirely by neutral and even hostile French, into a full-fledged British colony. Equally important, it prepared a series of reports on the difficulties in most of the major trouble spots in the colonies. The recommendations contained in these reports revealed that, despite the long era of accommodation and easy administration since the advent of Walpole, the members of the board and other colonial officials had not altered their notions about the proper relationship between the parent state and the colonies but slightly. Underlying all the recommendations was the assumption that it was absolutely "nec-

---

[48] Oliver M. Dickerson, *American Colonial Government, 1696–1765* (Cleveland, 1912), 39.

[49] Bedford to Newcastle, Aug. 11, 1748, Additional Manuscripts 32716, f. 38, British Library, London.

essary to revise the Constitutions of the Settlements abroad" and "to regulate them, that they may be usefull to, & not rival in Power and Trade their Mother Kingdom,"[50] and it was rumored in both London and the colonies that the ministry was at last "determined to settle a general plan for establishing the Kings Authority in all the plantations."[51] Except for the Nova Scotia enterprise, which received strong backing from the administration and, like the Georgia venture, large sums of money from Parliament, the board's recommendations were, however, virtually ignored by the administration. As James Abercromby, colonial agent for Virginia and North Carolina, later lamented, "matters of moment" were sometimes "delayed for years . . . after [Halifax] . . . had done his part."[52] Tired of waiting on the "Great Men," who "never want a pretence to protract the dispatch of Business,"[53] Halifax pushed very hard to have himself appointed a separate secretary of state with broad jurisdiction and full responsibility for the colonies. Although he failed in this effort because of the opposition of the king and the two older secretaries of state, he did succeed in securing enlarged powers for the Board of Trade in April 1752.

With its new powers, the board embarked upon a vigorous campaign to enforce the traditional ideals of British colonial policy and, especially, to reduce the authority and influence of the lower houses. It established a packet boat system to provide more regular communication with the colonies, urged each of the royal governors to secure a comprehensive revision of the laws in his colony and to send home copies of all public papers promptly, and enjoined the governors "strictly to adhere to your instructions and not to deviate from them in any point but upon evident necessity justified by the particular Circumstances of the case."[54] Although the board's programs were greeted in many places with enthusiasm by royal officeholders and others who had long been alarmed by the imbalance of the colonial constitutions caused by the lower houses' con-

---

[50]"Some Considerations Relating to the Present Conditions of the Plantations . . . ," [ca. 1748–51], Colonial Office Papers, 5/5, ff. 313–18, Public Record Office, London.

[51]Cadwallader Colden to George Clinton, Feb. 12, 1756, Clinton Papers, box 10, Clements Library.

[52]Abercromby to William Pitt, Nov. 25, 1756, Chatham Papers, Gifts and Deposits, 30/8/95, ff. 197–208, PRO.

[53]See John Catherwood to George Clinton, Mar. 1, 1751, Clinton Papers, box 11, Clements Library.

[54]Board of Trade to Governors, June 3, 1752, CO 324/15, 318–23, PRO.

stant "nibbling at the Prerogative of the Crown,"[55] they were, in general, adamantly opposed by the lower houses, whose members considered them attacks upon the established constitutions of the colonies. Because of "the great lenity shewn them these 50 Years past," one writer penetratingly observed, it seemed to be impossible to bring the colonies "under any other Dominion" than the one to which they had become accustomed.[56]

Even with its enlarged authority, the board could not deal effectively with opposition from the lower houses. The board could and did intimidate the governors into a strict observance of their instructions, but that only reduced their room for political maneuver when they needed all the latitude possible to accomplish the impossible tasks assigned to them. Thus, the board succeeded in its objectives only in New Hampshire, where Governor Benning Wentworth had put together a powerful political combination which monopolized all political power and stifled opposition, and in the new civil governments in Nova Scotia and Georgia, where the board took extraordinary pains "to check all Irregularities and unnecessary Deviations from the Constitution of the Mother Country in their Infancy."[57] By the time the outbreak of the Seven Years' War forced it to suspend its reform activities in 1756, the Board had realized that its general campaign was a failure. Increasingly, it had been driven to threaten the intervention of Parliament, and in 1757 the House of Commons actually did intervene for the first time in the domestic affairs of a colony when it censured the Jamaica assembly for making extravagant constitutional claims while resisting instructions issued from the board.

There was a sharp contrast between the colonial and metropolitan reactions to the experience of the Seven Years' War. The aggressive tactics of the lower houses, which used the need for defense funds to extort still more power from the governors, and the open violation of the Navigation Acts by merchants in the northern colonies, left no doubt in the minds of officials in London that some major reconstruction of colonial governance would have to be undertaken at the end of the war to put a stop, once and for all, to the extreme particularism of the colonies. The experience of Halifax in the prewar years made it clear, as a number of

---

[55] [Archibald Kennedy], *A Speech Said to Have Been Delivered...* (New York, 1755), 5.

[56] W. M. to Halifax, Mar. 10, 1756, Chatham Papers, 30/8/95, ff. 157–60, PRO.

[57] [John Pownall], "General Propositions . . . ," Shelburne Papers, 49:559–66, Clements Library.

new proposals for imperial reform emphasized, that much of that reconstruction would have to be undertaken by Parliament, because "no other Authority than that of the British Parliament" would "be regarded in the colonys or be able to awe them into acquiescence."[58]

Among the colonists, on the other hand, the conviction that the colonies had played a major part in the "glorious" British victory and a genuine appreciation of the extraordinary military effort made by the British in the colonies produced at once an expanded sense of self-importance and a surge of British nationalism. In the glow of the great British victories of 1758 and 1759 and the Treaty of Paris in 1763, few colonists even noted that in 1759, as soon as the victory over the French in Canada had been won and colonial support for the war effort was no longer vital, metropolitan authorities had renewed the campaign to bring the colonies under closer supervision. Proud to be a part of the most extensive empire in the world since the Roman Empire, they looked forward to a bright new era of peace and prosperity in which they would, because of the elimination of the French in North America, be freer than ever to pursue their several interests.

This euphoric state depended, of course, upon a considerable amount of metropolitan permissiveness, upon a lax enforcement of the Navigation Acts on the one hand and the continued ability of dominant colonial interests to exercise a major voice in colonial government through the lower houses on the other; and it was tempered by the same anxieties about their relations with the metropolitan government that had gnawed at colonials for the past century. What they needed to complete their happiness and to enable them to make their potential contribution to the future greatness of the empire were some assurances that their interests would not be sacrificed to those of the home islands, that they would not, as a New Yorker wrote, be deprived "of making use of those Means which Providence has been pleased to put into our Hands for the Ease and Comfort of Life, from what we raise and manufacture from our own Produce and Labour."[59] They needed as well some guarantee, as

---

[58] "Hints Respecting the Civil Establishment in Our American Colonies," [1763], Shelburne Papers, 49:508, Clements Library.

[59] [Archibald Kennedy], *Observations on the Importance of the Northern Colonies under Proper Regulations* (New York, 1750), 30–31.

the Virginia committee of correspondence declared in July 1764 in objecting to Parliament's proposed stamp duties, that their "just Liberties & Privileges as free born British Subjects" would be protected and
that they would not be arbitrarily subjected by the British government
to the full "*Plenitude of its Power.*"[60] That the constitutions of the colonies were "so imperfect, in numberless instances, that the rights of the
people lie, even now, at the mere mercy of their governours" was a source
of major concern.[61] Clearly, as one colonial had predicted a decade earlier,
the colonists would regard any parliamentary or ministerial restraints
upon the free pursuit of their own interests as "oppression; especially
such Laws, as according to the Conceptions . . . [they] have of *English
Liberty,* they have no Hand in the contriving or making."[62]

Increasingly aware that the colonies were "certainly the greatest part
of the Riches and Glory of these Kingdoms" and tormented—as they
had been since the 1690s—by the possibility that their extensive self-
governing powers would inevitably lead to "Notions of Indepen[den]cy
of their Mother Kingdom,"[63] imperial officials tried with the full assistance of Parliament to impose just such restraints in the years after 1763.
They attempted to confine the restless striving of the colonists into channels acceptable to British economic interests, to establish a stricter system of colonial administration, and to restrain the long-established self-
governing powers of the colonists. The response of the leaders of the
continental colonies, at least, was reluctantly to conclude that protection of their economic interests and security for their liberties could
never be achieved within the British Empire.

Removal of the tensions that had underlain the relationship between
the colonies and the mother country ever since 1660 came only with separation. In revolution and independence, the individualistic tendencies
that had been manifest in colonial life from the first establishment of
the colonies in America and that had been at the heart of metropolitan
administrative difficulties were finally given free rein. Tentatively elevated to the status of a right by the pursuit of happiness clause in the

---

[60] Virginia Committee of Correspondence to Edward Montagu, July 28, 1764, "Proceedings of the Virginia Committee of Correspondence," *Virginia Magazine of History and
Biography* 12 (1905): 8–14.

[61] William Smith, *History of New-York . . .* (Albany, 1814), 10.

[62] [Kennedy], *Observations on the Importance of the Northern Colonies,* 10.

[63] W. M. to Pitt, Nov. 16, 1756, Chatham Papers, 30/8/95, ff. 194–95, PRO; "Some
Considerations," [1748–51], CO 5/5, ff. 313–18, PRO.

Declaration of Independence, these tendencies would be transformed in the half century after 1776 into one of the central ideals of American life.

Under the title "Constitutional Tensions in the British Empire, 1660–1763," the earliest draft of this paper was presented at a session on "Constitutional Tensions in the American Empires during the Eighteenth Century," at the Eightieth Annual Meeting of the American Historical Association, San Francisco, California, December 29, 1965. With minor verbal changes, it is here reprinted with the permission of Harper Collins Publishers from Jack P. Greene, ed., *Great Britain and the American Colonies, 1606–1763* (New York: Harper & Row, 1970), xi–xlvii.

Four

The Glorious Revolution and the British Empire 1688–1783

ANY EXAMINATION of the meaning of the Glorious Revolution for the newest and most distant members of the vast extended polity that comprised the English Empire at the end of the seventeenth century must confront three related questions. First is the question of what precisely the Glorious Revolution was. Second is the question of the immediate context and impact of the Glorious Revolution in the colonies. Third is the question of the long-range significance of the revolution for the extending Anglophone or, after 1707, British Empire.[1]

Few historians of metropolitan Britain have much concerned themselves with either the second or the third of these questions, and most colonial historians who have interested themselves in the meaning of the Glorious Revolution for the colonies have concentrated upon the years immediately before and after it, upon the contemporary uprisings in Massachusetts, New York, and Maryland, and on relationships between metropolis and colonies during the decades immediately before and after. In the process they have neither sought to refine or to extend definitions of the revolution borrowed from historians of the metropolis nor showed much interest in exploring the long-term implications of the revolution and the revolutionary settlement for the proliferating polities of colonial British America. In the interest of trying to achieve some broader perspective on the Glorious Revolution and its meaning for the larger An-

---

[1] The argument and materials presented here are largely drawn from my recent book, *Peripheries and Center: Constitutional Development in the Extended Polities of the British Empire and the United States, 1607–1788* (Athens, Ga., 1986).

glophone world, this chapter focuses primarily upon those long-term implications.

Before launching into this extensive subject, however, it will be useful to explore some of the ramifications of the rather complex recent historiography on the immediate context and impact of the Glorious Revolution in the colonies. The view that seems to be emerging from this historiography is, for the most part, a success story—for the metropolis. In this interpretation the Glorious Revolution was little more than a stage in the successful effort, begun under Charles II, to consolidate the authority of the metropolitan government in the colonies.

The experiences of the two principal continental colonies have been cited to illustrate the wider dimensions and essential features of such an interpretation. Whereas Virginia, the oldest American colony, had already been forced fifteen years earlier in the wake of Bacon's Rebellion in 1676 to come to terms with post-Restoration English imperialism, Massachusetts, the most populous New England colony, was compelled in the immediate wake of the revolution to accept a charter which made the governor, who drew his authority from England, far more powerful than the elected House of Representatives, which drew its authority from the towns, a revolutionary development which significantly altered both the spiritual and the secular worlds of Massachusetts. Nor in either colony did the centralizing impulse stop at the colonial capitals. In Massachusetts, as a result of the new charter, the towns ostensibly lost authority to the provincial government. In Virginia the elected House of Burgesses and the localities its members represented apparently lost power to the royally appointed council.[2]

Still other developments seem to provide support for this emerging view. In the wake of 1688-89, New York, New Jersey, Pennsylvania, and Maryland, all formerly private colonies, came under the immediate control of the crown, albeit Pennsylvania rather quickly and Maryland within a generation reverted to their proprietary owners. A new navigation act in 1696 broadly extended central control over the external trade of the colonies, and London officials proved generally and often successfully resistant to most efforts by colonial legislatures to secure for their

---

[2] These developments are treated most extensively in Stephen Saunders Webb, *1676: The End of American Independence* (New York, 1984), and Richard R. Johnson, *Adjustment to Empire: The New England Colonies, 1675–1715* (New Brunswick, N.J., 1981).

constituents the principles of limited executive authority usually associated with the Glorious Revolution in England. Only where metropolitan
representatives obviously had acted in outrageously arbitrary ways, as
was the case in Jamaica with the duke of Albemarle in 1688, did the
crown show much concern for disciplining its agents for behavior that
appeared to locals to violate the rights usually thought to have been
confirmed to metropolitan English people by the Glorious Revolution.
Moreover, what the revolution and the revolutionary settlement left undone in this centralizing process, the wars of the next quarter century
apparently accomplished, for several scholars have emphasized how the
intercolonial wars of 1689-1713 heightened colonial dependence on the
center.[3]

From studies of these subjects as well as from a variety of analyses of
other aspects of metropolitan-colonial relations during earlier and later
periods can be constructed a broad interpretive framework which seems
to be gaining considerable scholarly support. According to this framework, an extraordinary devolution of authority outward to the new colonial peripheries during the first half of the seventeenth century was
followed by a gradual resumption of that authority between the Restoration and the middle decades of the eighteenth century as a result of several related developments: the imposition of the Navigation Acts, the
royalization of many private colonies, the establishment of successful
patronage networks running between the metropolis and the colonies,
the expansion of the royal bureaucracy, growing colonial dependence
upon the metropolis for defense, and what one scholar has referred to as
the "gradual and grudging adjustment [on the part of colonists] to imperial membership and monarchical rule." What had been a loose congeries
of political entities before 1660 slowly during the century thereafter became integrated into a large imperial framework with London at its center and the metropolitan political nation as its presiding force in a worldwide conflict of political empires.[4]

[3] David S. Lovejoy, *The Glorious Revolution in America* (New York, 1972); J. M. Sosin,
*English America and the Revolution of 1688: Royal Administration and the Structure of
Provincial Government* (Lincoln, Nebr., 1982); and I. K. Steele, *Politics of Colonial Pol-
icy: The Board of Trade in Colonial Administration, 1696-1720* (Oxford, 1968).

[4] On these developments, see, in addition to the works cited in note 3, A. P. Thornton,
West-India Policy under the Restoration (Oxford, 1956); Philip Haffenden, "The Crown
and the Colonial Charters, 1675-1688," *William and Mary Quarterly*, 3d ser., 14 (1958):
297-311, 452-66; Michael G. Hall, *Edward Randolph and the American Colonies, 1676-
1703* (Chapel Hill, N.C., 1960); Richard S. Dunn, "Imperial Pressures on Massachusetts
and Jamaica, 1675-1700," in Alison Gilbert Olson and Richard Maxwell Brown, eds.,

Although much can be said in favor of this line of interpretation, an examination of the long-range effects of the Glorious Revolution upon the wider British Empire suggests that it has been carried vastly too far. Such an examination first requires a general consideration of those domestic features of the revolution that seem to have had particular saliency for the wider imperial polity.

For English people, at least for those of a Whig persuasion, the Glorious Revolution more than anything else represented a victory for law and liberty, for limited and representative government. As a result of the revolution, the king's power within England was circumscribed and the principle of coordination, the idea of the king as one of three branches of Parliament, each with coordinate authority, was enshrined as the new orthodoxy. As Jennifer Carter has observed, England now "had a monarch depending on a parliamentary title, and a constitution based on law." The "two salient features of the post-Revolution constitution were, first, that however much it was disguised a parliamentary monarchy had replaced a divine right monarchy; and, secondly, [that] since 1689 the monarch had somehow learned to live with Parliament."[5]

Of course, as many scholars have emphasized, these developments were by no means a "foregone conclusion" at the time of the Glorious Revolution. Only gradually over the next half century did Parliament grow from what Burke subsequently called "a mere representative of the people, and a guardian of popular privileges for its own immediate constituents . . . into a mighty sovereign," from a body which was not simply "a control on the crown on its own behalf" to one that, as Burke put it, "communicated a sort of strength to the royal authority." As several historians have recently emphasized, the "concept of a sovereign parlia-

Anglo-American Political Relations, 1675–1775 (New Brunswick, N.J., 1970), 50–75; Stephen Saunders Webb, *The Governors-General: The English Army and the Definition of the Empire, 1569–1681* (Chapel Hill, N.C., 1979); J. M. Sosin, *English America and the Restoration Monarchy of Charles II: Trans-Atlantic Politics, Commerce, and Kinship* (Lincoln, Nebr., 1980); and James M. Henretta, *"Salutary Neglect": Colonial Administration under the Duke of Newcastle* (Princeton, N.J., 1972). The quotation is from Richard R. Johnson, "The Glorious Revolution in the Context of the Search for Atlantic Empire: The Example of John Nelson," paper presented at a conference on "The Glorious Revolution in America—Three Hundred Years After," College Park, Md., Apr. 30, 1988, 13.

[5] Jennifer Carter, "The Revolution and the Constitution," in Geoffrey Holmes, ed., *Britain after the Glorious Revolution, 1689–1715* (New York, 1969), 40, 47.

ment" had not been "reasonably foreseeable in 1689," was largely "a development of the mid-eighteenth century," and was only just "hardening into an orthodoxy" during the 1760s. By the latter date, however, this great constitutional change was virtually complete, and one of its primary effects, as Harry Dickinson has noted, was to transform the ancient "doctrine of non-resistance from a buttress of divine right monarchy into the strongest defence of an existing constitution, whatever form it might take."[6]

But the historians' conventional preoccupation with national events and central institutions and their focus upon the ascendancy of Parliament within Britain and the eventual triumph of the doctrine of parliamentary omnipotence during the mid-eighteenth century have perhaps tended to obscure a second important result of the Glorious Revolution and the broad political and constitutional settlement that came in its wake, a result which had particularly important implications for the governance of the most distant portions of the empire.

The rise of Parliament may have been the most important result of that revolution, but it was by no means the only one. Within Britain, as Carter has pointed out, another consequence of the revolution was "a distinct, though not complete, withdrawal of central authority from local affairs." Earlier in the seventeenth century, Charles I had undertaken an extensive effort to exert the authority of the central government over county and local affairs in both the civil and religious realms. Although this effort had been interrupted during the Civil War, the later Stuarts resumed it after the Restoration. "Perhaps nothing done in the 1680s by Charles II and James II," Carter has noted, "caused so much reaction against them as their interference with local privilege and the accustomed pattern of existing hierarchies—in counties, in corporations, or in university colleges."[7]

At least in the short run, the Glorious Revolution effectively put a brake upon this centralizing effort and thereby created the conditions necessary for "the typical eighteenth-century situation of gentry and

[6] Ibid., 55; Edmund Burke, "Letter to the Sheriffs of Bristol," *The Works of Edmund Burke*, 16 vols. (London, 1826), 3:188; H. T. Dickinson, "The Eighteenth-Century Debate on the Sovereignty of Parliament," Royal Historical Society, *Transactions*, 5th ser., 26 (1976): 189; and "The Eighteenth-Century Debate on the 'Glorious Revolution,'" *History* 61 (1976): 33, 39; Barbara A. Black, "The Constitution of the Empire: The Case for the Colonists," *University of Pennsylvania Law Review* 124 (1976): 1210–11; John Phillip Reid, *In Defiance of the Law: The Standing-Army Controversy, the Two Constitutions, and the Coming of the American Revolution* (Chapel Hill, N.C., 1981).

[7] Carter, "Revolution and the Constitution," 53.

aristocratic independence in the localities." Within Britain, the localities, along with the people who dominated them, enjoyed much less interference from the central government during the first half of the eighteenth century than they had at any time under the Stuart monarchy.
Especially under the Hanoverians, the establishment and cultivation of
extensive patronage networks by the center helped to mitigate the centrifugal tendencies that flowed out of this situation and to enhance the
power of London. But during the eighty years following the Glorious
Revolution, Britain may very well have experienced a significant redistribution of power—a devolution of authority—to the localities, as English, Welsh, and (after 1707) Scottish counties came close to resembling
what the sociologist Edward Shils in another context has referred to as
"pockets of approximate independence."[8]

To what extent and in what ways these two broad domestic results of
the Glorious Revolution affected the many outlying polities that composed the empire is not a subject that has received much attention from
historians. Recent literature on the immediate effects of the revolution
would seem to imply that they were by no means powerfully evident
outside the home islands. If the Glorious Revolution had guaranteed
that Britain would thenceforth have a constitution of principled limitation and government by consent, if it had made it clear that English
kings would thereafter, as the Massachusetts lawyer James Otis later
declared, be "made for the good of the people, and not the people for
them," the same apparently was not true for the king's American polities.[9]

That the revolution did little to stem the activities of an aggressive
metropolitan government bent upon consolidating English authority in

---

[8] Ibid., 53; T. H. Breen, *Puritans and Adventurers: Change and Persistence in Early
America* (New York, 1980), 4–24; Edward Shils, *Center and Periphery: Essays in Macro-
sociology* (Chicago, 1975), 10. See also Norma Landau, *Justices of the Peace, 1679–1760*
(Berkeley and Los Angeles, 1984), on the continuing independence of county elites in
regard to the internal affairs of the counties; and E. P. Thompson, "The Grid of Inheritance: A Comment," in Jack Goody, Joan Thirsk, and E. P. Thompson, eds., *Family and
Inheritance: Rural Society in Western Europe, 1200–1800* (Cambridge, Eng., 1976), 328–
60, on the "tenacity and force of local custom" in determining patterns of social and legal
relations in English local society.

[9] James Otis, *A Vindication of the Conduct of the House of Representatives of the Province
of Massachusetts-Bay* (Boston, 1762), 18.

the New World seems to be confirmed by that government's continuing insistence upon asserting a level of prerogative power in the colonies which, in the wake of the revolution, had been much eroded in England, where Parliament effectively acted to impose explicit restrictions upon royal authority. But metropolitan administrators never consented to extend those restrictions to the colonies. With Parliament taking no role in the internal governance of the colonies, crown officials were free to continue to claim wide prerogative powers there. Thus, long after the crown had given up its rights to veto laws, to prorogue and dissolve legislative bodies and determine the frequency of their meetings, to dismiss judges at pleasure, and to create courts in Britain itself, it continued to claim and in many cases actually to exercise such authority for its governors in the colonies.[10]

Yet the argument that the achievements of the Glorious Revolution did not apply to the colonies can be sustained only by ignoring a mass of evidence from the colonies. In 1688-89 the revolution was widely, if by no means exclusively, interpreted in the colonies as a victory for the security of the rights of Englishmen not just in the metropolis but throughout the English-speaking world, a victory, moreover, that some colonists, at least in Maryland, New York, and Massachusetts, had helped to gain through a common struggle against oppressive royal officials who, no less than their Stuart masters at home, appeared to have been agents of arbitrary government. Indeed, the revolution seems to have supplied a new intensity to efforts by colonial legislatures, previously stimulated by the centralizing efforts of the later Stuarts, to secure explicit written legal guarantees of their constituents' rights to English liberties and privileges. Between 1688 and 1696 the legislatures of at least seven colonies tried to pass measures in imitation of Parliament's 1689 Declaration of Rights.[11]

Notwithstanding the continuing resistance of crown officials to any efforts to limit the royal prerogative in the colonies, their behavior following the Glorious Revolution made it clear that the events of 1688-89 had effectively settled the question of representative government in the colonies in favor of the colonists. Although representative institutions

---

[10] See Bernard Bailyn, *The Origins of American Politics* (New York, 1968), 66–71.

[11] See Jack P. Greene, *Great Britain and the American Colonies, 1606—1763* (New York, 1970), xiii–xli [chap. 3 above]; A. Berriedale Keith, *Constitutional History of the First British Empire* (Oxford, 1930), 141–42; Lovejoy, *Glorious Revolution;* Nuala Zahadieh, "The Glorious Revolution in Jamaica," paper presented at a conference on "The Glorious Revolution in America—Three Hundred Years After," College Park, Md., Apr. 30, 1988.

had been an integral part of colonial governance since 1619, metropolitan officials under James II had moved strongly in the mid-1680s in the direction of abolishing them altogether by bringing all of the New England colonies together in the unrepresentative Dominion of New England. But the New Englanders had overthrown the dominion in 1689, and neither William III nor his advisers showed any disposition to revive it or to govern the colonies without representative assemblies. Not, in fact, until the nature of the empire changed in the nineteenth century did the home government again think of trying to govern settler colonies without representative institutions.

Other developments had similar results. Although the new Massachusetts charter of 1691 placed significant limitations upon the colony's traditional self-governing powers, it also provided the colony with greater self-governing privileges than were then enjoyed by any royal colony, and the return of Pennsylvania to William Penn in 1694 revealed both the new government's more respectful attitude toward charters and the limits of the metropolitan movement to royalize proprietary and corporate colonies. Following the Glorious Revolution, in fact, the campaign for a consolidated empire, for the retrenchment of local authority in the colonies through the elimination of private colonies, securing permanent revenues, and restricting the authority of colonial legislatures, was desultory, sporadic, unsustained, and, at best, only modestly successful.

Why this campaign was not more sustained and successful is a question which has a direct bearing upon the larger problem of the meaning of the Glorious Revolution for the peripheries of the empire. This question can be explained partly in terms of ideology and partly in terms of the necessary structure of governance within the empire. Within the metropolitan political establishment, the ideological commitment to limited governance and to the sanctity of private and corporate rights, a commitment which was reinforced by the conception of the British polity confirmed by the Glorious Revolution, obviously served as a powerful restraint upon metropolitan behavior toward the colonies.

Probably even more important were the nature and sources of metropolitan authority in those portions of the empire that lay outside the home islands. In the early 1720s in a passage in *Cato's Letters* that many writers on the colonies later found appropriate for quotation, John Trenchard and Thomas Gordon remarked that distant colonies could be kept dependent upon their parent states either "by Force" or by "using them well." Unlike most later and ostensibly similar political entities, however, the early modern British Empire was emphatically not held together by force. The few military units stationed in America before the mid-1750s were intended not to police but to defend the colonies, and British political society was strongly averse to paying for expeditionary forces to intervene in the colonies' domestic affairs. Bacon's Rebellion in 1676 was the last—and the only—time before the late 1760s that London authorities employed such an expedient. At least to some extent, British political society following the Glorious Revolution also found the use of force to intervene in local affairs ideologically uncongenial.[12]

Without a much larger force than it either had or could afford to have in the colonies, the British government thus had no choice in its efforts to maintain its authority there than, in Trenchard's and Gordon's words, to use them well. That "public opinion sets bounds to every government," that no government could function, as Burke put it, "without regard to the general opinion of those who were to be governed," was a truism among early modern political theorists; and although those people who were most closely involved in colonial administration in London often demanded tighter controls over the colonies, the metropolitan government never during the seven decades following the Glorious Revolution made a concerted effort to govern the colonies in ways that were at serious variance with colonial opinion.[13]

Just as the lack of troops in the colonies meant that metropolitan authority was heavily dependent upon provincial opinion in its relations with the colonies, the absence of elaborate and effective law enforcement agencies within the colonies, as well as the widespread distribution of the franchise, meant that provincial polities had to adopt a similarly consensual mode of governance toward the localities, a mode which was necessarily highly sensitive to local interests and opinions. Except in those few places where local governing functions were handled by the provincial governments, as was the case only in the smaller island colonies and in lowcountry South Carolina before the 1770s, enormous political responsibility—and authority—thus devolved upon local governing institutions. To a not insignificant degree, then, effective government in the empire resided not in London, and not even in the colonial capitals, but in local communities—just as it did in England itself. In the early modern British Empire, imperial government was thus very largely provincial and local government.

Moreover, the small size of the public realm in the colonies and the

---

[12] John Trenchard and Thomas Gordon, *Cato's Letters*, 4 vols. (London, 1724), 3:286.

[13] James Madison, "Public Opinion," Dec. 19, 1791, in *The Writings of James Madison*, ed. Gaillard Hunt, 9 vols. (New York, 1900–1910), 6:70; Burke, "Letter to the Sheriffs of Bristol," *Works* 3:179.

powerful resistance to taxation to pay for expanding that realm meant that leadership and officeholding were primarily volunteer rather than professional. In contrast to the situation in metropolitan Britain, the demands of war nowhere led either to the proliferation of civil and military offices nor to the development of elaborate systems of public credit presided over by an extensive and entrenched bureaucracy. For those reasons, the metropolitan patronage system in the colonies was not anywhere nearly so large as would seem to be suggested by the attention modern scholars have lavished upon it. There were fewer than 100 offices in the gift of the crown in the colonies in 1752 and, despite the creation of more than ten colonies during the intervening period, fewer than 200 in 1775. Failure to establish the sort of deep patronage networks that enabled London authorities to exert some degree of central control over localities in the home islands during the eighteenth century greatly inhibited a parallel development in the colonies.[14]

The scantiness of metropolitan coercive and utilitarian resources in the colonies necessarily meant that governance in the early modern British Empire was consensual and that metropolitan authority was heavily dependent upon whatever normative resources in the form of loyalty and patriotic attachment the crown could command. The intense British patriotism of the colonists throughout the American sections of the empire in the decades immediately before the American Revolution has been well documented. What has been much less studied is the great extent to which the strength of that patriotism in the colonies depended upon the continuing credibility of the colonists' belief that they shared in the legacy of the Glorious Revolution. Epitomized by the enjoyment of limited and representative government, by a high degree of local control over local affairs, and by a respect for the customary rights and privileges of corporate entities like the colonies, that legacy was chiefly what throughout the eighteenth century made English liberty not only the envy of much of the Western world but also the pride of Englishmen

---

[14] "List of Offices in the American Colonys the Nomination to Which Was Vested in the Board of Trade by Order in Council of the 11 of March 1752," Chatham Papers, Gifts and Deposits, 30/8/95, Public Record Office, London; A List of Offices in the North American and West Indian Colonies, 1775, William L. Clements Library, Ann Arbor, Mich. Among scholars who have stressed the importance of patronage in colonial political life are Alison Gilbert Olson, *Anglo-American Politics, 1660–1775: The Relationship between Parties in England and Colonial America* (New York, 1973); Stanley Nider Katz, *Newcastle's New York: Anglo-American Politics, 1732–1753* (Cambridge, Mass., 1968); John A. Schutz, *William Shirley: King's Governor of Massachusetts* (Chapel Hill, N.C., 1961); and Henretta, *"Salutary Neglect."*

wherever they resided within the vast extended polity of the British Empire.[15]

If the maintenance of this pride among colonists was the main source of strength for metropolitan authority in the colonies, then that authority depended very heavily upon the restraint of metropolitan officials in trying to exert it. To a significant degree, London officials following the Glorious Revolution managed to retain, probably even to enhance, the authority of the center in the peripheries of the empire by acquiescing in the devolution of considerable power to provincial governments. Like the central government in Britain itself during the same period, those governments in turn exercised that power in cooperation with and often in deference to the opinions of strategic elites within the localities.

Notwithstanding the undeniable preference among metropolitan officials for a more centralized imperial system, then, their commitment to the revolution's principles—to limited government, government by consent, and local control—and their weak resources of control dictated that the same flow of authority from the center to the localities that took place in England following the Glorious Revolution would also occur in the empire at large. At least over the long haul, the devolution of authority that had begun with colonization in the early seventeenth century was not seriously arrested before the American Revolution, and the extraordinary localization of authority that occurred in Ireland, the West Indies, and the North American colonies after 1688 ensured that, in contrast to contemporary Continental monarchies, Britain's expanding nation-state and overseas empire would emphatically not be founded on "methods of centralisation and absolutism."[16]

In both Ireland and the American colonies, the wide and highly selective application of English common law by provincial and local courts and the growth of parliamentary institutions during the eighteenth century symbolized this development. Before the Glorious Revolution, the Irish Parliament had convened only rarely. Though it met somewhat more frequently under Charles I, there were only three Irish Parliaments un-

---

[15] See Max Savelle, "Nationalism and Other Loyalties in the American Revolution," *American Historical Review* 67 (1962): 901–23; Paul A. Varg, "The Advent of Nationalism, 1758–1776," *American Quarterly* 17 (1964): 160–81.

[16] Carter, "Revolution and Constitution," 56.

der Elizabeth I and only one each under James I and Charles II. Between 1666 and 1692 it did not meet at all. Hence, as J. C. Beckett has noted, "the Irish parliament as we know it in the eighteenth century begins in 1692," when the ascendancy of the Protestant population as a result of the revolution enabled it "to take a more independent line than formerly," while the insufficiency of the Crown's hereditary revenues to meet the usual costs of government provided it with an opportunity "to assert its rights, even against England," in exchange for granting funds to make up the difference. As a result of these developments, the Irish Parliament beginning in 1692 both met regularly and developed a vigorous "spirit of independence." Comparable developments took place throughout the colonies in America. Just as was the case in Ireland with the Irish Parliament during these years, the local legislatures in the colonies became more and more essential to—and more and more the centerpieces of—provincial governance in every established colony.[17]

For the development of the British Empire as a whole, then, perhaps the most important results of the Glorious Revolution were the localization of power, the growth of parliamentary institutions, and the entrenchment of the associated traditions of principled limitation and government by consent, not just within Britain but also in Ireland and the American colonies. Notwithstanding important distinctions between the British and Irish Parliaments on the one hand and the colonial assemblies on the other, the growth in the power of all these bodies during the eighteenth century depended upon the same circumstance: the crown's inability to cover either the normal costs of government or extraordinary wartime expenses without formal grants from local legislative bodies.[18]

Contrary to recent historiography, moreover, war may have functioned to hasten this process, not to retard it. Although the involvement of Massachusets in the Seven Years' War was probably more extensive than that of any colony, local government there, as the legal historian John Phillip Reid has shown so forcefully, remained so strong that local authorities were repeatedly able to frustrate the designs of metropolitan officials during the 1760s and 1770s. To a very important extent, then, the British Empire in the 1760s and 1770s was still a loose congeries of

---

[17] J. C. Beckett, "The Irish Parliament in the Eighteenth Century," Belfast National History and Philosophical Society, *Proceedings*, 2d ser., 4 (1955): 18–20.

[18] See Jack P. Greene, *The Quest for Power: The Lower Houses of Assembly in the Southern Royal Colonies, 1689–1776* (Chapel Hill, N.C., 1963).

political entities, each of which enjoyed such extensive authority over local affairs as to be, practically speaking, almost self-governing states.[19]

The colonists' experience over the long period from 1688 to the 1760s had thus taught them that, as one Marylander put it in the late 1740s, "since the Settlement made at the *Revolution,*" the constitutions of the colonies, no less than that of Britain itself, had entered *"a new Aera"* in which "the main strong lines" of "the people's rights (including Americans)" had "been more particularly pointed out and established." In recent years several scholars have suggested that in resisting parliamentary authority during the 1760s and 1770s, the American colonies were "reject[ing] the results of" the Glorious Revolution. Far from rejecting the results of the Glorious Revolution, the colonists simply assumed that they were entitled to all its benefits. As a result of the revolution, they felt, their "Liberties & Constitution[s]" had been "secur'd & establish'd upon [just as] . . . firm and lasting [a] foundation" as had been those of Britain, and, in their view, an important foundation for that establishment had been the significant devolution of authority to provincial governments throughout the empire.[20]

Historians have often and accurately described the post-Glorious Revolutionary Anglophone world as an age of oligarchy. While this characterization is appropriate for all but the newest sociopolities in that world, it may well be misleading to the extent that it implies a cohesiveness or a centralization of authority within the larger extended polity of the empire. Even within Britain itself and certainly within each of the many polities in the periphery of the empire, oligarchies were segmented by space and identified powerfully with specific places and with the structures and customs of authority and privilege appertaining to those places. Perhaps as much as the familiar association of liberty with Englishness, this identification among locality, authority, and liberty had, in the wake of the Glorious Revolution, been encouraged and sustained in the outermost polities of the wider Anglophone world by the devolution process that did so much both to shape the separate polities in that world and to determine the character of relations among them.

---

[19] Alan Rogers, *Empire and Liberty: American Resistance to British Authority, 1755–1763* (Berkeley and Los Angeles, 1974); John Phillip Reid, *In a Defiant Stance: The Conditions of Law in Massachusetts Bay, the Irish Comparison, and the Coming of the American Revolution* (University Park, Pa., 1977).

[20] A Freeholder, *Maryland Gazette* (Annapolis), Mar. 16, 1748; Alison Gilbert Olson, "Parliament, Empire, and Parliamentary Law, 1776," in J. G. A. Pocock, ed., *Three British Revolutions: 1641, 1688, 1776* (Princeton, N.J., 1980), 289; C[hristopher] G[adsden],

To appreciate the deepest significance of this process in the era after the Glorious Revolution, it is useful, I would suggest, to understand that, in a fundamentally important sense, it extended well beyond the mere devolution of political authority from metropolis to provinces and from provinces to localities. By permitting individuals to exercise only lightly regulated control over their own lives and fortunes, it extended as well to individual freeholds and estates, even to individuals themselves, a development exemplified by the fetish for personal independence that was so powerful in eighteenth-century Britain and British America. It might even be suggested that this devolution of authority to the individual self went far deeper among the free population of America because of the much broader achievement of independence as a result of the wider dispersion of property among free people and the widespread diffusion of dependence through the proliferating institution of chattel slavery.

Not surprisingly in view of these developments, the metropolitan assertion of the doctrine of parliamentary supremacy as it was newly articulated in reference to the colonies in 1764-65 seemed, to many colonials, to represent "a total contradiction to every principle laid down at the time of the [Glorious] Revolution, as the rules by which the rights and privileges of every branch of our legislature were to be governed for ever." Indeed, by its insistence upon exerting a "*supreme* jurisdiction" over the colonies, Parliament seemed, to colonial spokesmen, not merely to be violating the most essential principles of the Glorious Revolution but actually to have assumed and to be acting upon precisely the same "high prerogative doctrine[s]" against which that revolution had been undertaken. Thus, the colonists believed, if by resisting Parliament they had become rebels, they were "rebels in the same way, and for the same reasons that the people of Britain were rebels, for supporting the [Glorious] Revolution."[21]

That is, they were merely acting to defend the rights they had long

South Carolina Gazette (Charleston), Dec. 17, 1764; *New York Gazette* (New York), Oct. 21, 1734.

[21] John Dickinson, *An Essay on the Constitutional Power of Great Britain over the Colonies in America* (Philadelphia, 1774), in Samuel Hazard et al., eds., *Pennsylvania Archives*, 138 vols. (Philadelphia and Harrisburg, Pa., 1852–), 2d ser., 3:565; *An Argument in Defence of the Exclusive Right Claimed by the Colonies to Tax Themselves* (London, 1774),

enjoyed as a result of the same devolution of authority to the localities, the same expansion of legislative power, and the same elaboration of customary legal traditions and institutions that had occurred in Britain itself following the Glorious Revolution. For the colonists, then, the Glorious Revolution signaled the rise not just of the British Parliament but of provincial parliaments in every polity within the empire. If, as the colonists and many people in the metropolis believed, the most important legacy of the Glorious Revolution was freedom from arbitrary government, then the metropolitan efforts of the 1760s and early 1770s seemed to be nothing less than an attempt to deprive the colonists of any share in that legacy.

Unrestrained by domestic and international circumstances that made the island colonies in the Atlantic and the Caribbean, Nova Scotia, Quebec, and the Floridas dependent upon the metropolis for defense, the leaders of the thirteen revolting colonies in 1776 could thus without the slightest logical legerdemain undertake an American Revolution in the conviction that it was necessary to secure for their inhabitants the guarantees of the Glorious Revolution, guarantees that were seen to be under assault from a British Parliament and an aggressive ministry bent upon governing the colonies in the arbitrary high-prerogative mode associated with the later Stuarts. In the historical circumstances that sustained this conviction, perhaps, lies the deepest meaning of the Glorious Revolution for the early modern British Empire, and especially for those colonies that seceded from that empire in 1776.

An early version of this paper was given as a closing comment at a conference on "The Glorious Revolution in America—Three Hundred Years After," sponsored by the Maryland Colloquium on Early American History, University of Maryland, College Park, April 30, 1988. The present version was developed for a conference on "The Glorious Revolution, 1688–89: Changing Perspectives," sponsored by George Washington University and the Folger Shakespeare Library, Washington, D.C., April 14, 1989. It is reprinted here with permission from Lois Schwoerer, ed., *The Revolution of 1688–89: Changing Perspectives* (Cambridge: Cambridge University Press, 1992), 260–71.

104; "An Apology for the Late Conduct in America," *London Gazeteer*, Apr. 7, 1774, in Peter Force, ed., *American Archives*, 9 vols. (Washington, D.C., 1837–53), 4th ser., 1:242; "To the Freemen of America: May 18, 1774," ibid., 336; [Hugh Baillie], *Some Observations on a Pamphlet Lately Published* (London, 1776), 2–3.

FIVE

The Gifts of Peace:
Social and Economic Expansion and Development in the Periodization of the Early American Past, 1713–63

AMERICAN HISTORIANS traditionally have concerned themselves largely with the description and exploration of great public events. The implications of this orientation for our understanding of early American history have been profound. For one thing, it has meant that a disproportionate amount of scholarly attention has been focused upon the two great events at either end of the colonial period: the settlement of the colonies during the seventeenth century and the origins and development of the American Revolution after 1760. It has also been in large part responsibile for the corresponding neglect of the long and relatively uneventful, if scarcely unimportant, years between the Glorious Revolution of 1689 and the end of the Seven Years' War in 1763, years during which each of the colonies seemed to settle down into a period of relatively self-contained development and during which, for the colonies as a whole, there was little common public history with the exception of the four intercolonial wars and the momentous series of spiritual explosions historians now call the Great Awakening. In the past, concern with these years has usually centered upon either the description of these important events or the exploration of some prominent general themes—the development of representative political institutions or of a common political culture—that seemed to have a direct bearing upon the coming of the American Revolution.

As American historians have to some extent moved away from event-oriented history over the past generation and especially during the last decades, an increasing number of scholars have produced a growing collection of monographs on many specific aspects of colonial life during these neglected years. But their studies have contributed almost as much to confuse us about the general picture as to enlighten us about detail. For what they have revealed is a tangle of seemingly discrete and idiosyncratic local developments and characteristics that have thus far largely defied systematic classification and comparison. The result is that we still do not have any firm grasp upon the period; we still have a clear sense neither of its general outline and underlying themes nor of whether it constituted a single, relatively undifferentiated unit of development or was rent by fundamental discontinuities. This chapter represents an effort to identify the main themes that characterized colonial life during the important formative years between 1713 and 1763 and to use those themes as the basis for developing a coherent scheme of periodization. In this scheme, not politics but the social and economic conditions that provided the central focus and context for public life receive primary emphasis.

In the British colonies of North America and the West Indies, the late summer and early fall of 1713 were punctuated by widespread public rejoicing over the signing of the Treaties of Utrecht and the successful conclusion of the War of the Spanish Succession earlier in the year. Colonial governors set aside special days of thanksgiving to enable the colonists to assemble in their local communities to give their "hearty thanks" to God for crowning the martial efforts of the British nation with such an "Honourable Peace." Meeting later that fall and winter, several of the colonial legislatures prepared formal addresses of thanks and congratulations to Queen Anne. Looking back over a difficult period now brought to a happy conclusion and forward to what would hopefully be a more tranquil and prosperous future, the colonists, in their prayers and addresses, pondered the meaning of this "great and valuable blessing" for themselves and their posterity.[1]

Whatever effect the peace of Utrecht might have upon the future, however lasting it might turn out to be, there was one sense in which its meaning was abundantly clear: it had finally provided a respite from what had been almost a quarter century of virtually uninterrupted mili-

---

[1] W. W. Hening, ed., *The Statutes at Large: Being a Collection of All the Laws of Virginia*, 13 vols. (Richmond, etc., 1809–23), 4:560, 561–62.

tary conflict among the nations of western and central Europe and their colonies. For Great Britain and its colonies, this conflict had begun in 1689 with the eight-year War of the League of Augsburg (King William's War in the colonies) and, after a brief interlude between 1697 and 1702, had continued for eleven more years through the War of the Spanish Succession (Queen Anne's War in the colonies). These wars, though in many ways economically beneficial to the home islands,[2] had placed very heavy demands upon their energies and resources. For the colonies they had been considerably less exacting. Nevertheless, recurrent fighting in the Caribbean and along the northern edges of New England and New York in both wars and along the Carolina frontier between Spanish Florida and French Louisiana in the second war had required burdensome outlays of men and money, especially by the colonies at the northern and southern extremities of the continental settlements.

The psychological costs of the wars are more difficult to assess, but the long period of conflict seems to have had a marked depressive effect upon the expansive energies of the colonies. The French and Indian threat in the north clearly impeded the advance into Maine, New Hampshire, northern and western Massachusetts, and northern New York, and relatively few new frontier areas were opened up for settlement.[3] Whether from a decline in immigration, birthrate, or both, the rate of population growth slowed perceptibly. Among colonists of European extraction, the growth rate dropped from 80.3 percent over the two decades from 1670 to 1690 to only 48.1 percent for the period between 1690 and 1710, the lowest percentage increase for any twenty-year period between 1670 and 1770. The decline in New England was most dramatic, from 66.9 percent to 30.8 percent, with the rate in Massachusetts falling from 60.7 percent to a mere 8 percent. But it also fell sharply in New York, and even the Chesapeake colonies, which were less directly involved in the fighting, had a significantly lower rate over the period from 1690 to 1710 than for any earlier or later comparable time span during the colonial period.[4] Because of the dearth of reliable trade statistics before 1697, the impact of the wars upon the overseas trade of the colonies cannot be measured precisely, though the rate of increase in the amount

---

[2] On this point, see A. H. John, "War and the English Economy, 1700–1763," *Economic History Review* 7 (1955): 329–44.

[3] See Douglas Edward Leach, *The Northern Colonial Frontier, 1607–1763* (New York, 1966), 109–25; Lois Matthews Rosenberry, *The Expansion of New England* (Boston, 1909), 58–63; Ruth L. Higgins, *Expansion in New York with Especial Reference to the*

of trade between the colonies and the British Isles, if not also in other branches of colonial trade, may have fallen significantly,[5] and a small decline in the rate of increase among the black population suggests less activity in the slave trade.[6]

The hope in 1713 was that the Utrecht settlement would be the first step in reversing these trends, and in this hope Britons both at home and in the colonies were not to be disappointed. For the settlement marked the beginning of a quarter century of peace and prosperity for the British Empire in general and of rapid and uninterrupted growth for the mainland colonies in particular. Far more than the unconnected political histories of individual colonies, this extensive growth in every sector of life provided the central theme of colonial British American history between 1713 and 1763. Equally important, it laid the territorial, demographic, and economic foundations for the period of intensive differentiation and development that followed during the thirty years beginning around 1730.

Of course, the peace of 1713–39 was always tenuous. Minor wars with Spain twice temporarily broke it, first in 1717–21 and then in 1728–29. Notwithstanding a recurring series of disputes over questions of succession and other dynastic ambitions and an intensification of commercial rivalries among the several colonial powers in America, however, "exhaustion after a quarter of a century of war," the waning of traditional religious rivalries, and the dedication of both France and Britain to the maintenance of peace combined to prevent the outbreak of a general war. The Triple Alliance by which Britain, France, and the Netherlands pledged to maintain the status quo as established at Utrecht served as a powerful deterrent to war for sixteen years after its signing in 1717, and the continued unwillingness of France to risk war by backing Spain in its

---

Eighteenth Century (Columbus, Ohio, 1931), 37–41, 47–52, 56–59; Verner W. Crane, *The Southern Frontier, 1670–1732* (Ann Arbor, Mich., 1929), 47–107; and, especially, David E. Van Deventer, *The Emergence of Provincial New Hampshire, 1623–1741* (Baltimore, 1976), 62–84.

[4] These rates were computed from the table of "Estimated Population of the American Colonies: 1610 to 1780," *Historical Statistics of the United States, Colonial Times to 1857* (Washington, D.C., 1960), ser. Z, 1–19, 756.

[5] See Phyllis Deane and W. A. Cole, *British Economic Growth, 1688–1959: Trends and Structure* (Cambridge, Eng., 1962), 86–88.

[6] Absence of reliable data makes it impossible to determine with any accuracy the changing volume of slave importations into the British continental colonies prior to 1690. For the years 1690 to 1710, however, see Philip D. Curtin, *The Atlantic Slave Trade: A Census* (Madison, Wis., 1969), 127–54.

commercial and territorial disputes with Britain, even after the rap-
prochement between the two Latin powers in the *pacte de famille* in 1733,
helped to stave off an Anglo-Spanish conflict for another six years.[7]

Within Britain, two central policy objectives operated to predispose
the government to try to avoid war through the long ministry of Sir
Robert Walpole from 1721 to 1742. The first was Walpole's determination
to achieve internal political stability. The settlement of the great religious controversies of the seventeenth century, the rejection of divine
right theory after 1688, and Walpole's own superb talents as a political
manager and as a contriver of informal mechanisms to control the large
and unruly British electorate helped—along with favorable international
and economic conditions—to guarantee his success. Yet the stability
achieved by Walpole could never be taken for granted because it always
seemed on the verge of disruption from many of the same sources that
had kept the English political system in a convulsed state for most of
the previous half century: the relentless "pressure from the Dissenters to
change the *status quo*," the lingering threat of the return of the violent
party strife that had rent English politics since the last years of Charles
II, and the apparent precariousness of the Protestant succession.

Indeed, the issue of the succession seemed to acquire an even greater
potential for disruption with the accession of the Hanoverians following
the death of Queen Anne in 1714. German-born and preoccupied with
Hanoverian affairs, neither George I (1714–27) nor George II (1727–60)
was ever so popular with his British subjects as to feel completely secure
upon the British throne as long as there was a potential alternative focus
of loyalty in the person of the Stuart Pretender, James III, son of the
Stuart deposed by William III and Parliament in the name of Protes-
tantism and liberty during the Glorious Revolution of 1688. The Pretender had enough supporters in the Scottish Highlands to raise a full-
scale rebellion in 1715 and to provoke additional scares of Jacobite risings
and plots to overthrow the government in 1717, 1718, 1719, and 1723.
Not until France formally renounced its support for the Pretender by
the Treaty of Aix-la-Chapelle in 1748 did the Stuart menace, which had
produced another, even larger, uprising in Scotland in 1745, cease to be
a source of deep anxiety for British ministers.

A new and seemingly equally dangerous destabilizing element was the

---

[7] W. F. Reddaway, "Rivalry for Colonial Power, 1714–1748," in J. Holland Rose, A. P.
Newton, and E. A. Benians, eds., *The Cambridge History of the British Empire*, vol. 1,
The Old Empire from the Beginnings to 1783 (New York and Cambridge, Eng., 1929),
346–70; Max Savelle, "The American Balance of Power and European Diplomacy, 1713–

emergence of a highly vocal and rancorous opposition beginning in the 1720s. Under the brilliant leadership of Henry St. John, first Viscount Bolingbroke, the ex-Tory minister who returned from exile in 1725, radical Whig and dissenting writers on the left and alienated Tory intellectuals on the right subjected Walpole to a murderous political crossfire as they hammered away at the central charge that his use of patronage and public funds to secure support for his government was part of a systematic "Robinarchical" conspiracy to subvert the constitution and destroy the moral fabric of British society.[8]

If Walpole's efforts to maintain political stability in the face of these many potentially disruptive elements led him to pursue a policy of peace, so also did his devotion to promoting British commerce. Persuaded that commerce was "the main riches of the nation,"[9] Walpole rarely lost an opportunity to encourage mercantile enterprise. To the great chagrin of Tory critics of the new economic order of "projecting," stockjobbing, continuing national indebtedness, and increased governmental influence for new financial institutions such as the Bank of England, Walpole actively promoted the projects of the new men of money and looked out for their interests, even to the extent of arranging a "parliamentary whitewash" of the South Sea Bubble in 1721.[10] No less than Walpole, British commercial interests were intent upon preserving the peace. For one thing, the memory of the adverse effects of the wars of 1689–1713 was always fresh in their minds. For another, the colonial trade quickly emerged as "the principal dynamic element" in British foreign trade following the settlement at Utrecht,[11] which proved so favorable to Britain in the colonial sphere as to make major expansion possible without military conflict.

Neither the territorial nor the commercial settlements secured at Utrecht could have been any better contrived for Britain's economic advantage. By the territorial settlement Britain secured title to St. Chris-

---

78," in Richard B. Morris, ed., *The Era of the American Revolution* (New York, 1939), 140–55.

[8] J. H. Plumb, *The Origins of Political Stability: England, 1675–1725* (Boston, 1967), 159–89; Archibald S. Foord, *His Majesty's Opposition, 1714–1830* (New York, 1964), 42–216; Reddaway, "Rivalry for Colonial Power," 347–54; Isaac Kramnick, *Bolingbroke and His Circle: The Politics of Nostalgia in the Age of Walpole* (Cambridge, Mass., 1968).

[9] Sir Robert Walpole, *Cautions to Those Who Are to Chuse Members to Serve in Parliament* (London, 1714), 2, as cited by Reddaway, "Rivalry for Colonial Power," 348.

[10] Kramnick, *Bolingbroke and His Circle*, 48–55; Michael Kammen, *Empire and Interest: The American Colonies and the Politics of Mercantilism* (Philadelphia, 1970), 60–71.

[11] Ralph Davis, "English Foreign Trade, 1700–1714," *Economic History Review* 15 (1962–63): 290.

topher's in the West Indies and Acadia, Newfoundland, and Hudson's Bay on the continent. These acquisitions not only reduced the possibilities for Anglo-French friction in the colonies by placing most of the areas of former conflict securely in British hands but also gave the British continental colonies abundant room for expansion without fear of coming into direct contact with the settlements of another major colonial power. By the commercial settlement, which was embodied in the Asiento Treaty, the British also acquired for the South Sea Company the right both to supply the Spanish colonies in America with slaves from Africa and to send an "annual ship" to engage in other forms of direct trade with those colonies. These privileges thus opened up to the British on a legal basis the still vast riches of the Spanish Empire in America and encouraged the development of a brisk illegal trade between the British West Indian colonies and Spain's American possessions. Although this contraband trade and the methods undertaken by the Spanish to suppress it were perpetual sources of tension between Britain and Spain, they were not in themselves of sufficient importance to provoke a war.[12]

For the British continental colonies in North America, the effects of a number of international and metropolitan conditions that obtained after the war—the continuance of peace, the achievement of domestic political stability within Britain, the home government's dedication to promoting overseas trade, and the favored position of Britain in the New World following the Utrecht settlement—were profound. For virtually the first time in their history, they were, for a long period, largely free from the anxieties and distractions of war. Even relations with the Indians were comparatively peaceful. In frontier areas where there was heavy commerce between whites and Indians or significant white encroachment upon lands claimed by powerful Indian tribes, notably in South Carolina and Maine, Indian-white relations were always tense and potentially explosive. But there were only two serious Indian wars during the quarter century following Utrecht, and both—the Yamassee War in South Carolina in 1715–16 and the Abenaki War in northern New England in 1722–26—were localized and did not represent a serious or lasting bar to the expansion of colonial settlement.[13] For a few years following the peace, former wartime privateers who, like "Blackbeard" (Ed-

---

[12] Savelle, "American Balance of Power," 140–55.

[13] See Howard H. Peckham, *The Colonial Wars, 1689–1762* (Chicago, 1964), 81–87; Max Savelle, *The Origins of American Diplomacy: The International History of Anglo-America, 1492–1763* (New York, 1967), 232–47, 262–69; Crane, *Southern Frontier,* 162–280; Leach, *Northern Colonial Frontier,* 126–56.

ward Teach or Thach), turned to piracy after the war inflicted heavy losses upon colonial commerce in both the Atlantic and the Caribbean. But the combined efforts of the colonial governments and the British navy had destroyed this menace by the early 1720s. Thereafter, ships engaged in the colonial trade moved with fewer dangers of seizure than at any time since the 1680s.[14]

Beginning in 1721 with Walpole's administration, moreover, there was a significant easing of tensions between the colonies and the metropolitan government. The usual press of domestic and international affairs inevitably meant that Walpole's government, like most of its predecessors, would have little time for colonial matters. Vastly more important was a marked tendency to permit the colonies to proceed on their own with little interference from Britain except in matters that were of serious and pressing concern to powerful interest groups in the home islands, the result of Walpole's dedication to promoting the economic well-being of the nation, to which the colonies were making an increasingly important contribution, and to avoiding political difficulties for the administration at home. Consequently, metropolitan authorities repeatedly sacrificed long-standing goals for bringing the colonies under closer supervision to immediate economic and political advantage whenever it seemed necessary and expedient to do so, and the colonists found themselves subjected to fewer pressures from the metropolitan government than at any period since the Restoration.[15]

This long span of peace and relaxation of pressure from the metropolitan government permitted the colonists to give free rein to their expansive energies, and the quarter century following the Utrecht settlement marked the beginning of a sustained period of territorial, demographic, and economic growth for the continental colonies that, except for a brief deceleration in the 1740s and 1750s, continued at a rapid pace until the end of the colonial period and, of course, on into the nineteenth century.

At the conclusion of Queen Anne's War in 1713, the colonists were still

---

[14] The effects of piracy upon colonial trade have never been adequately studied, but see Shirley C. Hughson, *The Carolina Pirates and Colonial Commerce, 1640–1740* (Baltimore, 1894), 1–134, and John F. Jameson, ed., *Privateering and Piracy in the Colonial Period: Illustrative Documents* (New York, 1923).

[15] For a more extensive discussion, see Jack P. Greene, *Great Britain and the American Colonies, 1606–1763* (New York, 1970), xxxi–xli [chap. 3 above].

clustered in a series of noncontiguous nuclei up and down the Atlantic seaboard. There were two large centers of settlement, one in Virginia and Maryland stretching all around Chesapeake Bay and another covering the coastal regions of eastern and southern New England and reaching up the valleys of the Connecticut and other major rivers. Two smaller concentrations of population fanned out from Philadelphia and New York, and there were isolated groups of settlements on the central Maine coast, on the upper Connecticut River valley in what is now southeastern Vermont, around Albany on the Hudson River, on the upper Delaware River in the vicinity of Easton, Pennsylvania, on the lower Delaware, at three widely dispersed points in tidewater North Carolina, and at Charleston and Port Royal in South Carolina. Over the next twenty-five years, population spread out in all directions from these nuclei until there was one long continuum of settlement stretching from Pamlico Sound in North Carolina north to southern Maine and reaching inland more than 100 miles from the New England coast and more than 150 from the Chesapeake and Delaware into the easternmost mountain valleys of Pennsylvania and Virginia. In the south there was a series of larger, if still noncontiguous, centers in southern North Carolina, South Carolina, and the new colony of Georgia, founded in 1733.[16]

This extraordinary expansion of settled area was accompanied by a rapid growth of population. During the three decades from 1711 to 1740, the number of white inhabitants in the continental colonies increased by over 160 percent, from 289,162 to 753,721.[17] By contemporary standards in either Europe or in the colonies of other European powers in America,[18] the decennial rates of growth were remarkably high: 38.8 percent from 1711 to 1720, 34.4 percent from 1721 to 1730, and 39.5 percent from 1731 to 1740. Over the whole thirty-year period, the rate of increase was most impressive in the Middle Colonies and in the Carolinas and

---

[16] See Fulmer Mood, "Studies in the History of American Settled Areas and Frontier Lines," *Agricultural History* 26 (1952): 16–34; Herman Ralph Friis, *A Series of Population Maps of the Colonies and the United States, 1625–1790* (New York, 1940); Leach, *Northern Colonial Frontier,* 126–43; Rosenberry, *Expansion of New England,* 76–107; Higgins, *Expansion in New York,* 47–69; Robert L. Meriwether, *The Expansion of South Carolina, 1729–1765* (Kingsport, Tenn., 1940), 3–30.

[17] These and subsequent data on population growth were derived from an adjusted version of the table on "Estimated Population of American Colonies," *Historical Statistics of the United States,* 756.

[18] See J. Potter, "The Growth of Population in America, 1700–1860," in D. V. Glass and D. E. C. Eversley, eds., *Population in History: Essays in Historical Demography* (Chicago, 1965), 631–46.

Table 5.1. Estimated number of immigrants by decade, 1711–40

1711–20		37,940
1721–30		25,533
1731–40		60,362
	Total	123,835

Georgia: 222.6 percent in Pennsylvania and Delaware, 175.1 percent in the Carolinas and Georgia, and 172.1 percent in New York and New Jersey. But the population of the New England and Chesapeake colonies also grew rapidly: 149.9 percent in the former and 125.6 percent in the latter. Regional variations in these rates from one decade to another reflected the general movement of population and changing patterns of international migration. Thus, between 1710 and 1720 the rate of increase was highest in New York and New Jersey (56.9%) and New England (48.3%), older colonies whose expansion had been checked by the long years of war between 1689 and 1713. By contrast, during the next two decades growth rates were highest in newer colonies in which vast new regions were just opening up for settlement, as the white population of Pennsylvania and Delaware increased by 75.8 percent in the 1720s and 73.1 percent in the 1730s while that of the Carolinas and Georgia grew by 45.8 percent in the 1720s and 69.9 percent in the 1730s.

A substantial portion of the total increase of the white population was the result of an expanding immigration from Great Britain and Europe. Exactly how high the proportion was cannot at present be determined with any certainty. There has been no comprehensive or systematic study of the problem, and accessible evidence is extremely fragmentary.[19] However, at least a rough idea of the volume of immigrants can be obtained by using available decennial estimates of the white population. Though the rate of natural increase among colonial whites obviously varied somewhat from place to place and from time to time according to a number of different variables, the average decennial rate of natural increase for the colonies as a whole appears to have been slightly over 28 percent,[20] the figure used to prepare table 5.1, showing the total estimated number of immigrants by decade between 1711 and 1740. Because this

---

[19] See Henry A. Gemery, "European Emigration to North America, 1700–1820: Numbers and Quasi-Numbers," *Perspectives in American History*, n.s., 1 (1984): 283–342; Robert V. Wells, *Population of the British Colonies in America before 1776: A Survey of Census Data* (Princeton, N.J., 1975).

[20] Potter, "Growth of Population in America," 645–46.

figure is, if anything, probably too low,[21] the totals are probably too high and represent the maximum rather than the minimum possible number of immigrants. If these totals are reasonably accurate, then only slightly more than a fourth of the total increase of the white population between 1711 and 1740 can be accounted for by first-generation immigrants.

Historians have traditionally emphasized the non-English character of this early eighteenth-century immigration. There had, of course, been non-English elements in the colonies during the seventeenth century. The English had inherited from 5,000 to 7,000 Dutch settlers and from 1,000 to 3,000 Swedes and colonists of still other nationalities with the conquest of New Netherlands in 1664.[22] Thereafter, the largest single group of foreigners to migrate to the colonies in the seventeenth century were the French Huguenots, 15,000 of whom immigrated in the twenty years following the ending of toleration for French Protestants by the revocation of the Edict of Nantes in 1685. Though they settled in every colony, the heaviest concentrations were in South Carolina, New York, and New England.[23] Finally, a small cluster of German Pietists had settled at Germantown in Pennsylvania in 1683, and a few Scots were scattered throughout the colonies.[24]

But non-English immigrants did not begin to appear in large numbers until the early decades of the eighteenth century. Scots, from both the lowlands and the highlands, came in significant numbers only after the Act of Union between England and Scotland in 1707, and even then they did not come in large numbers for the next thirty years, so that the total number of Scottish immigrants between 1707 and 1740 probably did not exceed 10,000.[25] Heavy German immigration began in 1708 with the migration of a small group of war refugees from the Palatinate to New

---

[21] Contemporary estimates ran much higher, and Potter thinks that it may have been as high as 30%. See ibid., 662.

[22] On the Dutch, see Thomas J. Condon, *New York Beginnings: The Commercial Origins of New Netherland* (New York, 1968), 177; Carl Wittke, *We Who Built America: The Saga of the Immigrant* (Cleveland, 1964), 14–22.

[23] Wittke, *We Who Built America*, 23–34; Arthur H. Hirsch, *The Huguenots of Colonial South Carolina* (Durham, N.C., 1928); Gilbert Chinard, *Les Réfugiés Huguenots en Amérique* (Paris, 1925). A recent work, Jon Butler, *The Huguenots in America: A Refugee People in New World Society* (Cambridge, Mass., 1983), 41–67, significantly revises these figures downward.

[24] Albert Bernhardt Faust, *The German Element in the United States*, 2 vols. (New York, 1927), 1:111–12; Ian Charles Cargill Graham, *Colonists from Scotland: Emigration to North America, 1707–1783* (Ithaca, N.Y., 1956), 9–17.

[25] See Graham, *Colonists from Scotland*, 25, 43–46, 105–27, 185.

York. In subsequent decades the ravages of war in their homelands, rising taxes, natural disasters, religious persecution, and the lures of enterprising colony promoters brought thousands of immigrants, primarily from the southwestern portions of Germany and the German-speaking cantons of Switzerland, to New York, North Carolina, New Jersey, and, in greatest numbers, to Pennsylvania and Delaware, from which, beginning in the 1730s, they moved south and west into Maryland, Virginia, and the Carolinas. According to the best available estimates, approximately 29,000 German-speaking people immigrated to the colonies between 1710 and 1740.[26] Starting in 1718, a series of natural calamities combined with rising rents, a mutable linen industry, and long-standing Presbyterian fears of Episcopal persecution to drive significant numbers of descendants of seventeenth-century Scottish colonists of northern Ireland to the colonies. From then until 1740, perhaps as many as 35,000 of these Ulster Scots migrated in successive waves that correlated closely with periods of adverse economic conditions in Ulster. The first of them went to New England, where they settled primarily in New Hampshire, and a few thousand migrated to South Carolina and New York, but as in the case of the Germans, the vast majority went to Delaware and Pennsylvania and from thence west and south into the Chesapeake colonies and the Carolinas.[27]

Even if these estimates are reasonably correct, however, and they rest on a very unsatisfactory base and may be considerably too high, the largest single group of immigrants of the period 1711–40 still came from England. The combined immigration totals of Scots, Germans, and Ulster Scots was only 74,000, and the number of people from other non-English groups migrating to the colonies at this time was statistically

---

[26] This estimate is based upon the data in Oscar Kuhns, *The German and Swiss Settlements of Colonial Pennsylvania* (New York, 1901), 30–61; Walter Allen Knittle, *The Early Eighteenth Century Palatine Emigration* (Philadelphia, 1936), 242–44, 282–303; Faust, *German Element in the United States* 1:73–262; Albert B. Faust, "Swiss Emigration to the American Colonies in the Eighteenth Century," *American Historical Review* 22 (1916): 43–44; Frank Spencer, ed., "An Eighteenth-Century Account of German Emigration to the American Colonies," *Journal of Modern History* 28 (1956): 57. An excellent recent work is Marianne S. Wokeck, "Harnessing the Lure of the 'Best Poor Man's Country': The Dynamics of German-Speaking Immigration to British North America, 1683–1783," in Ida Altman and James Horn, eds., *To Make America: European Emigration in the Early Modern Period* (Berkeley, Calif., 1991), 204–43.

[27] See, especially, R. J. Dickson, *Ulster Emigration to Colonial America, 1718–1775* (London, 1966), 1–59; James G. Leyburn, *The Scotch-Irish: A Social History* (Chapel Hill, N.C., 1962), 180–81.

insignificant. Thus, of the estimated total of 123,835 immigrants, at least 49,835, or almost 40 percent, were English.[28] Altogether, immigrants from the British Isles—Englishmen, Scots, and Ulster Scots—accounted for over 75 percent of the total immigration.

Despite the crudeness and the uncertainty of the estimates for either the total number of immigrants or their distribution according to national origins, it is reasonably clear that a very high proportion of the growth in the white population of the colonies during the long years of peace from 1713 to 1740 is attributable to natural increase rather than to immigration. If, as very crude estimates suggest, the number of immigrants was no more than 123,835 and the average decennial rate of natural increase was roughly 28 percent, almost three-fourths, or 346,081 of the total growth of 469,916, was the product of natural increase.

This phenomenal rate of growth, which, as one scholar has remarked, was "considerably higher than that to be found in England at any time in the eighteenth and nineteenth centuries" and which provided the basis for the population theories of the economist T. R. Malthus,[29] has never been adequately explained, in large part, like other aspects of the demographic history of the colonies, because of the dearth of relevant data or the difficulty of retrieving extant materials. Contemporaries such as Benjamin Franklin and Ezra Stiles attributed it to unusually early marriages for women, and this factor may have been an important one in newly settled or rapidly expanding areas in which the rate of natural increase probably greatly exceeded the assumed average of 28 percent. But newer studies of older, less dynamic, and more settled areas in New England reveal that marriages for women below the age of twenty were unusual and that the average age of marriage—between twenty and twenty-two—was only two or three years younger than in the eighteenth century, hardly a great enough difference to account for the wide disparity in rates of natural population growth between the colonies and Britain.[30]

---

[28] There has been little study of immigration from England before the 1770s. See Mildred Campbell, "English Emigration on the Eve of the American Revolution," *American Historical Review* 61 (1955): 1–20, and Clifford K. Shipton, "Immigration to New England, 1680–1740," *Journal of Political Economy* 44 (1936): 225–27.

[29] See Potter, "Growth of Population in America," 631–33; Alfred O. Aldridge, "Franklin as Demographer," *Journal of Economic History* 9 (1949): 25–44; James H. Cassedy, *Demography in Early America: Beginnings of the Statistical Mind, 1600–1800* (Cambridge, Mass., 1969), 148–79.

[30] See John Demos, *A Little Commonwealth: Family Life in Plymouth Colony* (New York, 1970), 151, 193; Philip J. Greven, Jr., *Four Generations: Population, Land, and the Family*

Although firm conclusions are impossible without extensive additional research, a more plausible explanation has been advanced by Jim Potter and has found some support in recent local studies. Potter's suggestion is that the rapid natural growth of the colonial population resulted from a "combination of a moderately high . . . fertility rate" of 45–50 per thousand and "a moderate death rate of 20–25 per thousand," with the death rate reflecting "astonishingly low infant mortality" for the eighteenth century. These phenomena, Potter suggests in accord with eighteenth-century students of the subject, are in turn explicable primarily in terms of the "high productivity of American agriculture." Sufficiently abundant to allow the "population to grow despite all the rigours of the climate and of pioneer life," the food supply, Potter concludes, "sustained the health of women of child-bearing age and thus kept low the infant mortality rate."[31] A "relatively low incidence of contagious diseases," presumably the result of the predominantly nonurban character of the colonies, is an additional possible explanation for this low death rate.[32]

Whatever the specific explanation, it is clear that the psychological inhibitions that acted as a brake upon reproduction in countries with less opportunity were much less powerful in the colonies, at least outside older settled areas. Something of the expansive response to the existence of so much space and opportunity was suggested by William Byrd of Westover in 1729. "Mrs. Byrd will hardly be in a travelling condition till she's towards 50," he wrote to a female friend in London in explaining why he could not visit England; "I know knothing but a rabit that breeds faster. It would [be] ungallant in a husband to disswade her from it, but it would be kind in you, to preach her upon that chapter as a friend. She was delivered of a huge boy in September last and is so unconscionable as to be breeding again, nay the learned say she is some months gone. The truth of it is, she has her reasons for procreateing so fast. She lives in an infant country which wants nothing but people."[33]

---

in *Colonial Andover, Massachusetts* (Ithaca, N.Y., 1970), 31–37; and especially, the more general study of Robert Higgs and H. Louis Stettler III, "Colonial New England Demography: A Sampling Approach," *William and Mary Quarterly*, 3d ser., 27 (1970): 282–93.

[31] Potter, "Growth of Population in America," 646, 663.

[32] See Warren S. Thompson, "The Demographic Revolution in the United States," American Academy of Political and Social Sciences, *Annals*, no. 262 (1949): 62.

[33] Byrd to Mrs. Jane Taylor, April 3, 1729, in Marion Tinling, ed., *The Correspondence of the Three William Byrds of Westover, Virginia, 1684–1776*, 2 vols. (Charlottesville, Va., 1977), 1:391.

The black population expanded even more rapidly over the same period, rising by almost 235 percent from 44,866 in 1710 to 150,024 in 1740. The decennial growth rate was high—54.4 percent—between 1711 and 1720, and, though it fell to 32.2 percent during the 1720s, it rose sharply during the 1730s to 64.8 percent, the highest growth rate for any decade between 1690 and 1770. Because the vast majority of the black population—perhaps as high as 98 or 99 percent—was slave, this dramatic increase reflects a major expansion of the institution of slave labor. The expansion was, therefore, especially rapid in the southern plantation colonies, where the black population mushroomed from just over 36,000 in 1710 to over 125,000 in 1740.

But the spread of slavery was by no means limited to the southern colonies. By 1740 there were still only about 24,000 blacks in the colonies north of Maryland, but this figure represented a moderately heavy increase of 172.5 percent from the 8,803 blacks in those colonies in 1710. Connecticut and New Jersey showed steady decennial increases in the number of blacks in each of the three decades, and Massachusetts and New York (which had the largest concentration of blacks outside the South) registered substantial increases between 1710 and 1720 and steady gains over the next two decades, while Rhode Island during both the 1720s and 1730s and Pennsylvania and Delaware during the 1730s had especially large increases for nonplantation or semiplantation colonies. Despite the declining rates of growth in Massachusetts and New York after 1720, slavery in 1740 was still an expanding, rather than a contracting, institution everywhere in the continental colonies with the exception of New Hampshire. The rate of expansion was, of course, much slower in the northern than in the southern colonies.[34]

In contrast to the white population, a much smaller proportion of the growth of the black population can be attributed to natural increase. Like the figures for white immigrants, those for the number of slaves imported into the continental colonies from the West Indies and Africa can only be estimated. But according to the best informed estimates, adjusted to include imports into the northern as well as the southern colonies and given in table 5.2,[35] 70,814 were imported between 1711 and

---

[34] These figures are based on the table of "Estimated Population of the American Colonies," *Historical Statistics of the United States*, 756.

[35] Curtin, *Atlantic Slave Trade*, 137–40. Importations into the northern colonies, which are not included in the estimates given in Curtin, were computed from the table of "Estimated Population of the American Colonies," *Historical Statistics of the United States*, 756, by assuming a rate of natural increase compared with that of the southern colonies.

Table 5.2. Estimated number of slaves imported by decade, 1711–40

1711–20		15,027
1721–30		11,836
1731–40		43,951
	Total	70,814

1740, over two-thirds of them in the 1730s. Assuming that these totals are not too far off, though they are almost certainly somewhat high, slave imports thus accounted for over 67 percent of the total increase in the black population, while immigrants, it will be recalled, accounted for only about a fourth of the total increase of the white population.

The geographical origins of these slaves is much more difficult to trace than the sources for the white population. Philip D. Curtin, the most careful student of the subject, has recently suggested on the basis of scattered evidence that almost all of the slaves imported into the northern colonies came from the West Indies, while the vast majority of those imported into the southern colonies—86 percent in Virginia and 96 percent in South Carolina—came directly from Africa. These figures are, however, based largely on information for the middle and later decades of the eighteenth century and may not be an accurate indication of the situation from 1711 to 1740.[36]

The ethnic origins of colonial blacks were considerably more diverse than those of the whites. Curtin has analyzed the geographical origins of the slaves imported into the colonies during the eighteenth century and finds that they were drawn from six different regions in Africa. The largest number came from Angola (24.5%) and the Bight of Biafra (23.3%), with the Gold Coast (15.9%), Senegambia (13.3%), and the Windward Coast (11.4%) also contributing substantial proportions and Sierra Leone (5.5%), the Bight of Benin (4.3%), and Mozambique-Madagascar (1.6%) much smaller ones. Each of these broad regional categories was in turn composed of several—in some cases, many—different ethnic groups, with the result that the ethnic composition of the black population was extraordinarily complex. The above percentages on regional origins refer to the black population as a whole, and individual colonies varied markedly from this general pattern of distribution ac-

If the rate of natural increase was indeed higher in the northern colonies, as it is usually assumed to have been, then my figures for total imports are somewhat high but probably by less than 5%.

[36] Curtin, *Atlantic Slave Trade*, 142–45.

cording to the geographical sources of slaves imported during the years of major importation and other idiosyncratic factors. This was especially true in South Carolina, where slaveholders showed a strong preference for slaves from Senegambia and the Gold Coast and an extreme aversion to those from the Bight of Biafra, which constituted the largest single element in the slave population of Virginia.[37]

However diverse the Africans in their regional and ethnic origins, the heavy importation of slaves was clearly a response not only to the rising demand for slave labor and the accumulation of sufficient capital to pay for it but also, to an important extent, to the low rate of natural increase among the black population. If the figures for total importations given above are not grossly distorted, then the average natural decennial growth rate for blacks between 1710 and 1740 was only 17.1 percent. Even if one allows for a somewhat smaller importation and a higher rate of natural increase among slaves in the northern colonies, where health and working conditions may have been better than in the South, it is doubtful that the average decennial rate of increase for all of the colonies could have been more than 20 percent in these early years of the eighteenth century.

Although this growth rate was almost certainly considerably higher than that for any other plantation society, whether Spanish, Portuguese, French, Dutch, or British, before the abolition of slavery, it was significantly below that for the white population of the British continental colonies, which, it will be recalled, was in the vicinity of 28 percent, or that for the black population of the United States in the postcolonial period. This low rate of natural increase reflected, though probably to a lesser degree, the operation of conditions that are usually thought to have retarded the natural growth of the black populations in all of the slave societies in the Americas: the heavy preponderance of males in the slave labor force, at least during the early years; the impermanency and instability of many slave families; high mortality rates, especially among infants; harsh working conditions; poor or inadequate diets; and a general lack of incentive for reproduction among a group which had been forcibly torn from its native roots and was condemned along with its posterity to perpetual bondage.[38]

The rapid territorial and demographic growth of the colonies was not the only indicator of the extraordinary expansive energies at work in the

---

[37] Ibid., 156–68; Daniel C. Littlefield, *Rice and Slaves: Ethnicity and the Slave Trade in Colonial South Carolina* (Baton Rouge, La., 1981).

[38] See Curtin, *Atlantic Slave Trade*, 89–93.

colonies during the quarter century following Utrecht. There was also a significant expansion in the volume of agricultural production and overseas trade as well as in urban growth.

The difficulties of writing about the expansion of colonial agricultural production in any very precise terms are enormous. For one thing, no figures are available for internal consumption for any single product, and all estimates must therefore be based solely upon the volume of exports. For another, the only two agricultural commodities for which export figures are readily accessible on an annual basis for the whole of the eighteenth century are tobacco and rice. However, together, these two commodities constituted a substantial proportion of the total value of colonial agricultural exports, as high as 55 percent in 1770[39] and probably even higher during the early and middle decades of the eighteenth century.

Moreover, they have the additional advantage of representing what are almost certainly the two extremes in rates of growth for agricultural products. Rice was a comparatively new crop, having only been introduced during the 1690s, and the amount exported increased at the phenomenal rates of over 350 percent between 1711 and 1720, over 210 percent during the 1720s, and almost 115 percent in the 1730s, figures that are probably comparable to those for Chesapeake tobacco between 1620 and 1660 and West Indian sugar between 1650 and 1690. If no other crop experienced such a boom during the period 1710–40, probably no other major agricultural commodity increased as slowly as tobacco, a well-established crop whose rate of growth was sharply limited by a relatively slowly expanding market in Britain and continental Europe. Yet even tobacco showed a marked increase: a modest expansion of about 4 percent between 1711 and 1720 but, for so ancient a commodity, a very substantial increase of 17.7 percent in the 1720s and 18.7 percent during the 1730s.

If these two sets of figures are a roughly accurate index to the increase in production—as opposed simply to the export—of rice and tobacco, and if they are in fact indicative of the upper and lower limits in the expansion of agricultural production between 1710 and 1740, then it is probable that the average decennial growth rate in the production of all agricultural commodities for export and for internal consumption was considerably higher than the figure given above for tobacco, almost certainly in excess of 30 percent and probably closer to 40 percent. At the

[39] "Value and Quantity of Articles Exported from British Continental Colonies, by Destination: 1770," *Historical Statistics of the United States*, 761.

very least, it seems reasonable to conclude that agricultural production kept pace with population growth and may even have exceeded it.[40]

Although they are also incomplete, existing data on colonial overseas trade reveal an impressive rise in the volume of exports and imports during the thirty years between 1711 and 1740. Exports to England increased sharply in every decade, from an annual average value of £265,480 in 1701–10 to £667,135 in 1731–40, an overall rate of expansion of over 150 percent or just over 36 percent per decade.[41] Of course, exports to Great Britain accounted for only part of colonial exports. In 1770, the only year for which evidence is readily available on total exports, just over half (50.9%) of the entire volume of exports went to Great Britain. The rest went to the West Indies (24.6%), southern Europe (20.1%), Ireland (3.4%), and Africa (0.6%).[42]

In the absence of any similar breakdown for the earlier years of the century, an estimate of the total value of colonial exports can be obtained by projecting the figures for 1770 backward. Assuming that the ratio between exports to Britain and those to other places remained fairly constant at 50:50 for the whole eighteenth century, the rates of increase in the value of total exports during the years 1710–40 would have been exactly the same as those for exports to Britain alone. However, if, as seems more likely, the proportion of colonial exports going to Britain was higher earlier in the century,[43] if, for instance, it decreased at a graduated rate from roughly 60 percent of the total in 1700–1710 to 50 percent in 1770, then the rate of increase in the annual value of total exports may have been as much as 6 to 7 percent higher than that for exports to Britain, and the annual average value of all colonial exports may have risen to as high as £1,270,717 during the decade 1731–40.[44] But even if my crude estimates are off by as much as 15 to 20 percent, which seems highly improbable, it is evident that colonial exports expanded at a remarkably rapid rate during the quarter century following the Utrecht

---

[40] "Tobacco Imported by England, by Origin: 1697 to 1775" and "Rice Exported from Producing Areas: 1698 to 1774," ibid., 765, 767–68.

[41] "Value of Exports to and Imports from England, by American Colonies: 1697 to 1776," ibid., 757.

[42] "Value and Quantity of Articles Exported from British Continental Colonies, by Destination: 1770," ibid., 761.

[43] It seems more likely only because exclusive trade with southern Europe probably developed somewhat later, in the 1720s and 1730s.

[44] As computed from "Value of Exports and Imports from England, by American Colonies," ibid., 761.

settlement, a rate considerably higher than that for any other comparable time span in the eighteenth-century history of the colonies.

Colonial imports also rose dramatically over the same period. Without
any breakdown in the origins of all colonial imports for any single year
during the colonial period, the value of total imports cannot be estimated. However, figures on imports from England (which almost certainly accounted for a far higher proportion of colonial imports than exports to England did for total colonial exports) rose from an annual
average value of £267,302 in 1701–10 to £646,192 in 1731–40, an overall
rate of increase of over 140 percent or a little more than 34 percent per
decade. Colonial imports from Britain thus increased at a rate of about
2 percent less per decade than their exports to Britain, with the result
that the colonies actually had a favorable balance of trade with Britain
in each of the three decades.[45] Because much, if not all, of the difference
was obviously being drained off to pay for the large importations of
slaves from Africa and the West Indies during these years, the colonies
probably did not have a favorable balance of trade overall. But the heavy
investment in slaves combined with the increasing value of imports from
England reveals a significant expansion in the buying capacity of the colonies.

A final, if much less impressive, indicator of colonial expansion during
the years 1713–40 is in the area of urban growth. Available estimates for
urban population increase are extremely rough and are limited only to
the five largest towns: Boston, Philadelphia, New York, Newport, and
Charleston. But they are probably sufficiently accurate to permit several
general and highly tentative observations. Most important, the rate of
increase for the urban population was significantly lower than that for
the population as a whole, and these five cities contained a steadily de-
creasing proportion of the total population of the colonies. These facts
are simply a more vivid indication of what can already be surmised from
the data discussed above: to a very large extent the rapid expansion of
the colonies in the early eighteenth century was characterized by extensive—as opposed to intensive—settlement.

Still, the rate of growth for these five towns was relatively high for a
society which was primarily rural and an economy which was largely
devoted to agriculture. In 1710 no town had as many as 10,000 people,
and only Boston, Philadelphia, and New York had over 5,000. By 1740
Boston contained over 15,000 inhabitants, Philadelphia and New York

---

[45] Ibid.

had more than 10,000, and Charleston and Newport had over 5,000. The total rate of growth for all five cities over the whole thirty-year period from 1710 to 1740 was about 100 percent, with Philadelphia growing by 160 percent, Charleston, Newport, and New York in the vicinity of 120 to 125 percent, and Boston, because of an abnormally small rate of expansion in the 1720s, by just under 90 percent.[46]

Each of these cities was, of course, primarily a center for external trade and, except for Newport, a distributing point for imports from Britain and elsewhere into a large hinterland, a fact which makes it abundantly clear that colonial urban growth was in large part a response to the rapid increase in the volume of agricultural and other production and of overseas trade. Whether other smaller towns that also engaged in overseas trade—Annapolis, Newcastle, Hartford, Providence, New Haven, Salem, Portsmouth—or an important inland trading center such as Albany increased at a comparable rate over the same period cannot be said without much further investigation, but it is probable that they also showed substantial growth, although, of course, from a much smaller base.[47] If the experience of southeastern Pennsylvania was typical, however, it is also probable that other kinds of towns—county seats, processing towns, transport towns, and religious centers—grew quite slowly until about midcentury.[48]

In its address of congratulations to Queen Anne upon the peace in 1713, the New Hampshire assembly had been happy simply to have achieved at last "a fair Prospect of sitting under our own Vines and Fig Trees [with] . . . none to make us afraid." But the assembly of Jamaica, whose constituents, unlike the farmers and woodsmen of New Hampshire, had already tasted the sweets of high prosperity during the economic boom that accompanied the sugar revolution in the British West Indian colonies during the last half of the seventeenth century, had a far more accurate vision of what the future might hold. So significant an

---

[46] The figures are taken from Carl Bridenbaugh, *Cities in the Wilderness* (New York, 1938), 303.

[47] All of the cities mentioned here probably had at least 2,000 people by 1740, and several of them seem to have doubled in size between 1710 and 1740. See the figures scattered through Evarts B. Greene and Virginia D. Harrington, *American Population before the Federal Census of 1790* (New York, 1932).

[48] See James T. Lemon, "Urbanization and the Development of Eighteenth-Century Southeastern Pennsylvania and Adjacent Delaware," *William and Mary Quarterly*, 3d ser., 24 (1967): 501–42.

extension of the crown's dominions in America as the one obtained at Utrecht, the Jamaica legislature predicted, was bound to "make them all Flourish."[49]

The peace thus set the stage for a period of remarkable growth for most of the British colonies in America and especially for those on the continent. During the next twenty-five years, the extent of settled territory, the size of the population, the volume of immigrants, the number of slaves imported, the volume of agricultural production, the amount of foreign trade, and the size of major urban centers—all increased at an unusually rapid rate. This previously unparalleled territorial, demographic, economic, and social expansion—these remarkable "Gifts of Peace,"[50] in the words of an anonymous poet—is clearly the most important element in the history of the continental colonies between 1713 and 1740. By transforming the colonies from relatively slowly growing units with mildly promising social and economic futures into dynamic entities, it put them for the first time upon a solid social and economic base, opened up previously unimagined possibilities for still greater expansion and development, and significantly enlarged the range and level of colonial aspirations.

The long interlude of relative peace and expansion gave way in 1739–40 to another extended period of war and uncertainty. In contrast to the earlier wars of 1689–1713, the conflicts of 1739–63 were, to a significant extent, the product of rivalries in America. Indeed, the prominence of the colonies and colonial considerations in these later wars provided powerful testimony to the extent to which colonial growth and the expansive energies that growth represented had both evoked metropolitan concern for their safety and exacerbated fears of Britain's growing commercial power among rival European imperial nations. Directly traceable to the one-sided settlement at Utrecht and to the dramatic shift in the balance of colonial power to Britain made possible by that settlement, these wars were rooted in the growing fear among the Spanish and French of British aggrandizement in America and an increasing appetite among the British for an even greater share of the riches that were being extracted from the New World. More immediately, the first of these wars, the War of

---

[49] *Boston News-Letter,* July 12–19, July 26–Aug. 2, 1714.

[50] *Georgia, a Poem* (London, 1736), 11.

Jenkins' Ear, so called because of the public outcry that followed the revelation by Robert Jenkins, a British sea captain, that Spanish *guardacostas* had boarded his ship and clipped his ear, resulted from the rapid deterioration of Anglo-Spanish relations in the 1730s.

Not that Anglo-Spanish relations had been very smooth at any time since Utrecht. Using the trading privileges they had obtained by the Treaty of the Asiento as a wedge, British merchants had quickly developed a brisk contraband trade with the Spanish colonies, and authorities in Madrid had retaliated by unleashing their *guardacostas* on illegal British traders. Inevitably, the *guardacostas* seized many ships that claimed to be engaged in legal trade as well as those involved in smuggling, and this situation had been a continuing source of friction throughout the period from 1713 to 1730. But tensions between Britain and Spain mounted even higher in the earlier 1730s as a consequence of two separate developments. The first was the joint Anglo-Spanish Declaration in February 1732 by which the Spanish government in effect purchased British support for its schemes in Italy by agreeing to assume responsibility for any damages arising out of unjust seizures of British ships by Spanish *guardacostas* off the coast of the colonies, an agreement which only made British contraband trade the easier. The second was the British decision in 1733 to establish the colony of Georgia on land that the Spanish regarded as legally theirs by virtue of prior occupation, rights the English had recognized in the Treaty of Madrid in 1670.[51]

Continued interference with British shipping by the *guardacostas* and the breakdown of attempts to negotiate a settlement of all outstanding issues between Spain and Britain in America finally created a situation in October 1739 in which the British Opposition could play upon English patriotic sentiments to force Walpole into a declaration of war against Spain. Subsequent British military and naval strategy made it abundantly clear, as Max Savelle has remarked, that for "Britain, the War of Jenkins's Ear was an imperialistic war, undertaken, in part at least, with a view to extending British colonial and commercial power in the New World" at the direct expense of Spain.[52] Despite the opposition of British West Indian sugar interests who, fearing competition on the British sugar market from the addition to the empire of any new sugar colonies,

---

[51] Savelle, "American Balance of Power," 150–54, and *Origins of American Diplomacy*, 326–50; John Tate Lanning, *The Diplomatic History of Georgia: A Study of the Epoch of Jenkins' Ear* (Chapel Hill, N.C., 1936); Richard Pares, *War and Trade in the West Indies, 1739–1763* (Oxford, 1936), 1–64.

[52] Savelle, "American Balance of Power," 154.

argued against further expansion in the Caribbean, British military plans all had as a primary objective not simply the reduction and sacking of key Spanish bases but the actual annexation of valuable pieces of Spanish territory or, at the very least, the independence of Spanish colonies under the benign protection of the British.

Expectations of easy and profitable victories followed Admiral Edward Vernon's almost bloodless capture of Porto Bello in November 1739, just a month after the formal declaration of war. But no comparable successes were forthcoming. In 1741 the government provided Vernon with a huge fleet to subdue the Spanish West Indies, and Admiral George Anson with a smaller force to "liberate" the Philippines. But Anson lost most of his ships on the voyage, and Vernon, supported by 8,000 men under General Thomas Wentworth, failed to take the Spanish stronghold of Cartagena, a fiasco which left little doubt, as one historian has put it, "that as a speculation the Spanish war had failed."[53] Except for an abortive attempt in 1740 by General James Oglethorpe, the moving spirit behind the Georgia enterprise, to capture St. Augustine, Spain's most northerly outpost in Florida, and a later unsuccessful attack on Georgia by the Spanish in 1742, all of the fighting was in the Caribbean.[54]

Spain had entered the war expecting help from France, the two countries having agreed to cooperate against common enemies in both Europe and America by the first *pacte de famille* in 1733. But the French refused to enter the war without some major commercial concessions from the Spanish, and before a satisfactory agreement could be worked out, the death of the Austrian emperor in 1740 touched off a general Continental war over the Austrian succession and diverted French attention from Britain's challenge to Spain in the New World. Not until events on the Continent forced them to seek the aid of the Spanish in 1743 did the French, in the second *pacte de famille,* agree to aid Spain in destroying Georgia and in retrieving all territory seized by Britain during the war. On March 15, 1744, France formally joined the Spanish in the war against Great Britain.

Fighting quickly spread to the North American continent, where the war became known as King George's War. As in the earlier wars, fighting was concentrated along the frontier between Canada and the northern continental colonies. The British and French used Indian allies to carry out raids along the borders in both Maine and New York, and a force of New Englanders, led by William Pepperrell, cooperated with a British

[53] Reddaway, "Rivalry for Colonial Power," 371.

[54] Pares, *War and Trade in the West Indies,* 65–127; Peckham, *Colonial Wars,* 89–95.

naval squadron, commanded by Admiral Peter Warren, to capture the strongly fortified settlement of Louisbourg on Cape Breton Island in the late spring of 1745. A much larger project to attack Quebec in the following year failed, however, when British regulars who had been intended for the expedition were diverted to an unsuccessful venture on the French coast, and in Europe the war quickly reached a stalemate, with the French making steady advances on land against the Low Countries and the British dominating the seas. By the Treaty of Aix-la-Chapelle, the belligerents agreed on October 18, 1748, to end the war and to restore the status quo *ante bellum,* France thereby abandoning its promise to help Spain destroy Georgia. The British returned Louisbourg to France, compensating its unhappy New England conquerors by reimbursing them for the money they had spent on the expedition.[55]

The next five years constituted a brief interlude of peace in which the French and the British endeavored to strengthen their positions in North America. Alarmed by the penetration of Pennsylvania fur traders into the Ohio country, to which they had long laid claim, the French erected a series of forts from the western end of Lake Ontario down to the Forks of the Ohio River at the present site of Pittsburgh, with the intention of eventually occupying the whole Ohio River valley and blocking British expansion into that area. For their part, the British concentrated upon strengthening their precarious hold on Nova Scotia by establishing, at considerable public expense, a military and naval base at Halifax in 1749 and, for the first time since they had acquired clear title to the colony in 1713, actively encouraging English and New England immigrants to settle in the colony. The activities of the French clearly revealed their determination not to permit the British to tip the balance of power in America any further in their favor, while the willingness of Parliament to vote such large sums of money for Nova Scotia was a clear indication of the growing importance attached by the British to its continental settlements in North America.[56]

At the same time that they were moving to shore up colonial defenses, British officials in London were also seeking to establish much tighter control over the colonies. Alarmed by reports of massive political disturbances in some colonies and by an increasing chorus of laments from

[55] Savelle, "American Balance of Power," 154–57, and *Origins of American Diplomacy,* 373–85; Peckham, *Colonial Wars,* 97–119.

[56] Savelle, *Origins of American Diplomacy,* 386–435; Peckham, *Colonial Wars,* 120–29. On the Nova Scotia enterprise, see John Bartlet Brebner, *New England's Outpost: Acadia before the Conquest of Canada* (New York, 1927), 166–202.

royal governors about their declining power in the face of the aggressive political tactics of local interests operating through the elected lower houses of assembly, they were obviously worried lest the crown should lose its hold over such valuable possessions as the colonies over the previous four decades had increasingly shown themselves to be. In 1748 they began to reverse the traditional laissez-faire policy of Walpole and thereafter attempted to administer the colonies with a degree of rigor and attention unknown since the earlier decades of the century. Under the vigorous direction of George Dunk, earl of Halifax, who became its president in 1748, the Board of Trade, the London agency principally concerned with the colonies, embarked upon an intensive campaign to enforce traditional ideals of British colonial policy as they had been worked out during the half century following the Restoration and, more particularly, to reduce the authority and influence of the colonial lower houses. Lack of cooperation by the ministry and opposition from the colonial legislatures combined to thwart most of the board's efforts, and the outbreak of war in the colonies in 1754 forced the board to suspend its activities in the interest of securing colonial cooperation against the French.[57]

The last of the eighteenth-century intercolonial wars, unlike earlier ones, began not in Europe or in the Caribbean but in the wilderness of the Ohio country. Virginia land speculators had been interested in the region ever since 1748, when a group of them had banded together to form the Ohio Company, which in turn had acquired a huge grant of land in the upper Ohio River valley. Rumors of French activities in the area spurred Lieutenant Governor Robert Dinwiddie of Virginia, himself an investor in the Ohio Company, to dispatch young George Washington in late 1753 to protest the French occupation. When Washington returned and reported that the French had refused to abandon the region, Dinwiddie sent him with a small force to build a fort at the Forks of the Ohio. Upon his arrival in May 1754, however, he discovered that the French had already constructed Fort Duquesne on that spot. Following a successful skirmish with a small French force which had been sent to intercept him, Washington and his men sought to erect a crude fort to give the Virginians a foothold in the area, but a large French force attacked him, forced him to capitulate, and sent him back across the Alleghenies to Williamsburg, leaving the French in undisputed possession of the Ohio country. This remote encounter was the beginning of the French

---

[57] See Jack P. Greene, "'A Posture of Hostility': A Reconsideration of Some Aspects of the Origins of the American Revolution," *American Antiquarian Society, Proceedings* 87 (1977): 27–68, for a more extensive discussion of this change in policy.

and Indian War, an undeclared colonial war in North America which broadened in 1756 into a worldwide conflict, with Britain and Prussia opposing France and Austria in what has since come to be known as the Seven Years' War.[58]

The only intercolonial conflict in which a significant portion of the fighting took place on the North American continent, the war went extremely badly for Britain and its colonies for the first four years. In 1755 a group of French and Indians surprised and routed a numerically superior British force under Edward Braddock which was on its way to destroy Fort Duquesne, thus opening the whole of the Virginia and Pennsylvania frontier to incursions by the Indians for the next three years. Two separate and smaller British forces did capture Fort Beauséjour in Acadia and defeat a French force on Lake St. George. But after a lull in the conflict in America in 1756, these small gains were more than offset by a series of French successes in 1757 and 1758. The French not only seized British posts on Lake Ontario and along the Lake Champlain–Lake George water route from Montreal to Albany but repulsed a large British assault on Fort Ticonderoga, which commanded the narrow neck of land that separated Lake George and Lake Champlain. For their part the British seemed unable even to launch a major campaign.

Under the vigorous war leadership of William Pitt, who came into power in June 1757 and began to pour large sums of money into the war effort, the tide of the war in America finally began to turn. In the summer of 1758 the British captured Louisbourg, Fort Frontenac at the eastern end of Lake Ontario, and Fort Duquesne. In 1759 they won several strategic victories; in the Caribbean, they captured the important sugar island of Guadeloupe, and on the continent they seized not only most of the important French forts along the route from Albany to Montreal and on the southern shores of Lake Ontario but also the great Canadian citadel and capital of Quebec. The following summer they captured Montreal, the one remaining French stronghold in Canada, and Detroit, from which they proceeded to take control of all French outposts on the Great Lakes.[59]

With the conflict in Africa and Asia going equally badly for France and the war in Europe at a stalemate, France opened negotiations for peace through Spain, which was fearful that British conquests in

---

[58] Peckham, *Colonial Wars*, 129–38; W. J. Eccles, *The Canadian Frontier, 1534–1760* (New York, 1969), 157–67.

[59] Peckham, *Colonial Wars*, 139–205; Eccles, *Canadian Frontier*, 167–91.

America, were they not returned to France, would so increase British power in the New World as to "threaten the Spanish Empire in America" and eventually perhaps even "reduce both France and Spain to the position of second-rate states in Europe."[60] But the British would not agree to French terms for the return of captured territory and, threatened by the possible entrance of Spain into the war on the side of France, themselves declared war on Spain in January 1762. Over the next nine months, they proceeded to capture the West Indian islands of Martinique, St. Lucia, and Grenada from the French and the city of Havana from the Spanish.[61]

These triumphs forced the French and Spanish to negotiate. In a position of overwhelming strength at the peace table, Britain won a settlement which far exceeded that gained at Utrecht almost exactly a half century earlier. The Treaty of Paris of February 1763 was a measure of rising British power in America. Seemingly as well, it was a harbinger of still greater power and prosperity in the future—power and prosperity in which the colonists on the continent and in the West Indies could be expected to share, perhaps even to a larger extent than they had benefited from the favorable conditions in the expansive decades that had followed the peace at Utrecht.

Indeed, colonial expansive energies had gained such an extraordinary momentum between 1713 and 1740 that, in contrast to the situation during the wars of 1689–1713, they were only temporarily slowed and by no means stopped by the wars of 1739–63. To be sure, the movement of settlers into previously unsettled areas was checked. In regions with the greatest military activity—in northern and western New England and northern and western New York during both wars, and along the westernmost frontiers of Pennsylvania, Maryland, and Virginia during the French and Indian War—it was even temporarily reversed.[62] But there was, concurrently, a great rush of population south from Philadelphia into western Maryland, Virginia, and North Carolina and west from the Carolina seacoast into the interior of both North and South Carolina. In

[60] Savelle, *Origins of American Diplomacy,* 448.

[61] Pares, *War and Trade in the West Indies,* 186–226, 556–95.

[62] Rosenberry, *Expansion of New England,* 77, 90, 108–9; Higgins, *Expansion in New York,* 70–84; Richard L. Morton, *Colonial Virginia,* 2 vols. (Chapel Hill, N.C., 1960), 2:675–90.

Virginia alone, ten new counties in the west and south were founded in the 1740s and ten more in the 1750s, while in North Carolina four new counties were created in the 1740s, eight in the 1750s, and two more in the early 1760s. In South Carolina, where the legislature was laggard in this regard, the extension of settlement cannot be measured in terms of the creation of new administrative units, but there was a sizable movement of population from and through the lowcountry into the piedmont in the 1740s and 1750s and a still heavier movement from the north into the backcountry beginning in the mid-1750s.[63]

Even in the northern colonies there was a considerable expansion of settlement into unsettled interior areas away from war zones. Between 1740 and 1763 most of the unoccupied areas within 100 to 150 miles of the coast from Philadelphia north to Portsmouth were filled in with new counties and towns, and during the interwar years between 1748 and 1754 in New York and New England there was even some extension of settlement north toward Canada and east into Maine and Nova Scotia. Following the British capture of Canada in 1759, the tempo of territorial expansion everywhere increased rapidly, as settlers from the older inhabited areas and a rising tide of immigrants from Britain and Europe moved into frontier areas and into the newer colonies of Georgia and Nova Scotia.[64]

The growth of the white population also continued to be steady. Between 1740 and 1770 it increased by almost 125 percent, from 753,721 to 1,689,583. Though the decennial rate of increase fell somewhat from what it had been in the previous three decades, temporarily stabilizing at around 30 percent,[65] it was still remarkably high by any contemporary

---

[63] See the maps for the distribution of population in 1740 and 1760 in Friis, *Series of Population Maps*, opp. 12; Morton, *Colonial Virginia*, 536–82; Harry Roy Merrens, *Colonial North Carolina in the Eighteenth Century: A Study in Historical Geography* (Chapel Hill, N.C., 1964), 27–29; Meriwether, *Expansion of South Carolina*, passim; and Lemon, "Urbanization and the Development of Eighteenth-Century Southeastern Pennsylvania and Adjacent Delaware," 501–42.

[64] See Rosenberry, *Expansion of New England*, 108–37; Stanley D. Dodge, "The Frontier of New England in the Seventeenth and Eighteenth Centuries and Its Significance in American History," Michigan Academy of Science, Arts, and Letters, *Papers* 28 (1951): 191–95; Andrew Hill Clark, *Acadia: The Geography of Early Nova Scotia to 1760* (Madison, Wis., 1968), 351–52, 368–69; and John Bartlet Brebner, *The Neutral Yankees of Nova Scotia: A Marginal Colony during the Revolutionary Years* (New York, 1937), 24–65, 92–221.

[65] The rates were 27.4% for the 1740s, 32.3% for the 1750s, and 32.9% for the 1760s. These and the figures on population growth that follow are based on an adjusted version of the

Table 5.3. Estimated number of immigrants by decade, 1741–70

1741–50		66,013
1751–60		65,426
1761–70		75,076
	Total	206,515

standards among either the societies of western Europe or their American colonies. Moreover, the rates of increase continued to be extremely high in newly settled colonies and sections of older colonies that were receiving heavy influxes of immigrants from earlier settlements and from Europe. Thus, the white population rose by almost 228 percent in the Carolinas and Georgia, over 160 percent in Pennsylvania and Delaware, and almost 149 percent in New York and New Jersey. In the earlier settled New England and Chesapeake colonies, presumably losing population to newer areas, growth rates were much lower: about 98 percent in New England and 92 percent in the Chesapeake. Even within these regions, however, there were pockets with high rates of increase. New Hampshire and Rhode Island showed high growth rates of around 170 percent and 140 percent, respectively, while Virginia registered an increase of nearly 120 percent, a substantial proportion of it undoubtedly in the newly formed western counties.

Again, as table 5.3 reveals, a large amount of this increase came from immigration.[66] The wars of 1739–63, and especially the Seven Years'

---

table on "Estimated Population of the American Colonies," *Historical Statistics of the United States*, 756.

[66] The method used to estimate the number of immigrants for the decades 1710–40—assuming a standard decennial natural increase of 28% and subtracting that figure from the total population increase—could not be used for the period 1740–70 because the total of existing and entirely plausible estimates of non-English immigrants exceeded the number obtained by that method without any allowances for English and Welsh immigrants. Two factors may account for this situation. Either decennial natural increase fell considerably below 28% to 23% or 22%, which seems unlikely, or the aggregate population figures for these decades are much too low. The latter seems to be more likely because I discovered that the totals for Virginia and Maryland were altogether too low, and there may have been similar errors elsewhere. For Maryland, see Arthur Eli Karinen, "Numerical and Distributional Aspects of Maryland Population, 1631–1840," Ph.D. diss., University of Maryland, 1958, 44, 107, 109–10, 195–202. Of course, a combination of these factors may explain the situation. As an alternative method, I simply totaled existing estimates for non-English immigrants and, on the assumption that the ratio between non-English and English immigrants remained at roughly 60% to 40% (as it seems to

War, acted as a slight brake upon immigration.[67] Still, the total number of immigrants during the three decades, approximately 206,515, represented almost a 40 percent increase over the previous thirty years. German immigrants came in very large numbers, particularly in the 1740s and early 1750s. Over all three decades, about 49,815 Germans came through Philadelphia alone and perhaps as many as 12,000 through other ports, especially Newcastle, Charleston, Savannah, and the North Carolina coastal towns.[68] Although there had been a few hundred Sephardic Jews from Spain and Portugal in the colonies by the early decades of the eighteenth century, there was a small immigration of perhaps as many of 1,000 to 1,500 in the years after 1740. The largest concentration was in Newport, Rhode Island, which had a Jewish population of almost 1,200 by 1776, but there were substantial Jewish communities in both New York and Charleston.[69] Together with a small number of Dutch, French, and other immigrants of Continental origins, the Germans and Jews probably constituted around 30 percent of the total immigration between 1740 and 1770.

By far the highest proportion of immigrants still came from the British Isles, however. Scottish immigrants from the Lowlands and the Highlands continued to come in modest numbers until 1763, the entire total for the twenty-three years beginning in 1741 probably not exceeding 7,700. But in the seven years between 1763 and 1770 as many as 14,000 entered the colonies, with North Carolina, South Carolina, Georgia, and New York being their principal destinations.[70] The most plausible esti-

---

have done between 1710 and 1740), calculated the total number of immigrants by adding 40% of the total to cover English and Welsh immigrants.

[67] Certainly, this was true for the Germans. From a high of 5,000 to 7,000 per annum, the number of Germans coming in through Philadelphia numbered only 90 from 1756 through 1762. See Kuhns, *German and Swiss Settlements,* 57.

[68] Ibid.; Faust, *German Element in the United States,* 145–285; Spencer, "Eighteenth-Century Account of German Emigration," 57.

[69] See Jacob R. Marcus, *Early American Jewry,* 2 vols. (Philadelphia, 1951–53); Hyman B. Grinstein, *The Rise of the Jewish Community of New York, 1654–1860* (Philadelphia, 1945); Barnett A. Elzas, *The Jews of South Carolina* (Philadelphia, 1905); Morris A. Gutkind, *The Story of the Jews of Newport: Two and a Half Centuries of Judaism, 1658–1908* (New York, 1936); and Daniel Snydacker, "Tradition in Exile: Quakers and Jews of New York and Newport in the New World Economy, 1650–1776," Ph.D. diss., The Johns Hopkins University, 1982.

[70] Graham, *Colonists from Scotland,* 21–22, 185–89; Duane Meyer, *The Highland Scots of North Carolina, 1732–1776* (Chapel Hill, N.C., 1961).

mate of the volume of Ulster Scots immigrating during these years places the total number at around 40,000, with very large numbers beginning to come in the late 1760s.[71] The number of immigrants from England and Wales can only be estimated, but if the ratio of English and Welsh immigrants to the entire volume of immigrants remained roughly the same as it had been during the period 1710–40—and there is no reason to suppose that it fell much below the approximately 40 percent proportion it seems to have been during those years—there may have been as many as 82,000.[72]

But these increasing numbers of immigrants accounted for a declining proportion of the total increase of the white population. Immigrants constituted almost one-fourth of the total growth between 1710 and 1740 but only about one-fifth between 1740 and 1770. Thus, almost 80 percent, or 727,822 of the total growth of 932,822, was the result of natural increase.

The black population and the institution of slavery also continued to expand at a much more rapid rate than the white population. The number of blacks increased by over 200 percent, from 150,024 in 1740 to 455,721 in 1770. The decennial growth rate averaged just over 45 percent, falling from a high of 54.8 percent in the 1740s to 40.5 percent in the 1750s and 39.8 percent in the 1760s. As in the previous thirty years, the most dramatic increases were in the colonies from Maryland south. As the institution of slavery fanned out in all directions from the Maryland and Virginia tidewater and the South Carolina lowcountry and as large sections of both North Carolina and Georgia adopted the slave plantation system, the black population of the southern colonies leaped from just over 125,000 in 1740 to almost 403,000 by 1770, an increase of over 278,000 in just thirty years! The black population also grew steadily in the colonies to the north, with Delaware, Pennsylvania, Rhode Island, and Massachusetts in the 1740s, Pennsylvania and New York in the 1750s, and Connecticut and Pennsylvania in the 1760s all showing decennial growth rates in excess of 30 percent. In absolute numbers, however, the black population in the northern colonies was small, and the proportion of the total black population of the colonies north of Maryland was declining continuously: the southern colonies contained

---

[71] Dickson, *Ulster Emigration to America,* 48–59.

[72] Indeed, in the 1770s English immigrants were coming at a rate of roughly 3,000 to 3,500 per year. See Campbell, "English Emigration on the Eve of the Revolution," 4; and Bernard Bailyn, *Voyagers to the West: A Passage in the Peopling of America on the Eve of the Revolution* (New York, 1986).

Table 5.4. Estimated number of slaves imported by decade, 1741–70

1741–50		64,360
1751–60		43,178
1761–70		69,459
	Total	176,997

80.4 percent of the black inhabitants in 1710, 83.3 percent in 1740, and 88.3 percent in 1770.

As was the case in 1711–40, a very large proportion of the increase in the black population resulted from heavy importations of new slaves from Africa and the West Indies. As table 5.4 shows, approximately 176,997 slaves were imported into the colonies between 1741 and 1770, with the 1740s and 1760s each showing importations that were nearly as high as those for the entire period between 1711 and 1740.[73] Slave importations thus accounted for around 57 percent of the total increase in the black population of the colonies between 1741 and 1770. As these heavy importations suggest, the rate of natural increase among the black population continued to be substantially lower than that for the white population. Whereas slave importations accounted for around 57 percent of the total increase in the black population of the colonies between 1741 and 1770, immigrants constituted only about 20 percent of the growth of the white population. The average natural decennial rate of growth for blacks again appears to have been only around 17 percent, about the same as it had been for the previous three decades.

Such massive importations of slaves clearly point to a marked expansion in colonial buying power during the period 1741–70 through either a growing accumulation of capital or an increasing reservoir of available credit from Britain or, what is more probable, some combination of the two. The figures for imports from Britain point in the same direction. The average annual value of imports from England rose very sharply from £646,192 in 1731–40 to £1,797,922 in 1761–70, an overall rate of increase of over 178 percent and an almost 40 percent rise over the rate for the previous thirty years. The decennial rate of growth showed a significant increase of almost 10 percent over the earlier period to 43.5

[73] These figures on importations were derived from Curtin, *Atlantic Slave Trade*, 133–45, and from an adjusted version of the table on "Estimated Population of the American Colonies," *Historical Statistics of the United States*, 756, by the method described in note 35 above.

percent, a growth rate which far exceeded that for either the white population or the population as a whole.[74]

Although the growth rates for the black population and colonial imports from England both suggest the continuation of the kind of rapid economic expansion that had characterized the period 1711–40, the figures for the volume of agricultural production and colonial exports point to a marked deceleration in the pace of economic expansion over the period 1741–70. As for the earlier period, there are no adequate figures on the volume of agricultural production as a whole. Nor are the export figures for tobacco and rice, used as the basis for speculations about the earlier period, such a satisfactory index for the later years. On the face of it, neither crop appears to have been in any sense typical of probable trends for agricultural exports as a whole. In the 1740s tobacco exports increased by over 20 percent, faster than during any previous or later decade during the eighteenth century. But the rate of increase fell to under 1 percent in the 1750s and actually declined by more than 6 percent in the 1760s. For the 1750s this falling growth rate can be explained in part by the closing or diminution during the Seven Years' War of the Continental market, to which much tobacco was reexported from Britain. But the continued decline in the 1760s after the war was over also suggests that the European market for tobacco had, at least temporarily, reached its upper limits under existing marketing arrangements.

In contrast to tobacco, rice exports continued to move upward throughout the whole period but at a much slower pace, which declined from almost 115 percent in the 1730s to about 28 percent in the 1740s, rising only slightly to just over 29 percent in the 1750s and much more rapidly to almost 65 percent in the 1760s. Of course, the sudden deceleration in the rate of rice exports from the boom years earlier in the century was to be expected, and the rising rate in the 1760s suggests that the low rates of expansion in the 1740s and 1750s can be explained by uncertain market conditions associated with the wars of 1739–63 and especially the presumed closing of the Spanish market from 1739 to 1748 during the War of Jenkins' Ear and King George's War. Although other American export crops were not so dependent upon a stable and open Continental market as a basis for expansion, the figures for rice exports are probably more nearly indicative of the situation for agricultural production as a whole than are those for tobacco. The growth rate in the volume of agricultural products may have decelerated between 1741 and 1770, but

---

[74] See "Value of Exports to and Imports from England, by American Colonies: 1697 to 1776," *Historical Statistics of the United States*, 757.

because of a growing internal market within the colonies as a whole and probably also in the West Indies, it is doubtful that it fell much below the rate of increase for the total population, which, white and black together, averaged about 33.5 percent per decade.[75]

Whatever the situation may have been with regard to the rate of expansion of agricultural production, one should not get the impression that the colonial economy as a whole was on a downward curve during the years 1741–70. The real figures for colonial exports reveal a substantial increase during every decade in the volume of total exports, from an annual average value of £1,270,717 in 1731–40 to £1,350,333 in 1741–50, £1,543,137 in 1751–60, and £2,085,238 in 1761–70.[76] Nevertheless, the growth rate in the volume of colonial exports decelerated sharply between 1741 and 1770. The total of exports continued to increase, of course, but at a vastly slower rate. Between 1711 and 1740 it increased by over 150 percent or just over 36 percent per decade, whereas between 1741 and 1770 it increased by only 64 percent overall or at an average decennial rate of just 18.5 percent. As in the case of agricultural export products, the wars of 1739–63 undoubtedly had an adverse effect upon the whole export sector of the colonial economy. But the fact that the rate of increase for exports fell so far behind that for imports from England and that the real value of imports from England greatly exceeded that of exports to England in all three decades (thus creating an adverse balance of trade with England) strongly suggests not only that colonial demand for English manufactures was rising at a much faster pace than colonial productive capacities but also that the rate of increase in those productive capacities was leveling off from the high rates achieved during the boom period from 1711 to 1740.

Like the volume of exports, the combined populations of the five largest urban centers increased at a strikingly decelerated rate during the years 1741–70, the overall growth rate falling from about 100 percent during the previous thirty years to slightly over 56 percent. But this aggregate percentage creates a distorted picture and is explainable by the facts that Boston actually declined in population from 17,000 in 1740 to 15,520 in 1770 and that the average decennial growth rates for Newport and Charleston were only 13.3 percent and 17.5 percent, respec-

---

[75] The figures for tobacco and rice exports are derived from "Tobacco Imported by England, by Origin: 1697–1775" and "Rice Exported from Producing Areas: 1698 to 1774," ibid., 765, 767–68.

[76] See "Value of Exports to and Imports from England, by American Colonies: 1697 to 1776," ibid., 757. The above discussion considers not simply exports to England but ex-

tively. By contrast, Philadelphia and New York continued to grow rapidly, the former at an average decennial rate of 32.7 percent and the latter at 26.3 percent, while Charleston, after two consecutive decades of slow growth, increased by nearly 60 percent during the 1760s. In addition, by 1770 New Haven had grown to about 8,000 inhabitants; Norwich and Norfolk to around 6,000; Salem and Baltimore, which was only a hamlet in 1750, to about 5,000; New London, Lancaster, Hartford, Middletown, Portsmouth, Marblehead, and Providence to around 4,000; and Albany, Annapolis, and Savannah to between 2,500 and 4,000.[77] Moreover, an investigation of southeastern Pennsylvania suggests that there was a significant acceleration of the process of urbanization—in the size of almost every type of town—in that area.[78] Much further study will be required before we can speak with confidence about the extent of urbanization among the colonies as a whole, but the rapid growth of Philadelphia, New York, Charleston, and the other towns referred to above, as well as the experience of southeastern Pennsylvania, suggests that urban growth, even though it was uneven and continued at a slower rate than that of the population as a whole, may have been more impressive during the years 1741–70 than during any comparable earlier time span.

The rapid increase in the volume of imports from Britain; the heavy importation of slaves; the deceleration in the rates of growth of the white population, of the volume of agricultural production, and of the size of the export sector of the economy; and the extent and character of urbanization during the years 1741–70—all suggest that a subtle change was

---

ports as a whole. For my method of calculating total exports to all places, see the discussion earlier in this chapter.

[77] The population figures are derived from Bridenbaugh, *Cities in the Wilderness*, 303, and *Cities in Revolt: Urban Life in America, 1743–1776* (New York, 1955), 5, 216–17; and W. S. Rossiter, *A Century of Population Growth* (Washington, D.C., 1909), 11. The figures for Philadelphia for which the above figures were computed probably are somewhat too high. In *The Private City: Philadelphia in Three Periods of Its Growth* (Philadelphia, 1968), Sam Bass Warner, Jr., argued convincingly that its population in 1775 was only 23,739 rather than the conventionally cited figure of 40,000. If Warner is right, then my figure for 1770 of 28,042, which was given by Rossiter as the population for 1769, is too high and the rates correspondingly so.

[78] Lemon, "Urbanization and the Development of Eighteenth-Century Southeastern Pennsylvania and Adjacent Delaware," 501–42.

taking place in the orientation of colonial life. During the previous thirty years, extraordinarily rapid extensive economic and demographic growth had easily been the single most important and most visible characteristic of colonial development. This growth continued to be impressive during the next three decades. To a far greater extent than during the earlier period, however, it was accompanied by a growing tendency toward intensive social and economic differentiation and development, especially in older settled areas. In retrospect, that tendency seems to stand out as perhaps the most important distinguishing feature of colonial British-American history during the years 1741–70.

This shift in emphasis was visible in many areas of colonial life. It was especially evident in the growing diversity of colonial society. The large influx of non-English immigrants and African slaves made the population increasingly heterogeneous, while the variety of religious beliefs among the new arrivals and the religious divisions arising out of the several spiritual upheavals that rent the colonies during the 1730s and 1740s resulted in a growing religious multiformity. At the same time, urbanization created an alternative style of living which diverged sharply from the character of life in the rural settlements in which a still rising share of the colonists continued to live. This growing gap between town and country was matched by an ever-widening gulf between the very wealthy and the least prosperous elements in colonial society, a concomitant of the greater social differentiation that had accompanied the accumulation of wealth—and status—by the most successful planters, merchants, and lawyers. Similarly, the dramatic expansion of slavery through all of the southern colonies created significant differences in socioeconomic configuration between them and the provinces to the north that depended largely on free or indentured labor. The reorientation in colonial development was evident as well in the growing complexity of colonial society. This complexity, most pronounced in the towns but also observable in older settled rural areas, was manifest in an increasing specialization in overall occupational structure as well as in business, trades, the professions, and perhaps even commercial farming.

But colonial society was becoming not only more diverse and more complex but also more coherent. For one of the most important elements in this process of intensive social differentiation and development was a movement toward social consolidation spearheaded by those emergent economic elites. At midcentury, those elites everywhere were seeking, with considerable success, to establish their political, social, and cultural predominance over the societies of the colonies. As improving communications, more extensive economic ties, and, especially during the last two intercolonial wars, greater military and political cooperation drew them ever more closely into the ambit of British culture, they more and more aspired to reproduce in the colonies the society and culture of Britain. To this end, they proceeded through legislation, voluntary associations, and personal actions to try to superimpose upon the colonies many of the institutions, cultural forms, traditions, and values of the mother country. To the very large extent that these efforts were successful, the societies of the colonies became more integrated in both their structures and their values, as non-elite elements sought to assimilate to the social ideals and patterns of behavior the elites admired.

The inevitable products of earlier and continuing material gains within the colonies, these tendencies toward diversity, complexity, and consolidation had their origins much earlier in the colonial period, but they came to fruition during the middle decades of the eighteenth century and especially during the three decades beginning in 1741. Extensive economic and demographic growth and intensive social and economic development were conjoint processes that were manifest throughout the era from 1713 to 1763. Extensive growth defined the first half of the period, while intensive development characterized the second. Not politics per se, then, but these two broader processes offer the most promising framework for a coherent history of colonial British America during these years.

This chapter was written in 1969–70 as the first chapter of a never-completed volume on *The American Colonies in the Eighteenth Century, 1713–1763* for the New American Nation Series. Parts of it were given as a lecture on "The Problem of Periodization in Early Eighteenth-Century Colonial History" at the Columbia University Seminar in Early American History and Culture, New York, May 9, 1972, and as a seminar at the David Bruce Center for American Studies, University of Keele, Keele, England, February 19, 1976. With considerable revision, it is published here for the first time.

Six

The Growth of
Political Stability:
An Interpretation of
Political Development in
the Anglo-American Colonies,
1660–1760

N O ASPECT OF Anglo-American colonial life has been more thoroughly studied than the political. In contrast to the situation in
France,[1] history in both Great Britain and the United States has been—
and continues to be—preeminently the history of politics and public life.
Equipped with an increasingly sophisticated conception of political history as not only the narrative of public events and institutional development but also the study of social context, structure, culture, process,
and function, scholars of early America have produced, especially over
the past twenty years, an impressive collection of monographs and specialized works on the several political systems of the colonies.[2] The vast
majority of these studies have, however, been local and segmental in nature, and there have been relatively few attempts to bring their conclusions together in an effort to discern general patterns in the direction
and character of change over time. The best general analysis presently
available[3] provides us with a static model of the colonial political process.

What is required is a developmental model capable of calling attention
to and revealing the interaction among the entire range of political activities within and among the several colonial societies. Such a model also

---

[1] Jacques Le Goff, "Is Politics Still the Backbone of History?" *Daedalus* 100 (1971): 1–4.

[2] Jack P. Greene, "Changing Interpretations of Early American Politics," in Ray A. Billington, ed., *The Reinterpretation of Early American History* (San Marino, Calif., 1966),
151–84.

[3] Bernard Bailyn, *The Origins of American Politics* (New York, 1968).

will need to take into account the relationship between the social and the political system, process as well as structure and content, and spatial and temporal variations throughout colonial political life. This short piece is obviously not the place to undertake an assignment of such magnitude. But it does provide a vehicle for exploring some tentative hypotheses about the nature of political development in colonial America with particular reference to the growth of colonial political resources and changing patterns in the structure, semiology, and character of politics during the period 1660 to 1760. Although illustrations are drawn from many of the colonies, the hypotheses are based largely upon the experiences of five of the largest and economically most important colonies: Virginia, Massachusetts, Pennsylvania, South Carolina, and New York.

Such an exploration should begin with a clear recognition of the importance of those basic properties or features of the political systems of the colonies that underlay and characterized political activity throughout the colonial period. Certainly among the most significant was the colonial status of the colonies. The fact that they were colonial rather than independent meant that they were socially and economically truncated, that the highest echelons of the economic and social systems to which they were tied lay in the parent state.[4] It also meant that the apex of authority—political, legal, moral, and cultural—rested there as well. The relationship between colonies and metropolis was thus of crucial significance. It bound the colonies within a system in which the ultimate determination of policy lay largely beyond their control. But it also gave them access to resources—to markets, credit, manufactures, staples, shipping, technical skills, military and naval protection, political rewards and preferment, status, and, perhaps most important of all, normative standards and models of behavior and an intimate connection with a great metropolitan tradition—which none of them could have commanded on their own.[5] Finally, the relationship also guaranteed, as J. G. A. Pocock has recently emphasized, that the colonies would be "subcultures within a single Anglophone world."[6] For colonial political

---

[4] E. J. Hobsbawm, "From Social History to the History of Society," *Daedalus* 100 (1971): 20–45.

[5] Jack P. Greene, "An Uneasy Connection: An Analysis of the Preconditions of the American Revolution," in Stephen G. Kurtz and James H. Hutson, eds., *Essays on the American Revolution* (Chapel Hill, N.C., 1973), 45–56.

[6] J. G. A. Pocock, "Virtue and Commerce in the Eighteenth Century," *Journal of Interdisciplinary History* 3 (1972): 122.

life, this meant that institutions of government, systems of law and justice, and patterns of behavior and perception would be, to one degree or another, clearly derivative from those of the mother country.

A second and equally important feature of colonial political life was that each colony constituted an almost wholly separate political environment. Many colonies were to some extent offshoots of older colonies: Maryland and North Carolina of Virginia; Rhode Island, Connecticut, New Hampshire, and Nova Scotia of Massachusetts Bay; the Leeward Islands, Jamaica, and South Carolina of Barbados; and Georgia of South Carolina. As such, they exhibited important similarities in political structure and culture to the colonies that had spawned them. Yet because each colony had its own distinctive patterns of economic activity, social and ethnic composition, religious organization, and urban development as well as its own peculiar body of traditions, customs, and experience, it manifested its own characteristic configurations of political activity. This individuality was reinforced by the fact that at least until the Seven Years' War and really until the pre-Revolutionary crises there was virtually no common political life among the colonies. Political contact among colonies was largely transitory and tangential to the central concerns of politics, and the political involvement of each colony with the metropolis was considerably greater than that with its neighboring colonies. Not even the metropolis had sufficient power to erode the peculiarities of the political systems of individual colonies, however, as metropolitan influences were received, modified, ignored, or discarded according to their relevance to local circumstances and their correspondence with local traditions.

A third characteristic of basic significance was that the political system itself was almost everywhere highly circumscribed in its operation. Because of the exigencies common to such new communities, provincial governments, as Bernard Bailyn has pointed out, engaged in a much wider range of activities than did the central government in Britain. They performed all of the normal functions of government: the symbolic function of affirming—and embodying—through actions and laws the values of society; the regulative functions, such as establishing the ground rules directing the allocation of land and the process of settlement, setting forth prescriptions governing individual conduct, and enforcing the law; and the protective functions of guaranteeing security of liberty and property and contributing to defense against alien attacks. But they also assumed responsibility, first, for initiating a wide range of social services and for conferring a variety of privileges, benefits, and exemptions upon groups or individuals charged with the provision of those services and, second, for fostering the economic well-being of the citizenry through regulations for improving the production of old staples or for establishing incentives to encourage the development of new ones.[7]

However wide the range of government activity in the colonies in comparison with that in Britain, by any modern standards, as Robert Zemsky has recently underlined in regard to early eighteenth-century Massachusetts, the colonists expected remarkably little from government, which was a minuscule, almost a shoestring, operation. Budgets—and taxes—were low; paid full-time public officials were few (Massachusetts had six); civil, judicial, and police establishments were small, part-time, and unprofessional; and, before the Seven Years' War, military establishments were small and usually temporary. Because most of the responsibility for maintaining order, enforcing laws, mediating conflicts, handling routine litigation, and performing public services devolved upon agencies of local government in counties, towns, and parishes, colonists had considerably more contact with formal components of the political system at the local level than with the small establishments at the provincial level. But at most times and places government weighed lightly upon the vast majority of colonists, whose usual involvement with the political system was limited largely to the payment of normally light taxes, the occasional performance of public service obligations such as road maintenance or militia musters, and except in Rhode Island no more than annual participation in elections and, in New England, town meetings. The results were that the political systems of the colonies both provided a rather small scope for the active involvement of citizens in the formal agencies of government and, as Zemsky has argued, "had in many respects become an archetype of the classical economic state." They placed few constraints on individual behavior; the public sphere was relatively small, and the private sphere was exceptionally large.[8]

A fourth important feature of the political systems of the colonies was that they were all basically exclusivist in their assumptions and operation. That is, full rights of participation in political society were denied most of the inhabitants, including women, children, servants, slaves, Catholics, Jews, nonnaturalized aliens, holders of no property, and, in many cases, even long-term tenants and older sons still living with their parents. Partly, this wide exclusion derived from the traditional conception that, just as membership in a corporation should be restricted to

---

[7] Bailyn, *Origins of American Politics*, 101–4.

[8] Robert Zemsky, *Merchants, Farmers, and River Gods: An Essay on Eighteenth Century American Politics* (Boston, 1971), 1–9.

those with a full legal share, so citizenship in a polity should be limited to those with a permanent attachment in the form of property.[9] More fundamental, however, and as yet insufficiently appreciated, was the assumption that full participation should be restricted, in the words of John Locke, to those people not "depending upon the wills of any other man" in ordering "their actions" and disposing "of their possessions, and persons as they think fit, within the bounds of the law of nature."[10] Those without property—which was equated with and thought to be requisite for independence—and those who because of religious, legal, or familial obligations were subject to the wills of others simply did not have the degree of autonomy necessary for full rights of participation. A corollary of this assumption, one that required the exclusion of women, minors, and slaves, was that groups with presumed emotional, physical, or "natural" disabilities were incapable of controlling themselves and, for that reason, also lacked the competence to be accorded full civil status in society.[11]

None of these basic properties of the colonial political systems—not their colonial status, their separation into largely discrete political environments, the circumscribed nature of their operations, nor their exclusivist character—remained wholly constant over time. Of the four, however, only the first varied in sufficiently important ways to produce major repercussions in colonial political life before the 1760s. Indeed, the changing intensity in the degree of colonial involvement with the parent society was one of three crucial variables affecting the character of colonial political development. In two sectors—the economic and the cultural—the direction of change in metropolitan-colonial relations was virtually linear. Although the rate of change was obviously not constant over time and the extent of change was not uniform throughout the colonies, between the middle of the seventeenth century and the middle of the eighteenth there was a powerful movement in both the economic and cultural realms toward an ever more intense involvement. From the initial implementation of the navigation system in the 1650s and the 1660s, the tendency everywhere—among the mainland colonies and in the West Indies—was toward a closer involvement with the economy of the home

---

[9] J. R. Pole, *Political Representation in England and the Origins of the American Republic* (New York, 1966), 25–26, 31, 36–37, 47–49, 53–56, 84, 88, 136–38, 143–47.

[10] Peter Laslett, *The World We Have Lost*, 2d ed. (London, 1971), 190.

[11] Michael Zuckerman, *Peaceable Kingdoms: New England Towns in the Eighteenth Century* (New York, 1970), 195–96. See also Jack P. Greene, *All Men Are Created Equal: Some Reflections on the Character of the American Revolution* (Oxford, 1976).

islands, until by the middle of the eighteenth century the economies even of the non-staple-producing New England colonies had become closely integrated with that of the metropolis.[12] This growing involvement, together with an increasing volume of contacts among individuals and the improved communications that accompanied it, drew the colonists ever closer into the ambit of British life during the eighteenth century, provided them with ever easier and more direct access to English, Irish, and, increasingly, Scottish ideas and models of behavior, and tied them ever more closely to metropolitan culture.[13]

In the political and military sectors, by contrast, there was no linear movement from lesser to greater involvement between colonies and metropolis. The degree to which the latter imposed upon the former ebbed and flowed over time according to the amount of metropolitan energy and attention applied to colonial supervision, and that depended upon a wide assortment of international and domestic, as well as colonial, considerations. After the Restoration, of course, levels of political involvement never sank below those of the first years of colonization. But two long periods of more or less intensive and systematic efforts by the metropolitan government to impose stricter controls on the political systems of the colonies—one lasting from the mid-seventeenth century to about 1710 and the other from 1748 to 1783—were separated by a period characterized by a much more casual posture toward the colonies.[14] Militarily, the mainland colonies were involved with the metropolis to a substantial degree only during the Seven Years' War between 1754 and 1763 and to a considerably smaller extent during the earlier intercolonial wars of 1689 to 1713 and 1739 to 1748. Even during periods of most intense metropolitan political activity, however, the extent to which the metropolitan political system imposed upon those of the colonies varied enormously from

[12] Stuart Bruchey, *The Roots of American Economic Growth, 1607–1861: An Essay in Social Causation* (New York, 1965), 66–67; Jere R. Daniell, *Experiment in Republicanism: New Hampshire Politics and the American Revolution, 1741–1794* (Cambridge, Mass., 1970), 3–33.

[13] John Clive and Bernard Bailyn, "England's Cultural Provinces: Scotland and America," *William and Mary Quarterly*, 3d ser., 11 (1954): 200–213. Jack P. Greene, "Search for Identity: An Interpretation of the Meaning of Selected Patterns of Social Response in Eighteenth-Century America," *Journal of Social History* 3 (1970): 189–220.

[14] Jack P. Greene, ed., *Great Britain and the American Colonies, 1606–1763* (New York, 1970), xiii–xlvii [chap. 3 above]; Ian K. Steele, *Politics of Colonial Policy: The Board of Trade in Colonial Administration, 1696–1720* (Oxford, 1968); James A. Henretta, *"Salutary Neglect": Colonial Administration under the Duke of Newcastle* (Princeton, N.J., 1972).

place to place according to the political vulnerability of each colony. The degree of a colony's vulnerability was in turn a function of several different local factors, including how dependent it was upon the mother country for external and internal defense; the longevity, strength, and character of local charters, traditions, customs, and institutions; the autonomy and self-consciousness of local leaders; the integration of the social with the political system; and the degree to which it was incorporated into the metropolitan patronage system. Together, these many local considerations, as they changed over time, were thus themselves a second crucial variable in determining the character of political development and patterns of political activity in individual colonies.

The third, and in many respects, the most important of these crucial variables was the changing social and economic circumstances of each colony. With the colonies, as with all societies, the ethnic, cultural, and religious composition of the population, the demographic and social structure, the organization of the system of production, the strength of community attachment, and the degree of social integration as they changed over time inevitably affected in profound ways the nature and direction of political development. And changes in many of these areas in most colonies came particularly rapidly as the colonists had to adapt themselves and their societies, first, to the conditions of the New World and, then, especially after about 1710, to the new problems and opportunities created by the sustained growth in population, agricultural production, overseas exports, buying power, and extent of settled territory.

This extraordinary expansion obviously was not uniform over the whole of the colonies. It proceeded at differential rates and produced varying effects. But it was everywhere one of the most salient features of colonial life between 1710 and 1760 and brought rapid and extensive changes in its wake. By enlarging the size of the polity and the pool of potential leaders and politically relevant members of the population; by stretching institutional structures; by increasing social stratification and occupational differentiation and thereby either undermining or reinforcing the degree of social integration or strength of community; and by significantly enlarging the range and level of colonial aspirations, the remarkable expansion of the colonies affected both the character of the political systems of the colonies and the rate and thrust of their political development. As I argue at greater length later, these changes were by no means always—or perhaps even usually—disruptive or destabilizing. Perhaps because this process of growth seems, at least through its early and middle stages, to have been characterized by a major expansion in mobility opportunities, the increase in social aspirations that accompanied it did not lead to deep or widespread social frustration and political and social mobilization,[15] though in a few cases, as indicated later, it did create either social contenders for power who resorted to open political conflict to achieve their ambitions or, among some aspiring segments of the population, persons with an acute sense of political deprivation and discrimination.

Within the context established by the basic properties discussed above, these three crucial variables—the degree of colonial involvement with the parent society, the specifically local circumstances of politics, and the changing conditions of social and economic life—interacted to shape colonial political development. Because there were considerable differences in the nature and operation of these variables from one political environment to another, there were significant variations in the form and character of that development among the several colonies. The contention of this essay is that notwithstanding these many important variations, the political development of each of the major colonies followed a generally similar pattern. A relatively long period of drastic, almost chronic, political disorder and flux began, in most cases, early in the period of settlement[16] and lasted through the first decades of the eighteenth century. This era of disorder was followed, beginning in the 1720s and 1730s, by an era of extraordinary political stability and in some places even relative public tranquillity that continued in most colonies at least into the 1750s and 1760s.[17]

---

[15] Samuel P. Huntington, *Political Order in Changing Societies* (New Haven, 1968), 53–55; Laslett, *World We Have Lost,* 166–77; Alan Tully, *William Penn's Legacy: Politics and Social Structure in Colonial Pennsylvania, 1726–1755* (Baltimore, 1977), 3–44.

[16] Massachusetts is, of course, the only exception among the major colonies. There, a long period of stability preceded a relatively short period of flux beginning in the 1680s and lasting until the 1720s.

[17] The widespread and largely uncritical use of the concepts *political instability* and *political stability* in recent literature on early American politics (e.g., Bailyn, *Origins of American Politics,* 59–105; Michael Kammen, *People of Paradox: An Inquiry concerning the Origins of American Civilization* [New York, 1972], 57–78; and Patricia U. Bonomi, *A Factious People: Politics and Society in Colonial New York* [New York, 1971]) strongly underlines the need for some attempt at definition. J. H. Plumb has developed an apparently satisfactory definition for England in *The Origins of Political Stability, England, 1675–1725* (Boston, 1967), xvi–xviii. But it is clearly not sufficient simply to adapt a series of specifications derived from the experience of an older, far more complex and structurally differentiated political society. Social and political conditions in the colonies differed radically from those in England, and the character and conditions of political stability differed accordingly. My contention, which hopefully will be refined by future discussion and consideration, is that for colonial America the concept of political stability

The history of Virginia, Britain's oldest, largest (in terms of both territory and people), and, on the mainland, economically most important
colony in America, is the most graphic example of this general pattern
of development. Throughout the seventeenth century the public affairs
of that colony had been riven with strife and discord, the stable situation
that obtained under Governor Sir William Berkeley between the Restoration in 1660 and Bacon's Rebellion in 1676 being only the exception
that proved the rule. The endless struggles for ascendancy in an extremely fluid social and economic environment that had characterized political life before the Restoration were supplanted, following Bacon's Rebellion, by a series of recurrent conflicts arising out of the crown's efforts
to assert tighter controls over the economic and political life of the colony. These conflicts both split the gentry—the leading tobacco magnates
and the colony's political elite—into warring factions and led to the expulsion or removal of one governor after another for the next fifty years.

Only at the end of the second decade of the eighteenth century when
Lieutenant Governor Alexander Spotswood reached an accommodation
with local leaders was this pattern finally broken. By carefully cultivating local leaders as well as the new Walpolean emphasis upon harmony
and cooperation among all branches of government, Spotswood's successors, Hugh Drysdale and, particularly, Sir William Gooch, who administered the colony from 1727 to 1749, managed both to extirpate "all Factions" and to achieve a new political stability which lasted for the
remainder of the colonial period. Pragmatic politicians both, Drysdale
and Gooch carefully avoided transgressing local interests and cherished
customs and traditions. In the process, they managed largely through
the force of their own moral and political leadership and with almost no
utilitarian resources at their disposal to achieve a situation in which the
vast majority of legislators routinely supported the administration and
thereby, in one of the very few instances in the whole of the colonial
experience, actually exhibited habits of obedience to the crown similar
to those displayed by the "average, uncorrupted or little corrupted M.P."

---

may be used to characterize any situation in which the following seven conditions obtained: (1) ordinarily low levels of collective violence and civil disorder; (2) the absence
or muting of longstanding issues that polarize or deeply divide the nation; (3) the routine
acceptance by political society of the existing institutional and leadership structure; (4)
the regularization of relations among the several branches and levels of government; (5)
low rates of turnover among leaders; (6) the orderly transfer of authority or leadership
through constitutional challenges without serious disruption of the polity; and (7) the
reduction of factional or party strife to levels at which it becomes either unimportant
and no longer dysfunctional or routinized and functional. Political stability does not

in Britain, whose normal posture was one of support for the administration. With the exception of Robert Dinwiddie during the first years of his tenure in the early 1750s, subsequent governors, including Francis Fauquier and Norborne Berkeley, Baron de Botetourt, obtained similar results by following the successful examples of Drysdale and Gooch.[18]

In forging this new stability, Drysdale and Gooch were, of course, aided by the new concern of metropolitan authorities after 1720 to achieve peace and order in the colonies, no matter what the cost, and by the fact that, in contrast to the situation in earlier years, Virginia was no longer tied so closely into the British patronage system. They were helped as well by a fortunate set of circumstances within Virginia, where a generally favorable economic situation, a homogeneity of economic and social interests among all regions and all social categories among the free population, a high degree of social and religious integration, and a community of political leaders so large as to make it impossible for a single group to monopolize political power discouraged sharp political divisions. Virginia politics during these years provides a classic example of what Samuel P. Huntington has described as a situation of "traditional stability" in which, in the absence of large or important urban centers, the countryside was dominant and the rural elite governed unchallenged by endogenous groups, with the tenantry and yeomanry assuming a passive or only marginally active political role and the weak intermediate class tending to ally itself with the dominant elite.[19]

A slightly different configuration of forces produced a very similar pattern of development in South Carolina, with the exception of Maryland the colony on the continent whose socioeconomic life was most like that of Virginia and, after 1746, probably the crown's wealthiest and

---

require: (1) social or political inertia; (2) complete public tranquillity or the absence of rivalry and contention within the political system; (3) permanency of membership in political factions or party groupings; (4) a high degree of cohesiveness or solidarity among the political elite; or (5) a monopoly of power by a single group within the elite.

[18] See Bernard Bailyn, "Politics and Social Structure in Virginia," in James Morton Smith, ed., *Seventeenth-Century America: Essays in Colonial History* (Chapel Hill, N.C., 1959), 90–115; John C. Rainbolt, "The Alteration in the Relationship between Leadership and Constituents in Virginia, 1620–1720," *William and Mary Quarterly*, 3d ser., 27 (1970): 411–34. The quotations are from a speech of Sir John Randolph, speaker of the House of Burgesses, Aug. 6, 1736, in Greene, *Great Britain and the American Colonies*, 247, and Paul Lucas, "A Note on the Comparative Study of the Structure of Politics in Mid-Eighteenth-Century Britain and Its American Colonies," *William and Mary Quarterly*, 3d ser., 28 (1971): 301–9.

[19] Huntington, *Political Order in Changing Societies*, 76.

most thriving (in terms of the per capita wealth of free citizens) possession on the continent. Settled over six decades after Virginia, South Carolina was the scene of violent political strife for much of its first fifty
years, during which merchants were arrayed against planters, immigrants from the West Indies against those who came directly from England, Britons against French Huguenots, churchmen against dissenters, town against countryside, and local political leaders against the
proprietors. This discordance culminated in the overthrow of the proprietors in 1719, but royal government did not immediately put an end to
the political turmoil. A demand for an increase in paper money, stimulated by a severe depression during the late 1720s, brought renewed
chaos, the provincial government broke down completely, and the colony
came dangerously close to civil war. Only after the permanent implementation of royal government in 1730 was this tumultuous pattern of politics broken.[20]

In contrast to the situation in Virginia, however, the moral leadership
of South Carolina's royal governors was not an important ingredient in
the new era of public stability that began to take shape during the 1730s
and continued to characterize the political life of the colony until the
Regulator troubles of the late 1760s. Although the prospects for this new
stability were enhanced by the lack of pressure emanating from the metropolitan government during the 1730s and 1740s, it was built primarily
upon the gradual integration of hitherto competing and disparate interests and groups during the "ever-increasing prosperity" enjoyed by the
colony through the middle decades of the eighteenth century. With prosperity came not only the muting of earlier religious and ethnic differences
but also what Robert M. Weir has referred to as an homogenization of
economic interests. The common pursuit of profit in this bustling staple
economy drew merchants and planters, town and country, into a symbi-
otic relationship and led to the development of close ties of consanguinity, a "consciousness of shared economic interests," and a consensus about
values and social and political priorities among the colony's emergent
elite, which included a rising professional class of lawyers as well as merchants and planters.

Reinforced by a growing sense of the need for the colony's small white,
free population, composed of a relatively large elite and a comparatively
small yeoman and artisanal class, to present a solid front against a bur-

---

[20] M. Eugene Sirmans, *Colonial South Carolina: A Political History, 1663–1763* (Chapel
Hill, N.C., 1966); Richard Waterhouse, *A New World Gentry: The Making of a Merchant
and Planter Class in South Carolina, 1670–1770* (New York, 1989).

geoning African slave majority, and by a series of minor crises during the late 1730s and early 1740s that underlined the necessity for internal political unity, this new unanimity "suffocated factionalism." After 1750 the multiplication of the number of English placemen in executive offices and on the royal council and the renewal of pressure from the metropolitan government created tensions between the local elite and metropolitan representatives in the administration. But these tensions, and the few open conflicts they generated, took on the character of "a contest between the united representatives of one society and the representatives of an outside power" and did not again split the colony's leaders into factions. What South Carolina politics represented after 1730 was thus a stable town-country alliance in which a tightly interlocked urban-rural elite with a common vision of socioeconomic and political goals governed with remarkable social and political harmony and without challenge from inside the society.[21]

A variation of the South Carolina pattern can be found in the experience of Pennsylvania, the newest of the five major continental colonies and, by the 1720s, already one of the most dynamic centers of demographic and economic growth in the whole of the Americas. Like South Carolina, Pennsylvania was fraught with social and political turmoil for most of its early history. Disagreements between proprietor William Penn and Quaker leaders in the colony over a variety of issues, the vigorous antiauthoritarianism of the predominant Quaker majority, and "the erosion of a sense of community among the Quakers" early split the colony's inhabitants into warring factions and established a pattern of political instability which persisted for almost a half century. No sooner did an antiproprietary clique composed largely of leading "Philadelphia Quaker merchants and their country allies" wrest power from Penn's supporters than they found "themselves challenged from below" by a coalition of lesser men organized into a loose "country party" under the leadership of David Lloyd. Although the first decade of the eighteenth century found Lloyd and his group in the ascendancy, "a new determination on the part of the leading merchants and land owners to put an end" to the disruptive activities of Lloyd, along with improving economic conditions and the gradual development of a sturdier set of governing institutions, opened up the prospect for the establishment of political peace after 1710. But two unfortunate choices as governor—Charles Gookin and Sir

---

[21] Robert M. Weir, "The Harmony We Were Famous For: An Interpretation of Pre-Revolutionary South Carolina Politics," *William and Mary Quarterly*, 3d ser., 26 (1969): 473–501.

William Keith—and bitter disagreements over proprietary power, conditions of land tenure, and paper currency kept the fires of faction alive for another fifteen years.[22]

Only after 1725 did this pattern finally begin to disappear. The tactful administration of Patrick Gordon for a decade after 1726, the disappearance of the old political issues, the death of Lloyd, and the emergence of Andrew Hamilton, a proponent of cooperation with the proprietor, as the colony's leading political leader, all worked to set the stage for a new era of stability in public life and the virtual extinction of factional politics. During the 1730s the failure of the proprietor to exploit favorable conditions for the development of a strong proprietary political interest left the "Quaker party," a tight coalition of city and country leaders which controlled the powerful assembly, in a dominant position in Pennsylvania politics. This position was strengthened by the failure in 1740–42 of a strong proprietary challenge led by Governor George Thomas over the issue of the Quakers' refusal to support the war effort against Spain, and for the next twelve years "conditions of peace and stability" prevailed, as Quaker control of the assembly went unchallenged. After 1750 the growth of a powerful proprietary interest—composed mainly of a growing body of wealthy Anglican merchants and proprietary officeholders in the city and some of the leaders of the Scotch-Irish and German settlers in the backcountry—along with the proprietor's attempt to shore up executive authority, secure exemption from taxation of proprietary lands, and gain financial support for the British war effort against the French, again brought factional politics to Pennsylvania in the mid-1750s, and the contention lasted for a decade. Significantly, however, the new factional competition did not produce the same sort of bitter and endemic conflict, civil disorder, and political breakdown that had marked the early years of Pennsylvania politics.

As in the case of South Carolina, the new stability in Pennsylvania depended quite as much upon socioeconomic as upon political developments. Unparalleled commercial and agricultural prosperity both turned the attention of the middle and lower strata away from the political to the economic realm and helped the nascent elite of merchants and landholders to consolidate its position in Pennsylvania society. The result, as Gary B. Nash and Alan Tully have argued, was that after 1725 "control of the political process slowly" passed to a tightly integrated group of wealthy Philadelphia merchants and country landholders. Unchallenged

---

[22]Gary B. Nash, *Quakers and Politics: Pennsylvania, 1681–1726* (Princeton, N.J., 1968), 110–11, 168–69, 179–80, 274–76, 305–8.

by a weak proprietary interest, this stable town-country alliance, sharing a remarkable consensus about political goals and socioeconomic priorities, monopolized political power and created a stable political environment, characterized by "a little contention and much good harmony."[23]

In Massachusetts, the oldest and largest of the New England colonies, a similar pattern of development is observable. The relatively unified dominance of the old Puritan leadership and the stable political world it provided were seriously undermined after 1670 by the combined efforts of metropolitan authorities, who hoped to expand English authority in New England, and a rising group of merchants in the coastal towns, who were unhappy with restraints imposed by the traditional Puritan leadership and wanted closer political ties to cement the economic alliances they were forming in the English mercantile world. For fifty years after 1680, conflict, intense and deeply divisive, was endemic to Massachusetts politics, conflict over the repeated attempts by royal governors Sir Edmund Andros, Joseph Dudley, Samuel Shute, and William Burnet, usually with the support of the Boston mercantile community if often only with token backing from the crown, to extend their prerogative powers against the determined opposition of the country party in the House of Representatives. There was conflict as well over the governors' insistence upon preserving the crown's monopoly of mast trees in the New England woods (to the direct economic disadvantage of the two Elisha Cookes, who headed the country party), the desirability of a land bank and an inflationary monetary policy, and a plethora of other issues.[24]

As Robert Zemsky has recently shown, however, the quarter century beginning in 1730 "was one of basic political stability" in Massachusetts. The contest "over the royal prerogative quickly abated" following a de facto constitutional compromise during the late 1720s which "granted a measure of independence" to both the governor and the assembly. In addition, the old rural-urban antagonism that had underlain much of the earlier factional strife became much less pronounced as representatives from the rural towns increasingly acquiesced under the leadership of a small, socially prominent elite from the maritime east—as long as it served the interests of the rural, agricultural majority. By working within and respecting this delicate balance of political forces, a governor

---

[23] Tully, *William Penn's Legacy,* 23–51.

[24] T. H. Breen, *The Character of the Good Ruler: A Study of Puritan Political Ideas in New England, 1630–1730* (New Haven, 1970), 165–67.

could count on cooperation from the legislature and, from the point of view of local leaders, a successful administration. That he did not, proved the eventual undoing of Jonathan Belcher. Despite a taste for compromise, he was unable during the land bank controversy in 1740–41 to walk the narrow line between the inflationary advocates in the colony and their opponents in Massachusetts and London. His successor, William Shirley, who governed the colony from 1741 to 1757, operated in this new political milieu far more successfully. With strong connections in Britain and a talent for conciliation, he made skillful use of the limited local patronage at his command as well as the many contracts and offices at his disposal as a result of the military operations in the northern colonies during King George's War to attach many of the colony's leading men to the administration and to gain their support for his legislative programs.

This administrative machine evoked fears of a "Robinarchical" corruption among his opponents and by the 1760s, after Shirley's departure, had become sufficiently narrow and restrictive as to call forth widespread charges of "oligarchy" from those who were not a part of it, charges that took on additional resonance from the perspective of the Revolutionary controversy. But it was never so strong as to be able to ignore the wishes of the rural majority. The urban-rural alliance in Massachusetts, which, like those in South Carolina and Pennsylvania, was crucial to the achievement of stability during the years from 1730 to 1760, was thus based less upon a homogenization of interests, as in South Carolina, or the workings of an interlocking elite which brought town and country together in pursuit of shared economic, political, and religious goals, as in Pennsylvania. Rather, it was an alliance born out of the necessity for compromise, in which, despite an occasional lack of congruence of interests or social goals, western rural votes joined with eastern urban expertise to fashion a stable political environment.[25]

Of the five major continental colonies, New York deviates most sharply from the pattern exhibited by the four colonies discussed above. From its very beginning, Patricia U. Bonomi has written, echoing a general consensus, New York politics was "peculiarly unstable and factious," and the tumultuous politics of the early years seem never to have given way to a period of stability. The "Leislerian conflict and its twenty-year

---

[25]Greene, "Changing Interpretations of Early American Politics," 166–67; Bernard Bailyn, *Ideological Origins of the American Revolution* (Cambridge, Mass., 1967), 114–17; Zemsky, *Merchants, Farmers, and River Gods,* xii and passim; John M. Murrin, "From Corporate Empire to Revolutionary Republic: The Transformation of the Structure and

aftermath, the commercial-landed rivalry of the 1720s, the Morris-Cosby dispute, the court-Assembly struggle of the mid-century years, and the rancorous campaigns of the 1760s"—all exhibited "a steadily rising intensity of competition among concerted factions for a share of public authority." Marked by ethnic, religious, economic, and sectional diversity, New York society was never able to achieve the same levels of socioeconomic and cultural integration that characterized Virginia and South Carolina. Despite ties of consanguinity, the split between the mercantile elite in the towns and the Hudson River landlords—between the commercial and the landed interest—was too deep to permit the development of the kind of close-knit elite that bound town and country so tightly together in Pennsylvania.

Never a large colony, New York, unlike Massachusetts, was not forced by the sheer complexity of social and economic circumstances to develop a differentiated political system which by consent of all parties placed power in the hands of an identifiable and responsive elite in the capital. More closely tied into the British patronage system than any of the other four colonies, including even Massachusetts, the political life of New York was always less self-contained and always more subject to the vagaries of British politics than those of the other colonies. In New York, moreover, politics seems to have continued to be looked upon as a source of economic gain for a much wider segment of the political leadership and for a much longer time than was the case in the other four colonies. Clearly, New York seems to have been an exception to the general pattern represented by the other important mainland colonies.

The question is what kind of exception. To be sure, New York never achieved, except perhaps for a brief period in the early 1740s, the diminution of factional strife that characterized the experiences of the other four colonies for much of the period between 1730 and 1760. But the political historian's understandable and traditional emphasis upon conflict and change, an emphasis which is especially apparent in the historiography of colonial New York politics, tends to obscure basic regularities and continuities in the political process, and the blatant factionalism of New York politics may have been less destabilizing than has been conventionally supposed. Indeed, Bonomi's work suggests that following the settlement of the Morris-Cosby dispute in the mid-1730s, New York politics may have moved slowly toward a less brittle state: the multiplicity of "interests" in the colony had become too great and too many interests

Concept of Federalism," paper read at the Annual Meeting of the American Historical Association, New York, Dec. 30, 1966.

had become too powerful and too assertive ever again to permit a governor to purchase political calm by systematically cultivating one interest
at the expense of all others, as governors Robert Hunter and William
Burnet had done between 1715 and 1730.

What seems to have developed beginning in the late 1730s was a new
mode of politics which may perhaps best be described as a model of tension within a broad framework of consent. The central feature of this
new mode was the vigorous—and functional—rivalry of this multiplicity
of interests within clearly defined—and agreed upon—political boundaries, a rivalry which routinized and, through the eventual creation of
loose parties, institutionalized competition at the same time that it discouraged or diminished the possibilities for explosive, open conflict, civil
disorder, and political disruption. Moreover, this rivalry gave expression
to occasional apologies for parties as legitimate agencies for the expression of interests in society, a development which is not found elsewhere
for another half century. If these surmises turn out to be correct, then
faction, in a complex political society such as that of New York, may
have operated as a necessary precondition for stability, and even New
York may have fashioned out of its own exceptionally diverse cultural
and economic materials a peculiar but appropriate form of political stability during the middle decades of the eighteenth century.[26]

The new stability that characterized the political life of Virginia,
South Carolina, Pennsylvania, Massachusetts, and, perhaps in a somewhat different way, even New York after 1725 depended upon a number
of interacting variables: the general relaxation of pressures from the metropolitan government, unparalleled prosperity for most sectors of the
free populations of most colonies, and, to one degree or another, the
functional integration of socioeconomic and political life within each of
the colonies. But it was the result as well of a major development of
political resources, a development which both defined or characterized
the new political stability and, by stimulating changes in the structure
and culture of politics, contributed to a significant increase in the capabilities of the colonial political systems. In the pages that follow, this
process is discussed as it was manifest in five principal areas: elite articu-
lation, institutional development, configurations of political consciousness, patterns of relations between the elite and other politically relevant
segments of society, and the expansion of the public realm.

---

[26] Bonomi, *A Factious People*, 55, 59, 133–34, 143, 280–86, and passim; Stanley N.
Katz, *Newcastle's New York: Anglo-American Politics, 1732–1753* (Cambridge, Mass.,
1968).

Stable, coherent, and acknowledged political and social elites were slow to emerge in the colonies. Of the five colonies under consideration, only Virginia and, to a much lesser extent, Massachusetts had what might with some semblance of credibility be described as reasonably thoroughly articulated elites by the beginning of the eighteenth century. Elsewhere, elites were unstable and inchoate and contained, as James Logan wrote in 1713, few "men of Parts & Learning."[27] In this situation, political leadership fell to men who were at best only partially equipped for their tasks. Not that they were all so ill-suited as the boisterous and ignorant assemblymen parodied by Governor Robert Hunter in *Androboros* in 1714.[28] But, as the historian William Smith, Jr., later complained in commenting on the character of the members of the assembly in the early days of New York, they were mainly "plain, illiterate, husbandmen whose views seldom extended farther than to the regulation of highways, the destruction of wolves, wildcats, and foxes, and the advancement of the other little interests of the particular counties, which they were chosen to represent."[29] And those few men of accomplishment who were available for public life had, as Logan remarked, to be "furnished with an Exteriour suited to take with the common humours of the Crowd."[30]

Smith was correct to emphasize the parochial and basically utilitarian or bread-and-butter orientation of most politicians. From the beginning, colonial politics had been expressive of a fundamental preoccupation with the protection and facilitation of group and local interests and individual enterprise. The colonists, Gooch wrote, assumed they had "a Natural Liberty of pursuing what may promote their own benefit," and they expected political society to encourage—or at least not to inhibit—them in that pursuit. Men went into public life in large part because it provided them with direct economic and social benefits in the form of easier access to land, special business or professional advantages, lucrative public offices, or higher social status.[31]

---

[27] Logan to Josiah Martin, Aug. 4, 1713, quoted in Nash, *Quakers and Politics*, 286.

[28] Robert Hunter, *Androboros: A Biographical Farce* (New York, 1714).

[29] William Smith, Jr., *The History of the Province of New York*, ed. Michael Kammen, 2 vols. (Cambridge, Mass., 1972), 1:259.

[30] Logan to Josiah Martin, Aug. 4, 1713, quoted in Nash, *Quakers and Politics*, 286; Rainbolt, "Alteration in the Relationship," 411–34.

[31] Sir William Gooch, "Some Remarks on a Paper Transmitted into America, Entitled a Short Discourse on the Present State of the Colonies in America with Respect to Great Britain," in William Byrd, *History of the Dividing Line, and Other Tracts*, 2 vols. (Richmond, 1866), 2:230; Greene, "An Uneasy Connection," 56–58.

But the character, quality, and orientation of political leadership changed markedly during the first half of the eighteenth century. By the 1730s and 1740s, the nascent elites had, in all of the important colonies, achieved considerable success in the "struggle . . . to establish" themselves "at the center of colonial life."[32] By European standards they were, in many respects, peculiar elites. At their core was to be found, in every case, a group of first families or descendants of first families who, having successfully established themselves during the first or second generations after settlement, managed to retain their wealth and social standing in the discordant years of the late seventeenth and early eighteeth centuries. But, especially in South Carolina, which experienced an extraordinary economic boom after 1740, and Pennsylvania and New York, where rapid commercial prosperity opened up widespread new opportunites in trade and the professions, the elites were, in some significant part, nouveau riche in composition; and even in older colonies like Virginia and Massachusetts, there was always room for the talented newcomer or upstart who managed to pull himself up the economic ladder.

Membership in the elite thus depended at least as much upon achievement and merit as upon traditional ascriptive criteria such as family or inherited status. As Bonomi has remarked in the case of New York, with such origins and with no "legally sanctioned sphere of influence," colonial elites, unlike their English model, never developed an exclusive function or that well-developed and secure sense of identity that derive from longevity and the illusion of permanence it creates.[33] To a large extent, colonial elites remained loose categories and never developed into sharply defined corporate groups.

But if the world lost in seventeenth-century England could not be recaptured in all its details in eighteenth-century America, these emergent elites did acquire a high degree of coherence and visibility in their respective societies. Through intermarriage and personal and social ties, they early developed those close family and personal relationships and "informal inter-elite communications patterns" that characterize elites in every society and, like their great estates and closer connections to metropolitan culture, helped to set them apart from men in other social categories. Like those of the English gentry, the imposing (by American

---

[32] Nash, *Quakers and Politics*, vii.

[33] Bonomi, *A Factious People*, 281; Zemsky, *Merchants, Farmers, and River Gods*, 39–98; Waterhouse, *New World Gentry;* Jack P. Greene, "Foundations of Political Power in the Virginia House of Burgesses, 1720–1776," *William and Mary Quarterly*, 3d ser., 16 (1959): 485–506 [chap. 10 below]; Dietmar Rothermund, *The Layman's Progress: Religious and*

standards) houses they built in increasing numbers through the first half of the eighteenth century in the country and in the towns expressed "in monumental form," so all could see, their accomplishments and standing.[34]

These cohering elites, spreading, as William Knox once remarked, in size and influence as the colonies became more wealthy,[35] provided a growing reservoir of political leaders. The progenitors of these elites— the men who between 1640 and 1720 had established and consolidated the positions of the elites in colonial life—had fulfilled themselves by acquiring estates, obtaining status in the community, and enhancing the family name. But their extraordinary success meant that their heirs who were just coming into manhood during the 1720s and 1730s—members of the second generation in South Carolina and Pennsylvania and of the third generation in Virginia, Massachusetts, and New York— had to look elsewhere to find a suitable outlet for their energies and talents.

For men whose wealth and security of position provided them with the necessary leisure to direct at least part of their attention into noneconomic channels, politics, as Bonomi has suggested, provided "the most satisfying"—the most exciting, challenging, and psychologically and publicly rewarding—opportunities in the mid-eighteenth-century colonies. Many men—for the most part first-generation arrivistes like the massachusetts merchant Thomas Hancock—still entered public life primarily "to advance their economic or material well-being, their income, their property, [or] their economic security." For a significant proportion of the established elite, however, and even many of the more thoroughly socialized among the new men, politics was becoming a primary activity, in many ways a profession. Within a decade on either side of 1730, the elite in each of the five colonies had, as Zemsky has shown in the case of Massachusetts, "transformed itself into a community of professional politicians," who, in contrast to men like Hancock, "enjoyed the power," "savored the responsibility," and "reveled in the opportunity" they found in the political arena.

Political Experience in Colonial Pennsylvania, 1740–1770 (Philadelphia, 1961), 140–41; Tully, *William Penn's Legacy.*

[34] Laslett, *World We Have Lost,* 179–81; Gabriel Almond and G. Bingham Powell, Jr., *Comparative Politics: A Developmental Approach* (Boston, 1966), 32–33.

[35] Jack P. Greene, ed., "William Knox's Explanation for the American Revolution," *William and Mary Quarterly,* 3d ser., 30 (1973): 293–306.

Twentieth-century Americans customarily think of professional politicians as devoted to the pursuit of "self-serving ends" which, in some measure, "deny the primacy of state and community." But in the eighteenth-century colonies, the ethic—the self-image as well as the public definition—of the professional politician was quite something else. The prevailing, almost universal, suspicion of men who hungered after power and office required that individual and particularistic goals be subordinated to, filtered through, and disguised by the predominant ideal of the public servant as the dedicated exponent of the common weal. Of course, the new professional elements in colonial politics pursued their own self-interest. Like most men, they can scarcely be supposed to have been exempt from the widespread tendency to interpret the common good in terms of individual ends. But the professional ethic, an ethic to which the professionals themselves were no less deeply committed than the members of the body politic at large and by which they interpreted their role and conduct for themselves quite as much as for their constituents, stressed the pursuit not of power or party goals or individual rewards but of the public welfare as it might best be discovered through accommodation, persuasion, debate, and manipulation amid the cross pressures and inevitably uncertain world of day-to-day politics.[36]

The majority of men in government—at both the local and, except perhaps in the case of the comparatively small South Carolina, New York, and Pennsylvania assemblies, the provincial levels—continued to be "men of narrower experience and vision whose interests and influence had only a limited sphere."[37] But the influence of the "professionals" was far out of proportion to their numbers. Everywhere, even when they were divided by personal or factional rivalry, as was especially true in New York, they belonged to "a remarkably close-knit community, a specialized group of men with remarkably similar social backgrounds and political interests." Exhibiting attitudes and values that were "peculiarly a product of the [special inside] roles they played within the political arena," they represented a world which to the outsider "was indeed mys-

---

[36] Bonomi, *A Factious People,* 281; Zemsky, *Merchants, Farmers, and River Gods,* 39–98, 209, 212; Tully, *William Penn's Legacy;* Waterhouse, *New World Gentry;* Michael G. Kammen, "Intellectuals, Political Leadership, and Revolution," *New England Quarterly* 41 (1968): 583–93.

[37] Bonomi, *A Factious People,* 9, 37–38; Zemsky, *Merchants, Farmers, and River Gods,* 10–38; Tully, *William Penn's Legacy;* Waterhouse, *New World Gentry;* Greene, "Foundations of Political Power," 485–506; Edward Marks Cook, Jr., "Local Leadership and the

terious, employing as it did its own rules, language, and measures of success." The source of their influence with backbenchers in the legislatures and men of lesser rank and knowledge in the localities was the expertise and connection that came from this tight little world: they were able to convert that expertise into actual power because they alone had the influence and ability to "give concrete form to ideas favored by a rank and file majority."[38]

Within the provincial governing structure, the professionals provided a conduit of information between the administration and the legislature, just as the legislators served as mediators between the provincial government and the localities, where, at least in the older settled counties and parishes in the colonies from New York to South Carolina and in the more dynamic and larger towns in Massachusetts, the elites helped to achieve political stability by providing the same sort of responsible, informed, and energetic leadership they offered at the provincial level. The emergence of the colonial elites, with a solid nucleus of men with a primary and professional commitment to politics, thus led to a significant differentiation and specialization of roles within the colonial political systems and represented an important example of political development in the most technical sense of that term.[39]

The appearance of these communities of professional politicians also produced important changes in the character of existing institutions. Although the royal and proprietary councils and even the judiciary were in most places through the first half of the eighteenth century local institutions in the sense that a large number of their members were drawn out of the colonial elites, the largest and most dynamic of the institutions at the provincial level were the lower houses of assembly. By the 1730s some of these bodies were a century old. The early colonists, as Michael Kammen has pointed out, had "acquired the *legal* right to representative forms of government from the Crown; but in actual practice they had discovered those forms anew for themselves." Absolute government, Herman Merivale declared in commenting on this development in the early nineteenth century, was "a thing quite contrary to the genius of our old colonial system, as well as to the spirit of British institutions." From the beginning, the assemblies were aggressive and simple institutions. Most of them displayed a marked tendency "to imitate the House of

---

Typology of New England Towns, 1700–1785," *Political Science Quarterly* 86 (1971): 586–608.

[38] Zemsky, *Merchants, Farmers, and River Gods*, 43–44, 60, 63–64, 169–70.

[39] Almond and Powell, *Comparative Politics*, 22.

Commons in London and insist upon every jot and tittle of parliamentary privilege" during the closing decades of the seventeenth century, and their role in the colonial political systems was augmented by the demands of the first two intercolonial wars between 1689 and 1713. But some of them still lacked the independence, the guarantees of regular meetings and frequent elections, and the intense self-consciousness that characterized the British House of Commons after, if not in large part also before, the Glorious Revolution.[40]

Under the guidance of the new political professionals through the early and middle decades of the eighteenth century, the lower houses consolidated their position in the colonial governments and acquired greater autonomy, as the growing complexities of the political process made them indispensable to the functioning of the colonial political systems. In their eagerness to cultivate metropolitan social models, the professionals in each colony sought to turn their lower house into an "epitome of the house of Commons." In the process, the lower houses developed a much more articulate sense of their corporate rights, defined their procedures more clearly, and otherwise sought to give substance to the ideal that the lower houses, as the sole givers of internal public law and as the presumed equivalents of the British House of Commons, were endowed with charismatic authority and held in trusteeship all of the sacred rights and privileges of the public.[41]

Other political institutions at both the provincial and local levels presumably underwent a similar process of corporate definition and consolidation of authority, especially in the localities, which with the rapid growth of the colonies during the eighteenth century seem to have assumed an ever higher burden of responsibility for maintaining social order.[42] In few colonies, however, does the accompanying process of ratio-

---

[40] Michael Kammen, *Deputyes and Libertyes: The Origins of Representative Government in Colonial America* (New York, 1969), 10, 57, 62–65; Herman Merivale, *Lectures on Colonies and Colonization* (London, 1841–42), 74, 96.

[41] Jack P. Greene, *Quest for Power: The Lower Houses of Assembly in the Southern Royal Colonies, 1689–1776* (Chapel Hill, N.C., 1963); Greene, "Political Mimesis: A Consideration of the Historical and Cultural Roots of Legislative Behavior in the British Colonies in the Eighteenth Century," *American Historical Review* 75 (1969): 337–60 [chap. 8 below]; Greene, "An Uneasy Connection," 36–37; John M. Murrin, "The Myths of Colonial Democracy and Royal Decline in Eighteenth-Century America," *Cithara* 5 (1965): 65–66. The quotation is from *The Privileges of the Island of Jamaica Vindicated* (London, 1766), 33–34.

[42] Tully, *William Penn's Legacy;* Waterhouse, *A New World Gentry;* Michael Zuckerman, "The Social Context of Democracy in Massachusetts," in Stanley N. Katz, ed., *Colonial*

nalization or secularization seem to have been so extensive as it was in Rhode Island.[43] In the area of specialized political infrastructure, the colonial political systems were relatively undeveloped. There were embryonic parties in New York and Pennsylvania, but they had no systematically cultivated base of popular support and only rudimentary organizations. Elsewhere, political groups, as in the case of Massachusetts, were "invariably small, close-knit and ephemeral." Even in New York, where an interest theory of representation was more thoroughly developed, there were no well-defined or reasonably permanent pressure groups, public associations, or other organizations to process demands and proposals from the citizenry.[44] The absence or rudimentary character of such an infrastructure meant, of course, that the political institutions of the colonies were not highly developed in modern terms. But they were as developed as necessary to cope with ordinary conditions of life in the colonies.

Within the context of the new political stability and under the influence of the new community of professional politicians, traditional configurations of political consciousness also underwent important changes as a result of a shift in those "agreed upon and unquestioned" premises that shape patterns of political perception, provide guidelines for acceptable political behavior and a moral basis for political action, and determine the "underlying propensities" of the political system.[45] Although political consciousness was not the exclusive preserve of the elite, it was concentrated in and most fully developed among that group. In the colonies, as in most societies, it was the elite, as Zemsky has recently underlined, who best understood and most consistently based its actions upon the "generally accepted" beliefs and values of the political systems.[46] Increasingly under the early Stuarts, Peter Laslett has written, politics in England began "to include the politics of intellectual difference, of argument about theory or something approaching it," with the result

America: Essays on Politics and Social Development (Boston, 1971); Zemsky, *Merchants, Farmers, and River Gods,* 322.

[43] Sydney V. James, "Colonial Rhode Island and the Beginnings of the Liberal Rationalized State," in Melvin Richter, ed., *Essays in Theory and History: An Approach to the Social Sciences* (Cambridge, Mass., 1970), 165–95, 275–79.

[44] Bonomi, *A Factious People;* Zemsky, *Merchants, Farmers, and River Gods,* 21–22; Almond and Powell, *Comparative Politics,* 46–47.

[45] Quotations from Almond and Powell, *Comparative Politics,* 23, 59.

[46] Zemsky, *Merchants, Farmers, and River Gods,* 249.

that there was a new "appreciation of political and constitutional issues in something like intellectual terms."[47]

This appreciation—which revolved around a conception of political life as a perpetual struggle between prerogative and privilege, between a grasping and arbitrary monarch and a beleaguered House of Commons fighting valiantly to preserve the rights of the people—was transferred to the colonies in the seventeenth century, where it was given additional power and a continuing hold on the minds of colonial legislators because of "the Crown's exaggerated claims for prerogative in the plantations."[48] In Britain under the later Stuarts and increasingly during the first half of the eighteenth century, fears of prerogative were increasingly supplanted by anxieties about corruption: "Court Influence or Ministerial Corruption," a "hydra-headed monster" whose heads were the standing army, "Placemen, Pensioners, National Debt, Excise, and High Taxation," came to be set in opposition to the ideal of the virtuous, uncorrupted, and independent (preferably landed) proprietor whose economic independence, active patriotism, and sense of civic responsibility were both the primary bulwarks against the subversion of liberty by the minions of corruption and, ideally, the prerequisites for the exercise of a voice in the political system.[49] For an aspiring political elite whose major claim to social position rested upon the amount of property at its command and for many of whom propertied independence was an undeniable reality, the appeal of this conception of politics was irresistible.

But the ideal of the vigilant, independent, and patriotic landholder struck far greater resonances—and had a deeper and more lasting impact upon colonial political consciousness—than did the fears of corruption. With no standing army and only a small civil establishment, without sinecures, pensions, secret service funds, or indeed, much patronage, colonial administrations simply lacked the means for effective corruption in the style of Sir Robert Walpole. As Richard Bushman has shown in the case of Massachusetts, colonial political leaders did indeed worry about corruption, but it was the more primitive form of corruption arising from the evil and avarice of individual governors and royal officials and not corruption deriving out of court or administrative "influence."

---

[47] Laslett, *World We Have Lost*, 175, 177.

[48] Greene, "Political Mimesis," 337–55.

[49] Pocock, "Virtue and Commerce," 119–24; J. G. A. Pocock, *Politics, Language, and Time: Essays on Political Thought and History* (New York, 1971), 120–45; Isaac Kramnick, *Bolingbroke and His Circle* (Cambridge, Mass., 1968).

Only in those places like Shirley's Massachusetts or proprietary Maryland, where the governors did have some patronage, did fears of "Ministerial Corruption" have some widespread appeal and frequency of expression.[50]

But there was an additional reason why this newer conception of politics as an adversary relationship between virtue and corruption did not achieve still wider acceptance and why the older notion of politics as conflict between privilege and prerogative lost some of its own appeal through the middle decades of the eighteenth century. With the gradual relaxation of pressure from London beginning in the 1720s, colonial politics, under the accommodative ministrations of men like Gooch, Shirley, Gordon, James Glen in South Carolina, George Clarke in New York, and Edward Trelawny in Jamaica, came to be seen more as a cooperative and less as an antagonistic process.

No longer faced with claims for excessive prerogative power from governors, many of whom were becoming increasingly domesticated, a rising community of professional politicians could feel free to cultivate a pragmatic concern for compromise and for accommodation with the executive in the pursuit of the public welfare. In Virginia and Massachusetts, where, for somewhat different reasons, political stability lasted for several decades, there even developed a vital tradition of such cooperation along with a habit of following executive leadership which was not too dissimilar from the tradition among the English parliamentary elite of routine obedience to the crown. With the revival of prerogative claims, first in New York during the late 1740s and then in Pennsylvania and South Carolina in the 1750s, such a tradition was seriously undermined. But to the extent that traditional attitudes gave way to a more rational, analytical, and pragmatic orientation during the period of stability in the mid-eighteenth century, the political systems of the colonies may be said to have gone at least partway through the developmental process referred to by political scientists as political secularization.[51]

---

[50] Robert M. Weir, "Bolingbroke, the Politics of Nostalgia, and the American South: A Review Essay," *South Carolina Historical Magazine* 70 (1969): 267–73; Zemsky, *Merchants, Farmers, and River Gods*, 21–22, 52–54; Greene, "Political Mimesis," 355–59; Richard L. Bushman, "Corruption and Power in Provincial America," in *The Development of a Revolutionary Mentality: Papers Presented at the First Library of Congress Symposium on the American Revolution* (Washington, D. C., 1972), 63–91; Breen, *Character of the Good Ruler*, 240–76.

[51] Almond and Powell, *Comparative Politics*, 24; Lucas, "Note on the Comparative Study of the Structure of Politics," 304–7; Zemsky, *Merchants, Farmers, and River Gods*, 68–70; Greene, "An Uneasy Connection," 65–74.

These changes in the character of leadership, institutions, and consciousness were accompanied by an alteration in the relationship between constituents and their leaders. Between 1675 and 1725 the deferential behavior that had formerly characterized Puritan Massachusetts and Berkeley's Virginia gave way to a political style in which the electorate played a large role and the relationship between leaders and the people, as John C. Rainbolt has said of Virginia, "was one of familiarity . . . [among] all orders and frequent subservience [on the part of the leaders] to the sentiments of the common planters." In the newer political societies of Pennsylvania, South Carolina, and New York, deferential attitudes had never been strong, while popular involvement and the responsiveness of the leadership had always been rather high.[52]

One of the most conspicuous features of the new era of political stability after 1725 was the contraction of the role of the electorate. Suffrage remained high. Within the limits imposed by the exclusivist assumptions on which were based, colonial political systems were extraordinarily inclusive: in comprehensiveness, they were "not approached by any other society then in existence."[53] The new relationship did not result from the systematic exclusion by the leadership of any portion of the traditional electorate; many voters merely withdrew from or neglected to participate in elections. Unless a vital public issue was involved, voters simply did not turn out to the polls in large numbers. As Nash has pointed out in the case of Pennsylvania, as long as "government did not threaten burdensome taxes, military duty, or religious restrictions" (and the issues varied with other colonies), "most of the people found no need to engage actively in politics." "The strength of the middle and lower strata, then," Nash argued, "was passive, consisting simply of the ability to thwart any political faction which might be so careless as to formulate programs which ignored the fundamental requirements of the people."[54]

There was a similar development with reference to office holding. The steady spread of settlement, growth of population, and creation of new political units meant that in absolute numbers more people had access to and actually held office. But it was a declining proportion of the total

---

[52] Rainbolt, "Alteration in the Relationship," 411–43, esp. 412; Nash, *Quakers and Politics*; Bonomi, *A Factious People*, 17–102.

[53] Bonomi, *A Factious People*, 281; Greene, "Changing Interpretations of Early American Politics," 156–59; Chilton Williamson, *American Suffrage: From Property to Democracy, 1760–1860* (Princeton, N.J., 1960).

[54] Nash, *Quakers and Politics*, 335–90; Zemsky, *Merchants, Farmers, and River Gods*, 39, 248; Bonomi, *A Factious People*, 115, 133, 162; Robert E. Brown and Katherine Brown,

political population. Moreover, the extension of political jurisdictions meant that of those people in peripheral areas only those with connections to the provincial capital did not live in a geographical isolation which effectively excluded them from access to office at the provincial level. In addition, growing social differentiation created a great social and "technical gap" between the elite and the rest of society, who lacked the expertise—and social prerequisites—for high office. The result was that a smaller and smaller percentage of the whole society could expect to hold important offices at either the provincial or local levels. Because this development was gradual, however, because the political societies of the colonies sank slowly rather than fell precipitously into it, few seem to have felt any serious sense of relative deprivation.[55]

The acquiescence of the broad body politic represented by the low level of participation in elections and the acceptance of the legitimacy and good policy of a more and more elitist leadership structure must be seen in part as the "result of political contentment or of satisfaction" with the government provided by the new professional politicians. This satisfaction was also revealed in the scope of support which the constituency regularly extended to the political system by paying taxes, obeying laws, and otherwise manifesting respect for and attachment to the political community and its symbols, institutions, and leaders. But the new acquiescence must also be seen as an indication of a growing degree of political socialization on the part of all segments of the free community, as they found their places within and became integrated into the political systems of the colonies.[56]

This satisfaction and degree of political socialization, along with the revival of deferential behavior that came with them, suggest, of course, that the colonial political systems under the new professionals were performing the tasks assigned to them extremely well. They were, as several scholars have argued for different colonies, both effective and responsive to the needs and wishes of their respective societies.[57] They had also de-

Virginia, 1705—1786: Democracy or Aristocracy? (East Lansing, Mich., 1964), 136–240; Tully, *William Penn's Legacy;* Waterhouse, *A New World Gentry.*

[55] Laslett, *World We Have Lost,* 183–85.

[56] Nash, *Quakers and Politics,* 335; Almond and Powell, *Comparative Politics,* 27–30, 63–64, 247; Edward Shils, "Political Development in the New States: II," *Comparative Studies in Society and History* 2 (1960): 387.

[57] Almond and Powell, *Comparative Politics,* 27–30, 63–64, 247; Zemsky, *Merchants, Farmers, and River Gods,* xii–xiii, 251–52; Tully, *William Penn's Legacy;* Charles Sydnor,

veloped a capacity to avoid or resolve conflicts. As in Britain, the localities were the primary "conflict arenas," and a variety of potentially explosive issues were raised and resolved at that level.

At the provincial level rivalry among leaders and the push and pull of politics were perpetual, but civil disorder became extremely rare. After 1715 it tended to break out only in certain specific kinds of situations: (1) where a government failed to perform its expected function, as in the South Carolina revolt against the proprietors in 1719; (2) where a government acted against the wishes of a large segment of the population, as in the New Jersey land riots of the late 1740s and early 1750s; (3) where the controlling leaders suffered a loss of public confidence because of a failure to act on an issue of great moment to some significant segment of the population, as in Pennsylvania during the exclusion crisis of 1756 or the Paxton uprising in 1764; (4) where the political machinery had been stretched too far to provide adequate government, as in the case of the North Carolina Regulators; (5) where a deadlock between more or less equal contending forces resulted in a serious breakdown of government, as in the representation controversies in North Carolina and New Hampshire during the late 1740s; or (6) where the traditional rights and privileges of the community were thought to be threatened by an "external power," as in the impressment riots in Boston in the 1740s.

Colonial political systems had difficulty in dealing with such irregular occurrences, but neither the volume nor the range of such phenomena were very great. The susceptibility of the political systems to demands, the general level of political trust by constituents in their leaders, and a new level of civility in the political arena—all helped to avoid or routinize conflict and to promote a conception of politics as an accommodative, rather than a discordant, process, in which the broad body of the people normally deferred to the leadership and decisions of a highly professional and competent political elite with confidence in its capacity to govern.[58]

A final area in which there were significant developments during the long period of stability was in the improvement of the instruments of communication and the emergence of nongovernmental institutions to provide political training and disperse political knowledge. These included a relatively vigorous, if not always entirely autonomous, press; a

---

Gentlemen Freeholders: Political Practices in Washington's Virginia (Chapel Hill, N.C., 1952).

[58] Laslett, *World We Have Lost,* 166–71, 194–95; Almond and Powell, *Comparative Politics,* 17–18, 54–56, 186; Shils, "Political Development in the New States," 383–87; Pau-

growing and increasingly sophisticated and competent legal profession; schools, including more institutions of higher learning; voluntary associations such as coffeehouse groups, clubs, chambers of commerce, and professional societies; and expanding networks of trade. Along with an increase in travel, literacy, and books and other printed materials, these developments contributed to erode much of the traditional localism of rural America, to provide easier access to metropolitan knowledge and technical skills, and to encourage the rapid development of human capital—in sum, to widen the cognitive map and augment the political potential of the colonists. More directly, despite the low level of participation in elections and the declining proportion of the population who could expect to hold public office, men at all levels of society routinely engaged in "an extraordinary number of public and private transactions," including land grants and litigation that involved contact with politics. These transactions gave the colonists "a range [and depth] of political competence that was elsewhere unknown" and helped to create a relatively broad and informed citizenry.[59]

But the political implications of the enormous expansion of the public realm represented by these developments remained largely latent before the 1760s. The emergence of a "public" and of increased participation in public affairs became much more manifest beginning with the Stamp Act crisis. Thereafter, the politicization of the colonists increased at an exponential rate, as British officials, an anonymous pamphleteer complained in London in 1774, "impoliticly kept [the colonists] in a state of continual training for nine successive years. Their Orators," he lamented, "have been furnished with topics for popular harangues, and the mass of the people have been taught politics, and the mode of being troublesome to Government."[60] The potential for such broad and deep politicization had been growing rapidly over the previous generation. But in the stable po-

line Maier, *From Resistance to Revolution: Colonial Radicals and the Development of American Opposition to Britain, 1765-1776* (New York, 1972), 3-26.

[59] Shils, "Political Development in the New States," 385-86; Shils, "Concentration and Dispersal of Charisma," *World Politics* 11 (1958-59): 19; Laslett, *World We Have Lost*, 209; Almond and Powell, *Comparative Politics*, 244-46; Bonomi, *A Factious People*, 281; Kammen, "Intellectuals, Political Leadership, and Revolution," 588-89; Lawrence A. Cremin, *American Education: The Colonial Experience, 1607-1783* (New York, 1970), 519-20, 548-49, 553, 555-56.

[60] Cremin, *American Education*, 545; Rothermund, *Layman's Progress*, 83; *A Letter to a Member of Parliament on the Present Unhappy Dispute between Great Britain and Her Colonies* (London, 1764), 7.

litical world that obtained in the major colonies for much of the period between the 1720s and the early 1760s, nothing occurred to bring it to full flower.

The stability that characterized the major colonies over much of the period from 1725 to 1760 obviously did not extend to all of the colonies. A case can be made that Maryland achieved a considerable degree of stability over that period of a type which was similar in some respects to that of Pennsylvania and in others to that of New York. The more primitive political societies of North Carolina, New Jersey, and New Hampshire were rarely free of tumult or contention during these years; and when New Hampshire did achieve some political harmony after 1752, it was a harmony which was much more akin to that experienced by Virginia under Berkeley almost a century earlier than to that of contemporary Virginia, South Carolina, or Massachusetts. In Connecticut and Rhode Island, where the crown did not intrude so thoroughly into provincial affairs at the end of the seventeenth century, the direction of development seems to have been precisely opposite from that found in the predominant pattern, as the relatively stable political structures that existed at the end of the seventeenth century and during the early decades of the eighteenth century were shattered by religious divisions, disagreements over monetary policy, and exigencies created by rapid expansion between 1730 and 1750.[61] Even the political stability achieved by the five leading colonies began to come apart after 1750 under pressures created by the Seven Years' War, a renewal of effort by the metropolitan government to impose tighter controls over the colonies, and a variety of internal stresses and strains.[62]

But the extensive political development that had taken place during earlier decades—development in leadership, institutions, political consciousness, the socialization of the electorate to their political systems, instruments of communication, and institutions of nongovernmental political training—was irreversible. The increased capabilities and re-

---

[61] Charles A. Barker, *The Background of the Revolution in Maryland* (New Haven, 1940); Donald L. Kemmerer, *Path to Freedom: The Struggle for Self-Government in Colonial New Jersey, 1703–1776* (Princeton, N.J., 1940); Daniell, *Experiment in Republicanism;* Richard L. Bushman, *From Puritan to Yankee: Character and the Social Order in Connecticut, 1690–1765* (Cambridge, Mass., 1967); David S. Lovejoy, *Rhode Island Politics and the American Revolution, 1760–1776* (Providence, 1958); Greene, "Changing Interpretations," 159–72.

[62] Greene, "An Uneasy Connection," 65–80.

sources that it had provided to the political systems of the colonies would prove indispensable in coping with the challenges that lay beyond 1760.

Initially entitled "The Development of Early American Politics," this chapter was written for a conference on "The American Revolution" at the James Ford Bell Library, University of Minnesota, Minneapolis, May 2, 1973. It was subsequently presented as a paper at a session on "Politics and Ideology" at a conference on "Atlantic Society, 1600–1800," at the University of Edinburgh, Edinburgh, Scotland, July 1, 1973; as the annual Society of the Cincinnati Lecture at the University of Richmond, Richmond, Virginia, November 1, 1973; and as a paper at The Seminar, Department of History, The Johns Hopkins University, Baltimore, Maryland, February 7, 1974. It is here reprinted, with some updating of the footnotes and a few verbal changes, by permission from John Parker and Carol Urness, eds., *The American Revolution: A Heritage of Change* (Minneapolis: James Ford Bell Library, 1975), 26–52.

SEVEN

The Role of the Lower Houses of Assembly in Eighteenth-Century Politics

THE RISE OF THE REPRESENTATIVE ASSEMBLIES was perhaps the most significant political and constitutional development in the history of Britain's overseas empire before the American Revolution. Crown and proprietary authorities obviously had intended the governor to be the focal point of colonial government with the assemblies merely subordinate bodies called together when necessary to levy taxes and ratify local ordinances proposed by the executive. Consequently, except in the New England charter colonies, where the representative bodies early assumed a leading role, they were dominated by the governors and councils for most of the period down to 1689. But beginning with the Restoration and intensifying their efforts during the years following the Glorious Revolution, the lower houses engaged in a successful quest for power as they set about to restrict the authority of the executive, undermine the system of colonial administration laid down by metropolitan and proprietary authorities, and make themselves paramount in the affairs of their respective colonies.

Historians have been fascinated by this phenomenon. For nearly a century after 1776 they interpreted it as a prelude to the American Revolution. In the 1780s the pro-British historian George Chalmers saw it as the early manifestation of a latent desire for independence, an undutiful reaction to the mild policies of the mother country.[1] In the middle of the

---

[1] George Chalmers, *An Introduction to the History of the Revolt of the American Colonies,* 2 vols. (Boston, 1845), 1:223–26 and 2:226–28, particularly, for statements of Chalmers's position.

nineteenth century the American nationalist George Bancroft, although more interested in other aspects of colonial history, looked upon it as the natural expression of American democratic principles, simply another chapter in the progress of mankind.[2] The reaction to these sweeping interpretations set in during the last decades of the nineteenth century, when Charles M. Andrews, Edward Channing, Herbert L. Osgood, and others began to investigate in detail and to study in context developments from the Restoration to the end of the Seven Years' War. Osgood put a whole squadron of Columbia students to work examining colonial political institutions, and they produced a series of institutional studies in which the evolution of the lower houses was a central feature. These studies clarified the story of legislative development in each colony, but this necessarily piecemeal approach, as well as the excessive fragmentation that characterized the more general narratives of Osgood and Channing, tended to emphasize the differences rather than the similarities in the rise of the lower houses and failed to produce a general analysis of the common features of their quest for power.[3] Among later scholars, Leonard W. Labaree in his excellent monograph *Royal Government in America* presented a comprehensive survey of the institutional development of the lower houses in the royal colonies and of the specific issues involved in their struggles with the royal governors, but he did not offer any systematic interpretation of the general process and pattern of legislative development.[4] Charles Andrews promised to tackle this problem and provide a synthesis in the later volumes of his magnum opus, *The*

---

[2] George Bancroft, *History of the United States*, 14th ed., 10 vols. (Boston, 1854–75), 3:1–108, 383–98, particularly.

[3] Herbert L. Osgood, *The American Colonies in the Seventeenth Century*, 3 vols. (New York, 1904–7), and *The American Colonies in the Eighteenth Century*, 4 vols. (New York, 1924–25). For Edward Channing's treatment, see *A History of the United States*, 6 vols. (New York, 1905–25), vol. 2. Representative of the studies of Osgood's students are William R. Shepherd, *History of Proprietary Government in Pennsylvania* (New York, 1896); Newton D. Mereness, *Maryland as a Proprietary Province* (New York, 1901); W. Roy Smith, *South Carolina as a Royal Province, 1719–1776* (New York, 1903); Charles L. Raper, *North Carolina: A Study in English Colonial Government* (New York, 1904); William H. Fry, *New Hampshire as a Royal Province* (New York, 1908); Edwin P. Tanner, *The Province of New Jersey, 1664–1738* (New York, 1908); Edgar J. Fisher, *New Jersey as a Royal Province, 1738–1776* (New York, 1911); and Percy S. Flippin, *The Royal Government in Virginia, 1624–1775* (New York, 1919).

[4] Leonard W. Labaree, *Royal Government in America* (New Haven, 1930), 172–311, particularly. Two other illuminating studies by Labaree's contemporaries are A. B. Keith, *Constitutional History of the First British Empire* (Oxford, 1930), which is legalistic in emphasis, and John F. Burns, *Controversies between Royal Governors and Their Assemblies in the*

Colonial Period of American History, but he died before completing that part of the project.[5]

As a result, some fundamental questions have never been fully answered, and no one has produced a comprehensive synthesis. No one has satisfactorily worked out the basic pattern of the quest; analyzed the reasons for and the significance of its development; explored its underlying assumptions and theoretical foundations; or assessed the consequences of the success of the lower houses, particularly the relationship between their rise to power and the coming of the American Revolution. This essay is intended to suggest some tentative conclusions about these problems, not to present ultimate solutions. My basic research on the lower houses has been in the southern royal colonies and in Nova Scotia. One of the present purposes is to test the generalizations I have arrived at about the southern colonies by applying them to what scholars have learned of the legislatures in the other colonies. This procedure has the advantage of providing perspective on the story of southern developments. At the same time, it may serve as one guidepost for a general synthesis in the future.

Any student of the eighteenth-century political process will sooner or later be struck by the fact that, although each of the lower houses developed independently and differently, their stories were similar. The elimination of individual variants, which tend to cancel out each other, discloses certain basic regularities, a clearly discernible pattern—or what the late Sir Lewis Namier called a morphology—common to all of them. They all moved along like paths in their drives for increased authority, and, although their success on specific issues differed from colony to colony and the rate of their rise varied from time to time, they all ended up at approximately the same destination. They passed successively through certain vaguely defined phases of political development. Through most of the seventeenth century the lower houses were still in a position of subordination, slowly groping for the power to tax and the rights to sit separately from the council and to initiate laws. Sometime during the early eighteenth century most of them advanced to a second stage at which they could battle on equal terms with the governors and councils and challenge even the powers in London if necessary. At that point the lower houses began their bid for political supremacy. The vio-

---

Northern American Colonies (Boston, 1923), which fails to tie together in any satisfactory way developments in the four colonies it treats.

[5] Charles M. Andrews, "On the Writing of Colonial History," *William and Mary Quarterly,* 3d ser., 1 (1944): 29–42. The line of interpretation that Andrews would probably

lent eruptions that followed usually ended in an accommodation with the governors and councils which paved the way for the ascendancy of the lower houses and saw the virtual eclipse of the colonial executive. By the end of the Seven Years' War, and in some instances considerably earlier, the lower houses had reached the third and final phase of political dominance and were in a position to speak for the colonies in the conflict with the metropolitan government that ensued after 1763.

By 1763, with the exception of the lower houses in the corporate colonies of Rhode Island and Connecticut, which had virtually complete authority, the Pennsylvania and Massachusetts houses of representatives were probably most powerful. Having succeeded in placing its election on a statutory basis and depriving the council of direct legislative authority in the Charter of Privileges in 1701, the Pennsylvania house under the astute guidance of David Lloyd secured broad financial and appointive powers during the administrations of Daniel Gookin and Sir William Keith. Building on these foundations, it gained almost complete dominance in the 1730s and 1740s despite the opposition of the governors, whose power and prestige along with those of the council declined rapidly.[6] The Massachusetts house, having been accorded the unique privilege of sharing in the selection of the council by the royal charter in 1691, already had a strong tradition of legislative supremacy inherited from a half century of corporate experience. During the first thirty years under the new charter, first the benevolent policies of Sir William Phips and William Stoughton and then wartime conditions during the tenures of Joseph Dudley and Samuel Shute enabled the house, led by Elisha Cooke, Jr., to extend its authority greatly. It emerged from the conflicts over the salary question during the 1720s with firm control over finance, and the crown's abandonment of its demand for a permanent revenue in the early 1730s paved the way for an accommodation with subsequent

---

have followed is briefly developed in his brilliant *The Colonial Background of the American Revolution: Four Essays in American Colonial History* (New Haven, 1924), 3–65.

[6] Developments in Pennsylvania may be traced in Shepherd, *Proprietary Government;* Richard Jackson, *An Historical Review of Pennsylvania* (London, 1759); Roy N. Lokken, *David Lloyd: Colonial Lawmaker* (Seattle, 1959); Sister Joan de Lourdes Leonard, *The Organization and Procedure of the Pennsylvania Assembly, 1682–1772* (Philadelphia, 1949); Winifred T. Root, *The Relation of Pennsylvania with the British Government, 1696–1765* (Philadelphia, 1912); and Theodore Thayer, *Pennsylvania Politics and the Growth of Democracy, 1740–1776* (Harrisburg, Pa., 1953). On Rhode Island and Connecticut, see David S. Lovejoy, *Rhode Island Politics and the American Revolution, 1760–1776* (Providence, 1958), and Oscar Zeichner, *Connecticut's Years of Controversy, 1754–1775* (Chapel Hill, N.C., 1949).

governors and the eventual dominance of the house under Governor William Shirley after 1740.[7]

The South Carolina Commons and New York House of Assembly were only slightly less powerful. Beginning in the first decade of the eighteenth century, the South Carolina lower house gradually assumed an ironclad control over all aspects of South Carolina government, extending its supervision to the minutest details of local administration after 1730 as a succession of governors, including Francis Nicholson, Robert Johnson, Thomas Broughton, the elder William Bull, and James Glen, offered little determined opposition. The Commons continued to grow in stature after 1750, while the council's standing declined because of the crown policy of filling it with placemen from England and the Commons's successful attacks upon its authority.[8] The New York House of Assembly began to demand greater authority in reaction to the mismanagement of Edward Hyde, Viscount Cornbury, during the first decade of the eighteenth century. Governor Robert Hunter met the challenge squarely during his ten-year administration beginning in 1710, but he and his successors could not check the rising power of the house. During the seven-year tenure of George Clarke beginning in 1736, the house advanced into the final stage of development. Following Clarke, George Clinton made a vigorous effort to reassert the authority of the executive, but neither he nor any of his successors was able to challenge the power of the house.[9]

---

[7] Useful studies on Massachusetts are Robert E. Brown, *Middle-Class Democracy and the Revolution in Massachusetts, 1691–1780* (Ithaca, N.Y., 1955); Martin L. Cole, "The Rise of the Legislative Assembly in Provincial Massachusetts," Ph.D. diss., State University of Iowa, 1939; Thomas Hutchinson, *The History of the Colony and Province of Massachusetts-Bay*, ed. Lawrence S. Mayo, 3 vols. (Cambridge, Mass., 1936); and Henry R. Spencer, *Constitutional Conflict in Provincial Massachusetts* (Columbus, Ohio, 1905).

[8] The best published study on South Carolina is Smith, *South Carolina as a Royal Province*. Also useful are David D. Wallace, *The Life of Henry Laurens* (New York, 1915); Jack P. Greene, *The Quest for Power: The Lower Houses of Assembly in the Southern Royal Colonies, 1689–1776* (Chapel Hill, N.C., 1963); and M. Eugene Sirmans, "The South Carolina Royal Council, 1720–1763," *William and Mary Quarterly*, 3d ser., 18 (1961): 373–92.

[9] Developments in New York can be followed in Carl L. Becker, *The History of Political Parties in the Province of New York, 1760–1776* (Madison, Wis., 1909); Milton M. Klein, "Democracy and Politics in Colonial New York," *New York History* 40 (1959): 221–46; Lawrence H. Leder, *Robert Livingston, 1654–1728, and the Politics of Colonial New York* (Chapel Hill, N.C., 1961); Beverly McAnear, "Politics in Provincial New York, 1689–1761," Ph.D. diss., Stanford University, 1935; Irving Mark, *Agrarian Conflicts in Colonial New York, 1711–1775* (New York, 1940); William Smith, *The History of the Late*

The lower houses of North Carolina, New Jersey, and Virginia developed more slowly. The North Carolina lower house was fully capable of protecting its powers and privileges and competing on equal terms with the executive during the last years of proprietary rule and under the early royal governors, George Burrington and Gabriel Johnston. But it was not until Arthur Dobbs's tenure in the 1750s and 1760s that, meeting more regularly, it assumed the upper hand in North Carolina politics under the astute guidance of Speaker Samuel Swann and treasurers John Starkey and Thomas Barker.[10] In New Jersey the lower house was partially thwarted in its spirited bid for power during the 1740s under the leadership of John Kinsey and Samuel Nevill by the determined opposition of Governor Lewis Morris, and it did not gain superiority until the administrations of Jonathan Belcher, Thomas Pownall, Francis Bernard, and Thomas Boone during the Seven Years' War.[11] Similarly, the Virginia Burgesses vigorously sought to establish its control in the second decade of the century under Alexander Spotswood, but not until the administrations of Sir William Gooch and Robert Dinwiddie, when first the expansion of the colony and then the Seven Years' War required more regular sessions, did the Burgesses finally gain the upper hand under the effective leadership of Speaker John Robinson.[12]

Among the lower houses in the older colonies, only the Maryland House of Delegates and the New Hampshire House of Assembly failed to reach the final level of development in the period before 1763. The Maryland body made important advances early in the eighteenth cen-

---

Province of New York, 2 vols. (New York, 1829); and Charles W. Spencer, *Phases of Royal Government in New York, 1691–1719* (Columbus, Ohio, 1905).

[10] Useful analyses of North Carolina are Raper, *North Carolina*, and Desmond Clarke, *Arthur Dobbs, Esquire, 1689–1765* (Chapel Hill, N.C., 1957).

[11] New Jersey developments can be traced in Donald L. Kemmerer's excellent study, *Path to Freedom: The Struggle for Self-Government in Colonial New Jersey, 1703–1776* (Princeton, N.J., 1940).

[12] Among the more useful secondary works on Virginia are Flippin, *Royal Government;* Bernard Bailyn, "Politics and Social Structure in Virginia," in James M. Smith, ed., *Seventeenth-Century America: Essays on Colonial History* (Chapel Hill, N.C., 1959), 90–115; Lucille Blanche Griffith, *The Virginia House of Burgesses, 1750–1774* (University, Ala., 1968); Ray Orvin Hummel, Jr., "The Virginia House of Burgesses, 1689–1750," Ph.D. diss., University of Nebraska, 1934; David J. Mays, *Edmund Pendleton, 1721–1803*, 2 vols. (Cambridge, Mass., 1952); Charles S. Sydnor, *Gentlemen Freeholders: Political Practices in Washington's Virginia* (Chapel Hill, N.C., 1952); Thomas J. Wertenbaker, *Give Me Liberty: The Struggle for Self-Government in Virginia* (Philadelphia, 1958); and David Alan Williams, "Political Alignments in Colonial Virginia, 1698–1750," Ph.D. diss., Northwestern University, 1959.

tury while under the control of the crown and aggressively sought to extend its authority in the 1720s under the leadership of the older Daniel Dulany and again in the late 1730s and early 1740s under Dr. Charles Carroll. But the proprietors were usually able to thwart these attempts, and the Delegates failed to pull ahead of the executive despite a concerted effort during the last intercolonial war under the administration of Horatio Sharpe.[13] In New Hampshire the house had exercised considerable power through the early decades of the eighteenth century, but Governor Benning Wentworth effectively challenged its authority after 1740 and prevented it from attaining the extensive power exercised by its counterparts in other colonies.[14] It should be emphasized, however, that neither the Maryland nor the New Hampshire lower house was in any sense impotent, and along with their more youthful equivalent in Georgia, they too gained dominance during the decade of debate with Britain after 1763. Of the lower houses in the continental colonies with pre-1763 political experience, only the Nova Scotia assembly had not reached the final phase of political dominance by 1776.[15]

The similarities in the process and pattern of legislative development from colony to colony were not entirely accidental. The lower houses faced like problems and drew upon common traditions and metropolitan precedents for solutions. They all operated in the same broad imperial context and were affected by common historical forces. Moreover, family, cultural, and commercial ties often extended across colony lines, and newspapers and other printed materials, as well as individuals, often found their way from one colony to another. The result was at least a general awareness of issues and practices in neighboring colonies, and occasionally there was even a conscious borrowing of precedents and traditions. Younger bodies such as the Georgia Commons and the Nova Scotia assembly were particularly indebted to their more mature counterparts in South Carolina and Massachusetts Bay.[16] On the executive

---

[13] On Maryland, see two excellent studies, Charles A. Barker, *The Background of the Revolution in Maryland* (New Haven, 1940), and Aubrey Land, *The Dulanys of Maryland* (Baltimore, 1955).

[14] New Hampshire developments can be followed in Fry, *New Hampshire,* and Jeremy Belknap, *History of New Hampshire,* 3 vols. (Boston, 1791–92).

[15] On Georgia, see W. W. Abbot, *The Royal Governors of Georgia, 1754–1775* (Chapel Hill, N.C., 1959), and Albert B. Saye, *New Viewpoints in Georgia History* (Atlanta, 1943). John Bartlet Brebner, *The Neutral Yankees of Nova Scotia* (New York, 1937), is the best study of developments in that colony.

[16] On this point, see Abbot, *Royal Governors,* and Brebner, *Neutral Yankees.*

side the similarity in attitudes, assumptions, and policies among the governors can be traced in large measure to the fact that they were all subordinate to the same central authority in London, which pursued a common policy in all the colonies.

Before the Seven Years' War the quest was characterized by a considerable degree of spontaneity coupled with a lack of awareness that activities of the moment were part of any broad struggle for power. Rather than consciously working out the details of some master plan designed to bring them liberty or self-government, the lower houses moved along from issue to issue and from situation to situation, primarily concerning themselves with the problems at hand and displaying a remarkable capacity for spontaneous action, for seizing any and every opportunity to enlarge their own influence at the executives' expense, and for holding tenaciously to powers they had already secured. Conscious of the immediate issues in each specific conflict, they were largely unaware of and uninterested in the long-range implications of their actions. Virginia governor Francis Fauquier correctly judged the matter in 1760. "Whoever charges them with acting upon a premeditated concerted plan, don't know them," he wrote of the Virginia burgesses, "for they mean honestly, but are Expedient Mongers in the highest Degree."[17] Still, in retrospect it is obvious that throughout the eighteenth century the lower houses were engaged in a continuous movement to enlarge their sphere of influence. To ignore that continuity would be to miss the meaning of eighteenth-century colonial political development.

One is impressed with the rather prosaic manner in which the lower houses went about the task of extending their authority, with the infrequency of dramatic conflict. They gained much of their power in the course of routine business, quietly and simply extending and consolidating their authority by passing laws and and establishing practices whose implications escaped both colonial executives and metropolitan authorities and were not always fully recognized by the lower houses themselves. In this way they gradually extended their financial authority to include the powers to audit accounts of all public officers, to share in disbursing public funds, and eventually even to appoint officials concerned in collecting and handling local revenues. Precedents thus established soon hardened into fixed principles, "undoubted rights," or "inherent powers," changing the very fabric of the colonial constitutions. The notable absence of conflict is perhaps best illustrated by the none-too-surprising

[17] Fauquier to Board of Trade, June 2, 1760, Colonial Office Papers, 5/1330, ff. 37–39, Public Record Office, London.

fact that the lower houses made some of their greatest gains under those governors with whom they enjoyed the most harmony, in particular Keith in Pennsylvania, Shirley in Massachusetts, Hunter in New York, and the elder and younger Bull in South Carolina. In Virginia the House of Burgesses made rapid strides during the 1730s and 1740s under the benevolent government of Gooch, who discovered early in his administration that the secret of political success for a Virginia governor was to reach an accord with the plantation gentry.

One should not conclude that the colonies had no exciting legislative-executive conflicts, however. Through the middle decades of the eighteenth century the governors repeatedly tried to enhance their authority: Clinton to weaken the financial powers of the New York house, Samuel Shute and William Burnet to gain a permanent civil list in Massachusetts, Benning Wentworth to extend unilaterally the privilege of representation to new districts in New Hampshire, Johnston to break the extensive power of the Albemarle counties in the North Carolina lower house, Dinwiddie to establish a fee for issuing land patents without the consent of the Virginia Burgesses, and Boone to reform South Carolina's election laws. Each attempt provoked a storm of controversy which brought local politics to a fever pitch.[18] But such conflicts were the exception and usually arose not out of the lower houses' seeking more authority but from the executives' attempts to restrict powers already won. Impatient of restraint and jealous of their rights and privileges, the lower houses responded forcefully and sometimes violently when executive action threatened to deprive them of those rights. Only a few governors, men of the caliber of Henry Ellis in Georgia and to a lesser extent William Henry Lyttelton in South Carolina and Bernard in New Jersey, had the skill to challenge established rights successfully without raising the wrath of the lower houses. Clumsier tacticians—Pennsylvania's William Denny, New York's Clinton, Virginia's Dinwiddie, North Carolina's Dobbs, South Carolina's Boone, Georgia's John Reynolds—failed when pursuing similar goals.

Fundamentally, the quest for power in both the royal and the proprietary colonies was a struggle for political identity, the manifestation of the political ambitions of the leaders of emerging societies within each colony. There is a marked correlation between the appearance of eco-

---

[18] The details of these disputes can be traced in Smith, *History of New York* 2:68–151; Hutchinson, *History of Massachusetts Bay* 1:163–280; Labaree, *Royal Government,* 180–85; Lawrence F. London, "The Representation Controversy in Colonial North Carolina," *North Carolina Historical Review* 11 (1934): 255–70; Jack P. Greene, ed., "The Case

nomic and social elites produced by the growth in colonial wealth and population on the one hand and the lower houses' demand for increased authority, dignity, and prestige on the other. In the eighteenth century colonies a group of planters, merchants, and professional men either had attained or were rapidly acquiring wealth and social position. The lower houses' aggressive drive for power reflects the determination of this new elite to attain through the representative assemblies political influence as well. In another but related sense, the lower houses' efforts represented a movement for autonomy in local affairs, although it is doubtful that many of the members recognized them as such. The lower houses wished to strengthen their authority within the colonies and to reduce to a minimum the amount of supervision—and associated uncertainties—that royal or proprietary authorities could exercise. Continuously nourished by the growing desire of American legislators to be masters of their own political fortunes and by the development of a vigorous tradition of legislative superiority in imitation of the metropolitan House of Commons, this basic principle of local control over local affairs got part of its impetus, in some cases, early in the lower houses' development from an unsatisfactory experience with a despotic, inefficient, or corrupt governor such as Thomas, Lord Culpeper, or Francis, Lord Howard of Effingham, in Virginia, Lionel Copley in Maryland, Sir Edmund Andros in Massachusetts, Seth Sothell in North Carolina, or the infamous Cornbury in New York and New Jersey. Clearly, the task of defending men's rights and property against the fraud and violence of tyrannical executives fell most appropriately to the representatives of those whose rights and property demanded protection.

But the quest for power involved more than the extension of the authority of the lower houses within the colonies at the expense of the colonial executives. After their initial stage of evolution, the lower houses learned that their real antagonists were not the governors but the proprietors or crown officials in London. Few governors proved to be a match for the representatives. A governor was virtually helpless to prevent a lower house from exercising powers secured under his predecessors, and even the most discerning governor could fall into the trap of assenting to an apparently innocent law which would later prove damaging to the royal or proprietary prerogative. Some governors, for the sake of pre-

---

of the Pistole Fee: The Report of a Hearing on the Pistole Fee Controversy before the Privy Council, June 18, 1754," *Virginia Magazine of History and Biography* 46 (1958): 399–422, and "The Gadsden Election Controversy and the Revolutionary Movement in South Carolina," *Mississippi Valley Historical Review* 46 (1959): 469–92 [chap. 13 below].

serving amicable relations with the representatives or because they thought certain legislation to be in the best interest of a colony, actually conspired with legislative leaders to present the actions of the lower houses in a favorable light in London. Thus, Jonathan Belcher worked with Massachusetts leaders to parry the crown's demand for a permanent revenue in the 1730s, and Fauquier joined with Speaker John Robinson in Virginia to prevent the separation of the offices of speaker and treasurer during the closing years of the Seven Years' War.

Nor could metropolitan authorities depend upon the colonial councils to furnish an effective check upon the representatives' advancing influence. Most councillors were drawn from the rising social and economic elites in the colonies. The duality of their role is obvious. Bound by oath to uphold the interests of the crown or the proprietors, they were also driven by ambition and a variety of local pressures to maintain the status and power of the councils as well as to protect and advance their own individual interests and those of their group within the colonies. These two objectives were not always in harmony, and the councils frequently sided with the lower houses rather than with the governors. With a weakened governor and an unreliable council, the task of restraining the representative assemblies ultimately devolved upon the home government. Probably as much of the struggle for power was played out in Whitehall as in Williamsburg, Charleston, New York, Boston, or Philadelphia.

Behind the struggle between colonial lower houses and metropolitan authorities were two divergent, though on the colonial side not wholly articulated, concepts of the constitutions of the colonies and in particular of the status of the lower houses. To the very end of the colonial period, metropolitan authorities persisted in the views that colonial constitutions were static and that the lower houses were subordinate governmental agencies with only temporary and limited lawmaking powers— in the words of one metropolitan official, merely "so many Corporations at a distance, invested with an Ability to make Temporary By Laws for themselves, agreeable to their respective Situations and Climates."[19] In working out a political system for the colonies in the later seventeenth century, metropolitan officials had institutionalized these views in the royal commissions and instructions. Despite the fact that the lower houses were yearly making important changes in their respective constitutions, the crown altered neither the commissions nor the instructions

---

[19] Sir William Keith, "A Short Discourse on the Present State of the Colonies in America with Respect to the Interest of Great Britain" (1729), CO 5/4, ff. 170–71, PRO.

to conform with the realities of the colonial political situation and throughout the eighteenth century continued to maintain that they were the most vital part of the constitutional structure of the royal colonies. The Pennsylvania proprietors and to a lesser extent those of Maryland were less rigid, although they also insisted upon their theoretical and political supremacy over the lower houses.

Colonial lower houses had little respect for and even less patience with such a doctrinaire position, and whether or not royal and proprietary instructions were absolutely binding upon the colonies was the leading constitutional issue in the period before 1763. As the political instruments of what was probably the most pragmatic society in the eighteenth-century Western world, colonial legislators were unlikely to be restrained by dogma divorced from reality. They had no fear of innovations and welcomed the chance to experiment with new forms and ideas. All they asked was that a thing work. When the lower houses found that instructions from metropolitan authorities did not work in the best interests of the colonies, that they were, in fact, antithetic to the very measures they as legislatures were trying to effect, they openly refused to submit to them. Instructions, they argued, applied only to officials appointed by the crown. "Instructions from his majesty, to his governor, or the council, are binding to them, and esteemed as laws or rules; because, if either should disregard them, they might immediately be displaced," declared a South Carolina writer in 1756 while denying the validity of an instruction stipulating that colonial councils have equal rights with the lower houses in framing money bills. "But, if instructions should be laws and rules to the people of this province, then there would be no need of assemblies, and all our laws and taxes might be made and levied by an instruction."[20] Clearly, then, instructions might bind governors but never the elected branch of the legislature.

Even though the lower houses, filled with intensely practical politicians, were concerned largely with practical political considerations, they found it necessary to develop a body of theory with which to oppose unpopular instructions from Britain and to support their claims to greater political power. In those few colonies that had charters, the lower houses relied upon the guarantees in them as their first line of defense, taking the position that the stipulations of the charters were inviolate, despite the fact that some had been invalidated by English courts, and could not be altered by executive order. A more basic premise, equally applicable to all colonies, was that the constituents of the lower houses,

---

[20] *South Carolina Gazette* (Charleston), May 13, 1756.

as inhabitants of British colonies, were entitled to all the traditional rights of Englishmen. On this foundation the colonial legislatures built their ideological structure. In the early charters the crown had guaranteed the colonists "all privileges, franchises and liberties of this our kingdom of England[,] . . . any Statute, act, ordinance, or provision to the contrary thereof, notwithstanding."[21] Such guarantees, colonials assumed, merely constituted recognition that their privileges as Englishmen were inherent and unalterable and that it mattered not whether they stayed on the home islands or migrated to the colonies. "His Majesty's Subjects coming over to America," the South Carolina Commons argued in 1739 while asserting its exclusive right to formulate tax laws, "have no more forfeited this their most valuable Inheritance than they have withdrawn their Allegiance." No "Royal Order," the Commons declared, could "qualify or any wise alter a fundamental Right from the Shape in which it was handed down to us from our Ancestors."[22]

One of the most important of these rights was the privilege of representation, on which, of course, depended the very existence of the lower houses. Metropolitan authorities always maintained that the lower houses existed only through the consent of the crown,[23] but the lower houses insisted that an elected assembly was a fundamental right arising out of an Englishman's privilege to be represented and that they did not owe their existence merely to the king's pleasure. "Our representatives, agreeably to the general sense of their constituents," wrote New York assemblyman William Smith in the 1750s, "are tenacious in their opinion, that the inhabitants of this colony are entitled to all the privileges of Englishmen; that they have a right to participate in the legislative power, and that the session of assemblies here, is wisely substituted instead of a representation in parliament, which, all things consid-

---

[21] For instance, see the provision in the Maryland charter conveniently published in Merrill Jensen, ed., *English Historical Documents: American Colonial Documents to 1776* (New York, 1955), 88.

[22] James H. Easterby and Ruth S. Green, eds., *The Colonial Records of South Carolina: The Journals of the Commons House of Assembly*, 8 vols. (Columbia, S.C., 1951–61), *1736–1739*, 720 (June 5, 1739).

[23] This view was implicit in most thinking and writing about the colonies by metropolitan authorities. For the attitude of John Carteret, Lord Granville, an important figure in colonial affairs through the middle decades of the eighteenth century, see Benjamin Franklin to Isaac Norris, Mar. 19, 1759, as quoted by William S. Mason, "Franklin and Galloway: Some Unpublished Letters," American Antiquarian Society, *Proceedings*, n.s., 34 (1925): 245–46. Other examples are Jack P. Greene, ed., "Martin Bladen's Blueprint for a Colonial Union," *William and Mary Quarterly*, 3d ser., 17 (1960): 516–30, by a promi-

ered, would at this remote distance, be extremely inconvenient and dangerous."[24]

The logical corollary to this argument was that the lower houses were equivalents of the House of Commons and must perforce in their limited spheres be entitled to all the privileges possessed by that body in Great Britain. Hence, in cases where an invocation of fundamental rights was inappropriate, the lower houses frequently defended their actions on the grounds that they were agreeable to the practice of the House of Commons. Thus in 1755 the North Carolina lower house denied the right of the council to amend tax bills on the grounds that it was "contrary to Custom and Usage of Parliament."[25] Unintentionally, crown officials encouraged the lower houses to make this analogy by forbidding them in the instructions to exercise "any power or privilege whatsoever which is not allowed by us to the House of Commons . . . in Great Britain."[26]

Because neither fundamental rights nor imperial precedents could be used to defend practices that were contrary to customs of the mother country or to the British constitution, the lower houses found it necessary to develop still another argument: that local precedents, habits, traditions, and statutes were important parts of their particular constitutions and could not be abridged by a royal or proprietary order. The assumptions were that the legislatures could alter colonial constitutions by their own actions without the active consent of metropolitan officials and that once the alterations were confirmed by usage they could not be countermanded by the British government. They did not deny the power of the governor to veto or of the Privy Council to disallow their laws but argued that metropolitan acquiescence over a long period of time was tantamount to consent and that precedents thus established could not be undone without their approval. The implication was that the American colonists saw their constitutions as living, growing, and constantly changing organisms, a theory which was directly opposite to the metropolitan view. To be sure, precedent had always been an important element in shaping the British constitution, but crown officials were unwilling to concede that it was equally so in determining the fundamental

---

nent member of the Board of Trade, and [Archibald Kennedy], *An Essay on the Government of the Colonies* (New York, 1752), 17–18, by an official in the colonies.

[24] Smith, *History of New York* 1:307.

[25] Journals of the Lower House, Jan. 4–6, 1755, in William L. Saunders, ed., *The Colonial Records of North Carolina*, 10 vols. (Raleigh, N.C., 1886–90), 5:287.

[26] Leonard W. Labaree, ed., *Royal Instructions to British Colonial Governors, 1670–1776*, 2 vols. (New York, 1935), 1:112–13.

law of the colonies. They willingly granted that colonial statutes, once formally approved by the Privy Council, automatically became part of the constitutions of the colonies, but they officially took the position that both royal instructions and commissions, as well as constitutional traditions of the mother country, took precedence over local practice or unconfirmed statutes.[27] This conflict of views persisted throughout the period after 1689, becoming more and more of an issue in the decades immediately preceding the American Revolution.

If metropolitan authorities would not grant the validity of the theoretical arguments of the lower houses, neither, after 1689, did they make any systematic or concerted effort to force a rigid compliance with official policies. Repressive measures, at least before 1763, rarely went beyond the occasional disallowance of an offending statute or the official reprimand of a rambunctious lower house. General lack of interest in the routine business of colonial affairs and failure to recognize the potential seriousness of the situation may in part account for this leniency, but it is also true that official policy under both Walpole and the Pelhams called for a light rein on the colonies, on the assumption that contented colonies created fewer problems for the administration. "One would not Strain any point," Charles Delafaye, secretary to the lords justices, cautioned South Carolina's Governor Francis Nicholson in 1722, "where it can be of no Service to our King or Country." "In the Plantations," he added, "the Government should be as Easy and Mild as possible to invite people to Settle under it."[28] Three times between 1734 and 1749 the ministry failed to give enthusiastic support to measures introduced into Parliament to ensure the supremacy of instructions over colonial laws.[29] In general, the proprietors were equally lax, as long as there was no encroachment upon their land rights or proprietary dues, though the Calverts were somewhat more insistent upon preserving their proprietary prerogatives.

Metropolitan organs of administration were in fact inadequate to deal effectively with all the problems of the empire. Since no special govern-

---

[27] For a classic statement of the metropolitan argument by a modern scholar, see Lawrence H. Gipson, *The British Empire before the American Revolution,* 10 vols. (Caldwell, Idaho, and New York, 1936–61), 3 (rev.):275–81.

[28] Delafaye to Nicholson, Jan. 22, 1722, in Papers concerning the Governorship of South Carolina, bMs Am 1455, item 9, Houghton Library, Harvard University, Cambridge, Mass.

[29] For a discussion of these measures, see Bernhard Knollenberg, *Origin of the American Revolution, 1759–1766* (New York, 1960), 49.

mental bodies were created in England to deal exclusively with colonial affairs, they were handled through the regular machinery of government—a maze of boards and officials whose main interests and responsibilities were not the supervision of overseas colonies. The only body sufficiently informed and interested to deal competently with colonial matters was the Board of Trade, and it had little authority, except for the brief period from 1748 to 1761 under the presidency of George Dunk, earl of Halifax. The most useful device for restraining the lower houses was the Privy Council's right to review colonial laws, but even that was only partly effective, because the mass of colonial statutes annually coming before the Board of Trade made a thorough scrutiny impossible. Under such arrangements no vigorous colonial policy was likely. The combination of metropolitan lethargy and colonial aggression virtually guaranteed the success of the lower houses' quest for power. An indication of a growing awareness in metropolitan circles of the seriousness of the situation was Halifax's spirited, if piecemeal, effort to restrain the authority of the lower houses in the early 1750s. Symptomatic of these efforts was the attempt to make Georgia and Nova Scotia model royal colonies at the time royal government was established by writing into the instructions to their governors provisions designed to ensure the continued supremacy of the executive and to prevent the lower houses from going the way of their counterparts in the older colonies. However, the outbreak of the Seven Years' War forced Halifax to suspend his activities and prevented any further reformation until the cessation of hostilities.

Indeed, the war saw a drastic acceleration in the lower houses' bid for authority, and its conclusion found them in possession of many of the powers held less than a century before by the executive. In the realm of finance they had imposed their authority over every phase of raising and distributing public revenue. They had acquired a large measure of independence by winning control over their compositions and proceedings and obtaining guarantees of basic English parliamentary privileges. Finally, they had pushed their power even beyond that of the English House of Commons by gaining extensive authority in handling executive affairs, including the right to appoint executive officers and to share in formulating executive policy. These specific gains were symptoms of developments of much greater significance. To begin with, they were symbolic of a fundamental shift of the constitutional center of power in the colonies from the executive to the elected branch of the legislature. With the exception of the Georgia and Nova Scotia bodies, both of which had less than a decade of political experience behind them, the houses by 1763 had succeeded in attaining a new status, raising themselves from dependent lawmaking bodies to the center of political authority in their respective colonies.

But the lower houses had done more than simply acquire a new status in colonial politics. They in a sense had altered the structure of the constitution of the British Empire itself by asserting colonial authority against metropolitan authority and extending the constitutions of the colonies far beyond the limitations of the charters, instructions, or fixed notions of metropolitan authorities. The time was ripe for a reexamination and redefinition of the constitutional position of the lower houses. With the rapid economic and territorial expansion of the colonies in the years before 1763 had come a corresponding rise in the responsibilities and prestige of the lower houses and a growing awareness among colonial representatives of their own importance, which had served to strengthen their long-standing, if still imperfectly defined, impression that colonial lower houses were the American counterparts of the British House of Commons. Under the proper stimuli, they would carry this impression to its logical conclusion: that the lower houses enjoyed an equal status under the crown with Parliament. Here, then, well beyond the embryonic stage, was the theory of colonial equality with the mother country, one of the basic constitutional principles of the American Revolution, waiting to be nourished by the series of crises that beset metropolitan-colonial relations between 1763 and 1776.

The psychological implications of this new political order were profound. By the 1750s the phenomenal success of the lower houses had generated a soaring self-confidence, a willingness to take on all comers. Called upon to operate on a larger stage during the Seven Years' War, they emerged from that conflict with an increased awareness of their own importance and a growing consciousness of the implications of their activities. Symptomatic of these developments was the spate of bitter controversies that characterized colonial politics during and immediately after the war. The Gadsden election controversy in South Carolina, the dispute over judicial tenure in New York, and the contests over the pistole fee and the Two-Penny Acts in Virginia gave abundant evidence of both the lower houses' stubborn determination to preserve their authority and the failure of crown officials in London and the colonies to gauge accurately their temper or to accept the fact that they had made important changes in the constitutions of the colonies.

With the shift of power to the lower houses came the development in each colony of an extraordinarily able group of politicians. The lower houses provided excellent training for the leaders of the rapidly maturing colonial societies, and the recurring controversies prepared them for the problems they would be called upon to meet in the dramatic conflicts after 1763. In the decades before independence there appeared in the colonial statehouses John and Samuel Adams and James Otis in Massachusetts Bay; William Livingston in New York; Benjamin Franklin and John Dickinson in Pennsylvania; Daniel Dulany the younger in Maryland; Richard Bland, Richard Henry Lee, Thomas Jefferson, and Patrick Henry in Virginia; and Christopher Gadsden and John Rutledge in South Carolina. Along with dozens of others, these men were thoroughly schooled in the political arts and primed to meet any challenge to the power and prestige of the lower houses.

Britain's "new colonial policy" after 1763 provided just such a challenge. It precipitated a constitutional crisis in the empire, creating new tensions and setting in motion forces different from those which had shaped earlier developments. The new policy was based upon concepts both unfamiliar and unwelcome to the colonists, such as centralization, uniformity, and orderly development. Yet it was, for the most part, an effort to realize old aspirations. From Edward Randolph in the last decades of the seventeenth century to the earl of Halifax in the 1750s, colonial officials had envisioned a highly centralized empire with a uniform political system in each of the colonies and with the metropolitan government closely supervising the subordinate governments.[30] But because they had never made any sustained or systematic attempt to achieve these goals, there had developed during the first half of the eighteenth century a working arrangement which permitted the lower houses considerable latitude in shaping colonial constitutions without requiring crown and proprietary officials to give up any of their ideals. That there had been a growing divergence between metropolitan theory and colonial practice mattered little so long as each refrained from challenging the other. But the new policy threatened to upset this arrangement by implementing the old ideals long after the conditions that produced them had ceased to exist. Aimed at bringing the colonies more closely under metropolitan control, this policy inevitably sought to curtail the influence of

---

[30]On this point, see Charles M. Andrews, *The Colonial Period of American History,* 4 vols. (New Haven, 1934–38), 4:368–425; Michael Garibaldi Hall, *Edward Randolph and the American Colonies, 1676–1703* (Chapel Hill, N.C., 1960); Arthur H. Basye, *Lords Commissioners of Trade and Plantations, 1748–1782* (New Haven, 1925); and Dora Mae

the lower houses, directly challenging many of the powers they had acquired over the previous century. To protect gains they had already made and to make good their pretensions to greater political significance, the lower houses thereafter no longer had merely to deal with weak governors or casual metropolitan administrators; they now faced an aggressive group of officials bent upon using every means at their disposal, including the legislative authority of Parliament, to gain their ends.

Beginning in 1763, one metropolitan action after another seemed to threaten the position of the lower houses. Between 1764 and 1766 Parliament's attempt to tax the colonists for revenue directly challenged the colonial legislatures' exclusive power to tax, the cornerstone of their authority in America. A variety of other measures, some aimed at particular colonial legislatures and others at general legislative powers and practices, posed serious threats to powers that the lower houses either had long enjoyed or were trying to attain. To meet these challenges, the lower houses had to spell out the implications of the changes they had been making, consciously or not, in the structures of their respective governments. That is, for the first time they had to make clear in their own minds and then to verbalize what they conceived their respective constitutions in fact to be, and what they should be. In the process, the spokesmen of the lower houses laid bare the wide gulf between metropolitan theory and colonial practice. During the Stamp Act crisis in 1764–66, the lower houses claimed the same authority over taxation in the colonies as Parliament had over it in England, and a few of them even asserted an equal right in matters of internal policy.[31] Although justified by the realities of the colonial situation, such a definition of the lower houses' constitutional position within the empire was at marked variance with metropolitan ideals and only served to increase the determination of the home government to take a stricter tone. This determination

Clark, *The Rise of the British Treasury: Colonial Administration in the Eighteenth Century* (New Haven, 1960).

[31] See the sweeping claim of the Virginia House of Burgesses to the "Inestimable Right of being governed by such Laws respecting their internal Polity and Taxation as are devised from their own Consent" in objecting to Grenville's proposed stamp duties (H. R. McIlwaine and John Pendleton Kennedy, eds., *Journals of the House of Burgesses of Virginia*, 13 vols. [Richmond, 1905–15], *1761–65*, 302–4 [Dec. 18, 1764]). The protests of all the lower houses against the Stamp Act are conveniently collected in Edmund S. Morgan, ed., *Prologue to Revolution: Sources and Documents on the Stamp Act Crisis, 1764–1766* (Chapel Hill, N.C., 1959), 8–17, 46–69.

was manifested after the repeal of the Stamp Act by Parliament's claim in the Declaratory Act of 1766 to "full power and authority" over the colonies "in all cases whatsoever."[32]

The pattern over the next decade was, on the part of the home government, one of increasing resolution to take a firmer tone with the colonies and, on the part of American lawmakers, a heightened consciousness of the implications of the constitutional issue and a continuously rising level of expectation. In addition to their insistence upon the right of Parliament to raise revenue in the colonies, metropolitan officials also applied, in a way which was increasingly irksome to American legislators, traditional checks like restrictive instructions, legislative review, and the suspending clause, which required prior crown approval before laws of an "extraordinary nature" could go into effect. Finally, Parliament threatened the very existence of the lower houses by a measure suspending the New York assembly for refusing to comply with the Quartering Act in 1767 and by altering the substance of the Massachusetts constitution in the Massachusetts Government Act in 1774. In the process of articulating and defending their constitutional position, the lower houses developed aspirations much greater than any they had had in the years before 1763. American representatives became convinced in the decade after 1766 not only that they knew best what to do for their constituents and the colonies and that anything interfering with their freedom to adopt whatever course seemed necessary was an intolerable and unconstitutional restraint but also that the only security for their political fortunes was to abandon their attempts to restrict and define parliamentary authority in America and instead to deny Parliament's jurisdiction over them entirely by asserting their equality with Parliament under the crown. Suggested by Richard Bland as early as 1766, such a position was openly advocated by James Wilson and Thomas Jefferson in 1774 and was officially adopted by the First Continental Congress, when in its declarations and resolves it claimed for Americans "a free and exclusive power of legislation in their several provincial legislatures, where their right of representation can alone be preserved, in all cases of taxation and internal polity."[33]

[32] Danby Pickering, ed., *The Statutes at Large from Magna Carta to the End of the Eleventh Parliament of Great Britain, Anno 1761, Continued to 1806,* 46 vols. (Cambridge, Eng., 1762–1807), 27:19–20.

[33] Worthington C. Ford et al., eds., *Journals of the Continental Congress,* 34 vols. (Washington, D.C., 1904–37), 1:68–69 (Oct. 14, 1774).

Parliament could not accept this claim without giving up the principles it had asserted in the Declaratory Act and, in effect, abandoning the traditional British theory of empire and accepting the colonial constitutional position. The First Continental Congress professed that a return to the status quo of 1763 would satisfy the colonies, but Parliament in 1774–76 was unwilling even to go that far, much less to promise them exemption from parliamentary taxation. Besides, American legislators now aspired to much more and would not have been content with a return to the old, unarticulated, and undefined pattern of accommodation between metropolitan theory and colonial practice that had existed through most of the period between 1689 and 1763. Rigid guarantees of colonial rights and precise definitions of the constitutional relationship between the mother country and the colonies and between Parliament and the lower houses on American terms, that is, metropolitan recognition of the autonomy of the lower houses in local affairs, would have been required to satisfy them.

Between 1689 and 1763 the lower houses' contests with royal governors and metropolitan officials had brought them political maturity, a considerable measure of control over local affairs, capable leaders, and a rationale to support their pretensions to political power within the colonies and in the empire. The British challenge after 1763 threatened to render their accomplishments meaningless and drove them to demand equal rights with Parliament and autonomy in local affairs and eventually to declare their independence. At issue was the whole political structure forged by the lower houses over the previous century. In this context, the American Revolution becomes in essence a war for political survival, a conflict involving not only individual rights, as historians of the event have traditionally emphasized, but assembly rights as well.

This chapter was written for presentation at a session on "Early American Politics: Practice and Theory," at the 44th Annual Meeting of the Mississippi Valley Historical Association, Detroit, Michigan, April 20, 1961, and originally was entitled "The Quest for Power: An Interpretation of Colonial Legislative Development." Reprinted here with permission and minor verbal changes from the *Journal of Southern History* 27 (1961): 451–74, it has been reprinted many times, in Grady McWhiney and Robert Weibe, eds., *Historical Vistas: Readings in United States History,* 2 vols. (Boston, 1963), 1:123–44; Sidney Fine and Gerald S. Brown, eds., *The American Past,* 2 vols., 2d ed. (New York, 1965), 1:66–84; ibid., 3d ed. (1970), 1:74–93; ibid., 4th ed. (1976), 1:88–107; Paul Goodman, ed., *Essays in American Colonial History* (New York, 1967), 425–43; Abraham S. Eisenstadt, ed., *American History: Recent Interpretations,* 2 vols. (New York, 1969), 1:80–100; Trevor Colbourn and James T. Patterson, eds., *The American Past in Perspective,* 2 vols. (Boston, 1970), 1:74–99; Marvin Myers and J. R. Pole, eds., *The Meanings of American History: Interpretation of Events, Ideas, and Institutions,* 2 vols. (Glenview, Ill., 1971), 1:103–14; Frank Otto Gatell, Paul Goodman, and Allen Weinstein, eds., *The Growth of American Politics: A Modern Reader* (New York, 1972), 1:33–58; James Kirby Martin, ed., *Interpreting Colonial America: Selected Readings* (New York, 1973), 290–309; Tiziano Bonazzi, ed., "Il ruolo delle camere basse nella politica settecentesca," in *La rivoluzione americana* (Bologna, 1977), 155–73; and Peter Charles Hoffer, *Early American History,* 18 vols. (New York, 1988), vol. 8, *Planters and Yeomen: Selected Articles on the Southern Colonies,* 20–43.

—EIGHT—

Political Mimesis:
A Consideration of the Historical and Cultural Roots of Legislative Behavior in the British Colonies in the Eighteenth Century

U NTIL COMPARATIVELY RECENTLY, most investigations of government and politics in the eighteenth-century American colonies
concentrated upon recurrent contests between governors and elected
lower houses of assembly and "the growth of colonial self-government"
as reflected in the repeated triumphs of the assemblies in those struggles.
There was an almost total consensus, as Charles M. Andrews wrote in
1943 after a lifetime of study, that "the most conspicuous feature" of "the
political and institutional aspects . . . of the eighteenth century . . . was
the rise of the colonial assembly with its growth to self-conscious activity
and *de facto* independence of royal control."[1] Perhaps because the focus
in these studies was primarily upon institutional development and the
process by which the assemblies increased their authority, none of the
studies made much attempt to handle the problem of motivation, to
explain in any detail why the assemblies acted as they did. The early
assumption of nineteenth-century patriotic American historians that the
assemblies, obviously representing the natural desire of all men to be
free, were fighting for liberty and democracy against executive oppression and tyranny simply gave way to the equally vague and untestable
supposition of H. L. Osgood, Andrews, and their students. They contended that the assemblies, responding to environmentally induced so-

---

[1] The quotations are from Charles M. Andrews, *The Colonial Background of the American
Revolution: Four Essays in American Colonial History* (New Haven, 1924), 30, and "On
the Writing of Colonial History," *William and Mary Quarterly*, 3d ser., 1 (1944): 39.

cial and intellectual tendencies that diverged sharply from those of the mother country, were seeking to secure as much self-government as possible, to attain, in the words of one writer, "the largest measure of local home rule compatible with whatever might be necessary to retain the advantages of the British connection."[2]

Around the beginning of this century, a few historians adopted a more promising line of investigation by focusing upon the political divisions that existed in almost every colony at many points during their history and that invariably cut across institutional boundaries. Because these historians often sought to explain those divisions in terms of a crude social dichotomy between upper and lower classes, the earliest of their studies did not much advance our understanding of the psychology of colonial politics. But they did show, as Andrews acknowledged late in his career, that any complete explanation of colonial political life required an "understanding of the social and propertied interests involved, class distinctions and personal rivalries, the motives of majorities, and the ambitions of political leaders."[3] Despite the often fragmentary records of colonial politics, many detailed studies written during the past twenty-five years have provided a wealth of solid information on the nature of political rivalries, the social, economic, and religious motivation that lay behind those rivalries, and the substantive issues in dispute. In the process they have shifted attention almost entirely away from the emergence of the assemblies, but they have revealed that rivalries were so diverse, motivation so complex, and issues so varied—not only from colony to colony but also from time to time within colonies—that it has been extremely difficult to construct an alternative general framework of interpretation which has so comprehensive an applicability.[4]

---

[2] See Andrews, "On the Writing of Colonial History," esp. 40–41, and Charles M. Andrews, "The American Revolution: An Interpretation," *American Historical Review* 31 (1926): 219–32. For more extensive discussion of these traditions and citations to some of the principal works, see Jack P. Greene, *The Quest for Power: The Lower Houses of Assembly in the Southern Royal Colonies, 1689–1776* (Chapel Hill, N.C., 1963), vii–ix, 4–7, and Greene, review of F. G. Sprudle, *Early West Indian Government: Showing the Progress of Government in Barbados, Jamaica, and the Leeward Islands, 1660–1760* (Palmerston, N.Z., 1963), in *William and Mary Quarterly*, 3d ser., 22 (1965): 147–48. The quotation is from Charles Worthen Spencer, "The Rise of the Assembly, 1691–1760," in Alexander C. Flick, ed., *History of New York State*, 10 vols. (New York, 1933–37), 2:196.

[3] Andrews, "On the Writing of Colonial History," 40.

[4] For an extended discussion of these works, see Jack P. Greene, "Changing Interpretations of Early American Politics," in Ray A. Billington, ed., *The Reinterpretation of Early American History* (San Marino, Calif., 1966), 151–72.

Bernard Bailyn has considered this problem at some length in his recent studies of the relationship among society, politics, and ideology in the eighteenth-century colonies. Earlier writers had described many of the central ingredients of colonial political thought and had pointed out the remarkable degree to which they were "a proudly conscious extension of political thought in England,"[5] but Bailyn was the first to try to show which strands of English political thought were most important in the colonies and how those strands affected colonial political behavior. In the introduction to the first volume of his *Pamphlets of the American Revolution*, he analyzed in greater detail than any previous scholar the intellectual content of American arguments against British policy between 1763 and 1776. He found that, although Americans drew heavily upon the heritage of classical antiquity, the writings of Enlightenment rationalism, the tradition of the English common law, and the political and social theories of New England Puritanism, it was the writings of "a group of early eighteenth-century radical publicists and opposition politicians in England who carried forward into the eighteenth century and applied to the politics of the age of Walpole the peculiar strain of anti-authoritarianism bred in the upheaval of the English Civil War" that dominated Revolutionary political thought, "shaped it into a coherent whole," and, to a remarkable degree, determined the ways American leaders interpreted and responded to British regulatory and restrictive measures after 1763.[6] In a new and expanded version of this work, Bailyn argued on the basis of an investigation of earlier political writings that this same "configuration of ideas and attitudes . . . could be found [in the colonies] intact—completely formed—as far back as the 1730s" and "in partial form . . . even . . . at the turn of the seventeenth century."[7]

That this opposition vision of politics—this pattern of thought that viewed contemporary Britain "with alarm, 'stressed the dangers to England's ancient heritage and the loss of pristine virtue,' studied the processes of decay, and dwelt endlessly on the evidences of corruption . . . and the dark future these malignant signs portended"[8]—was the single

---

[5] The most important is Clinton Rossiter, *Seedtime of the Republic: The Origin of the American Tradition of Political Liberty* (New York, 1953), 139–47; the quotation is from 140.

[6] Bernard Bailyn, *Pamphlets of the American Revolution, 1750–1776,* 1 vol. to date (Cambridge, Mass., 1965–), 1:20–89; the quotations are from ix, 28.

[7] Bailyn, *The Ideological Origins of the American Revolution* (Cambridge, Mass., 1967), xi, 45–52.

[8] Ibid., 46.

most important intellectual ingredient in "American politics in its original, early eighteenth-century form," Bailyn has subsequently contended in a series of recent essays. He seeks to explain why this conception of politics acquired in the colonies a place in public life far more significant than it had ever had in England, why it became so "determinative of the political understanding of eighteenth-century Americans" that it formed the "assumptions and expectations" and furnished "not merely the vocabulary but the grammar of thought, the apparatus by which the world was perceived." In constructing an answer to this question, Bailyn managed to weave "into a single brief statement of explanation" his own findings on political ideology, many of the discoveries of those writers who stressed the rise of the assemblies, and the conclusions of the students of internal political divisions. What gave the opposition view of politics a "sharper relevance" in America, according to Bailyn, was the "bitter, persistent strife" that characterized colonial politics, strife between executives and legislatures and, infinitely more important, among the chaotic and continually shifting factions that, he suggested, were endemic to colonial life. This strife was rooted in two anomalies. First, while the theoretical powers of colonial executives were greater than those of their English counterparts, their actual powers were much smaller because they had at their disposal few of the "devices by which in England the executive" exerted effective political control. Second, the intense competition for status, power, and wealth generated by an unstable economic and social structure made what in England were only "theoretical dangers" appear in the colonies to be "real dangers" that threatened the very essentials of the constitution and created an atmosphere of suspicion and anxiety which made the opposition vision of politics seem especially appropriate.

Although the interpretation presented by Bailyn in *The Origins of American Politics* accommodates more aspects of colonial political life than any previous explanation, it is not, by itself, a sufficient explanation. Above all, it is insufficient because it does not fully take into account or put in clear perspective one of the main features of colonial political life, the very feature almost invariably singled out for comment by contemporaries in the colonies and subsequently treated as the central theme of colonial political development by so many later historians: the persistent preoccupation of colonial legislators with the dangers of prerogative power. Bailyn was, to be sure, at some pains to show the excessiveness, by English standards, of the governors' assigned powers. But he paid little attention to the colonial response to this situation. Instead, he stressed the executive weakness and the economic and social instability that made public life so brittle as presumably to give the opposition's frenzied charges of influence, conspiracy, and ministerial corruption such extraordinary explanatory power in the colonies. But this neglect and this emphasis were, in large measure, predetermined by Bailyn's research design. Limiting his investigation mostly to pamphlets and newspaper essays and ignoring other relevant sources such as legislative journals, he approached his study of early eighteenth-century political thought in search of the intellectual origins of the American Revolution and the origins of mid-eighteenth-century American politics, and he found precisely what he was looking for: instances of colonial use of the writings of John Trenchard and Thomas Gordon, Viscount Bolingbroke, and other writers of the opposition to Sir Robert Walpole and the colonial conditions that made the message of those writers so congenial. The result of this focus is that his study is both incomplete and, to the extent that it does not give adequate attention to other, perhaps more central aspects of early eighteenth-century politics, anachronistic. Specifically, in relation to the subject of this chapter, it does not consider changes in the nature and content of colonial political thought over time. It neither explores older intellectual and political traditions that preceded colonial acceptance of the Walpolean opposition conception of politics nor seeks to explain under what conditions and to what extent newer conceptions replaced those older traditions. What Bailyn has failed to do for the early eighteenth century is thus precisely what he has correctly accused earlier writers of not doing for the Revolutionary era: he has not been sensitive to what colonial political leaders "themselves . . . professed to be their own motivations." He has not considered the importance of how they saw themselves and how they conceived of the dimensions and function of the political roles into which they were cast.[9]

It is this problem as it specifically relates to the behavior of colonial legislators during the eighteenth century that I shall attempt to explore. My argument is that colonial legislative behavior was initially and deeply rooted in an older political tradition. I shall try to identify and explain the nature of that tradition, the sources and ways through which it may have been transmitted to the colonies, the intellectual and institutional imperatives it required of its adherents, the internal political and social circumstances that contributed to its acceptance and perpetuation in the colonies long after it had spent most of its force in England, and

---

[9] Bernard Bailyn, *The Origins of American Politics* (New York, 1968), esp. the preface and chaps. 1 and 2. This work was previously published in *Perspectives in American History* 1 (1967): 9–120. The quotations are from ix, 10, 53, 63, 96, 160.

the extent to which it continued to inform and shape colonial legislative behavior right down to the American Revolution.

The older political tradition to which I refer is, of course, the seventeenth-century tradition of opposition to the crown as it developed out of the repeated clashes between the first two Stuarts and their Parliaments during the first half of the century and, even more important because it occurred during a formative period in colonial political life, out of the Whig opposition to Charles II and James II in the 1670s and 1680s. Initially emerging from attempts by James I to challenge some of the "ancient Privileges" of the House of Commons, this tradition, as Thornhagh Gurdon remarked in the early eighteenth century, was a product of the "Apprehensions and Fears" among "Parliament and People . . . that instead of the ancient Constitution of *England,* a Monarchy limited by original Contract, between the ancient Princes and their People, established, and known by Custom and Usage," James "aimed at a . . . despotick Government." The ensuing "Strife and Debate," as eighteenth-century opposition writers were fond of pointing out, could be interpreted, fundamentally, as another effort in behalf of liberty in its age-old struggle against arbitrary power from whatever source it emanated. But because the crown in this instance was the offending party and the House of Commons was still conceived of as the chief bulwark of the people's liberties, the contest became a fight by the House of Commons to restrain the prerogative of the king, an attempt by the Commons to define what one later writer described as "the just Limits between Prerogative and Privilege."[10] The specific issues in dispute changed from Parliament to Parliament under the early Stuarts, but the debate over them was almost invariably cast in this form. Even after the contest had escalated in the early 1640s to the point where the ultimate issue became whether king or Parliament would exercise sovereign power, parliamentary leaders tended to see and to justify their actions as necessary protests or preventive measures against arbitary use of royal prerogatives.[11]

[10] Thornhagh Gurdon, *The History of the High Court of Parliament,* 2 vols. (London, 1731), 2:415–16, 506–8.

[11] For discussions of the varied content of opposition thought under the first two Stuarts, see Margaret Atwood Judson, *The Crisis of the Constitution: An Essay in Constitutional and Political Thought in England, 1603–1645* (New Brunswick, N.J., 1949).

In part because Parliament itself had been so obviously guilty of abusive use of governmental power during the Civil War and Interregnum and in part because Parliament's existence no longer appeared to be in jeopardy, the conditions under which Charles II returned to the throne created strong pressures toward cooperation between king and Parliament. For a decade and a half after the Restoration, the opposition talked not about the dangers of excessive prerogative but about the potential evils of royal influence in the second Long Parliament. But as the "prerogative reached unparalleled heights"[12] in the late 1660s and as the very existence of Parliament increasingly seemed to the emerging Whig opposition "to be far too precarious and desperately in need of stronger protection,"[13] the "uneasy co-operation of the first few years after the Restoration gave way in the 1670s to a series of charges by the Commons that the king was acting unconstitutionally." It was widely assumed, as a later speaker declared, that the King had had "a surfeit of Parliaments in his father's time, and was therefore extremely desirous to lay them aside."[14]

Moved by the same old fears that had plagued its predecessors during the first half of the century, the House of Commons once again "leapt at any chance to question the royal prerogative" and to demand "constitutional safeguards . . . to protect the role of Parliament."[15] As Betty Kemp has pointed out, the last six years of the reign of Charles II "and the whole reign of James II, showed that the more fundamental dangers of dissolution and absence of parliament had not passed," with the significant result that the Commons was "recalled . . . from a seemingly premature concern with influence to their earlier concern with prerogative."[16] Opposition writers reminded their readers that the history of relations between crown and Commons had been a "Series of . . . Invasions upon the *Privileges of Parliaments*" by the crown[17] and dilated upon the theme that, in the later words of Thomas Hanmer, it was not coopera-

---

[12]Caroline Robbins, *The Eighteenth-Century Commonwealthman: Studies in the Transmission, Development, and Circumstance of English Liberal Thought from the Restoration of Charles II until the War with the Thirteen Colonies* (Cambridge, Mass., 1961), 26.

[13]J. H. Plumb, *The Origins of Political Stability: England, 1675–1725* (Boston, 1967), 32.

[14]Betty Kemp, *King and Commons, 1660–1832* (London, 1957), 3 n. 21.

[15]Plumb, *Origins of Political Stability,* 50–51.

[16]Kemp, *King and Commons,* 23–24.

[17]See, e.g., the title to part 2 of William Petyt, *Jus Parliamentarium: or, The Ancient Power, Jurisdiction, Rights, and Liberties, of the most High Court of Parliament, Revived and Asserted* (London, 1739). This work was first published in 1680.

tion with but "distrust of the executive" that was the chief "principle on which the whole of our Constitution is grounded."[18]

Although the conviction that "serious restrictions" had to be imposed "on the King's prerogative in relationship to Parliament" was inextricably intertwined with fears of popery and concern over the crown's arbitrary interference with all sorts of established institutions, and although it was held in check by vivid memories of what happened when Parliament went too far in its assault upon the crown in the 1640s,[19] it was central to Whig and parliamentary opposition under the last two Stuarts and was one of the primary justifications for the Revolution of 1688.[20] Once these restrictions had been achieved by the settlement of 1689, they provided the basis for working out in the eighteenth century those methods "for co-operation between King and Commons" described by Betty Kemp, J. H. Plumb, and others.[21] Though the fear of prerogative always lurked not far beneath and occasionally even appeared above the surface of political life, it ceased to be an animating force in English politics. Opposition writers concerned themselves instead with the dangers of ministerial influence and corruption.[22]

In the colonies, by contrast, the seventeenth-century opposition tradition, with its overriding fear of prerogative power and its jealous concern with protecting the privileges and authority of the House of Commons, continued to occupy a prominent place in politics at least until the middle of the eighteenth century and did not entirely lose its force until after the Declaration of Independence.

---

[18] As quoted in Kemp, *King and Commons*, 4–5.

[19] O. W. Furley, "The Whig Exclusionists: Pamphlet Literature in the Exclusion Campaign, 1679–81," *Cambridge Historical Journal* 13 (1957): 19–36; J. R. Jones, *The First Whigs: The Politics of the Exclusion Crisis* (London, 1961). The quotation is from Kemp, *King and Commons*, 8.

[20] For the Whig opposition program, see Betty Behrens, "The Whig Theory of the Constitution in the Reign of Charles II," *Cambridge Historical Journal* 7 (1941): 42–71, esp. 61–63. A clear analysis of events is provided by Clayton Roberts, *The Growth of Responsible Government in Stuart England* (Cambridge, Eng., 1966), 197–244.

[21] Kemp, *King and Commons*, 8; Plumb, *Origins of Political Stability.*

[22] Robbins, *Eighteenth-Century Commonwealthman*, 56–319; Bailyn, *Ideological Origins*, 34–54; and Isaac Kramnick, *Bolingbroke and His Circle: The Politics of Nostalgia in the Age of Walpole* (Cambridge, Mass., 1968).

Any explanation for this phenomenon must at this point be highly tentative. A partial explanation is to be found, however, in the powerful mimetic impulses within colonial society. At work to some extent in all areas of colonial life from the beginning of English colonization, these impulses are another example of the familiar tendency of provincial societies to look to the cultural capital for preferred values and approved models of behavior. If, as Peter Laslett has remarked, English colonization contained within it a strong urge to create in America "new societies in its own image, or in the image of its ideal self,"[23] the impetus among the colonists to cast their societies in that same ideal image was (except in places like Massachusetts Bay, where men actually hoped to improve upon and not merely to duplicate English patterns) infinitely more powerful. Conditions of life in new and relatively inchoate and unstable societies at the extreme peripheries of English civilization inevitably created deep social and psychological insecurities, a major crisis of identity, that could be resolved, if at all, only through a constant reference back to the one certain measure of achievement: the standards of the cultural center. The result was a strong predisposition among the colonists to cultivate idealized English values and to seek to imitate idealized versions of English forms and institutions.[24]

These mimetic impulses, which became increasingly intense through the eighteenth century and, ironically, were probably never greater than they were on the eve of the American Revolution, were given more power and made more explicit by two simultaneous developments in the late seventeenth and early eighteenth centuries. The first was the emergence of recognizable and reasonably permanent colonial elites with great political influence, whose economic activities carried them directly into the ambit of English society and thereby subjected them, to an even greater degree than earlier colonials, to the irresistible pull of English culture.[25] The second was the extensive expansion of English governmental influence into the colonies after the Restoration and the largely successful attempt by metropolitan authorities to substitute something resembling

---

[23] Peter Laslett, *The World We Have Lost* (New York, 1965), 183.

[24] There is no adequate treatment of this phenomenon during the early phase of European expansion, but see Ronald Syme, *Colonial Elites: Rome, Spain, and the Americas* (London, 1958).

[25] There is no comprehensive study of this subject, but see Louis B. Wright, *The First Gentlemen of Virginia: Intellectual Qualities of the Early Colonial Ruling Class* (San Marino, Calif., 1940); Bernard Bailyn, *The New England Merchants in the Seventeenth Cen-*

an English model of government for a welter of existing political forms that had grown up in the colonies.[26]

That this model was only superficially English, that the analogy between king, Lords, and Commons in England on the one hand and the governors, councils, and assemblies in the colonies on the other was so obviously imperfect, only stimulated the desire of colonial political leaders to make it less so.[27] Nowhere was this desire more manifest than in the behavior of the lower houses of assembly and of the men who composed them. Because the governors and councils so clearly rested upon a less independent foundation, they might never be more than "imperfect" equivalents of their English counterparts. But the lower houses had so "exact" a "resemblance" to "that part of the British constitution" which they stood for in the colonies that it was entirely plausible to entertain the heady possibility that each of them might indeed come to be the very "epitome of the house of Commons." Because they were "called by the same authority," derived their "power from the same source, [were] instituted for the same ends, and [were] governed by the same forms," there was absolutely no reason why each of them "should not have the same powers . . . and the same rank in the system of" its "little community, as the house of Commons" had "in that of Britain."[28]

In their attempt to convert this possibility into reality, to model their lower houses as closely as possible after the English House of Commons, colonial legislators had a wide range of sources to draw upon. They had, to begin with, some of the proceedings of the House of Commons as published, for the period from 1618 to the execution of Charles I, along with many other relevant documents, in John Rushworth's eight-volume *Historical Collections* (London, 1659–1701) and, for the 1670s and 1680s, in the separately printed journals of each session of the House. They had, as well, much of the vast literature of the Whig opposition to the later Stuarts, including both the major philosophical disquisitions of

---

tury (Cambridge, Mass., 1955); and Frederick B. Tolles, *Meeting House and Counting House: The Quaker Merchants of Colonial Philadelphia* (Chapel Hill, N.C., 1948).

[26] On this point, see esp. A. P. Thornton, *West-India Policy under the Restoration* (Oxford, 1955); and Michael Garibaldi Hall, *Edward Randolph and the American Colonies, 1676–1703* (Chapel Hill, N.C., 1960).

[27] The power of this analogy is discussed, perhaps in somewhat exaggerated form, in Bailyn, *Origins of American Politics*, 59–65.

[28] The quotations are from *The Privileges of the Island of Jamaica Vindicated with an Impartial Narrative of the Late Dispute between the Governor and House of Representatives*

Henry Neville, Algernon Sydney, and John Locke (each of which carefully defined the functions of the House and elaborated the proper relationship between prerogative and Parliament), and many of the vast
number of occasional pieces, some of which were reprinted following the
Glorious Revolution in the two-volume collection of *State Tracts* (London, 1689–93) and others of which were later issued together in the
sixteen-volume edition of *Somers Tracts* (London, 1748–52).[29] Finally,
they had such terse and comprehensive statements of Whig theory as
Henry Care's *English Liberties: or, The Free-Born Subject's Inheritance*
(London, 1682), which was reprinted several times in the colonies; the
Whig contributions to the extensive debate over the antiquity of Parliament;[30] early Whig histories, especially that of Paul de Rapin-Thoyras,
the Huguenot who sailed with William of Orange and who interpreted
the events of the seventeenth century from the perspective of the most
radical wing of Whig thinkers;[31] and, probably most important of all, the
several parliamentary commentaries and procedural books published in
the seventeenth century, including those of William Hakewill,[32] Sir Edward Coke,[33] Henry Scobell,[34] Henry Elsynge,[35] and, most significantly,
George Petyt.[36] Petyt's work was reprinted by Andrew Bradford in 1716

(London, 1766), 33–34. Similar statements are scattered throughout the literature of
colonial politics.

[29] The best analyses of the content of this literature will be found in Behrens, "Whig
Theory of the Constitution"; Furley, "Whig Exclusionists"; and Robbins, *Eighteenth-
Century Commonwealthman*, 22–87. The best discussion of Locke's ideas is in the introduction to Peter Laslett's edition of *Two Treatises of Government* (Cambridge, Eng.,
1960).

[30] The standard discussion of these writings is J. G. A. Pocock, *The Ancient Constitution
and the Feudal Law: A Study of English Historical Thought in the Seventeenth Century*
(Cambridge, Eng., 1957).

[31] Paul de Rapin-Thoyras, *The History of England, as Well Ecclesiastical as Civil*, trans.
Nicholas Tindal, 15 vols. (London, 1725–31), is the first English edition.

[32] William Hakewill, *The Manner of Holding Parliaments in England* (London, 1641).

[33] Sir Edward Coke, *The Fourth Part of the Institutes of the Laws of England* (London,
1644).

[34] Henry Scobell, *Memorials of the Method and Manner of Proceedings in Parliament in
Passing Bills* (London, 1656).

[35] Henry Elsynge, *The Ancient Method and Manner of Holding Parliaments in England*
(London, 1660).

[36] George Petyt, *Lex Parliamentaria: or A Treatise of the Law and Custom of the Parliaments of England* (London, 1689).

in both New York and Philadelphia and was the last such treatise of major proportions until John Hatsell published his four-volume work in 1781.[37]

As Petyt remarked in his preface, these procedural books served as a comprehensive introduction to *"the admirable method of* Parliamentary Proceedings; *the Exactness and Decency of their* Orders; *the Wisdom and Prudence of their* Customs; *the Extent of their* Powers; *and the Largeness of their* Privileges."* They adumbrated in detail and cited appropriate precedents concerning mechanics of conducting elections, the necessary qualifications for members and electors, the methods of examining election returns and deciding disputed elections, the power of the House over its own members, the method of electing a speaker and the correct way for him to conduct his office, the ways of selection and the roles of other House officers, the proper procedures for passing bills and conducting debates, the several categories of committees and the structure and function of each, the customary form of a session, the privileges of members, and the usual distribution of function and patterns of relationship among the three branches of Parliament.

The importance of such manuals in the exportation of parliamentary government to distant plantations can scarcely be overemphasized. If, as Anthony Stokes later remarked, "the Journals of the Houses of Parliament" were "the precedents by which the Legislatures in the Colonies conduct[ed] themselves,"[38] these manuals provided a convenient distillation of the several pertinent matters in those journals. The extent to which colonial legislators probably used them in the process of taking, as the Pennsylvania speaker David Lloyd phrased it, "their rules from the *House of Commons,"* of copying its forms and procedures, may be inferred from the work of several earlier scholars, most notably Mary Patterson Clarke,[39] and requires no further comment here.

---

[37] John Hatsell, *Precedents of Proceedings in the House of Commons,* 4 vols. (London, 1781). Among the few pieces of literature of this genre to appear in the eighteenth century were Gurdon's *History of the High Court of Parliament* and Giles Jacob, *Lex Constitutiones: or, The Gentleman's Law* (London, 1719), esp. chap. 3. For a discussion of the changing nature of the interest in such matters from the seventeenth to the eighteenth century, see J. Steven Watson, "Parliamentary Procedure as a Key to the Understanding of Eighteenth Century Politics," *Burke Newsletter* 3 (1962): 108–28.

[38] Anthony Stokes, *A View of the Constitution of the British Colonies in North America and the West Indies, at the Time the Civil War Broke Out on the Continent of America* (London, 1783), 243–44.

[39] Mary Patterson Clarke, *Parliamentary Privilege in the American Colonies* (New Haven, 1943), esp. 1–13. The bibliographical note (270–87) refers to several other specialized

What has been much less clearly perceived, however, and what, in fact, has been largely missed by earlier writers is the remarkable extent to which these parliamentary commentaries and the later Stuart opposition literature shaped not merely the form and procedure of the lower houses but also the understanding and behavior of their members. For, in addition to spelling out the method and manner of parliamentary proceedings, they prescribed explicitly and in detail a whole set of generalized and specific institutional imperatives for representative bodies, a particular pattern of behavior for their members, and a concrete program of political action.

The central assumptions behind this prescription were, first, that there was a natural antagonism between the "King's Prerogative" and the "Rights, Liberties and Properties of the People," and, second, that the primary function of the House of Commons, as Henry Care declared, was "to preserve inviolable our Liberty and Property, according to the known Laws of the Land, without any giving way unto or Introduction of that absolute and arbitrary Rule practised in Foreign Countries."[40] To that end the House was expected always to be careful never to relinquish possession of the "Keys to unlock People[']s Purses" and always to be on the alert for any indications of arbitrary government in order that they might be checked before they could "wound the Body Politick in a vital Part." The role of the House of Commons was thus essentially negative and defensive. To "redress Grievances, to take notice of Monopolies and Oppressions, to curb the Exorbitances of great Favourites, and pernicious Ministers of State, to punish such mighty Delinquents, who are protected by the King, that they look upon themselves too big for the ordinary reach of Justice in Courts of Common Law, to inspect the conduct of such who are intrusted with the Administration of Justice, and interpret the Laws to the prejudice of the People, and those who dispose the publick Treasure of the Nation"—these were the many grave and weighty responsibilities that fell to and could only be handled by that "great Assembly." The House was the subject's single most important governmental hedge against "arbitrary Violence and Oppression" from the prerogative or any other source, and the final guarantor

works touching on this point. The quotation is from [David Lloyd], *Remarks on the Late Proceedings of Some Members of Assembly at Philadelphia* (Philadelphia, 1728). Among many similar statements, see [Thomas Nairne], *A Letter from South Carolina* (London, 1710), 21–22.

[40]Gurdon, *History of the High Court of Parliament,* 415–16; Henry Care, *English Liberties,* 4th ed. (London, 1719), 164. All citations to Care are to this edition.

of the liberty that was the peculiar and precious "Birth-right of En-glishmen."[41]

Such extraordinary responsibilities required both a strong House of Commons and a membership devoted to maintaining that strength. Voters had, therefore, always to be especially careful to elect to Parliament only men who had sufficient "Wisdom and Courage" that they could "not be hectored out of their Duties by the Frowns and Scowls of Men" and who were "resolved to stand by, and maintain the *Power and Privileges of Parliaments*," which were the very "Heart-strings of the Common-Wealth." It was incumbent upon all men elected to "*that honourable Station*" to make sure that they were "*thoroughly skill'd in* Parliamentary Affairs, *to know their own* Laws *and* Customs, *their* Powers *and* Priviledges, *that they may not at any time suffer Invasions to be made upon them, by what plausible* Pretences *soever.*"[42]

Because many—perhaps most—of those "Invasions" could be expected to derive directly from and even to be protected by the excessive "Privileges and Prerogatives" invested in the crown, it was absolutely necessary that the House of Commons have sufficient powers and privileges to contest the crown on equal, perhaps even superior, grounds. The House had to have legal guarantees that it would meet frequently, have full investigative powers, and have complete control over its own officers.[43] Its members must have freedom of speech and debate, freedom from arrest during sessions, and exemption from punishment outside the House for anything said or done in or on behalf of the House. In short, the House had to be a law unto itself, responsible only to its constituents and to its own special law, the "Lex & Consuetudo Parliamenti."[44]

Bent upon turning their lower houses into "epitomes of the House of Commons," "so fond," as one Jamaica governor reported, "of the notion to be as near as can be, upon the foott of H[is] M[ajesty's] English subjects that the desire of it allmost distracts them,"[45] and prone, like all provincials, to take the ideals of their cultural capital far more seriously

---

[41] Care, *English Liberties*, 4, 122, 138–39; Petyt, *Lex Parliamentaria*, 19, 24.

[42] Care, *English Liberties*, 164–67; Petyt, *Lex Parliamentaria*, preface.

[43] Petyt, *Lex Parliamentaria*, 3, 13, 16, 30–31, 132. Petyt was clearly unhappy with the king's prominent role in the choice of speaker, noting that the selection must have been "anciently free to the *Commons*, to choose whom they would of their own House" (ibid., 132).

[44] Ibid., 9, 36–37, 81–82, 87, 139.

[45] Duke of Portland to [Lord Carteret?], Dec. 7, 1723, in William Noel Sainsbury et al., eds., *Calendar of State Papers, Colonial*, 43 vols. (London, 1860–), *1722–23*, 385.

than they were ever taken in the capital itself, colonial representatives adopted in toto this entire system of thought and action, along with its patterns of perception and its cluster of imperatives, roles, and conventions. This system supplied them with a special frame of reference, an angle of vision which helped them to put their own problems and actions in historical, seemingly even cosmic, perspective, gave them a standard of behavior, determined how they conceived of the lower houses and of their own political roles, and, most important, shaped into predictable and familiar forms their perceptions of and responses to political events.

So deeply was this system of thought and action imbedded in their political culture that the remembrance of the terrible excesses of Stuart despotism, of those infamous times "when prerogative was unlimited, and liberty undefined," and "arbitrary power, under the shelter of unlimited Prerogative was making large strides over the land," was throughout the eighteenth century always near the surface of political consciousness. Colonial representatives scarcely needed to be reminded of "what extraordinary Progress was made" in the attempt "to raise Royalty above the Laws and Liberties of the People, by the chimerical Ideas of Prerogative" during the "three last hereditary Reigns of the *Stuarts*, what Toil, what Fatigue, what Slaughter the Nation underwent before the Delirium of *Charles* the 1st, could be vanquished. What Lengths were run, what large Compliances made under *Charles* the Second, . . . how near fatal the Blow was to Freedom and Liberty under his Brother *James*," and how all of these evil efforts were defeated only because they were "constantly and strictly opposed by Parliament" under the leadership of those noble House of Commons men—Sir John Eliot, Sir Edward Coke, Edward Littleton, John Pym, John Hampden, William Jones—"who stood forth at that critical period, in defense of the Constitution."[46]

With such vivid memories always before them, colonial legislators had a strong predisposition to look at each governor as a potential Charles I or James II, to assume a hostile posture toward the executive, and to define with the broadest possible latitude the role of the lower house as "the main barrier of all those rights and privileges which British subjects enjoy."[47] Ever ready to stand "in the gap against oppression," they were,

---

[46] *Privileges of the Island of Jamaica Vindicated,* 8, 11, 13, 28, 36, 66; A New England Man, *A Letter to the Freeholders and Qualified Voters, Relating to the Ensuing Election* (Boston, 1749), 2.

[47] Pennsylvania Assembly, *To the Honourable Patrick Gordon, Esq., Lieut. Governor* (Philadelphia, 1728), 6, as quoted by Lawrence H. Leder, *Liberty and Authority: Early American Political Ideology, 1689–1763* (Chicago, 1968), 87.

in the best tradition of seventeenth-century English opponents of the crown, constantly worried lest *"Prerogative"* gain "a considerable Advantage over *Liberty"* or a governor extend "his Power, beyond what any King in *England* ever pretended to, even in the most despotick and arbitary Reigns."[48] Especially sensitive to any encroachments "upon their jurisdiction" that might "(if submitted to) strip them of all authority, and [thereby] disable them from either supporting their own dignity or giving the people . . . that protection against arbitrary power, which nothing but a free and independent Assembly" could "give," they invariably, in imitation of the English House of Commons, opposed all attempts to make innovations "contrary to . . . the constant Practice of all English Assemblies" or "to Govern otherwise than according to the Usage and Custom of the Country since the first Settlement thereof." In the words of Elisha Cooke, Jr., they "Warily observed and tim[or]ously Prevented" any precedents that might, by making "little Changes in Fundamentals," lead to the collapse of the whole constitution.[49] In their determination to discover and root out all examples of arbitrary executive power, they were particularly concerned "to enquire into the abuses and corruptions of office, the obstructions of public justice, and the complaints of subjects, oppressed by the hand of power, and to bring the offenders in such cases to justice."[50]

The governors of the colonies themselves encouraged colonial representatives in this conception of the function of the lower houses and the mode of behavior it implied. For the legislators were not the only group imprisoned by the rhetoric, anxieties, and peculiar political myopia of Stuart England. Like the Stuart monarchs and their supporters and occupying similar roles in the political order, governors could scarcely avoid interpreting any questioning of executive actions and any opposition to gubernatorial programs or metropolitan directives as at least a covert challenge to the essential prerogatives of the crown or proprietors.

---

[48] *Privileges of the Island of Jamaica Vindicated,* 42; Americanus, *A Letter to the Freeholders and Other Inhabitants of the Massachusetts-Bay Relating to Their Approaching Election of Representatives* ([Boston], 1729), iii; *A Second Letter from One in the Country to His Friend in Boston* ([Boston], 1729), 2.

[49] *Privileges of the Island of Jamaica Vindicated,* 2; *The Remonstrance of Several of the Representatives for Several Counties of the Province of New York Being Members of the Present Assembly* (New York, 1698), 1; Resolutions of the Maryland House of Delegates, Oct. 22, 1722, in St. George Leakin Sioussat, *The English Statutes in Maryland* (Baltimore, 1903), 75; Elisha Cooke, *Just and Seasonable Vindication Respecting Some Affairs Transacted by the Late General Assembly at Boston, 1720* [Boston, 1720], 14.

[50] *Privileges of the Island of Jamaica Vindicated,* 51.

From every colony came charges from the governors and their adherents that the lower houses were "exceeding their due and reasonable Bounds; strengthening themselves with pretences of publick Good and their own Privileges as the Representatives of the People." Everywhere, the executives complained that the lower houses were declaring "themselves a House of Commons," assuming "all the Privileges of it, and" acting "with a much more unlimited Authority." It was widely echoed, and believed, that the lower houses, like the first Long Parliament in the "Period that every good Man wishes could be struck out of our Annals," were actually endeavoring "to wrest the small Remains of Power out of the Hands of the Crown," "to assume the Executive Power of the Government into their own Hands," and perhaps even "to weaken, if not entirely to cast off, the Obedience they owe to the Crown, and the Dependance which all Colonies ought to have on their Mother Country." From the governors' chairs, the leaders of the legislative opposition appeared to be, not patriots struggling in the glorious cause of liberty, but exactly what the leaders of the House of Commons had seemed to the Stuarts: "designing and malicious Men imposing upon, and deluding the People" until they were "so far infatuated, as to seem insensible of their . . . true interest."[51] Every recalcitrant lower house appeared to be bent on pursuing "the example of the parliament of 1641," and every leader to be "a great Magna-Carta Man & Petition-of-Right-maker" determined to persuade his fellow legislators "to dance after the Long Parliament's pipe."[52] Both sides, then, were playing out roles and operating within a conception of

---

[51] The quotations are from *The Representation and Memorial of the Council of the Island of Jamaica to the Right Honourable the Lords Commissioners for Trade and Plantations* (London, 1716), ii, iv, 14; Governor James Glen to Commons House, Sept. 20, 1755, Journals of the South Carolina Commons House, Jan.–May 1754, Colonial Office Papers, 5/472, ff. 6–7, Public Record Office, London; and a speech of Governor Jonathan Belcher to the Massachusetts General Assembly, Oct. 2, 1730, reprinted in *Extracts from the Political State of Great Britain, December 1730* [Boston, 1731], 4–5. For many similar characterizatons of the lower houses and their leaders by governors and their supporters, see Sir William Beeston to Board of Trade, Aug. 19, 1701, *Cal. St. Papers, Col., 1701,* 424–25; Lord Cornbury to Board of Trade, Nov. 6, 1704, Feb. 19, 1705, ibid., *1704–5,* 308–9, 386; Samuel Shute to Crown, [Aug. 16, 1723], ibid., *1722–23,* 324–30; Henry Worsley to Duke of Newcastle, Aug. 4, 1727, ibid., *1726–27,* 325–26; *The Honest Man's Interest as He Claims Any Lands in the Counties of New-Castle, Kent, or Sussex, on Delaware* [Philadelphia, 1726], 1.

[52] Francis Lord Willoughby to King, Aug. 8, 1665, CO 1/19, no. 92, PRO, as quoted in Thornton, *West-India Policy,* 65; Lewis Morris to Board of Trade, June 10, 1743, *The Papers of Lewis Morris,* New Jersey Historical Society, *Collections,* 14 vols. (Newark, N.J., 1852–1965), 4:162.

politics which derived directly from the revolutionary situation in Stuart England, a conception which conditioned them to view politics as a continuing struggle between prerogative and liberty, between executive and legislative power.

For governors and legislators alike, this conception of their behavior and their disagreements gave them an enlarged purpose which transcended the narrow bounds of their several localities and, by investing their actions with national—not to say, universal—meaning, linked them directly to their cultural inheritance as Englishmen, gave them a more secure sense of who and what they were, and helped to satisfy their deepest mimetic impulses. Equally importantly, at least in the case of the legislators, that enlarged purpose also supplied them and their institutions with the prestige, standing, and political power within their respective communities that seem to be essential to meet the psychological needs of emergent elites.

The fact that this specific conception of politics had a powerful hold on men's minds in England at exactly the same time that colonial legislators were self-consciously beginning to cultivate English political values and to imitate the procedures and behavior of the House of Commons does not completely account for the adoption of that conception in the colonies. What does account for its adoption as well as for its continuing vitality in the colonies—long after it had become in England little more than a series of political clichés and hackneyed constitutionalisms that were largely irrelevant to the realities of political life—was the survival in the eighteenth-century colonies of the very conditions and circumstances that had initially spawned the conception in seventeenth-century England. For, as Bailyn has recently reminded us,[53] explicit restrictions of the kind Parliament successfully imposed upon the prerogative in England following the Glorious Revolution were never achieved in the colonies. As a result, the institutional cooperation made possible by the revolutionary settlement in England was rarely attainable in the colonies, and the specter of unlimited prerogative thus continued to haunt colonial legislators.

For legislators "in love with . . . [the English] Constitution," striving diligently to achieve a "form of government" which resembled "that of

---

[53] Bailyn, *Origins of American Politics*, 66–71.

England, as nearly as the condition of a dependent Colony" could "be brought to resemble, that of its mother country," and culturally programmed to be ever on guard against the dangers of unlimited prerogative,[54] this situation was a source of perpetual anxiety. Not only did it directly frustrate their mimetic impulses by blatantly reminding them of the great gap between their aspirations and reality, it also put them into continual fear lest some evil governor employ his excessive power to introduce the most pernicious form of tyranny. It seemed absolutely inexplicable, as an anonymous Jamaican declared in 1714, "that in all the Revolutions of State, and Changes of the Ministry" in England since the Restoration "the several Colonies which compose the *British* Empire in *America*" and were inhabited by supposedly freeborn Englishmen "should . . . lye still so much neglected, under such a precarious Government and greivous Administration, as they have, for the most part, labour'd under, both before and since the late signal Revolution."[55] Indeed, from the perspective of that revolution in which the rights and privileges of subjects in England had been so fully "confirmed; and the knavish Chicanes, and crafty Inventions, that were introduced to deprive the Subject of his Rights . . . abolished," it seemed especially grievous—and frighteningly dangerous—"that a Governour of any Colony . . . so far distant from the Seat of Redress . . . should be vested with a Power to govern, in a more absolute and unlimited manner there, than ever the Queen herself can, according to Law, or ever did attempt to exercise in *Great Britain*," or that a lower house should have "less Sway and Weight" in a colony "than the *House of Commons* had in *Great Britain*."[56]

The dangers of this situation were not merely imaginary. They were vividly confirmed by the many "Instances" in which both royal and proprietary governors, lacking in many cases even a remote sense of identity of interests with the colonists, had used their preponderant powers "to gripe and squeeze the People . . . for [no] . . . other Reason, than their own private Gain," "usurped more Authority than [even theoretically] belonged to them," and attempted to exercise "Arbitrary Power, unknown in our Mother-Country since the glorious Revolution of 1688." It was well known "that all [of the many] Contentions and Animosities . . .

[54] Fayer Hall, *The Importance of the British Plantations in America to the Kingdom* (London, 1731), 24; *Privileges of the Island of Jamaica Vindicated,* 31.

[55] *The Groans of Jamaica, Express'd in a Letter from a Gentleman Residing There, to His Friend in London* (London, 1714), iv.

[56] Daniel Dulany, *The Right of the Inhabitants of Maryland to the Benefit of the English Laws* (Annapolis, 1728), 17; *Second Letter,* 2; *Groans of Jamaica,* vi.

between the Governour and Inhabitants of" the colonies took "their first
Rise, from some grievous and intolerable Acts of Oppression, in the Administration." As Richard Jackson remarked, it was the governors who
always acted the "*offensive Part*," who "set up unwarrantable Claims" and
employed "Snares, Menaces, Aspersions, Tumults, and every other unfair Practice" in an attempt either to bully or to wheedle "the Inhabitants out of Privileges they were born to." Like the House of Commons,
the lower houses thus always acted "on the *defensive only*"; their members
courageously struggled with true British patriotism against the wicked
machinations of "hungry, ignorant, or extravagant" governors and their
"crafty, active, knavish . . . , servile, fawning" adherents, the very
"trash of mankind," who alone would enter into such unsavory alliances
against the people's rights and liberties as represented by the lower
houses.[57]

Whatever images they held of themselves, however, colonial representatives could not, in the situation, act "on the *defensive only*." Precisely
because the king's governors claimed to "be more Absolute in the Plantations than" the king himself was "in England," because some governors
actually sought to use their exorbitant powers to increase the prerogative
at the expense of liberty, and because, as a Barbadian complained in
1719, it was not always possible to secure redress against such grievances
in London in the face of the governors' superior influence with men in
power—for all of these reasons so "generally [well] Known in *America*,"
the lower houses found themselves—and were frequently and correctly
accused of—trying to secure checks on the prerogative and power over
executive affairs well beyond any exercised by the House of Commons.
It was "a received opinion" that "Right without Power to maintain it, is

---

[57] The quotations are from *An Essay upon the Government of the English Plantations on
the Continent of America* (London, 1701), written by an anonymous Virginian and reprinted in a modern edition by Louis B. Wright (San Marino, Calif., 1945), 11, 21; A
New England Man, *Letter to the Freeholders*, 5; *Groans of Jamaica*, iv–v; [Richard Jack-
son], *An Historical Review of Pennsylvania from Its Origin* (Philadelphia, 1812), 378–79;
*A Representation of the Miserable State of Barbadoes under the Arbitrary and Corrupt Ad-
ministration of His Excellency, Robert Lowther, Esq; the Present Governor* (London, 1719),
esp. 22–23; "Considerations of the Present Benefit and Better Improvement of the English Colonies in America," [1690s], in Historical Manuscripts Commission, *Report of the
Manuscripts of the Duke of Buccleuch and Queensberry*, 3 vols. (London, 1899–1926), 2,
pt. 2:737; Morris to Secretary of State, Feb. 9, 1707, in Edmund B. O'Callaghan and
Berthold Fernow, eds., *Documents Relative to the Colonial History of the State of New York*,
15 vols. (Albany, 1853–87), 5:37.

the Derision and Sport of Tyrants."[58] To defend such deviations from the metropolitan norm, colonial legislators were forced to fall back upon that ultimate defense of the seventeenth-century House of Commons, *"Perpetual Usage"* and "established custom," and to claim that, like the Commons, each legislature had a "Lex & Consuetudo Parliamenti" of its own.[59]

Despite the depth and genuineness of their imitative impulses, the mimesis of the House of Commons by the colonial lower houses and of the metropolitan government by the several provincial governments could never be exact, if only because of the Crown's exaggerated claims for prerogative in the plantations and the immoderate responses those claims evoked from the legislatures. The result, a source of amusement, derision, and amazement among the metropolitan administration's supporters in the colonies, was the ironic spectacle of men who were determined to form their "Assemblies . . . on the Plan of an *English* Parliament," forced into defending their peculiar practices on the obvious grounds that it was "altogether . . . absurd to prescribe [exactly] the same form of government to people differently circumstanced."[60]

The lower houses in most colonies were able through such innovative practices to bridle the governors, both because, unlike the king, the governors were never protected from attack by the aura of the concept that the king could do no wrong and because, as Bailyn has so fully and effectively argued, most governors did not have at their command those "devices by which in England the executive" was able to exert its control over politics and secure its goals. But this ability to restrain the governors never completely allayed the colonial legislators' fears of prerogative power and arbitrary government. As long as the crown or proprietors refused to abandon their claims to such extravagant powers for their

---

[58] *Essay upon Government,* 17; *Representation of the Miserable State of Barbadoes,* 32–33; [Nairne], *Letter from South Carolina,* 21–22, 26–27; A New England Man, *Letter to the Freeholders,* 5.

[59] Examples may be seen in Cooke, *Just and Seasonable Vindication,* 3, 9; and Henry Wilkinson, "The Governor, the Council and Assembly in Bermuda during the First Half of the Eighteenth Century," *Bermuda Historical Quarterly* 2 (1945): 69–84, esp. 81–81.

[60] The quotations are from [Lloyd], *Remarks on the Late Proceedings,* as quoted by Roy N. Lokken, *David Lloyd: Colonial Lawmaker* (Seattle, 1959), 230; and *Pennsylvania Gazette Letter from South Carolina* (Philadelphia), Mar. 28, 1738, as quoted by Leder, *Liberty and Authority,* 103; see also [Nairne], *Letter from South Carolina,* 21–22, 25–26; and Lewis Evans, "A Brief Account of Pennsylvania," 1753, in Lawrence Henry Gipson, *Lewis Evans* (Philadelphia, 1939), 131–34.

governors or to recognize the actual limitations imposed upon the prerogative by the lower houses, there was always the terrifying possibility
that metropolitan authorities might unleash the unlimited might of the
parent state to enforce its claims, perhaps even by bringing the force of
Parliament itself against the lower houses.[61] Although some colonial
leaders wishfully hoped that "*that August Assembly*, the Protectors of
English Liberties," might actually side with its sister institutions in the
colonies, there was an uneasy awareness as well of "how deeply" parliamentary intervention might "enter into our *Constitution* and affect our
most *valuable priviledges*." Such extreme vulnerability meant, of course,
that colonial legislators could never feel entirely secure "against the as-
saults of arbitrary power . . . [upon] their lives, their liberties, or their
properties."[62]

The resulting anxiety, only partly conscious and appropriately expressed through the classic arguments of the seventeenth-century opposition to the Stuarts, ensured that, at least until such a time as the colonies were granted "a free Constitution of Government" equivalent to
that enjoyed by Englishmen at home, those arguments would continue
to be especially relevant to colonial politics and to give form and coherence to much of its outward appearance. However, because those arguments and the conception of politics from which they derived were seemingly so explanatory of the peculiar circumstances of colonial politics and
apparently so well suited to meet the psychological needs produced by
these circumstances, they became so integral a part of colonial political
culture and so determinative of the sensibilities of colonial politicians
that they ran far "deeper than the Surface of things."[63] They ran so deep,
in fact, that they created a strong predisposition to interpret virtually
all political conflict as struggles between prerogative and liberty. Even
factional fights over tangible economic issues that obviously cut across
institutional lines and had nothing ostensible to do with constitutional
questions were perceived as, and thereby to some extent actually con-
verted into, such struggles.

---

[61] Bailyn, *Origins of American Politics*, 70–105; Greene, review of Spurdle, *Early West Indian Government*, 149.

[62] *A Letter to a Gentleman Chosen to Be a Member of the Honourable House of Representatives to Be Assembled at Boston* [Boston, 1731], 7–8, 14–15; *Privileges of the Island of Jamaica Vindicated*, 27–28, 45.

[63] The quotations are from *Essay upon Government*, 20; and Isaac Norris, *Friendly Advice to the Inhabitants of Pennsylvania* (Philadelphia, 1710), 2.

It is important, of course, to keep in mind that in colonial as in all politics there was commonly a considerable difference between the ostensible and the real; any comprehensive interpretation will have to distinguish between and describe both "the dress parade of debate" and "the program of opportunist political tactics" and the concrete social and economic interests that lay behind that debate.[64] But it is equally important to comprehend the powerful hold of this older opposition political conception upon the minds of colonial politicians and the remarkable extent to which it conditioned them to conceive of and to explain—even to themselves—behavior and actions arising out of the most self-interested and sordid ambitions as essential contributions to the Englishman's heroic struggle against the evils of unlimited prerogative.

But the hold of this older political conception upon colonial politicians was not so powerful as to prevent them from receiving and employing later English conceptions. Through the middle decades of the eighteenth century, the economies of the home islands and the colonies became ever more tightly connected, the last two intercolonial wars provided a new and compelling focus of common attention,[65] and the colonial elites developed an increasing cultural and political self-consciousness and became more aware of the great social gulf between the colonies and Britain.[66] As a result, the attractive force of English culture and the explicit desires of the elites to cultivate English styles and values and to anglicize their societies greatly intensified. Under certain conditions this intensification of colonial mimetic impulses led to the supplementation and,

---

[64] The quotations are from Spencer, "Rise of the Assembly," 197.

[65] The role of the intercolonial wars in intensifying British patriotism and a concern for things British among the colonists is described by Max Savelle, *Seeds of Liberty: The Genesis of the American Mind* (New York, 1948), and Richard L. Merritt, *Symbols of American Community, 1735–1775* (New Haven, 1966).

[66] See the perceptive reflection by [Sir Egerton Leigh], *Considerations on Certain Political Transactions in the Province of South Carolina* (London, 1774), 27, upon "what slow advances *Infant Societies* of Men make towards Regularity or Perfection; that in the first outset they are occupied in providing for their necessary wants, and securing their protection; the niceties and punctilios of Public Business never enter their heads, till they have brought their Colony to such an outward state that they feel some *Self-conceit* has crept into their hearts; then it is that Men begin to give polish to their Acts, and to be emulous of Fame."

in a few cases, the virtual submersion of the older seventeenth-century political tradition by either, or parts of both, of two newer systems of political thought imported directly from Walpolean England. This process of supplementation and submission was rendered especially easy because of the close similarity among the older and newer traditions of basic assumptions about human nature, the corrosive effects of unbridled power, the functions of governments and constitutions, and the preferred qualities for rulers.

The first of these traditions, which Bailyn has labeled "mainstream thought," was developed by administrative supporters in the half century after the Glorious Revolution and especially during Walpole's ministry. Within the House of Commons itself, this tradition was fostered by and epitomized by the behavior of Arthur Onslow, who was speaker continuously from 1727 to 1761. He enjoyed a great reputation in both Britain and the colonies and served as a model for speakers of the colonial lower houses. The nuances of this tradition cannot be described here, but its central imperative was the desirability of institutional cooperation among all branches of government.[67] Governors and administrative supporters in all the colonies cultivated this ideal in every sort of political situation. But the ideal could only become the dominant political tradition—among legislators as well as among the administration—in colonies where there was no threat from the prerogative, either through the direct challenges of governors intent upon exercising the full range of their assigned powers, or through the corruption or manipulation of the legislature by the use of patronage.

Among the mainland colonies, at least, such a situation existed only in Virginia. There, Lieutenant Governor William Gooch had practically no patronage at his disposal to raise fears of undue executive influence and had sufficiently strong connections at home to keep the Board of Trade from insisting that he take steps to obtain legislative recognition of his assigned prerogative powers. By cooperating closely with Sir John Randolph and John Robinson, two speakers of the House of Burgesses who were obviously inspired by and frequently compared to the great Onslow, Gooch managed both to extirpate faction in the colony and to gain such widespread acceptance of the ideal of institutional cooperation as to avoid almost all conflict with the legislature and seriously to under-

---

[67] This tradition has never been fully analyzed, but Kramnick, *Bolingbroke and His Circle*, 111–36, is a good brief introduction.

mine the older conception that politics was a struggle between prerogative and liberty.[68]

The second tradition was, of course, that of the Walpolean opposition,
which has been so fully and penetratingly analyzed by Bailyn, J. G. A.
Pocock, Caroline Robbins, Isaac Kramnick, and others that it requires
little elaboration here.[69] What I would like to call attention to, however,
is the emphasis in this tradition upon the necessity of maintaining a clear
separation of powers and upon the dangers of executive influence in the
House of Commons. To some degree, of course, the theory of balanced
government was integral to every English political tradition from the
middle of the seventeenth to the early part of the nineteenth century,
and colonials had conventionally employed it in political arguments.
Even such a militant antiprerogative politician as Elisha Cooke, Jr., sub-
scribed to it. In 1720 he wrote that "the King's Prerogative when rightly
used, is for the good & benefit of the People, and the Liberties and Properties of the People are for the Support of the Crown, and the King's
Prerogative when not abused."[70]

Significantly, however, most colonial legislators, like Cooke, seem to
have employed the idea of balance primarily as a defense of liberty and
property against prerogative.[71] Confronted as they were with executive
claims for such extensive prerogative powers, they manifested little interest in imposing any restraints upon their own legislative powers. Indeed, as Corinne Comstock Weston has implied in her revealing study,
English Constitutional Theory and the House of Lords, 1556–1832, that
theory seems to have been attractive primarily to groups whose powers

---

[68] For contemporary statements, see the speeches of Randolph, Aug. 24, 1734, Aug. 6,
1736, in H. R. McIlwaine and John Pendleton Kennedy, eds., *Journals of the House of
Burgesses of Virginia, 1727–40* (Richmond, 1910), 175–77, 241–43.

[69] Bailyn, *Ideological Origins,* 22–93; J. G. A. Pocock, "Machiavelli, Harrington, and
English Political Ideologies in the Eighteenth Century," *William and Mary Quarterly,* 3d
ser., 22 (1965): 547–83; Robbins, *Eighteenth-Century Commonwealthman,* esp. 271–319;
Kramnick, *Bolingbroke and His Circle,* esp. 84–110, 137–87, 205–60.

[70] Cooke, *Just and Seasonable Vindication,* 18.

[71] It is probably also true that the balance that interested colonial legislators most was
not the classic English mixture of monarchy, aristocracy, and democracy, which, because
of the absence of any social base for an aristocratic branch of government in the colonies,
was of doubtful applicability, but, as one anonymous South Carolinian phrased it, the
"proper [for the colonies] balance of power between the crown and people" (*South Carolina
Gazette,* [suppl.], May 13, 1756). Among many other expressions of a similar idea from
widely varying sources, see Thomas Foxcraft, *God the Judge, Putting Down One, and*

or prerogatives were under attack and who were operating from a position of practical political weakness. Just as Charles I, seeking to stem the assault of the first Long Parliament, was chiefly responsible for popularizing and thrusting into the center of political consciousness the doctrine of balanced government in England during the seventeenth century,[72] so in the colonies during the eighteenth century, governors and various administrative adherents in places where the executive was unusually weak—men such as Cadwallader Colden and Archibald Kennedy in New York and James Logan and the Reverend William Smith in Pennsylvania—were its earliest and most vociferous exponents and were most deeply committed to it.[73]

Among the colonial political community at large, however, it appears to have received primary emphasis only where the threat of administrative corruption of the legislature was sufficiently great to make the desirability of a strict separation of powers especially obvious. Such a situation seems to have existed in Maryland, where the proprietor always had extensive patronage at his command;[74] in New Hampshire, where after 1750 Governor Benning Wentworth established a powerful patronage machine;[75] in New York, where in the 1740s and 1750s James De Lancey, first as chief justice and then as lieutenant governor, managed to achieve such an invulnerable position in the government that he was able to establish a system very much resembling a "Robinarchical" corruption;[76] and, preeminently, in Massachusetts, where William Shirley, governor from 1741 to 1756, put together a peculiar combination of superb talents for political management, strong connections in Britain, and local patronage sufficient to enable him to secure an effective "influence" over the Massachusetts legislature.[77]

Setting Up Another (Boston, 1727), iii; *The Crisis* ([Boston], 1754); and Lewis Evans, "A Brief Account of Pennsylvania," 1753, 131–34.

[72] Corinne Comstock Weston, *English Constitutional Theory and the House of Lords, 1556–1832* (New York, 1965), esp. 5–6, 26–28, 32–33.

[73] See Savelle, *Seeds of Liberty,* 298–304.

[74] See Donnell M. Owings, *His Lordship's Patronage: Offices of Profit in Colonial Maryland* (Baltimore, 1953).

[75] Jere R. Daniell, "Politics in New Hampshire under Governor Benning Wentworth, 1741–1767," *William and Mary Quarterly,* 3d ser., 23 (1966): 76–105.

[76] Bailyn, *Origins of American Politics,* 107–14.

[77] John M. Murrin, "From Corporate Empire to Revolutionary Republic: The Transformation of the Structure and Concept of Federalism," paper read at the Annual Meeting of the American Historical Association, New York, Dec. 30, 1966.

In such a situation the real danger of "Subversion and Change of the Constitution" derived not from "the Wantonness and Violence of Prerogative," but from "the Power of the People trusted with their Representatives," and the charges of conspiracy, corruption, and influence associated with the Walpolean opposition and the whole system of thought connected with them took on a heightened relevance. Shirley's Massachusetts provided real substance to the charge that there was a *"deep Plot"* among "all the Men *in the P—v—ce of the Massachusetts* that have grown very remarkably Rich and Great, High, and Proud, since the Year 1742," who "by Cunning, and by Power; through Lust of Power, Lust of Fame, Lust of Money," and "love of *Prerogative*"; "through Envy, Pride, Covetousness, and *violent* Ambition" were intent upon "killing . . . our CONSTITUTION," destroying the very "Freedom, the Liberty and Happiness of the People of *New-England*." In such a situation, in which a grasping administration was intent upon corrupting the whole legislature, the legislature could no longer be trusted to safeguard the constitution. That responsibility then fell directly upon the people, who were urged to bind their representatives by positive and inflexible instructions to prevent them from selling their constituents' liberty for pelf or position.[78]

The extraordinary flowering in Shirley's Massachusetts of political literature cast in the intellectual mold of the Walpolean opposition suggests the possibility that before 1763 the ideas of that opposition were fully relevant to and predominant in only those colonial political situations that bore some reasonable resemblance to that of Walpole's England. These were situations in which the administration actually had at its command many of the devices of the informal constitution that Walpole had used to give his administration its effective influence over Parliament and to achieve that "high degree of public harmony" and "peaceful integration of political forces" which, much to the chagrin and worry of the opposition, accounted for the stability and marked the success of his ministry. If this suggestion turns out to be true, if the acceptance and widespread utilization of the political conceptions of the Walpolean opposition before 1763 were concentrated in, or even limited to, those places where the governors had enough practical political power to enable them to dominate the lower houses and where an informal constitution similar to the one that existed in England was most fully devel-

---

[78] A New England Man, *Letter to the Freeholders*, 6; Vincent Centinel, *Massachusetts in Agony: or, Important Hints to the Inhabitants of the Province* (Boston, 1750), 4, 8, 9, 12; *A Letter to the Freeholders and Other Inhabitants of This Province* ([Boston], 1742), 8.

oped, then Bailyn's arguments that the Walpolean opposition tradition became dominant everywhere in the colonies during the decades before the Revolution and that the "swollen claims and shrunken powers" of the executive were among the most important sources of that development may have to be substantially qualified.[79]

I would suggest, in fact, that before the 1760s in most colonies both Walpolean traditions, mainstream and opposition, supplemented rather than supplanted the older tradition of the seventeenth-century opposition to the Stuarts. The older tradition had been so institutionalized in colonial politics and so internalized among colonial politicians that it could never really be displaced until the conditions that had given rise to and nourished it had disappeared, until "the principles of the British constitution" had been fully extended to the colonies and, as James Otis remarked as late as 1762, "all plantation Governors" had resolved to "practice upon those principles, instead (as most of them do) of spending their whole time in extending the prerogative beyond all bounds."[80] In Virginia, even while Randolph was praising Lieutenant Governor Gooch for his mild administration and dilating upon the necessity and virtues of cooperation between legislature and executive, he worried about "those Governors" elsewhere "who make Tyranny their Glory." How close the fears of unlimited prerogative remained to the surface of Virginia politics was dramatically revealed during the early 1750s in the pistole fee controversy, when Gooch's successor, Robert Dinwiddie, tried to levy a fee without the consent of the House of Burgesses.[81] Similarly, in Shirley's Massachusetts the Walpolean opposition fear of the administration's influence, of "an ambitious or designing Governour" who might "be able to *corrupt* or *awe* your Representatives," was often—and probably usually—combined with the older concerns about the "large Strides Prerogative" was "daily making towards absolute and despotick Power,"[82] much in the same way that, earlier in the century, apprehensions of prerogative had frequently been accompanied by complaints that avaricious court-

---

[79] Bailyn, *Origins of American Politics,* 63, 96.

[80] James Otis, *A Vindication of the Conduct of the House of Representatives of the Province of the Massachusetts-Bay* (Boston, 1762), 51.

[81] Speech of Randolph, Aug. 6, 1736, in *Journal of the House of Burgesses of Virginia, 1727–40,* 242. On the pistole fee controversy, see Jack P. Greene, "The Case of the Pistole Fee: The Report of a hearing on the Pistole Fee Controversy before the Privy Council, June 18, 1754," *Virginia Magazine of History and Biography* 46 (1958): 399–422.

[82] See, e.g., A New England Man, *Letter to the Freeholders;* L. Quincius Cincinnatus, *A Letter to the Freeholders and Other Inhabitants of the Massachusetts Bay* (Boston, 1748); *A*

iers were assisting prerogative in its unending efforts to "compleat" its "Conquest . . . over Liberty."[83]

What finally led to the submersion of the older opposition tradition and rendered the Walpolean mainstream tradition wholly irrelevant was the series of restrictive measures taken by crown and Parliament against the colonies after 1763. Even farther removed from the center of politics than the English opposition, the colonists, as Bailyn has so brilliantly and convincingly argued, could only interpret British behavior in opposition terms. Even then, however, it was not the corruption of local legislatures by local executives about which they primarily worried. Nor was it the relevance of the message of the Walpolean opposition to local politics that made it so attractive to them. Rather, it was the corruption of Parliament by the ministry and the extraordinary extent to which that corruption seemed to explain what was being done to the colonies by the metropolitan government. Even after 1763, the submersion of the older opposition tradition by the newer Walpolean one was never total. Because so many of the objectionable measures of the British government between 1763 and 1776 stemmed directly from the crown and were immediate challenges to the customary powers of the colonial lower houses, the old fears of unlimited prerogative persisted. The Declaration of Independence can and must be read as an indictment of not merely a corrupt Parliament under the influence of a wicked king but also of the unjust and arbitrary misuse of the royal prerogative to undermine the liberties of the people and their lower houses.[84]

The degree to which this seventeenth-century conception of politics as a continual struggle between prerogative and liberty was fundamental to the political system of the old British Empire is perhaps best indicated by the fact that the conception continued to exercise a powerful sway over men's minds and to have an important influence in political life in those colonies that did not revolt, as long as the old pattern of political and constitutional relationship persisted. Over sixty years after the American Revolution it was still true, as Lord Durham reported in 1839,

---

Letter to the Freeholders (1742), 9; and *The Crisis*. The quotations are from Americanus, *A Letter to the Freeholders* (1739), 5, 11. This pamphlet is an excellent example of the uneasy and even awkward superimposition of the new opposition fears of influence upon the older opposition apprehensions about prerogative.

[83] Among many examples, see *Samuel Mulfords Speech to the Assembly at New-York* ([New York], 1714), esp. 6–7. The quotation is from *A Letter to the Freeholders* (1742), 4.

[84] See Greene, *Quest for Power*, ix-x, 438–53; and, for a similar argument, Edward Dumbauld, *The Declaration of Independence and What It Means Today* (Norman, Okla., 1959).

that "it may fairly be said . . . that the natural state of government in all these colonies is that of collision between the executive and representative body."[85] That such collisions were the "natural state of government" in the older colonies in the eighteenth century as well was the reason why the tradition of the seventeenth-century opposition to the Stuarts continued down to the early 1760s to be a primary element in colonial political culture and a profound shaping influence upon the behavior of colonial legislators.

This chapter was prepared for presentation at a conference of the International Commission for the History of Representative and Parliamentary Institutions in London, July 19, 1968. It was subsequently presented at The Seminar, Department of History, The Johns Hopkins University, Baltimore, Maryland, November 4, 1969. It has been reprinted as no. H-395 in the Bobbs-Merrill Reprint Series in American History (Indianapolis, 1972) and in Earl Latham, ed., *The Declaration of Independence and the Constitution* (Lexington, Mass., 1976), 33–57, 61–65; and Peter Charles Hoffer, *Early American History*, 18 vols. (New York, 1988), vol. 12, *American Patterns of Life: Selected Articles on the Provincial Period of American History*, 110–33. It is here reprinted with permission from the *American Historical Review*, 75 (1969), 337–67.

[85] As quoted by Sir Alan Burns, "The History of Commonwealth Parliaments," in Sir Alan Burns, ed., *Parliament as an Export* (London, 1966), 20.

—NINE—

Legislative Turnover in Colonial British America, 1696 to 1775: *A Quantitative Analysis*

T HE ONGOING INVESTIGATION of political development in Britain's American colonies has produced many excellent monographs on specific colonies during particular periods of their history, as well as a few hypothetical general essays.[1] From these works two competing lines of argument have emerged concerning the character and direction of political change during the eighteenth century. One group of studies has suggested that the political systems of the several colonies were coming apart; the other, that they were coming together. The absence of comparable data for many colonies in several areas has perhaps discouraged the sort of systematic comparative analysis necessary for the evaluation of these arguments. Because they can be computed for most of the period between 1696 and 1775 for each of Britain's twenty-two American colonies that had functioning legislatures before 1763, legislative turnover rates can serve as one reasonably firm quantitative base from which such an analysis may proceed.[2]

---

[1] See, especially, Bernard Bailyn, *The Origins of American Politics* (New York, 1968), and Jack P. Greene, "The Growth of Political Stability: An Interpretation of Political Development in the Anglo-American Colonies, 1660–1760," in John Parker and Carol Urness, eds., *The American Revolution: A Heritage of Change* (Minneapolis, 1975), 26–52 [chap. 6 above].

[2] These turnover rates have been computed from legislative membership lists compiled from the following sources. Antigua: Colonial Office Papers, 91/1–9, 12, 14, 19–20, 22, 24–25, 27–29, 31, 33–35, 38–39, and CO 155/1–2, Public Record Office, London. Bahamas: *House of Assembly Journal from . . . 1729 to . . . 1786*, 5 vols. (Nassau, Bahamas, 1910–12). Barbados: CO 31/1–3, 5–10, 12–13, 16–18, 20, 22, 24, 26, 29, 32, 36, 39, 41. Ber-

The turnover rates used in this chapter consist of the percentage of re-placements from one legislature to the next, calculated according to the following formula:[3]

---

muda: CO 40/1–3, 5–6, 8–9, 11–12, 15, 18, 20. Connecticut: J. Hammond Trumbull and Charles J. Hoadly, eds., *The Public Records of the Colony of Connecticut . . . [1636–1776]* (Hartford, 1850–90), vols. 3–15. Delaware: Josiah Granville Leach, "Members of the Assembly of the 'Three Lower Counties upon Delaware,'" Genealogical Society of Pennsylvania, *Publications* 5 (1914): 245–56. Georgia: Allen D. Candler, ed., *The Colonial Records of the State of Georgia,* 21 vols. (Atlanta, 1904–16), vols. 13–15. Jamaica: *The Journals of the Assembly of Jamaica . . . 1663–(1826),* 14 vols. (Kingston, Jamaica, 1811–29). Maryland: Edward C. Papenfuse et al., comps., *A Biographical Dictionary of the Maryland Legislature, 1635–1789* 1 (Baltimore, 1979): 30–67. Massachusetts: for 1693–1715, *The Acts and Resolves, Public and Private, of the Province of the Massachusetts Bay . . .* (Boston, 1869–1922), vols. 7–9; for 1715–71, *Journals of the House of Representatives of Massachusetts,* 49 vols. (Boston, 1919–80); and, for 1772–75, *Journal of the Honorable House of Representatives of . . . Massachusetts-Bay* (Boston, 1772–76). Montserrat: CO 155/1–2, 6–7, and CO 177/1–4, 7–10, 12, 15. Nevis: CO 154/5, 155/1–5, and 186/1–3, 5–7. New Hampshire: Nathaniel Bouton et al., eds., *Provincial and State Papers: Documents and Records Relating to the Province and State of New Hampshire* (Concord, N.H., 1867–1943), vols. 3–7. New Jersey: "A List of the Members of Assembly," New Jersey Historical Society, *Proceedings,* 1st ser., 5 (1850–51): 24–33. New York: Patricia U. Bonomi, *A Factious People: Politics and Society in Colonial New York* (New York, 1971), 295–311. North Carolina: John L. Cheney, Jr., ed., *North Carolina Government, 1585–1974: A Narrative and Statistical History,* rev. ed. (Raleigh, N.C., 1975), 25–59. Nova Scotia: the manuscript and contemporaneously printed assembly journals in the Nova Scotia State Papers, D 1–15, and transcripts of records from the Public Record Office, in the Public Archives of Nova Scotia, Halifax. Pennsylvania: Gertrude MacKinney et al., eds., *Pennsylvania Archives,* 8th ser., 8 vols. (Harrisburg, Pa., 1931–35). Rhode Island: John Russell Bartlett, ed., *Records of the Colony of Rhode Island and Providence Plantations, in New England* (Providence, 1856–65), vols. 3–7. St. Kitts: CO 155/1, 4–7, and 241/1–12, 14–15, 18. South Carolina: Walter B. Edgar and Inez Watson, eds., *Biographical Directory of the South Carolina House of Representatives,* 2 vols. (Columbia, S.C., 1974–77). Virginia: H. R. McIlwaine and John Pendleton Kennedy, eds., *Journals of the House of Burgesses of Virginia,* 13 vols. (Richmond, 1905–15). The data for New Jersey from 1722 to 1776 were supplied to me by Dr. Thomas L. Purvis. Modified to make them comparable to the data for other colonies, the Pennsylvania figures are derived from Richard Alan Ryerson, *The Revolution Is Now Begun: The Radical Committees of Philadelphia, 1765–1776* (Philadelphia, 1978), 259. Dr. Margaret Rouse-Jones compiled the legislative lists for Antigua, Barbados, Bermuda, Montserrat, Nevis, and St. Kitts. Dan Thorp and Keith Mason helped to compile and analyze the data for Connecticut, Massachusetts, and Rhode Island.

[3]Though developed independently, this formula is the same as that used in Morris P. Fiorina et al., "Historical Change in House Turnover," in Norman J. Ornstein, ed., *Congress in Change: Evolution and Reform* (New York, 1975), 28.

$$\text{Percentage of replacements} = \frac{(\text{No. of new members}) - (\text{No. of new seats})}{(\text{No. of seats}) - (\text{No. of new seats})}$$

A replacement is any man who was not a member of the immediately previous legislature at the time of its expiration, whether or not he had earlier been a member; a carryover is any man who had been a member, whether or not he had served through the entire period of its existence or had been only recently returned at a by-election following the death, disability, resignation, or expulsion of a member.[4]

Table 9.1 presents the results of these calculations by decade with column 1 indicating the number of elections in each decade, column 2 the mean rate of turnover for those elections, and column 3 the median rate.[5] As this table reveals, there was wide variation among the colonies in both rates. Among the twenty colonies with legislatures that had been in existence for more than two decades in 1775, the mean (for all elections) ranged from 61.5 percent in Rhode Island to 21.6 percent in Delaware, with a median (among the means) of 41.1 percent.

Table 9.2 provides for each colony the deviations from the mean for all elections by decade and represents an effort to illustrate more clearly the relative magnitudes of change in mean turnover from decade to decade. It also gives the percentage of change from the first to the last decade and the percentage of variation from the highest to the lowest decade. Figure 9.1 in turn illustrates the average decennial decrease in mean turnover for all legislatures. Figures 9.2 through 9.23 provide for each colony a histogram which shows actual turnover for each election for which data are available and indicates through the smoothing lines the direction of change over time.[6]

The most impressive fact to emerge from these tables and graphs, a

---

[4] To give a concrete illustration: the rounded percentage of replacements (35%) for the Pennsylvania election of 1729 is obtained by subtracting the number of new seats (4) from both the number of new members (13) and the number of seats (30), and then dividing the results of the former (9) by those of the latter (26).

[5] In the overwhelming number of cases, variations between mean and median rates are insignificant. Both, however, have been included in table 9.1 to call attention to such variations wherever they occur.

[6] The histograms and graphs were drawn with a program known as Top Drawer, developed by SLAC at Stanford University for the specific purpose of drawing plots and graphs. To obtain the smoothing lines, the program employs a nonlinear algorithm which uses a technique of interpolation that supposes that known values are from a histogram of equally spaced bins. This technique is relatively insensitive to fluctuations in individual points.

Table 9.1. Turnover Rates by Decade, 1696–1775

Colony	1696–1705			1706–15			1716–25			1726–35			1736–45		
	1	2	3	1	2	3	1	2	3	1	2	3	1	2	3
Antigua	4	56.2	47.5	9	41.8	43.0	3	45.3	48.0	2	42.0	32.5	1	36.0	36.0
Bahamas										1	67.0	67.0	3	41.3	38.0
Barbados	10	23.9	22.0	10	44.1	27.5	10	25.4	22.0	9	18.3	14.3	10	12.4	18.0
Bermuda	1	67.0	67.0	5	42.0	38.0	2	51.5	46.5	2	51.0	42.5	3	35.7	43.8
Connecticut	20	52.9	53.5	18	53.3	50.5	20	49.0	49.5	20	46.3	46.5	20	43.2	42.2
Delaware										6	29.8	28.0	10	15.0	17.0
Georgia															
Jamaica	7	54.1	51.0	8	45.6	41.5	6	48.5	43.5	5	40.4	44.0	1	46.0	46.0
Maryland	3	56.7	48.0	4	47.2	54.5	4	52.7	46.5	3	39.3	43.8	4	28.5	28.0
Massachusetts	10	65.1	65.0	10	51.2	52.0	12	52.3	56.5	12	42.7	43.5	11	43.4	45.0
Montserrat	3	71.3	63.3	1	25.0	25.0				1	50.0	50.0	1	75.0	75.0
Nevis	7	36.0	39.8	7	38.0	39.8	8	44.1	40.5	5	21.2	20.3	9	34.9	33.3
New Hampshire	6	48.9	38.4	3	50.1	42.8	4	32.9	21.4	8	30.1	30.1	6	39.0	32.5
New Jersey	1	43.0	43.0	4	60.2	57.5	2	81.0	79.5	2	54.5	42.5	5	38.6	41.8
New York	5	46.8	37.0	6	27.8	26.5	1	38.0	38.0	3	26.7	19.0	4	32.5	26.5
North Carolina				4	84.0	82.5	3	63.7	63.0	7	36.0	50.0	6	39.5	46.0
Nova Scotia															
Pennsylvania	2	62.0	62.0	10	45.4	57.8	10	48.0	54.0	10	30.4	30.5	10	16.9	13.4
Rhode Island	10	72.9	73.0	17	76.6	76.3	19	59.1	65.5	12	54.2	54.5	10	60.1	56.5
St. Kitts				4	71.0	67.5	8	44.6	42.5	9	43.4	46.0	9	41.8	42.3
South Carolina	5	58.4	53.0	7	69.1	69.8	5	61.0	58.0	8	46.1	44.0	4	69.7	66.5
Virginia	6	51.0	51.5	2	56.3	69.0	3	39.0	38.0	1	55.0	55.0	2	64.5	59.5

1: Number of elections.   2: Mean.   3: Median.

Table 9.1 (*Cont.*)

Colony	1646–55			1756–65			1766–75			All elections		
	1	2	3	1	2	3	1	2	3	1	2	3
Antigua	1	28.0	28.0	3	22.7	12.0	1	24.0	24.0	28	41.1	36.5
Bahamas	5	43.0	44.0	2	48.5	42.5	5	20.2	17.3	16	37.7	33.5
Barbados	9	7.2	5.4	10	12.9	13.8	9	13.2	13.6	101	22.9	18.1
Bermuda	4	40.2	45.5	4	38.7	37.5	8	40.2	39.5	32	40.7	41.5
Connecticut	20	46.3	46.2	20	48.2	45.0	20	41.9	41.5	172	47.8	46.9
Delaware	10	20.7	21.8	10	25.6	28.2	10	20.4	17.1	46	21.6	21.8
Georgia				4	49.7	53.5	5	47.4	52.0	9	48.4	52.8
Jamaica	6	30.2	27.5	3	40.7	39.3	3	35.7	40.0	56	46.3	44.5
Maryland	4	33.7	38.5	4	37.5	31.5	3	47.3	47.0	33	45.3	45.0
Massachusetts	10	44.3	43.5	10	37.0	35.5	10	33.6	31.0	90	46.7	45.0
Montserrat	1	38.0	38.0	1	0.0	0.0	3	25.3	25.0	14	45.8	49.8
Nevis	7	39.1	36.0	5	26.8	27.0	10	29.2	27.5	68	35.7	33.4
New Hampshire	3	35.3	28.0	3	40.7	38.0	4	30.2	29.5	42	39.3	41.1
New Jersey	4	36.2	29.5	1	29.0	29.0	2	50.0	46.5	21	48.7	46.3
New York	3	22.3	25.8	2	44.5	26.5	2	35.0	22.5	30	34.4	27.5
North Carolina	4	40.5	31.5	5	44.8	44.0	6	40.0	35.5	36	47.0	49.5
Nova Scotia				3	61.3	55.5	1	74.0	74.0	4	64.5	55.5
Pennsylvania	10	19.6	17.5	10	22.3	22.5	10	17.6	15.5	72	29.8	25.5
Rhode Island	10	56.8	55.5	11	55.4	56.0	11	49.8	52.5	104	61.5	62.2
St. Kitts	9	35.2	38.5	9	30.7	29.0	9	43.2	42.3	61	40.7	41.9
South Carolina	7	62.4	68.0	6	43.5	46.0	6	34.7	25.5	49	55.5	54.0
Virginia	2	44.5	40.5	3	41.3	39.0	5	29.4	32.0	29	47.4	47.0

Table 9.2. Deviation from colony means by decade

Colony	1696–1705	1706–15	1716–25	1726–35	1736–45	1746–55	1756–65	1766–75	% Change first to last decade	% Variation highest to lowest
Antigua	15.1	0.7	4.2	0.9	-5.1	-13.1	-18.4	-17.1	-32.3	-33.5
Bahamas	0.8	21.2		29.3	3.6	5.3	10.8	-17.5	-46.8	-46.8
Barbados	26.3	1.3	2.5	-4.6	-10.5	-15.7	-10.0	-9.7	-10.5	-36.9
Bermuda	5.1	5.5	10.8	10.7	-5.0	-0.5	-2.0	-0.5	-36.0	-36.0
Connecticut			1.2	-1.5	-4.6	-1.5	0.4	-5.9	-11.0	-11.4
Delaware				8.2	-6.6	-0.9	4.0	-1.2	-9.4	-14.8
Georgia							1.3	-1.0	-2.3	-2.3
Jamaica	7.8	-0.7	2.2	-5.9	-0.3	-16.1	-5.6	-10.6	-18.4	-23.9
Maryland	11.4	1.9	7.4	-6.0	-16.8	-11.6	-7.8	2.0	-9.4	-28.2
Massachusetts	18.4	4.5	5.6	-3.9	-3.2	-2.4	-9.7	-13.6	-32.0	-31.5
Montserrat	25.5	-20.8		4.2	29.2	-7.8	-45.8	-20.5	-46.0	-75.0
Nevis	0.3	2.3	8.4	-14.5	-0.8	3.4	-8.9	-6.5	-6.8	-29.7
New Hampshire	9.6	10.8	-6.4	-9.2	5.8	2.1	7.5	-3.0	-12.6	20.0
New Jersey	-5.7	11.5	32.9	5.8	-10.1	-12.5	-19.7	1.3	7.0	-52.6
New York	12.4	-6.6	3.6	-7.7	-1.9	-12.1	10.1	0.6	-11.8	-24.5
North Carolina		37.0	-16.7	11.0	-7.5	-6.5	-2.2	-7.0	-44.0	-44.5
Nova Scotia							-3.2	9.5	12.7	12.7
Pennsylvania	32.2	15.6	18.2	0.6	-12.9	-10.2	-7.5	-12.2	-44.4	-45.1
Rhode Island	11.4	15.1	-2.4	-7.3	-1.4	-4.7	-6.1	-11.7	-23.1	-26.8
St. Kitts	30.3	30.3	3.9	2.7	1.1	-5.5	-10.0	2.5	-27.8	-40.3
South Carolina	2.9	13.6	5.5	-9.4	14.2	6.9	-12.0	-20.8	-23.7	-35.0
Virginia	3.6	8.9	-8.4	7.6	17.1	-2.9	-6.1	-18.0	-21.6	-35.1
Decennial aggregate average decrease		2.6	4.2	3.7	1.3	4.5	1.1	0.9		

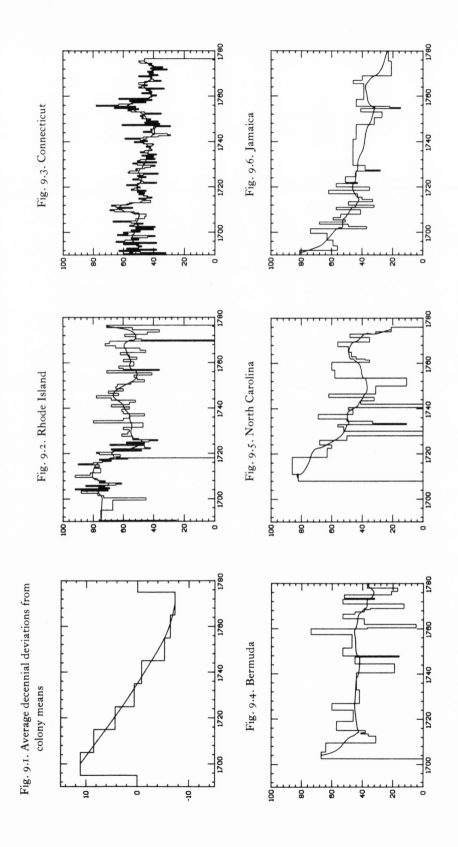

Fig. 9.1. Average decennial deviations from colony means

Fig. 9.2. Rhode Island

Fig. 9.3. Connecticut

Fig. 9.4. Bermuda

Fig. 9.5. North Carolina

Fig. 9.6. Jamaica

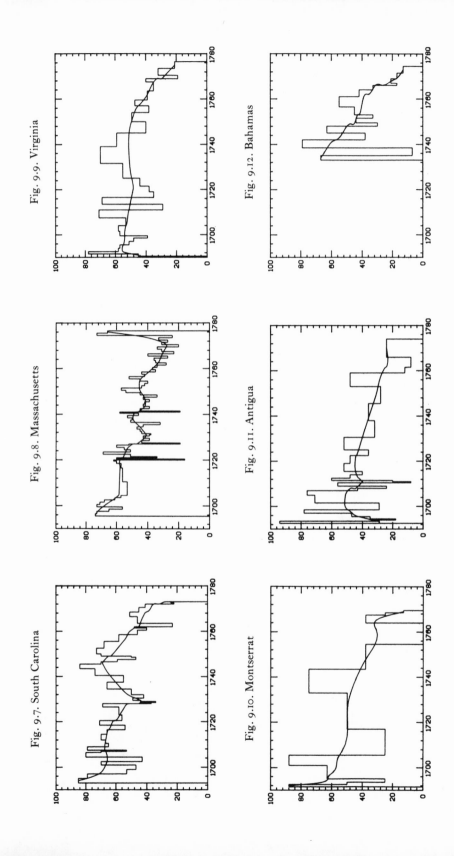

Fig. 9.7. South Carolina

Fig. 9.8. Massachusetts

Fig. 9.9. Virginia

Fig. 9.10. Montserrat

Fig. 9.11. Antigua

Fig. 9.12. Bahamas

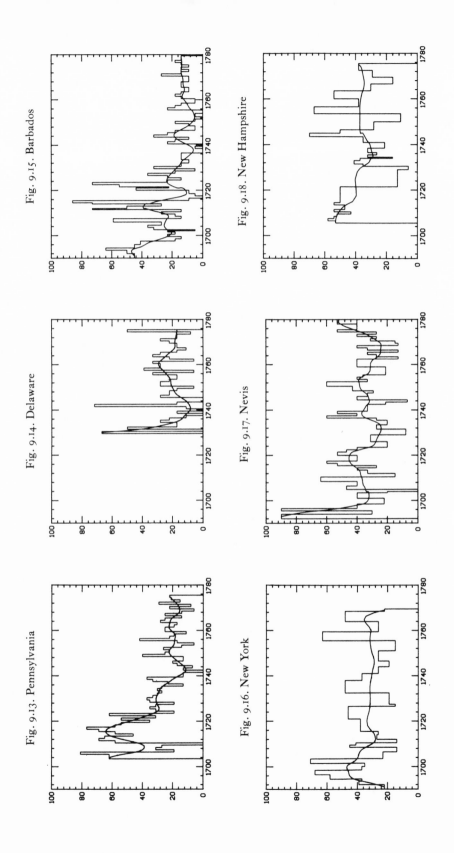

Fig. 9.13. Pennsylvania

Fig. 9.14. Delaware

Fig. 9.15. Barbados

Fig. 9.16. New York

Fig. 9.17. Nevis

Fig. 9.18. New Hampshire

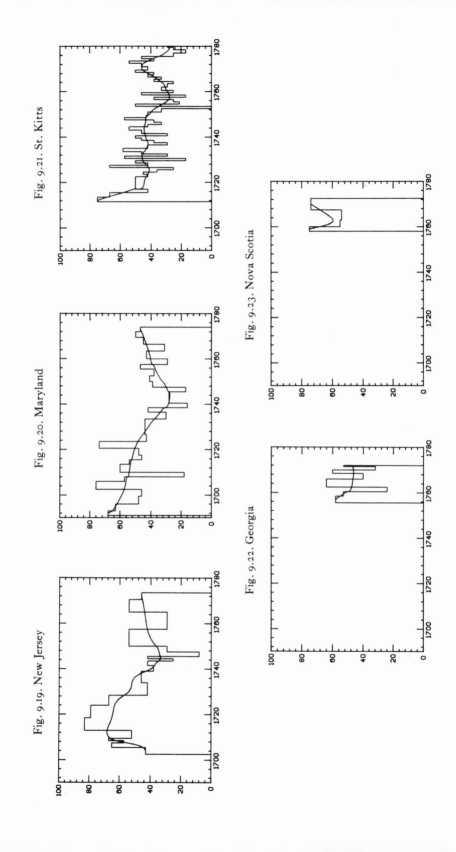

Fig. 9.19. New Jersey

Fig. 9.20. Maryland

Fig. 9.21. St. Kitts

Fig. 9.22. Georgia

Fig. 9.23. Nova Scotia

fact dramatically illustrated by figure 9.1, is the steady long-term decline in turnover for the colonies as a whole during the eight decades covered by this study, with the most pronounced drops occurring in the decades 1716–25, 1726–35, and 1746–55. This aggregate pattern is reflected in the experiences of twenty-one of the twenty-two colonies. Of those twenty-one, the Bahamas, with 46.8 percent, registered the greatest decline, and Nevis, with 6.8 percent, and Georgia—a colony which did not have a legislature until 1755—with 2.3 percent, the smallest. The median decline among these twenty-one colonies was 18.4 percent.[7] Only Nova Scotia, which, like Georgia, did not acquire a legislature until the 1750s and did not therefore have time to establish a clear trend by the late colonial period, did not conform to this pattern.

What, precisely, this widespread decline in turnover tells us about British colonial American political development is a question without a clear answer. In recent years a few scholars have used legislative turnover as an instrument of analysis in specialized studies of the political life of individual colonies.[8] But they have lacked the comparative material necessary to determine whether the specific patterns of turnover they observed were high or low or what these patterns might reveal about larger political trends. The data presented in this note, as well as available evidence for other British and American legislatures, can help to resolve this problem.

Data comparable to those offered here for the colonial legislatures exist for two other bodies: the eighteenth-century British House of Commons and the United States House of Representatives. Table 9.3 shows the percentage of new members coming into the House of Commons for each election from 1715 to 1780.[9] Because the data for 1715 through 1747

---

[7] New Jersey actually shows a rise from the first to the last decade of 7%. But if one takes the second decade as a base for New Jersey, it registered a fall of over 10%.

[8] See, in particular, Robert J. Dinkin, *Voting in Provincial America: A Study of Elections in the Thirteen Colonies, 1689–1776* (Westport, Conn., 1977), 68–69; John M. Murrin, "Review Essay," *History and Theory* 9 (1972): 266; Thomas L. Purvis, *Proprietors, Patronage, and Paper Money: Legislative Politics in New Jersey, 1703–1776* (New Brunswick, N.J., 1986) 102–5; Ryerson, *Revolution Now Begun*, 12–14, 259; Alan Tully, *William Penn's Legacy: Politics and Social Structure in Provincial Pennsylvania, 1726–1755* (Baltimore, 1977), 181–82; and Michael Zuckerman, *Peaceable Kingdoms: New England Towns in the Eighteenth Century* (New York, 1970), 21–212, 278–80.

[9] Table 9.3 was prepared from material in Romney Sedgwick, *The House of Commons, 1715–1754*, 2 vols. (New York, 1970), 1:115, and Sir Lewis Namier and John Brooke, *The House of Commons, 1754–1790*, 2 vols. (New York, 1964), 1:98. Neither Sedgwick nor

Table 9.3. Percentage of new members in the eighteenth-century British House of Commons

Year	%	Year	%
1715	36.0	1754	27.9
1722	37.0	1761	27.6
1727	35.5	1768	31.2
1734	35.5	1768	31.2
1741	37.0	1780	29.7
1747	37.0		

include not only new members chosen at general elections but also all those returned at all by-elections between then and the following general election, they obviously overstate actual replacement rates by some unknown percentage. The astonishingly narrow scope of fluctuation exhibited in subsequent elections and the absence of any reason to suppose that early eighteenth-century elections differed to any marked degree from those held later in the century make it unlikely, however, that this overstatement is greater than 5 to 10 percent. If this surmise is correct, then average turnover in the House of Commons appears to have been remarkably stable from 1715 to 1780, moving up and down within an extremely limited range of 27 to 35 percent.

Turnover for the United States House of Representatives was much less stable and remained at notably higher levels for most of the period between 1790 and 1898. After fluctuating from 37 to 54 percent between 1790 and 1800, turnover dropped slightly over the following decade and then rose steadily until the 1860s, when it began a long-term decline which has continued to the present and has produced quite low levels that have not exceeded 30 percent since 1948.[10] As table 9.4 reveals, turnover exceeded 50 percent in more than two-fifths of all elections until 1900, was under 40 percent in fewer than one-fifth of those elections,

Namier and Brooke define precisely what they mean by "new member": whether that term refers only to those who had never previously sat in the Commons or, as in the case of my colonial data, to all replacements. If the former is the case, then the figures in table 9.3 are probably somewhat low because the number of replacements both in colonial legislatures and in the United States House of Representatives has often exceeded the number of members who had not formerly served. See Fiorina, "Historical Change," 28–31.

[10] These trends are graphically represented in Nelson W. Polsby, "The Institutionalization of the U.S. House of Representatives," *American Political Science Review* 42 (1968): 147.

Table 9.4. Distribution of turnover in elections to United States House of Representatives, 1790–1970

% range	No. of elections	% of elections	First election in range	Last election in range
A. 1790–1899				
Over 70	1	2	1843	1843
60–69	5	9	1817	1875
50–59	18	33	1801	1895
40–49	21	38	1791	1897
30–39	10	18	1793	1899
Total	55	100		
B. 1900–1970				
30–39	8	22	1903	1949
20–29	17	47	1901	1965
10–19	10	28	1927	1971
0–9	1	3	1969	1969
Total	36	100		

and never once fell below 30 percent. By contrast, during the first thirty-six elections of the twentieth century, turnover never rose above 40 percent and was below 30 percent in more than three-fourths of the elections.[11]

At least three general observations can be made on the basis of a comparison of turnover for these three groups of legislatures. First, existing data do not enable us to determine whether the House of Commons, like the colonial legislatures during the early eighteenth century and the House of Representatives during its first century, had a higher turnover at some earlier period and, if so, when that turnover began to decline, at what rate, and according to what pattern. Nevertheless, along with the generally downward trend of the colonial legislatures and, after the middle of the nineteenth century, of the House of Representatives, the relatively low and stable turnover in elections to the House of Commons during the eighteenth century strongly implies that in established governmental frameworks within an Anglo-American setting there has been a marked tendency for electoral turnover to decline over time.

Second—and far more important for the analysis of British-American colonial politics—within the general context established by these three sets of data, turnover rates of from 25 to 35 percent were clearly not

---

[11] Table 9.4 is constructed from the data in Fiorina, "Historical Change," 29–31.

so exceptional as some historians have suggested.[12] Rather, they were remarkably similar to those turnover rates characteristic of the contemporary metropolitan electoral process and of the United States House of Representatives after it had been in existence for more than a century.

Third, and correlatively, although most colonial legislatures experienced considerably more volatility in turnover than did the eighteenth-century House of Commons (though little if any more than the nineteenth-century House of Representatives), all those that had been functioning for any length of time appear by the middle decades of the eighteenth century to have been moving powerfully in the direction of patterns similar to those displayed by their metropolitan counterpart at the same time. As table 9.1 and figures 9.2 through 9.23 make clear, turnover rates had fallen to the level of those of the House of Commons by 1716–25 in Barbados and New Hampshire; 1726–35 in Delaware, Nevis, New York, and Pennsylvania; 1736–45 in Maryland; 1746–55 in Antigua and Jamaica; 1756–65 in New Jersey and St. Kitts; and 1766–75 in the Bahamas, Massachusetts, Montserrat, South Carolina, and Virginia. Of the four older colonies in which turnover never dipped below 35 percent for any decade, Bermuda, Connecticut, and North Carolina all had rates hovering around 40 percent in 1766–75, while Rhode Island was the only colony with a long-established legislature in which turnover never declined well below 50 percent.

The meaning of this drop in colonial turnover and the assimilation to metropolitan norms it represented must at this point remain highly conjectural. Students of the House of Representatives have interpreted declining turnover in that body as an indication of growing institutionalization. As entry to and exit from the House became less easy and frequent, they have posited, membership became more stable and leadership more continuous, professional, and difficult of access. Rising continuity, they have argued, in turn resulted in increasing legislative competence, as both leaders and other members had more experience and, presumably, more commitment to their duties as legislators.[13] There is no reason to suppose that declining turnover did not contribute to produce similar results in the colonial legislatures. Indeed, the turnover

---

[12] See, for instance, Zuckerman, *Peaceable Kingdoms,* 211–12, and Dinkin, *Voting in Provincial America,* 68.

[13] Polsby, "Institutionalization of the U.S. House," 145–46; Fiorina, "Historical Change," 56; H. Douglas Price, "Congress and the Evolution of Legislative 'Professionalism,'" in Ornstein, *Congress in Change,* 2–4.

figures on which this chapter is based undoubtedly understate the extent to which both continuity and competence increased over time. In at least some colonies by the middle decades of the eighteenth century, some substantial proportion of replacements represented not wholly "new" members without previous legislative experience but men returning to the legislature after a break in service. The systematic analysis necessary to calculate the magnitude of this phenomenon has not been done. But Alan Tully has recently shown that roughly three out of every eight replacements in the Pennsylvania assembly between 1726 and 1755 had previously served in that body.[14]

Equally interesting is the question of what declining turnover indicates about shifting relations between constituents and representatives. Until considerably more work has been done to reconstruct the electoral histories of some representative number of the more than 650 legislative constituencies that existed in British colonial America by the 1770s, answers to this question will also have to be hypothetical. In the meantime, we may speculate that declining turnover was a manifestation of at least some of the following developments within the several colonial polities:

1. sharper definitions of and greater agreement upon the social, economic, and cultural attributes necessary for legislators;

2. clearer identification of those individuals who could credibly claim to have those attributes and more widespread acceptance within the electorate of the legitimacy of those claims;

3. a corresponding narrowing of the range of people whose claims to the necessary attributes would be recognized by the electorate to be legitimate;

4. declining electoral competition and a growing tendency for electoral turnover to be voluntary through resignation or retirement of old members or, as seems to have been the case in some New England towns, to operate according to some recognized principle of rotation;

5. weak or limited development of political parties and factions, given the usual association of low levels of organized electoral competition with primitive political infrastructures;

6. declining levels of dissatisfaction on the part of constituents with respect to the legislative performance of their representatives, in view of the comparatively large numbers of adult males who could meet franchise requirements and the reputed independence of voters;

---

[14] Tully, *William Penn's Legacy,* 181–82. Similar calculations by Thomas L. Purvis (letter to the author, Sept. 15, 1980) reveal, however, that this was not the case in New Jersey, where fewer than one in five replacements had previously served in the legislature.

7. a consequent depoliticization of the electorate as measured by decreased participation in routine elections; and

8. declining levels of political conflict involving the mobilization of constituents by leaders of opposing groups within the legislatures.[15]

If, like that of the metropolis, electoral politics throughout British America was indeed becoming more settled, coherent, and predictable in these and other ways during the first three quarters of the eighteenth century, it is also important to identify and consider some broad patterns of differentiation suggested by the data in tables 9.1 and 9.2 and figures 9.1 through 9.23. Of course, the record of each colony was unique, and one of the most useful purposes of the data is the specification of points at which significant departures from established trends occurred in particular colonies. But every one of the twenty colonies with legislatures that had been in existence for at least twenty-five years before 1775 seems to have conformed at least roughly to one or another of three general patterns. The first exhibited a consistently (but not monotonic) downward trend over the whole period. The second displayed a dramatic fall to low or low-medium levels that thereafter remained relatively stable to the end of the colonial period. The third took the form of an inverted bell curve with a long-term decline followed by a rise at the end of the period. The first two of these general patterns exhibited important variants.

The eleven colonies that experienced a consistent decline in turnover (hereafter referred to as Group I) can be broken down into four categories. Table 9.5 distributes the colonies by these and other categories developed below. Initially, all colonies in each of the four categories in Group I had comparatively high turnover of 50 to 84 percent. Rhode Island and Connecticut compose the first category (I-A). They experienced a modest rate of decline with comparatively low levels of fluctuation and wound up in 1766–75 with relatively high turnover, 49.8 percent for Rhode Island and 41.9 percent for Connecticut. Bermuda and North Carolina form a second category (I-B). They also ended up with turnover rates in the upper tercile, 40.2 percent for Bermuda and 40 percent for North Carolina. But they exhibited much sharper rates of decline and considerably higher levels of variation than the two colonies in Group I-A. Jamaica, South Carolina, Massachusetts, and Virginia represent a

---

[15] For evidence that many of these developments did in fact characterize several colonies, see Purvis, "'High-Born, Long Recorded Families': Social Origins of New Jersey Assemblymen, 1703 to 1776," *William and Mary Quarterly,* 3d ser., 37 (1980): 592–615; Tully, *William Penn's Legacy,* 79–102; Richard Waterhouse, *A New World Gentry: The Making*

Table 9.5. Colonies categorized according to turnover rates

Group I

A	B	C	D
Rhode Island	Bermuda	Jamaica	Montserrat
Connecticut	North Carolina	South Carolina	Antigua
		Massachusetts	Bahamas
		Virginia	

Group II		Group III
A	B	
Pennsylvania	New York	New Jersey
Delaware	Nevis	Maryland
Barbados	New Hampshire	St. Kitts

third category (I-C), in which turnover fell at modest rates, and with only medium levels of variation, to still lower levels in 1766–75 of 35.7 percent for Jamaica, 34.7 percent for South Carolina, 33.6 percent for Massachusetts, and 29.4 percent for Virginia. The fourth category in this group (I-D) includes Montserrat, Antigua, and the Bahamas. They experienced much more dramatic declines in turnover, respectively to 25.3 percent, 24 percent, and 20.2 percent, and showed medium to high levels of fluctuation.

Six colonies (hereafter referred to as Group II) followed a second general pattern. In Pennsylvania, Delaware, and Barbados (II-A), turnover ranged from high to medium in the early years and declined very sharply in the 1720s and 1730s—to 16.9 percent in Pennsylvania, 15 percent in Delaware, and 7.2 percent in Barbados—before leveling off at somewhat higher rates and exhibiting comparatively low levels of fluctuation down to the mid-1770s. In these colonies, turnover rose slightly in 1766–75— by 0.7 percent in Pennsylvania, 5.4 percent in Delaware, and 6 percent in Barbados—from the lowest levels reached in earlier decades. But it must be emphasized that all three still had exceptionally low rates. Indeed, they rank with the Bahamas as the four colonies with lowest turnover in that decade. Three other colonies, New York, Nevis, and New Hampshire (II-B), initially had medium turnover ranging from 36 percent (Nevis) to 48.9 percent (New Hampshire). During the early and middle decades of the eighteenth century their rates dropped rapidly to

---

of a Merchant and Planter Class in South Carolina, 1670–1770 (New York, 1989); and Dinkin, *Voting in Provincial America*, 144–80.

low or low-medium levels (21.2 percent in Nevis, 22.3 percent in New York, and 30.1 percent in New Hampshire), and then, fluctuating over a wider range than was characteristic of colonies in category II-A, rose somewhat during the last two decades of the colonial period. But they still remained at medium levels of 35 percent for New York, 30.2 percent for New Hampshire, and 29.2 percent for Nevis.

Three other colonies, New Jersey, Maryland, and St. Kitts, compose Group III. Each of them had high turnover in 1696–1705 that declined to medium levels—around 30 percent—during at least one decade between 1736 and 1765 before climbing thereafter far more steeply than in any of the other colonies to high rates of 43.2 percent for St. Kitts, 47.3 percent for Maryland, and 50 percent for New Jersey.

Why the colonies in Groups II and III began to deviate from the generally downward movement of turnover after 1750 can only be suggested here. Preliminary efforts at visual correlation of turnover patterns with the data set forth in table 9.6 strongly indicate, however, that none of several obvious variables—longevity of the legislature, frequency and regularity of elections, level of party development, regional situation, and type of political system—would seem to be of major importance in distinguishing the colonies in Group I from those in Groups II and III. Thus, of the six colonies with legislatures established before 1640, Virginia, Bermuda, Massachusetts, and Connecticut fall into Group I, Barbados into Group II, and Maryland into Group III. Similarly, among the eight colonies with annual or (in the case of Rhode Island before 1727 and Connecticut) semiannual elections, Connecticut, Massachusetts and Rhode Island are in Group I; Barbados, Delaware, Nevis, and Pennsylvania are in Group II; and St. Kitts is in Group III.

In such relatively primitive or traditional political societies, medium to high levels of factional or party development might be expected to have produced more electoral competition and thereby to have contributed to greater turnover. Of the six colonies that seem to have experienced significant party development during the late colonial period, however, three (Rhode Island, Connecticut, and Massachusetts) are in Group I, two (Pennsylvania and New York) are in Group II, and one (Maryland) is in Group III. With regard to regional situation, four small island colonies, four southern plantation colonies, and three northern mainland colonies belong to Group I; one southern plantation colony, four northern mainland colonies, and one small island colony to Group II; and one small island colony, one southern plantation colony, and one northern mainland colony to Group III. Nine royal colonies and both corporate colonies fall into Group I; four royal colonies and two proprie-

Table 9.6. Selected variables among colonial legislatures

Colony	Date established	Election frequency	Level of party development by 1750s	Regional situation	Type of government by 1750s
Antigua	1644	I	L	Is	R
Bahamas	1729	I	L	Is	R
Barbados	1639	A	L	SP	R
Bermuda	1620	I	L	Is	R
Connecticut	1637	A	M	NM	C
Delaware	1704	A	L	NM	P
Georgia	1755	I	L	SP	R
Jamaica	1664	I	L	SP	R
Maryland	1635	I	H	SP	P
Massachusetts	1634	A	M	NM	R
Montserrat	1654	I	L	Is	R
Nevis	1658	A	L	Is	R
New Hampshire	1680	I	L	NM	R
New Jersey	1668	I	L	NM	R
New York	1683	I	H	NM	R
North Carolina	1665	I	L	SP	R
Nova Scotia	1758	I	L	NM	R
Pennsylvania	1682	A	M	NM	P
Rhode Island	1647	A	H	NM	C
St. Kitts	1642	A	L	Is	R
South Carolina	1671	I	L	SP	R
Virginia	1619	I	L	SP	R

Key: I = Irregular H = High Is = Small Island R = Royal
A = Annual or M = Medium NM = Northern Mainland C = Corporate
Semiannual L = Low SP = Southern Plantation P = Proprietary
Dates for the establishment of the legislatures are taken from Michael Kammen, *Deputyes and Libertyes: The Origins of Representative Government in Colonial America* (New York, 1969), 11–12. For a review of some of the literature on which the classification of the levels of party government is based, see Jack P. Greene, "Changing Interpretations of Early American Politics," in Ray Allen Billington, ed., *the Reinterpretation of Early American History* (San Marino, Calif., 1966), 151–184.

tary colonies into Group II; and two royal colonies and one proprietary colony into Group III. From these observations on the data in table 9.6 one can conclude little more than that corporate and southern plantation colonies tended to exhibit Group I patterns of turnover, and northern mainland and proprietary colonies Group II or Group III patterns.

But data presented in table 9.7 suggest that at least for the mainland colonies and Jamaica, a combination of size of legislature and ratio of representatives to potential voters may well have been a far more sig-

Table 9.7. Size of legislatures and ratio of representatives to adult white males, 1700–1770

Colony	1700 M	1700 R	1730 M	1730 R	1770 M	1770 R	% of change 1700–1730	% of change 1731–70	% of change 1700–1770
Nevis	10	1:22	15	1:17	15	1:13	−22	−23	−40
St. Kitts	12	1:27	24	1:30	24	1:15	11	−50	−44
Bahamas			24	1:7	24	1:16		128	
Antigua	21	1:27	25	1:32	25	1:20	18	−37	−25
Bermuda	36	1:20	36	1:28	36	1:32	40	14	60
Montserrat	8	1:38	8	1:26	8	1:32	−31	23	−15
Jamaica	35	1:40	41	1:37	41	1:62	−7	67	55
Georgia					25	1:102			
Nova Scotia					27	1:103			
Barbados	22	1:146	22	1:164	22	1:147	12	−11	0
Rhode Island	26	1:43	30	1:102	65	1:167	137	63	288
South Carolina	30	1:21	38	1:52	51	1:192	147	269	814
Connecticut	47	1:108	79	1:187	138	1:258	73	37	138
North Carolina	22	1:94	31	1:154	81	1:315	63	104	235
New Hampshire	13	1:74	17	1:124	34	1:363	67	192	390
Massachusetts	80	1:137	91	1:244	125	1:368	78	50	168
Delaware	18	1:25	18	1:96	18	1:374	284	289	1396
Virginia	44	1:191	58	1:289	118	1:439	51	51	129
Maryland	46	1:114	50	1:295	58	1:478	158	62	319
New Jersey	23	1:114	24	1:287	24	1:910	151	217	698
New York	20	1:168	26	1:320	27	1:1065	90	232	533
Pennsylvania	26	1:134	30	1:336	36	1:1301	150	287	870

The ratios (R) in this table have been computed by dividing the number of representatives (M), taken from the sources mentioned in n. 2 above, by the number of adult white males in the population, a figure that was in turn obtained by dividing the total white population by five. For the thirteen colonies that established the United States, I have used the figures in the table of estimated population in U.S. Bureau of the Census, *Historical Statistics of the United States, Colonial Times to 1957* (Washington, D.C., 1960), 76. For the remaining nine colonies, figures come from censuses for the dates closest to 1700, 1730, and 1770, from several sources. The figures for Bermuda, the Bahamas, Antigua in 1700, Montserrat in 1700 and 1730, Nevis in 1700 and 1730, St. Kitts in 1700 and 1730, Jamaica in 1730 and 1770, and Barbados in 1730 and 1770 are taken from Robert V. Wells, *The Population of the British Colonies in America before 1776: A Survey of Census Data* (Princeton, N.J., 1975), 173, 183, 196, 209, 212, 238. Those for Antigua in 1730 and 1770, Montserrat in 1770, Nevis in 1770, and St. Kitts in 1770 are derived from Richard B. Sheridan, *Sugar and Slavery: An Economic History of the British West Indies, 1623–1775* (Baltimore, 1973), 159, 164, 174, 194. Those for Jamaica and Barbados in 1700 come from Frank Wesley Pitman, *The Development of the British West Indies, 1700–1763* (New Haven, 1917), 372–73. The Jamaican figure for 1700 is obtained by dividing the slave population given by Pitman by the black-white ratio for that year given by Sheridan, *Sugar and Slavery,* 217. Those for Nova Scotia are derived from John Bartlet Brebner, *The Neutral Yankees of Nova Scotia: A Marginal Colony during the Revolutionary Years* (New York, 1937), 94–95.

nificant variable than either regional situation or type of government. For what the northern mainland colonies and one of the two southern plantation colonies—colonies that, in conformity to Group II or III patterns, began to show at least a slight upturn in turnover rates sometime after 1750—had in common were legislatures of relatively small and slowly increasing size and a steeply rising ratio of representatives to constituents. The ratios of the six mainland colonies in Groups II and III, with the possible exception of New Hampshire, rose very sharply between 1700 and 1730. With the exception of Delaware and Maryland, which demonstrated a marked slowing in their rates of increase after 1730, they also continued to register high rises after 1730. By 1770 they constituted six out of the seven colonies with the highest ratios of constituents to legislators. Conversely, the ratios for the mainland colonies in Group I increased at a much slower rate, even when, as was the case with Virginia, they remained relatively high over the entire period to 1775. If the distance between voters and representatives was widening in every colony except the four Leeward Islands, it was widening most rapidly and becoming greatest in those mainland colonies which experienced an increase in legislative turnover during the last decades of the colonial period.[16]

This discovery suggests that the legislatures of the mainland colonies in Group I may have been considerably more responsive to the interests and needs of their constituents and far less resistant to sharing power with new political units and new groups of people than the assemblies of those colonies in Groups II and III. Indeed, far from making any effort to concentrate political power in the hands of people in older constituencies by limiting the size of the legislature, the legislatures in Group I colonies routinely extended or, in the case of South Carolina, tried to extend representation to new political divisions as fast as they were created, despite the opposition of metropolitan authorities after 1745. Why the legislatures of the mainland colonies in Groups II and III did not do the same seems to have varied from one colony to the next.[17] For whatever reasons, however, they added very few members to a small base

---

[16] This explanation obviously cannot account for the similar upturn in Barbados and two of six small island colonies, Nevis and St. Kitts, all of which continued to have low and either, as in the case of Barbados, relatively slowly increasing ratios or, as in the case of Nevis and St. Kitts, even declining ones.

[17] A possible explanation may lie in the increasingly heterogeneous populations of many of the colonies in Groups II and III. Certainly, Maryland, Pennsylvania, Delaware, New Jersey, and New York were characterized by considerable and growing ethnic and reli-

despite a six- to ten-fold increase in the adult white male population between 1700 and 1770. The greater and rapidly widening gap between voters and legislators in so many of the colonies in Groups II and III also strongly suggests that their legislatures may not only have been less representative and less in touch with their constituents' needs than legislatures in colonies in Group I but also, as a function of their small size, less able to absorb new people with political ambitions.

By the 1760s and 1770s, the established political systems of the mainland colonies in Groups II and III may thus have been markedly less able than those of colonies in Group I to satisfy either the ambitions of aspiring leaders in normal times or the demands of the citizenry in periods of crisis. One consequence of this development may have been an increase in legislative turnover. In all probability not coincidentally, these same colonies were the ones in which support for the resistance to Britain in 1775–76 was most problematic and independence was accompanied by the highest levels of apprehension, political conflict, and upheaval. For several of the mainland colonies in Group I, on the other hand, the long-term downward trend in legislative turnover through the middle decades of the eighteenth century actually accelerated significantly during the 1760s and 1770s, as voters responded to the deepening crisis with Britain by returning their old representatives to office at an increasingly higher rate. The result was that the established political systems of those colonies, at least as they were represented by the elected branches of the legislature, became more—not less—continuous, experienced, coherent, and stable as the controversy with Britain developed and exhibited less internal disunity and political displacement in 1775–76.

If this line of argument is correct, these diverging patterns of electoral turnover during the last quarter of the eighteenth century would seem to shed some light on the relationship between the internal political sociology of individual colonies and American resistance to Britain. But for comprehending the long-term political development of the colonies it would be a mistake to emphasize this divergence too heavily. The most vivid impression to emerge from inspection of the graphs in this chapter remains the gradual decrease of electoral turnover during the eighteenth

---

gious diversity, and that diversity may have made leaders wary of expanding the political systems of those colonies in ways that might encourage broader and more diverse participation. But the leaders of South Carolina and Jamaica, whose populations were similarly heterogeneous, did not display a similar caution, perhaps because their large black slave populations made it imperative that they incorporate as many white inhabitants into the political system as possible.

century to levels roughly approximating those of the metropolitan House of Commons. This decrease occurred throughout British America and was almost certainly indicative of, first, the emergence within the colonies of more settled, coherent, and stable political systems with more continuous, experienced, and secure leadership and, second, greater political socialization among the electorate as represented by apparently declining levels of voter discontent with leaders. With a growing volatility in electoral turnover, several colonies, notably those in Groups II-B and III, exhibited at least a short-term departure from these trends after 1746. Right through the great crises in metropolitan-colonial relations between 1763 and 1776, however, a majority of colonies experienced a continuation, and some of them even an intensification, of the long-term tendency toward closer conformity with metropolitan norms of electoral turnover.

This chapter was written in 1980 for the journal in which it appeared. It is reprinted with permission from *William and Mary Quarterly*, 3d ser., 38 (1981): 442–63.

TEN

Foundations of Political Power in the Virginia House of Burgesses, 1720–76

ISTORIANS HAVE DEVOTED more attention to the Virginia House of Burgesses than to any other lower house in the continental colonies. They have treated its internal development, its part in royal government, its procedure, and its personnel. They have assessed its role in developing the leaders of the Revolutionary generation and traced its part in the "struggle for liberty." Yet no one has attempted to analyze the structure of power within the Burgesses in the half century before the American Revolution.

The first question to be asked in such an analysis is how power was distributed in the house. Was it spread more or less equally among all members, or was it generally concentrated in the hands of a few? The answer to this question lies in the committees where the work of the house was done and where the real decisions were made. The only way one can hope to determine the pattern of the distribution of power in the eighteenth-century house is by a qualitative analysis of committee posts, that is, by a study which takes into account not only the number of committee posts held by each member but also the varying degrees of importance of the committees themselves.[1]

I have undertaken such an analysis and used my findings as a yardstick to measure the influence or power of individual burgesses. The results indicate that relatively few members played significant roles in the proceedings of the house: of the 630 men who sat in that body between

---

[1] See table of leaders, and for the criteria used, see the Note on Method and Sources, both at the end of this chapter.

1720 and 1776, some 520 can safely be eliminated from consideration, because only 110 members belonged at one time or another to the select few who dominated the proceedings of the house. Of these few, some, of course, were more powerful than others. In fact, the leaders as a whole may be divided into those of first and second rank. In any given session the top level was composed of the speaker, who made appointments to all committees, and from two to perhaps seven or eight others, including, as a rule, the chairmen of the standing committees. Men of somewhat less importance, usually five to ten in number, constituted the second level. In the 1736 session, for example, five men at the top level handled about a third of the committee assignments while seven others at the second level handled another fourth. Altogether these twelve burgesses—one-sixth of the total membership—occupied more than half of the committee seats. Until 1742 it was not uncommon for as many as one-third to one-half of the burgesses to serve on no committees at all; then, for reasons that are not now entirely clear, the size of the standing committees was enlarged and nearly three-fourths of the members were given assignments. Beginning in 1748, the speaker adopted the practice of giving each member at least one post on a standing committee, but this diffusion of assignments does not appear to have affected the structure of power in the house; in 1752 somewhat less than one-fifth of the members handled over half of the business of the house, with the six most powerful men occupying a fourth of the committee posts and eleven others holding another fourth. This pattern did not change significantly for the rest of the colonial period. It was modified slightly after 1766, when Peyton Randolph succeeded John Robinson as speaker. Randolph further increased the size of the standing committees and, more importantly, sprinkled the major assignments among a greater number of members, with the result that the number of men at both levels of power increased slightly.

These men of power provided the house with a certain continuity of leadership from 1720 until well after the Declaration of Independence. Some of them died, some retired, some were defeated at the polls, but never at any time was there a wholesale turnover in leadership. This continuity, plus the lack of evidence of any major dissatisfaction with the leadership or of the existence of any group intent upon challenging it, emphasizes the fact that organized political parties did not exist in colonial Virginia. There was often disagreement on specific issues, but as St. George Tucker later suggested to William Wirt when the latter was preparing his biography of Patrick Henry, the disagreements were "only such as different men, coming from different parts of our extensive

Country might well be expected to entertain." Tucker had never witnessed anything in the House of Burgesses "that bore the appearance of
party spirit."[2]

The discovery of the fact that the House of Burgesses was dominated
by the few rather than the many immediately raises some important
questions about the leaders. What were their professional and economic
interests, their social and family backgrounds and connections, their political experience and education, their national origins and religious
affiliations, and their geographical distribution?

Most of these men were comparatively wealthy. While it is usually
impossible to determine the extent of a man's wealth at any given time,
at least a general idea of the land and slave holdings of most of the 110
may be culled from existing wills, inventories, tithable and tax lists, and
personal records. Information on landholdings is available for all but
ten. Nearly three-fourths of the 100 for whom such information is available had large holdings, that is, holdings in excess of ten thousand acres.
At least seven, and perhaps ten, owned more than forty thousand acres;
and the holdings of forty-six, certainly, and as many as sixty-four, perhaps, exceeded ten thousand acres. A dozen possessed from one to five
thousand acres. Only one man is thought to have owned fewer than five
hundred acres. Records of slaveholdings are more difficult to find, but
reasonably exact information is available for over half of the 110, and
most of the others are known to have possessed some slaves. Quite naturally, the larger landowners—men like John Robinson, Charles and Landon Carter, Benjamin Harrison, and Archibald Cary—also owned the
greater numbers of slaves. Eleven of those for whom records are available owned more than three hundred slaves—a staggering number for
the times. Twenty-five possessed from fifty to three hundred slaves;
twenty-two others had more than ten. Land and slaves were, of course,
not the burgesses' only assets. Livestock, plantation dwellings and out-
buildings, farm equipment, and town houses must be added to their
riches. Some men, like the Nelsons and Richard Adams, had large mercantile establishments; and a few dabbled in mining and manufacturing.

Most of the 110 leaders of the house were, of course, planters. Indeed,
at least ninety-one were directly involved in planting and raising tobacco, although a third of these engaged in planting only as a secondary
occupation. The lawyers—most of whom were planters on the side—
were the next most numerous professional or occupational group.

---

[2] St. George Tucker to William Wirt, Sept. 25, 1815, *William and Mary Quarterly,* 1st
ser., 22 (1914): 252–57.

Thirty-nine of the 110 were practicing lawyers, but they were far more significant than their number would indicate. The services of trained lawyers were invaluable to the house. They had precisely those talents required in framing legislation and carrying on the business of the Burgesses, and throughout the period under consideration, they were conspicuous by their presence at the top level of power. Of the four men who served as speaker, three—John Holloway, Sir John Randolph, and Peyton Randolph—were lawyers. Other occupational groups were less prominent. Of the thirteen men not accounted for above, ten were merchants, two were physicians, and one was a teacher.

Nearly all of the leaders of the house had secondary economic interests. It has already been pointed out that the majority of the lawyers were planters, too. So also were the merchants, one of the physicians, and the teacher. Similarly, most of those who were primarily planters had other interests. Their most important secondary occupation was land speculation. Over two-fifths, and perhaps more, speculated in western lands—a profitable avocation. A dozen participated in some form of mercantile activity. Three were engaged in mining; four were part-time surveyors; four were part-time soldiers; and one was a part-time teacher. Archibald Cary might even be classed a manufacturer, for one of his many secondary interests was an ironworks.

Historians from the time of William Wirt to the present have considered family an important ingredient of political power in eighteenth-century Virginia. Bernard Bailyn has recently put forward the provocative thesis that a new ruling class emerged out of an immigration to Virginia which began in the late 1630s or early 1640s and continued through the 1660s. According to Bailyn, this ruling class supplanted the leaders of the earlier immigrants, secured more or less permanent control first of the county institutions and then of the House of Burgesses, and supplied much of the political leadership of the eighteenth century.[3] My own investigations of the family backgrounds of the Burgesses' leaders indicate that this thesis is only partly valid. Certainly, the generation that came to Virginia between 1635 and 1670 contributed more leaders than any other generation. Forty-nine of the 110 were descendants of that generation. Only seven derived from the pre-1635 immigrants. However, fifty others—nearly half of the leaders who dominated the Burgesses from 1720 to 1776—descended from the several generations that came to

---

[3] Bernard Bailyn, "Politics and Social Structure in Virginia," in James Morton Smith, ed., *Seventeenth-Century America: Essays on Colonial History* (Chapel Hill, N.C., 1959), 98–102.

the colony after 1670.[4] This fact is significant, for it indicates that the earlier immigrants did not have a monopoly on political power or a very tight control over the House of Burgesses. In fact, families still comparatively new on theVirginia scene in 1720 supplied a significant proportion of the Burgesses' leadership during the fifty years preceding the Revolution. Nearly one-fifth of the 110 were drawn from families that arrived in Virginia between 1690 and 1720, and another tenth from those that came after 1720. Some of the newcomers, of course, found marriage into an established family a convenient avenue to social and political power, but many, like Speaker John Holloway, John Clayton, and James Power, acquired wealth, position, and political power without the advantages of connections with older families—an indication that social lines were still fluid and that political power was still attainable for the ambitious and gifted among the newly arrived.

It should not be inferred, however, that family connections were unimportant. Over half of the leaders were connected either through blood or marriage to one of the great eighteenth-century families, and only a conspicuous few reached the top level of power without such a connection. Indeed, certain families—notably the Randolphs, Carters, Beverleys, and Lees—supplied an unusually large proportion of the leaders of the house. Including descendants through both male and female lines, the Randolphs provided eleven, the Carters nine, the Beverleys eight, and the Lees six. The Blands, Burwells, and Corbins each furnished four, and the Blairs, Harrisons, Ludwells, and Nelsons three. These seven families were connected through marriage with other leading burgesses: six had marriage ties with the Carters, five with the Randolphs, and four with the Beverleys. Membership in, or alliance with, one of these families was certainly an important political asset, although, to keep the matter in proper perspective, from one-third to one-half of the leaders were not related to any of these families, and not every member so related attained political power.

In religion and nationality the leaders were remarkably homogeneous. Of the 80 percent ascertainable, all were Anglicans. It seems likely that those about whom information is not available were also Anglican, although it is entirely possible that several adhered to other Protestant faiths. In national origins the vast majority were English, and if there were a few Scots, some Welsh, and even an occasional Irishman, still they all were Britons.

The educational level of the 110 leading burgesses appears to have

---

[4]No information was found on the dates of arrival of the ancestors of four of the 110.

been remarkably high. At least fifty had some education at the college or university level. Some forty attended the College of William and Mary, but others journeyed to England for at least a part of their formal schooling. Richard Henry Lee and Robert Munford studied at Wakefield Academy in Leeds; Charles and Landon Carter at Solomon Low's School, near London; Gabriel Jones at the Blue Coat School in Christ's Hospital, London; and four others at unknown schools in the British Isles. Ten others read law at the Inns of Court—for whatever that may or may not have been worth. A few matriculated at the universities; two at Oxford, another at Cambridge, and one, possibly two, at Edinburgh. Of those who had the benefits neither of an English education nor of study at William and Mary, many, like Francis Lightfoot Lee, were taught at home by a private tutor. Others, like George Washington, got their education in parish schools conducted by local clergymen. No fewer than seventeen of those without university training successfully undertook the study of law; they proceeded either, like Edmund Pendleton and Paul Carrington, under the watchful eye of a practicing attorney or, like Patrick Henry, on their own. From the records at hand it is impossible to determine whether the educational attainments of the leaders were higher than those of their fellow burgesses, or just how much higher their educational level was than the general level in Virginia. In all likelihood, however, they were at least as well educated as any men in the colony.

The leaders' formal education was supplemented by practical experience at the county and parish levels. In fact, a record of active county and parish service was in the background of almost every burgess. The late Charles S. Sydnor, in his study of eighteenth-century Virginia politics, found that posts on the county courts, the parish vestry, and the county militia were important milestones on the pathway to political power.[5] My own investigation amply supports his findings. Either before or during their service in the house, well over four-fifths of the Burgesses' men of power between 1720 and 1776 served as gentlemen justices of the peace. Over half were vestrymen, and nearly two-fifths were officers of the county militia. A few had also been clerks, king's attorneys, sheriffs, surveyors, and coroners in the counties. Some had served as town officials; no fewer than five had been mayors of Williamsburg. Five others combined burgessing with the colony's attorney generalship. Each of these posts—military, judicial, civil, and ecclesiastical—gave the prospective burgess an opportunity to develop the sort of leadership that

[5] Sydnor, *Gentlemen Freeholders: Political Practices in Washington's Virginia* (Chapel Hill, N.C., 1952), 78–93.

would prove useful in the house, to gain an intimate knowledge of his future constituents, and to learn something of the obligations and responsibilities of political office and political power.

An analysis of the geographical distribution of the leaders shows that no one section had a monopoly on political power within the house. Neither does there appear to have been any attempt by representatives from the older counties in the tidewater to exclude from places of importance those burgesses who came from the newer areas. On the other hand, it appears that leadership and geographical origins were not unrelated, for leaders were rarely drawn from sections settled for less than a generation. During the period under consideration, more leaders came from the tidewater, in particular from the region extending from the south side of the James River northward to the Rappahannock and from the western rim of Chesapeake Bay westward to the fall line, than from any other section; in fact, until 1730 most of the leaders were tidewater men. However, from 1705 on, representatives from the Northern Neck, that area lying between the Rappahannock and Potomac rivers and stretching westward to the mountains, played an increasingly important role in the affairs of the house and by 1730 equaled the tidewater in supplying the house with leaders. In the 1730s the counties around the fall line also began to contribute a significant number of leaders. This development was, after all, a logical one, especially because the social and economic patterns of the tidewater were extended not only to the Northern Neck and the fall line area but also into the piedmont,[6] and because family ties cut across geographical lines. From 1689 to the end of the colonial period, there appears to have been an almost continuous shift of the geographical center of power northward and westward, following the frontier by about a generation. Thus, the house did not draw leaders from the piedmont until the late 1740s, nearly twenty-five years after the first settlement of that region. Similarly, although the occupation of the Shenandoah Valley and mountain area farther west began in the 1740s, none of their representatives rose to positions of authority until the late 1760s.

Why these particular 110 men acquired places of power rather than their colleagues is a question of fundamental importance. As individuals they exhibit most of the "qualifications" I have discussed. They were wealthy, derived part of their income from planting, were often related to the great Virginia families, were Anglicans, were of English (or at least

[6] See Carl Bridenbaugh, *Myths and Realities: Societies of the Colonial South* (Baton Rouge, La., 1952), 2–6.

of British) origin, had attained a high educational level for the time and place, were experienced in local politics, and came from areas settled for at least a generation. These were the tangibles upon which political power was based, although the lack of any one, two, or even three of these qualifications might not necessarily bar a man from a position of power. The more essential elements were wealth, family, and education; but even a generous helping of all three would not guarantee a position among the leaders of the house. Otherwise William Byrd III, Robert Wormeley Carter, Charles Carter, Jr., Richard Bland, Jr., and others would have been assured of such a place. In the long run the capacity to put these elements to effective use—call it political acumen, sagacity, the quality of political leadership—was probably decisive, although it is not susceptible of analysis in a study of this nature. But to secure the support of the electorate and the confidence of his colleagues and to exercise leadership in the Virginia House of Burgesses, 1720–76, a man had to have some measure of the tangible "qualifications," as well as the capacity to use them.

Table 10.1. The 110 leaders of the Virginia House of Burgesses, 1720–76

The 110, selected on the basis of the quantitative analysis described in the Note on Method and Sources below, include any member who performed a significant portion of the Burgesses' committee business at any one session between 1720 and 1776. I have treated several short sessions as single sessions. The three between February 20, 1746, and April 18, 1747, are referred to as *1746–47;* the three between February 14 and November 2, 1754, as *1754;* the three between May 1 and November 8, 1755, as *1755;* the two between March 25 and September 8, 1756, as *1756;* the two between April 14, 1757, and April 12, 1758, as *1757–58;* the two between September 14 and November 11, 1758, as *1758;* the two between February 22 and November 21, 1759, as *1759;* the three between March 4, 1760, and April 1, 1761, as *1760–61;* the three between November 3, 1761, and April 7, 1762, as *1761–62;* the two between October 30, 1764, and June 1, 1765, as *1764–65;* the two between November 6, 1766, and April 11, 1767, as *1766–67;* and the two between November 7, 1769, and June 28, 1770, as *1769–70.*

Name and primary occupation	Service and constituency	Sessions in first rank	Sessions in second rank
Acrill, William (lawyer)	**1736: Charles City**	**1736**	
Adams, Richard (merchant)	**1752-65: New Kent** **1769-76: Henrico**		**1769-70**
Alexander, John (planter)	**1766-75: Stafford**		**1772**
Aylett, William (planter)	**1736-40: Westmoreland**		**1738**
Baker, Richard (lawyer)	**1768-71: Isle of Wight**		**1769-70**
Banister, John (lawyer)	**1766-68, 1769-76:** **Dinwiddie**		**1769-70; 1772;** **1775**
Barradall, Edward (lawyer)	**1738-42: College of** **William and Mary**	**1740; 1742**	**1738**
Beverley, William (planter)	**1734-40: Orange** **1742-49: Essex**	**1744; 1746-47;** **1748-49**	**1736; 1738;** **1740; 1742**

Name and primary occupation	Service and constituency	Sessions in first rank	Sessions in second rank
Blair, Archibald (physician)	1718, 1727-34: Jamestown		May 1718; 1720; 1722; 1730; 1732
	1720-26: James City		1736; 1738
Blair, John, Sr. (merchant)	1734: Jamestown		
	1736-40: Williamsburg		
Blair, John, Jr. (lawyer)	1766-70: College of William and Mary	1766-67; 1769-70	1768; 1769
Bland, Richard (lawyer)	1742-76: Prince George	1746-47; 1748-49; 1752; 1753; 1754; 1755; 1756; 1757-58; 1758; 1759; 1760-61; 1762; 1763; 1764-65; 1766-67; 1768; 1769-70; 1771; 1772; 1773; 1774; 1775	1761-62; 1769
Bolling, Robert (merchant)	1723-34: Prince George	1732	1734
Braxton, Carter (planter)	1761-71, 1775-76: King William	1775	1766-67
Braxton, George, Jr. (planter)	1742-49, 1758-61: King & Queen	1746-47; 1748-49	1742
Burwell, Carter (planter)	1742-55: James City	1754; 1755	1746-47; 1748-49; 1752; 1753
Burwell, Lewis of Kingsmill (planter)	1758-74: James City		1764-65; 1766-67; 1769-70
Burwell, Nathaniel (planter)	1710-12: Jamestown		1720
	1720: Gloucester		
Carrington, Paul (lawyer)	1765-76: Charlotte		1769-70; 1772; 1775
Carter, Charles of	1734-64: King George	1742; 1744;	1736; 1758;

Name and primary occupation	Service and constituency	Sessions in first rank	Sessions in second rank
Cleve (planter)		1746-47; 1748-49; 1752; 1753; 1754; 1755; 1756; 1757-58; 1759; 1760-61	1761-62
Carter, Charles of Corotoman (planter)	1758-76: Lancaster		1769-70
Carter, Landon (planter)	1752-68: Richmond	1752; 1754; 1755; 1756; 1757-58; 1759; 1766-67	1758; 1760-61; 1762; 1764-65
Cary, Archibald (planter)	1748-49: Goochland 1756-76: Chesterfield	1762; 1764-65; 1766-67; 1769-70; 1772; 1775	1757-58; 1758; 1760-61; 1768; 1769; 1773; 1774
Chiswell, John (planter)	1742-55: Hanover 1756-58: Williamsburg		1755
Claiborne, Augustine (lawyer)	1748-53: Surry		1753
Clayton, John (lawyer)	1715: Jamestown 1720-26: James City 1727-34: Williamsburg	1720; 1722; 1728; 1730; 1732; 1734	1715
Conway, Edwin (planter)	1710-18, 1723-55: Lancaster	1736; 1738; 1740; 1742; 1744; 1746-47	1712; 1715; 1730; 1732; 1734; 1752
Corbin, Gawin, Sr. (planter)	1698-1705, 1718-22: Middlesex 1715: King & Queen	1715; May, 1718; 1720	1703; 1704; 1705; Nov., 1718; 1722
Corbin, Gawin, Jr. (planter)	1734-40: King & Queen 1742-47: Middlesex	1736	1738; 1744; 1746-47
Corbin, Richard (planter)	1748-49: Middlesex		1748-49
Dandridge, Bar-	1772-76: New Kent		1775

Name and primary occupation	Service and constituency	Sessions in first rank	Sessions in second rank
tholomew (planter)			
Digges, Dudley (lawyer)	1752-76: York	1775	1754; 1755; 1756; 1757-58; 1769-70; 1772
Digges, William (planter)	1752-71: Warwick		1754; 1755; 1757-58; 1760-61
Eskridge, George (lawyer)	1705-14, 1718-34: Westmoreland	1728; 1730; 1732	1710; 1712; 1713; May 1718; Nov. 1718; 1734
Eyre, Littleton (merchant)	1742-61: Northampton		1752
Eyre, Severn (lawyer)	1766-73: Northampton	1769-70	1766-67; 1772
Fitzhugh, Henry (planter)	1734-42: Stafford	1736; 1738; 1740; 1742	1734
Fitzhugh, William (planter)	1772-76: King George		1772
Fleming, John (lawyer)	1756-67: Cumberland		1764-65; 1766-67
Fry, Joshua (teacher)	1746-54: Albemarle	1753	1748-49; 1752
Gray, Edwin (planter)	1769-76: Southampton		1774
Grymes, John (planter)	1718-22: Middlesex		May 1718; Nov. 1718; 1720
Harmar, John (merchant)	1742-47: Williamsburg		1742
Harrison, Benjamin, Sr. (planter)	1736-45: Charles City	1744	1738; 1740; 1742
Harrison, Benjamin, Jr. (planter)	1748-76: Charles City	1769-70; 1772	1753; 1755; 1757-58; 1759; 1760-61; 1762;

Name and primary occupation	Service and constituency	Sessions in first rank	Sessions in second rank
Harrison, Henry (planter)	1715-30: Surry	May 1718	1764-65; 1766-67; 1768; 1769; 1773; 1774 1722; 1723; 1728; 1730
Harwood, William (planter)	1742-76: Warwick		1774
Hedgman, Peter (planter)	1732-40: Prince William 1742-58: Stafford		1748-49
Henry, Patrick (lawyer)	1765-68: Louisa 1769-76: Hanover	1769-70	1766-67; 1772
Holloway, John (lawyer)	1710-14: King & Queen 1720-22, 1727-34: York 1723-26: Williamsburg	1710; 1712; 1713; 1714; 1720; 1722; 1723; 1726; 1728; 1730; 1732	1711-12
Holt, James (lawyer)	1772-76: Norfolk County		1772
Jefferson, Thomas (lawyer)	1769-76: Albemarle		1775
Johnson, Philip (planter)	1752-58: King & Queen 1761-65: James City		1753; 1755; 1757-58
Johnston, George (lawyer)	1758-65: Fairfax		1759; 1762
Jones, Gabriel (lawyer)	1748-53: Frederick 1756-58, 1769-71: Augusta 1758-61: Hampshire		1757-58; 1769-70
Jones, Joseph (lawyer)	1772-76: King George	1775	1772
Jones, Robert (lawyer)	1748-55: Surry		1748-49; 1752; 1753
Kemp, Matthew (lawyer)	1723-30: Middlesex	1730	1728
Lee, Francis	1758-68: Loudoun		1766-67; 1775

Name and primary occupation	Service and constituency	Sessions in first rank	Sessions in second rank
Lightfoot (planter)	1769-76: Richmond		
Lee, Henry (lawyer)	1758-76: Prince William	1775	1766-67; 1769-70; 1772
Lee, Richard of Lee Hall (planter)	1757-76: Westmoreland		1769; 1769-70; 1774
Lee, Richard Henry (planter)	1758-76: Westmoreland	1762; 1766-67; 1769-70; 1772; 1774	1759; 1760-61; 1761-62; 1764-65; 1769; 1771; 1773
Lee, Thomas (planter)	1726-33: Westmoreland	1732	
Lomax, Lunsford (planter)	1742-55: Caroline		1744; 1746-47; 1752; 1754; 1755
Ludwell, Philip (planter)	1742-49: Jamestown	1748-49	1744; 1746-47
McCarty, Daniel, Sr. (planter)	1705-6, 1715-23: Westmoreland	1715; May 1718; Nov. 1718	1705; 1722; 1723
McCarty, Daniel, Jr. (planter)	1734-44: Westmoreland		1738
Martin, John (merchant)	1730-34, 1738-40: Caroline 1752-56: King William		1734; 1740; 1752; 1753; 1754; 1755
Mason, David (planter)	1758-76: Sussex		1774
Mason, Thomson (lawyer)	1766-71: Stafford 1772-74: Loudoun		1766-67
Mercer, George (planter)	1761-65: Frederick		1762
Mercer, James (lawyer)	1762-76: Hampshire	1775	1766-67; 1769-70
Meriwether, Nicholas (planter)	1705-20: New Kent 1722-34: Hanover	1712	1710; 1714; 1715; 1730; 1732; 1734]

Name and primary occupation	Service and constituency	Sessions in first rank	Sessions in second rank
Munford, Robert (planter)	1765-76: Mecklenburg	1775	
Nelson, Thomas (1716-87) (lawyer)	1745-49: York	1746-47	1748-49
Nelson, Thomas (1738-89) (merchant)	1761-76: York	1775	1769-70; 1772
Nelson, William (merchant)	1742-45: York	1744	1742
Norton, John (merchant)	1749-55: York		1755
Nicholas, Robert Carter (lawyer)	1756-61: York 1766-76: James City	1756; 1757-58; 1760-61; 1769-70; 1772; 1774; 1775	1758; 1759; 1766-67; 1768; 1773
Page, John (lawyer)	1752-68: Gloucester		1754; 1755; 1756; 1757-58
Pendleton, Edmund (lawyer)	1752-76: Caroline	1754; 1755; 1756; 1757-58; 1760-61; 1764-65; 1766-67; 1768; 1769-70; 1772	1752; 1753; 1758; 1759; 1761-62; 1762; 1769; 1773; 1774
Power, James (lawyer)	1742-47: King William 1752-58: New Kent	1754; 1755; 1756	1746-47; 1752
Randolph, Beverley (planter)	1744-49: College of William and Mary		1746-47
Randolph, Isham (planter)	1738-40: Goochland		1740
Randolph, Sir John (lawyer)	1734-36: College of William and Mary	1734; 1736	
Randolph, John, Jr. (lawyer)	1769: Lunenburg 1774-76: College of William and Mary		1775
Randolph, Peter (planter)	1749: Henrico		1748-49

Name and primary occupation	Service and constituency	Sessions in first rank	Sessions in second rank
Randolph, Peyton (lawyer)	1748-49, 1761-75: Williamsburg 1752-61: College of William and Mary	1748-49; 1752; 1753; 1755; 1756; 1757-58; 1758; 1759; 1760-61; 1761-62; 1762; 1764; 1764-65; 1766-67; 1768; 1769; 1769-70; 1771; 1772; 1773; 1774; 1775	
Randolph, Richard (planter)	1727-48: Henrico	1734; 1742; 1746-47	1730; 1732; 1736; 1740; 1744
Randolph, William, Sr. (planter)	1715-26: Henrico	1726	May 1718; 1720; 1723
Randolph, William, Jr. (planter)	1752-61: Henrico	1757-58	1753; 1754; 1756; 1759
Reade, Clement (lawyer)	1748-54, 1758-63: Lunenburg		1752; 1753; 1759
Riddick, Lemuel (planter)	1736-68, 1769-75: Nansemond		1742; 1744; 1748-49; 1752; 1755; 1764-65; 1769-70; 1772
Robinson, Christopher (planter)	1752-58: Middlesex		1753
Robinson, John (planter)	1727-65: King & Queen	1732; 1734; 1736; 1738; 1740; 1742; 1744; 1746-47; 1748-49; 1752; 1753; 1754; 1755; 1756;	

Name and primary occupation	Service and constituency	Sessions in first rank	Sessions in second rank
Ruffin, John (planter)	1754-55: Surry	1757-58; 1758; 1759; 1760-61; 1761-62; 1762; 1763; 1764; 1764-65	1755
Starke, Bolling (lawyer)	1769-72: Dinwiddie		1769; 1769-70
Tabb, Thomas (merchant)	1748-58, 1761-69: Amelia		1766-67
Tayloe, John (planter)	1727-32: Richmond		1730; 1732
Walker, Thomas (physician)	1752-54: Louisa 1756-61: Hampshire 1761-76: Albemarle		1757-58; 1764-65; 1769-70
Waller, Benjamin (lawyer)	1744-61: James City	1746-47; 1748-49; 1752; 1754; 1755; 1756; 1757-58; 1760-61	1744; 1753; 1758; 1759
Waller, William (lawyer)	1742-53, 1756-60: Spotsylvania		1748-49; 1752
Washington, George (planter)	1758-65: Frederick 1766-76: Fairfax		1769-70; 1772
Whiting, Beverley (lawyer)	1738-55: Gloucester	1746-47; 1748-49; 1752; 1753	1744
Whiting, Thomas (planter)	1755-76: Gloucester		1775
Willis, Francis (planter)	1727-40, 1745-49: Gloucester		1732; 1734; 1738
Wood, James (planter)	1766, 1769-76: Frederick		1775
Woodson, John (planter)	1768-76: Goochland		1772; 1774

Name and primary occupation	Service and constituency	Sessions in first rank	Sessions in second rank
Wormeley, Ralph (planter)	1742-64: Middlesex		1748-49
Wythe, George (lawyer)	1754-55: Williamsburg 1758-61: College of William and Mary 1761-68: Elizabeth City	1764-65; 1766-67	1754; 1755; 1759; 1760-61; 1761-62; 1762

NOTE ON METHOD AND SOURCES

In preparing the above chapter and table, I have established seven categories of committees according to their relative importance and the nature of their work and, for lack of a better device, assigned numerical values to each. Five categories apply to committees appointed to handle the regular work of the legislative session. They are, in descending order of importance, standing committees, extraordinary committees, committees of the whole house, major committees, and routine committees. The standing committees and the committees of the whole house were so designated by the Burgesses. By the end of the colonial period there were six standing committees: privileges and elections, propositions and grievances, public claims, courts of justice, trade, and religion. They handled the bulk of house business and for that reason were certainly the most important. Chairmanships of the standing committees were, next to the speakership, the most honored posts in the house. I considered as extraordinary committees all those involved in determining matters of broad policy both in regard to internal affairs in Virginia and to Virginia's relations with the mother country, particularly during the years of crisis after 1763. The remaining committees I divided into two groups, those handling purely routine business and those concerned with matters of somewhat greater importance. The latter group I called major committees; the former, routine committees. In addition, the Burgesses occasionally appointed what might be called extrasessionary committees, that is, committees created to perform legislative or sometimes even executive tasks when the Burgesses was not in session. They included those to correspond with the London agent and those to supervise military expenditures.

To differentiate between the relative importance of these seven categories, I have assigned the following numerical values to the memberships and chairmanships of each: chairman, standing committee—15; member, standing committee—5; member, major extrasessionary committee—8; member, minor extrasessionary committee—6; chairman, extraordinary committee—7; member, extraordinary committee—4; chairman, committee of the whole—3; chairman, major committee—5; member, major committee—3; chairman, routine committee—3; member, routine committee—2.

I have ranked the individual burgesses for each session between 1720 and 1776 by counting up their total number of committee posts in each category, assigning them the stated values for each post, and in turn adding up those values. Obviously, this system is not entirely satisfactory, but it seems to me to reflect more accurately the value of each man's committee work than would a simple quantitative tabulation of the total number of his assignments.

The House of Burgesses has exercised a curiously powerful appeal for historians, perhaps both because it was the first representative assembly in the English colonies and because it played such an important part in the politics of a colony at the forefront of the Revolutionary movement. Two Columbia University dissertations later published in book form, Elmer I. Miller's *The Legislature of the Province of Virginia* (New York, 1907) and Percy Scott Flippin's *The Royal Government in Virginia, 1624-1775* (New York, 1919), provided pioneer studies of the Burgesses' internal development and its role in royal government. Stanley M. Pargellis described its procedure in "The Procedure of the Virginia House of Burgesses," *William and Mary Quarterly*, 2d ser., 7 (1927): 73–86, 143–57; and Ray Orvin Hummel, Jr., in his doctoral dissertation, "The Virginia House of Burgesses, 1689-1750," University of Nebraska, 1934, carried the study of its institutional development considerably beyond Miller. The years since the Second World War have seen the publication of several additional works that deal at least partly with still other aspects of the Burgesses. Most delightful of these perhaps is the late Charles S. Sydnor's study of the practices and patterns of Virginia politics in the late colonial period, *Gentlemen Freeholders: Political Practices in Washington's Virginia* (Chapel Hill, N.C., 1952), which particularly emphasizes the Burgesses' role in developing the leaders of the Revolutionary generation.

Other more general studies have attempted to explore the social forces that shaped colonial Virginia politics. These include Carl Bridenbaugh's *Myths and Realities: Societies of the Colonial South* (Baton Rouge, La., 1952), 1–52, and *Seat of Empire: The Political Role of Eighteenth-Century Williamsburg* (Williamsburg, Va., 1950); Daniel J. Boorstin's *The Americans: The Colonial Experience* (New York, 1958), 99–143; and Bernard Bailyn's "Politics and Social Structure in Virginia," in James Morton Smith, ed., *Seventeenth-Century America: Essays on Colonial History* (Chapel Hill, N.C., 1959), 90–115. Lucille Blanche Griffith, *The Virginia House of Burgesses, 1750-1774* (University, Ala., 1968), has provided an excellent and much needed account of the composition and personnel of the Burgesses in the quarter century before the Revolution, and Thomas Jefferson Wertenbaker has added to his long and distinguished list of writings on colonial Virginia *Give Me Liberty: The Struggle for Self-Government in Virginia* (Philadelphia, 1958), a study of the Burgesses' role in what he calls the struggle for liberty. I treat the same topic for the middle years of the eighteenth century from a considerably different point of view in *The Quest for Power: The Lower Houses of Assembly in the Southern Royal Colonies, 1689-1776* (Chapel Hill, N.C., 1963). David Alan Williams's doctoral dissertation, "Political Alignments in Colonial Virginia, 1698-1750" (Northwestern University, 1959), covers the origins of factions in both the Burgesses and council in the early years of the eighteenth century.

The following materials were most useful in obtaining information about the 110 leaders. Especially valuable were the *Virginia Magazine of History and Biography* and the *William and Mary Quarterly*, both conveniently indexed up to and including the 1930 issues by the *Virginia Historical Index*, ed. Earl G. Swem (Roanoke, 1934–36). Also helpful were some of Virginia's printed official records, particularly the *Executive Journals of the Council of Colonial Virginia, 1680-1754*, ed. Henry R. McIlwaine and Wilmer L. Hall (Richmond, 1925–45), and *The Statutes at Large, 1619-1792*, ed. William W. Hening (Richmond, etc., 1809–23). The *Encyclopedia of Virginia Biography*, ed. Lyon G. Tyler (New York, 1915), yielded much useful information, as did such county and local histories at T. E. Campbell, *Colonial Caroline* (Richmond, 1954), and Ralph T. Whitelaw, *Virginia's Eastern Shore* (Richmond, 1951). The several *Virginia Gazettes* used in conjunction with the *Virginia Gazette Index, 1736-1780*, ed. Lester J. Cappon and Stella F. Duff

(Williamsburg, Va., 1950), were also valuable. Biographies exist for a few of the 110 and were a prime source of information. These include Walter R. Wineman, "Calendar of the Landon Carter Papers in the Sabine Hall Collection and a Biographical Sketch of Colonel Landon Carter," Ph.D. diss., University of Pittsburgh, 1956; Robert K. Brock, *Archibald Cary of Ampthill: Wheelhorse of the Revolution* (Richmond, 1937); Lois Fell Jackson, "Colonel Joshua Fry, Albemarle's Soldier Statesman," Ph.D. diss., University of Virginia, 1945; Robert D. Meade, *Patrick Henry: Patriot in the Making* (Philadelphia, 1957); Dumas Malone, *Jefferson the Virginian* (Boston, 1948); John Carter Matthews, "Richard Henry Lee and the American Revolution," Ph.D. diss., University of Virginia, 1939; Emory G. Evans, "The Nelsons: A Biographical Study of a Virginia Family in the Eighteenth Century," Ph.D. diss., University of Virginia, 1957; David J. Mays, *Edmund Pendleton, 1721–1803* (Cambridge, Mass., 1952); Douglas Southall Freeman, *George Washington* (New York, 1948–52); and William E. Hemphill, "George Wythe, the Colonial Briton," Ph.D. diss., University of Virginia, 1937. Personal papers, both printed and in manuscript, were particularly helpful, including *The Papers of Thomas Jefferson*, ed. Julian P. Boyd (Princeton, N.J., 1950–); *Letters of Richard Henry Lee*, ed. James C. Ballagh (New York, 1911–14); *Writings of George Washington*, ed. J. C. Fitzpatrick (Washington, D.C., 1931–44); Carter Family Papers, Swem Library, College of William and Mary; Paul Carrington and Ludwell-Lee Papers, Virginia Historical Society; Richard Henry Lee and Sabine Hall Collections, University of Virginia Library; Thomas Walker Papers, Library of Congress; and Fairfax Family Papers, Henry E. Huntington Library. In this connection, I should also point out that microfilms of most of these manuscripts as well as a sizable percentage of all manuscript materials relating to eighteenth-century Virginia are included in the excellent research collections of Colonial Williamsburg's Research Department.

Still other sources provided information about particular aspects of the 110. Jackson T. Main, "The One Hundred," *William and Mary Quarterly*, 3d ser., 11 (1954): 354–84, and *The Quit Rents of Virginia*, comp. Annie Laurie Wright Smith (Richmond, 1957), contain valuable material concerning the land and slave holdings of many burgesses. But the bulk of such material must be culled from wills, inventories, and tithable and tax lists among the existing county records preserved on microfilm at the Virginia State Library and Archives. A convenient guide to both wills and inventories in those records is *Virginia Wills and Administrations, 1632–1800*, comp. W. Clayton Torrence (Richmond, 1931). The best sources for information about family backgrounds are the numerous printed genealogies, to which Robert Armistead Stewart, *Index to Printed Virginia Genealogies* (Richmond, 1930) is a satisfactory key. In determining what members attended the College of William and Mary, *A Provisional List of Alumni, Grammar School Students, Members of the Faculty, and Members of the Board of Visitors of the College of William and Mary in Virginia from 1693 to 1888* (Richmond, 1941) is invaluable. Similarly, *Justices of the Peace of Colonial Virginia, 1757–1775*, Virginia State Library, Bulletin, no. 14 (Richmond, 1921), is a handy tool for discovering what burgesses served on the county bench in the late colonial period.

Under the title "Political Leadership in the House of Burgesses, 1720–1775," this chapter was given at a session on "Politics in Eighteenth Century Virginia," at the 29th Annual Meeting of the Southern Historical Association, Nashville, Tennessee, November 6, 1958. It appeared with its current title in the *William and Mary Quarterly*, 3d ser., 16 (1959):485–506, and is reprinted here with permission. It has been previously reprinted as "Group Structure and Career-Line Analysis," in Edward N. Saveth, ed., *American History and the Social Sciences* (New York, 1964), 167–74; as no. H-274 in the Bobbs-Merrill Reprint Series in American History (Indianapolis, 1967); in John Lankford and David Reiners, eds., *Essays on American Social History* (New York, 1970), 39–44; and in T. H. Breen, ed., *Shaping Southern Society: The Colonial Experience* (New York, 1976), 215–31.

ELEVEN

Society, Ideology, and Politics:
An Analysis of the Political Culture of Mid-Eighteenth-Century Virginia

OVER THE PAST TWO CENTURIES, few commentators on the era of the American Revolution have failed to appreciate Virginia's preeminent contribution of political talent to that period, a contribution which has perhaps never been equaled by any other state at any other point in American history. What has been less appreciated and only imperfectly understood, however, is that this extraordinary flowering of talents was not simply an accident of history and that the high quality of Virginia political leadership derived quite as much from a viable political culture as from the individual talents of its practitioners. The brilliant assemblage of gifted politicians associated with Revolutionary Virginia—Patrick Henry and George Washington, George Mason and Thomas Jefferson, James Madison and John Marshall are only the most conspicuous examples—brought much more than their own individual geniuses to the momentous events between 1763 and 1789.

Trained in a functional political system which had been tested and refined by a century and a half of experience and coming out of a tradition of superior political leadership which was of more than two generations' standing, they brought as well an intimate knowledge of day-to-day politics in a society where politics was an old and laudable pursuit. Perhaps of equal importance, they came with a deep commitment to a code of political behavior and a political ideology which was peculiarly well suited to meet the demands of a revolutionary situation. That commitment governed their relationships with one another and with leaders from other places and determined to a remarkable extent the nature of their responses to the successive problems of their generation. To identify the code and the ideology to which they were committed—the rules of the game of politics as it had come to be played in mid-eighteenth-century Virginia—and to elaborate the social circumstances and political conditions that underlay them are necessary first steps toward understanding Virginia's extraordinary contribution to the foundation of the American nation.

The key to any comprehension of the politics of colonial Virginia is that unusual group referred to by contemporaries as the "Virginia gentry." In its largest meaning the term *gentry* referred to a broad and miscellaneous category of people: old families and new, those of great and only modest wealth, mannered gentlefolk and crude social upstarts, the learned and the ignorant. As the dissenter James Reid, an obscure but effective social satirist, said of the gentry of King William County in the 1760s, any person who had "Money, Negroes and Land enough" was automatically considered a gentleman, so that even a person "looked upon as . . . unworthy of a Gentleman's notice because he had no Land and Negroes" could, if he "by some means or other, acquired both," become "a Gentleman all of a sudden." What Reid's remarks underline is that the only common denominator among all of the members of the broad social category of gentry was possession of more than ordinary wealth.[1]

Within that broad category, however, was a much smaller, cohesive, and self-conscious social group, at the core of which were about forty interrelated families who had successfully competed with other immigrants for wealth and power through the middle decades of the seventeenth century and consolidated their position between 1680 and 1730. Initially, their fortunes had been derived from a wide variety of sources—planting, shipping, commerce, land development, public office, the law—but by the early decades of the eighteenth century, plantation agriculture—specifically, tobacco culture—had become the most prestigious economic pursuit. Members of this inner gentry continued to engage in a variety of subsidiary or auxiliary enterprises, and some even spent more of their energies in commerce or at the bar than in managing their

---

[1] James Reid, "The Religion of the Bible and Religion of K[ing] W[illiam] County Compared," [1769], in Richard Beale Davis, ed., *The Colonial Virginia Satirist: Mid-Eighteenth-Century Commentaries on Politics, Religion, and Society* (Philadelphia, 1967), 48.

estates. But almost all of them were heavily involved in planting, and although by the 1740s and 1750s antiquity of family was also becoming of some consequence, possession of large holdings of land and slaves was perhaps the most visible symbol of membership in the group. Because wealth in a rapidly expanding economy was available to most enterprising men and, especially after 1730, to the lawyers who were needed in large numbers to handle an ever-increasing volume of land and business transactions, the inner gentry was continuously replenished from below and without, and the social structure remained open throughout the colonial and Revolutionary periods. There was always room for the ambitious, talented, and successful from among both new immigrants and scions of the older yeomanry, and frequent marriages between families with new wealth and those of the older gentry meant that assimilation was quick and easy.[2]

The gentry dominated virtually every phase of life in the colony. Its members created with the use of slaves and large units of production a disproportionate amount of the colony's wealth, frequently served as entrepreneurs for smaller producers in their immediate areas, and stimulated the growth of the colony by their activities in land development. In politics, they early assumed leadership, filling almost all posts of responsibility at every level of government from the governor's council and the elective House of Burgesses down to the county courts and the parish vestries. In social and intellectual life, they were the unquestioned leaders, defining the preferred social roles and the dominant values, setting the style of life to which all ambitious Virginians aspired, providing, as the young New Jersey tutor Philip Fithian observed in 1773, "the pattern of all behaviour."[3]

Although the gentry was preeminent in Virginia life and was probably,

---

[2] Bernard Bailyn, "Politics and Social Structure in Virginia," in James M. Smith, ed., *Seventeenth-Century America: Essays in Colonial History* (Chapel Hill, N.C., 1959), 90–115; Jack P. Greene, *The Quest for Power: The Lower Houses of Assembly in the Southern Royal Colonies, 1689–1776* (Chapel Hill, N.C., 1963), 22–24, and "Foundations of Political Power in the Virginia House of Burgesses, 1720–1776," *William and Mary Quarterly*, 3d ser., 16 (1959): 485–506 [chap. 10 above]; Robert E. and B. Katherine Brown, *Virginia, 1705–1786: Aristocracy or Democracy?* (East Lansing, Mich., 1964), 7–31; Hugh Jones in Richard L. Morton, ed., *The Present State of Virginia* (Chapel Hill, N.C., 1956), 81.

[3] *Journal and Letters of Philip Vickers Fithian, 1773–1774: A Plantation Tutor of the Old Dominion*, ed. Hunter D. Farish (Williamsburg, Va., 1943), 35; Carl Bridenbaugh, *Myths and Realities: Societies of the Colonial South* (Baton Rouge, La., 1952), 1–53, and *Seat of*

as the English traveler J. F. D. Smyth noted in the 1780s, more numerous than its counterparts in other colonies, it never constituted more than a small percentage of the total population. If the category is defined as the larger plantation owners and their families—a definition which would include all of the larger merchants and the wealthier and more important lawyers—it probably did not comprise much over 2 to 5 percent of the total white inhabitants, with the inner gentry group comprising no more than a fraction, perhaps a fifth, of the whole category. Beneath the gentry was a numerous miscellany of free white people whom contemporaries customarily divided into two ranks—a very large middle rank consisting of the less affluent planters, independent yeoman farmers, and rural artisans and tradesmen, who together with their families seem to have comprised the bulk of the white population in every Virginia county, and an apparently smaller lower rank of landless overseers and agricultural laborers, many of them young or just out of their indentures, who, according to travelers, were seldom miserable and were fewer "in number, in proportion to the rest of the inhabitants, than perhaps [in] any other country in the universe."[4]

If there was little real poverty among white people in colonial Virginia, there were nonetheless great extremes in wealth, and traveler after traveler was impressed, as was Smyth, by the "greater distinction supported between the different classes of life" in Virginia than in most of the other colonies. Just how this distinction affected the inner dynamics of Virginia society, the relations between various social groups, is not an easy matter to determine. Smyth thought that that "spirit of equality, and levelling principle" which pervaded "the greatest part of America" did not "prevail to such an extent in Virginia," and Fithian testified in the early 1770s that the "amazing property" of the gentry so tended to blow "up the owners to an imagination, which is visible in all, but in various degrees according to their respective virtue, that they are ex-

---

Empire: The Political Role of Eighteenth-Century Williamsburg (Williamsburg, Va., 1950); Louis B. Wright, *The First Gentlemen of Virginia: Intellectual Qualities of a Colonial Ruling Class* (San Marino, Calif., 1940); Charles S. Sydnor, *Gentlemen Freeholders: Political Practices in Washington's Virginia* (Chapel Hill, N.C., 1952); Daniel J. Boorstin, *The Americans: The Colonial Experience* (New York, 1958), 99–143; and Greene, "Foundations of Political Power," 485–506.

[4] See especially John Ferdinand D. Smyth, *A Tour in the United States of America*, 2 vols. (London, 1784), 1:65–69; Thomas Anburey, *Travels through the Interior Parts of America*, 2 vols. (Boston and New York, 1923), 2:215–17; Marquis de Chastellux, *Travels in North America in the Years 1780, 1781 and 1782*, ed. Howard C. Rice, Jr., 2 vols. (Chapel Hill, N.C., 1963), 2:437; and Brown and Brown, *Virginia, 1705-1786*, 32–59.

alted as much above other Men in worth & precedency, as blind stupid fortune has made a difference in their property."[5]

To many outsiders Virginia seemed to be patently aristocratic. The Massachusetts lawyer Josiah Quincy, Jr., found that Virginia in 1773 was diffused with an "aristocratical spirit and principle," and the marquis de Chastellux, an officer in the French forces during the War for Independence, was convinced that "the national character, the very spirit of government" in Virginia was and would "always be aristocratic."[6]

Though members of the gentry seem neither to have described nor to have thought of themselves as aristocrats—a word they held in the utmost abhorrence because of its pejorative connotations of rule by a small, legally privileged group for their own private ends—there is no lack of evidence that they consciously asserted their social superiority over and marked themselves off from the rest of society by their fine dress, splendid "equipages," stately houses, "polish'd conversation," genteel bearing, and, increasingly, sumptuous lifestyle. The gentry invariably "rode in Coaches, or Chariots, or on fine horses," and "the very elevated sort" wore finery imported from London, or "Perukes." Virginians of all classes might take pride in their celebrated hospitality to friends and strangers. But only the wealthy could afford the "lavish entertainments, often lasting for days," to which the gentry turned for diversion.[7]

Moreover, frequent references to the lower rank as the "vulgar herd," "common herd," or "ignorant Vulgar" suggest that the gentry shared the traditional disregard for the abilities and worth of the poorer segments of society that was so universal among western European elites before and even after the elevation of "the people" by the French Revolution. Although they might not all have approved his characteristically intemperate choice of language, few of his equals in Virginia or elsewhere would probably have disagreed with the judgment of Colonel Landon Carter of Sabine Hall, one of the leading members of one of the largest and most respected Virginia families, that there was little about the generality of mankind to be admired and that some of them were "but Idiots."[8]

---

[5] Smyth, *Tour* 1:65–69; Fithian, *Journal and Letters*, 211–12. On poverty in Virginia, see Chastellux, *Travels* 2:437.

[6] Mark A. De Wolfe Howe, ed., "Journal of Josiah Quincy," Massachusetts Historical Society, *Proceedings* 49 (1916): 467; Chastellux, *Travels* 2:435–36.

[7] See St. George Tucker to William Wirt, Sept. 25, 1815, *William and Mary Quarterly*, 1st ser., 22 (1914): 252–53; "Observations in Several Voyages and Travels in America," July 1746, ibid., 16 (1907): 158–59. A superb exploratory discussion of the "social style"

Whether this attitude was matched at the other end of society by that envy of the rich that modern social analysts have come to expect from the poor is less easy to establish. The lower sort, obviously, left few records of their aspirations and resentments, but there was at least some suspicion among the gentry that, as Landon Carter phrased it in response to a poetic election attack on him, there was "something in a good Estate, which those who don't enjoy, will ever hate." There were also some poorer sorts like the Reverend Devereux Jarratt, a carpenter's son, who remembered in his old age that as a small boy he had regarded the "*gentle folks*, as beings of a superior order" and "kept off at a humble distance." Still others who, like the growing group of dissenting Baptists after 1760, found the lifestyle of the more crude and dissolute segments of the gentry thoroughly reprehensible, reviled the gentry as "men brought up in ignorance, nourished in pride, encouraged in luxury, taught inhumanity and self conceit, tutored in debauchery, squandering youth either in idleness, or in acquiring knowledge which ought to be forgot, illiterate, untinctured by sentiment, untouched by virtues of humanity."[9]

Most remaining evidence, however, indicates that deference and respect, not envy and resentment or fear and obsequiousness, were the conventional attitudes of the rest of Virginia society toward the gentry. How many people shared the pride in the gentry exhibited by the York County blacksmith—and erstwhile poet—Charles Hansford is not clear. "Who can but love the place that hath brought forth / Such men of virtue, merit, honor, worth?" rhymed Hansford in 1752:

---

of the gentry is in Rhys Isaac, "Evangelical Revolt: The Nature of the Baptists' Challenge to the Traditional Order in Virginia, 1765–1775," ibid., 3d ser., 31 (1974): 348–53. See also Charles Hansford, "My Country's Worth," [1752], *The Poems of Charles Hansford*, ed. James A. Servies and Carl R. Dolmetsch (Chapel Hill, N.C., 1961), 57.

[8] See, for instance, James Maury to John Camm, Dec. 12, 1763, in H. R. McIlwaine and John Pendleton Kennedy, eds., *Journals of the House of Burgesses of Virginia*, 13 vols. (Richmond, 1905–15), *1761–65*, li–liii; James Wood to George Washington, July 7, 1758, in Stanislaus M. Hamilton, ed., *Letters to Washington and Accompanying Papers*, 5 vols. (Boston and New York, 1898–1902), 3:149; Jack P. Greene, ed., *The Diary of Colonel Landon Carter of Sabine Hall, 1752–1778*, 2 vols. (Charlottesville, Va., 1965), Feb. 12, 1774, 2:795; and [John Randolph], *Considerations on the Present State of Virginia* ([Williamsburg, Va.], 1774), 3.

[9] Landon Carter's Reply to Election Poem, Nov. 1, 1768, Sabine Hall Collection, University of Virginia Library, Charlottesville; *The Life of Reverend Devereaux Jarratt* (Baltimore, 1806), 16; Reid, "Religion of the Bible," 57.

The gentry of Virginia, I dare say,
For honor vie with all America.
Had I great Camden's skill, how freely I
Would celebrate our worthy gentry.[10]

Economic inequality does not, however, seem to have resulted in any deep or widespread social or political antagonisms toward the gentry, at least not before the 1760s. A remarkably wide franchise which extended even to tenants who rented the requisite amount of land;[11] a fluid social structure with a vital upper stratum which not only was always eager to receive but also was constantly searching out new talents and new abilities; the mixing of tenants, yeomen, small planters, and gentlemen amongst one another in every section of the colony; and frequent interchanges among people of all social classes at church, court days, horse races, cockfights, militia musters, and elections—all seem both to have precluded the development of a rigidly stratified social system and to have promoted free and easy intercourse among all groups in the society. Moreover, the fact that tobacco was the lifeblood of the entire economy and every segment of society meant that disparity of economic interests among people of various social categories was rare. Richard Bland, perhaps the most impressive political thinker in mideighteenth-century Virginia and also a member of an old gentry family, accurately characterized the situation when he wrote in 1745 that he would "always act to the utmost of my capacity for the good of my electors, whose interest and my own, in great measure, are inseparable."[12]

The traditional portrait of colonial Virginia as dominated by a small body of privileged aristocrats who ruled by overawing and closely controlling the rest of society derives, one suspects, less from the society itself than from the romantic writings of later historians like Edmund Randolph and, especially, William Wirt. Committed to a post-1789 Jeffersonian view of the American Revolution which had borrowed its language and symbolism from the French, rather than the American, Revolution, they felt compelled to show that their revolution had been

---

[10] Hansford, "My Country's Worth," 56–57.

[11] Brown and Brown, *Virginia, 1705–1786*, 136–50.

[12] Bland to Theodorick Bland, Sr., Feb. 20, 1745, *The Bland Papers*, ed. Charles Campbell, 2 vols. (Petersburg, Va., 1840–43), 1:4.

revolutionary, too, that, like the French Revolution, it had unleashed the people by breaking the hold of a privileged aristocracy.[13]

But even while Randolph and Wirt were writing, older Virginians recognized the inaccuracy of their characterization. One of these was Judge St. George Tucker, who had immigrated to Virginia from Bermuda in the early 1770s and had become a leading figure at the bar. He objected vigorously in 1815 to Wirt's "exaggerated" portrait of colonial Virginia society, denying that there was any "such thing as Dependence" of the rest of society upon the gentry "except in the case of overseers" and declaring that he had never found any "expression of *Jealousy* towards the rich" among "what is called the *yeomanry.*" Rather, he observed the "rich . . . never failed to pull off their hats to a poor man whom they met, and generally, appear'd to me to shake hands with every man in a Court-yard, or a Church-yard, and as far as I could judge[,] the planter who own'd half a dozen negroes felt himself perfectly on a level with his rich neighbor that own'd an hundred." If the Virginia gentry were aristocrats, he emphasized, they were certainly *"harmless aristocrats"* in no sense *"embodied"* and without any "Inclination, to do any political Injury."[14]

Tucker's observations accord with the impressions of most contemporary travelers, who, even when, like Chastellux, they were impressed with the aristocratic character of Virginia, never remarked upon either any explicit conflict among the several social categories or the "dependence" of the middle and lower ranks upon the gentry. Chastellux, in fact, found the freedom and independence of the ordinary white, property-owning Virginian one of the most striking features of the society. "A Virginian," he noted, "never resembles a European peasant: he is always a free man, who has a share in the government, and the command of a few Negroes." By thus uniting "in himself the two distinct qualities of citizen and master," the Virginian, Chastellux thought, enjoyed a place in society far above that of the bulk of men throughout the rest of the world and closely resembled those "individuals who formed what were called *the people* in the ancient republics." Unlike their counterparts in the Old World, the vast majority of adult white males in Virginia and, for that matter, all of British colonial America were neither

---

[13] Edmund Randolph, *History of Virginia,* ed. Arthur H. Shaffer (Charlottesville, Va., 1970), 178–83; and, esp., William Wirt, *Sketches of the Life and Character of Patrick Henry* (Philadelphia, 1818), esp. 32–67.

[14] Tucker to Wirt, Sept. 25, 1815, *William and Mary Quarterly,* 1st ser., 22 (1914): 252–53.

burdened with poverty nor deprived of a right to participate in government.[15]

Some of the cement of this relatively harmonious relationship between the gentry and the rest of society was supplied by the related concepts of stewardship and order. Frequent observations by travelers and Virginians alike on the indolence of the lesser gentry and the middle and lower ranks in the colony, with their fondness for society and their addiction to pleasure, suggest that apathy may have been the primary reason why men from those ranks failed to play a more prominent role in political life.[16]

But a factor of enormous importance was the widespread belief among Virginians at all levels of society that government should be reserved for and was the responsibility of enlightened and capable men. "The happiness of mankind," the Reverend David Griffith, Anglican rector of Shelburne Parish, declared in a sermon before the Virginia Convention in 1776, "depends, in a great measure, on the well ordering of society," while order, in turn, depended upon a necessary "subordination in society." However complex the economic and social divisions in colonial Virginia, there were only two orders in politics. All society was divided between the rulers and the ruled, and although the line of separation was neither very sharply nor very rigidly drawn, the habit of equating the rulers with "Gentlemen of Ability and Fortune" had the sanction of a long tradition which stretched back well beyond the original settlement of the colonies to antiquity.[17]

Although the gentry never pretended to have an "exclusive title to common sense, wisdom or integrity" and insisted upon the "right" of all

[15] Chastellux, *Travels* 2:397. See also Johann David Schoepf, *Travels in the Confederation* [1783–84], trans. and ed. Alfred J. Morrison, 2 vols. (Philadelphia, 1911), 1:63–65, for similar observations.

[16] See, for instance, Hugh Jones, *Present State of Virginia*, 84; Andrew Burnaby, *Burnaby's Travels through North America*, ed. Rufus Rockwell Wilson (New York, 1904), 53–55; Thomas Jefferson, *Notes on the State of Virginia*, ed. William Peden (Chapel Hill, N.C., 1955), 164; Chastellux, *Travels* 2:435–36; and Reid, "Religion of the Bible," 45–68.

[17] David Griffith, *Passive Obedience Considered* (Williamsburg, Va., [1776]), 6, 12; William Stith, *The Sinfulness and Pernicious Nature of Gaming* (Williamsburg, Va., 1752), 14–15.

"orders of men" to "assume the character of politicians," men of "High Birth and Fortune," as one anonymous writer, perhaps the Reverend Jonathan Boucher, pointed out in 1774, did have "the solid and splendid advantages of education and accomplishments; extensive influence, and incitement to glory." Because they also had "a greater Stake in the Country" and enjoyed a "larger Property," the Reverend William Stith of the College of William and Mary declared in a sermon before the House of Burgesses in 1752, they were naturally "bound . . . to be more studious of that Country's Good." The conclusion followed almost irresistibly that they were, therefore, the proper persons to entrust with the political leadership of the country.[18]

On the other hand, those in the middle and lower ranks, who, it was assumed, lacked the talent, wisdom, training, time, or interest for politics, were expected, as Lieutenant Governor William Gooch put it in the early 1730s, to live as honest men, mind their own business, fear God, honor the king, make good tobacco, shun those "given to Noise and Violence," and "Submit . . . to every Law." The liberty of the governed depended, in fact, declared the Reverend James Horrocks, also of the college, in 1763, upon "a dutiful Obedience to the Laws of our Country, and those [of] our Superiors, who have the Care of them." The alternative, he suggested, was no less than complete licentiousness, a state in which those handmaidens of the happy state—"Liberty and public Safety"—actually became enemies instead of allies to each other. There was, then, in society no antagonism but, as David Griffith observed, *"a mutual obligation . . . between the governed and their rulers. "* That obligation consisted in a reciprocal promise, a kind of covenant, to which all free white inhabitants were party, by which the rulers—those "virtuous and enlightened citizens" whose numbers were small in every community—were to provide good government, and the governed were to obey them.[19]

Government by the "virtuous and enlightened" was not only the ideal but also, to a remarkable degree, the habit of colonial Virginians. Members of the native gentry occupied almost all important appointive posts. Right up to 1776, the crown regularly chose them for all crown offices

---

[18] Stith, *Sinfulness of Gaming,* 14–15; [John Randolph], *Considerations,* 22–23; Jonathan Boucher, *A Letter from a Virginian* ([New York], 1774), 7–8.

[19] Sir William Gooch, *A Dialogue between Thomas Sweet-Scented, William Orinoco, Planters, . . . and Justice Love-Country* (Williamsburg, Va., 1732), 17; James Horrocks, *Upon the Peace* (Williamsburg, Va., 1763), 8; Griffith, *Passive Obedience,* 13. For instances of

except the governorship and lieutenant governorship as well as for its twelve-man council, which throughout the middle decades of the eighteenth century was for the most part "composed of some very respectable characters." Similarly, governors invariably selected the gentry for justices of the peace, sheriffs, militia officers, and other positions in county government.[20]

Within the counties, the critical areas where the values of the community were enforced, the gentlemen justices of the peace had complete authority to administer the laws and dispense justice. Particular status and responsibility attached to membership in the quorum, that inner circle of justices designated by the governor from among the most esteemed men in the county, whose presence was required in all "Matters of Importance." Charged with the heavy responsibility of doing "equal Right to all Manner of People, Great and Small, High and Low, Rich and Poor, according to Equity, and good Conscience, and the Laws and Usages of . . . Virginia, without Favour, Affection, or Partiality," all magistrates, and especially members of the quorum, said the handbook which described and directed them in the execution of their responsibilities, were supposed to be:

> Men of Substance and Ability of Body and Estate; of the best Reputation, good Governance, and Courage for the Truth; Men fearing God, not seeking the Place for Honour or Conveniency, but endeavouring to preserve the Peace and good Government of their Country, wherein they ought to be resident; Lovers of Justice, judging the People equal[l]y and impartially at all Seasons, using Diligence in hearing and determining Causes, and not neglecting the Public Service for private Emploiment, or Ease; of known Loialty to the King, not respecting Persons, but the Cause; and they ought to be Men of competent Knowledge in the Laws of their Country, to enable them to execute their Office and Authority to the Advancement of Justice, the Benefit of the People, and without Reproach to themselves.

---

questioning the political abilities and wisdom of the middle and lower sorts, see James Wood to George Washington, July 7, 1758 in Hamilton, *Letters to Washington* 3:149; [Randolph], *Considerations*, 22–23; Chastellux, *Travels* 2:435–36; and [Boucher], *Letter from a Virginian*, 7–8.

[20]Greene, *Quest for Power*, and "Foundations of Political Power"; Sydnor, *Gentleman Freeholders;* Tucker to Wirt, Sept. 25, 1815, *William and Mary Quarterly*, 1st ser., 22 (1914): 253.

Moreover, the freeholders regularly exercised their liberty of choice to select gentlemen to represent them in Williamsburg in the elective House of Burgesses, the only institution of government elected by the voters in Virginia and by the 1750s certainly more powerful and perhaps more prestigious even than the royal council.[21]

Because the small size of the council excluded all but a few from a seat on it, the pinnacle of success for most of the politically ambitious among the gentry was a position of leadership in the House of Burgesses. To reach such a position a man had to go through a process of rigorous selection. First, he had to have the approval and the backing of the leading local gentry. Individuals without such approval often sought and occasionally won election, but because of the long and vital tradition of gentry leadership, the sanction of community leaders was usually a decisive advantage. Moreover, the gentry tended to select from among its numbers not the gamesters or the spendthrifts, not those whom the Reverend John Camm, the contentious Anglican rector of Yorkhampton Parish, derisively referred to as "decayed gentry" or James Reid cruelly lampooned as "Assqueers," but the men they most admired; and those they most admired were those who most successfully adhered to the most cherished and deeply held values of the group. The man who was "best esteemed and most applauded," Fithian found, was the one who attended "to his business . . . with the greatest diligence," and it was not only diligence but a whole congeries of related qualities—honesty and generosity, "probity and great Integrity," moderation and humility, courage and impartiality, learning and judgment, "Circumspection & frugality"—that recommended a gentleman to his neighborhood peers.[22]

The broad body of freeholders, the next hurdle on the path to political preferment, seem routinely to have looked for the same qualities. Of course, few candidates, no matter how impressive their other qualities,

---

[21] George Webb, *The Office and Authority of a Justice of the Peace* (Williamsburg, Va., 1736), 200–202.

[22] John Camm, *A Review of the Rector Detected* (Williamsburg, Va., 1764), 7; Reid, "Religion of the Bible," 56–57; Fithian, *Journal and Letters*, 35; [Randolph], *Considerations*, 22–27; [Gooch], *Dialogue*, 14; Landon Carter's essay on refusal of councillors to join the Association, [1775?], Sabine Hall Collection, University of Virginia Library; Landon Carter to George Washington, Feb. 12, 1756, in Hamilton, *Letters to Washington* 1:195; Robert Carter Diary, July 5, 1723, vol. 12, Virginia Historical Society, Richmond; *Virginia Gazette* (Williamsburg), Sept. 29, 1752. For an insight into the influence of the leading men in a county on the nomination of burgesses, see Theodorick Bland, Jr., to John Randolph, Jr., Sept. 20, 1771, Bryan Family Papers, University of Virginia Library.

could expect to secure election if they were personally disagreeable to the voters. Only the most secure candidate did not find it necessary "to lower himself a little" to secure election. "Swilling the planters with bumbo," "Barbecues," and other forms of "treating" paid for by the "friends" of the candidates—for candidates themselves were prohibited by law from engaging openly in such activities—were common practices at elections. "At an election," said one caustic observer, "the merits of a Candidate are always measured by the number of his treats; his constituents assemble, eat upon him, and lend their applause, not to his integrity or sense, but [to] the quantities of his beef and brandy." But character and distinction rather than "Bribery" or a willingness to "cajole, fawn, and wheedle" before the populace seem to have been the characteristics that most frequently recommended men to the electorate.[23]

The freeholders understood, as a popular handbook for justices of the peace put it, both that the House of Burgesses was "one of the main Fundamentals of our Constitution, and the chief Support of the Liberty and Property of the Subject," and that, "considering the great Trust reposed in every Representative of the People in General Assembly," "every Freeholder" should "give his vote for Persons of Knowledge, Integrity, Courage, Probity, Loialty, and Experience, without Regard to Personal Inclination or Prejudice." Enjoined by the election law to choose "Two of the most fit and able Men" among them for their representatives, the freeholders regularly returned the same men whom the leading gentry also found most suitable.[24]

Perhaps the best contemporary analysis of the "Humours of a Virginia Election," of voting behavior and voter preferences, is *The Candidates*, a didactic farce written in 1770 by Robert Munford, himself a burgess for Mecklenburg County. In this play there are five candidates. The freeholders initially seem to be most favorably disposed toward the three who themselves most "love[d] diversion": Sir John Toddy, a likable sot and a vivid example of Camm's "decayed gentry," as well as Strutabout and Smallhopes, a pair of ignorant and ostentatious social upstarts who seek to secure votes by keeping "the liquor . . . running." When all of the votes are tallied, however, the freeholders have chosen the two obviously superior candidates: Worthy, a gentleman of unquestionable distinction,

[23] Sydnor, *Gentleman Freeholders*, 39–59; Reid, "Religion of the Bible," 50–51, 54; Robert Munford, *The Candidates*, ed. Jay B. Hubbell and Douglass Adair (Williamsburg, Va., 1948), 17, 20, 24, 40.

[24] Webb, *Office and Authority*, 17–18; *The Acts of Assembly* (Williamsburg, Va., 1752), 51.

and Wou'dbe, a "man of sense, and . . . larning." Worthy is clearly one of those men celebrated by Charles Hansford,

> whose genius seems design'd
> For legislators and to keep mankind
> Within the bounds of reason and justice.
> This is a province which is very nice
> And difficult, yet of the greatest use;
> For men too often liberty abuse.
> Bounds must be set to mankind, or else they
> From justice and morality will stray.
> 'Tis difficult to make such laws, be sure
> That vice be punish'd, liberty secure.
> But yet Virginia yieldeth some of these
> Whose penetrating judgment searches, sees
> As far as human prudence will extend,
> Good laws to make, and people's morals mend.[25]

Not every county had a Worthy to send to Williamsburg, but all had sober and sensible gentlemen of good parts like Wou'dbe. Of course, *The Candidates* was clearly inspired by instances in which the freeholders had not behaved in the prescribed manner and was intended to recall them to a proper sense of their responsibilities. Most of the time, however, Virginia's real freeholders, like Munford's imaginary ones, seem to have borne out the judgment of the Scottish philosopher David Hume that the "lower sort of people and small proprietors are good judges enough of one not very distant from them" and would, therefore, in local elections "probably chuse the best, or nearly the best representative." By one means or another, lesser men might occasionally win election. But only men of unusual merit and responsibility could expect to continue to enjoy the long-term support of their constituents.[26]

After a man had obtained election, he underwent an even more exacting scrutiny within the House of Burgesses. Of the many called to that

---

[25] Munford, *Candidates*, 20–21, 32; Hansford, "My Country's Worth," 60–61.

[26] David Hume, *Essays* 1:487, as quoted in Douglass Adair, "'That Politics May Be Reduced to a Science': David Hume, James Madison, and the Tenth *Federalist*," *Huntington Library Quarterly* 20 (1956–57): 352. For three divergent views on the nature of Virginia elections, see Sydnor, *Gentlemen Freeholders*, 11–59; Brown and Brown, *Virginia, 1705–1786*, 145–242; and Lucille Blanche Griffith, *Virginia House of Burgesses, 1750–1774* (Northport, Ala., 1963), 53–79.

body, only a few were chosen for leadership. In the Burgesses, as in most large assemblies or societies, a few men, as the German traveler Johann David Schoepf found in the 1780s, led the debate and thought and spoke for the rest. The Burgesses was the theater for political talents, and only those who turned in superb performances could expect to secure a leading role. Men with special qualities or skills that set them off from their fellows had a decided advantage, and it was usually those with thorough legal training, good education, and clear and refined ideas, an impressive command of language, a brilliant oratorical style, a capacity for business, unusual personal charm, or some combination of these characteristics who played the most active and influential roles, who were singled out by their fellows, the demands of the institution, and their own qualities for the pinnacle of Virginia political life.[27]

The very ideal of government by extraordinary men imposed an enormous obligation upon the ruling group in colonial Virginia. Acceptance of the office of burgess—of the designation as one of the "ablest" in the community—meant, for instance, that one accepted the responsibility not only to represent his constituents but also to work, as Munford put it in *The Candidates,* "for wholesome laws" and his "country's cause." To be sure, some men sought office simply to gratify their ambition—which in the eighteenth century generally connoted an insatiable thirst for wealth and power. Like the unnamed object of attack in the anonymous Virginia political tract *A Defense of Injur'd Merit Unmasked,* they were "swayed by avarice, and spurr'd on in" their "ambitious views to obtain a place of profit, whereby to gratify that insatiable passion[,] . . . avarice." Even the most devoted public servants could scarcely be expected to ignore the direct economic and social benefits, in the form of access to public lands, special business or professional advantages, lucrative public offices, or higher social status, that might be the by-products of political office. The point is that those benefits were incidental, and by the mid-eighteenth century were becoming increasingly so. However important such consideration may have been in the gentry's formative period from 1660 to 1730, most of the older gentry families were so well established by 1740 that they could have obtained whatever economic benefits they sought through social and family connections without tak-

---

[27]Shoepf, *Travels* 1:56–57; Greene, "Foundations of Political Power," 485–506. On the importance of oratory, see Randolph, *History of Virginia,* 192, and *Diary of Landon Carter,* May 14, 1755, 1:120. For an extended analysis of the ingredients of political leadership in colonial and Revolutionary Virginia, see Jack P. Greene, "Character, Persona, and Authority: A Study of Alternative Styles of Political Leadership in Revolutionary

ing on what Munford's character Wou'dbe correctly described as the "troublesome and expensive employment" of public office. And it was the older families that set the pattern of behavior for the rest of the gentry. Clearly, one has to look elsewhere for the primary motives that impelled the gentry into politics in the late colonial and Revolutionary periods.[28]

Perhaps the most important element in the gentry's assumption of political leadership was their commitment to the notion built into the concept of stewardship that it was not merely the right but the duty of the social and economic leaders of society to exercise the responsibilities of government. In the best tradition of the English country gentleman, the Virginia gentry labored tirelessly at the routine and tedious business of governing in the county courts, the parish vestries, the House of Burgesses, and various local offices—offices that were "Attended with a certain Expense and trouble without the least prospect of gain"—not primarily to secure the relatively small tangible economic rewards they derived from their efforts but rather to fulfill the deep sense of public responsibility thrust upon them by their position in society. That all good men should concern themselves with the welfare of their country lay at the very center of the value structure of the gentry, and when George Washington expressed his strong "Sense of Obligations to the People" to do everything in his "power for the Hon'r and Welfare of the Country," upon his first election to the House of Burgesses from Frederick County in 1758, he was merely subscribing to a time-honored belief. "*It surely is the duty of every man who has abilities*," observed Wou'dbe in *The Candidates*, "to serve his country, to take up the burden, and bear it with patience."[29]

Nor were the gentry's burdens limited to the chores of government. Upon them fell the task of providing social models and moral leadership for their respective communities. As the magistrates for the counties, the gentry were obligated, Governor Gooch declared, to give the rest of the people "all the Light they" could "into the Intent and Meaning" of the laws, which were "the People[']s Direction in moral Actions." As "Gentlemen and Persons of Distinction," they were expected, William

---

Virginia," in W. Robert Higgins, ed., *The South during the American Revolution: Essays in Honor of John R. Alden* (Durham, N.C., 1976).

[28] Munford, *Candidates*, 24, 43; *The Defence of Injur'd Merit Unmasked* (n.p., 1771), 9.

[29] George Washington to James Wood, [July 1758], *The Writings of George Washington*, ed. John C. Fitzpatrick, 39 vols. (Washington, D.C., 1931–44), 2:251; Munford, *Candidates*, 38; [Mercer], "Dinwiddianae," [1754–57], in Davis, *Colonial Virginia Satirist*, 23.

Stith declared in a sermon against gaming in 1752, "by their Example to lead" the "lower people . . . on to every thing, that is virtuous and honest, and with the utmost Severity of the Law to restrain and punish" vice and dishonesty. Nothing would ever affect "the Generality of the People," he added, if it were "contradicted by the Lives and Conversations . . . of their rich and powerful Neighbors." Landon Carter agreed that it was the obligation of the "polite and more considerable part" of society to set "Patterns and examples" for and give "Prudent advice and assistance to" the rest of the community, and he was convinced that there was nothing more commendable than "to let men see our good works that they may take example by them in their conduct to each other and to the happiness and safety of their Country."[30]

Charles Hansford underlined the importance and spelled out the nature of this obligation in verse in the early 1750s:

> A gentleman is placed so that he
> In his example cannot neuter be:
> He's always doing good or doing harm.
> And should not this a thinking man alarm?
> If he lives ill, the vulgar will him trace;
> They fancy his example theirs will grace.
> Many are fond to imitate a man
> That is above their class; their little span
> Of knowledge they consult not. In the way
> Their betters walk, they think they safely may.
> Thus, both are wrong but may, perhaps, be lost,
> And all God's goodness disappointed, cross'd.
> For, sure, His goodness always should be prais'd
> By those He hath above the vulgar rais'd.
> 'Tis most ungrateful not to bless that hand
> By which we are plac'd above the crowd to stand.
>
> Contrariwise, when gentry do live well,
> Their bright example is a kind of spell
> Which does insensibly attract the crowd
> To follow them in virtue's pleasant road.

---

[30] [Gooch], *Dialogue*, 14–15; Stith, *Sinfulness of Gaming*, 14–15, 24; Landon Carter to Purdie and Dixon, Fall 1769, Carter Family Papers, Swem Library, College of William and Mary, Williamsburg; *Diary of Landon Carter*, Nov. 6, 1771, Oct. 6, 1774, Mar. 15, 1776, Feb. 15, 23, 1777, 2:638, 866–67, 1001–2, 1084.

> In such a way who would not take delight
> To see gentry and commons both unite?
> This would true honor to our gentry bring,
> And happiness to all would flow and spring.
> We find example is of greater force
> Than the most famous clergyman's discourse.
> None will deny the assertion to be true:
> Example always precept will outdo.[31]

How widely diffused and generally accepted these notions were is indicated by the remarks of the Presbyterian divine Samuel Davies, the most influential dissenting minister in Virginia in the 1750s and himself only on the fringes of the colony's establishment, to the Hanover volunteers during the Seven Years' War. Emphasizing the obligation of the gentleman-officers to "enforce Religion and good Morals by your Example and Authority" and to "suppress the Contrary," he argued that "Such a Conduct" would render them "popular among the Wise and Good" and would bring them no other censure than "the senseless Contempt of Fools."[32]

Among the gentry, fathers sought to instill this strong sense of social duty—this powerful commitment to public service—in their sons from a very young age. They took deliberate care to transmit the political values, ideals, and attitudes of the group and to nurture that devotion to the public good that was the mark of all gentlemen of distinction. One of the most important elements in the education of young gentlemen was the constant exposure to the inner workings of governmental institutions and their early involvement in discussions of political and judicial affairs. Their study was purposely oriented toward politics and the law. Because laws, one writer said in the *Virginia Gazette* in 1745, were "the Ties of harmonious Society, and Defence of Life, Liberty, and Property against arbitrary Power, Tyranny, and Oppression," they were obviously worth intensive study. The gentry, wrote one unfriendly observer, "diligently search the Scriptures; but the Scriptures which they search are the Laws of Virginia: for though you may find innumerable families in which there is no Bible, yet you will not find one without a Law-book." "Bring [up] any Subject from Mercer's abridgement [of the laws of Virginia], and

---

[31] Hansford, "My Country's Worth," 63–64.
[32] Samuel Davies, *The Curse of Cowardice* (Woodbridge, N.J., 1759), 21.

the youngest in Company will immediately tell you how far a grin is actionable."[33]

Thus did fathers encourage their sons to prepare themselves for their public responsibilities. Landon Carter urged his son Robert Wormeley to study the laws of the colony so that he might ready himself for the day when he would be "in a Capacity to lend a hand towards their improvement or support." By the time they had reached manhood, sons of the gentry had an intimate knowledge of the Virginia political process and a thorough preparation for the tasks of government and community leadership, and the politically ambitious among them looked forward with eagerness to the time when they could assume their duties. "It is in our Power, if we be not wanting to ourselves," declared William Leigh exuberantly in a student oration at the College of William and Mary in 1771, "to support with Dignity the Cause of Religion, to sustain with Firmness the Rights of Society, and to interpret with Precision the Laws of our Country." Each of his classmates, he remarked, had it in his power to make of himself "an Honor to this Temple of Science, a Blessing to the State, and an Ornament to Humanity."[34]

These were aspirations of the highest order, and they suggest still another motive for gentry participation in politics: the opportunities for diversion and distinction in public life. The give-and-take of politics was the most exciting and challenging activity in the life of rural Virginia, and the gentry enjoyed it thoroughly. Even if they proved unequal to the challenge it presented, politics still offered an escape from the isolated and sometimes enervating life of the large plantations. For the most part gentry families were widely dispersed among the counties, and neighboring with equals was neither easy nor frequent. Even men of a bookish turn, like Landon Carter or Richard Bland, longed for the conversation and company of people with similar interests and aspirations. "In Virginia," Landon Carter complained in his diary in 1762, "a man dyes a month sooner in a fit of any disorders because he can't have one soul to talk to."[35]

---

[33] "Common Sense," *Virginia Gazette*, Oct. 3, 1745; Reid, "Religion of the Bible," 51–52.

[34] Dedication of Landon Carter to Robert Wormeley Carter, 1753, in copy of *A Collection of All the Acts of Assembly, Now in Force, in the Colony of Virginia* (Williamsburg, Va., 1733) in the library of Sabine Hall, Warsaw, Va.; William Leigh, *An Oration in Commemoration of the Founders of William and Mary College* (Williamsburg, Va., 1771), 8; Charles S. Sydnor, *Political Leadership in Eighteenth-Century Virginia* (Oxford, 1951), 3.

[35] *Diary of Landon Carter*, Nov. 23, 1762, 1:242.

Yet it was not so much the possibility for diversion that pulled them into politics as the desire to excel. Their fathers and grandfathers—the men who had between 1640 and 1740 established and consolidated the position of the gentry in Virginia life—had fulfilled themselves by acquiring landed estates, enhancing the family name, and obtaining status and wealth in the community. But their extraordinary success in realizing these ambitions meant that members of the third generation, who were just coming into manhood in the 1720s and 1730s, had to look elsewhere to find a proper outlet for their talents. Whereas the desire of the first and second generations to outdistance their fellows had led them primarily into the pursuit of wealth and status and only incidentally into politics, the third generation found that their desire to excel could best be realized in the public sphere; hence they entered into politics with the same avidity and the same devotion that their ancestors had shown in carving out a place for their families in the New World environment. Increasingly in the decades after 1725, politics became the chief road to individual distinction. The public arena was where men could test their mettle in discussion and debate, employ their talents for the benefit of the community as they had been taught they were supposed to, perhaps even attain real praiseworthiness, that elusive and rare quality that set extraordinary men off from the rest of mankind and obtained for them the respect and admiration of society. Perhaps because the stakes were so high, the gentry learned to play the game very well.

At least in part because of the gentry's devotion to politics and because of the relatively high quality of government it provided through the middle decades of the eighteenth century, the concept of stewardship retained its vitality and meaning in Virginia long after it apparently began to break down elsewhere in the British colonies. In Virginia it was not just an anachronistic tradition, an empty ideal which no longer conformed to reality; it was a fact of social life. The result was a relatively harmonious political relationship between the gentry and the rest of society, the central feature of which was the routine acquiescence of the middle and lower ranks in gentry government. "From the experience of nearly sixty years in public life," the politically powerful Edmund Pendleton, one of the foremost lawyers in Virginia, wrote in 1798, "I have been taught to . . . respect this my native country for the decent, peaceable, and orderly behaviour of its inhabitants; justice has been, and is duly and diligently administered—the laws obeyed—the constituted authorities respected, and we have lived in the happy intercourse of private harmony and good will. At the same time by a free communication between those of more information on political subjects, and the classes who have not otherwise an opportunity of acquiring that knowledge, all were instructed in their *rights* and *duties* as freemen, and taught to respect them."[36]

The strength of this relationship between the gentry and the rest of society is perhaps nowhere better illustrated than in the story told to Chastellux by Benjamin Harrison of Brandon. On Harrison's departure for the First Continental Congress in the early fall of 1774, "a number of respectable but uninformed inhabitants" waited upon him and said: "You assert that there is a fixed intention to invade our rights and privileges; we own we do not see this clearly, but since you assure us that it is so, we believe it. We are about to take a very dangerous step, but we have confidence in you and will do anything you think proper." It was just such an extraordinary confidence of the governed in their governors, repeatedly demonstrated in day-to-day political relationships, at elections, and at points of crisis throughout the era of the American Revolution, that was the distinguishing feature of the Virginia political system. What the Anglican minister Jonathan Boucher said of Virginia's delegates to that first Congress might well have been said, albeit in somewhat more moderate language, of the leadership at large: that "the general opinion of your knowledge, abilities, and virtues" caused the colony to "look upon you as the oracles of our country; your opinions . . . have the effect of laws, on the mind of the people."[37]

This impressive harmony was symptomatic of the general tranquillity of Virginia public life through the middle decades of the eighteenth century. None of the disruptive forces—sectional hostility, religious conflict, factional strife, institutional rivalry between executive and legislature—that disturbed other colonies was present to a sufficient degree in Virginia to overturn established patterns of politics. There was no wide social, economic, or political gulf between the tidewater and the piedmont. The latter was in general simply an extension of the former. Many

---

[36] Pendleton to Citizens of Caroline County, Nov. 1798, *The Letters and Papers of Edmund Pendleton, 1734–1803*, ed. David J. Mays, 2 vols. (Charlottesville, Va., 1967), 2:650.

[37] Chastellux, *Travels* 2:428; [Boucher], *Letter from a Virginian*, 7. Other examples of similar feelings toward the gentry may be found in Hansford, "My Country's Worth," 50–59; and Roger Atkinson to Samuel Pleasants, Oct. 1, 1774, in A. J. Morrison, ed., "Letters of Roger Atkinson, 1769–1776," *Virginia Magazine of History and Biography* 15 (1908): 354–57.

younger sons of old tidewater inhabitants settled in the piedmont, and it always had close ties with the eastern region and almost precisely the same economic, social, and political structure. Only after 1750, when the Appalachian and transmontane regions began to fill up with Ulster Scot and German immigrants spilling south from Pennsylvania, was a heterogeneous element introduced into the colony. Eschewing the plantation system and Negro slavery for the smaller family farm, the new immigrants established a society which was markedly different from that in the older regions. But economic bonds with the East were strong, representation in the House of Burgesses was not seriously disproportionate, and sectional tensions never developed during the colonial and Revolutionary periods.[38]

The same situation prevailed in the colony's religious life. Before the late 1740s Virginians were overwhelmingly Anglican, the Church of England being the established church. Not only was Anglicanism generally moderate in its traditions, "equally distant," said the Reverend William Dawson of the College of William and Mary, "from Superstition on the one Hand, and Enthusiasm on the other," but the Anglican laity in Virginia had long been notorious for its lack of interest in theology and its mildness in religious matters. "As they have little or no Religion," said James Reid, "they have no religious quarrels." Moreover, the Anglican tradition of outward conformity not only encouraged individual dissent in theology but contributed to an easy toleration of religious diversity. As was the case in Britain, "Positive statutes," as Edmund Randolph later wrote, "were still scourges to the preaching and assembling of dissenters," small in number though they were, "but a spirit of mildness was an antidote to the licensed severity of laws."[39]

Long before the Great Awakening and the migrations from Pennsylvania had begun to add perceptibly to the dissenting elements in the colony during the 1740s, liberty of conscience, at least for Protestants, had become a convention of Virginia society, with the result that the great increase in Presbyterians and other dissenters after 1750, though it thor-

---

[38] For a more extended discussion of this point, see Greene, *Quest for Power*, 22–31; Bridenbaugh, *Myths and Realities*, 1–53; and Robert Detweiler, "Politics, Factionalism, and the Geographic Distribution of Standing Committee Assignments in the Virginia House of Burgesses, 1730–1776," *Virginia Magazine of History and Biography* 80 (1972): 267–85.

[39] See esp. Schoepf, *Travels* 1:62–63; *Diary of Landon Carter*, Mar. 10, 1752, 1:81; Randolph, *History of Virginia*, 158; William Dawson to Virginia Clergy, Jan. 15, 1746, *Virginia Gazette*, Jan. 9–16, 1746; Reid, "Religion of the Bible," 54.

oughly alarmed the Anglican clergy and even some of the more devout members of the laity and produced demands from the dissenters for more precise legal guarantees of toleration, initially neither upset most of the Anglican laity nor created serious political discord. With virtually no support among the leading gentry, the Presbyterians, who had in any case adopted an extremely conciliatory posture toward the existing religious establishment, simply did not appear to represent a formidable political challenge. Only after 1765 did religious issues intrude deeply into the public realm, as the more militant Baptists began to make significant inroads in the Virginia countryside. By their visibly different lifestyle, their vigorous condemnations of the Anglican establishment, their appeals to slaves as well as freemen, and their seemingly uncontrolled enthusiasm, they clearly challenged in fundamental ways many traditional social mores; by their belligerent demands for full toleration and separation of church and state, moreover, they thrust religion into the political arena, where it remained an issue of substance for over two decades.[40]

Equally impressive was the absence of significant political tensions. Virginia political leaders managed to maintain a remarkable degree of unanimity both among themselves and with royal administrators. There was some competition between rival speculating groups over western lands after 1745, and temporary cliques occasionally formed around the leading men in the House of Burgesses over specific issues, but there was never any issue of sufficient force to create deep or lasting political divisions. As a result, colonial Virginia was largely free from "party spirit," as St. George Tucker later remarked, and such divisions as there were arose merely from "differences of opinion" which "different men, coming from different parts of" an "extensive Country might well be expected to entertain." Even the rivalry between council and lower house that was so characteristic of politics in some other colonies failed to materialize in Virginia, where the council and the House of Burgesses were bound by close family and social ties.[41]

Nor were there the traditional antagonisms between the Burgesses

---

[40] The standard account of Virginia religious development is George Maclaren Brydon, *Virginia's Mother Church*, 2 vols. (Richmond, 1947–52). For the development of religious "discord" in Virginia, see Brown and Brown, *Virginia, 1705–1786*, 243–70; and, esp., Rhys Isaac, "Religion and Authority: Problems of the Anglican Establishment in Virginia in the Era of the Great Awakening and the Parsons' Cause," *William and Mary Quarterly*, 3d ser., 30 (1973): 3–36, and "Evangelical Revolt," 345–68.

[41] Tucker to Wirt, Sept. 25, 1815, *William and Mary Quarterly*, 1st ser., 22 (1914): 253.

and the royal lieutenant governors. The failure of a vigorous attempt by Lieutenant Governor Alexander Spotswood (1710–22) to lessen the powers of the Virginia council and the enormous amount of discord and animosity it provoked taught him an important lesson about Virginia politics: success and tranquillity depended in large measure upon the governor's reaching an accord with the native gentry. By following this course during his last years, Spotswood finally succeeded in putting a stop to the strife and discord that had characterized the colony's political life for much of its early existence.[42]

This lesson was not lost on either of Spotswood's immediate successors, Hugh Drysdale (1722–26) and Sir William Gooch (1727–49). During his long twenty-two-year tenure, Gooch, in fact, became the principal architect of a system of political stability which remained essentially intact for the rest of the colonial period. Like his contemporary English model, Sir Robert Walpole, Gooch was a pragmatic and judicious politician who emphasized the virtues of conciliation, harmony, and compromise in the public arena. Carefully avoiding transgressing against local interests and cherished customs and traditions, he in effect made himself the prime minister of the local gentry. With the cooperation of three powerful and immensely popular speakers of the House of Burgesses— John Holloway (1720–34), Sir John Randolph (1734–38), and John Robinson (1738–66)—Gooch managed largely through the force of his own scrupulous moral leadership—with almost none of the patronage that had provided the principal cement for Walpole's comparable achievement in Britain—to establish a modus vivendi with the gentry in which the vast majority of legislators routinely supported the administration and thereby, in one of the very few such instances in the whole of the Anglo-American colonial experience, actually exhibited habits of obedience to the crown similar to those displayed by the "average, uncorrupted or little corrupted M.P." in Britain, whose normal posture was one of support for the administration.[43]

"By discountenancing Public Animosities," Gooch also "extirpated all Factions," something that even the great Walpole was unable to do. The result, as Speaker Randolph told the Burgesses in 1734, was a "Happiness, which seems almost peculiar to our selves, of being under none of

[42] Jack P. Greene, "The Opposition to Lieutenant Governor Alexander Spotswood, 1718," *Virginia Magazine of History and Biography* 70 (1962): 35–42.

[43] Paul Lucas, "A Note on the Comparative Study of the Structure of Politics in Mid-Eighteenth-Century Britain and Its American Colonies," *William and Mary Quarterly*, 3d ser., 28 (1971): 305.

the Perturbations which we see every where else arising from the different Views and Designs of Factions and Parties." As an aspiring poet put
it in the *Virginia Gazette* two years later,

> Now Wars and Tumults wholly cease,
> And all the Land enjoys sweet Peace.
> Just Order holds its curbing Reins,
> And wild Licentiousness restrains,
> Vice out of Countenance is fled,
> And Virtue rises in its Stead,
> With Pleasure, Honour'd Sir, we view
> Our Country flourish under You.
> And whilst You with Impartial Hand,
> Distribute Justice through the Land:
> No private Broils shall Feuds create,
> No Civil Wars disturb the State.[44]

In achieving this extraordinarily stable political situation, Gooch was,
of course, aided by a new concern among metropolitan authorities under
Walpole to achieve peace and order in the colonies, no matter what the
cost, and by the fact that, in contrast to the situation in earlier years,
Virginia was no longer tied so closely into the British patronage system.
He was helped as well by a fortunate set of social circumstances within
Virginia, some of which have been referred to earlier and all of which
discouraged sharp or enduring political divisions: a generally favorable
long-term economic situation beginning in the 1730s; a homogeneity of
economic and social interests among the free population, which was increasingly feeling pressures to unite in the face of a rising tide of alien
black African slaves; a high degree of social and religious integration;
and a community of political leaders so large as to make it virtually impossible for a single small group to monopolize political power.

Within Virginia, however, Gooch reaped most of the credit for the new
political tranquillity. Writers and speakers widely heralded Gooch for his
"disinterested and unprejudic'd PATRIOTISM," comparing him favorably
to George I and Augustus. His "love and good will to the people of this
Country, and . . . readiness" to "exert it upon all occasions" had, as
Speaker Randolph told Gooch in August 1736, "given universal satisfac-

---

[44] Randolph's speeches, Aug. 24, 1734, Aug. 6, 1736, in *Journals of the House of Burgesses
of Virginia, 1727-40,* 175-76, 241-42; David Mossum, Jr., "Ode," *Virginia Gazette,* Nov.
26, 1736.

tion to the people under your government." By refusing to be "intoxicated with . . . power," Gooch had shown himself to be "a faithful trustee of the public good" and had convinced Virginians that he had learned the "art of governing well"—the "most abstruse, as well as the usefullest science in the world"—"to some degree of perfection."[45]

John Markland expressed the prevailing sentiment in 1730 in an ode extolling Gooch for his role in bringing printing to Virginia:

> He came, He saw, and was belov'd;
> Like Lightening, quick but strong,
> An universal Gladness mov'd
>   Throughout th' admiring Throng.
>   No sooner was He seen,
>   His calm, yet awful Look,
>   Majestic, yet serene,
> The very Pow'r of Prejudice remov'd,
>   And ev'n His *Silence* spoke.
>   But when His graceful *Tongue,*
> Copious of reason, did display
> To Happiness, or nearest, surest Way,
>   Ev'n Party-Rancour dy'd away,
>   And private Spleen.
>   We found whence *Britain* is so blest,
>   Which had so much our Envy bore,
> We found—and griev'd we found it not before—
> We found, that when by Love and Peace,
>   A Prince has fix'd his Throne
>   In ev'ry Subject's loial Breast,
> No wonder Factions end, and Murmers cease,—
> Since now, what GEORGE is there, GOOCH here has amply shewn.[46]

To be sure, Gooch purchased this "universal satisfaction" at a price which was somewhat more than metropolitan officials ideally would have liked to pay, a price which included acceptance by the crown's chief official of strong local institutions with sufficient power even to counterbalance royal authority in the colony. In the bargain, however, he gained

---

[45] John Markland, *Typographia: An Ode on Printing* (Williamsburg, Va., 1730), iii, 9–10; and Randolph's speech, Aug. 6, 1736, *Journals of the House of Burgesses of Virginia, 1727–40*, 241–42.

[46] Markland, *Typographia*, iii, 9–10.

enormous personal influence in legislation. Thus, he managed in the mid-1730s, in a great individual triumph, to secure an effective tobacco inspection law for the first time in the colony's history, and against much opposition from rank-and-file planters. Equally important, his conciliatory and judicious behavior helped to mitigate that deep suspicion of executive authority traditionally exhibited by colonial legislators and was essential in gaining acceptance within the Virginia legislature of the ideal of institutional cooperation in pursuit of the common good. Indeed, the Burgesses even took pride, as Speaker Randolph noted in the speech just quoted above, in not pretending to be any "more than the Representative Body of a Colony, naturally and justly dependent upon the Mother Kingdom, whose Power is circumscribed by very narrow Bounds, and whose Influence is of small extent. All we pretend to is to be of some Importance to those who send us hither, and to have some Share in their Protection, and the Security of their Lives, Liberties, and Properties." What a sharp contrast to the lower houses in most other colonies, where insistence upon a rigid adherence to metropolitan claims for an overblown prerogative and patently self-interested behavior by governors caused legislators to become suspicious of all executive authority and to regard it as their solemn duty to undermine gubernatorial power wherever possible![47]

That the Burgesses' actual power was far greater than Randolph's remarks would suggest and that the Burgesses was willing to pretend to less authority at the very time when most of its counterparts were doing precisely the opposite provide a striking indication of the success of Gooch's policy of pragmatic compromise and institutional cooperation. "But oh! much more extended is the Pow'r," said Markland in his poem,

> Than o'er the Length of boundless Land,
> Or o'er the Sea's remotest Strand,
> Where Goodness and paternal Care
> The Sovereign's native Vertues are,

---

[47] Randolph's speech, Aug. 6, 1736, *Journals of the House of Burgesses of Virginia, 1727–40*, 241–42. For the normal pattern of executive-legislative relations in the colonies, see Jack P. Greene, "Political Mimesis: A Consideration of the Historical and Cultural Roots of Legislative Behavior in the British Colonies in the Eighteenth Century," *American Historical Review* 75 (1969): 337–60 [chap. 8 above]. For Gooch's ideas on the proper stance of governors toward local establishments, see his remarks on Sir William Keith, "A Short Discourse on the Present State of the Colonies in America," [ca. 1730], in Jack P. Greene, ed., *Great Britain and the American Colonies, 1606–1763* (New York, 1970), 196–214.

And Subjects Hearts with Loialty run o'er:
  Where envious Thoughts abortive die,
  Nor Malice rowls her low'ring Eye:
  Where, with contending Zeal,
  The *Prince* and *People* strive,
  The *Prince* to make his *People* thrive,
    Their Grievances to heal;
  And all good and adverse Fortune shares;
    They, in Return to *Him*,
  Pay mutual Rev'rence and Esteem,
  And all his Pow'r his Honour, Happiness, is theirs.[48]

Moreover, this same policy seems to have been in considerable part responsible for Virginia's intense British patriotism and loyalty to the crown through the middle decades of the eighteenth century. Probably no other colony had so high a regard for things English as Britain's "eldest Foreign Care." "Every political sentiment, every fashion in Virginia," wrote Edmund Randolph later, "appeared to be imperfect unless it bore a resemblance to some precedent in England," and this "almost idolatrous deference to the mother country" made Virginians willing even to bear serious violations of their rights by the metropolis "upon a mere reluctance to quarrel with the mother country." Virginians delighted in conceiving of the colony as "the most dutiful and loyal" of the crown's overseas dominions, "the happy retreat," as the Reverend Hugh Jones phrased it, "of true Britons."[49]

Though it provoked a violent political hassle, pushed the House of Burgesses into that grasping posture it had not openly assumed since the middle years of Spotswood's administration, and ultimately resulted in a concerted and successful drive by the Burgesses to establish its political supremacy within the colony, not even the ill-conceived attempt in 1753–54 by Robert Dinwiddie (1752–58) to charge without the Burgesses' consent a fee of a pistole for signing and sealing patents for land could lessen the goodwill toward the crown that Gooch had so carefully cultivated. In fact, Dinwiddie's experience only reaffirmed the wisdom of his predecessor, and he tried thereafter to steer a similar course. The

---

[48] Markland, *Typographia*, 7.
[49] Ibid., 8; Randolph, *History of Virginia*, 116, 176; Jones, *Present State of Virginia*, 82–83; Philo Patria [Richard Bland] to George Washington, 1756, in Hamilton, *Letters to Washington* 1:394.

antagonisms created by the pistole fee incident were so strong that he never overcame them during the remaining four years of his administration. But his two successors, Francis Fauquier (1758–68) and Norborne Berkeley, Baron de Botetourt (1768–70), cast themselves in the Gooch mold and won the esteem of Virginia political leaders. With governors like Gooch and Fauquier—patriot governors who, as James Horrocks said of Fauquier, were friends to liberty, protectors of the constitution, and promoters of the colony's welfare—it was no wonder that the Virginia governors at the close of the Seven Years' War had, as various commentators noted, more extensive powers and were more independent of the lower house than governors of other colonies, or that the colony was and had been for over thirty years a model of dutiful and affectionate loyalty.[50]

That a group so devoted to politics should have produced so little theoretical writing on political matters has puzzled many later historians. But the imperatives of Virginia political life as well as the values of the gentry dictated that other qualities should be more admired than the speculative. In Virginia, as elsewhere in the English colonies, politics had already assumed that functional and pragmatic character that has been so predominant a feature of subsequent American politics, and Virginians were wary, as Jonathan Boucher noted, of "the false refinements of speculative men, who amuse themselves and the world with visionary ideas of perfection, which never were, nor ever will be found, either in public or in private life." The man of action, the man with a capacity for business who addressed himself directly to problems at hand, rather than the philosopher, was the sort of person Virginians most admired.[51]

Many of the older gentry families and many of the new professional men, especially among the lawyers, had large libraries and seem to have read widely. One English traveler reported in the 1740s that many of the gentlemen were "a most agreeable Set of Companions, and possess a

---

[50] Horrocks, *Upon the Peace*, iii–iv; [Landon Carter], *A Letter to the Right Reverend Father in God, the Lord B——p of L——n* (Williamsburg, Va., 1760), 35. A conventional assessment of executive power in Virginia during the late 1750s may be found in Memorial of James Abercromby, read by Board of Trade, Nov. 21, 1759, Colonial Office Papers, 5/1329, ff. 343–49, Public Record Office, London.

[51] [Boucher], *Letter from a Virginian*, 9–10.

pretty deal of improving Knowledge; nay, I know some of the better sort, whose Share of Learning and Reading, would really surprize you, considering their Educations." But the Reverend Hugh Jones's characterization of Virginians as "more inclinable to read men by business and conversation, than to dive into books" seems to describe the vast majority of the gentry, who, Jones reported, were "generally diverted by business or inclination from profound study, and prying into the depths of things." Virginia's was essentially an oral culture whose predominant orientation was toward action. The gentry valued "mental acquirements" and paid "particular Respect to Men of Learning," but they appreciated other traits, including industry, polish, good character, and affability, even more and preferred that men demonstrate their "clear and penetrating powers of mind" in their deeds or in conversation and speaking rather than in writing. Men with a strong scholarly or speculative bent, such as Landon Carter and Richard Bland or, in a later generation, Thomas Jefferson and James Madison, were not quite the "biological sports" one writer has suggested, but they were the exception rather than the rule among the leading Virginia politicians.[52]

Lack of concern for political theory and speculation did not mean, however, that Virginians did not operate within a clear, if nowhere systematically articulated, framework of assumptions and perceptions about politics and society. This framework was wholly conventional and almost entirely English, albeit it contained a heavy infusion of ideas from the classics. It was drawn from a wide variety of English sources: the Anglican literature of piety, such as Richard Allestree's *The Whole Duty of Man;* popular works of civility, including Henry Peacham's *Compleat Gentleman,* Richard Braithwaite's *English Gentleman,* and Allestree's *Gentleman's Calling;* mainstream English political thought, especially as expressed in contemporary English periodicals, which quickly found their way to Virginia and frequently were pirated by the editors of the several *Virginia Gazette*s; English legal theorists, particularly Coke and, later, Blackstone; seventeenth-century Whig opposition writers like Milton, Harrington, Sydney, and Locke; Tory Augustan or "country" opposition writers, most heavily Addison, Pope, Swift, and Bolingbroke; and—to a much lesser extent—radical Whig thinkers such

---

[52]"Observations in Several Voyages and Travels in America," [1746], *William and Mary Quarterly,* 1st ser., 16 (1907): 158; Jones, *Present State of Virginia,* 80–82; Fithian, *Journal and Letters,* 211; Landon Carter, *The Rector Detected* (Williamsburg, Va., 1764), 24; Schoepf, *Travels* 1:61–62, 91–95; Horrocks, *Upon the Peace,* 12.

as Trenchard and Gordon.[53] However derivative in origin and however commonplace in content, this framework of political and social ideas played a powerful role in Virginia politics. It underlay and informed virtually all political behavior. It was, moreover, above debate. No important Virginia politician rose to challenge it at any point between 1720 and 1790, and this consensus was an important factor in both the absence of speculative political philosophy and Virginia's unanimity in the face of the repeated political crises between 1760 and 1789.

At the heart of that framework was the conventional belief in the imperfection of man. Man was not depraved or innately sinful, but he was weak, shortsighted, fallible in his judgments, perpetually self-deluded, prone to favor his own errors, and a slave to his vanity, interests, prejudices, and passions. *"Humanum est errare"* ("to be human is to err") was the Reverend David Griffith's succinct expression of this belief, and the most frequent source of man's errors, he noted in a sermon in 1775, was his "Selfishness and ambition." The pursuit of self was behind man's "insatiable passion of . . . avarice" and his "Fondness for Power incontroulable." His inability to resist those desires, which, as Landon Carter observed in his diary in 1770, "increased like a dropsical thirst . . . the more they are indulged," led him into corruption and ultimately into that state of complete depravity where "power and self aggrandizement" became the sole "object of . . . pursuit," ambition and passion ruled unrestrained, and, as Richard Bland put it in 1764, a man would "trudge, with Might and Main, through Dirt and Mire, to gain his Ends." The natural weakness of all men and the conscious malevolence of some meant that they could never be left entirely to their own devices or to the mercy of one another, for it was virtually certain, as Landon Carter pointed out, that sooner or later some of them would "fall into such Depravations of Mind, as to become more cruel than the most savage Beast of Prey." The good of every individual and of society in general demanded, therefore, that man's weak and evil tendencies be restrained; and the function of government was to protect man from himself and his fellows, to neutralize his passions by checking them against those of other men, to "restrain vice and cherish virtue," and to promote order

---

[53] See esp. Wright, *First Gentlemen of Virginia*; Robert Manson Myers, "The Old Dominion Looks to London: A Study of English Literary Influences upon the *Virginia Gazette* (1736–1766)," *Virginia Magazine of History and Biography* 54 (1946): 195–217; and Elizabeth Christine Cook, *Literary Influences in Colonial Newspapers, 1704–1750* (New York, 1912), 179–229.

and happiness by securing the life, liberty, and property of every individual.[54]

This was a large order. Because they were necessarily composed of imperfect men, all governments, no matter how benevolent the intentions of the rulers, could be expected to be fallible, to be continually, if inadvertently, inflicting injustice and injury upon the very society they were trying to serve. It was in the very "nature of men in authority," it seemed to Richard Henry Lee, "rather to commit two errors than to retract one." An even greater difficulty arose from the probability that there would always be some among the rulers who would be unable to resist their grosser passions. That "more determinations of government have proceeded from selfishness and ambitions, than from disinterested and benevolent measures," noted David Griffith, was a lamentable fact of history, and the paramount danger to any state was man's unquenchable thirst for power. Virginia politicians were wary of the possibility that someone or some group might eventually acquire what Richard Bland called a "Leviathon of Power" and introduce the worst sort of arbitrary and despotic polity. Clearly, the governed had to be protected from the baser tendencies of their governors, and the main instrument for their protection was the constitution.[55]

To the Virginia gentry, *constitution* was the most hallowed term in their political vocabulary. The constitution was the guarantor of their rights, liberties, and property. The "most valuable Part of our Birthright as Englishmen," Richard Bland asserted, was the "vital Principle in the

---

[54] Examples of this conception of human nature and the function of government are [Carter], *Letter to B——p of L——n*, 6, 17, 43; *A Letter from a Gentleman in Virginia, to the Merchants in Great Britain, Trading to That Colony* (London, 1754), 5, 16; *Maryland Gazette* (Annapolis), Oct. 28, 1754; *Letter to a Gentleman in London from Virginia* (London, 1759), 15, 20–21; *Diary of Landon Carter*, Sept. 28, 1770, Sept. 11, 1775, 1:505, 2:940–42; Common Sense [Richard Bland], *The Colonel Dismounted or the Rector Vindicated* (Williamsburg, Va., 1764), 13; [Gooch], *Dialogue*, 13; *Defence of Injur'd Merit*, 9; [Nicholas], *Considerations on the Present State of Virginia Examined*, 24–25; Griffith, *Passive Obedience*, 6–14, 18–19, 23; speech of Sir John Randolph, Aug. 6, 1736, *Journals of the House of Burgesses of Virginia, 1727–40*, 241–42.

[55] [Carter], *Letter to a Gentleman in London*, 20–21, *Letter to B——p of L——n*, 6, 46, 55, and *Rector Detected*, 16, 22; Camm, *Review of Rector Detected*, 16; [Bland], *Colonel Dismounted*, 14; Richard Henry Lee, Introduction to John Dickinson and Arthur Lee, *The Farmer's and Monitor's Letters to the Inhabitants of the British Colonies* (Williamsburg, Va., 1769), i; [Nicholas], *Considerations*, 28–29; [Boucher], *Letter from a Virginian*, 9–10; Griffith, *Passive Obedience*, 12; George Mason to George Washington, Sept. 15, 1756, in Kate Mason Rowland, *The Life of George Mason, 1725–1792*, 2 vols. (New York, 1892), 1:66.

Constitution" that "all men" were "only subject to Laws made with their own Consent." That principle provided the primary security for the "liberty and Property for every Person," placed them beyond the reach of the "highest EXECUTIVE Power in the State" as long as they lived in "Obedience to its Laws," and ensured that they would live under a government of impartial laws rather than partial men. For, although laws made by fallible legislators could never be entirely satisfactory to everyone in society, they were infinitely preferable to the "voluntary Mercy" or "charitable Disposition" of men.[56]

Every branch of government was bound by this principle, but the House of Burgesses, as the predominant force in the legislative process and as the agency through which the governed gave their consent to laws, was the "natural" guardian of their rights. It had a special obligation to keep a sharp eye out for any transgressions of the law and to oppose every measure that had "the least tendency to break through the legal Forms of government," because, as Bland argued, "a small spark if not extinguished in the beginning will soon gain ground and at last blaze out into an irresistible Flame." The rule of law had to be absolute. "LIBERTY & PROPERTY" were "like those previous Vessels whose soundness is destroyed by the least flaw and whose use is lost by the smallest hole."[57]

The House of Burgesses itself, of course, was a potential threat to the liberty, property, and basic rights of its constituents. The house, said Edwin Conway, a representative from Northumberland County, in 1737, was like "the *Lion* . . . in the Fable who" was "stronger in Power than any single Subject in the Colony." Precisely because of this great power, both the constituency and the members of the house had to be ever watchful lest a conspiracy of evil or misguided men capture the house and seek to subvert or destroy the rule of law. One protection against such a development was the customary prohibition within the Anglophone world against legislative tinkering with those traditional and fundamental rights of individuals, such as trial by jury and the right to a writ of habeas corpus, that were firmly rooted in English com-

---

[56] [Carter], *Letter from a Gentleman in Virginia*, 29, 35, and *Letter to B——p of L——n*, 29, 35; [Bland], *Colonel Dismounted*, 21–23, and *A Fragment on the Pistole Fee, Claimed by the Governor of Virginia, 1753*, ed. Worthington C. Ford (Brooklyn, N.Y., 1891), 36–37.

[57] Bland, *Fragment on the Pistole Fee*, 37–38; [Gooch], *Dialogue*, 13; [Carter], *Letter from a Gentleman in Virginia*, 12, 19, 22–23, *Letter to B——p of L——n*, 44, and *Letter to a Gentleman in London*, 14, 19–20.

mon law and had been guaranteed by the Revolutionary Settlement of 1688.[58]

Another check against the legislature, of course, was the requirement of periodic elections. Although there was no law in Virginia requiring elections at stated intervals, eighteenth-century governors followed English practice and never tried to keep a legislature in existence beyond the seven-year limit. No matter how frequent the elections, however, representatives, by deliberately deceiving and playing upon the emotions of their constituents, could always secure their support for the worst species of legislative tyranny. "In all free governments, and in all ages," Jonathan Boucher observed in 1774, there would always be "Crafty, designing knaves, turbulent demogogues, quacks in politics and imposters in patriotism" who sought to overturn the constitution while pretending to defend it.[59]

The ultimate safeguard against such a threat was a balanced constitution, that "ingenious" contrivance that most of the eighteenth-century British world regarded as the secret of a successful polity. By mixing the various elements of the polity together in such a way as to keep them in a constant state of equilibrium, so that each would serve as a countervailing force against the others and harmful tendencies would thereby be checked or neutralized, a balanced constitution was the device through which imperfect men could live together in a state of relative harmony. Before the 1770s no Virginian spelled out exactly what was balanced by the constitution—whether the governors were balanced against the governed, the gentlemen against the commoners, the prerogative against local interests, or each of the three branches of government (the legislative, judicial, and executive) against one another. But Virginians were thoroughly persuaded that "in every state" it was absolutely "necessary for the publick weal that as just an equilibrium as possible should be preserved." That the preservation of the whole polity depended upon maintaining a proper balance and a distinct separation of functions between its several parts was, as Robert Carter Nicholas declared in 1774, an article of faith, and the fact that the House of Burgesses, even after it had gained the ascendancy in Virginia politics in the mid-1750s, did not attempt a significant extension of its authority over executive affairs after the fashion of its counterparts elsewhere in the colonies is in part a

---

[58] See Edwin Conway to Mr. Parks, *Virginia Gazette*, June 24, 1737.

[59] [Boucher], *Letter from a Virginian*, 7–10.

testimony to the continuing devotion of Virginia politicians to the ideal of a well-balanced constitution.[60]

This ideal, with its emphasis upon the subordination of the several parts of society to the interests of the whole, was closely related to another "fundamental . . . Rule of the *English* Constitution": the doctrine of *salus populi est suprema lex*. Landon Carter and Richard Bland employed that doctrine extensively between 1759 and 1764 as a defense, first of Virginia's wartime paper money emissions against the opposition of British merchants and then of the Two-Penny Acts, which enabled people to pay their public obligations in money instead of tobacco in two years of extremely short crops, against the attacks of the clergy, the prime victims of the acts. As defined by Carter and Bland, the doctrine meant simply that anything that was "absolutely necessary for the Good of the Community," that is, the corporate welfare of the society, was "therefore just in itself," other constitutional rules or individual interests to the contrary notwithstanding. Not the disadvantages to a few individuals but "the Advantages . . . to the People in general" were the "principal Consideration with legislatures in forming Laws," Bland asserted in defending the Two-Penny Acts, and Carter thought it was a "great Absurdity" to suggest that the interests of any man or group of men were more important than the preservation of the "community, which they compose." Even the king's prerogative, great and powerful as it was, Bland argued in writing against the crown's disallowance of laws the Virginia legislature thought necessary for the welfare of the colony, could "only be exerted . . . for the Good of his People, and not for their Destruction"; and Carter contended that the constitution itself, which in normal circumstances should be kept "as sacred as possible," might have to be "aided, extended or qualified . . . to support and preserve the Community." Everything had to give way before the public good.[61]

---

[60] Alexander Spotswood to Sir John Randolph, *Virginia Gazette*, Dec. 10, 1736; speech of Sir John Randolph, Aug. 6, 1736, *Journals of the House of Burgesses of Virginia, 1727–40*, 241–42; [Nicholas], *Considerations*, 24–25; Randolph, *Considerations*, 5–8; *Virginia Gazette* (Purdie), June 27, 1766; [Bland], *Colonel Dismounted*, 14.

[61] Richard Bland, *A Letter to the Clergy of Virginia* (Williamsburg, Va., 1760), 15–16, 18; Bland to John Camm, Oct. 25, 1763, in [Bland], *Colonel Dismounted*, ii; and [Carter], *Letter to a Gentleman in London*, 20–21, *Letter to B——p of L——n*, 6–7, 19, 46, 50–51, and *Rector Detected*, 30. For a report of a similar argument by Patrick Henry, see James Maury to John Camm, Dec. 12, 1763, *Journals of the House of Burgesses of Virginia, 1761–65*, liii.

To make sure that the welfare of the entire community would always be its central concern, government, Virginians felt strongly, had to be especially careful not to grant to any group within it—and particularly to no group among the rulers—any special status, privileges, exemptions, or benefits. However salutary such a grant might appear at the time it was given, and however virtuous the men to whom it was given might be, "Ambition and lust of power above the laws" were, as Jonathan Boucher asserted, "such predominant passions in the Breasts of most men, even of men who escape the infection of other vices," that they could never be trusted not to try to turn it to their own selfish ends, perhaps even to attempt the establishment of a despotism, or what Landon Carter disapprovingly called "a mere Aristocratic power," that "Arbitrary and Oppressive" form in which men governed for their own private ends rather than for the common good. So pronounced was the tendency of a few to try to extend their power in any state that the legislature had to be constantly on the alert, Landon Carter declared, to protect the "greater Number of Individuals against an almost certain Oppression from the lesser Number," and the only certain way to prevent the polity from degenerating into an aristocracy was to preserve the absolute equality of all freemen within it. That "Subjects have not Pretence to Immunities, one more than another," was, therefore, a first principle with Virginia political leaders.[62]

The evils of an excessively popular government were similar. The people, as young James Madison, cousin of the fourth president, and later bishop of the Episcopal church in Virginia, said in a Phi Beta Kappa oration at the College of William and Mary in 1772, were "the original Springs of Government." But they entrusted at each election part of their liberty to the men they chose for representatives, thereby giving them a large measure of independence and freeing them from the necessity to cater to the whims or act according to the sentiments of their constituents. Except in cases that "related particularly to the interest of the Constituents alone" and on which he had the "express Instructions of . . . Constituents," a representative had to "be Governed" not by the collective "sentiments of his Constituents" but by "his own Reason and Conscience," so that, in consultation with his fellow legislators, he could act on behalf of the good of the colony as a whole and not simply in the narrow interest of a particular constituency. The alternative, that a

---

[62] [Boucher], *Letter from a Virginian,* 9–10, 15; *Diary of Landon Carter,* May 9, 1774, 2:808; and [Carter], *Letter to a Gentleman in London,* 10, 19, *Letter to B——p of L——n,* 29, and *Rector Detected,* 22.

representative was bound by the wishes of his constituents in all cases, was unacceptable largely because it placed responsibilities on the people at large that they had neither the breadth of perspective nor the capacity to bear and perhaps even paved the way for their inevitable domination and manipulation by a small band of demagogues who could be expected to play upon the "credulity of the well-meaning, deluded multitude" for their own selfish ends and to introduce, under the guise of democracy, "an Aristocratic Power." The electorate was simply too restricted in its vision and too prone to be misled by men who could appeal to the passions or humors of the moment to be trusted to act in the best interests of the community at large.[63]

To prevent the degeneration of the polity into either aristocracy or democracy and to preserve the constitution in its "due Poise," Virginians depended upon the stewardship of the "real Patriot." A patriot could never be a man who was indolent, "ambitious of power," "proficient in the arts of dissimulation," or governed by "self and gain alone." Rather, he had to be an impartial and disinterested man whose "first principle," his "Ruling Passion," was "love of . . . Country"—a determination "to act under all appointments relative to the Public" and for no "Interest less than that of a whole Country." He had to be a man who would always "view the whole ground and persevere to the last," and one who would constantly adhere rigidly to the commands of the Burgesses' oath and upon "all Things proposed . . . deliver" his "Opinion faithfully, justly, and honestly, according to" his "best Understanding and Conscience, for the general Good, and Prosperity of this Colony, and every Member thereof; and to do" his best "endeavours to prosecute That, without mingling therewith, the particular Interest of any Person or Persons whatsoever." He could not "value" himself upon "Titles and Honors" or other "empty Things . . . of no intrinsic Worth" or "exchange his Duty and Integrity for Civilities" or other blandishments from the hand of power. He had to be, as the epitaph of William Byrd II of Westover declared he was, "the constant enemy of all exorbitant power, and hearty friend to the liberties of his country," an "honest Man" chosen, as an anonymous writer said in the *Virginia Gazette*, "to represent his County, or Borough, from the Knowledge his Constituents have of his Worth. He believes no Party can ever be in the Right, or always in the Wrong: He votes and

---

[63] James Madison, *An Oration in Commemoration of the Founders of William and Mary College* (Williamsburg, Va., 1772), 6; [Boucher], *Letter from a Virginian*, 9–10; [Randolph], *Considerations*, 3–5, 22–23; Conway to Parks, *Virginia Gazette*, Nov. 17, 1738; *Diary of Landon Carter*, Oct. 17, 1754, 1:116–17.

speaks as he judges best for the Service of his Country, and when the Session ends, returns, like *Cincinnatus,* to the Plough." He could not attach himself to any party because parties, Virginians were convinced, were the instruments of partial men whose devotion to factional ends necessarily robbed them of their independence of judgment and prevented them from considering the welfare of the entire country impartially. Finally, he had to concern himself primarily with keeping "Society moving on its proper Hinges" and to be willing to justify unpopular "public Measures when he thinks them necessary," to renounce the "people when he thinks them wrong," and to "call the first Connexions to an Account" whenever they acted unjustly or injuriously to the public.[64]

The two most essential qualities for the patriot, and ideally for all men, were virtue and independence. Virtue required a devotion to truth, honesty, moderation, and reason, a "Behavior . . . above every Appearance of Evil," and a determination both to guard against one's weaknesses by a constant exercise in self-control—a virtuous man could never be "a Slave to his own Ill-nature"—and to attempt to ennoble one's life by "real Goodness." "Whoever does not take care to govern his Passions, they will soon govern him," wrote James Reid, "and lead him into labyrinths of vice, error, prejudices, and immoralities from whence he will find it very difficult to extricate himself; for in time he will become fortified and impregnable against common sense and the dictates of right reason." "Virtue," the Reverend William Stith asserted, was the "grand Fountain of publick Honour and Felicity," and no man, as Robert Carter Nicholas once remarked, could "be safely trusted" with public office who

---

[64] *Defence of Injur'd Merit,* 7; *Diary of Landon Carter,* Mar. 21, 1752, Jan. 31, 1776, Aug. 8, 1777, 1:89, 2:970, 1121–22; [Carter], *Letter from a Gentleman in Virginia,* 3–5, 21–22, 27, 35, *Maryland Gazette,* Oct. 28, 1754, *Letter to a Gentleman in London,* 6–7, 9, 14, 27, *Letter to B——p of L——n,* 5, 10, 53, *Rector Detected,* 24; and Landon Carter to Councillors, [1774–75], Sabine Hall Collection, University of Virginia Library; Richard Bland's poem to Landon Carter, June 20, 1758, in Moncure D. Conway, *Barons of the Potomack and Rappahannock* (New York, 1892), 138–41; [Randolph], *Considerations,* 7–8; George Washington to Mrs. Mary Washington, Aug. 14, 1755, to Speaker John Robinson, Dec. 1756, and to Governor Robert Dinwiddie, Sept. 15, 1757, *Writings of Washington* 1:159, 532–33, 2:133; Robert Carter Nicholas to Washington, Aug. 18, 1756, Philo Patria [Richard Bland] to Washington, 1756, and John Robinson to Washington, Nov. 15, 1756, in Hamilton, *Letters to Washington,* 1:338, 391, 394–95, 2:1–2; epitaph of William Byrd, n.d., in *The Writings of "Colonel William Byrd of Westover in Virginia Esqr.,"* ed. John Spencer Bassett (New York, 1901), xli; Randolph, *History of Virginia,* 273; Burgesses' Oath, *Virginia Gazette,* Nov. 24, 1738; Sir John Randolph to Alexander Spotswood, ibid., Oct. 29, Dec. 17, 1736; essay on "an honest Man," ibid., Sept. 29, 1752.

did "not act upon *solid, virtuous* Principles" and would not "sacrifice every sinister, selfish Consideration" for the "True Interest" of "his Country." Only men who were "conscious of the Uprightness and Integrity of their Actions" and were therefore "not easily dismayed," Richard Bland explained, could be expected to "stand firm and unshaken" against the imperfections of themselves and other men; and Landon Carter was convinced that chaos could frequently be reduced to "order and comfort" by "the appearance only of some good man."[65]

Independence was no less important than virtue. Perhaps because their constant exposure to black slavery impressed upon them how miserable and abject a slave could be, Virginians took great pride, as Wou'dbe inferred in *The Candidates*, in thinking that a spirit of personal independence was particularly strong among them. In Virginia, Edmund Randolph later remarked, "a high sense of personal independence was universal": "disdaining an abridgment of personal independence," he declared, was one of the most essential "manners which belonged to the real Virginian planter and which were his Ornament!" Foreign travelers and internal social critics alike were repeatedly impressed with this strong sense of independence among Virginians. A Virginia gentleman, said James Reid, had such overweening pride as to regard anything that seemed to deprive "him of his free agency" as "an imposition which is not to be put up with in a land of Liberty. It would be making him a piece of Clock work, a mere lump of mechanism, and a cypher of no value. It would be changing one who was born a Gentleman into a vile slave, and depriving him of that freedom which nature has vested him with." For the aspiring patriot, independence was especially important. It was, as Landon Carter wrote in 1769, the "base or footstool on which Liberty can alone be protected," and without liberty, without complete

---

[65] *Diary of Landon Carter,* Mar. 6, 9, 13, 1752, Feb. 15, 1770, June 6, 1773, May 10, 1774, 1:75–78, 84–85, 357–58, 2:755–56, 808–9; [Carter], *Letter to a Gentleman in London,* 12, 27–28, *Letter to B——p of L——n,* 1, 8, 40; Landon Carter to "My Friend," n.d., and to Councillors, [1774–75], Sabine Hall Collection, University of Virginia Library; Landon Carter to Purdie and Dixon, Fall 1769, Carter Family Papers, folder 3, Swem Library, College of William and Mary; Stith, *Sinfulness of Gaming,* 11–12, 25; [Randolph], *Considerations,* 3; [Nicholas], *Considerations,* 37–38; Bland, *Letter to Clergy,* 9; Burnaby, *Travels,* 20; Schoepf, *Travels* 1:55; William Nelson to Washington, Feb. 22, 1753, Landon Carter to Washington, Oct. 7, 1755, in Hamilton, *Letters to Washington* 1:1, 108; Randolph, *History of Virginia,* 178, 193, 197; The Monitor, "On Good Nature," *Virginia Gazette,* Jan. 28, 1737; essay on "an honest Man," ibid., Sept. 29, 1752; Reid, "Religion of the Bible," 55, 60–61.

freedom to act impartially and independently, no man could fulfill the obligations of the patriotic public servant.[66]

Within this broad consensus of working political assumptions there was considerable room for maneuver, and what divided the political leadership within the House of Burgesses was a disagreement not over the rules of the game but rather over how the game should be played. By the 1740s and 1750s, and perhaps even earlier, there had emerged two poorly delineated but recognizable postures or styles of leadership. One style may best be described as responsible. The conspicuous minority who assumed this posture insisted upon a strict adherence to the traditional ideals of politics. They were the disinterested patriots par excellence, the ideologues of virtue and independence. They prided themselves upon their personal virtue, their willingness to sacrifice even friendship for truth and justice, and their elevation above the clamour of the multitude. It was not praise they sought but praiseworthiness; it was not enough for them just to seem—they had to be—men of distinction. Like Worthy in *The Candidates*, they professed to have "little inclination to the service" and an "aversion to public life." Far from courting the favor of their constituents, they had the "troublesome office" of burgess thrust upon them. Rather than part with an ounce of their virtue, they preferred to withdraw from public life. They were fond of quoting Cato's lines from Joseph Addison's play *Cato:* "When vice prevails and impious men bear sway / The post of honour is a private station."[67]

Epitomized by such men as Landon Carter, Richard Henry Lee, George Washington, and George Mason, the "responsible" men were often more rigid in their professions than in their practice. But they were

---

[66] Randolph, *History of Virginia*, 178, 193, 197; Reid, "Religion of the Bible," 55, 60–61; Landon Carter to Purdie and Dixon, Fall 1769, Carter Family Papers, folder 3, Swem Library, College of William and Mary.

[67] See Munford, *Candidates*, 38, 40, 43; [Nicholas], *Considerations*, 37–38; [Randolph], *Considerations*, 3, 5–8; *Diary of Landon Carter*, Mar. 14, 1770, 1:368; Anburey, *Travels*, 2:200–201; *Defence of Injur'd Merit*, 8; Bland's poem to Carter, June 20, 1758, in Conway, *Barons of the Potomack and Rappahannock*, 138–41; Washington to Speaker John Robinson, Dec. 1756, *Writings of Washington* 1:532–33; Edmund Randolph, *An Oration in Commemoration of the Founders of William and Mary College* (Williamsburg, Va., 1771), 6; Landon Carter to Dixon and Hunter, [May 1776], Sabine Hall Collection, University of Virginia Library.

the consciences of Virginia politics, the idealists who were devoted to the goal of impersonal and impartial government, the visionaries who insisted that man should strive to be perfect in spite of his imperfections and in the face of almost certain failure. They were the vigorous public servants who stood for activity, energy, and resolution in times of crisis.

The second style was more representative—more flexible—in its orientation. Those who exhibited it showed no disposition to oppose the conventional ideals of politics, but they were willing to interpret them more loosely than the men of the more responsible style and to deviate from them somewhat if there was no obvious danger in doing so. They were the pragmatic politicians, whose primary emphasis was upon accommodation, moderation, deliberation, and control, and whose most fundamental commitment was to the continuing stability of the polity. Although they were careful never to "fawn or cringe" before the freeholders and did not violate the gentleman candidate's rule not to solicit votes openly, they believed, like Wou'dbe in *The Candidates,* that "the Prudent candidate who hopes to rise, / Ne'er deigns to hide it, in a mean disguise." They had few scruples about courting the freeholders and, though they often found it distasteful, were not too proud to mingle with the voters in order to reinforce through ties of affection the relationship between themselves and their constituents.[68]

Within the House of Burgesses they were the amiable and assiduous men of business with "sound political Knowledge" who were ever willing to arrange a compromise in order to avoid a convulsive struggle among contending interests. Inclined to be more concerned with the wishes of the electorate than with the preservation of their own unsullied virtue, they were—in the interests of preserving control and maintaining stability—willing to tailor their behavior and even to employ what Landon Carter derisively called a "low popular argument" to suit the "humour of the Plebians." They were the realists of Virginia politics, who took politics on its own terms. They accepted man's limitations and the fact that he would often err, and were not disposed to fret if the political system became somewhat personal and partial as long as no gross evils seemed to result. Exemplified by Sir John Randolph and John Robinson, the latter the very "Darling of the Country" for twenty-eight years during his tenure as speaker of the Burgesses between 1738 and 1766, Peyton Randolph, Edmund Pendleton, Archibald Cary, and Benjamin Har-

[68] Munford, *Candidates,* 24–25, 36–38, 41, 43.

rison, the men of the representative style provided the responsive and practical element in Virginia politics.[69]

The existence of the two styles and a measure of difference between them was revealed in two important debates during the 1750s. The first, lasting only a few hours and recorded only in Landon Carter's private minutes of the session, concerned the nature of representation and the function of a representative. Men of the representative style, the "favourers of Popularity," headed by Speaker John Robinson, argued that a representative was "to Collect the sentiments of his Constituents and whatever that Majority willed ought to be the rule of his Vote," that he was, in fact, "obliged to follow the direction of his Constituents" even "against his own Reason and Conscience." Men of the responsible style— those who considered themselves "Admirers of Reason and Liberty of Conscience"—took the position that "reason and Good Conscience should direct" except in cases "where the matter related particularly to the interest of the Constituents alone."[70]

The second and more important debate concerned the extent and nature of Virginia's contribution to the Seven Years' War and seems to have lasted throughout the period from 1754 until the demands on Virginia became lighter after the war took a turn for the better in 1757. Although the evidence is sketchy and the details of motivation are by no means certain, one of the main issues clearly was whether the House of Burgesses, as Landon Carter and Richard Bland insisted, should "give, freely and liberally, such Supplies, as will enable the Government, to act with Spirit and Resolution" or should follow the more popular course, advocated primarily by Robinson and his friends, of making less of an effort and thereby pleasing an apparently large segment of the public which was grumbling about paying such heavy taxes.[71]

The importance of these divergent styles in the day-to-day politics of Virginia should not be overemphasized. Their existence seems to have been only dimly perceived by contemporaries, who had neither defined their character nor identified their tendencies clearly. Perhaps no politician fitted precisely or wholly into either of the models just described.

---

[69] Randolph, *History of Virginia*, 173; *Diary of Landon Carter*, Apr. 1, 6, 14–15, 17, 1752, Aug. 22, 1754, May 14, 1755, 1:91, 93, 100–105, 107–14.

[70] *Diary of Landon Carter*, Oct. 17, 1754, 1:116–17.

[71] Landon Carter to Washington, [Apr. 1756], George William Fairfax to Washington, May 9, 13, 1756, Philo Patria [Richard Bland] to Washington, 1756, and Bland to Washington, [June 1757], in Hamilton, *Letters to Washington* 1:236, 251, 256–57, 391, 394–95, 3:87–89; *Diary of Landon Carter*, Aug. 22, 1754, 1:107–14.

Responsible men like George Washington, Landon Carter, and Richard Henry Lee could resort to treating at a crucial election or to acting the *"Babbling Dog"* and *"the angry Man in the Lobby"* if they thought it necessary to win public support for a measure they favored. Similarly, representative types like Peyton Randolph and Edmund Pendleton by no means ignored their consciences in the blind pursuit of the whims of their constituents and could upon occasion insist on the strictest devotion to the rules of the game, especially in the face of an external challenge.[72]

But the push and pull between these two orientations within a large framework of consent provided still another element of balance within the Virginia political system and supplied much of the energy that made it function so effectively. It ensured that there would usually be both responsibility and responsiveness, wisdom and practicality, strength and adaptability, a concern for virtue and talent among the rulers and for the liberty and sentiments of the constituents. This concern for both virtue and liberty prevented the political system from becoming a closed corporation and gave it both an amazing capacity for assimilating new men and a strength, effectiveness, and responsiveness to the electorate which won for it the confidence of the public at large.

These several qualities were revealed most clearly during crises, and they became especially manifest in the decade immediately preceding the debate with Great Britain over Parliament's right to tax the colonies and the nature of constitutional relationships within the empire. Between 1752 and 1763 the Virginia political system had not only to meet the heavy demands of the Seven Years' War but also to cope with its first serious challenges since Alexander Spotswood's frontal assault on it four decades earlier. The contests over the pistole fee, the legal tender status of wartime paper money issues, and the Two-Penny Acts put the system to a series of demanding tests. In each case, it proved its essential viability, as it demonstrated an ability to cope with political crises while at the same time preserving an overall political stability in the colony and a high degree of unanimity among its leaders and retaining the support of the electorate at large—all testimonies to the caliber of its leadership, the strength of the relationship between the leadership and the constituency, and the vitality of its traditional political ideals. In addition, the

---

[72]Camm, *Review of Rector Detected,* 25; Sydnor, *Gentlemen Freeholders,* 39–59.

three crises vividly underlined for Virginia political leaders the necessity for a vigorous and jealous cultivation of those ideals.

In all three controversies, the central issue was the same: some individual or group was trying to extend its power or gain some private advantage at the expense of the whole community. Dinwiddie's behavior in the pistole fee incident left no doubt that he was "an avaritious and designing Delegate" who was attempting by "illegal and arbitrary" means to introduce a "branch of Power" unsanctioned by law which would lead straight to "that Hydra Oppression." The complaining British merchants were obviously "men of low and selfish Notions," "very *inhumane Principles*," "governed . . . wholly by Avarice," and "no otherwise *interested* in the Country, than in the dirty Demands" they had "against it." The opposing clergymen were clearly "avaritious, merciless" men without a grain of patriotism, "who, in Defiance of the Truth, stick at no Artifice to bring their evil Machinations to Perfection."[73]

Such behavior provided ample confirmation of the validity of the Virginians' traditional conception of human nature and of their conviction that the general good required that all men be placed under strict legal and constitutional restraints. The Reverend William Stith's ringing toast, *"Liberty & Property and no Pistole,"* dramatically reaffirmed for Virginians what could never have been far from the thoughts of men in a society where the possession of land was so important, namely that there was an intimate connection between liberty and property and that the chief security for both was the rule of law, guarded by the elective House of Burgesses. Each contest, in fact, only convinced Virginia political leaders that the Burgesses was the only body that could be trusted to act in the best interests of the colony.[74]

What continued to bother those leaders, however, what became distressingly clear during these three crises, was the one important defect in the Virginia political system: no matter what kind of workable balance of power they might attain within the colony, they could never, because

---

[73] Bland, *Fragment on the Pistole Fee,* 25, *Letter to Clergy,* 3, 5, and *Colonel Dismounted,* 13; Carter, *Letter from a Gentleman in Virginia,* 3–5, *Maryland Gazette,* Oct. 28, 1754, *Letter to a Gentleman in London,* 6–7, 9, 11, 14, 22, 25, 27, *Letter to B——p of L——n,* 5, 53, and *Rector Detected,* 5, 25, 27–28, 33; and Bland's poem to Carter, June 20, 1758, in Conway, *Barons of the Potomack and Rappahannock,* 138–41.

[74] See Greene, *Quest for Power,* 159–65, and "The Case of the Pistole Fee: The Report of a Hearing on the Pistole Fee Controversy before the Privy Council, June 18, 1754," *Virginia Magazine of History and Biography* 66 (1958): 406–22. Stith's toast and comments are in his letter to the Bishop of London, Apr. 21, 1753, Fulham Palace MSS, Virginia (second box), 13 Lambeth Palace, London.

of their colonial status and the vague constitutional arrangements that prevailed at the time, be sure that the metropolitan government would not upset it.

These fears did not inhibit Virginia political leaders to any noticeable degree. In each crisis the House of Burgesses acted with extreme boldness, branding anyone who paid Dinwiddie his pistole "a Betrayer of the Rights and Privileges of the People," refusing to comply with a royal order to remove the legal tender requirement from its paper money on the grounds that it "would be an Act of Injustice" to its constituents, and arguing with metropolitan authorities over portions of their ruling in the hassle over the Two-Penny Acts. Moreover, the house never once had to back down completely in the face of metropolitan power. Crown officials upheld the constitutionality of the pistole fee, but they also made important concessions to the house, exempting certain land patents from the fee and requiring Dinwiddie to reappoint Peyton Randolph, agent for the house against Dinwiddie in London, to the attorney generalship from which Dinwiddie had removed him. The Burgesses' stand on the paper money question was one of the chief considerations in prompting metropolitan officials to obtain parlimentary prohibition of legal tender paper money in the Currency Act of 1764, but again the house was pleased that the act only prohibited future issues and required the prompt retirement of old emissions at the times stipulated in the issuing acts and did not alter the legal tender status of old bills. Finally, although the crown disallowed the Two-Penny Acts, it did not yield to the clergy's demand that the acts be declared null and void from their first passage, so that the disallowance had no practical effect because both laws had long since expired. That the Burgesses had achieved some degree of victory in each of these contests did not mean, however, that house leaders regarded the resolution of any one of them as ideal.[75]

The primary cause for their anxiety was the potential threat to the colony from two potent weapons in the royal arsenal: legislative review and the royal instructions. By the first, metropolitan authorities could disallow colonial laws. By the second, they could, by forbidding the governor to pass certain kinds of measures, prevent the Burgesses from legislating in those areas, no matter how pressing the need, and thus actually exercise legislative power in the colony without the consent of the

---

[75] See Thad W. Tate, "The Coming of the Revolution in Virginia: Britain's Challenge to Virginia's Ruling Class, 1763-1776," *William and Mary Quarterly*, 3d ser., 19 (1962): 324-35; *Journals of the House of Burgesses of Virginia, 1752-58*, Nov. 21-28, Dec. 4, 1753, 129, 132, 136, 141; Greene, "Case of the Pistole Fee," 406-22; Representation of Virginia

people's representatives in the Burgesses. Virginia leaders did not fear that the crown under ordinary circumstances would use these weapons deliberately to oppress the colony, but they were concerned lest it unintentionally injure the colony by taking the wrong advice.

When it came to Virginia affairs, at least, the house was in full agreement with Dinwiddie's sarcastic comment during the pistole fee contest that it thought itself "more Wise than any other Body of People upon the Face of the Earth," and the house regarded it as preposterous that Dinwiddie, British merchants, or a few of the Virginia clergy should presume to set their judgment against that of the Burgesses, the representatives of the entire colony. For metropolitan officials to listen to such "selfish and interested" parties and to make decisions even partly in accord with their demands was a source of considerable discomfort. Initially, to prevent such developments the Burgesses sought to secure the right to keep an agent of its own choosing in London to explain its position on any questions that might come up. But even that safeguard, which the Burgesses obtained in 1759, would be insufficient if the direction of metropolitan affairs fell into the hands of evil men. As long as "An Act of Assembly" was such "a trifling thing," both legislative review and the royal instructions could, as Landon Carter bitterly remarked in 1752 when he heard of the crown's disallowance of ten laws from a careful revisal of 1749, be employed "in a Clandestine manner" to introduce "All imaginable Bribery."[76]

Fear of precisely just such a development as well as the desire to establish the Burgesses' competence in local legislation and to remedy what Virginian leaders considered a glaring flaw in the Virginia constitution led the Burgesses, especially Richard Bland and Landon Carter, to seek, during the controversy over the Two-Penny Acts, some precise constitutional arrangement that would limit the crown's use of these two powers while at the same time providing Virginia with permanent protection against the unlimited might of the parent state.

Specifically, this search was prompted by the Privy Council's 1759 instruction to Governor Fauquier threatening him with recall if he did not obey the royal instruction forbidding him to assent either to acts of less

---

Burgesses to Francis Fauquier, May 1763, Shelburne Papers, 49:455–66, William L. Clements Library, Ann Arbor, Mich.

[76] Dinwiddie to Board of Trade, Dec. 29, 1753, CO 5/1328, ff. 77–78, 81–82, PRO; *Diary of Landon Carter,* Apr. 8, 1752, 1:95. On the agency question, see Greene, *Quest for Power,* 280–84.

than two years' duration or to acts that repealed laws already confirmed by the king unless they contained a clause suspending them until the royal pleasure should be known. The potential dangers of that instruction were spelled out by Landon Carter's brother, Charles Carter of Cleve, next to Speaker John Robinson the most powerful member of the House of Burgesses, in a letter to a correspondent in England. "By a late revival of an old Instruction," he wrote, "we cannot alter or amend any Law before Application is made to his Majesty, which has taken away our Constitution." Unless the London agent could "get an Alteration," he predicted, "we in all Probability may be ruined, as no body of men is infallible, and all Laws are found by Experience deficient."[77]

In an opening round of pamphlets in 1759–60, Landon Carter and Bland argued that by preventing the enactment of laws that were "absolutely necessary" for the preservation of the colony, such a "Rule strictly adhered to must, sooner or later, prove the Destruction of the . . . State." Obviously, no instruction could be permitted to operate in such a way as to "destroy the Country," and Bland insisted that it was a "clear and fundamental . . . Rule of the *English Constitution*" that any "pressing Necessity" justified "any Person for infringing them," for deviating from them "with Impunity." "The Royal Prerogative," Bland argued, could "only be exerted while in the Hands of the best and most benign Sovereign, for the Good of his People, and not for their Destruction," and it was "impossible that any Instruction to a Governour" could "be construed so contrary to the first Principles of *Justice* and *Equity*, as to prevent his Assent to a Law for relieving a Colony in a Case of . . . general Distress and Calamity."[78]

Although Carter had argued that "instructions" were "neither Laws of publick Authority, nor Rules of Constitution," the 1759–60 tracts in general tended to question the wisdom rather than the constitutionality of the instruction; but the refusal of metropolitan officials to take seriously a formal protest from the House of Burgesses against the instruction in question demonstrated just how frail such arguments were as a protection against the preponderant power of the metropolitan govern-

---

[77] Tate, "Coming of the Revolution in Virginia," 326–32; Charles Carter to Peter Wyche, [ca. 1760], Guard Book, vol.6, no. 48, Royal Society of Arts, London, as cited in Gwenda Morgan, "Anglo-Virginia Relations 1748–1764," M.A. thesis, University of Southampton, 1969, 75–76.

[78] Bland, *Letter to Clergy*, 15–18; [Carter], *Letter to B——p of L——n*, 6, 19–20, 29, 43–47, 50–51, 59, and *Rector Detected*, 23, 30.

ment. A rigid observance of that instruction, the Burgesses had pleaded, repeating the contentions of Bland and Carter, would "involve the Colony in the most insuperable Difficulties."[79]

The necessity for some clearly defined constitutional restraints upon metropolitan use of instructions was now more obvious than ever, and Richard Bland attempted to work out what such restraints ought to be in *The Colonel Dismounted*, published in late 1764 at the end of the Two-Penny Acts controversy. "Under an *English* Government," Bland argued, all men were born free and were "only subject to Laws made with their own Consent." Because Virginians had not lost the "Rights of Englishmen" by their removal to America, they were protected by the same rule, which required that Virginia have "a legal Constitution, that is, a Legislature, composed, in Part, of the Representatives of the People," without whose consent no "Laws for the INTERNAL Government of the Colony" could be made. Drawn up by people at a distance, with insufficient knowledge of conditions in the colony, and kept secret from the colonial political community, instructions could therefore be only "Guides and Directions for the Conduct of Governors" and never law, because the people had not consented to them through their representatives. To make them law, said Bland, would be "at once, to strip us of all the Rights and Privileges of *British* Subjects, and to put us under the despotick Power of a *French* or *Turkish* Government." "Submission, even to the supreme Magistrate," he argued, "is not the whole Duty of a Citizen. . . . Something is likewise due to the Rights of our Country, and to the Liberties of Mankind."[80]

The difficulty with such constitutional speculations, of course, was that they were doomed to failure by the very problem they were contrived to solve. There was absolutely no way for Virginians to force metropolitan authorities to observe them; voluntary action by the metropolitan government was the only hope for acceptance. But the metropolitan government was clearly not even interested in them, much less willing to accept them. The resulting anxiety at this inability to achieve some precise limitations upon metropolitan authority, to repair such a glaring deficiency in their political system, haunted Virginia political leaders through the early years of the 1760s and fed a rising suspicion of metropolitan intentions and a fear that they would be unable to preserve them-

---

[79] [Carter], *Letter to B——p of L——n*, 44–47.

[80] [Bland], *Colonel Dismounted*, 21–23, 26. For Patrick Henry's more extreme use of the same argument, see Maury to Camm, Dec. 12, 1763, in *Journals of the House of Burgesses of Virginia, 1761–65*, li–liii.

selves and their constituents against an unintentional or corrupt exertion of the unlimited power of the home government.

Despite this anxiety, many of the leading Virginia political leaders exhibited a curious smugness in the early 1760s. Having found, averred a satiric poet, probably the Stafford County lawyer John Mercer,

> this loyal land in peace
> nor striving nor contending
> than how to prove 'its loves increase
> tow'rds one of George's sending,

Dinwiddie had raised the specter of arbitrary royal power in the colony for the first time in over thirty years and had inaugurated a long series of controversies through which "Virginians hitherto distinguished for their Loyalty" were repeatedly and "shamefully traduced, were Oppressed, Insulted, & treated like rebells, by the very persons from whom they" had been so "long taught to Expect Succour." But the luxuriant British patriotism so carefully nurtured by Gooch and then, after Dinwiddie, by Fauquier was too strong to be quickly stunted. Metropolitan behavior in the disputes of the 1750s and early 1760s weakened but by no means destroyed Virginians' affection for the parent state. Jubilant over the great British victory over the French and Spanish in the Seven Years' War and the Treaty of Paris in 1763, they were proud of the conspicuous part they themselves had acted in defending the frontiers of the empire and looked forward to a grand new era of expansion and liberty under the "admirable Constitution" of Great Britain, a constitution, as James Horrocks observed, that Britons had "Preserv'd . . . pure and uncorrupted thro' all the Struggles of Ambition and the most dangerous Attacks of Power."[81]

Indeed, Virginians virtually wallowed in professions of affection to the king and mother country. "Our Dependence upon Great Britain," the House of Burgesses told Lieutenant Governor Fauquier upon hearing of the peace, "we acknowledge and glory in, as our greatest Happiness and only Security." That the source of their greatest happiness should also be the cause of their deepest political frustration was ironic. But as long as that frustration was assuaged by the mildness of crown officials, as long

---

[81] [Mercer], "Dinwiddianae," 21, 27; Horrocks, *Upon the Peace,* 6; [Carter], *Letter to a Gentleman in London,* 25, and *Letter to B——p of L——n,* 38, 54; Robert Carter Nicholas to Washington, Jan. 23, 1756, in Hamilton, *Letters to Washington* 1:178–79; Bland, *Fragment on Pistole Fee,* 35.

as it arose from an anticipated rather than from a felt danger, they could easily push it to the backs of their minds. Besides, over the past decade, they had succeeded, if not in defeating, at least in checking, the malignant designs, in turn, of a "mercenary" and corrupt governor, an influential group of selfish merchants, and a small knot of scheming clergymen (while simultaneously making a major contribution toward the destruction of a powerful union of bloodthirsty savages and cunning papists). Also, the concessions they had won from the metropolitan government in these several disputes helped to perpetuate their belief in the essential justice of the mother country and its basic goodwill toward Virginia. Moreover, they had the satisfaction of knowing that they had behaved throughout these disputes with a "loyalty debased by no servile compliance and . . . a patriotic watchfulness never degenerating into the mere petulance of complaint." They hoped, as Edmund Randolph later phrased it, that "to know when to complain with truth and how to complain with dignity was . . . ample for the only end which could then be projected" within a beneficent political system such as the first British Empire.[82]

The most pressing, perhaps, but not all, or ultimately even the most important, sources of anxiety to the Virginia political community were external, however. Throughout the middle decades of the eighteenth century, the internal state of Virginia society was a source of persistent concern. Part of this concern was endemic to a largely one-crop economy and derived from the enduring fear that if the bottom ever fell out of the world tobacco market, Virginia's prosperity would quickly go down the drain. Thus, the *Virginia Gazette* might celebrate the virtues of tobacco by equating it with the rural virtues of peace, ease, and freedom:

> Sing ye Muses, Tobacco, the Blessing of Peace,
> Was ever a Nation so blessed as this?
>
> . . . . .
>
> Let foreign Climes the Vine and Orange boast,
> While wastes of war deform the teeming Coast;
> Britannia, distant from each hostile Sound,
> Enjoys a Pipe, with Ease and Freedom crown'd;

[82] Representation of Virginia Burgesses to Fauquier, May 1763, Shelburne Papers, 49:455, Clements Library; Randolph, *History of Virginia*, 160–61, 163.

E'en restless Faction finds itself most free,
Or if a Slave, a Slave to Liberty.

. . . . .

Tell, if ever you have seen
Realms so quiet and serene.[83]

But the limited success of repeated attempts to encourage agricultural diversification through legislation rendered the colony's economy especially vulnerable to sudden fluctuations in the demand for tobacco. Through most of the period between 1725 and 1775, the world tobacco market was expanding, almost even bullish, the result to a great extent of a growing tobacco market in France. But a major economic downturn at the end of the Seven Years' War vividly reminded Virginians of the disadvantages of too heavy a concentration upon a single crop. Tobacco prices were low and falling, and credit was especially tight. Invariably, in such periods of concentration the normal indebtedness of the planters—in flush times a major economic resource—seemed to be an overwhelming burden. Also, with a large public debt arising out of the heavy military expenditure made by the colony during the war and a contracting money supply caused by the successful offensive of British merchants against the colony's fund of paper currency, the economic picture by 1763 seemed especially bleak.[84]

As Arthur Lee wrote to his brother Philip Ludwell Lee from Britain in November 1763, Virginia was "a country overburdened with debts," both private and public, "threatened with the horrors of a [renewal of] savage War [brought on by Pontiac's uprising in the west]: her produce sinking universally in its value; without funds, trade or Men"—a "truly miserable" situation that required "the utmost Exertions, of the few able & patriotic Men among you, to save the state from sinking." The causes of this seemingly desperate and, unknown to him, short-term situation were numerous. But Lee thought a major part of the problem was traceable to the colony's excessive dependence upon tobacco. "Tobacco, your present Staple," he declared, "seems to be [a] very precarious commodity; its culture appears to be falling continually & shoud the same consumption continue, yet as the Colony becomes more populated, the

---

[83] *Virginia Gazette,* May 30, 1751.

[84] The best treatment of economic conditions in Virginia at the close of the Seven Years' War is Joseph Albert Ernst, "Genesis of the Currency Act of 1764: Virginia Paper Money and the Partition of British Investments," *William and Mary Quarterly,* 3d ser., 22 (1965): 34–59.

produce must of course overstock the Markets & reduce its value." It was "therefore incumbent" on Virginians to develop a diversified agricultural economy.[85]

Nor was the excessive vulnerability of a one-crop economy the only evil attributable to "that baneful weed tobacco." It had, said Edmund Randolph, "riveted two evils in the heart of Virginia, the declension of that agriculture which is the most safe and most honorable [i.e., mixed agriculture], and the encouragement of slavery, the most base of human conditions." Furthermore, as was becoming increasingly clear by the 1750s, tobacco was also exhausting "the fertility of our soil" and swallowing "up in its large plantations vast territories, which if distributed into portions were best adapted to favor population."[86]

As Randolph's recitation of the malicious effects of the race for tobacco profits suggests, black slavery, which had expanded so dramatically as a result of increasingly heavy importations of new slaves after 1720, was a second internal source of social unease among white Virginians. Every state has "an internal Weakness, or Distemper," said an anonymous writer in the *Virginia Gazette* on April 3, 1752: "I take the *Slavery* established here to be . . . a greater Fund of Imbecility to the State, than the old English *Villainage*, or the late *Clanship* of Scotland," a "poison," said another writer, which had diffused itself "in a variety of destructive shapes." The mad "Rage" for these "innumerable black Creatures" not only "swallow'd up" all of the liquid resources, the rich "Treasure" bestowed upon the colony by nature and industry, declared an anonymous correspondent in a trenchant allegory in the *Virginia Gazette* in 1738, but it also introduced a powerful internal enemy of incalculable danger. "Having no Enemy from without," said the allegorist, "this simple People are madly fond of securing one in their own Bowels," an enemy, another writer pointed out, who might, if a consistent vigilance were not maintained, at any time rise in conspiracy and end up "cutting our T[hroa]ts."[87]

Along with the "propitious" natural environment, which was too "luxuriant" to "generate the noble art of living upon little," slavery had also discouraged art, industry, and a respect for labor, other observers lamented. Nor was the diminution of the industry of whites the only "ill

---

[85] Arthur Lee to Philip Ludwell Lee, Nov. 5, 1763, Arthur Lee Papers, 1:2, bMS Am 811F, Houghton Library, Harvard University, Cambridge, Mass.

[86] Randolph, *History of Virginia*, 71, 202.

[87] *Virginia Gazette*, Apr. 21, 1738, Apr. 3, 1752; Randolph, *History of Virginia*, 96; [Mercer], "Dinwiddianae," 32.

Effect" slavery had "upon the Morals & Manners of our People." It also gave rise to such "Habits of Pride, and Cruelty in . . . Owners" as to make it unclear whether, as James Reid remarked, a "vicious, rich" slaveowner differed in any respect from "his . . . vicious, poor Negro, but in the colour of his skin, and in his being the greater blac[k]-guard of the two" and to raise the question of whether every such master should not in justice "be punished in hell by his own slaves."[88]

Tobacco and the excessive avarice it generated had thus "stained the country with all the pollutions and cruelties of slavery," and it was almost universally known, as George Mason, the learned Fairfax County planter and future author of the Virginia Declaration of Rights, pointed out in 1765, that "one of the first Signs of the Decay, & perhaps the primary Cause of the Destruction of the most flourishing Government that ever existed was the Introduction of great Numbers of Slaves—an Evil very pathetically described by the Roman historians." Some observers hoped that the evils of slavery might yet be mitigated if further importations of slaves were inhibited by high duties and "proper Encouragement" were offered "to white persons to settle the Country." "The Policy of encouraging the Importation of free People & discouraging that of Slaves has never been duly considered in the Colony," Mason complained, "or we shou'd not at this Day see one Half of our best Lands in most parts of the Country remain unsetled, & the other cultivated with Slaves." But the "blessings" to be expected from such a policy, another writer had bitterly remarked in the mid-1750s, were probably "too great" either "for the consent of a British Mother, or for the Option of a people already Infatuated & Abandoned."[89]

The fear that Virginians were indeed growing increasingly "Infatuated & Abandoned" was still a third—and infinitely the most powerful—internal source of social anxiety. Beginning in the late 1730s, a growing number of Virginians complained about the decline of the old values of industry, thrift, and sobriety; certain signs, they predicted, of the moral declension of Virginia society. Particularly disturbing was the exorbitant growth of luxury. Increasingly, after 1740, travelers and thoughtful members of the gentry alike remarked upon the "extravagance, ostentation, and . . . disregard for economy" in the colony, particularly among the

[88] Randolph, *History of Virginia*, 216; Mason, "Scheme for Replevying Goods . . . ," Dec. 23, 1765, *The Papers of George Mason*, ed. Robert A. Rutland, 3 vols. (Chapel Hill, N.C., 1970), 1:61–62; *Virginia Gazette*, Apr. 10, 1754; Reid, "Religion of the Bible," 49.

[89] Randolph, *History of Virginia*, 202; Mason, "Scheme for Replevying Goods . . . ," Dec. 23, 1765, *Papers of George Mason* 1:61–62; [Mercer], "Dinwiddianae," 30; Hansford,

wealthy, and Lieutenant Governor Francis Fauquier expressed alarm in 1762 at the planters' rising indebtedness to British merchants, which he attributed to the planters' unwillingness to "quit any one Article of Luxury." Certain it was that a growing number of gentlemen planters, including William Byrd III, Benjamin Grymes, and other scions of old gentry families, were rapidly bringing "ruin upon themselves by their extravagance" and were able to "screen themselves from ignominy only by the ostentation and allurements of fashionable life," which they could keep up only by plunging themselves ever further into debt.[90]

The ultimate consequences of this rising addiction to luxury were well known. "There are two pernicious Things in the Government of a Nation, which are scarce ever remedied," warned Mentor in the *Virginia Gazette* in 1752: "the first is an unjust and too violent Authority in Kings: the other is Luxury, which vitiates the Morals of the People." Of the two, luxury was more to be dreaded. Whereas "too great an Authority [only] intoxicates and poisons Kings," "Luxury poisons a whole Nation," as it

> habitates itself to look upon the most superfluous Things, as the Necessaries of Life; and thus every day brings forth some new Necessity of the same Kind, and Men can no longer live without Things, which but thirty years ago were utterly unknown to them. This Luxury is called fine Taste, the Perfection of Arts, and the Politeness of a Nation. This Vice[,] which carries in its Womb an infinite Number of others, is commended as a Virtue; it spreads its Contagion from the Great down to the very Dregs of the People: The Lowest Rank of Men would pass for greater than they are; and every one lives above his Condition, some for Ostentation, and to make a Shew of their Wealth; others through a mistaken Shame, and to cloak their Poverty. Even those who are so wise as to condemn so great a Disorder, are not so wise as to dare, to be the first to stem the Tide, or to set contrary Examples. Thus, a whole Nation falls to Ruin; all Conditions and Ranks of Men are confounded; an eager Desire of acquiring Wealth to support a vain Expence corrupts the purest minds; and when Poverty is accounted infamous, nothing is minded but how to grow rich. . . . Even those who have no Fortune, will appear and spend as

---

"My Country's Worth," 65–67; "Observations on Several Voyages . . . ," [1746], *William and Mary Quarterly*, 1st ser., 16 (1907): 6–9.

[90] Burnaby, *Travels*, 55; Fauquier to Board of Trade, Nov. 3, 1762, CO 5/1330, ff. 339–40, PRO; [Carter], *Letter from a Gentleman in Virginia*, 28–29; Randolph, *History of Virginia*, 279–80.

if they had, and so they fall to borrowing, cheating, and using a Thousand mean Arts to get Money. But who shall remedy these Evils? The Relish and Customs of a whole Nation must be changed; new Laws must be given them. And who shall attempt this unless the Great Men should prove to be so much of Philosophers, as to set an Example of Moderation themselves, and so, to put out of Countenance all those, who love a pompous Expence, and at the same Time, encourage the Wise, who will be glad to be authorized in a virtuous Frugality.

In his sermon on the peace in 1763, James Horrocks warned his listeners against too "great a Tendency amongst us to Extravagance and Luxury" and admonished them to eschew the "insignificant Pride of Dress, the empty Ambition of gaudy Furniture, or a splendid Equipage . . . which must undoubtedly serve more for Ostentation and Parade, than any real Use or valuable Purpose."[91]

But luxury was not the only sign of moral decay in mid-eighteenth-century Virginia: drunkenness and swearing seemed to be increasing at an alarming rate, and, beginning in the 1740s, a rampant "spirit of gaming" had broken "forth . . . in ways [equally] destructive of morals and estates." By the early 1750s gaming had become so "very fashionable among the young Men" of the colony that William Stith preached a sermon before the House of Burgesses on *The Sinfulness of Gaming,* and the pages of the *Virginia Gazette* contained numerous warnings on its evil effects.[92]

Charles Hansford spelled out the magnitude of the problem in verse in the early 1750s.

> For, oh, my country, it would not be right
> Nor just for me only to show thy bright
> And shining side! I fear thou hast a dark
> And gloomy one. Attend thee! Do but hark!
> The dice-box rattles; cards on tables flow.
> I well remember, fifty years ago
> This wretched practice scarcely then was known.
> Then if a gentleman had lost a crown

---

[91] *Virginia Gazette,* Dec. 29, 1752; Horrocks, *Upon the Peace,* 9–10, 14. See also the extended essay on the same theme, "The Virginia Centinal, No. X," in *Virginia Gazette,* Sept. 3, 1756.

[92] Randolph, *History of Virginia,* 61; *Virginia Gazette,* Feb. 28, Mar. 28, Sept. 5, 1751; Stith, *Sinfulness of Gaming.*

> At gleek or at backgammon, 'twere a wonder,
> And rumbled through the neighborhood like thunder.
> But many now do win and lose pistoles
> By fifties—nay, by hundreds. In what shoals
> Our gentry to the gaming tables run!
> Scoundrels and sharpers—nay, the very scum
> Of mankind—joins our gentry, wins their cash.
> O countrymen! This surely would abash
> Our sleeping sires! Should one of them arise,
> How would it shock *him*! How would it surprise
> An honorable shade to see his boy
> His honor, time, and money thus employ![93]

"What a damned situation our Country is in," complained James Mercer in 1754. "No money to be got but at Horseraces & Gaming Tables & that not sufficient to open the Eyes of the People who frequent those places & are worse than selling their Wives & Children." But it was not just that the rage for gambling, as Hansford put it, did "much harm / To some estates; 'tis like a spell or charm"; it also had devastating effects upon the character of the gamesters. The "prevailing Passion and Taste for Gaming[,] . . . Racing, Cards, Dice and all other such Diversions," warned James Horrocks, carried with them a "fatal Tendency" that ate away at the very foundations of Virginia society. Said Hansford,

> Honour, it stabs! religion it disgraces;
> It hurts our trade, and honesty defaces.
> But, what is worse, it so much guilt does bring,
> That many times distraction thence does spring.[94]

What was infinitely more frightening, however, was the increasing possibility that Virginians were already too far abandoned even to feel any guilt, that they had already proceeded too far along the road to corruption traveled by Rome to avoid the inner decay and destruction that were the ultimate fate of that once mighty empire. Indeed, so prevalent was the addiction to luxury and pleasure that the very character of Virginia society seemed to be changing. "I have observed," wrote "A

---

[93] Hansford, "My Country's Worth," 62–64.

[94] Ibid.; James Mercer to Daniel Parke Custis, May 31, 1754, Custis Papers, folder 1754–55, Virginia Historical Society; Horrocks, *Upon the Peace,* 9–10, 14.

Gentleman" to the *Virginia Gazette* in 1751, "that the Majority of those that claim" the "term GENTLEMAN . . . have abandoned themselves to such trifling or vicious Practices, and glory in them as their peculiar Badge and Characteristic, that I am afraid the unfashionable Minority who sustain the same Denomination, will not be able to preserve it in its original Reputation, especially since their Number and Influence seem [to be] daily declining. I am already," he added, "somewhat uneasy, when I am complimented with the Character; and indeed could not bear it, did I not take the Liberty to abstract from it the modern Ideas crowded under it, and assure the Company I am not a *Gamester, Cock-Fighter,* or *Horse-Racer* by Trade; that I speak *English,* not *Blasphemy;* that I drink to quench my Thirst, not to quench my *Reason;* &c."[95]

In the new scheme of things, "Learning and good sense; religion and refined morals; charity and benevolence" seemed to have "nothing to do in the composition" of a gentleman. To be sure, there were still a "discerning few" among the gentry in every county in whom "good sense abounds." Such men were truly "an honour to humanity, a glory to the Colony, and the luminaries of the County." But could this "unfashionable Remnant of Gentlemen of this antique Stamp" possibly stem the tide of fashion, the corrosive "degeneracy in morals which is so conspicuous all around us" and had already struck deep roots in Virginia society?[96]

For that degeneracy, various observers noted, proceeded from the very conditions of life in Virginia, from the ease, affluence, and indulgence and the lax—some said, vicious—"manner of Education" they promoted. "For the Youth" of Virginia, observed one English traveler, "partake pretty much of the *Petit Maitre* Kind, and are pamper'd much more in Softness and Ease than their Neighbours more Northward," with the result that "young Fellows" were "not much burden'd with Study" and, in sharp contrast to their fathers, learned to spend more of their "Time and Money in modish Recreations than in furnishing" their libraries "with valuable Collections, in charitable Distributions, or intellectual Improvements."[97]

Complained James Reid:

> Before a boy knows his right hand from his left, can discern black
> from white, good from evil, or knows who made him, or how he exists,

---

[95] *Virginia Gazette,* July 11, 1751.

[96] Ibid.

[97] Ibid.; "Observations on Several Voyages . . . ," 15–16; Reid, "Religion of the Bible," 48, 52, 53–57.

he is a Gentleman. Before he is capable to be his own master, he is told that he is Master of others; and he begins to command without ever having learned to obey. As a Gentleman therefore it would derogate greatly from his character, to learn a trade; or to put his hand to any servile employment. His dog & horse are his favourite companions, and a negro about his own age, stature & mental qualifications, whom he abuses and kicks for every trifle, is his satelite. He learns to dance a minuet, that is, to walk slowly up and down a room with his hat on, and look wondrous grave, which is an affectation of the body to hide the defects of the mind. He is taught too how to skip and caper when ever he hears a few horse hairs rubbed with rozin, scraped across the guts of a cat, and he procures a competent skill in racing and cock-fighting. With these accomplishments, and a small knowledge in cards and dice, he becomes a gentleman of finished education, of consummate politeness, that is impudence & ignorance, consequently he is fit to enter into gay company, and to be a companion, humble admirer, & favourite of the fair-Sex. There is no matter whether he can read or not, such a thing has nothing to do in the composition. He has money, land and negroes, that's enough. These things procure him every honour, every favour, every title of respect.[98]

How could men thus "brought up" possibly reverse the precipitous moral decline that seemed to have seized the colony? For Virginians, in common with all western Europeans, had been taught—most vividly by the example of Rome—that "revolutions of life" were inexorable: "Obscurity and indigence are the Parents of vigilance & economy; vigilance and economy of riches and honour; riches and honour of pride and luxury; pride & luxury of impurity and idleness; and impurity and idleness again produce indigence and obscurity." Were Virginians really on the downward turn in this irreversible wheel of fortune? "We need only to open our eyes," wrote James Reid, "to behold this in the most glaring colours. The father toils his body, vexes his mind, hurts his soul, & ruins his health to procure riches for his son, who not knowing the trouble of acquiring them, spends them without prudence, and sinks into his original obscurity with contempt, disgrace and mortification."[99]

Clergymen of all persuasions seconded Reid's opinion. During the Seven Years' War, the Presbyterian Samuel Davies developed at great

---

[98] Reid, "Religion of the Bible," 56.

[99] Ibid., 55–57.

length in a series of blistering sermons the proposition that the war was God's punishment for the colony's sins. The roots of Virginia's troubles, he announced, were its "Riches." Excessive wealth had produced so great a "deluge of Luxury and Pleasure" that wherever one looked he found not virtue but a surfeit of drunkenness, swearing, avarice, craft, oppression, prodigality, vanity, sensuality, gaming, and disobedience to superiors: the catalogue of Virginia's sins was endless. "O VIRGINIA! a Country happy in Situation, improved by Art, and hitherto blessed of Heaven," he cried in 1756, "but now undermined and tottering by thy *own sins*," sins so great that it could be said of the "Men of *Virginia*, as well as those of *Sodom, They are wicked, and Sinners before the Lord exceedingly.*"[100]

Anglican clergymen from James Blair in the late 1730s to William Stith in the early 1750s and James Horrocks in the early 1760s echoed these sentiments, albeit in the more moderate and less impassioned tones befitting their religious persuasion. "The Vice and Wickedness of a Nation," Stith had counseled the Burgesses in 1752, "are the certain Forerunners and Cause of its Disgrace and Destruction," and both Davies and Horrocks agreed that all signs suggested that the destruction of Virginia was imminent. Davies believed that the situation called for nothing less than "A THOROUGH NATIONAL REFORMATION" marked with "Repentance, Reformation and Prayer," and Horrocks, that a permanent return to the solid virtues of Virginia's forefathers was needed. In such an enterprise, responsibility fell heavily on those men of solid virtuous principles, that increasingly "unfashionable Remnant," which still in the early 1760s dominated both the House of Burgesses and the other major political institutions of the colony. How or even whether they could fulfill that responsibility was a question of crucial importance that Virginia society would soon have to confront.[101]

In the early 1760s—on the eve of the great political and emotional crisis that preceded the American Revolution—the Virginia political commu-

---

[100] Samuel Davies, *Virginia's Danger and Remedy* (Williamsburg, Va., 1756), 12, 16, 20–21, 23, 25, 28, 48, *Curse of Cowardice*, 8, 14–15, 33–34, *Religion and Patriotism* (Philadelphia, 1755), 10–12, 27–35, and *The Crisis: or, The Uncertain Doom of Kingdoms at Particular Times, Considered* (London, 1756), 28–35.

[101] Stith, *Sinfulness of Gaming*, 11–12, and *The Nature and Extent of Christ's Redemption* (Williamsburg, Va., 1753), 31; Horrocks, *Upon the Peace*, 9–10, 14; Camm, *Review of*

nity thus faced the future with an uncertain blend of anxiety and confidence. It was anxious over the unhealthy state of the tobacco market, the pernicious effects of black slavery upon white society, the disturbing crisis in moral behavior, and, more than at any time since the very first decade of the century, the colony's constitutional security within an empire whose leaders were showing disturbing signs of a growing disregard for the political welfare of its peripheral members. But it was also confident in the basic stability, responsiveness, effectiveness, and virtue of the Virginia political system and in the colony's long-term future within an empire which enjoyed so great a blessing, so great a security to liberty and property, as the British constitution. Over the next quarter of a century, this peculiar combination of anxiety and confidence would in considerable measure shape the responses of the Virginia political community to a series of political challenges of a magnitude undreamed of in 1763.

The earliest draft of this chapter was written in the summer of 1964 for a book Keith Berwick and I planned on the politics of Revolutionary Virginia. I gave it as a lecture entitled "The Conditions and Assumptions of Virginia Politics on the Eve of the American Revolution" at the University of Michigan at Ann Arbor on October 14, 1964, and at the History Faculty Seminar at Dartmouth College, Hanover, N. H., on March 8, 1965. An abbreviated version of the present draft was presented on April 5, 1973, at Miami University of Ohio, Oxford, Ohio, as one of the "McClellan Lectures on the American Revolution" under the title "Virtue and Liberty: A Case Study of the Revolution in Virginia," and, under the present title, at the Anglo-American Conference of Historians in London on July 9, 1976; at the English Institute of the University of Lyon, Lyon, France, March 19, 1977; and at the English Institute of the University of Bordeaux, Bordeaux, France, March 22, 1977. It was one of three papers on eighteenth-century Virginia politics considered at a seminar held in the Department of History at La Trobe University, Bundoora, Victoria, Australia, August 20, 1976. It is here reprinted with corrections and minor editorial changes from Richard M. Jellison, ed., *Society, Freedom, and Conscience: The Coming of the Revolution in Virginia, Massachusetts, and New York* (New York: W. W. Norton & Co., 1976), 17–76, 191–200.

Rector Detected, 20; Davies, *Virginia's Danger and Remedy,* 12, 16, 20–21, 23, 25, 28, 48, *Curse of Cowardice,* 8, 14–15, 33–34, *Religion and Patriotism,* 10–12, 27–35, and *The Crisis,* 28–35. See also "Robert Dinwiddie's Proclamation for a Fast," Aug. 28, 1775, *Virginia Gazette,* Sept. 12, 1755.

TWELVE

The Attempt to Separate the Offices of Speaker and Treasurer in Virginia, 1758–66:
An Incident in Imperial Conflict

THE PERIOD FROM 1740 TO 1776 was in many respects the golden age of Virginia politics. Those years witnessed the political ascendancy of the House of Burgesses and the emergence of that talented group of politicians who played such a prominent role both in effecting the separation of the colonies from Great Britain and in guiding the new nation through its first half century of independence. No man was more important in these developments than John Robinson, speaker of the Burgesses and treasurer of the colony. He filled those two posts for twenty-eight years, from 1738, two years after he had first entered the house at the age of thirty-two as a representative from the county of King and Queen, to his death in 1766.[1] Beginning in 1723 the Burgesses customarily combined the offices of speaker and treasurer. The treasurer was responsible for receiving from collectors all revenues arising from provincial laws and disposing of those revenues upon the Burgesses' order and the governor's warrant. Appointed to the post by an act of the legislature, the treasurer, in lieu of any established salary for the speakership, received a commission of 4 percent of all money passing through his office until 1748 and 5 percent after that date. Virginia speaker-treasurers were always powerful, and Robinson by virtue of his long tenure and immense popularity was unusually so, occupying a place second only to the lieutenant governor, the crown's chief representative in the

---

[1] The best biographical sketch of Robinson is William M. Dabney, "John Robinson, Speaker of the House of Burgesses and Treasurer of Virginia," M.A. thesis, University of Virginia, 1941.

colony. The attempt by metropolitan authorities between 1758 and 1766 to lessen the authority of both Robinson and the Burgesses by separating the offices of speaker and treasurer has never received the attention it deserves.[2]

Robinson was probably the most powerful native politician in eighteenth-century colonial Virginia. Some historians have attributed his enormous influence to his control over the treasury. Examination of his accounts after his death revealed that he had loaned large sums of public as well as private money to burgesses and councillors alike. This revelation gave rise to the assertion that he had made opportune loans to gain votes and influence in both chambers of the legislature. But the absence of any evidence of irregularity in his accounts before 1765 renders the validity of such an assertion doubtful. Indications are that the deficiencies in his accounts discovered in 1766 were of relatively recent origin.[3] Rather, it would seem that his power grew out of his tremendous reputation, as Edmund Randolph later pointed out, "for sound political knowledge and an acquaintance with parliamentary forms, a benevolence, which created friends and a sincerity which never lost one."[4] Lieutenant Governor Francis Fauquier paid Robinson high tribute in 1759 when he described him as "a Man of Worth, Probity and Honor; the most beloved both in his public and private Character of any Man in the Colony," and again in 1761 as "the Darling of the Country, as he well deserves to be for his great integrity, assiduity and ability in business."[5] He ran the Burgesses with an iron hand, brooking no opposition. "Whatever he agreed to was Carryed," Landon Carter confided to his diary in 1752, "and whatever he Opposed dropt."[6]

Both lieutenant governors William Gooch, who administered the col-

---

[2] Brief treatments of this attempt may be found in Percy S. Flippin, *The Royal Government in Virginia, 1624-1775* (New York, 1919), 212-13, 276; Thomas J. Wertenbaker, *Give Me Liberty: The Struggle for Self-Government in Virginia* (Philadelphia, 1958), 28, 210; and Richard L. Morton, *Colonial Virginia*, 2 vols. (Chapel Hill, N.C., 1960), 2:749-50.

[3] See George Chalmers, *An Introduction to the History of the Revolt of the American Colonies*, 2 vols. (Boston, 1845), 2:353-54; David J. Mays, *Edmund Pendleton, 1721-1803: A Biography*, 2 vols. (Cambridge, Mass., 1952), 1:176-77, 184.

[4] Edmund Randolph, *History of Virginia*, ed. Arthur H. Schaffer (Charlottesville, Va., 1970), 173.

[5] Francis Fauquier to Board of Trade, Apr. 10, 1759, and May 12, 1761, Colonial Office Papers, 5/1329, ff. 303-6, and 5/1330, ff. 129-35, Public Record Office, London.

[6] Jack P. Greene, ed., *The Diary of Colonel Landon Carter of Sabine Hall, 1752-1778*, 2 vols. (Charlottesville, Va., 1965), Mar. 12, 1752, 2:83.

ony from 1728 to 1749, and Fauquier, who assumed the governorship in 1758, got along well with Robinson. On the other hand, Robert Dinwiddie, who served as lieutenant governor from 1752 to 1758, disliked Robinson because of his opposition to Dinwiddie's imposition in 1752—without the consent of the House of Burgesses—of a fee of a pistole for signing and sealing patents for land. Robinson not only opposed Dinwiddie during the exciting pistole fee controversy in 1753–54 but actually proposed—without the approval of the governor and council—to pay Attorney General Peyton Randolph £2,500 to act as agent for the house against Dinwiddie in London.[7] Dinwiddie reported that Robinson had "behaved with great Warmth and ill Manners" to him during that controversy. From that time on it was his intention to break Robinson's power by separating the offices of speaker and treasurer. He was determined, he wrote agent James Abercromby in October 1754, "on calling a new Assembly to regulate it [the combined offices of speaker and treasurer] for the Future in a more Constitutional Method."[8]

Robinson's display of power during the Seven Years' War intensified Dinwiddie's dislike. Chalmers's observation that "in a practical view of government, Dinwiddie ruled on ordinary occasion[,] . . . But Robinson acted as dictator on all emergencies" was not much of an exaggeration.[9] Dinwiddie was forced to depend upon the Robinson-controlled Burgesses for supplies and men with which to wage war against the French. And when the Burgesses reappointed Robinson after the 1756 election, Dinwiddie was forced to consent to the appointment. Still, he had not abandoned his conviction that the offices of speaker and treasurer should be separated, although the necessity of securing military appropriations and of getting along with the Burgesses during the course of the war precluded any possibility of separating them at that time, as any attempt to do so would have certainly alienated both Robinson and the house. But Dinwiddie continued his campaign for separation in England after he stepped down as lieutenant governor. He brought the matter to the attention of the Board of Trade, which directed his successor, Fauquier, "to disunite the offices of Treasurer and Speaker if it could be done

---

[7] For a discussion of the pistole fee controversy, see Jack P. Greene, ed., "The Case of the Pistole Fee: The Report of a Hearing on the Pistole Fee Dispute before the Privy Council, June 18, 1754," *Virginia Magazine of History and Biography* 66 (1958): 399–422.

[8] Dinwiddie to Board of Trade, May 10, 1754, and to James Abercromby, Oct. 23, 1754, *The Official Records of Robert Dinwiddie*, ed. Robert A. Brock, 2 vols. (Richmond, 1883–84), 1:160–62, 373–76.

[9] Chalmers, *History of the Revolt* 2:353–54.

without prejudice to his Majesty's Service." In order to give the new governor some latitude in this "delicate Affair," the board did not make this direction a formal instruction.[10]

The "Eyes of the Country," Fauquier later learned, were upon him when he arrived in the colony in late spring of 1758. On the same ship came letters from Dinwiddie "publickly" proclaiming that he had procured an instruction to Fauquier ordering him to separate the offices of speaker and treasurer and exalting "it as a Victory gained over the Speaker." How Fauquier handled this matter could determine the success or failure of his whole administration. The course he followed was well chosen to please local political leaders. Shortly after his arrival, he submitted the board's direction both to the members of the council and to Attorney General Peyton Randolph, who "were all of Opinion that this could not be effected without the most manifest prejudice to his Majestie's Service and that the very attempting it might throw the Country into a Flame." Accordingly, Fauquier wrote the board that the "affair your Lordships recommended to me in regard to the Treasurership being annexed to the Speakers place, I am afraid will meet with great Difficulty, as it has been a Custom of so long standing and the present Gentleman is so popular and so sure of the Chair."[11] Further consultation with "many of the principal people" convinced Fauquier that it would be unwise to attempt to carry out the board's direction at that time. He learned that Robinson was "the most popular Man in the Country: beloved by the gentlemen, and the Idol of the people," and also that it was "an established Custom at least of long Date, though not from the beginning of the Colony, that the Assembly have elected their own Treasurer for all Monies by them raised for any publick Service: to be accountable to them, for the Disbursement of it."

These findings contributed to his decision not to attempt an immediate separation of the two offices. But the strong probability that such an attempt would invite retaliatory measures from the Burgesses was the primary consideration in that decision. Money was needed to fulfill obligations already incurred in the Seven Years' War and to pay for additional men and supplies, and Fauquier was informed that "not a penny" of it would be granted unless Robinson was allowed to continue as both

---

[10] W. W. Hening, ed., *The Statutes at Large: Being a Collection of All the Laws of Virginia* (Richmond, etc., 1809–23), 7:33–35; Fauquier to Board of Trade, Apr. 10, 1759, CO 5/1329, ff. 303–6, PRO.

[11] Fauquier to Board of Trade, June 11, 1758, Apr. 10, 1759, CO 5/1329, ff. 171–73, 303–6, PRO.

speaker and treasurer. Had Fauquier attempted to divorce the treasurership from the speakership, on one hand, he would have offended the Burgesses and would have forfeited any chance to secure more money for the war. On the other hand, failure to make such an attempt would likely have incurred the displeasure of London authorities. Faced with this dilemma, Fauquier decided to postpone any effort to divide the two offices until after the next session of the Burgesses "was over, the Money raised and the present Turn sewed."[12]

Having decided upon this course of action, Fauquier sought to win support from both the Burgesses and the Board of Trade. Suspecting that Robinson would learn of his inquiries and fearing that "he might take Umbrage at it and a Jealousy might arise, which might be detrimental to his Majestie's Service," Fauquier went directly to Robinson "and in the frankest Manner talked to him of it." This bold stroke had beneficial consequences. Robinson was highly pleased with Fauquier's candor, and Robinson's friends assured Fauquier that the openness of his behavior had firmly attached the speaker to him. In an effort to win the Board of Trade's approval, Fauquier sent a very frank relation of his conduct. He justified his decision to postpone any attempt at separation on the grounds that it would have prevented passage of additional military appropriations.[13]

But the board was not completely pleased with Fauquier's handling of the affair. It did not actually censure him but was obviously concerned about his inability to accomplish its direction. Thoroughly unsympathetic with the position of Robinson and the Burgesses, the board reiterated its opinion in January 1759 "that this practice, however warranted by long usage or the acquiescence of the Crown in the Acts which have been passed since 1738, for uniting those Offices, is both irregular and unconstitutional, and that a Governor ought not to give his assent to any such Acts for the future if it can be refused without manifest prejudice to His Majesty's Service." But in September 1758, before the board's reply was written in January, Fauquier at his first encounter with the newly elected Burgesses followed his original intentions and gave his assent to a measure to reappoint Robinson treasurer. The board's January letter reached him the following April, and he immediately replied in an effort to justify his conduct and to point out its beneficial results. He still believed that it would be impolitic to divide the two offices during Rob-

---

[12] Fauquier to Board of Trade, June 28, 1758, ibid., ff. 175–78, PRO.
[13] Ibid.

inson's lifetime, but if the board insisted, he offered to obey its directions.[14]

Fauquier's arguments persuaded crown officials not to disallow the law, but the Board of Trade was far from pleased with it. The board cautioned Fauquier not to pass such a law again. In addition, it emphasized the fact that it remained "convinced of the irregularity and impropriety of annexing the Office of Treasurer to the person of the Speaker by an express Clause in the Act contrary to the former practice and Custom of the Colony"—a conviction without foundation, for, as Fauquier later pointed out, the act was identical to the ones passed earlier by Gooch and Dinwiddie.[15]

Despite the board's objections, the wisdom of Fauquier's policy was soon evident. In September 1758 Fauquier reported that the "Step I took in Regard to the Speaker, has done me much Service as it has given him [Robinson] and all his Friends a great Opinion of the Openness of my Conduct." "I am if possible more and more convinced," he wrote, "that it will always be impracticable to separate the Offices of Speaker and Treasurer during the Life of Mr. Robinson, perhaps even after his Decease." Similarly, he wrote the board the following April that "I owe the Supply I have obtained this Year of Men and Money to the strong Support of himself [Robinson] and his Friends, for I am afraid the Disposition of the House in General was against encreasing the Debt of the Colony." Taken out of context and divorced from its aspersive implications, Chalmers's observation that Fauquier "entered into a league with Robinson, to divide the powers of government between them and to rule with equal sway" was in large part correct. Fauquier found, as had Gooch, that the secret of governing successfully in Virginia was to work closely with the group in power. The close relationship Fauquier established with Robinson on his arrival in the colony continued until the speaker's death and gave rise to a harmonious spirit which pervaded his entire administration.[16]

But the question came up again in 1761. George II's death prompted Fauquier to dissolve the Burgesses in mid-April of that year, and the

---

[14] Board of Trade to Fauquier, Jan. 14, 1759, CO 5/1367, 350–54; Fauquier to Board of Trade, Apr. 10, 1759, CO 5/1329, ff. 303–6, PRO; Hening, *Statutes* 7:242–44.

[15] Board of Trade to Fauquier, Nov. 20, 1759, CO 5/1367, 397–98; Fauquier to Board of Trade, Mar. 13, 1760, CO 5/1329, ff. 399–403, PRO.

[16] Fauquier to Board of Trade, Sept. 23, 1758, Apr. 10, 1759, CO 5/1329, ff. 185–90, 303–6, PRO; Chalmers, *History of the Revolt* 2:354.

treasurer issue had to be reopened by the newly elected house. He wrote the Board of Trade on May 12—a month after he had called for new elections—that the question would come up again in November and that he felt obliged to consent to Robinson's reappointment unless he received special instructions prohibiting it.[17] Fauquier sent the letter early enough so that with dispatch the board conceivably could have answered it by the following November, but the odds were against any rapid action. British administrative machinery normally moved slowly, a fact of which Fauquier was aware, and it is quite likely that he purposely waited to write until mid-May, a time which made it not impossible but highly improbable for the board to reply by early November. Fauquier well knew that to attempt a separation either with or without the crown's special instruction would have alienated the Burgesses and would have dashed his hopes to obtain money for the war. Yet he also knew that to pass another treasurer act without first asking permission of the board would incur its extreme displeasure. If the board was given ample warning and did not get its prohibition to him before he had passed the act, he could hardly be blamed for his action, especially in view of the pressing need for military appropriations.

If Fauquier had such calculations in mind, his timing was perfect. The Board of Trade, acting with relative dispatch on this occasion, still did not reply until September 10, when it repeated the sentiments that the treasurership should be detached from the speakership at the first opportunity. But Fauquier had already passed a new treasurer bill on November 14, before the board's letter arrived in Williamsburg. In February, Fauquier wrote apologetically to the board that he had again consented to Robinson's reappointment as treasurer. He explained that the board's letter had arrived after he had passed the act, but admitted that even if the letter had arrived in time he would "not have judged it proper to have tried the Experiment when it was mighty probable His Majesty would have required the Assistance of his Colonys to prosecute the war with Vigour."[18]

Fauquier had no further opportunity to divide the two offices until he again dissolved the house in May 1765, after it passed Patrick Henry's

---

[17] Fauquier to Board of Trade, May 12, 1761, CO 5/1330, ff. 129–35, PRO.

[18] Board of Trade to Fauquier, Sept. 10, 1761, CO 5/1368, 186–89; Fauquier to Board of Trade, Feb. 24, 1762, CO 5/1330, ff. 219–22, PRO; H. R. McIlwaine and John Pendleton Kennedy, eds., *Journals of the House of Burgesses of Virginia* (Richmond, 1906–15), *1761–65*, 26–27 (Nov. 14, 1761); Hening, *Statutes* 7:466–69.

resolutions against the Stamp Act. At that time he expressed his determination to consent to Robinson's reappointment to the treasurership if he was again chosen as speaker. Fauquier considered Robinson's opposition to Henry's radical measures sufficient justification for permitting him to continue in both offices, although the Board of Trade still insisted upon a separation if it could be accomplished without provoking a major altercation.[19] With Robinson's death in the spring of 1766 came the disclosure of his loans of large sums of public money to his indebted friends.[20] This revelation convinced the Burgesses that uniting the two offices placed too much power in the hands of a single individual, and the house solved Fauquier's problem by voluntarily detaching the treasurership from the speakership, appointing Robert Carter Nicholas as treasurer and Peyton Randolph as speaker. To compensate Randolph for the loss of income involved in the speaker's losing the treasurer's office, the Burgesses granted him an annual salary of £500, which was later raised to £600.[21] The Burgesses continued to follow this arrangement for the remainder of the colonial period.

This series of incidents clearly indicates the enormous power of both John Robinson and the Virginia House of Burgesses during the middle decades of the eighteenth century. By the 1750s and 1760s it was simply impossible to govern Virginia without the active cooperation of the Burgesses. To have attempted to alter, without the Burgesses' consent, a constitutional practice of such long standing in the colony as the union of these two offices would have created serious repercussions in Virginia politics, and Fauquier recognized that the success of his administration depended more upon his ability to get along with Robinson and the house than to carry out the Board of Trade's directive. As a part of the concerted assault on the power of colonial lower houses spearheaded by the earl of Halifax during his presidency of the Board of Trade from 1748 to 1761, the attempt to separate the offices of speaker and treasurer

[19] Fauquier to Board of Trade, June 5, 1765, CO 5/1331; Board of Trade to Fauquier, July 22, 1766, CO 5/1368, PRO.

[20] Mays, *Pendleton* 1:174–208, 358–85, gives an excellent analysis of this affair.

[21] See Hening, *Statutes* 8:210–14, 394–95, 587–88; *Journals of the House of Burgesses of Virginia, 1766–69*, 11 (Nov. 7, 1766); Robert Carter Nicholas to Colonel William Preston, May 21, 1766, Preston Papers, Draper MSS, 2 QQ 97, State Historical Society of Wisconsin, Madison; Fauquier to Board of Trade, May 11, 1766, and to Earl of Shelburne, Nov. 18, 1766, CO 5/1331, 5/1345, PRO; Dunmore's Answers to Board of Trade Queries, 1774, CO 5/1352, PRO; William Nelson to Edward and Samuel Athawes, Nov. 13, 1766, William Nelson Letter Book, Virginia State Library and Archives, Richmond.

might well have provoked a major controversy and become a serious element in the unfolding Revolutionary movement in Virginia. That it did not is a tribute to Fauquier's political deftness. Although metropolitan officials were never altogether pleased by his handling of the matter, they were perhaps fortunate to have a man of his talent on the job.

This chapter was written in 1962 for the journal in which it appeared. It is reprinted with minor changes and permission from the *Virginia Magazine of History and Biography* 71 (1963):11–18.

THIRTEEN

The Gadsden Election Controversy and the Revolutionary Movement in South Carolina

I N THE QUARTER CENTURY before the American Revolution the tempo of the almost continuous contest for power between the lower houses of colonial legislatures and the metropolitan organs of control increased perceptibly. For over a hundred years the lower houses had been gradually, and at times dramatically, whittling away at the powers of metropolitan officials, forging new principles of representative government, and developing an able group of political leaders. By the middle of the eighteenth century they had succeeded in almost every colony in shifting the center of political power from royal and proprietary authorities to themselves and had become remarkably sophisticated institutions. Called upon to operate on an even larger stage during the French and Indian War, they emerged from that conflict with an increased awareness of their own importance, at once more impatient of restraint and more tenacious of their powers and privileges. Symptomatic of these developments was the growing number of bitter controversies that characterized colonial politics during and immediately after the war. Fundamentally, these disputes resulted in large measure from the stubborn refusal of many crown officials to accept the new political order in the colonies or to admit that the lower houses were anything more than subordinate governmental agencies with only temporary and limited lawmaking powers. Such was the case with South Carolina's Gadsden election controversy. Provoked by Governor Thomas Boone's attempt to reform the colony's election practices, this controversy was the most heated political contest in the over forty years since the crown had assumed control of the colony. It kept South Carolina in turmoil for over nineteen months and was fraught with significance for the approaching Revolutionary movement.[1]

Fresh from a successful eighteen-month tour as governor of New Jersey, Boone had arrived in Charleston in December 1761 to assume the post of "His Majesty's Governor and Captain-General of South Carolina."[2] Carolinians greeted him warmly, and in his first months in Charleston he seemed to establish cordial relations with its people. A descendant of the Colletons, one of the oldest and most influential families in South Carolina, Boone was only thirty-one when he became governor of the colony. Educated at Eton and at Trinity College, Cambridge, he had first come to South Carolina in 1752, not long after his twenty-first birthday, to take over estates that he and his brother Charles had inherited from the widow of his uncle, Joseph Boone—long a leading figure in South Carolina's political and economic life. After two years in the colony, Boone returned to England, where he remained until 1759, when he once again came out to South Carolina. During this second visit he married a native of the colony, Sarah, the daughter of Thomas Tattnall and widow of Samuel Peronneau. Not long after his marriage, toward the end of 1759, he was appointed governor of New Jersey.[3]

Understandably, South Carolinians were generally enthusiastic over having a former resident for governor. During the initial weeks, the Commons House of Assembly and the council, the South Carolina Society and the Charleston merchants, the Charleston Library Society and the Charleston Artillery Company, and the Anglican and Presbyterian clergies showered him with formal addresses filled with warm congratu-

---

[1] Historians have never adequately treated the Gadsden election controversy. Joseph Johnson first dealt with it in his *Traditions and Reminiscenses, Chiefly of the American Revolution in the South* (Charleston, S.C., 1851), 5–13, but he compiled his cursory account from limited sources without reference to official records. Later historians, notably E. I. Renick in his essay "Christopher Gadsden," Southern History Association, *Publications* (Washington, D.C.), 2 (1898): 245–46, and Edward McCrady in his book *The History of South Carolina under the Royal Government, 1719–1776* (New York, 1899), 354–75, followed Johnson's account and added little to it, although McCrady made some use of materials in the *South Carolina Gazette* for the first time. W. Roy Smith used official records extensively in his *South Carolina as a Royal Province, 1719–1776* (New York, 1903), 339–49, to produce what is perhaps the best published account. Lewis B. Namier has presented much valuable new information in his articles "Charles Garth and His Connexions," *English Historical Review* 44 (1939): 443–70, and "Charles Garth, Agent for South Carolina," ibid., 632–52, which deal with Garth's role in the dispute.

[2] *South Carolina Gazette* (Charleston), Dec. 26, 1761.

[3] A brief account of Boone's life is in Namier, "Charles Garth and His Connexions," 462–70.

lations and "expressions of joy." Boone demonstrated his appreciation by presenting St. Michael's Church with a fine set of plate and St. Philip's with a gift "of equal value."[4] His relations with the council were amicable, and his dealings with the Commons House were not unpleasant. It seemed unlikely, even after half a year, that any controversy would arise to cloud this harmonious atmosphere.

Boone's effort to challenge the authority of the Commons House of Assembly interrupted the tranquillity of his administration.[5] Traditionally, some of the most wealthy, influential, and capable men in South Carolina were members of the Commons House, and by the middle of the eighteenth century that body had become the most powerful force in the politics and government of the colony. In its quest for increased authority during the first half of the century it had secured ironclad control over the colony's finances. Ingenious use of that control had won for it a variety of powers, including the right to nominate and appoint many public officers, among them supervisors of all public works and services; to exercise a fairly extensive control over its own composition and proceedings; and even to share in no small degree in the formation and administration of executive policy.[6] Among its most cherished powers was the right to determine the validity of the elections of its own members.

This power was essential to the Commons' control over its membership. It had been successfully asserted by the English House of Commons in 1604 in the cases of Goodwin and Fortescue and had been exercised freely by colonial lower houses from their inceptions. In South Carolina the Commons House had assumed this power at least as early as 1692, when it appointed a special committee to review some disputed elections, and by 1711 it had created a standing committee on privileges and elections.[7] But vagueness in the wording of a clause requiring members to take a state oath before the governor seemed to make it possible for him to refuse the oath to members whose credentials he did not ap-

---

[4] *South Carolina Gazette*, Dec. 26, 1761, Jan. 2, 9, 23, Feb. 6, 27, Mar. 6, 1762.

[5] Twenty years later William Bull II testified that Boone had been sympathetic to the governor and council in their disputes with the Commons during his earlier residences in the colony. William Bull II to Commissioners for American Claims, Mar. 15, 1785, Audit Office Papers, 13/125, Public Record Office, London.

[6] For a general treatment of the Commons' quest for power and the degree of its success, see Jack P. Greene, *The Quest for Power: The Lower Houses of Assembly in the Southern Royal Colonies, 1689–1776* (Chapel Hill, N.C., 1963).

[7] Mary Patterson Clarke, *Parliamentary Privilege in the American Colonies* (New Haven, 1943), 132–72, esp. 140–41.

prove, and thus a governor might conceivably usurp the power to determine the validity of elections.[8] Before Boone's administration, however, the only serious attempt by a governor to interfere with the exercise of that power by the Commons House had been the refusal by Francis Nicholson in 1725 to administer the oath to James Atkin, elected from the parishes of St. Thomas and St. Dennis, on the grounds that a bill of indictment was pending against him. The representatives immediately protested. "We are," they declared, "the Sole judges of our own priviledges & of the Qualifications of our own Members"; and in reply to a demand from Nicholson that they cite a precedent for this case from the proceedings of the British House of Commons, they showed that during the reign of Queen Elizabeth a member of Parliament, indicted for felony, had been allowed to retain his seat until convicted.[9] After a delay of almost a month—during which time he may have been acquitted—Atkin was allowed to take the oath; and no further executive intrusion upon the Commons' power to determine the eligibility of its own members occurred until the Gadsden controversy of 1762.

Governor Boone dissolved the Commons House that was in session when he arrived in the colony because it had been elected under a 1759 election law which had subsequently been disallowed by British authorities and issued writs for a new election to be held on January 26 and 27, 1762.[10] The newly elected Commons House, which first met Boone on February 6, 1762, was composed of forty-eight members. A much smaller number regularly occupied its major committee posts and dominated proceedings. Destined to assume the leading roles in this house were eleven men, most of them absentee or part-time planters and all of them men of considerable influence in the colony. Benjamin Smith (the speaker), Isaac Mazyck, Thomas Middleton, William Wragg, Robert Pringle, and William Roper were also among the most opulent merchants in Charleston; Rawlins Lowndes, Charles Pinckney, Peter Manigault, and James Parsons were successful and able lawyers; and Peter Taylor had earlier served the colony as commissary general. Taylor, Mazyck, and Middleton had been members of the Commons intermittently for over twenty years; Smith and Lowndes, for nearly fifteen; Pringle, Pinckney, Manigault, and Roper, for more than five; and Wragg was a

---

[8] Thomas Cooper and David J. McCord, eds., *The Statutes at Large of South Carolina*, 10 vols. (Columbia, S.C., 1836–41), 3:135–40.

[9] Journals of the Commons House of Assembly, Apr. 16, 1725, Colonial Office Papers, 5/428, 25, 27–28, PRO.

[10] *South Carolina Gazette*, Dec. 26, 1761.

former member of the council. For all their years of legislative experience, most of these men were relatively young. Pinckney and Parsons were still in their thirties; Smith, Middleton, Manigault, and Lowndes were all just over forty, five years younger than Wragg; Pringle and Roper were in their early fifties. The only leaders over sixty years of age were Mazyck and Taylor.

The new Commons House was elected under a statute of 1721 which established the qualifications of both voters and assemblymen, designated constituencies, apportioned representation, and regulated election procedure. The parish was the unit of representation, and church wardens were the election officials. They were to execute election writs issued by the governor and council, making sure that public notice was given at least two weeks before the election and that the polls were kept open for two successive days between 9:00 A.M. and 4:00 P.M. In addition, all election officials were required to take an oath before a justice of the peace for the faithful execution of the writs.[11]

The disallowance in London of the 1759 attempt to amend this electoral statute of 1721 gave Boone cause to examine it rather closely. He found it "so loose and general, so little obligatory on the Church Wardens, and so difficult in prescribing the forms to be observed" that on March 19, 1762, he recommended that the Commons enact a new measure. The committee to which this recommendation was referred received it unfavorably. Committee chairman Thomas Middleton reported on March 23 that no "bad consequence" or "objection" to the existing statute had been found, and the following morning the Commons informed Boone that it did not consider it "necessary at this time, to alter that Law."[12]

Boone's displeasure at the Commons' summary rejection of his recommendation led him to seize the first opportunity to demonstrate the error of their decision. When, in April 1762, Charles Lowndes declined the seat in the Commons to which he had been elected by the parish of St. Paul, Boone complied with a request from that body that he call a special election to fill the vacancy. In that election Christopher Gadsden, a thirty-six-year-old Charleston merchant-planter who had been a member of the Commons from 1757 to 1761, received nearly 80 percent of the votes in a three-way contest.[13] When the Commons reconvened in Sep-

---

[11] *Statutes at Large of South Carolina* 3:135–40.

[12] Commons House Journals, Mar. 19, 23, 24, 1762, CO 5/480, 41, 44, PRO.

[13] Ibid., Apr. 21, 1762, 72; Christopher Gadsden to the Gentlemen Electors of the Parish of St. Paul, Jan. 25, 1763, *South Carolina Gazette*, Feb. 5, 1763.

tember after a two-month recess, it found a blank election return from the churchwardens of St. Paul. In response to an inquiry by the Commons, the wardens declared that Gadsden had been duly elected. Upon further investigation, the Commons found that the wardens had neglected to take the oath for the faithful execution of the election as required by the statute of 1721—a discovery which it failed to enter upon its minutes. Still, although the letter of the law had been violated, the spirit obviously had not. The election had been carried on without any other irregularity, and Gadsden was the overwhelming choice of the St. Paul electors. Furthermore, in the past the Commons had occasionally admitted members returned as the result of elections in which the churchwardens had not been properly sworn. On September 13, therefore, the Commons declared Gadsden elected. Later in the day the necessary oaths in the house were administered to him, and two members were appointed to accompany him to the executive chamber to witness his taking of the state oath before the governor.[14]

Boone, however, had no intention of tendering Gadsden the state oath. While the debate over the St. Paul election was in progress in the Commons, he had asked that body to come to the council chamber with any bills it had ready to present for his approval. The Commons asked leave to be excused from attending the governor until it had finished its debate. Boone granted this request, but, curious to learn the subject of the debate, he examined the Commons' journals and found that the house had been considering the St. Paul election. Upon further inquiry into private sources, he learned that the churchwardens of St. Paul had not taken the oaths required by law. Expressing his astonishment that the Commons had admitted Gadsden, he quickly took advantage of the opportunity that this action afforded to prove the wisdom of his recommendations that the election act be revised. He refused to administer the state oath to Gadsden, charged the Commons with an "undeniable . . . infraction of the election act," and precipitately dissolved it.[15]

Later in the same day, September 13, Boone issued writs for the election of a new Commons House; and on the following day he wrote the Board of Trade of the dissolution, reporting that the representatives seemed "desirous of determining themselves the sole Judges of an Act of Assembly, under which they must be elected."[16] A month later, on Octo-

---

[14] Commons House Journals, Sept. 10, 13, 1762, CO 5/480, 154–58, PRO.

[15] Ibid., Sept. 13, 1762, 158–59.

[16] Boone to Board of Trade, Sept. 14, 1762, CO 5/377, ff. 157–58, PRO.

ber 12 and 13, the South Carolina voters responded by reelecting thirty-seven of the forty-eight members of the previous house. Of the earlier group of leaders, only Middleton, Taylor, and Pringle were missing. Of the eleven new men, seven had seen previous service in the house, among them Gadsden—who was returned by the electors of St. Paul by an "almost unanimous vote"—Henry Laurens, Richard Beresford, and Thomas Drayton. Laurens was one of the most affluent merchants in Charleston, and Beresford and Drayton were large planters. Perhaps the most prominent among those elected for the first time was James Moultrie, a rising young lawyer. Like most of their colleagues, these men possessed the additional advantage of membership in prominent South Carolina families. After a brief meeting in late October at which Benjamin Smith was again elected speaker, Boone prorogued the session for a month.[17]

When the Commons reconvened on Monday, November 22, it proceeded to business in the usual manner.[18] After the minutes of the last day of the preceding session had been read, the representatives proceeded to the council chamber at the request of the governor to hear his opening address. Boone restricted his speech to formalities, cheering the successes of the king's arms in Canada and Havana, pointing with pride to the tranquillity along the frontier, and recommending the amendment of laws relating to the militia and to Charleston buildings. The Commons spent the rest of Monday and all the following day in routine business and in preparing a reply to the governor's address. The task of composing that reply fell by tradition to a committee of the more important members. Accordingly, the speaker appointed Peter Manigault, Henry Laurens, Charles Pinckney, Isaac Mazyck, Christopher Gadsden, William Wragg, and David Oliphant to this committee. On Tuesday morning Chairman Manigault submitted the committee's mild and dutiful answer, which was amended slightly by the house, engrossed, and presented to the governor the following morning, November 24.[19]

Immediately after presenting its response, however, the Commons, instead of embarking upon the business recommended by the governor,

[17] Gadsden to Electors of St. Paul, Jan. 25, 1763, *South Carolina Gazette*, Feb. 5, 1763; Commons House Journals, Oct. 25–26, 1762, CO 5/480, 1–3, PRO.

[18] For a description of the opening of the house, see Mark De Wolfe Howe, ed., "Journal of Josiah Quincy, Junior, 1773," Massachusetts Historical Society, *Proceedings* 49 (1915–16): 451–52.

[19] Commons House Journals, Nov. 22–23, 1762, CO 5/480, 4–8, PRO.

turned its attention to the Gadsden election case of the previous September. It appointed a committee on privileges and elections, composed of John Rutledge, Rawlins Lowndes, Peter Manigault, Christopher Gadsden, David Oliphant, Charles Pinckney, William Scott, William Wragg, and Thomas Ferguson, to consider "the proceedings of the late Commons House of Assembly on the 13th of September last" and to report "whether by the said Proceedings the Election Act hath been Violated or Infringed." The Commons also charged the committee to consider "the Liberties and Privileges of this House, with regard to the right of determining their own Elections," and the governor's speech "at Dissolving the last General Assembly."[20]

On Tuesday, November 30, after six days of deliberation, the committee presented its report, which the Commons then debated most of the following Thursday and, on Friday morning, accepted with minor amendments. In the report the Commons asserted that "it is the undeniable fundamental and inherent Right & Privilege of the Commons House of Assembly . . . solely to examine and finaly determine the Elections of their own Members." Dismissing Boone's charge that it had violated the election law in the Gadsden case, the Commons argued that because churchwardens were sworn to execute the duties of their office at the time of their appointment, they were not expressly required to take special oaths for each election. The report also pointed out that inasmuch as Gadsden had been elected by a large majority and there had been no complaints about the election from the voters of St. Paul, the governor's charge that the Commons had attempted to dispense with the election act had no valid foundation. Further, the Commons denied that "the existence of the body of the People Representatives, either is, or ought to be owing to the Election Act; much less to a rigid Execution thereof," as Boone had implied in his dissolution speech. Instead, it asserted, "the right of the Inhabitants of this Province to be represented in the Legislature, is undeniably founded, not upon that Act, but in the known and ancient Constitution of our Mother Country, therefrom Originally derived, and always to have appertained to, and been exercised by them, as British Subjects, which right is confirmed to them by Charter"—an unmistakable declaration that the right of representation was one of the traditional rights of Englishmen and as such was an inherent right of the freemen of South Carolina. The Commons concluded its report with four resolutions modeled closely after those which had been

---

[20] Ibid., Nov. 24, 1762, 13.

adopted by the English House of Commons in 1702 in the case of *Ashby* v. *White.*[21]

The resolutions adopted by the South Carolina Commons declared that the right to determine validity of elections belonged solely and absolutely to the representatives of the people; that constitutionally the governor could take notice of only such actions of the house as were formally set before him; that Boone's refusal to administer the state oath to Gadsden after he had been declared duly elected by the Commons "was a breach of . . . Privileges"; and "that the abrupt and Sudden dissolution of the last Assembly, for matters only Cognizable by the Commons House, was a most precipatate, unadvised unprecedented Procedure; of the most dangerous Consequence, being a great Violation of the Freedom of Elections, having a Manifest Tendency to Subvert and destroy, the most Essential and invaluable rights of the People, & reduce the Power and Authority of the House to an Abject dependence on, & Subserviency of the Will, & Opinion of a Governor."[22] On Monday, December 6, the whole house waited on Boone with the report and resolutions, together with a remonstrance prepared by the committee on privileges and elections which appealed to the governor to support the Commons in "that essential and fundamental privilege of Solely examining and determining the Validity of the Election of their own Members."[23]

Boone was ready with his reply the following day. Haughtily refusing to give ground, he continued to hold that Gadsden had not been elected because the churchwardens had not taken the required oaths. He refused to acknowledge the Commons' contention that the churchwardens' initial oath of office qualified them to execute the writs of election and pointed out the difference between the two oaths. The governor argued that the Commons House existed only by the election act and that if that act was disallowed the people would be without representation. He also denied that the house had the sole power to determine its own elections, both because the governor was required by his commission to supervise elections and because of the danger that a lower house might determine an election contrary to law. Boone explained that the "last Commons house of Assembly . . . having endeavoured to give Validity

[21] Ibid., Nov. 30–Dec. 3, 1762, 19–27. The resolutions of the English House of Commons in the case of *Ashby* v. *White* may be found in Thomas P. Taswell-Langmead, *English Constitutional History,* 10th ed. (Boston, 1946), 301–2.

[22] Commons House Journals, Dec. 3, 1762, CO 5/480, 27–29, PRO.

[23] Ibid., Dec. 4–6, 1762, 31–33.

to an Election which the law did not warrant, Violated that law, and assumed a power they had no right to." Applauding himself "for having checked Constitutionally so dangerous an Usurpation," he informed the Commons that it had "a good and gracious Sovereign ever ready to discountenance oppression, and to brush [aside] an arbitrary and imperious Governor that dares to trampel on the people's liberties," and suggested that it refer its "Complaints to the Royal Ear."[24]

The Commons immediately ordered its committee on privileges and elections to prepare a reply and suspended business in the house until one could be drafted. The committee labored all day Wednesday, and on Thursday Gadsden submitted its effort to the house. Public interest in the controversy was great, and during the debate over the reply, observers crowded the doors of the Commons and milled about outside the State House.[25] By late Friday the Commons had decided to accept the committee's statement without change, and on Saturday, December 11, it instructed the committee to deliver the response to Boone.

In this reply the Commons reasserted its former contention that Gadsden's election was valid and again denied that the existence of the Commons House depended on the election law. It argued that if the present election law was disallowed, the Commons House would be elected by the previous election law and so on retrogressively to the proprietary charter itself. In fact, the Commons maintained, the charter merely confirmed "the natural right of the *Freemen* of this Province to be Represented." The Commons also reiterated its right to review elections of its members, observing that "we are far from thinking that Your Excellency has prov'd the last House guilty of any, much less a 'Dangerous Usurpation[,]' which we humbly apprehend ought to have been done before Your Excellency coud with any Propriety applaud yourself for having Constitutionally check'd it."[26]

Boone continued, however, to deny satisfaction to the Commons, and on December 16, after a three-day adjournment, the assembly resolved by a vote of 24 to 6 to do no further business with the governor until he had apologized for violating its rights and privileges.[27] This action was taken despite formidable opposition from William Wragg and probably

---

[24] Ibid., Dec. 7, 1762, 36–38.

[25] See Gadsden to Electors of St. Paul, Jan. 25, 1763, *South Carolina Gazette*, Feb. 5, 1763.

[26] Commons House Journals, Dec. 9, 1762, CO 5/480, 39–46, PRO.

[27] Ibid., Dec. 16, 1762, 48–49.

Henry Laurens, who sided with the house on the constitutional question but thought it unwise to put a complete stop to public business.[28] The Commons also directed the joint committee of correspondence, composed of four councillors and eighteen assemblymen, to transmit a full account of the dispute to the colony's London agent, Charles Garth. Because the number of assemblymen far exceeded the number of councillors and because the presence of the councillors was not required to conduct business, this committee was completely controlled by the representatives. Among the members from the Commons were Pinckney, Manigault, Rutledge, and Gadsden—the most active members of the committee on privileges and elections—as well as such other leaders as Speaker Smith, Mazyck, Lowndes, Laurens, Parsons, and Wragg.[29]

The report of this committee was not completed until February 14, 1763, and in the meantime some of its members became deeply involved on opposing sides of a newspaper argument concerning the controversy. While the Commons' reply was being presented to the governor on December 11, Peter Timothy's *South Carolina Gazette* came off the press with a short satiric advertisement by "Auditor Tantum," announcing the forthcoming publication of a treatise which would prove the rights and privileges of the people to be "ultimately *permissive*, not *inherent*" and would advance "another altogether new and important discovery," namely, that "the foundation of the present El——n of any M——r of A——y is in a *particular* oath of the Ch—— W——n, and not in the choice of the freemen of the pa——sh."[30] Another month passed, however, before the controversy in the press began in earnest. The main issue was whether the Commons had sufficient cause to justify putting a complete stop to public business. Those who held that the cause was not sufficient were headed by William Wragg and aired their views in bookseller Robert Wells's *South Carolina Weekly Gazette*. The defenders of the Commons' action, led by Gadsden, found an outlet in Peter Timothy's paper.

---

[28] See William Wragg's letter to the Electors of St. John's Parish, Colleton County, Dec. 13, 1762, *South Carolina Gazette*, Feb. 5, 1763.

[29] The other members from the Commons were William Roper, Thomas Lynch, David Oliphant, Thomas Wright, Richard Beresford, James Moultrie, John Beale, and Ebenezer Simmons. See Commons House Journals, Nov. 24 and Dec. 24, 1762, CO 5/480, 15–16, 50, PRO. For a study of the winning of control by the Commons over the colonial agent and the committee of correspondence see Greene, *Quest for Power*, 267–72.

[30] *South Carolina Gazette*, Dec. 11, 1762. The similarity in language and style of this piece to Gadsden's later letters to the press suggests that he was the author.

Wragg initiated the argument. He had headed those in the Commons who opposed the decision to suspend business, and in the January 5, 1763, issue of the *South Carolina Weekly Gazette* he published a letter addressed to the electors of his constituency—St. John, Colleton—justifying his opposition. Pointing out that Boone's adamant refusal to change his position meant that the final settlement of the dispute would have to be made by officials in England, he argued that a complete suspension of business by the Commons would gain the colony nothing. On the contrary, he contended, it would result in a number of ill consequences, including destruction of the public credit, withdrawal of the garrison at Fort Prince George on the frontier, interference with the application of South Carolina's London agent for its share of the parliamentary grant to the southern colonies, and failure of the house to replace money borrowed from the township fund for the purpose of encouraging the settlement of Protestants in the colony. It was even possible, Wragg further suggested, that the crown would approve Boone's stand.[31]

Gadsden answered Wragg in the February 5 issue of the *South Carolina Gazette*. In an open letter to the "Gentlemen Electors of the Parish of St. Paul," he countered Wragg's objections and vigorously defended the Commons' actions. He declared that the Commons' decision to cease business was "absolutely necessary" and the "only step that a *free* assembly, *freely* representing a *free* people, that have any regard for the preservation of the happy constitution handed down to them by their ancestors . . . could *freely* take." Gadsden built his case on two premises: that representatives ought to be freely chosen by the voters and that election returns ought to be freely examined by the representatives so chosen. Writing that "*free* men . . . have an *inherent* not *permissive* right to be so," he contended that individual freedom depended upon the freedom of the lower house and that the right to determine elections "is so unalienable and inherent in the people, that they can be no longer denominated a free people when it is parted with; because all their *freedom* as British subjects most essentially depends on it." This right, he argued, was the sine qua non of the legislative body, conceded to Parliament by the Act of Settlement and brought by English emigrants to America. No free Briton, he declared, would, "like Esau," sell his "birth-right for a mess of pottage."

Gadsden's assertions that the dispute could "be constitutionally decided only by a British parliament," and that before English subjects

---

[31] No copy of the paper in which this letter was first published is extant, but it was reprinted in *South Carolina Gazette*, Feb. 5, 1763.

could be deprived of the rights and liberties of their birthright, "they must be tried and condemned *by their peers*," were designed to counter Wragg's suggestion that the crown might favor Boone; and they seemed, as Boone later interpreted them, "to acknowledge . . . no other authority than the Parliaments" and to "expressly deny . . . the King's power to determine in matters of . . . privilege."[32] At the very least, these assertions suggested a marked reluctance to admit the right of London officials to rule on questions of parliamentary privilege. In addition, Gadsden proposed that the colonies unite in appointing one general agent to protect the "*natural* privileges" of British subjects in America; and he also gave early expression to an attitude his countrymen were to use frequently two years later. By asserting that the right of representation was a "natural right" and that because Americans did not vote for members of Parliament they could be represented only in their own legislative assemblies, he was in effect rejecting the British theory of virtual representation and anticipating the arguments used by Americans during the Stamp Act crisis.

Gadsden's letter did not end the battle in the press. On February 28 former chief justice William Simpson and merchant-assemblyman Henry Laurens published anonymous replies to Gadsden's letter in the *South Carolina Weekly Gazette.* Simpson's brief letter accused Gadsden of having been motivated by a "passion for popularity" and, supporting Boone's contention that the Commons had violated the election act in the Gadsden case, questioned the wisdom of the Commons' dispensing with laws.[33] No copy of Laurens's letter now exists, but it was apparently the result of a long-standing conflict with Gadsden and seems to have been largely a personal attack on him. The March 12 issue of the *South Carolina Gazette* carried Gadsden's reply, which identified Simpson and Laurens as the authors of the two anonymous letters and parried their attacks without adding to his earlier arguments. The newspaper war continued for another two months, as anonymous writers debated the wisdom of the Commons' decision to suspend business with the governor.[34]

---

[32] *South Carolina Gazette*, Feb. 5, 1763. For Boone's comments on Gadsden's letters, see his letters to the Board of Trade, Mar. 29 and Sept. 15, 1763, CO 5/377, ff. 213–14, 233–35, PRO.

[33] Simpson's letter, dated Feb. 9, 1763, was reprinted in *South Carolina Gazette*, Mar. 12, 1763.

[34] On Mar. 26, 1763, "By-Stander" wrote in support of Gadsden in Timothy's *South Carolina Gazette* and on Apr. 23 was defended in the same paper—by "By Stander's

While the battle in the press was going on, news of the controversy reached London. On March 9 the Board of Trade received a letter from Boone, presenting his side of the controversy and complaining of the Commons' action.[35] Although the board offered the opinion that Boone's September dissolution of the Commons was "without sufficient reason," it ignored the question of whether he had violated the Commons' power to determine the validity of elections of its members, and it handed down no official censure of either side.[36] On February 14 the Commons' committee of correspondence completed a long report on the controversy, which included all official documents pertaining to it and Gadsden's letter to the St. Paul electors. Significantly, Wragg and Laurens, both of whom had opposed the Commons' decision to discontinue business with Boone, did not sign the completed report. The committee sent the report to agent Charles Garth, in London, who arranged for its publication as a pamphlet entitled *A Full State of the Dispute betwixt the Governor and the House of Assembly.* At the direction of the committee, Garth distributed copies of the pamphlet to the other colonial agents resident in England and, in all probability, circulated it among some colonial officials, but he did not submit it officially to the Board of Trade until July 1764.[37] Indeed, Garth was in an awkward position. Governor Boone, who was his first cousin, had been largely responsible for obtaining the South Carolina agency for him, and he now found himself compelled by his position—to the disadvantage of his relative and benefactor—to do the bidding of the Commons House.

Standby"—from an attack by "Man in the Moon," which had been printed in Wells's *South Carolina Weekly Gazette.* On Apr. 30 Timothy published an unsigned letter praising the Commons' conduct in the controversy and deploring any action "to obtain peace at the expense of freedom"—this in response to an adverse communication appearing in the *Weekly Gazette* of Apr. 20. On July 2 Timothy printed two unsigned pieces complaining about the Commons' refusal to proceed to business at a time when action was needed to meet a growing smallpox epidemic.

[35] Boone to Board of Trade, Dec. 17, 1762, CO 5/377, ff. 171–72, PRO.

[36] *Journal of the Commissioners for Trade and Plantations,* 14 vols. (London, 1920–38), 11 (*1759–63*):342 (Mar. 9, 1763).

[37] See South Carolina Committee of Correspondence to Garth, Sept. 29, 1763, and his reply, Jan. 7, 1764, Garth Letter Book, as cited in Namier, "Charles Garth and His Connexions," 466. Despite several attempts I was unable to gain access to the one extant copy of this letter book that is now in private possession. Copies of the pamphlet, *A Full State of the Dispute,* may be found in CO 5/377, ff. 373–414, and in Treasury Solicitor Papers, bundle 5158, PRO; among the Hardwicke Papers, Additional Manuscripts 35910, ff. 251–91, British Library, London; and in the New-York Historical Society, New York.

Back in South Carolina, relations between Boone and the Commons had not improved. The Commons rigidly adhered to its resolution of December 16 and refused to meet at the governor's command, although it was technically in session to December 28, 1762, and from January 24 to March 28 and April 6 to 19, 1763. But a quorum did not appear until Boone called the house together in early September 1763, with a fervent appeal for measures to check recent attacks by the Creek Indians.[38]

Despite the apparent urgency of the situation, the Commons showed little inclination to resume business with Boone. Nor was the situation improved when the governor attempted to make innovations in the traditional procedure for qualifying new representatives. Several newly elected members, chosen in special elections to fill vacancies in the house, appeared at this session to take their seats. Normally, after new members had taken the necessary oaths in the house, they were sent to the governor to take the state oath. Customarily, two previously qualified members accompanied them to serve as witnesses. Accordingly, on September 5, the speaker sent Gadsden and James Moultrie to see Sir John Colleton, returned for St. John's Parish, Berkeley County, take the state oath. Boone's refusal to administer the oath to Colleton until Gadsden and Moultrie had retired was deeply resented by the Commons, which admitted Colleton only after he had presented satisfactory proof that he had taken the oath.[39] A week later Boone further offended the house by refusing to tender the oath to four other newly elected representatives until he had checked the Commons' journals to see if they had qualified as members. This last action aroused a storm of protest in the Commons, which declared it "a New Insult to & breach of Priviledge of the House."[40]

Even before these incidents, the Commons had again turned its attention to the Gadsden election dispute. On September 3 it appointed a committee composed of Gadsden, Manigault, Pinckney, Rutledge, Parsons, Thomas Wright, and Thomas Drayton to prepare an address to the crown on the causes of the controversy.[41] The first four of these were members of the committee on privileges and elections that had reported against the governor the previous December, and, as might have been expected, the address that this new committee submitted to the house

---

[38] Commons House Journals, Sept. 2–3, 1763, CO 5/478, 14–15, PRO.

[39] Ibid., Sept. 5–12, 1763, 17–23, 27.

[40] Ibid., Sept. 12–13, 1763, 28–29.

[41] Ibid., Sept. 3, 1763, 16.

on September 10 was a wholesale denunciation of Boone. It accused him of "taking upon himself to be the sole Judge of Elections" and of having dissolved the house "for no other reason but because their Determination was not agreeable to his Sentiments." The right "solely to Judge and finally determine the Validity of the Election of their own Members," the committee asserted, was "the most Valuable of our Priviledges[,] . . . the possession or want whereof We humbly conceive must denominate us to be either Freemen or Slaves." The address further declared that Boone's refusal to apologize for violating that right had been responsible for the interruption of public business for over eight months and asked redress from the crown. The Commons' acceptance of this address on September 13, 1763, exactly one year after Boone's precipitate dissolution of the previous house, was followed by the retirement of many members to their homes, and the house was again unable to meet for want of a quorum.[42]

To counteract the Commons' address to the crown, Boone wrote immediately to the Board of Trade. His earlier letters, in March and May 1763, had acquainted the board with the Commons' continued refusal to meet and had attempted to justify his conduct in the dispute.[43] In his letter of September 15 he reiterated his charges, complaining particularly of the Commons' having condemned him "for exerting the authority which the King had invested [him] . . . with." He warned that "if a Governor is to be called to an Account by a subsequent Assembly, for dissolving a former one even supposing him to be mistaken[,] . . . there is an End to the Exercise of this branch of the Prerogative in America" and added that "it seems . . . absurd that the inferior, offending, corrected party, should have the power of Judging the Conduct of the superior correcting Magistrate." Denying that the Commons' privilege to examine and determine the election of its own members could "operate against a positive law," he pointed out that "in the famous Case of Ashby & White the Resolutions of the House of Commons were qualified by the very material words 'in all cases not otherwise provided for by Act of Parliament.'"[44]

Boone's letter arrived at the Board of Trade on December 1, 1763. Two weeks earlier the Commons' address to the crown had reached Garth, who submitted it to the Privy Council on November 18. Upon the advice

---

[42] Ibid., Sept. 10, 13, 1763, 25–26, 30.

[43] See letters of Boone to Board of Trade, Mar. 29, 1763, and May 31, 1763, CO 5/377, ff. 213–14, 215–16, PRO.

[44] Boone to Board of Trade, Sept. 15, 1763, ibid., ff. 233–35.

of the Board of Trade, the Privy Council's committee on plantation affairs decided to postpone consideration of it until the governor could return to England.[45] Although Boone had been granted leave to return home at the time of his transfer from New Jersey to South Carolina, he had decided not to take advantage of the leave at that time, and because of the "doubtfull situation of So. Carolina" he continued to postpone his return.[46] As a result, London authorities took no further action until June 1764, when Boone finally decided to take his leave.

In the meantime, Boone made two further efforts to reestablish a working relationship with the members of the South Carolina Commons. Following a Creek Indian raid on the backcountry settlement at Long Canes on Christmas Eve, he reconvened the Commons in early January 1764. He opened the session with an urgent request for measures to protect the frontier settlements and was careful to say nothing that would offend the house. He even administered the necessary state oath to new representatives according to the traditional procedure, with two previously qualified members as witnesses. Still, the Commons would not resume business with the governor. A motion to discharge the resolution of December 16, 1762, failed to pass on January 6, 1764, and the members again dispersed.[47] In a letter to the Board of Trade deploring the representatives' inaction, Boone charged that "the Members of the Commons house of Assembly having their plantations near the Sea Coast, & in a state of Security, are deaf to the Cries of the back Settlers."[48] A subsequent attempt, in April, to persuade the Commons to provide for

---

[45] W. L. Grant and J. Munro, eds., *Acts of the Privy Council of England, Colonial Series,* 6 vols. (London, 1908–12), 4:612 (Nov. 18, 1763); Garth to South Carolina Committee of Correspondence, Jan. 7, 1764, Garth Letter Book, as cited in Namier, "Charles Garth and His Connexions," 466.

[46] Namier, "Charles Garth and His Connexions," 463–64.

[47] Commons House Journals, Jan. 4–6, 1764, CO 5/481, 2–6, PRO.

[48] Boone to Board of Trade, Jan. 21, 1764, CO 5/377, ff. 427–28, PRO. Writing about the same time, Henry Laurens complained that "one poor rash head-long Gentleman [unquestionably Christopher Gadsden] who has been too long a ringleader of people engaged in popular quarrels, lately declared in full Assembly that he would rather submit to the distruction of one half of the Country than to give up the point in dispute with the Governor . . . but it happens that he lives within the Walls of Charles Town if he was a settler at long Canes or even had one Thousand pounds at stake there he would sing a different note. Our Frontier inhabitants are not very much obliged to him for his tenderness altho the Indians may be." Laurens to Captain Christopher Rowe, Feb. 8, 1764, Laurens Papers, Historical Society of Pennsylvania, Philadelphia.

settling some newly arrived French Protestants also failed,[49] and the house did not transact any business until after Boone had left the colony in May.

Having received no decision from the London authorities relative to the controversy between him and the Commons, Boone wrote the Board of Trade on April 19, 1764, that he intended to make use of his leave of absence to return to England, and on May 11 he departed from the colony without ceremony, leaving the government in the hands of Lieutenant Governor William Bull II.[50] He arrived in Britain on June 28, nearly three weeks after the earl of Halifax had officially ordered him home to give an account of the controversy.[51]

Three days before Boone's arrival in London, Garth had asked the Privy Council's committee on plantation affairs for action on the Commons' address of September 1763 to the crown. The committee referred the matter to the Board of Trade, and on July 2 Garth sent a copy of the *Full State of the Dispute* to the board and asked to be heard in behalf of the Commons.[52] At the hearing, held on July 13, Boone appeared on his own behalf without counsel, while Garth and John Dunning, member of the Middle Temple and one of the most famous pleaders of his time, presented the case for the Commons. For six hours the case was argued before the board,[53] and on July 16 the board presented its report to the Privy Council. The board decided that "the Governor appears . . . to have taken up the matter in dispute with more Zeal than prudence and . . . to have been actuated by a degree of Passion and Resentment inconsistent with good Policy, and unsuitable to the dignity of his Situation," but at the same time it found the conduct of the Commons in neglecting the public business censurable. To "quiet the Minds of the People, & to prevent Disputes of the same nature from arising for the future," the

---

[49] Commons House Journals, Apr. 19–23, 1764, CO 5/481, 7–10, PRO.

[50] Boone to Board of Trade, Apr. 19, 1764, and Bull to Board of Trade, May 16, 1764, CO 5/377, f. 433, PRO.

[51] Charles Garth's Memorial to Board of Trade, July 2, 1764, CO 5/377, ff. 371–72; Earl of Halifax to Boone, June 9, 1764, CO 5/390, f. 34, PRO.

[52] Charles Garth's Memorial to Privy Council, June 25, 1764, Order in Council, June 26, 1764, Garth's Memorial to Board of Trade, July 2, 1764, CO 5/377, ff. 364–65, 367, 371–72, PRO.

[53] *Journal of the Commissioners for Trade and Plantations*, 12 (*1764–67*):99 (July 13, 1764); Garth to South Carolina Committee of Correspondence, July 20, 1764, Garth Letter Book, as cited in Namier, "Charles Garth and His Connexions," 469.

board recommended that the governor be instructed to appoint deputies to administer the state oath.[54] The following day the Privy Council accepted this report, ordering copies of it given to both Boone and Garth.[55] At a subsequent hearing before the Privy Council, on July 28, Charles Yorke, lawyer and later lord chancellor, appeared in Boone's defense; but the Privy Council did not countermand the board.[56]

The board's report was clearly unsympathetic to Boone's position. Because it did not uphold the governor in his attempts to usurp the power of determining the validity of elections from the Commons, this decision, coupled with the metropolitan authorities' replacement of Boone by Lord Charles Greville Montagu in 1766, represented a victory for the lower house. Thereafter no one questioned the Commons' exclusive power to determine the validity of elections of its own members. Future governors hesitated to revive a dispute which had broken one of their predecessors. So long as Lieutenant Governor Bull remained at the head of the colony, the Commons was content to allow the governor to administer the state oath in accordance with former practice. In fact, not until July 1769 did the Commons remind Governor Montagu of the board's recommendation and ask him to appoint deputies to administer the oath, a request he willingly granted by appointing six leading members of the house.[57]

Only one question remained to be settled: Boone's unpaid salary from the colony. Normally the Commons granted an annual stipend of £500 sterling to its governor to supplement his salary of £1,000 sterling paid by metropolitan authorities, but as a result of his dispute with the house, Boone had received no salary at all from the province during the period of his service in the colony. After his return to England, therefore, he submitted a memorial to colonial officials asking for £1,250, the usual "country salary" for two and a half years, to be paid out of the South Carolina quitrents.[58] The Board of Trade referred the request to the

---

[54] Board of Trade to Privy Council's Plantation Affairs Committee, July 16, 1764, CO 5/404, 226–29, PRO.

[55] *Acts of the Privy Council, Colonial* 4:612 (July 17, 1764).

[56] Ibid., 4:612 (July 28, 1764). The brief prepared by Boone's solicitor for Yorke's use in this hearing, entitled "Governor Boone's State of the Dispute between Himself & the Commons House of Assembly in South Carolina," is in the Hardwicke Papers, Add. MSS 35910, ff. 233–50, British Library.

[57] Commons House Journals, July 11, 13, 1769, 38:43, 51–52, South Carolina Archives Department, Columbia.

[58] Boone's Memorial to Lords of Treasury, Nov. 25, 1765, CO 5/378, ff. 15–16, PRO.

Privy Council's committee on plantation affairs, which agreed with the board that the Commons' action in withholding Boone's pay was unjust and a precedent which might "operate to the prejudice and discouragement of Your Majesty's Service . . . by awing and deterring . . . Governors from the due and faithful execution of their duty." Further, the committee directed the board to issue an additional instruction to the governor of South Carolina to ask the Commons to make good the arrears of salary due to Boone.[59] The board acted accordingly, and Lord Montagu, Boone's successor, submitted the instruction to the Commons in 1766. Although it denied that it had erred in withholding Boone's pay, the Commons, elated over the recent repeal of the Stamp Act, acceded to the royal instruction and closed the case by providing for the former governor—in part, perhaps, as a reward for his services in lobbying for the repeal.[60]

To construe the Gadsden election controversy as a precursor or a cause of the American Revolution would be to interpret it in terms of later developments rather than in the context in which it occurred. The dispute was simply a further incident, perhaps more intense than most, in the century-long struggle for power between the South Carolina Commons and the executive, and it left no residual grievances. While the metropolitan authorities' final decision contained no forthright declaration upholding the colonial representatives' right to determine the validity of elections of their own members, this right was never again contested in South Carolina.

Still, the significance of this controversy to the Revolutionary movement should not be overlooked. Primarily, it provided an opportunity for influential South Carolina representatives to develop further in political leadership and to acquire an important type of political experience—the waging of a political war of attrition in defense of what they felt were their constitutional rights. The men who led the Commons through this controversy were in the front rank of those who would guide the colony through the controversy with Britain during the decade after 1765 and through the War for Independence into statehood. Christopher Gadsden became one of the most ardent protagonists of the American cause, a formidable opponent of the Stamp Act and later measures, a delegate to

---

[59] *Acts of the Privy Council, Colonial* 4:743–44 (Feb. 1766).

[60] Smith, *South Carolina as a Royal Province,* 348–49. For Boone's part in the repeal of the Stamp Act, see Garth to South Carolina Committee of Correspondence, Feb. 22, 1766, Garth Letter Book, as cited in Namier, "Charles Garth and His Connexions," 470.

Boone spent the rest of his life in relative obscurity. Although he retained considerable

the Stamp Act and Continental Congresses, the organizer of the Charleston mechanics and tradesmen in support of the patriot cause, and an officer in the South Carolina armed forces. Like Gadsden, John Rutledge was a delegate to the Stamp Act and Continental Congresses, and he also served as governor of South Carolina during the most critical years of the war. In 1787 he was a delegate to the Federal Convention. Rawlins Lowndes rendered valuable services to the Revolutionary cause as speaker of the South Carolina house from 1764 to 1765 and from 1772 to 1775 and as president of the state in 1778 and 1779. Henry Laurens, though in disagreement with the majority of the Commons in the Gadsden election case, later distinguished himself as a leader in the movement for nonimportation leveled against the Townshend Acts in 1769, president of the First Provincial Congress as well as the council of safety, president of the Continental Congress from 1777 to 1780, and, later, American minister to Holland. Charles Pinckney and James Parsons, who with Rutledge were South Carolina's most enterprising lawyers in the 1760s and 1770s, also did yeoman service by opposing British policies and playing important roles in the formation of the new state government. Both were members of the provincial congresses and officers in the South Carolina military forces. Parsons was speaker of the first House of Representatives elected under the new state constitution of 1776; Pinckney was an important member of the legislative council, although he later turned loyalist. Many other members, too numerous to mention by name, were important members of the provincial congress or of the council of safety, or rendered valuable services in opposing the Stamp Act and the Townshend duties.

In addition, the techniques and arguments employed by the Commons and its protagonists in this contest were to be useful in the following decade. The principle of nonintercourse used by the Commons against Boone was applied against British manufacturers in the crisis over the Townshend Acts. The traditional method of seeking redress of grievances through formal appeals to British authorities adopted by the Commons in 1763 was again used to protest the Stamp Act and other measures of Parliament. The actions taken in the Gadsden case by the Commons' appointees to the committee of correspondence were independent and without the consent of the council's appointees to the commit-

---

property in South Carolina until it was confiscated in 1782, he never returned to the colony. Following service as a commissioner of customs from 1769 to 1805, he retired to his parental home in Kent at Lee, where he died in 1812. Namier, "Charles Garth and His Connexions," 470.

tee—a practice common to subsequent controversies. Similarly, the arguments advanced by the Commons and particularly by Gadsden were repeatedly revived after 1765. Gadsden's emphasis upon the inalienability of natural and inherent rights and his rejection of the idea of virtual representation would be used by South Carolinians and other Americans not only against the Stamp Act but throughout the constitutional debate with Britain. His proposal for the appointment of a general agent for all colonies was a harbinger of his appeal for united action at the Stamp Act Congress and his general sentiment for union in the 1770s.

Finally, this bitter and stirring contest attracted the interest and consumed the energies of the most important politicians in South Carolina for nearly two years. Carried on with great intensity, the case was responsible for arousing a spirit of opposition and shaping a climate of opinion among those leaders conducive to resistance at a critical time. Just as the Gadsden election case was being concluded, authorities in Britain were beginning to tighten the reins and to initiate a policy of parliamentary taxation of the colonies through the Sugar and Stamp Acts. The Commons' success in this dispute increased its confidence and made it less hesitant to embark upon troubled waters in the future. The hostility toward Governor Boone and the enthusiasm for the defense of constitutional rights and privileges displayed by the South Carolina Commons between 1762 and 1764 were easily transferred to Parliament and its Stamp Act in 1765. Assuredly, like the contests over the writs of assistance in Massachusetts Bay and the parsons' cause in Virginia, the Gadsden election controversy helped to set the stage for the Revolutionary movement in South Carolina.

This chapter was written in 1957 for the journal in which it appeared. It is reprinted with minor editorial changes and permission from the *Mississippi Valley Historical Review* 46 (1959):469–92.

—FOURTEEN—

The Jamaica Privilege Controversy, 1764–66: *An Episode in the Process of Constitutional Definition in the Early Modern British Empire*

O N JULY 4, 1766, the free inhabitants of Jamaica put on an extravagant public celebration. "The towns were splendidly illuminated," reported the historian Bryan Edwards, who himself was a participant in the occasion; "the shipping in the ports were dressed in their gayest colours, and such joy and satisfaction appeared in every countenance, as we may imagine were displayed by the English Barons on receiving *magna charta* from the reluctant hand of King John."[1] For the past few months, similar happenings had occurred in most of the continental colonies to the north following receipt of news of Parliament's repeal of the Stamp Act earlier in the year, and notification of Parliament's action had only reached Jamaica shortly before this celebration.[2] But the joyous events of July 4 marked not the repeal of the Stamp Act but the end of a bitter local controversy over the nature, extent, and sources of the parliamentary privileges of the Jamaica assembly.

The most profound constitutional crisis in Jamaica since at least the early 1720s, the prolonged privilege controversy was one of many similar incidents during which men on opposite sides of the Atlantic had for more than a century been hammering out constitutional arrangements

---

[1] Bryan Edwards, *The History of the British Colonies in the West Indies,* 3d ed., 3 vols. (London, 1801), 2:428n.

[2] Roger Hope Elletson to Henry Seymour Conway, July 7, 1766, and to Grey Cooper, July 8, 1766, in H. P. Jacobs, ed., "Roger Hope Elletson's Letter Book," *Jamaican Historical Review* 1 (1946): 205–6.

within the sprawling extended polity of the early modern British Empire. Perhaps as well as any such event, the controversy that disrupted Jamaican political life for more than eighteen months beginning in December 1764 provides a dramatic illustration of the process by which constitutional arrangements were defined in the early modern British Empire and the depth and character of constitutional conflict during the early stages of the imperial crisis that led to the American Revolution.[3]

The controversy erupted after the Jamaica legislature had been in quiet session for just over two months. On December 8 John Olyphant, since 1756 a representative from the parish of St. Elizabeth and a second-tier leader in the assembly, complained to the house that Richard Thomas Wilson, an officer of the provost marshal, had, in violation of house rules, executed a writ of seizure against his coach horses while Olyphant was attending the session. Those rules protected each member from arrest and any possessions "necessary for his accom[m]odation" from seizure while the house was "actually sitting for dispatch of business." Routinely, the house voted Wilson's action a breach of privilege and ordered Edward Bolt, its messenger, to take Wilson into custody. When the members examined Wilson at the bar of the house on December 14 and 15, they discovered that he had acted in response to directions from Lachlan McNeil, deputy marshal of Spanish Town, who was carrying out a court judgment obtained against Olyphant by Pierce Cooke, "a Shopkeeper in Spanish Town" and himself a former assistant to the provost marshal's officer. Voting both McNeil and Cooke "guilty of a breach of privilege of this house," the assembly then ordered Bolt to take them into custody and to bring each of them to the bar of the house to answer for this breach of privilege. Acting on the basis of a warrant signed by house speaker Charles Price, Jr., according, as several members of the

---

[3] Mary Patterson Clarke, *Parliamentary Privilege in the American Colonies* (New Haven, 1943), 252–60, and George Metcalf, *Royal Government and Political Conflict in Jamaica, 1729–1783* (London, 1965), 160–72, provide the fullest published accounts of the Jamaica privilege controversy. The Metcalf volume also contains a useful narrative of Jamaican political history for the half century before the conclusion of the American War for Independence. T. R. Clayton, "Sophistry, Security, and Socio-Political Structures in the American Revolution; Or, Why Jamaica Did Not Rebel," *Historical Journal* 29 (1989): 325–27, provides a short gloss on Metcalf's account.

house later said, "to the constant form and method of proceeding in the Assembly," Bolt thereupon took McNeil and Cooke into custody.[4]

Had McNeil and Cooke followed traditional procedure, petitioned the house, "and denied their Intention of offending the House," that body, unwilling, as some of its members later affirmed, "to be diverted from the more important business of the session" and having "no desire to be troubled with this case," would immediately have discharged them. But they took a very different course, applying instead to Governor William Henry Lyttelton in his capacity as chancellor of the Court of Chancery for a writ of habeas corpus to set them free.[5]

Lyttelton was an experienced administrator who had been governor of South Carolina during the late 1750s and had served without serious complaint as governor of Jamaica for more than three years. As soon as Cooke informed him of his intentions, the governor conferred privately with three house leaders—Price, Chief Justice Thomas Fearon, and Attorney General Gilbert Ford—in an effort to avoid an altercation over this matter. Lyttelton presented them with his royal instruction concerning assembly privileges, which he interpreted as forbidding protection of any legislator's goods from judicial seizure, and told them that if Cooke applied to him "*as Chancellor,* to grant him a Writ of Habeas Corpus," he would have to grant the writ as a matter "of Course." Even more serious, he pointed out, such an action "wou[l]d bring on a Judicial examination before" him "in Chancery touching the legality of the Commitment and the Nature of the Privileges which the House of Assembly claimed." To avoid such an examination, Lyttelton recommended that the house release Wilson, refrain from committing McNeil and Cooke, and "proceed no further in the matter." Lyttelton came away from these discussions thinking that house leaders had "acquiesce[d]" in his strategy "as the most prudent course."[6]

But the house ignored his recommendation and had its messenger take McNeil and Cooke into custody. When the prisoners immediately petitioned for a writ of habeas corpus, he issued it. Again, however, he tried

[4] *Journals of the House of the Assembly of Jamaica,* 7 vols. (Kingston, 1798), Dec. 8, 13–15, 1766, 5:508, 515, 518; Charles Price, Jr., et al., to Stephen Fuller, Dec. 1764, Lyttelton Papers, BA 5806/12 (iii), 926, Worcester Record Office, Worcester, Eng.; William Henry Lyttelton to Board of Trade, Dec. 24, 1764, Colonial Office Papers, 137/33, f. 180, Public Record Office, London.

[5] Price et al. to Fuller, Dec. 1764, Lyttelton Papers, BA 5806/12 (iii), 926, Worcester Record Office; Lyttelton to Board of Trade, Dec. 24, 1764, CO 137/33, f. 180, PRO.

[6] Lyttelton to Board of Trade, Dec. 24, 1764, CO 137/33, ff. 180–81, PRO.

to contain the controversy. With the advice of his council, he prorogued the assembly on December 18 for one day, "in consequence of which," as he wrote his superiors in London, "the Persons in Custody were of course set free, without having been brought before me, or any decisions having been given, whether the Commitment of them, was legal or not." At the same time, Lyttelton took "no little pains . . . to prevail with the Assembly to let the matter drop there, and not to revive it when they met again."[7]

But Lyttelton's efforts again "proved ineffectual." No sooner had the assembly reconvened in new session on December 19 than it began to dig in its heels. As a result of Lyttelton's implicit questioning of the extent of assembly privileges, several house leaders subsequently testified, "What was before only a light matter became now a serious one." Regarding the assembly as having "a superior jurisdiction" to the Court of Chancery, house members denied that the governor, "as chancellor," had "any right to judge of the commitments of the assembly." "Seeing themselves thus desperately attacked, their Authority in a way of being an[n]ihilated and their plainest priviledges questioned," they "thought it their indispensable Duty to assert their Rights and vindicate their injured Priviledges, and did upon their Meeting come to Resolutions . . . asserting their Priviledges and ordering the Delinquents again into Custody."[8]

In ten resolutions, every one of which passed without a dissenting vote, the house made it clear that it would define its own privileges and had no intention of permitting any other agency to do so. The first resolution asserted its members' right to privileges "against arrests and imprisonments, in such manner as has been heretofore used and accustomed." The next three carefully specified the areas in which such privileges did not apply. These included cases of treason, felony, and other major crimes, actions involving property not essential for a member's accommodation during sessions, and obligations to pay public taxes. In three more resolutions, the house laid down a line and defied Lyttelton to cross it, declaring that it would regard any reflections on its proceedings or its members as "a high violation" of its rights and privileges, any misrepresentations of its proceedings as "a breach of privilege, and destructive of the freedom of this house," and any assertion that it

[7] Ibid., f. 181.

[8] Ibid.; Price et al. to Fuller, Dec. 1764, Lyttelton Papers, BA 5806/12 (iii), 926, Worcester Record Office; [Nicholas Bourke], *The Privileges of the Island of Jamaica Vindicated* (London, 1766), xiv.

had "no power of commitment" as a "subversion of the constitution of the house." An eighth resolution asserted that no person committed for a breach of privilege should be discharged except by vote of the house. A ninth ordered Cooke, Wilson, and McNeil to be retaken into custody, and a tenth pledged the house to assist and protect messenger Edward Bolt in the execution of its commitment order. By ordering these resolutions published in the newspapers, the house made sure that its position on this issue was announced to the public at large.[9]

Lyttelton could scarcely back away from this public challenge. As soon as Bolt, following the house directions, again remanded Cooke and McNeil on December 20, they again applied for a writ of habeas corpus. Lyttelton granted the writ and agreed to hear their case the following morning. Upon learning "that their Priviledges were the next Day to be publickly argued at the Bar of the Court of Chancery," the assembly, several members subsequently reported, "was struck with astonishment[;] . . . everybody was in the utmost suspence, and nobody . . . imagined that the Governor wou[l]d take upon himself as Chancellor to strip the Representative Body of the People of their undoubted and inherent Priviledges which they had uninterruptedly enjoyed through such a long Series of Years and which can never be taken from them without depriving them of every Right we are entitled to as free Britons."[10]

After "a full hearing," however, Lyttelton freed both Cooke and NcNeil and himself threw down the gauntlet—and escalated the controversy—by decreeing that "it did not appear to him from the words of any Act of Parliament Or of any Act of the Governor[,] Council and Assembly of this Island Or of His Majesty's Commission of Instructions to His Excellency as Governor of this Island Or by any other meanes whatsoever that," as the governor subsequently phrased it, "the Commitment of the Parties then brought into Court was legal." By confining his decree "entirely . . . to the Case" at hand and by neither extending it "to the Privileges *at large* claimed by the House of Assembly" nor deciding that the house had "no power to *commit generally,*" Lyttelton intended to avoid a major confrontation with the legislature.[11]

Yet again, however, the governor had miscalculated, the house's response revealing the extent to which he had gravely underestimated the

---

[9] *Assembly Journals,* Dec. 19, 1764, 5:520–21.

[10] Price et al. to Fuller, Dec. 1764, Lyttelton Papers, BA 5806/12 (iii), 926, Worcester Record Office.

[11] Lyttelton to Board of Trade, Dec. 24, 1764, and Entry from the Register of the Court of Chancery, Dec. 21, 1766, CO 137/33, ff. 180–81, 189, PRO.

depth of feeling over this issue. By examining and then discharging its commitment of McNeil and Cooke, Lyttelton, in the house's view, had not only opened "a door" to similar applications in the future but had endeavored, "as much as in him lay, to bring the authority of that house into an unconstitutional dependence upon the court of chancery, and into contempt with the people." Thus, as soon as the assembly learned from its messenger that Lyttelton had "suffer'd our Privileges and the Speaker's Warrant to be argued by Lawyers fee'd by the Delinquents, and [had] actually discharged them declaring that there was no authority in the Assembly to commit them," the house proceeded "vigorously to vindicate" its "injured jurisdiction," falling, in Lyttelton's opinion, "into *the greatest heats*" and passing a series of what he regarded as "very violent Resolutions" in defense of its privileges and in condemnation of his actions.[12]

With these five resolutions the house went well beyond those adopted two days earlier. By a vote of 18 to 4, it charged Lyttelton with "a flagrant breach, contempt, and violation, of the privileges of this house, and the liberties of the people." Unanimously, it voted not to do any further business until it had been "righted in its privileges" and "received ample reparation for the indignity" it had suffered by Lyttelton's actions and, explicitly registering its contempt for Lyttelton's authority over such issues, yet again resolved to take Cooke and McNeil into "close" custody for "contempt and breach of the privileges of this house." By a vote of 19 to 4, it resolved to appoint a committee to prepare an address to the crown to defend its privileges and to ask the king to restrain Lyttelton's "arbitrary exercise of power as chancellor" and thereby protect Jamaica "from such open and manifest violations, destructive of our rights, and subversive of our constitution." As with the resolutions passed two days earlier, the house ordered the first four of these printed in the public newspapers.[13]

Quickly acting on the last of these resolutions, Speaker Charles Price, Jr., appointed himself and five other members, including four of the most active house leaders, John Edwardes, Chief Justice Thomas Fearon, Nicholas Bourke, and Edward Long, to prepare the address to the crown. The committee acted with dispatch, but the house had no opportunity to consider its efforts. As soon as Lyttelton got wind of the resolu-

---

[12] Price et al. to Fuller, Dec. 1764, Lyttelton Papers, BA 5806/12 (iii), 926, Worcester Record Office; Lyttelton to Board of Trade, Dec. 24, 1764, CO 137/33, ff. 180–83, PRO; [Bourke], *Privileges*, xiv.

[13] *Assembly Journals*, Dec. 21, 1764, 5:523.

tions, he prorogued the assembly and then on December 24, with the unanimous advice of the council, dissolved it and issued writs for the election of a new assembly to meet the following March 5.[14]

The broad political and constitutional context in which this controversy took place is a familiar one to students of the early modern British Empire. The terms in which the debate over the privileges of the Jamaica house took shape—privilege versus prerogative, liberty versus arbitrary government, local rights versus metropolitan power, law versus executive decrees or instructions—were scarcely new to British colonial governance and certainly not to Jamaican political life. From the middle of the seventeenth century on, colonial leaders and metropolitan administrators had disputed endlessly over the sources and extent of colonial legislative authority, the nature of colonial constitutions, and the limits of royal prerogative in the colonies. As was the case in the very first stages of the privilege controversy, these disputes had often turned around such issues as the authority of local custom and whether royal instructions bound local communities as well as the officials to whom they were given.[15]

In Jamaica these issues had a long history. In the late 1670s Jamaican legislators had led the fight against metropolitan efforts to establish in the colonies Poynings' Law, which required prior metropolitan approval for all Irish legislation. For the next fifty years their successors steadfastly refused to vote a permanent revenue until free Jamaicans had been formally guaranteed by statute their rights to the protection of all English laws.[16]

Much more recently, the house had stood firm against new metropolitan efforts, beginning in 1748, to restrict the scope of colonial legislative

[14] Ibid.; Price et al. to Fuller, Dec. 1764, Lyttelton Papers, BA 5806/12 (iii), 926, Worcester Record Office; Lyttelton to Board of Trade, Dec. 24, 1764, CO 137/33, ff. 181–83, PRO.

[15] In this connection, see the general discussion in Jack P. Greene, *Peripheries and Center: Constitutional Development in the Extended Polities of the British Empire and the United States, 1607–1788* (Athens, Ga., 1986), 7–54.

[16] See Agnes M. Whitson, *The Constitutional Development of Jamaica, 1660–1729* (Manchester, Eng., 1929).

authority and to enhance that of royal instructions.[17] Notwithstanding considerable pressure from the Board of Trade in London, it absolutely refused throughout the 1750s to insert into any law a clause suspending its operation until it had been approved by metropolitan officials.[18] When pressed upon this question by Governor Charles Knowles in connection with a revenue bill in October 1753, the house resolved that it had an inherent right to raise and to apply public monies in any way it saw fit, pointed out that it had never inserted suspending clauses in any public act, and declared such clauses to "be a very great Alteration of the Known and established Constitution of this Island" and "derogatory to the undoubted Right of the Subject" to propose "Laws to the Crown."[19] Denounced by Knowles as the "most extraordinary . . . ever . . . entered into by any assembly in His Majesty's Colonies,"[20] these resolutions eventually in May 1757 elicited a major constitutional pronouncement from the British House of Commons which effectively declared, as one colonial official later put it, that the colonies had "no Constitution," but "that the mode of Government in each of them" depended "upon the good pleasure of the King, as expressed in his Commission, and Instructions to his Governor."[21]

But such pronouncements carried no authority in distant colonies unless local political leaders through their behavior accepted them, and the "High-Spirited and Oppulent Planters" who "constantly composed" the Jamaica assembly, men, as one governor said, of "the best abilities and greatest weight in the Community,"[22] had no intention of settling for any constitutional arrangement that left their liberties on what appeared to them to be such a precarious foundation. If to metropolitan officials they

[17] Jack P. Greene, "'A Posture of Hostility': A Reconsideration of Some Aspects of the Origins of the American Revolution," American Antiquarian Society, *Proceedings* 87 (1977): 27–68.

[18] See Edward Trelawny to Board of Trade, Mar. 25, 1752, Charles Knowles to Board of Trade, June 27, Sept. 13, 1753, CO 137/25, ff. 235–37, 375–77, 137/26, ff. 5–11, PRO.

[19] Board of Trade to Privy Council, Oct. 15, 1754, CO 138/20, pp. 41–79, PRO.

[20] Knowles to Board of Trade, Jan. 12, 1754, CO 137/27, ff. 1–20, PRO.

[21] *Journal of the House of Commons* (London, 1757), 27:910–11 (May 23, 1757); Thomas C. Barrow, ed., "Project for Imperial Reform: 'Hints Respecting the Settlement for Our American Provinces,' 1763," *William and Mary Quarterly*, 3d ser., 24 (1967): 117.

[22] Knowles to Duke of Newcastle, Jan. 29, 1754, Newcastle Papers, Additional Manuscripts 32734, ff. 86–89, British Library, London; Knowles to Board of Trade, June 27, 1753, CO 137/25, ff. 375–77, PRO.

appeared to be people of an "ungovernable Spirit" who had such a power-ful "sense . . . of being Independent" that neither crown nor Parliament would long have any "share in the Government . . . without Force to support it,"[23] Jamaicans vastly preferred to have "the Character of a tur-bulent ungovernable People," a people of "passion, perversity, and futil-ity" whose "darling passion" was "Contention," than to stand idly by while some minions in or from the metropolis were "tearing to pieces the Ancient Frame of a well-constituted G——n—t."[24]

Lyttelton was no stranger to such a mindset when he came to take up the governorship of Jamaica late in 1761. When he became governor of South Carolina five years earlier, he immediately found South Carolina legislators "always perfectly agreed in one Principle, that the Power of the Governor ought . . . to be an object of Jealousy . . . & have accord-ingly from time to time done their utmost to reduce it, within as narrow limits as possible." As a result, he complained to the earl of Halifax, who as president of the Board of Trade had charged him to try to alter the balance of power in South Carolina, the governorship had been wholly "divested of that Authority & Influence which ought to Accompany it." Unable to "discover any adequate Means to restore it to its proper Weight," Lyttelton predicted that he would "meet with a most Strenuous Opposition whenever" he had "any point to Carry which may seem to favour the prerogative" and cautioned that the authority of the governor would always "be insufficient for his Master's Service" until it was "en-larg'd . . . in proportion as others Shall have Succeeded in their At-tempts to weaken it."[25]

Having already been provided by London officials with a large bound volume containing most of the principal documents pertaining to Jamai-ca's many political difficulties during the 1750s,[26] Lyttelton could not have been surprised to find the same problems in Jamaica. For nearly a

[23] Knowles to Board of Trade, Jan. 12, May 7, June 24, 1754, CO 137/27, ff. 1–20, 196–98, 137/28, f. 25, PRO.

[24] William Lewis to Rose Fuller, Jan. 17, 1758, Edward Clarke to Rose Fuller, Oct. 24, Dec. 20, 1755, Fuller Papers, 19/3, East Sussex Record Office, Lewes, Eng.; Thomas Pinnock to ——, June 26, 1756, Miscellaneous Manuscripts 490, Institute of Jamaica, Kingston.

[25] Lyttelton to Earl of Halifax, Oct. 18, 1756, William Henry Lyttelton Letter Book, 1757–59, Lyttelton Papers, BA 5806, 705:104, Worcester Record Office; Jack P. Greene, "South Carolina's Colonial Constitution: Two Proposals for Reform," *South Carolina Historical Magazine* 62 (1961): 71–81.

[26] This volume is in Lyttelton Papers, 7(1), Worcester Record Office.

year, however, he managed, as he had done throughout his tenure in South Carolina, to avoid a direct confrontation with local leaders. But when in October 1762 the assembly announced that it would never "Submit" its "Sentiments to the Determination of" the Board of Trade, the primary metropolitan board for colonial matters, "nor . . . suffer them in any Respect, to direct or influence" its "Proceedings by any Proposition or Decision whatever," and threatened to appeal to the crown against the board,[27] Lyttelton seized the occasion to impress upon his London superiors the weak state of royal authority in Jamaica.

Reminding the Board of Trade of the assembly's "constant & steady refusal to insert a [suspending] clause, in any Act they pass," Lyttelton in two long letters interpreted the assembly's attack upon the board as merely the latest expression of "an eager desire to be freed from those restraints, which the wisdom of His Majesty's Councils has put them under in common with the rest of the Colonies in the great point of Legislation," and "of the opinion which the people of this Island have form'd of the Constitution of this Government & of their Rights & Privileges." "Whatever powers" the assembly "was meant to have by His Majesty's Commission & Instructions to His Governors," Lyttelton explained, an inspection of its journals quickly revealed that its members had "for some years last past considered the House of Commons of Great Britain as their Model & have assum'd & exercis'd the powers thereof as nearly as the circumstances of the Country cou'd allow of, apprehending themselves to have an inherent Right so to do as English Subjects, entitled to the use & benefit of the Laws of England of which the Custom of Parliament makes a part, rather than by virtue of His Majesty's Commission to His Governor." In accord with this position, Lyttelton wrote, "whatever the Assembly have found upon consulting the Journals of the House of Commons to have been constitutionally done there, they have judged to be a sufficient authority to them to proceed in the same manner here."[28]

This "aspiring endeavour to acquire in their Assemblies & within the Sphere of their activity the same Powers and Priveleges as are enjoy'd by a British House of Commons," Lyttelton reported, was "universal[ly] . . . espous'd by the Inhabitants" and "too deeply rooted & founded upon Doctrines & Practises of too high & complicated a nature to be removed or much lessen'd by any means in my power." Any effort on his part to deny "the validity" of the assembly's pretensions, he predicted,

---

[27] Jamaica Assembly's "Answer," Oct. 1762, CO 137/32, ff. 221, PRO.

[28] Lyttelton to Board of Trade, Oct. 13, Oct. 24, 1762, CO 137/32, 207–11, 212–15, PRO.

would only throw Jamaica "into a state of the greatest Confusion & distraction," and he suggested that the board initiate a ministerial inquiry into "the Affairs of this Country." Only "a solemn Declaration of the Crown, not to say the Parliament also, of such a sort as may bring back the Government to it's first principles again," he observed, could possibly remedy these evils and enable the king's governor "to maintain the Honour & Dignity of His Government in this difficult Station."[29]

With this analysis Lyttelton was pursuing a strategy which had worked for him in South Carolina. By identifying the problems that prevented him from governing according to metropolitan rules and confessing his impotence to resolve them on his own, he effectively transferred responsibility for those problems to his superiors in London. For a time, this strategy also worked for Lyttelton in Jamaica. Making no effort to "thwart the prevailing passions of" Jamaicans, he never made himself vulnerable to "the effects of their resentment."[30] When London authorities chose to ignore the Jamaica assembly's challenge to the Board of Trade's authority and no ministerial inquiry was forthcoming,[31] Lyttelton settled down into nearly two years of what he himself described as a state of "great tranquility." He had little apprehension, he wrote a friend, "of being oblig'd to quit" his "American post . . . by the workings of popular discontent."[32]

But the failure of London authorities to take any action against the assembly for its behavior in October 1762 might well have taught him that, no matter how politically well-connected he may have been, he could expect little help from that quarter in any controversy arising out of any ostensible infringement of the assembly's rights. Given this earlier experience, it is surprising that Lyttelton did not tread even more carefully in December 1764 and that he so confidently expected, as he wrote William Knox, that the Board of Trade would provide him with effective support against the assembly.

[29] Ibid. See also Lyttelton to George Grenville, Jan. 11, 1763, Stowe Papers, box 22 (64), Henry L. Huntington Library, San Marino, Calif.

[30] Lyttelton to Grenville, Jan. 11, 1763, Stowe Papers, box 22 (64), Huntington Library.

[31] After reviewing the documents submitted by Lyttelton, the Privy Council did solicit legal advice "in regard to the most proper method to be taken by the Government upon this occasion." W. L. Grant and J. Munro, eds., *Acts of the Privy Council of England, Colonial Series*, 6 vols. (London, 1908–12), 4:520 (Mar. 3, 1763).

[32] Lyttelton to William Knox, July 22, 1764, Knox Papers, William L. Clements Library, Ann Arbor, Mich.

Lyttelton's dissolution on December 24 brought the first, most intense, and shortest phase of the privilege controversy to an end. During the second stage of the contest, between late December 1764 and August 1765, the protagonists on each side pursued three complementary and concurrent strategies. First, they endeavored to articulate and elaborate the constitutional arguments for their respective positions. Second, they sought to elicit political support in Britain and Jamaica. Third, they went head-to-head in two brief meetings of the legislature, the first in March and the second in August 1766.

In its resolve to address the crown on December 21, the house briefly set down the broad outlines of its constitutional position on privilege as it applied to the dispute at hand. Declaring that the Jamaica assembly had, "from the earliest establishment of civil government in this colony, enjoyed all the rights and privileges inherent in them, as the representative body of the people," the house contended that "the privilege of freedom from arrest, both of persons, and goods necessary for their accom[m]odation during their session," was both "essential" to protect the dignity and authority of any "free assembly" and had been "uninterruptedly enjoyed" by the Jamaica house for nearly a century. Along with its "other rights and privileges," the house rested its claim to this privilege on three foundations: first, the "reason and nature of their election and foundation"; second, "the grace, grants, and concessions, of his majesty's royal predecessors"; and, third, "prescriptive right and custom."[33]

During the three days between Lyttelton's prorogation and his dissolution of the assembly, his leading opponents from the house, operating as the committee to correspond with Jamaica's London agent, Stephen Fuller, elaborated the case against Lyttelton in a long letter. This letter did not focus only on the privilege controversy. Indeed, it began with an attack on the ministry's recent proposal for a parliamentary levy of stamp duties on the colonies. The fullest expression of Jamaican legislative opinion on this subject, this attack reiterated the conventional colonial view of the basis of the colonists' claims to the rights of "free Britons." Arguing that the right to no taxation without representation was the "most essential" of those rights and that taxing Jamaicans by "any other manner" than "by their Consent given by their Representatives in

---

[33] *Assembly Journals,* Dec. 21, 1764, 5:523.

Assembly" would "strip us of our Birthright as Britons," the committee instructed Fuller to do everything within his power "to obviate and prevent this alarming Measure." The committee also complained that the governor's sending on an expedition to Honduras a large number of the troops stationed in Jamaica to protect the free inhabitants had left the island "almost defenceless" against its slaves and asked Fuller to endeavor to secure a ruling to prevent similar "drafts in the future." Not surprisingly, however, the committee reserved most of its attention for a discussion of the privilege controversy.[34]

Because it struck so deeply "at the very Vitals of our Constitution," this controversy seemed to the committee to be "a Subject of more importance than either" the stamp duties or the reduction in troops. Suspecting that Lyttelton would, as a house partisan later suggested, use the dispute "to procure an alteration in the Constitution of this Island . . . in favor of his darling prerogative," the committee devoted special attention to Lyttelton's decree questioning the house's power to commit Cooke and McNeil, dismissing as scarcely needing refutation his suggestion that an act of either Parliament or the Jamaica assembly might be the source of its power to commit for breaches of privilege. "To attempt to divest the Assembly of a Power exercised by every Court of Quarter Sessions," the committee declared, was "extraordinary," and it pointed out that the "power of Commitment for Contempt" was "a Power every court possesses [as a matter] of Course, as essentially necessary to its existence." Lyttelton's suggestion that royal instructions might be the basis for assembly privileges seemed to the committee to be far "more dangerous" and far more worthy of denial. Such a suggestion, it wrote, might, if accepted, "render all Determinations in the Court of Chancery liable to be governed by Instructions." Arguing that "All Courts that govern themselves by any other Rule than those of Law and Equity" were "unconstitutional," the committee observed that "Property as well as Liberty" would have "very little Security in a Country where so high a Court as the Court of Chancery thinks itself bound in its Determination to follow Instructions."[35]

---

[34] Price et al. to Fuller, Dec. 1764, Lyttelton Papers, BA 5806/12 (iii), 926, Worcester Record Office. Because fourteen of the fifteen signatories to this letter were assembly members and the fifteenth had earlier been a member, this letter undermines the contention of T. R. Clayton in "Why Jamaica Did Not Rebel," 325, that "the Jamaican lower house remained silent on the constitutional implications of the Stamp Act."

[35] Price et al. to Fuller, Dec. 1764, Lyttelton Papers, BA 5806/12 (iii), 926, Worcester Record Office; Robert Graham to Chaloner Arcedeckne, Apr. 21, 1765, Vaneck Papers, 2/1, Cambridge University Library, Cambridge, Eng.

In closing, the committee expressed considerable pessimism that the controversy could be settled locally. Noting that the "Assembly was composed of Gentlemen of the best Interest and the greatest Fortunes and Abilities in the Island" and that "all the Resolutions about this matter except two or three were come to unanimously, and in those two or three, there were but three or four dissenting Voices," the committee expressed the opinion that, however long he resorted to "the desperate Course of Dissolutions," Lyttelton would never manage to "get an Assembly chosen so base as to act with him in raising money upon the People until he has made thorough Reparation for the Violation of the Priviledges and given full Assurance that they shall not be violated for the future." Because it also thought that Lyttelton was "not of a Temper to repair the Injury he has done to us," the committee thought that there was "no other Way to obviate the Calamities which this Gentleman's obstinate and arbitrary Conduct is likely to bring upon us, but by throwing ourselves at His Majesty's Feet and imploring his gracious Interposition against such a daring violation of our Rights." Accordingly, it directed Fuller to represent the house's case to either the Board of Trade, the secretary of state, or "by Petition to His Majesty in Council as you shall judge most proper . . . to procure us Redress for our violated Priviledges and Security against any future Invasions of our Rights and Liberties."[36]

Fifteen prominent Jamaicans, all but one of whom had been members of the dissolved assembly and all of whom had sat in that body, signed this letter. In addition to the speaker, Charles Price, Jr., the signatories included most of the legislators who had taken the most prominent role in committee assignments during the more than three years the dissolved assembly had been in existence: Nicholas Bourke, John Edwardes, Stephen Richard Redwood, Archibald Sinclair, Edward Long, Thomas French, George Paplay, Rose Price, William Gordon, George Bonner, Jasper Hall, and Thomas Brooks. Collectively, the fifteen signees had 113 years of legislative experience in the house. Of the leading house members, only Chief Justice Thomas Fearon and Attorney General Gilbert Ford, the last of whom had been recently appointed to the council, did not sign this letter.

Against such formidable opposition, Lyttelton knew that he had little chance of resolving the dispute locally. Persuaded that it would be "impossible, as well as unfit" for him "to make any reparation" for his decree "without which the late Assembly thought proper to declare they wou[l]d

---

[36] Price et al. to Fuller, Dec. 1764, Lyttelton Papers, BA 5806/12 (iii), 926, Worcester Record Office.

not do any business" and having "the greatest reason to apprehend that that [new] Assembly when chosen, will adopt the Doctrines and perhaps the identical Resolutions of the former," Lyttelton had little hope that he would "find . . . or be able to bring" a new assembly to a different "temper." Hence, he lost no time in sending his London superiors an account of "the late event" that had "so unfortunately interrupted" the harmony he had previously enjoyed with the assembly. In letters of December 24 and January 3 to the Board of Trade, he provided a narrative of events, pointed out the problems that would arise if a prolonged dispute prevented the assembly from voting supplies for the troops stationed in the island, and requested that the crown "make some Order of Declamation upon the matter" at the earliest possible moment.[37]

To try to make sure that such an order would be in his favor and to make it clear to the board that, as Lyttelton put it in a letter to a friend, "if the weather here is threatening & should grow stormy it has not been in my power consistently with my duty to prevent it," he sought both to counter the assembly's constitutional claims and to justify his own behavior. Taking particular exception to the house's declaration in its resolutions of December 21 that its "Rights and Privileges" were "*inherent* in them, as the Representative Body of the People," which he referred to the board for its consideration, he also denied its assertion that royal grants and custom supported its claims. "They never had any Charter, Grant, or Concession whatever from the Crown," he assured the board, "except a Proclamation of King Charles the 2d in the 13th Year of his Reign . . . by which it is declared that all Children of natural born Subjects of England . . . born in Jamaica" should "be reputed to be free Denizens of England, and . . . have the same Privileges to all intents and purposes, as free born Subjects of England." Those words, Lyttelton suggested, were merely "intended to prevent any such Children from being consider'd as Aliens" and could never "be construed to give any Privileges to the Assembly." "With respect to the prescriptive Right and Custom," Lyttelton asked the board to consider "how far" such an argument could be "admitted in a Colony, the civil Government of which is of not more ancient establishment, than the Reign of King Charles 2d, especially in Cases where the Prerogative of the Crown, the

---

[37] Lyttelton to Board of Trade, Dec. 14, 1764, Jan. 3, 1765, CO 137/33, ff. 183, 137/34, ff. 28–29, PRO; Lyttelton to William Knox, Jan. 10, 1765, Knox Papers, Clements Library; Lyttelton to William Bull, Dec. 28, 1764, Letter Book, 1762–65, f. 295, Lyttelton Papers, 2 (ii), Worcester Récord Office.

Course of Publick Justice, and the liberty of the Subject may be affected by it."[38]

By contrast, Lyttelton argued, his own behavior had throughout been both legal and "consonant to" his instructions from the crown. In his view the assembly's claim to protection for "such Goods and Chattels, as they may judge necessary for their accommodation" was "expressly contrary" to those instructions. In taking this position Lyttelton was of course merely subscribing to an old metropolitan view which had been given renewed emphasis by London authorities after 1748 and had been the source of many contentions with colonial political establishments during the 1750s and early 1760s: the view that royal instructions carried greater authority than local custom, common law rights, or charters in determining what was legal and constitutional in the colonies.[39]

Expressing his deep resentment that he had been so "grossly ill . . . treated for having done a Judicial Act as the King's Chancellor, or Keeper of His Seal of this Island, and in conformity to the Oath I took, when I enter'd upon my Office, *duely and impartially* to administer Justice to all His Majesty's Subjects," he cast himself as a disinterested defender of individual liberty against a tyrannical assembly dominated by would-be monopolizers of power and privilege, pointing out "how dangerous a Tyranny may be exercised in this Country by the Assemblies," if, as the house claimed, people committed by it had no right to apply for a writ of habeas corpus. "Any Determination of the nature and extent in general of the Powers or Privileges of the House of Assembly," he suggested, should not be left to "any Tribunal here" but ought to be settled by "the Decision of the Crown." In his view the crown, not the assembly, was the ultimate authority in all questions about colonial governance.[40]

By the time Lyttelton met a new assembly on March 19, 1765, he had not of course had any response from London. The Jamaican electorate had returned twenty-five of forty-one members of the previous house, just over 60 percent, about average for a Jamaica election, including all of the old leaders except John Edwardes of Port Royal and Nicholas Bourke from Portland. As a later writer remarked, the new assembly was thus, like the old, "composed . . . of men zealous for the constitution

---

[38] Lyttelton to William Knox, Jan. 10, 1765, Knox Papers, Clements Library; Lyttelton to Board of Trade, Dec. 24, 1764, CO 137/33, f. 182, PRO.

[39] Lyttelton to Board of Trade, Dec. 14, 1764, Jan. 3, 1765, CO 137/33, f. 183–84, 137/34, ff. 28–29, PRO.

[40] Ibid.

and liberties of their country." If the composition of the house and its selection of Charles Price, Jr., again to be its speaker did not bode well for Lyttelton's hopes to avoid a renewal of the privilege controversy, the scene at the traditional presentation of the speaker for the governor's confirmation shattered them altogether. Instead of asking the governor in a general way to confirm its freedom of speech and debate, its access to the governor, and freedom from arrests, as had long been customary in Jamaica, Price demanded these privileges in "a manner more specifick than ordinary," indeed, in precisely "the same manner," a house supporter later reported, "as they were asked by Speaker Williams in Queen Elizabeth's Reign[,] by the Late Speaker Onslow on his first presentation, And by Severall Others." Somewhat taken aback by this departure from custom and not knowing that Price's request had been "copied mutatis mutandis from one of the printed Journals of the House of Commons of Great Britain," Lyttelton responded that he would "grant the privileges which you have desired, so far as they are agreeable to law, and not repugnant to his majesty's commission and instruction to me." By this response he reiterated the view, implicit in his earlier ruling on privilege, that instructions carried greater legal weight than local custom or inherited tradition and served notice that he had not altered the stand he had taken the previous December.[41]

Nor did relations improve following this incident. "Unwilling . . . to revive the business of privilege," the assembly initially passed over Lyttelton's response "in silence" and did not again seek to take McNeil and Cooke into custody. Yet, when later the same day the governor reopened the contest by sending a copy of his instruction relating to privilege to the house, it ordered the instruction to "lie upon the table," resolved itself into a committee of the whole to consider "the state of the island," and, following a report from that committee, adopted nine resolutions on the subject of privilege. Passed unanimously, the first eight were exactly the same as those the previous house had adopted on December 19. Approved by an overwhelming majority of 31 to 4, the ninth provided for a committee to prepare an address to Lyttelton stating its objections to his chancery ruling on its privileges, pointing out the "inconveniencies, arising from the deficiency of money in the treasury, occasioned by the expiration of all the money-bills" following the dissolution of the pre-

---

[41] *Assembly Journals*, Mar. 19, 1765, 5:524; "A Summary Account of the Proceedings between the Governor and Assembly of Jamaica, 1764 & 1765," [after Aug. 17, 1765], Long Papers, Add. MSS. 22676, ff. 154–59, British Library; Lyttelton to Board of Trade, Mar. 24, 1765, CO 137/33, f. 212, PRO; [Bourke], *Privileges*, xv.

vious December, and asking the governor to expunge his ruling from the record so that, "consistent with" its "rights and privileges" and the "honour and dignity of the house," it might proceed to remedy those inconveniences.[42]

By this request house members made it clear that so long as "the chancellor's determination still remain'd, as a yoke about their necks," they "could not with dignity to themselves or justice to their constituents, proceed to any business." In a political society which attached so much significance to precedent, such a dangerous one could not be permitted to stand. According to one of its partisans, the house also hoped "that time and reflection had brought the governor to a just sense of the injury he had done the constitution" and that its request for him "to vacate and annul" his decree, "grounded" as it was "on the Vacate of a record which was made by Order of King Charles 2d in the Case Skinner & the East India Company," would offer him a way out. "To acknowledge errors, upon conviction, and make reparation for injuries" seemed to the house to be in "no way below the dignity of any man."[43]

Sent to Lyttelton the next day, this address left no doubt that the breach over privileges was still wide. On March 22 the governor called the house before him, denounced its address as "extraordinary," and denied that any judge could legally expunge a court record. Charging the house with responsibility for any problems Jamaica might experience as a result of having no tax laws, he prorogued it until the following September.[44]

House leaders attributed this deepening impasse largely to Lyttelton's stubbornness and conceit. Having permitted "His Sentiments of his [own] superior Abilitys & Judgement [to] carry him too far" at the beginning of the controversy, he was "too opinionated," they thought, to understand that, although Jamaicans, as one house member put it, were "rather high flyers, and obstinate, a little art & soothing would soon bring us down. We may be led," he observed, "but do not care to be trod upon."[45]

Lyttelton took another view. Writing to the Board of Trade on the same day he prorogued the assembly, he condemned the house's behavior

---

[42] *Assembly Journals*, Mar. 19, 1765, 5:527; [Bourke], *Privileges*, xv.

[43] [Bourke], *Privileges*, xv–xvi; "A Summary Account of the Proceedings," Long Papers, Add. MSS., 22676, ff. 154–59, British Library.

[44] *Assembly Journals*, Mar. 22, 1765, 5:528.

[45] Graham to Arcedeckne, Apr. 21, 1765, Vaneck Papers, 2/1, Cambridge University Library.

as yet another example of Jamaica's "lawless Spirit." He could not possibly have put an end to the controversy, he told the board, unless he had "sacrificed the most essential Duties of my Station, both Civil, and Judicial, to Pretensions as boundless, as they appeared to me to be illegal, and have suffer'd the Assemblies under a notion of Parliamentary Powers inherent in them, to treat the King's Instructions with contempt, and to exercise a Tyranny as oppressive to Individuals in obstructing the course of Publick Justice and restraining the liberty of their Persons by Commitments for pretended breach of Privileges as the Authority they have assumed in this Country is injurious to the Rights of the Crown, and destructive of the just Influence of His Majesty's Prerogative." Still, Lyttelton predicted that with metropolitan support he might yet restore "the tranquility and good Order of the Government," and three weeks later he "flatter[ed]" himself that by providing the occasion for the "interposition of your Lordships," his behavior in the privilege controversy would "be introductive of" the "good Order" that was "necessary for" Jamaica's "permanent Peace and Wellfare."[46]

At the very time Lyttelton was meeting the new assembly, London officials were already moving to provide him with support. Acting with what must have been record dispatch, the Board of Trade, having received Lyttelton's December 24 account of the controversy just two weeks earlier, on March 15 both brought the dispute to the attention of the Privy Council and wrote the governor its "entire Approbation" of his "Conduct upon these extraordinary Proceedings of the Assembly," conduct it regarded "as becoming and temperate as theirs has been indecent and violent." A mere five days later, the Privy Council indicated the crown's high displeasure with the assembly's resolutions "in support of certain pretended Priviledges" and expressed its conviction that a new assembly would "not adopt the Doctrines & Principles of the former Assembly" but would "in every respect proceed with Temper and Moderation in carrying on the Business of the Publick" in passing the bills necessary to raise the money to defray public expenses and support the troops. In the event that it did not, the Privy Council, in a patent attempt at intimidation, threatened "to lay the whole of the matter before the Parliament of Great Britain, in order that they may take such measures for raising the usual Supplies within the said Island, and for providing for the Publick Service and the Security of his Majesty's Subjects there as so unbecoming a Proceeding in the Assembly will render unavoidably

---

[46] Lyttelton to Board of Trade, Mar. 24, Apr. 12, 1765, CO 137/33, ff. 214–15, 137/34, 32–33, PRO.

necessary." In turn, the Board of Trade passed along this threat of parliamentary intervention and taxation to Lyttelton, authorizing him to make such use of it as he might think "expedient for His Majesty's Service."[47]

Following receipt of this letter on June 17, Lyttelton dissolved the assembly and issued writs for new elections to be held on August 13. "Anxious . . . to gett an Assembly to his mind," Lyttelton sponsored a vigorous campaign "to exclude the old members" from the assembly. Candidates favorable to him contested elections "in almost all the parishes," and one of his adherents "promised to return 20 Members" who would take his side in the privilege controversy.[48] "With great confidence, during the elections," an adherent of the house reported, Lyttelton's supporters told voters "that his M—— in Council had determined against us, and that, if a new assembly should adopt the maxims of the old, we should lose our legislature," and charged "that the members of the two last assemblies only meant to elude their creditors, and that the contest between the governor and them, was merely about a privilege from arrests" for paying their just debts.[49]

Lyttelton was confident of victory. To the Board of Trade he wrote that he expected the new Assembly to have many new members and to "meet in such a Temper . . . that the Public Business" would "be carried on in a manner conformable to His Majesty's expectations."[50] To William Knox on July 14, Lyttelton wrote ecstatically about the crown's approval of his conduct. "With this support" and with the help of the "many new Persons" who would be elected, he told Knox optimistically, he expected the new assembly to "have a little more temper & discretion than their Predecessors have shewn" and "that the necessary supplies" would "be voted & the factious humours subside."[51]

---

[47] Board of Trade to Lyttelton, Mar. 15, Mar. 21, 1765, CO 138/22, ff. 297–99, 304–5, PRO; Privy Council to Lyttelton, Mar. 20, 1765, CO 137/33, ff. 198–203, PRO.

[48] Simon Taylor to Chaloner Arcedeckne, July 11, 1765, Vaneck Papers, 2/1, Cambridge University Library.

[49] [Bourke], *Privileges*, xvi.

[50] Lyttelton to Board of Trade, June 18, 26, 1766, CO 137/33, ff. 220–22, PRO.

[51] Lyttelton to Knox, July 14, 1765, Knox Papers, Clements Library; Lyttelton to Stephen Fuller, July 14, 1765, Stephen Fuller Letter Book, Manuscript Department, William R. Perkins Library, Duke University, Durham, N.C.

In these expectations Lyttelton found himself "very much disappointed." He greatly overestimated both the turnover in the assembly and the weight of Privy Council pronouncements with Jamaican legislative leaders. No list of legislators for the August 1765 session survives, and we cannot, therefore, calculate the rate of persistence among old members. But house partisans reported that "the Old members" had easily "gain[ed] the Majority" and that the house contained "a very great majority . . . of men determined to support and vindicate the constitution."[52]

An indication of the temper of the new assembly could have been predicted from the contents of a remarkable pamphlet which appeared in Kingston on the eve of its convocation. Finished on August 10, 1765, published under the title *A Letter concerning the Privileges of the Assembly of Jamaica*, and thrice reprinted in London in 1765–67 in an enlarged edition with the title *The Privileges of the Island of Jamaica Vindicated*,[53] this work appeared anonymously but has been attributed to Nicholas Bourke on the basis of a contemporary manuscript notation in the copy in the Goldsmiths' Library at London University.[54]

Bourke was an Anglo-Irishman who about 1740 emigrated to Jamaica, where his uncle, Andrew Arcedeckne, was a prominent lawyer. An obviously able and enterprising young man, Bourke quickly established himself as a successful planter and in 1748 married a daughter of Chief Justice Thomas Fearon. For much of the time beginning in 1754, he was a member of the assembly, serving first for Kingston in 1754–56, then for Portland in 1757–64, and finally for his home parish of Clarendon in 1766–70. One of the most active committee members in the house, he

---

[52] Taylor to Arcedeckne, July 11, 1765, Vaneck Papers, 2/1, Cambridge University Library; [Bourke], *Privileges*, xvi–xvii.

[53] Thomas R. Adams, *The American Controversy: A Bibliographical Study of the British Pamphlets about the American Disputes, 1764–1783*, 2 vols. (Providence, 1980), 1:22–23, 41–42. The three London reprintings include two independent editions. The third reprinting was in John Almon, *A Collection Of the Most Interesting Tracts, Lately Published in England and America, on the Subjects of Taxing the American Colonies, and Regulating Their Trade*, 2 vols. (London, 1767), 2: no. 11. A "third" edition of the pamphlet, with additions covering the later stages of the privilege controversy and a later breach of privilege from November 1808 to April 1809, was published in Jamaica in 1810. This work was one of "Numberless . . . Papers printed both for and against the Conduct of the Assembly" at this time but is probably the only one still extant. Taylor to Arcedeckne, July 11, 1765, Vaneck Papers, 2/1, Cambridge University Library.

[54] The notation reads: "Written by Mr. Nicholas Bourke at that time a member of Assembly of Jamaica."

briefly served as speaker in 1770. By the time of his death on December 11, 1771, he had acquired a large estate, valued at nearly £34,000 and including two sugar plantations, two cattle pens, a house in the capital at Spanish Town, and 497 slaves.[55]

Bourke's library included 440 volumes,[56] and his pamphlet was a work of extraordinary learning in British parliamentary history. Drawing upon the journals of the House of Commons, parliamentary histories, and judicial reports, Bourke obviously intended to give the "antiprivilegians" in Jamaica a stern lesson in "the history and . . . the laws and constitution of England." He devoted nearly half his pamphlet to recapitulating incidents and decisions ranging from the early sixteenth century to as late as the 1750s in which the House of Commons had exercised its power of commitment. In the process Bourke overwhelmed his readers with evidence "that the house of Commons hath at all times enjoyed and exercised, the sole Right of judging of its own Privileges, and of punishing for breach of Privilege"; that the principal English courts, including the Court of Chancery, had never "presume[d] to discharge a commitment by the house of Commons"; and that there were neither English nor Jamaican precedents to support Lyttelton's determination of the previous December. That determination, he argued, was therefore "a dangerous violation of" the assembly's "privileges, and such an encroachment upon their jurisdiction, as would (if submitted to) strip them of all authority, and disable them from either supporting their own dignity or giving the people of this Colony that protection against arbitrary power, which nothing but a free and independent Assembly can give."[57]

Bourke's larger purpose was to demolish the "absurd, false, and wicked" assertions, implicit in Lyttelton's ruling and since made explicit by his supporters, that the assembly had "not the Privileges of the house of Commons," that the king could give his colonial subjects "what measure of Liberty, and what form of Government, he" pleased, and that the assembly therefore had "no Privilege, but what the King is pleased to allow us." As colonial spokesmen had long argued in opposition to such doctrines, Bourke contended that the colonists were "all British subjects" who were "entitled to the laws of England, and to its Constitution, as their inheritance" and who possessed "their Rights and Privileges, by

[55] Philip Wright, *Monumental Inscriptions of Jamaica* (London, 1766), 99; Estate Inventories, 51:102–8, Archives of Jamaica, Spanish Town, Jamaica; Wills, 40, ff. 64–67, Island Record Office, Spanish Town.

[56] Estate Inventories, 51:102–8, Archives of Jamaica.

[57] [Bourke], *Privileges*, 2, 14–15, 24–25, 28, 43.

as free and certain a tenure, as that, by which they hold their lands, as that, by which the King holds his crown." For that reason, Bourke continued, the "King could not give any other form of civil government or laws, than those of England."[58]

This requirement necessarily meant that "the form of government" and the constitution of the colonies resembled those "of England, as nearly as the condition of" dependent colonies could "be brought to resemble, that of . . . a great and independent empire." Like other British colonies, Jamaica, Bourke argued, had "enjoyed this constitution ever since civil government was first established here." "Upon this foundation," he affirmed, the "house of Assembly of Jamaica" necessarily held "the same rank in our little system as the house of Commons does, in that of our mother country," and "the court of Chancery and all the courts of justice" stood "in the same degree of subordination and inferiority to it, as those courts in England do to the house of Commons." "The power, the authority, and superiority over ministers and courts of justice, which the constitution" gave "to the house of Commons" was indeed, in Bourke's view, "the chief bulwark of the constitution" for "security against the oppression of ministers, and the corruption of judges." As such, it was "the birthright and inheritance of every Briton," no matter in which "part of the British Empire" he resided, "and the only form of government to which he can be made subject, without his consent."[59]

The doctrines advocated by Lyttelton and his adherents seemed to Bourke thoroughly to invert this constitution. Those doctrines did not deny that the colonists were "freemen" who held "their lands, their lives and liberties, under the security of the laws of England," and had "a right to justice administered in the same forms, and by the same rules, as in England," or that their courts derived "their existence from the same source," had "the same powers, and" stood "in the same degree of subordination to one another, as the courts of justice do in England." However, by asserting "that the representative body of the people, a court, by the laws of England, superior in rank, in power, and importance, to all those courts" was "in this Colony . . . placed below them," they at the same time denied the colonists "those powers and privileges, without which" their "rights and possessions" could not be secured, thereby, Bourke wrote indignantly, at once "mocking us with the sound of Liberty and Property, and robbing us of the substance."[60]

---

[58] Ibid., 27–28, 31.

[59] Ibid., 28, 31, 42, 47.

[60] Ibid., 44–46.

Denouncing such doctrines as "downright impudent nonsense," the intent of which was only "to prove us slaves," Bourke argued that the suggestion that the colonies had "no constitution . . . but what the king is pleased to give us" was "subversive of every thing, that should be dear to a Briton." "If our lives, liberties, and properties are not our inheritance, secured to us by the same laws, determined by the same jurisdictions, and fenced in and defended by the same constitution, as the wisdom of our ancestors found it necessary to establish, for the preservation of these blessings in our mother country," he wrote, "then, are the subjects of the Colonies, not freemen but slaves; not the free subjects, but the outcasts of Britain; possessing those invaluable blessings, only as tenants at will, the most uncertain and wretched of all tenures; and liable to be dispossessed, by the hand of power." No such form of government, he declared, could "be imposed upon us against our consent, without actually degrading us from the rank of Englishmen, and reducing us to a condition of slavery." If colonists were actually "freemen, and not slaves," he insisted, then their "liberties," including the constitutional superiority of "the representatives of the people" as the principal "fence" that secured "to the subject those invaluable blessings," were "as much" their "inheritance, as" their "lands." By no means "concessions from the crown," the privileges for which the Jamaican assembly contended thus "derived . . . from their Constituents" and were "the right and inheritance of the people."[61]

Throughout his pamphlet, Bourke set the context of the Jamaica privilege controversy within the framework of the seventeenth-century struggles of Parliament against the crown, when "arbitrary power, under the shelter of unlimited Prerogative, was making large strides over the land." He recalled how the Stuart monarchs had "carried the notions of kingly RIGHT and kingly POWER to such a blasphemous height and set so little value on the liberties of the people" that "nothing could" have been "more obnoxious [to them] than the House of Commons," to which they offered "many . . . affronts." He celebrated Parliament's refusal "to submit to affronts, or to yield up their privileges to the dictates of an undeserving monarch, or the attempts of a profligate court" and praised "those great men" in the House of Commons "who stood forth at that critical period, in defense of the Constitution." Stressing the "respect and deference" that have "ever be[en] shewn to the sentiments of opinions, and much more to the determinations" of men like Sir John Eliot, Sir Edward Coke, Sir Edward Littleton, Sir Robert Phelips, Sir William

---

[61] Ibid., 2, 44–47.

Jones, "and many others recorded in the histories of those times," Bourke held up the behavior of such "venerable patriots" as the only reason why "the Subjects of Britain" were "not at this day as much enslaved as those of France and Spain."[62]

Against the example of this glorious English tradition of parliamentary opposition to arbitrary government, Bourke addressed the arguments then circulating in Jamaica "to frighten us out of our freedom." "We are told, for instance, in the public papers, we are told it in private," Bourke reported, "that if the Assembly" did "not proceed to business, (their privileges unvindicated)," Jamaicans would lose their legislature and that the king-in-council had "determined against us, and has given us to understand, that if we insist on our privileges," the crown would apply "to his Parliament, to make laws for us." If it existed, such an order, Bourke argued, could only be regarded "an abuse of his Majesty's name and authority, by his ministers, and such an attack upon the people of this Colony, as, if submitted to, or forced upon them, proclaims them slaves." Like instructions to governors, resolutions of the Privy Council, Bourke declared, were "not laws: and if they" were "against law, no subject" was "obliged to obey them." By thus denying the finality of Privy Council decisions, Bourke, in this declaration, fundamentally challenged metropolitan theories of colonial governance.[63]

Somewhat surprisingly, in view of the House of Commons' 1757 resolutions denying the constitutional validity of an earlier Jamaican assembly's assertion of its rights, Bourke showed no disposition to question parliamentary authority. Rather, he acknowledged that the Jamaica assembly's authority was "subordinate to that of a British Legislature, which" was, "and must, in the nature of things, be supreme over all the British dominions." "Every subject throughout" those dominions, he wrote, owed "the highest respect and reverence" to Parliament and "obedience" to its "laws." Yet he expressed confidence that Parliament would reject, "as a daring attempt to degrade them, from the glorious title of protectors of British liberty, to the base purposes of oppression," any effort by the ministry to disfranchise Jamaicans because they would "not yield to the dictates of a minister, in a point of the last consequence to their freedom."[64]

---

[62] Ibid., 8–9, 11–12, 28.

[63] Ibid., 59–61.

[64] Ibid., 46–47, 61.

In conclusion, Bourke referred his readers to two widely different models: his native Ireland and Jamaica during the early years of its existence as an English colony. "Inhabited and possessed by the children of England and of those who conquered it," Ireland had been "once free," but now, as a result of submitting to Poynings' Law and of systematic corruption by English ministers, its people enjoyed "less liberty than any other subjects in the British dominions." Charging that ministers had "been long endeavouring to adorn the Colonies with" the same "fate and condition" to which their predecessors had brought Ireland, he praised early Jamaican legislators for preventing the imposition of Poynings' Law in the colony during the late 1670s and for refusing for more than a half century to establish a permanent revenue until they had secured the king's assent to Jamaica's "great charter," a 1728 statute guaranteeing Jamaicans the benefit of English laws.[65]

In Bourke's view contemporary Jamaicans could find no better example to follow. Only because "no threats could frighten, no bribes could corrupt, no arts or arguments could perswade" more than two generations of Jamaican legislators "to consent to laws, that would enslave posterity," he thought, were Jamaicans still free. If their "ancestors, in the infancy of this Colony, in the arbitrary reigns of a Charles and a James, and when prerogative was unlimitted, and liberty undefined, thus nobly withstood every attempt to enslave us," surely, Bourke admonished his readers, the "present generation," living in an era "when liberty is established, and prerogative limitted," could do no "less for posterity." He called upon the new assembly to continue to stand fast against Lyttelton's "irregular and unconstitutional" ruling and neither "to submit to Oppression" nor "to suffer ourselves to be frightened out of our liberties." By insisting that Jamaicans could not be made "slaves . . . without our consent," Bourke not only cautioned against submitting to such arbitrary actions but also made explicit the major underlying assumption behind emerging colonial theories about constitutional arrangements in the early modern British Empire, the assumption that those arrangements could not be changed by administrative fiat from the center but required colonial consent.[66]

That the new assembly would heed Bourke's advice and not depart significantly from its two predecessors was immediately revealed when it met on August 13 and once again unanimously elected Charles Price,

---

[65] Ibid., 63–66.
[66] Ibid.

Jr., to the speakership. Lyttelton would have liked to reject Price, but, showing far more regard for local custom than he had in the privilege case the previous December, he approved him. "How clearly soever it is the right of the Crown to do it," he wrote to the Board of Trade, there was no precedent for such a rejection in Jamaica, and he knew that the "Advocates of Privilege" would regard it as a "new breach" of privilege and persevere in reelecting Price until he would be forced into still another dissolution.[67]

Even with Price as speaker, Lyttelton still hoped that the Privy Council's ruling, which he had Attorney General Gilbert Ford, a former house member, show privately to leading legislators, would deter the house from again taking up the matter of privilege. To the governor's dismay, however, Price's behavior at the time of his presentation dramatically kept the controversy alive. Persisting in his opinion that the assembly's privileges did "not flow from the grace of the King, but" were "Rights inherent in them" and wishing to make a powerful symbolic statement in denial of the Privy Council's authority to rule on such questions, Price decided that he would not "ask them from the Crown at all." Accordingly, "instead of making any application of Privileges," Price simply "stood silent," and, when Lyttelton asked him if he had anything more to say, he replied, "No Sir." Not knowing how to respond, Lyttelton simply adjourned the assembly for three days until he had obtained an explanation for the speaker's behavior.[68]

What he learned was that Price's behavior was merely the first part of a bold effort to challenge the authority of the crown by going over the heads of the Privy Council directly to Parliament. Charles Price, Sr., an old foe of prerogative and former speaker who had come out of retirement for the occasion, proposed and a majority of the house agreed to petition the British "House of Commons against the measures of the King and his Ministers." To prevent the assembly from pursuing this plan, Lyttelton on August 16 recalled the house and asked the speaker if he would now apply for privileges. After Price answered that he did "not think there" was "any occasion for it," the governor asked again, only to be told that Price did "not intend it." Having recently been empowered to draw upon the metropolitan treasury to support the troops on the Jamaican military establishment while no taxes were being collected, Lyttelton felt no pressure to tolerate such a blatant defiance of

---

[67] Lyttelton to Board of Trade, Aug. 20, 1765, CO 137/33, f. 224, PRO.

[68] Ibid., ff. 224–26.

the crown's authority and on the spot dissolved his third assembly in less than seven months.[69]

With this dissolution, the privilege controversy entered a long but uneventful third phase which lasted for the next ten months until June 1766. As house leaders assessed the situation, they had little hope of a successful appeal to the metropolitan government. Not only was Lyttelton's "Interest . . . strong at Court" but also, as the Stamp Act seemed so powerfully to suggest, the climate of metropolitan opinion appeared to be running strongly against the colonies. "The ever memorable ministry who so far infringed the Constitutions of our Country as to tax a part of the people without the Consent of their representatives," one Jamaican legislator declared, seemed to be determined to reduce colonial liberty. The Stamp Act appeared merely the first step in a process by which "the spirit of freedom which formerly animated & supported Brittons in the most inhospitable Climates" in the colonies would be gradually "suppressed & extinguished." "Can we here," asked one Jamaican, "or Can the Colonys settled on the northern Continent, be now look'd upon as enjoying the benefits of the British Constitution? Does it not appear by the sentiments & proceedings of a late ministry, that our rights as Brittains are extinguish[e]d & done away so soon as we leave that Island?" "Hardly a Century ago," he observed, actions and resolutions of the kind the Jamaican house had adopted in the privilege controversy "would have been considered meretorious" but were "now from the Venality of the times & the Corruptness of a certain house, deem'd almost criminal."[70]

Perhaps hoping that the new British administration would be "more favourable . . . for America," the "Majority of the Late House," acting "as *private Subjects*," applied to the House of Commons for redress. By this action, house members may have intended, as one of them cynically noted in April 1765, simply to make it clear that Jamaicans thought it "better to be Slaves to a British parl[iamen]t than to the dependant of a Minister." Even if some of them did indeed privately fear that Parliament was "determined to suppress all Liberty in America," house leaders

[69] Ibid. See also, Taylor to Arcedeckne, Sept. 2, 1765, Vaneck Papers, 2/1, Cambridge University Library.

[70] Graham to Arcedeckne, Sept. 20, 1765, Vaneck Papers, 2/1, Cambridge University Library.

in this application, nevertheless expressed their faith that the Commons, as "the Constitutional Judges of the Rights of British Subjects, however remotely Scituated from their Mother Country," would "decide in a Constitutional Manner . . . the Nature and Extent of their Privileges." At the same time, individual House members urged Jamaican landowners resident in Britain to mobilize to prevent the colony's constitution from being overturned.[71]

The house's refusal to acknowledge the authority of the Privy Council in matters of privilege left Lyttelton few options. Now able to provide for the soldiers out of royal funds, he determined not to call another assembly until he had received the board's reaction to the assembly's action. After "all the late Assemblies" had "ended so unfruitfully," he wrote the Board of Trade, he had no reason to think that the members of still another assembly would "abate in their pretensions to excessive Privileges" until they had learned how the House of Commons had ruled on their petition. When Lyttelton learned that Chief Justice Thomas Fearon, who had taken "a large share in all the violent and illegal Resolutions of the last two Assemblies," was one of twenty-one members who signed the application to the House of Commons, however, he got a measure of vengeance by removing Fearon from his judgeship, a step that provoked Nicholas Bourke, Fearon's son-in-law and author of the pamphlet discussed above, to resign from his post as assistant judge.[72]

Throughout the fall and winter of 1765–66, Lyttelton had every reason to expect that the Privy Council would carry through on its threat to place the privilege controversy before Parliament and seems to have expected that Parliament would take his side. Indeed, the intensity of the opposition to the Stamp Act in the continental colonies during the spring and summer of 1765 encouraged him to believe that the metropolitan government would act in "an exemplary manner" to "maintain the Authority not [only] of the Crown but indeed of the King & Parliament"

[71] Taylor to Arcedeckne, Sept. 2, 1765, Jan. 24, 1767; Graham to Arcedeckne, Apr. 21, 1765, Vaneck Papers, 2/1, 2/2, Cambridge University Library; Lyttelton to Board of Trade, Aug. 20, 1765, CO 137/33, f. 227, PRO; "A Summary Account of the Proceedings," Long Papers, Add. MSS., 22676, ff. 154–59, British Library.

[72] Lyttelton to Board of Trade, Aug. 20, 1765, CO 137/33, ff. 227–29, PRO; "A Summary Account of the Proceedings," Long Papers, Add. MSS., 22676, ff. 154–59, British Library; Taylor to Arcedeckne, Sept. 2, Nov. 11, 1765, Vaneck Papers, 2/2, Cambridge University Library.

over all the colonies.[73] Following receipt of Lyttelton's report on his experiences with the assembly in August, the Privy Council in late November actually did order copies of all papers relating to the dispute laid before Parliament. Pending the results of a parliamentary inquiry, the Board of Trade left it up to Lyttelton whether or not he would call yet another assembly.[74]

But metropolitan officials were so consumed with the Stamp Act crisis that they had little time to consider "the unhappy Divisions subsisting" in Jamaica. The agent Stephen Fuller assured the committee of correspondence in late February 1766 that he had "never for one moment lost sight of this grand & important object" and reported that "immediately after the Business of the Stamp Act was over" the members of Parliament from Jamaica had resolved to "do every thing in their Power to reestablish the harmony, and Tranquility of the Island."[75] Waiting to hear what was happening in England, Lyttelton, in the meantime, managed, despite a slave uprising in St. Mary Parish in November and December, both to preserve "the good Order of the Government" and to enforce the Stamp Act, this last accomplishment perhaps having been made easier by the absence of an assembly.[76]

But members of the Jamaican political community deplored the "confusions we Continue in, about the affair of Privilege," and rumors that Lyttelton had asked to be recalled did not allay their discontent over his failure to call an assembly.[77] When on the last day of February 1766 the grand jury of Middlesex County addressed Lyttelton on this subject, no assembly had sat for more than a few days for over fourteen months. Considering the "present declining State of . . . Jamaica," worried about the government's failure to pay its creditors for so long, and anxious lest the fall slave rebellion might be the harbinger of an even larger one, this body urged Lyttelton to call an election and asked him to exert "his share of prerogative . . . in remedying as much as possible, the present

---

[73] Lyttelton to Knox, Oct. 20, 1765, Knox Papers, Clements Library.

[74] William Sharpe to Board of Trade, Nov. 29, 1765, CO 137/33, ff. 242–43, PRO; Board of Trade to Lyttelton, Dec. 20, 1765, CO 138/22, ff. 328–29, PRO.

[75] Fuller to Jamaica Committee of Correspondence, Feb. 22, 1766, Lyttelton Papers, Clements Library.

[76] Lyttelton to Stephen Fuller, Dec. 12, 1765, Fuller Letter Book, Perkins Library, Duke University; Lyttelton to Board of Trade, Dec. 24, 1765, CO 137/34, f. 48, PRO.

[77] Zachary Bayly to Chaloner Arcedeckne, Sept. 26, 1765; Taylor to Arcedeckne, Dec. 9, 1765, Vaneck Papers, 2/1, Cambridge University Library.

Misfortunes of our Country, and averting that Ruin and Desolation with which it was threatened."[78] A month later, Lyttelton finally issued writs for the election of an assembly to meet on May 13, at which time he was determined to make "a new trial . . . whether" this "Obstinate People" would "do the business they are convened for or ride testy as their Predecessors have done on the points of Privilege."[79]

The results of the election were not encouraging for Lyttelton, however. The "Sentiments and Disposition of those who" were going to "have the greatest weight in the Assembly" did not lead Lyttelton to expect that it would act any differently from previous ones, and he decided to postpone meeting with them until he had learned what his London superiors had determined about the controversy. In early May he still hoped, as he told the Board of Trade, that Parliament would take measures in response to the Stamp Act crisis "concerning the Government and Pretensions of His Majesty's American Dominions in general" that would put an end to "the Difficulties which obstruct the Settlement of the Peace of this Island."[80]

But Lyttelton's hopes were dashed on May 22 when he received a letter written on March 13 from Secretary of State Henry Seymour Conway and a member of the Rockingham administration that was then moving not to provoke but to quiet contention between metropolis and colonies. Instead of supporting Lyttelton, Conway urged him to seek some "Mode of Conciliation . . . there, without the Interference of Government," thereby confessing the metropolitan government's inability or unwillingness to enforce measures in the colonies without the consent of the local political establishment.[81] Well before he had received Conway's crushing letter, Lyttelton, long persuaded that "America [was] . . . a part of the world which . . . there is no reason to be in love with,"[82] had requested a leave of absence. In late May, probably in the same packet with Conway's letter, he received word that metropolitan officials had granted his request and had appointed Roger Hope Elletson as lieutenant governor to assume the governorship. Within ten days, on June 2, Lyttelton, no doubt taking solace in the conviction that he had at least

---

[78] Address of the Grand Jury of Middlesex, Feb. 28, 1766, Lyttelton Papers, 13 (i), Worcester Record Office.

[79] Lyttelton to Knox, Mar. 30, 1766, Knox Papers, Clements Library.

[80] Lyttelton to Board of Trade, May 12, 1766, CO 137/34, f. 24, PRO.

[81] Conway to Lyttelton, Mar. 13, 1766, Lyttelton Papers, 11 (i), 578, Worcester Record Office.

[82] Lyttelton to Knox, Mar. 30, 1766, Knox Papers, Clements Library.

preserved himself "from censure," even if he had not been able "to obtain . . . compliance with the Instructions of the Crown on the part of the People," embarked for London, leaving Jamaica and its obstinate legislative leaders behind him.[83]

With Lyttelton's departure, the privilege controversy entered a fourth and final phase. Scion of an old Jamaica family, a member of the Jamaica council since 1757, and politically well-connected in England, the new lieutenant governor had himself been a member of the Jamaica assembly in the 1750s, representing Port Royal in 1752–53 and 1756–57 and St. Andrew in 1754–56. One of Elletson's first acts was to call the assembly that had been elected on May 13 to meet on June 24.[84] Almost 54 percent (22 of 41) of the representatives who had sat in the last organized assembly in March 1765 had been reelected. Of the nineteen members who had not been in that body, eight had previously served in the assembly. Of those eight, three, Nicholas Bourke, John Edwardes, and Thomas Williams, had been in the assembly in December 1764 when the privilege controversy began, and Bourke and Edwardes had been active leaders in that body. Indeed, almost all of the legislators who had taken a prominent role in opposing Lyttelton, including Charles Price, Jr., Edwardes, Bourke, Thomas Fearon, Edward Long, Jasper Hall, Thomas French, George Bonner, Stephen Redwood, Francis Dennis, and George Paplay, remained in the house.

But this high persistence of leaders did not prevent the assembly from taking a conciliatory first step. In selecting a speaker, it passed over Charles Price, Jr., and selected William Nedham, albeit it subsequently formally thanked Price for "his steady, impartial, and faithful, discharge of the high and important office of speaker of this house, during the late assemblies," commended him for "supporting, on every occasion, the honour and dignity of the crown, and the rights and privileges of the people," and presented him with a piece of silver worth £300 sterling. Son of a longtime former speaker who had previously represented the parish of Vere in 1754–57 but had not been a member of the house during

---

[83] Elletson to Board of Trade, June 5, 1766, in Jacobs, "Elletson's Letter Book," *Jamaican Historical Review* 1 (1946): 195; Lyttelton to Knox, Mar. 30, 1766, Knox Papers, Clements Library.

[84] Elletson to Conway, June 5, 1766, in Jacobs, "Elletson's Letter Book," *Jamaican Historical Review* 1 (1946): 195–96.

the earlier stages of the controversy, Nedham at his confirmation requested privileges in the way that had been customary before the privilege controversy. Regarding these actions as an indication that the assembly was in a cooperative mood, Elletson called upon the house to
put old disputes behind it and take care of all the business that had
accumulated in the eighteen months since it had last met long enough
to enact any legislation.[85]

In accord with "the Temper of People without Doors," however, house
members showed no disposition to "forego entering again upon their late
disputes."[86] Immediately following Elletson's opening speech, they
passed seven of the eight resolutions adopted on December 21, 1764, and
March 19, 1765, asserting their privileges. Two days later, on June 26,
the house voted Pierce Cooke, who in May 1765 had sued its messenger
Edward Bolt for false imprisonment at the start of the privilege controversy, and his attorney, George MacCulloch, "in breach of the known
privileges of this house," ordered them taken into custody, and, before
discharging them the next day, forced both to apologize and thereby to
acknowledge its power of commitment. On June 28 it ordered George
Ramsay, register of the Court of Chancery, to lay the chancery record
containing Lyttelton's December 1764 ruling about its privileges before
the house.[87]

This last action was the first step in an effort to persuade Elletson to
do what Lyttelton had refused in March 1765: formally and explicitly to
void the offensive chancery decree. It provided the foundation for twelve
resolutions, adopted unanimously on July 1. In these resolutions, the
house defined the nature of its privileges and the terms on which it held
them. Denying either that any Jamaican court had authority to "examine, explain, limit, or in any wise determine upon" its privileges or that
any Jamaican judge was "competent . . . to controul the jurisdiction of
this house," the assembly, in making its principal constitutional point,
asserted that its privileges were founded neither "on acts of parliament,
nor on royal or ministerial instructions," but were "birth-rights inherent
in . . . the commons of this island" and "founded on the law of parliament, which," as "part of the common law of England," was "their rightful, lawful, and undoubted inheritance."[88]

---

[85] *Assembly Journals,* June 24, 28, 1766, 5:531–33, 540.

[86] Elletson to Conway, July 7, 1766, in Jacobs, "Elletson's Letter Book," *Jamaican Historical Review* 1 (1946): 204.

[87] *Assembly Journals,* June 24, 26–27, 28, 1766, 5:533–34, 536, 538–39, 540.

[88] Ibid., July 1, 1766, 5:542.

Declaring that anyone who, like Lyttelton, interfered with its exclusive jurisdiction over its privileges was "a violator of the constitution," a "subverter of the just and inherent birth-rights of the people," and "an enemy to the peace, welfare, and good government, of this island," the house denounced Lyttelton's behavior as "fundamentally subversive of the happy constitution of this colony, and of the rights, liberties, and privileges of the people," and voted that his decree should "be vacated, cancelled, and rendered void and damned, to all intents and purposes." To that end, the house called for an address to ask Elletson to cancel that decree "in such a way, that no traces may remain of so wicked and dangerous a precedent" and by that act to vindicate "the honour and dignity of this house, and the rights, liberties, and privileges, of the people, from the dangerous and unconstitutional doctrine which the said record is calculated to inculcate." Chaired by Nicholas Bourke, a committee immediately prepared such an address, which drew heavily upon Bourke's pamphlet and which the house presented to Elletson the next day.[89]

Elletson employed this address as a device whereby he might, as Conway had directed, resolve the privilege controversy in Jamaica "without the Interposition of the Government at home." He immediately referred the address for advice to the council, which, after "much debate, and very much consideration," on July 4 declared Lyttelton's decree "irregular and unprecedented" and requested Elletson to "order a Vacatur to be enter'd, and all the proceedings to be made null and void." Elletson thereupon called both the council and the assembly together and, "in the presence of a thousand spectators," ordered the decree "solemnly annuled and vacated." The register of the Court of Chancery then "deface[d] and obliterate[d] the said orders and determinations, by drawing cross-lines, with a pen, upon the same; and did cancel, tear, and destroy, the several petitions, affidavits, warrants, writs of *habeas corpus*, and returns thereon, filed in the same cause."[90]

The "general triumph and enthusiasm which prevailed on that occasion amongst all ranks of people" produced the celebrations described in the first paragraph of this chapter. Though it had required "a long and arduous struggle" of more than eighteen months, which had seen the dissolution of three assemblies because they had "refused to raise sup-

[89] Ibid., July 1–2, 1766, 5:542–44.

[90] Elletson to Conway, July 7, 1766, in Jacobs, "Elletson's Letter Book," *Jamaican Historical Review* 1 (1946): 204–5; Elletson to Board of Trade, July 7, 1766, CO 137/34, ff. 52–53, PRO; Edwards, *History* 2:428n; *Assembly Journals*, July 4, 1766, 5:544.

plies, unless satisfaction was given them" on the question of their privileges, this outcome, as one participant in these events later recalled, represented a "great victory" for "the people of Jamaica," and the assembly
sent its "cordial thanks" to Elletson. For his part the lieutenant governor,
as Jamaican legislators recognized at the time, had no option but to comply with the assembly's demand. As one house member evaluated the
situation, it was "very certain that he never would have got an Assembly
to do business with him had he not" erased the record "so [that] it was
rather a matter of force on him than his own Choice." Nevertheless, Elletson put the best face possible on the situation. Exulting that Jamaica
had "at last got rid of our Stumbling block *Privilege*," he congratulated
the legislature "on the fair prospect now before us of public Unanimity &
concord being restored and of the business of the Country being carried
on to the Satisfaction of all parties."[91]

But Elletson had not reckoned with the intensity of the assembly's
resentment or the depth of its anxieties over Lyttelton's actions. The
great victory it had achieved on July 4 did not bring the privilege controversy to an end. Immediately thereafter, the house did indeed embark
upon other business, but on July 22 it went on the attack, resolving to
appoint a committee "to inquire into the conduct of William Henry Lyttelton" during his governorship. Chaired by Edward Long and composed
of Nicholas Bourke, Charles Price, Jr., Jasper Hall, Robert Graham,
George Paplay, and John Ellis, this committee worked for more than
two weeks accumulating and analyzing evidence of Lyttelton's misbe-
havior in office.[92]

The exceedingly thorough eighty-page report it submitted to the
house on August 12 reviewed every aspect of Lyttelton's conduct in
office. It accused him of extorting fees through his secretary, of selling
military commissions to incompetent people, of displacing judicial and
militia officers who opposed him without assigning cause, of letting
chancery cases accumulate, of taking inadequate steps to quell the slave
uprising of December 1765, and, through his rapacious seizures of Spanish vessels, of interrupting trade with the Spanish colonies. Most important, the report charged that evidence found in three of Lyttelton's
early letters to the Board of Trade, copies of which agents of the assem-

[91] Edwards, *History* 2:428n; *Assembly Journals,* July 1, 16–17, 1766, 5:544–45, 557–58;
Taylor to Arcedeckne, Jan. 24, 1767, Vaneck Papers, 2/2, Cambridge University Library;
Elletson to Stephen Fuller, July 8, 1766, in Jacobs, "Elletson's Letter Book," *Jamaican
Historical Review* 1 (1946): 207.

[92] *Assembly Journals,* July 22, 1766, 5:565.

bly in London had obtained from the board, made it clear that he was engaged in a deliberate "design of Subverting the Constitution of our Government" by systematically "Debasing and Abolishing Assemblys."[93]

Whether he "brought [it] with him to the Island, or adopted [it] very soon after his Arrival here," this plan, the report charged, was early manifest in Lyttelton's insistence that the Jamaican "Constitution (of which we and our Ancestors have been in Possession ever since the first Settlement of this Colony)" flowed "no[t] from our being Englishmen, but from Concessions of the Crown, which were revokable at pleasure and that our Legislature, tho' it has ever Enjoyed and exercised the highest and most important . . . powers of Legislation[,] . . . had no better Foundation for it's rights and Privileges, than the will and pleasure of the Sovereign, nor could exercise any Powers but what it derived from his Majesty's Commission and Instructions to his Governor." Because he soon learned that the assembly was the "principal Obstruction" to this "plan of Power," the report surmised, Lyttelton early developed "an aversion to that body" and formulated "a design either to abolish Assembly's or[,] by Rendering them entirely dependant on the will and Pleasure of a Governor, to make them Subservient to his arbitrary purposes."[94]

In pursuit of this project for the "utter Abolition" of assemblies in Jamaica, Lyttelton, according to the report, took a number of carefully calculated measures. First, he misrepresented the constitution of the colony and the loyalty of its inhabitants to the Board of Trade, thereby artfully laying the foundation for his next step, which was to persuade London authorities to empower him to draw upon the royal treasury to subsist the king's troops in Jamaica. By this last measure, the report suggested, Lyttelton intended merely "to pave the way more effectually for the introduction of arbitrary power" by eliminating the "Necessity for calling . . . assemblies." Finally, the report concluded, Lyttelton had taken advantage of the cases of Cooke and McNeil to forward his project "to free himself from the Vigilance of . . . Assemblies" by destroying their privileges and bringing the assembly into public contempt. The "obscure Condition of these two men," the report observed, made it impossible that they would have had on their own "the Temerity and Imprudence to Oppose themselves to the Just power of the Constitution, unless they had Encouragement given them of protection from another Quarter." That Lyttelton "was the person that Encouraged" them "to act in that manner" the authors of the report had "not the Least doubt." Only

[93]"Assembly Journals," Aug. 12, 1766, CO 140/50, 215, PRO.

[94]Ibid.

the assembly's vigorous "assert[ion of] their priviledges" and stubborn "Reject[ion] of the Yoke, which he had fabricated for them," they affirmed, prevented him from succeeding in the "destructive Schemes which he had meditate[d] against our Constitution."[95]

In three days of debate in committees of the whole, the house condensed this report into thirty-four resolutions, thirty of which it passed on August 16. Like the document from which they were drawn, these resolutions depicted Lyttelton as a grasping and devious governor with high notions of prerogative, whose "illegal, arbitrary, violent, and unconstitutional proceedings" had earned him a black reputation as "an inciter of discord, an innovator of our happy constitution, and a violater of the rights, franchises, liberties, and privileges of the people; a promoter of arbitrary government, and an enemy to our gracious sovereign, and the welfare and prosperity of this island." The final resolution called for an address to the crown to vindicate Jamaica from "the calumnies and insinuations" Lyttelton had "disingenuously thrown upon them."[96]

Twenty-six of the resolutions passed by an overwhelming majority: nine of them passed unanimously, five others by a margin of at least four to one, ten by a ratio of at least two to one, and two more by a margin of three to two. These resolves included all of the most vehement denunciations of Lyttelton. The eight resolves decided by one or two votes, four of which did not pass, involved questions about whether Lyttelton's displacement of judicial and military officers constituted an abuse of the prerogative and whether those removals had had harmful public effects. The issue here, as the assembly subsequently revealed, was whether in appointments to offices governors were accountable only to the crown, as the minority insisted, or "also to the laws of this country," as the majority believed.[97]

The house recorded division lists on eleven of these votes as well as on two others on related questions two days later. These lists reveal that of the thirty people present and voting, a core group composed of fourteen people who voted on the winning side on every question and two people who voted with the winners twelve out of thirteen times constituted a majority which carried every question. This core group included five of the top eight legislative leaders as determined by an analysis of committee assignments: John Edwardes, Jasper Hall, Edward Long, James

[95] Ibid., 216, 219, 221–22, 227.

[96] *Assembly Journals*, Aug. 16, 1766, 5:638–43.

[97] Ibid., Aug. 16, 21, 1766, 5:638–43, 645.

Lewis, Nicholas Bourke, and Stephen Redwood. Of the fourteen people who voted in the minority, only two, Charles Price, Jr., and Thomas Gordon, were among the top eight leaders. This group displayed much less cohesion than the majority. Only one, Thomas Gordon, voted on the losing side every time; seven departed from him on at least three, and six on at least five, votes. But the dissidence of most of the fourteen people in opposition by no means extended much beyond the few questions that were determined by margins of one or two votes. Of a total of thirty votes on which there were no division lists, no more than nine people ever voted in the negative, and more than six voted in opposition on only eleven occasions. Among house members, the opposition to Lyttelton was thus extensive. He had few supporters among the membership at large and fewer still among their leaders, and that support was only on a few, mostly constitutionally ambiguous issues.[98]

Thinking that expunging Lyttelton's decree had put the privilege controversy behind him, Elletson found the scope, character, and constitutional implications of these resolutions perplexing. At least one councillor, Thomas Iredell, thought they represented such an "unwarrantable . . . assumption of power" that they demanded still another dissolution. Indeed, he believed that they "clearly prove[d]" what Lyttelton had suggested to the Board of Trade early in his administration in the letters the assembly had used so effectively to condemn him, "that unless some stop" were "put to the boundless pretensions of the House, it" would "be impossible to carry on Government." These latest resolutions, he suggested, had shown that even the "powers of a Brittish House of Commons" would "not satisfie them, were they granted their claim much higher," and that unless they were "suffered to usurp this Prerogative of the Crown, make a Cypher of the Council, and hold the King's representative in a State of bondage," they would "raise no money, the Troops" would "starve[,] and everything must tend to Anarchy and confusion."[99] Especially because the assembly had not yet voted money for the troops, however, Elletson behaved far more circumspectly, charging it with having taken measures that were "injurious to the right and prerogative, and derogatory of the honour and dignity, of his majesty's crown," but merely proroguing it for a day.[100]

---

[98] Ibid., 638–43, 644–45.

[99] Thomas Iredell to Lyttelton, Sept. 24, 1766, Lyttelton Papers, Clements Library; Elletson to Board of Trade, Sept. 29, 1766, in Jacobs, "Elletson's Letter Book," *Jamaican Historical Review* 1 (1946): 332.

[100] *Assembly Journals,* Aug. 20, 1766, 5:643.

When the house reconvened on August 21, it quickly acted to answer Elletson's charge. In seven resolutions it denied that any of its members had ever intended to infringe the royal prerogative and asserted that the house always thought itself obliged to oppose any measures that either encroached on the prerogative or "anywise trench[ed] upon and impeach[ed] the just rights, liberties, and privileges of the people." Most significantly, it declared that governors, "like all other ministers, to the king, were "accountable . . . to the laws of his country" for "every exorbitant act of power, or abuse of the prerogative" that they might commit. With this declaration, the house spelled out the constitutional assumptions that underlay its investigation into Lyttelton's conduct. It could not impeach a man who had already left office, but it could through its investigative powers call him into public account for any misconduct or violations of Jamaican law and thereby perhaps deter his successors from similar behavior.[101]

Notwithstanding the uncompromising tone of these resolutions, the house did not renew its investigation of Lyttelton and proceeded to prepare a bill to raise the money to pay its share of the current costs for the troops. On August 30, however, it did instruct a committee to draw up a complaint to the crown about Lyttelton's conduct. Composed mostly of members who had been more sympathetic to Lyttelton during the earlier investigation, this committee brought in a short but by no means exonerating memorial on September 12, which the house adopted. At the same time, the house instructed the committee of correspondence to write the colony's London agent instructing him to vindicate "the late and present assembly" from any misrepresentations in England and to recover for "the public of this island, the amount of monies" collected in Jamaica as a result of Lyttelton's successful enforcement of the Stamp Act. Although Elletson found these last measures "extraordinary" and objected to several provisions in the revenue bill, he concluded the assembly on September 12 by signing that and several other bills, thereby enacting the first legislation in Jamaica for nearly twenty-one months.[102]

Metropolitan officials showed no disposition to quarrel with the settlement of the privilege controversy reached by Elletson and the assembly. Indeed, on May 28, even before Lyttelton had left Jamaica, the Privy Council approved an additional instruction to the governor "allowing"

---

[101] Ibid., Aug. 21, 1766, 5:644–45.

[102] Ibid., Aug. 30, Sept. 12, 1766, 5:654, 662; Elletson to Board of Trade, Sept. 29, 1766, in Jacobs, "Elletson's Letter Book," *Jamaican Historical Review* 1 (1946): 333–34. A copy of the assembly's memorial is in the Lyttelton Papers, Clements Library.

Jamaican legislators for six days before and after sessions "a further Privilege from Arrests, in all Civil Suits, for such Servants and Equipage" as were "necessary for the personal Accom[m]odation of the said members in attending their respective Duties in General Assembly."[103] Once Lyttelton had returned, moreover, metropolitan authorities seemed perfectly happy to do "nothing further" in the matter,[104] and Fuller reported to his correspondents in Jamaica that the ministry was pleased that the controversy had been settled "without their being put to the trouble of determining upon points pregnant with innumerable & almost insuperable difficulties." Fuller predicted that the administration would thenceforth "let the matter sleep, rather than throw the whole Island again into fresh Distractions, & themselves into a complication of distinctions of so very great nicety, that after all it is impossible to draw the Line, & ever will be so."[105]

By the time Elletson next met the assembly in November 1766, he had received the crown's additional instruction expanding Jamaican legislative privilege, which he sent to the assembly on November 19. As Elletson reported privately to Stephen Fuller, that body promptly and unanimously passed a resolution which revealed that it was "not in the least disposed to avail themselves of it."[106] In that resolution the house reiterated its oft-repeated claim that, "as the representatives of the people of this island," it had "all the privileges that the house of commons hath as the representatives of the people of Great-Britain; and that any instruction from the king and his ministry, can neither abridge [n]or annihilate the privileges of the representative body of the people of this island."[107] The assembly had long since concluded "that it became them better to assert their own rights & liberties themselves by [their own] resolutions . . . than to refer them to the decision of any third party, even of the Crown itself."[108] With this declaration, the house announced once again

---

[103]Order in Council, May 28, 1766, CO 137/34, ff. 9–10, PRO; Duke of Richmond to Stephen Fuller, July 3, 1766, Lyttelton Papers, Clements Library; Fuller to Richmond, July 9, 1766, Stephen Fuller Letter Book, MS 6001, Boston College Library, Boston.

[104]Notation on Board of Trade to Privy Council, Aug. 1, 1766, Privy Council Papers, 1/52/57A, PRO.

[105]Fuller to Elletson, Oct. 2, 1766, and to Charles Price, Jr., Oct. 2, 1766, Stephen Fuller Letter Book, MS 6001, Boston College Library.

[106]Fuller to Elletson, Dec. 31, 1766, in Jacobs, "Elleston's Letter Book," *Jamaican Historical Review* 2 (1949): 78.

[107]*Assembly Journals*, Nov. 19, 1766, 6:4.

[108]Lyttelton to Board of Trade, Oct. 24, 1762, CO 137/32, 212–17, PRO.

that it had no intention of letting any metropolitan executive agency define its privileges.

Resentment against Lyttelton lingered for several months. "Nothing but the injustice of not complying with a Law of the Assembly's own making & the apprehension of the shock it would give to all publick Faith & honor," the legislator Simon Taylor observed in May 1767, had prevented the house from blocking payment of £4,000 Jamaica owed Lyttelton in back salary. At the same time, however, the privilege controversy rapidly lost steam. "All our Politicks are now at an end as if there never had been any such thing," Taylor wrote, "the impeachment against Lyttelton dropt & no more mention of him here than if there never had been any such person."[109]

Whether the assembly would replenish money Lyttelton had drawn from the royal treasury to support the troops during the privilege controversy lingered as an issue in Jamaican politics until the metropolitan government abandoned the fight in 1771. With this capitulation, the privilege controversy, as a modern historian has remarked, "finally ended with a complete victory for the Jamaican Assembly." Throughout the years from 1767 to 1771, the assembly hearkened back to that controversy by insisting that repaying the treasury would constitute an invitation for a subsequent governor to follow Lyttelton's example and attempt to govern without assemblies. Nothwithstanding these later reverberations, the assembly's resolution of November 19, 1766, on the additional instruction effectively gave it the last word in the Jamaica privilege controversy.[110]

This controversy provides a clear window into the state of constitutional play in the early modern British Empire on the eve of the American Revolution. It shows that, even as a new constitutional conflict which pitted Parliament against parliaments was beginning to emerge, the ongoing battles between crown and local powerholders that had characterized metropolitan-colonial relations since early in the seventeenth century continued unabated. As the Jamaican incident reveals, these older-style conflicts arose out of and revolved around opposing views of constitutional arrangements within the empire.

---

[109] Taylor to Arcedeckne, May 2, 1767, Vaneck Papers, 2/2, Cambridge University Library.

[110] Metcalf, *Royal Government and Political Conflict in Jamaica*, 170–76, quotation on 176.

Lyttelton's view grew out of a broader effort stretching back to the Restoration but reanimated after 1748 through the efforts of various imperial reformers to give metropolitan authorities a greater role in shaping colonial—and imperial—constitutional development. Underlying that effort was the argument articulated by both Lyttelton and his London supporters that colonial constitutions derived from royal grace and that royal commissions, instructions, and administrative and judicial decrees were authoritative in the colonies, overriding practices or considerations based on the larger rights of Englishmen, local custom, local need, or even local statutes. Following logically out of directives he had received from his London superiors, Lyttelton's actions in the privilege controversy, like those of other governors operating under the same directives at the same time, were, as he perceived the situation, nothing more than an episode in a larger project to restore colonial constitutions to their original condition.

That this project, as many colonial defenders understood, was based upon a profound misunderstanding of the history of constitutional development in the colonies, where metropolitan authorities had never had a free hand or even always a dominant one, only made it seem all the more subversive, and colonial political leaders quickly recognized that it represented a fundamental challenge to their conception of the constitutions under which they lived, conceptions that dated back to the middle decades of the seventeenth century. As Jamaican legislators made abundantly clear during the privilege controversy, that conception started with the assumption that colonials had the constitutions they had, not because they had been given them by the Crown, but because they had first inherited and then developed them by virtue of their status as native or naturalized Britons. In this view, those constitutions, fundamentally British in their form and especially in their representative assemblies, were the instruments through which colonists enjoyed their inherited rights as Britons. To live under a British constitution, with the same guarantees of government by consent and rule by law enjoyed in the home islands, was, for colonials residing in the remoter parts of the British world, essential to the maintenance of their identity as a British people, and the astonishing intensity and determination with which Jamaicans articulated and defended this view during the privilege controversy was a measure of the extraordinary importance that they attached to that crucial feature of their identity.

As self-conscious Britons and as surprisingly erudite students of English constitutional history, Jamaicans, like their opponents and like other colonials, conceived of their disputes in terms supplied by the great constitutional battles of the seventeenth century, as struggles between prerogative and privilege, power and rights, will and law. By deliberately using this language, they situated their conflicts in the mainstream of British constitutional conflict and thereby invested them with high significance.

The tension between these competing views of colonial constitutions, in no incident better illustrated than in the Jamaica privilege controversy, was unsusceptible to easy resolution in the early modern British Empire. The empire was not a highly centralized entity in which the metropolis enjoyed a monopoly of uncontested constitutional authority. Metropolitan decrees did not command automatic deference in the peripheries, and metropolitan officials had neither the coercive resources to implement their decisions nor a tradition sanctioning the use of what limited force they did have. As a consequence, whenever local power holders defied rulings from the capital or its representatives, metropolitan officials had little to fall back on except threats, and when threats did not work, as in the privilege controversy, they had to yield.

As the Jamaica privilege controversy so vividly reveals, local consent was crucial to the implementation of metropolitan initiatives. Regardless of theory, in practice, metropolitan power extended into the peripheries only so far as powerful local political establishments like the Jamaica legislature found acceptable. In the early modern British Empire, authority did not flow outward to distant dependent polities. Rather, authority derived out of—and was constituted through—an intricate, often contentious, and more or less continuous process of negotiation between metropolitan officials in both London and the colonies, on the one hand, and local political power holders in the colonies, on the other. Authority, in other words, was negotiated and consensual. In any given situation, what both parties were willing to accept defined what was— or was not—authoritative.

The Jamaica privilege controversy did not change this process of constitutional negotiation. By thwarting Lyttelton's effort to redefine the Jamaica constitution, the assembly did indeed during the mid-1760s prevent the implementation in Jamaica of the metropolitan view of imperial constitutional arrangements. But it did not manage to obtain explicit metropolitan endorsement for its own view of those arrangements. At the beginning of the great imperial controversy that would precede the American Revolution, constitutional authority within the British Empire remained fluid, unresolved, and the subject of a continuing process of negotiation.

But the Jamaica privilege controversy was considerably more than simply another, if perhaps more intense and prolonged, example of traditional constitutional conflict within the empire. Colonial legislatures had frequently resisted royal governors and succeeded in either bringing them to heel or, as in the case of the Gadsden election controversy in South Carolina, getting them removed. By so openly and so determinedly defying the Privy Council, however, the Jamaican assembly carried defiance of royal authority to an entirely new level, a level which had not been reached for many decades but which would be regained in the early 1770s during the Wilkes fund controversy in South Carolina and the dispute over the removal of the capital in Massachusetts. More importantly, by specifically denying the authority of Privy Council decisions that were against law (that is, Jamaican law) and by suggesting that such decisions did not have to be obeyed and might be appealed over the head of the Privy Council to the House of Commons, Jamaican leaders significantly expanded the colonial view of how the imperial constitution ought to work. In the process, they provided a striking example of constitutional definition at work in the early modern British Empire.

This chapter, on a subject about which I have been collecting material for over thirty years, is reprinted with permission and additions from the *Journal of Imperial and Commonwealth History* 22 (1994): 16–53.

FIFTEEN

Bridge to Revolution:
The Wilkes Fund Controversy in South Carolina,
1769–75

❀

IN ORIGINS as well as in results the American Revolution was an enormously complex phenomenon. Certain issues—parliamentary taxation and the tightening of the navigation system—were important in all of the colonies. But not each of the long catalogue of grievances listed in the Declaration of Independence was so universally felt. Many of the grievances arose out of attempts by metropolitan authorities to make the political systems of the colonies conform to metropolitan precedents and policies. Because those attempts were piecemeal and often ad hoc responses to glaring discrepancies in the practice of a particular colony, or in some cases two or three colonies, their impact—even if they were applied generally—varied from colony to colony. The result was that the specific causes of the Revolution and the particular pattern of the Revolutionary movement were different in every colony. To be sure, there was an American Revolution which was greater than the sum of its parts and had a character of its own; but there were also thirteen separate revolutions, each with its own peculiar characteristics, each with a list of grievances somewhat differently arranged. With few exceptions, local issues were contributory rather than decisive and must be relegated to a distinctly secondary position in any graduated classification of the causes of the American Revolution. An important exception is the Wilkes fund controversy in South Carolina. Coming during the five crucial years between 1769 and 1775, it furnished abundant testimony to the seriousness of the metropolitan challenge and helped to crystallize Revolutionary sentiment among the colony's political leaders.[1]

American protests against the Townshend revenue program coincided with the most intense phase of the demonstrations in London inspired by the celebrated and indomitable radical John Wilkes. Since his attack on George III's speech from the throne, in *North Briton* no. 45 on April 23, 1763, Wilkes had been popularly associated with the cause of liberty. After his return from exile in France in 1768, "Wilkes and Liberty" became the slogan of a numerous miscellany of supporters in Middlesex, London, and elsewhere in Britain. With his trial in early 1768 for various misdemeanors including libel against the government, his conviction on June 8, and his subsequent imprisonment, he became the martyr of English liberty.[2]

Americans as well as Englishmen were infatuated with Wilkes's cause. To Americans, the ministry's harassment of Wilkes and Parliament's attempts to tax the colonies were part of the same general assault upon liberty. In the colonies no less than in the heart of London, Wilkes became the symbol of liberty and "45" the charmed number of patriotism. Americans vied with English radicals in heaping encomium upon him. Wilkes, said one American newspaper, was the "unshaken colossus of freedom; the patriot of England, the rightful and legal representative of Middlesex; the favourite of the people; the British Hercules, that has cleaned a stable fouler than the Augean."[3] He was "not merely the idol of the mob," declared an article in the *South Carolina Gazette*, "but a

---

[1] The only more or less contemporaneous account of the Wilkes fund controversy is the brief section in John Drayton, *Memoirs of the American Revolution*, 2 vols. (Charleston, S.C., 1821), 1:91–114. There is no satisfactory modern account, though brief summaries are scattered through most of the general studies of colonial South Carolina, including Edward McCrady, *The History of South Carolina under the Royal Government, 1719–1776* (New York, 1899), 659–744; W. Roy Smith, *South Carolina as a Royal Province, 1719–1776* (New York, 1903), 368–87; and David D. Wallace, *South Carolina: A Short History, 1520–1948* (Chapel Hill, N.C., 1951), 243–46. Easily the best published account is Wallace's *The Life of Henry Laurens* (New York, 1915), 159–76, even though Henry Laurens (hereinafter Laurens) was not in the colony during much of the period of the controversy.

[2] An excellent recent study of the Wilkite movement in London is George Rudé, *Wilkes and Liberty: A Social Study of 1763 to 1774* (Oxford, 1962).

[3] *South Carolina Gazette* (Charleston), Mar. 15, 1770.

man whose very intrepid public conduct is thought deserving universal applause by the most candid, sensible, and prudent."[4]

With such great applause from the colonies, it is not surprising that Wilkes's English supporters turned to Americans for money when in early 1769 they formed the Society of the Gentlemen Supporters of the Bill of Rights to "defend and maintain the legal, constitutional Liberty of the subject" and, more immediately, to pay Wilkes's sizable debts.[5] Relatively few Americans were willing to translate their enthusiasm for Wilkes into more tangible favors, however. The Friends of Liberty in Boston sent their wishes for his restoration to his liberty, family, friends, and country, but no money. In Maryland and Virginia two different groups of planters each contributed forty-five hogsheads of tobacco.[6] The only official governmental body to respond was the South Carolina Commons House of Assembly.

Among the colonists solicited by the society was Christopher Gadsden, forty-five-year-old wealthy merchant and veteran politician, delegate to the Stamp Act Congress, staunch opponent of parliamentary taxation, and acknowledged leader of the Charleston radicals. The society's request arrived in the fall of 1769, when South Carolina was in the midst of a heated political hassle over the justice of the nonimportation agreements against the Townshend Acts.[7] South Carolina patriots were particularly sensitive to the charge, made by the critics of nonimportation, that they were "servilely" imitating their northern neighbors, waiting—as young William Henry Drayton later wrote—"till in the Northern Hemisphere, a *light* appeared to show the political course we were to steer."[8]

---

[4] Ibid., Dec. 28, 1769.

[5] Rudé, *Wilkes and Liberty*, 61–62.

[6] *South Carolina Gazette*, Dec. 28, 1769; *St. James Chronicle; or, British Evening Post* (London), Feb. 10, 1770; Boston Friends of Liberty to John Wilkes, Nov. 4, 1769, Wilkes Papers, Additional Manuscripts 30870, ff. 223–24, British Library, London. The Virginia hogsheads probably were never sent, the official collector, Miles, appearing to have sold them and applied the money to his own use. See George Mason to ____, Dec. 6, 1770, in Kate Mason Rowland, *The Life of George Mason, 1725–1792*, 2 vols. (New York, 1892), 1:150.

[7] *South Carolina American and General Gazette* (Charleston), Dec. 13, 1769; Robert Morris to John Wilkes, Feb. 6, 1770, Wilkes Papers, Add. MSS 30871, f. 7, British Library. On the debate over the Townshend Acts in South Carolina, see McCrady, *South Carolina under Royal Government*, 644–58.

[8] *South Carolina Gazette*, Sept. 21, Dec. 28, 1769.

To South Carolina patriots the society's request suggested an action which would at once demonstrate their boldness and their originality. There was no more conspicuous and dramatic way to display their devotion to American liberty than to vote a sum for the support of liberty in Britain. On December 8, 1769, they made their proposal to the Commons House, which voted overwhelmingly to accept it. Without the consent of either the council or Lieutenant Governor William Bull II, the house ordered Treasurer Jacob Motte to advance £1,500 sterling to a committee which was to send it to the Bill of Rights Society.[9] The committee promptly executed the Commons' order, stipulating to the Society that the money be used "for supporting such of our Fellow Subjects who by asserting the Just Rights of the People, have or shall become obnoxious to administration, and suffer from the hand of Power"—a clear indication that the Commons intended the grant to be used to support Wilkes.[10] For once, South Carolina patriots had acted independently of and more boldly than their northern counterparts. "In this instance," Peter Timothy proudly proclaimed in the Charleston *South Carolina Gazette*, "it cannot be said *we* have followed the Example of the Northern Colonies."[11]

Just how bold this action was will be apparent when it is recalled that since the seventeenth century the crown had stipulated in instructions to its governors that money be issued from colonial treasuries only upon warrants signed by the governors.[12] During the early years of royal government in South Carolina, the executive as well as both houses of the legislature had complied with this instruction.[13] But after 1750 the Commons increasingly resorted to the practice of borrowing money from the treasury for a particular service without the consent of either governor

[9] Journals of the Commons House of Assembly, 38:215 (Dec. 8, 1769), South Carolina Archives Department, Columbia.

[10] Committee to Robert Morris, Dec. 9, 1769, in "Correspondence of Charles Garth," *South Carolina Historical and Genealogical Magazine* 31 (1930): 132–33; Committee to Messrs. Hankey and Partners, Dec. 9, 1769, in John Almon, ed., *The Correspondence of the Late John Wilkes with His Friends*, 5 vols. (London, 1805), 5:42–43.

[11] *South Carolina Gazette*, Dec. 8, 1769.

[12] Leonard W. Labaree, ed., *Royal Instructions to British Colonial Governors, 1670–1776*, 2 vols. (New York, 1935), 1:203–4.

[13] See William Bull II to Earl of Hillsborough, Sept. 8, 1770, Transcripts of Records Relating to South Carolina in the British Public Record Office, 32:320–30, S. C. Archives Department.

or council and repaying the money later by an appropriation in the annual tax bill.[14] The Commons probably did not at first realize the implications of this practice, which enabled the Commons to order money from
the treasury by its single authority. Because the Commons had effectively denied the right of the governor and council to amend money
bills,[15] the only way the executive could hope to put a stop to the practice
was to reject an entire tax bill which appropriated money to repay the
treasurer for a sum advanced on the Commons' order. Such action not
only would have provoked a serious political dispute but also might have
put the colony in severe financial straits. Consequently, as long as the
Commons limited its orders to routine services to which the executive
had no serious objection, both the governor and council let the matter
pass without comment. Even when the Commons voted £600 sterling to
defray the cost of sending delegates to the Stamp Act Congress in New
York in 1765, both Lieutenant Governor Bull and the council, though
neither approved, allowed it to pass "sub silentio," as Bull later remarked, rather than provoke a violent dispute.[16]

But neither Bull nor the council could allow the Wilkes vote to pass
sub silentio. Wilkes was too much the center of attention in London for
the Commons' action not to come to the notice of metropolitan authorities. Bull could have publicly indicated his disapproval by dissolving the
Commons, but he was never one to act rashly. As a former speaker of the
Commons and as an experienced and astute politician, he well knew that
such a move might throw the colony into turmoil and seriously impair
his harmonious relationship with the house. Had there been any sizable
opposition to what the Commons had done, the risk might have been
worth taking, but the indications are that there was not. Merchant
Henry Laurens—absent from the Commons on a tour of the backcountry on the day of the vote—thought the measure too radical and predicted that "these Chaps will get a rap o' the knuckles for this,"[17] and
William Henry Drayton in the *South Carolina Gazette* congratulated the

---

[14] Committee of Correspondence to Garth, Sept. 6, 1770, "Garth Correspondence," *South
Carolina Historical and Genealogical Magazine* 31 (1930): 244–53.

[15] For a study of this development, see Jack P. Greene, *The Quest for Power: The Lower
Houses of Assembly in the Southern Royal Colonies, 1689–1776* (Chapel Hill, N.C., 1963).

[16] Commons Journals, 37:97 (Aug. 2, 1765), 194 (June 27, 1766), S. C. Archives Department; Bull to Hillsborough, Sept. 8, 1770, Transcripts of South Carolina Records,
32:320–30, ibid.

[17] Laurens's Petition to Ministry, June 23, 1781, Emmet Collection, New York Public
Library, as quoted in Wallace, *Henry Laurens,* 379.

colony on its "sudden increase" in wealth and snidely complimented "those of our patriots, who were most active in promoting a measure . . . to defray the *bills* of a *certain club* of patriots, at the *London Tavern*";[18] but most South Carolina politicians appear to have favored the grant. Only seven members of a full house voted against it, and Timothy's newspaper reported that had the order been for only £1,000 sterling the "Vote would have been *unanimous*" and that some were inclined to increase the sum to £2,000.[19] Moreover, the committee charged with transmitting the money to Wilkes consisted of seven of the ten most important members of the house, men with economic and social position who had, for the most part, been prominent in the Commons for over a decade and were the leading politicians in the colony. Peter Manigault, James Parsons, and John Rutledge were wealthy lawyers, Christopher Gadsden and Benjamin Dart large merchants, and Thomas Ferguson and Thomas Lynch successful planters.[20]

Because he could not avoid reporting the matter to authorities in London, Bull decided to leave the choice of retaliatory measures to them and immediately sent the colonial secretary, Lord Hillsborough, an account of the affair. To excuse himself and to explain his inability to prevent the Commons' sending the money, he noted that from "the great religious and Civil indulgences granted by the Crown to encourage Adventurers to settle in America, the Government of the Colonies has gradually inclined more to the democratical than regal side" and that "since the late unhappy discontents and the universal extension of the Claims of the American Commons" the power of the South Carolina Commons had "risen to a great Heighth." So extensive was its power, Bull reported, that the house had adopted the practice of ordering money out of the treasury by its single authority "as less liable to obstruction from the Governor or Council" to its "pursuing any favorite object."[21]

News of the grant to Wilkes got a mixed reception in London, where

---

[18] *South Carolina Gazette*, Dec. 28, 1769.

[19] Ibid., Dec. 8, 1769.

[20] The importance of members was determined by an analysis of committee assignments for the entire period, 1769–75. The other three most important leaders in this house were merchant Henry Laurens, lawyer Charles Pinckney, and planter Rawlins Lowndes, who later became speaker. In subsequent houses lawyers Thomas Bee, Thomas Heyward, Jr., and Charles Cotesworth Pinckney and merchant Miles Brewton also played prominent roles.

[21] Bull to Hillsborough, Dec. 12, 16, 1769, Transcripts of South Carolina Records, 32: 132–36, S. C. Archives Department.

it received considerable attention from the press.[22] Wilkes himself was annoyed because the Commons had sent the money to the society instead of directly to him for his private use. In a marked display of his well-known dislike for Americans, he personally responded to the committee not with appreciation but with a peevish letter which, he contended "was admirably calculated for the Meridian of South-Carolina." But the society rejected this letter, thanked the Commons, and pledged its support in maintaining the rights of all Britons.[23] William Henry Drayton, who had left South Carolina for London in early January, published a satirical attack on the South Carolina Commons in which he congratulated its members for having "broke loose from the shackles of their constitution, and the imperious restrictions of a royal commission and instructions."[24] But London merchant William Lee thought the Commons had "done nobly," and another London correspondent wrote that the vote to Wilkes had "given a greater Shock to the mini[steria]l Operations, for binding Liberty in Fetters, than any one Act of the Americans since the Stamp-Act bounced out of Pandora's Box" and predicted that South Carolina would "be revered, and considered, as the first in America," though he warned South Carolina patriots that "you *must expect* every Engine will be set to work to engage you to *rescind* that Vote."[25]

The timeliness of the warning was immediately discernible in the reaction of metropolitan authorities. When they received Bull's letter, they were both indignant and astonished. The Commons' audacity in voting money to support the ministry's most violent and effective critic deeply offended them, and they were amazed to learn that the Commons had acquired the power to order money out of the treasury without the con-

[22] See *Daily Advertiser* (London), Feb. 7, 1770; *London Chronicle*, Feb. 6–8, 1770; and *Middlesex Journal, or Chronicle of Liberty* (London), Feb. 10–13, 13–15, 15–17, 1770.

[23] John Horne, "Relation," *Controversial Letters of John Wilkes, Esq., the Reverend John Horne, and Their Principal Adherents* (London, 1771), 156–59; *South Carolina Gazette*, Aug. 23, 1770.

[24] R[obert] M[orris] to Speaker of South Carolina Commons, Feb. 23, 1770, *Lloyd's Evening Post* (London), Mar. 19–21, 1770. This letter, which was widely reprinted, apparently first appeared in the *Publick Advertiser* (London), Mar. 20, 1770. See *South Carolina American and General Gazette*, May 23, 1770. For the attribution of the letter to Drayton, see extract of a letter from London, Mar. 30, 1770, *South Carolina Gazette*, May 17, 1770. On Drayton's going to England, see *South Carolina Gazette and Country Journal* (Charleston), Jan. 9, 1770.

[25] William Lee to Richard Henry Lee, Feb. 6, 1770, Brock Collection, box 4, Henry E. Huntington Library, San Marino, Calif.; extract of a letter from London, Mar. 30, 1770, *South Carolina Gazette*, May 17, 1770.

sent of the executive. Moving with unusual alacrity, they sought an opinion from Attorney General William De Grey, who reported early in February 1770 that the Commons could not "by the Constitution" order money from the treasury without the consent of the governor and council. The Commons' exercise of that power, he declared, was contrary to the governor's commission and instructions and could not "be warranted by the modern practice of a few years, irregularly introduced, and improvidently acquiesced in." The assumptions were that the Commons could not alter the constitution of South Carolina or acquire new powers by usage and that both royal instructions and commissions took precedence over local practice. De Grey also questioned whether the Commons could vote money for other than purely local services and whether it could divert to different purposes money already appropriated by law. He concluded that the Commons' grant to Wilkes was illegal and suggested that "preventive measures for the future . . . to protect the subject from the Repetition of such exactions" should be taken, either "by the Parliament here, or by Instructions to the Governor."[26]

The Privy Council agreed with De Grey, and upon its order the Board of Trade prepared in early April an instruction which embodied the substance of his report. Threatening the governor with removal if he passed any bill raising money for other than local services, the instruction stipulated that he assent to no revenue measures that did not appropriate the money arising from it to specific purposes and that did not expressly limit the use of that money to the services for which it was appropriated. The instruction also directed that all money bills contain a clause subjecting the treasurer to permanent exclusion from public office and a penalty of triple the sum involved if he issued money from the treasury solely upon the Commons' order. After the Privy Council had formally approved the instruction, Hillsborough transmitted it to Bull on April 14, 1770, along with a letter expressing his hope that it would prevent further abuses.[27] But Hillsborough's hopes were soon disappointed. Far from solving the problem, the instruction only served to aggravate an already tense political situation in South Carolina.

Indeed, while the Board of Trade was preparing the additional instruction in London, the South Carolina council was challenging on its own the Commons' right to order money from the treasury without the

---

[26] Report of De Grey, Feb. 13, 1770, Transcripts of South Carolina Records, 32:166–81, S. C. Archives Department.

[27] Orders in Council, Apr. 3, 5, 1770, and Hillsborough to Bull, Apr. 14, 1770, ibid., 233–34, 241–48, 253–55; Labaree, *Royal Instructions* 1:208–9.

consent of the other two branches of the legislature. In early April 1770 the council objected to the Commons' inclusion of an item in the annual tax bill to repay the Wilkes grant to the treasury. Declaring that the grant was a tacit affront to "His Majesty's Government" and in no "sense honourable, fit, or decent," the council denied that the Commons could legally appropriate money for uses that did not directly concern the colony.[28]

The reply of the Commons—drawn up by a committee headed by Thomas Lynch and including James Parsons, Christopher Gadsden, Henry Laurens, Thomas Ferguson, and Benjamin Dart—outlined the position it would tenaciously adhere to for the next four years. It contended, somewhat speciously perhaps, that to grant money to support "the Just and Constitutional Rights and Liberties of the People of Great Britain and America" could hardly be "disrespectful or Affrontive to His Majesty, the great patron of the Liberty and Rights of all His Subjects." The Commons also pointed out that the council's insinuation that there were limitations upon its authority to appropriate money inferred that some power could raise money on the inhabitants "other than their own Representatives." That "Seditious Doctrine," the Commons declared, "must manifestly tend, to increase the Discontents and Disorder which have but too long subsisted in his Majesty's American Dominions." Upon the central point at issue—whether or not it could issue money from the treasury by its sole authority—the Commons resolved that it had always "exercised a Right of Borrowing monies out of the Treasury," that no governor had ever attempted to abridge that right, and that it had always "faithfully and punctually" repaid the money. Here, the Commons was arguing that it could alter the constitution of South Carolina by its own action, and that local precedents, habits, traditions, and statutes were important parts of that constitution—views directly opposite to those put forth by De Grey in London just two months earlier. From this vigorous defense the Commons took the offensive by pointing out "the inconsistency and absurdity" of the council's acting as both an upper house of the legislature and an advisory council and resolved to ask the crown to appoint a separate upper house "composed of independent men, and men of Property." This request, in part the consequence of the crown's recent policy of filling the council with placemen who were not natives of the colony, was the logical culmination of the long-standing rivalry between the Commons and the council that had seen the council

---

[28] Commons Journals, 38:382, 387–88 (Apr. 7–9, 1770), S. C. Archives Department.

continuously decline in status and in political influence within the colony.[29]

This altercation, if anything, intensified the ardor of South Carolina patriots for "Wilkes and Liberty." News of the activities of Wilkes and his London supporters frequently appeared in detail in Charleston newspapers, and his South Carolina admirers lost no opportunity to make a public display in his support.[30] The numbers 45, 92 (the number of Massachusetts representatives who had voted not to rescind the Massachusetts circular letter in June 1768), and 26 (the number of South Carolina representatives who had adopted resolutions approving the refusal of the Massachusetts assembly to withdraw the circular letter) were part of the standard ritual on all such occasions. On Wednesday, April 18, 1770, the day of Wilkes's release from prison, South Carolinians celebrated by ringing church bells, displaying colors, and illuminating over 150 houses in Charleston, "many of them with Forty-five Lights." "Ninety-Two Members of CLUB FORTY-FIVE," preceded by "26 Candles," met at "45 Minutes after Seven o'Clock" for "a most elegant Entertainment" at the house of Robert Dillon, and after drinking forty-five "loyal and patriotic Toasts" broke up at "45 Minutes past 12." Among the toasts were "May the Endeavours of John Wilkes, Esq; be rewarded as those of Junius were by the Romans" and "The patriotic Supporters of the Bill of Rights." This celebration, Peter Timothy's *Gazette* declared, indicated the "great . . . Regard we pay to those, who suffer in the Cause of Liberty, by a resolute and steady Opposition, to the arbitrary and tyrannical Attempts, of such wicked and corrupt Ministers as would overturn the English Constitution."[31] A similar demonstration followed the erection of a statue of William Pitt, earl of Chatham, in Broad Street on July 5.

One of the forty-five toasts on this last occasion—"Firmness and Perseverance in our Resolutions, not to flinch a single inch"—gave ample

[29] Ibid., 382, 387–92 (Apr. 7–10, 1770); Bull to Hillsborough, Apr. 15, 1770, Transcripts of South Carolina Records, 32:256–59, ibid. On the decline of the council, see M. Eugene Sirmans, "The South Carolina Royal Council, 1720–1763," *William and Mary Quarterly*, 3d ser., 18 (1961): 373–92.

[30] See *South Carolina Gazette*, Apr. 12, 19, July 5, 1770; *South Carolina Gazette and Country Journal*, Apr. 10, 24, July 10, 1770; and *South Carolina American and General Gazette*, Apr. 6, 1770.

[31] *South Carolina Gazette*, Apr. 19, 1770; *South Carolina Gazette and Country Journal*, Apr. 24, 1770.

warning of the position the Commons would take on the crown's additional instruction.[32] That instruction had reached Charleston before the
Commons met again on August 14. Anticipating the storm it would
raise, Lieutenant Governor Bull chose to lay it casually before the Commons rather than risk impairing his good relations by making too great
an issue of it. He was under no illusion that the house would compliantly
recede from its position even in the face of a royal mandate.[33] That he
had gauged the temper of the Commons correctly was apparent early in
the session.

The Commons quickly adopted a report—prepared by a committee
headed by John Rutledge and Thomas Lynch and including Christopher
Gadsden, Henry Laurens, John Mackenzie, Rawlins Lowndes, and
Charles Cotesworth Pinckney—that defied the additional instruction.
Declaring that the instruction was based upon "false, partial and insidi-
ous" information, the Commons denied that it had recently assumed the
power to order the treasurer to advance money without consulting the
governor or council. It pointed out that it had for some time exercised
and would continue to exercise that power, repaying the money later in
the annual tax bill. Far from being unconstitutional, the vote of funds
to the Bill of Rights Society was, the Commons asserted, "agreeable to
the usage and practice both ancient and Modern of the Commons House
of Assembly"—again clearly implying that precedent and custom were
important elements in the constitution of the colony and that no mandate from the crown could supersede them. Categorically rejecting the
instruction's contention that the South Carolina legislature could grant
money only for local uses, the Commons affirmed its "undoubted Right"
to vote funds for whatever services it thought fit and emphasized its
disapproval of the instruction's requiring an insertion of specific clauses
in money bills by flatly declaring that "Ministers dictating how a Money
Bill shall be framed, is an Infringement of the Privileges of this House;
to whom alone it belongs to Originate and prepare the same, for the
concurrence and Assent of the Governor and Council without any Alteration or Amendment whatsoever." Finally, the Commons dared to suggest that its actions would not have been considered dangerous "if the
Money borrowed had not been applied towards frustrating the unjust
and unconstitutional measures of an Arbitrary and Oppressive Ministry" and declared its intention of endeavoring to obtain the withdrawal

---

[32] *South Carolina Gazette,* July 5, 1770.

[33] Bull to Hillsborough, Aug. 23, 1770, Transcripts of South Carolina Records, 32:316–19,
S. C. Archives Department.

of the instruction by presenting the affair in a true light to the home officials through its London agent.[34]

That the Commons did not intend to confine its actions to mere parliamentary assertions of its rights was indicated when it once again tried to pass a tax measure containing an article to repay the treasurer the controversial £1,500, only to have the council again turn it down. Further disagreement between the two houses arose over a bill to appoint a treasurer. The death of Treasurer Jacob Motte the previous June had interjected a new element into the dispute. With the consent of the council, Bull had appointed Assistant Treasurer Henry Peronneau to fill the office until the legislature met, when, according to law, a permanent treasurer should have been formally appointed by statute. But the insistence of the council upon including the clauses required by the additional instruction, penalizing the treasurers for advancing money without the consent of the entire legislature, prevented passage of an appointing statute.[35]

These proceedings left Bull with little hope for settling the matter without some concession from metropolitan authorities. To Hillsborough he ventured to suggest that the additional instruction did not specifically preclude his assenting to a tax bill containing provision to repay the grant to Wilkes. In addition, he wisely counseled Hillsborough that the Commons would "very tenaciously adhere to" its two "grand points": the right to order money from the treasury by its single authority and the right to appropriate money to any purposes it thought proper, whether local or not.[36] But Hillsborough, no less adamant than the Commons, showed no disposition to yield. Replying that the instruction prohibited the passing of any measure that authorized repayment of the Wilkes fund, he declared that the Commons' resolutions were "ill founded" and "unbecoming" and directed Bull to veto money bills that did not comply with the additional instruction.[37]

---

[34] Commons Journals, 38:430–33 (Aug. 29, 1770), ibid.; Committee of Correspondence to Garth, Sept. 6, 1770, "Garth Correspondence," *South Carolina Historical and Genealogical Magazine* 31 (1930): 244–46.

[35] Commons Journals, 38:422–23, 440–41, 449–50, 453–56 (Aug. 23, 30, Sept. 6–7, 1770), S. C. Archives Department; Bull to Hillsborough, July 16, 1770, Transcripts of South Carolina Records, 32:297–98, ibid.; *South Carolina Gazette and Country Journal,* June 19, 1770.

[36] Bull to Hillsborough, Aug. 23, Sept. 8, 1770, Transcripts of South Carolina Records, 32:316–30, S. C. Archives Department.

[37] Hillsborough to Bull, Oct. 19, Nov. 15, 1770, ibid., 339–40, 353.

The Commons' attempt to secure revocation of the instruction produced the same results. Shortly before Bull prorogued the Commons in September 1770, its committee of correspondence directed the colony's London agent, Charles Garth, to secure removal of the instruction on the grounds that it had been issued as a result of misinformation. The committee emphasized that in the Wilkes vote the Commons had not diverted money appropriated to other purposes but had only followed the long-established practice of borrowing surplus funds from the treasury with a promise to repay them in the next annual tax bill. The committee admitted that "in Britain Votes of Credit only follow a Royal Requisition" but asserted that it was "not therefore necessary or proper that it should do so in America, for the distance must make the King's immediate Requisition impracticable on emergent Occasions, and if it were left to the Governor, a weak, ignorant or Corrupt one, might suffer the Public safety to be greatly endangered, or even lost before he would take the necessary steps to avert the Dangers which threatened it." Predicating its assertion upon the premise that the South Carolina Commons' right to grant its constituents' money stood "upon the same ground as that of the House of Commons," the committee pointed out that "it was never heard that the Commons, could not give unasked."[38]

In compliance with the committee's directions, Garth petitioned the Privy Council in late November 1770 to withdraw the instruction. Incorporating the committee's objections, he emphasized that the Commons regarded any such "Dictate or Direction" as a violation of its "first and essential Privilege . . . to originate and prepare . . . all Money Bills." Early in December the Privy Council referred the agent's petition to the Board of Trade for a report.[39] Despite Garth's endeavors, the board at a formal hearing on March 25 echoed Hillsborough's sentiments and steadfastly maintained that money could be ordered from the treasury only upon consent of all three branches of the legislature. The board denied that the instruction was intended to interfere "with the Privilege of the House in originating Money Bills" and declared ambiguously that its stipulations did not constitute an "Interposition in the Mode of raising or granting to His Majesty," but merely directions to the governor

---

[38] Committee of Correspondence to Garth, Sept. 6, 1770, "Garth Correspondence," *South Carolina Historical and Genealogical Magazine* 31 (1930): 244–53.

[39] Garth to Committee of Correspondence, Nov. 24, Dec. 17, 1770, and Garth's Petition to Crown, Nov. 22, 1770, ibid., 33 (1932): 117–24; Order in Council, Dec. 9, 1770, Transcripts of South Carolina Records, 32:420–28, S. C. Archives Department.

from which he was not to depart. On the board's recommendation, the Privy Council rejected Garth's petition.[40]

If London authorities were unyielding, so was the South Carolina Commons. In January and February 1771, while Garth's petition was awaiting action from the Board of Trade, the Commons tried to inveigle Bull into recognizing its right to order money from the treasury without executive consent by adopting the apparently innocent measure of ordering Treasurer Peronneau to pay Bull £7 current money for each of a number of recent poor Irish Protestant immigrants in order to help settle them. But Bull was not ensnared; he declined to accept the money unless it was provided for by an ordinance passed by all three branches of the legislature. Nor did he change his mind when the Commons ingeniously distinguished between unappropriated surplus monies and appropriated funds and contended that the additional instruction applied only to appropriated funds, which left it free to dispose of surplus funds by its sole authority.[41]

This session also failed to produce a tax bill, although it avoided the disagreement that arose during the previous session over the bill to appoint a treasurer. After Bull had arranged to include in the treasurer's bond the penalty clauses required by the additional instruction, the council no longer insisted upon their being in the bill of appointment. An ordinance passed in late February formally appointed as joint treasurers Henry Peronneau and Benjamin Dart, the former the candidate of Bull and the council and the latter—a "warm" patriot who had demonstrated "violent Opposition to Acts of Parliament in 1765 and 1770"—the nominee of the Commons.[42]

A decline in enthusiasm for Wilkes in both London and South Carolina followed the repeal of the bulk of the Townshend duties in the early 1770s

[40]Garth to Committee of Correspondence, Mar. 27, 1771, and Board of Trade to Privy Council Committee on Plantation Affairs, Mar. 27, 1771, "Garth Correspondence," *South Carolina Historical and Genealogical Magazine* 33 (1932): 125–29, 130–31.

[41]Commons Journals, 38:474, 476, 481–82, 487–88, 497–500 (Jan. 31, Feb. 7, 9, 15, 26, 1771), S. C. Archives Department.

[42]Ibid., 462, 466–67, 476–78, 494 (Jan. 27–28, Feb. 7, 23, 1771); Thomas Cooper and David J. McCord, eds., *The Statutes at Large of South Carolina*, 10 vols. (Columbia, S.C., 1836–41), 4:326–27; Laurens to John L. Gervais, Dec. 28, 1771, [Henry] Laurens Letter

and the subsequent collapse of the nonimportation agreements,[43] but the additional instruction of April 5, 1770, continued to be the cause célèbre of South Carolina politics. Returning from a two-year stay in Great Britain in September 1771, Governor Lord Charles Greville Montagu used argument, pressure, and intimidation to persuade the Commons to comply with the instruction; but it steadfastly resisted, preferring, it declared, to submit to the public and private calamities that might result from not having any tax bill rather than to adopt a measure which was inconsistent with "the established mode of Proceedings, and the proper Rights of the People." The moderate Henry Laurens, who beginning in late 1771 observed the dispute from London, correctly expressed the views of the colony's leading politicians when he wrote that he would rather "have no Tax Bill for seven Years" or even "forfeit my whole Estate and be reduced to the necessity of working for my Bread" than "give up that important point." The issue, as he saw it, was "Nothing less than the very Essence of true Liberty." The "*Right* of the People to give and grant voluntarily in mode and in Quantity free from the Fetters of ministerial Instructions, restrictive, or obligatory," was "indubitable," and the instruction was no less a threat to that right than the "Stamp Act or Internal Duties." For the members of the Commons to submit would be to "sell the Birth Right and dearest Privilege of their Constituents," to "incur the Hatred and Detestation of the present Age," and to brand themselves "in all future Ages with the infamous Characters of Betrayers of the Trust reposed in them by the People."[44]

Even a deft and subtle politician would have found it difficult to make headway against such determined opposition; Montagu's clumsy efforts failed completely. For a brief period after he met the Commons on September 17, 1771, he was optimistic. Along with Bull he hoped that the ministry's firm stand would discourage the Commons from further opposition. Late in September he wrote Hillsborough that there were "scarcely above Two Members in the House" who did not privately con-

Book, 1771-72, 142-44, 146, Laurens Papers, South Carolina Historical Society, Charleston.

[43] See, for examples, Laurens to Thomas Franklin and to James Laurens, both Dec. 26, 1771, Laurens Letter Book, 1771-72, 130-31, S. C. Historical Society.

[44] Commons Journals, 38:522 (Sept. 19, 1771), S. C. Archives Department; Laurens to James Habersham, Apr. 10, 1770, to William Williamson, Nov. 28, 1771, to John Rose, Dec. 5, 1771, to James Laurens, Dec. 12, 1771, to Alexander Garden, May 24, 1772, Laurens Letter Book, 1767-71, 492, 1771-72, 74-79, 93-104, 286-93, S. C. Historical Society; *South Carolina Gazette*, Sept. 19, 1771; *South Carolina Gazette and Country Journal*, Oct. 8, 1771.

demn the Commons' earlier actions, although he added that "a certain kind of Pride" might well prevent them from receding "from Orders they have so Publickly made." By mid-October, however, Montagu had had time to appraise the situation more realistically, and he warned Hillsborough that the dispute might not be settled for some time.[45]

Subsequent events indicated that Montagu's change of opinion was well warranted. Garth's failure to secure the withdrawal of the instruction had convinced many South Carolina political leaders that it was futile for the Commons to continue demanding recognition of its power to issue money from the treasury by its sole authority. Peter Timothy reported that "all the *Patriots* and *principal Speakers*" in the house were willing for political reasons to admit that the vote to Wilkes "was irregular."[46] They were not, however, willing to comply with the instruction or to abandon the attempt to repay the £1,500. They merely devised an expedient to obtain by guile what they had not been able to get by direct action. The Commons inserted in the annual tax bill an item providing for the payment of a certain sum to the estate of Jacob Motte for money he had advanced to pay bounties to Irish immigrants, provide for a survey of the colony, encourage silk culture, and provide "for other services." When the council examined the bill, it quickly recognized that the "other services" included the Wilkes grant and refused to pass the measure until the item was omitted and the clauses required by the instruction were included. The Commons acidly replied that it would never "regard any Ministerial Instruction in the framing of a Money Bill, nor alter any part of the Schedule upon your requisition." Neither body would yield. For the fourth consecutive session the debate over the additional instruction prevented passage of a tax bill.[47]

The Commons at this session reasserted its claim to the power to order surplus funds from the treasury on its sole authority by ordering the treasurers to advance £3,000 Carolina currency to the commissioners for silk manufacturing to purchase South Carolina silk for sale in Britain. The Commons probably expected Treasurer Dart as a former house

---

[45] Montagu to Hillsborough, Sept. 26, Oct. 20, 1771, Transcripts of South Carolina Records, 33:84, 87, S. C. Archives Department.

[46] Peter Timothy to Benjamin Franklin, Oct. 20, 1771, Franklin Papers, American Philosophical Society, Philadelphia; Commons Journals, 38:556 (Oct. 11, 1770), S. C. Archives Department.

[47] Commons Journals, 38:577–78 (Nov. 4, 1771), S. C. Archives Department. An indication of the pressure on the council to pass the tax bill is in *South Carolina Gazette*, Oct. 24, 1771.

leader to comply with its order, but neither he nor Perroneau would honor the commissioners' request for money. When the Commons demanded an explanation, the treasurers defended their behavior on the grounds that Montagu and the council had ordered them not to comply with the order and that to have done so would have been to violate their bonds and lay themselves open to legal action. The Commons had no sympathy for the treasurers' dilemma. After the treasurers admitted that the treasury contained sufficient unappropriated funds to cover its order, the Commons declared them "guilty of a violation and Contempt of the Authority and Privileges of this House" and with "but one dissenting Voice" boldly ordered them committed to the Charleston jail. However, Montagu dissolved the house before the commitment order could be carried out.[48]

London authorities wholeheartedly approved Montagu's dissolution. George III, it was reported from London, had "set his Face against that £1500" and was determined to see "*his Instructions* obeyed"; and Hillsborough directed Montagu in January 1772 to dissolve the house again if it continued to reject the additional instruction. Indeed, Henry Laurens heard from "a Gentleman of good Intelligence" that Hillsborough, who seemed to have "a Mist before his . . . Eyes" and to be "disposed to believe every evil of and to do every Evil in his Power to us," had said that he "wished for a continued Opposition to the Instruction, in order . . . to enable him to get a Law made for us."[49]

But Montagu's dissolution had so stiffened the Commons' opposition that not even the threat of parliamentary action could soften it. With the strong endorsement of the electorate, which had indicated its approval of the former house's position by returning the majority of the members who had chosen to stand for reelection, the new house that met in April 1772 refused either to submit to any "Ministerial Instructions, dictating the manner in which Money-Bills must be framed" or to do business until there was some hope of passing a tax bill on its own terms. The Commons believed with Henry Laurens that it had "Justice and the Constitution" on its side and was prepared to "Elect-Suffer Dissolution—and Reelect-Stand firm." When it became apparent that the Com-

---

[48]Commons Journals, 38:543, 579–84 (Oct. 2, Nov. 4–5, 1771), S. C. Archives Department; *South Carolina Gazette,* Nov. 7, 1771; *South Carolina American and General Gazette,* Nov. 11, 1771; Laurens to Gervais, Dec. 28, 1771, in Laurens Letter Book, 1771–72, 142–44, 146, S. C. Historical Society.

[49]Hillsborough to Montagu, Jan. 11, 1772, Transcripts of South Carolina Records, 33:105–8, S. C. Archives Department; Laurens to John Hopton, Jan. 29, 1771, to Wil-

mons intended to stick to its resolution, Montagu impatiently charged it with seeking to encroach upon the crown's "just Prerogative" and again dissolved it.[50]

Before the second dissolution, the Commons, encouraged by Henry Laurens's reports from London that prospects were favorable for removing "the Stumbling Block in the way of our Carolina Tax Bills,"[51] again ordered the committee of correspondence to direct Garth to procure the recall of the instruction. No Commons House, the committee wrote Garth, could consent to that instruction "without, at the same time, absolutely surrendering" its "most fundamental Right of Originating all Grants to his Majesty." The committee maintained that the "House [was] fully justified by long usage and a multitude of Precedents, in ordering the Treasurers to pay that Money in the Manner" that it did but added that even if the house had erred, it was inconceivable that any Commons House would submit "to so unconstitutional a remedy as that insisted on by the Instruction." The Commons had now shifted its argument and was endeavoring to effect a recall of the instruction not because it was contrary to the house's right to order surplus monies from the treasury without executive approval but because it violated the house's exclusive right to frame money bills. The committee ridiculed the Board of Trade's contention that the instruction was not intended to interfere with the Commons' privileges with regard to money bills. "This superlatively nice political refinement, tho' perhaps intelligible and distinguishable at St. Omers, and capable of being made so consistent with the Rights of the People thereabouts as to give it an easy passage amongst them," the committee declared, "we are well Assured, Notwithstanding . . . all its gilding, that the Freemen of this province will suffer the greatest Extremities before they can be brought to stomach it."[52]

---

liamson, Nov. 28, 1771, to Rose, Dec. 5, 1771, to James Laurens, Dec. 12, 1771, Laurens Letter Book, 1767–71, 594–97, 1771–72, 74–79, 93–108, S. C. Historical Society.

[50] Montagu to Hillsborough, Apr. 27, 1772, Transcripts of South Carolina Records, 33:140–41, S. C. Archives Department; *South Carolina Gazette,* Nov. 7, 1771, Mar. 26, Apr. 9, 16, 1772; *South Carolina American and General Gazette,* Feb. 25, 1772; Laurens to Garden, May 24, 1772, Laurens Letter Book, 1771–72, 286–93, S. C. Historical Society.

[51] See Laurens to William Williamson, Nov. 28, 1771, to Rose, Dec. 5, 1771, to James Laurens, Dec. 12, 1771, Feb. 28, 1772, to James Habersham, Dec. 20, 1771, to Gabriel Manigault, Mar. 2, 1772, Laurens Letter Book, 1771–72, 74–79, 93–108, 116–20, 198, 202–6, S. C. Historical Society.

[52] Committee of Correspondence to Garth, Apr. 10, 1772, "Garth Correspondence," *South Carolina Historical and Genealogical Magazine* 33 (1932): 136–38.

Garth did persuade metropolitan authorities to yield slightly. The letter from the committee of correspondence reached him at the end of May 1772, when the ministry was ready to accept "a Drawn Game." In a memorial to the crown he argued that the instruction "oppugned" the Commons' "most fundamental Right of originating all Grants to His Majesty." Hillsborough replied that it was intended only to prevent the Commons from ordering money from the treasury without consulting the governor or council and not to interfere with its privileges in regard to money bills. He confided that he would favor a revision "if the Point in view could be effectuated in a way less exceptionable to the Commons House." The rest of the ministry shared Hillsborough's sentiments. Later in June he informed Garth that the ministry had agreed to revoke that part requiring the insertion of certain provisions in all money bills if the Commons would pass a permanent declaratory law stipulating "that no Monies in the Treasurers Hands . . . be at any Time issued by Order of any one Branch of the Legislature singly and alone." By this concession the ministry hoped to remove the Commons' grounds for complaining that the instruction interfered with its rights concerning money bills.[53]

That this slight concession would have satisfied the Commons' leaders is doubtful, but Governor Montagu's actions in South Carolina prevented whatever good effect it might have had. Before he received notice of the ministry's concession, Montagu had decided that the Commons would never accept the instruction as long as it sat in Charleston, where the members who most heatedly opposed it lived. He wrote Hillsborough in July 1772 that he was considering calling the Commons to meet at Beaufort in the southern part of the colony. Probably suggested by Governor Thomas Hutchinson's similar tactics with the Massachusetts house, this action was a scarcely veiled attempt at intimidation. It would be not only a marked display of the political weapons at Montagu's command but also a dramatic indication of his extreme disapproval of the Commons' conduct and his annoyance at the colony's failure to find a suitable house for him in Charleston. More importantly, Montagu hoped that the Charleston members would remain at home and that the southern members attending would be more moderate and comply with

[53]Garth to Committee of Correspondence, June 3, 25, 1772, and Garth's Memorial to Crown, [June 2, 1772], ibid., 238–44; Laurens to Peter Mazyck, Apr. 10, 1772, Laurens Letter Book, 1771–72, 245–47, S. C. Historical Society; Hillsborough to Montagu, July 1, 1772, Transcripts of South Carolina Records, 33:164, S. C. Archives Department.

the instruction. Accordingly, despite the fact that he had by that time received news of the ministry's concession on the instruction, he issued writs for the election in mid-September of a new house to meet on October 8, 1772, at Beaufort.[54]

Montagu could scarcely have made a more serious political blunder. He might have foreseen the results by considering the tempest raised by Hutchinson in Massachusetts. South Carolina newspapers had followed that dispute with interest, one writer charging that, like the additional instruction, it was simply another attempt "to make even the mandate of the minister superior, in effect, to any American law."[55] This sentiment expressed what now became the position of South Carolina political leaders. They made every effort to frustrate Montagu's intentions by securing the election of representatives who would make the trip to Beaufort. In the *South Carolina Gazette and Country Journal,* Z.Z. warned the electorate that "the present Juncture of Public Affairs in this Province is critical and somewhat alarming," predicted that the "*Beaufort-Assembly*" might be "as important in its Consequences . . . as that of any assembly this Country ever saw," and urged that "your own Welfare, the Welfare of Generations yet unborn, may in a great Measure depend on the Counsels and Conduct of the ensuing Assembly." The *South Carolina Gazette* reported that because "the Existence of the *Beaufort-Assembly,* in all Probability, will be as *short* as, it is presumed, their Resolutions will be *spirited,*" the electors seemed "determined . . . to vote for no Gentlemen but who are on the Spot and can give their personal Attendance—the present Crisis being looked upon as the most improper, to make the Choice a mere Compliment." "No Measure of any Governor," it declared, "was ever more freely and generally condemned."[56] The election resulted in another overwhelming endorsement of the Commons' opposition to the additional instruction. All but nine of the members of the dissolved April house were returned. At an informal caucus in Charleston the newly elected representatives resolved neither to pass a declaratory act nor to agree to a tax bill which either mentioned the additional

---

[54] Montagu to Hillsborough, July 27, 1772, Transcripts of South Carolina Records, 33:167, S. C. Archives Department; *South Carolina Gazette,* Sept. 3, 1772.

[55] See *South Carolina Gazette,* Nov. 15, 1770, and *South Carolina American and General Gazette,* Aug. 20, Sept. 24, 1770.

[56] *South Carolina Gazette,* Sept. 3, 17, Oct. 8, 1772; *South Carolina Gazette and Country Journal,* Sept. 15, 1772.

instruction or failed to provide for the repayment of the Wilkes fund.[57]

That Montagu had seriously misgauged the length to which Charleston leaders would go to prevent the Commons from accepting the additional instruction was apparent when it assembled at Beaufort. The Charleston members attended in force and, already highly incensed, regarded it, as the Commons later declared, as "adding Insult to Injury" when Montagu kept the house sitting for three days before he formally received it and then prorogued it to meet at Charleston ten days later. Unknown to the Commons, Hillsborough had ordered Montagu to encourage it to proceed to business as quickly as possible, and the prorogation for the return to Charleston was intended as a conciliatory measure. It had precisely the opposite effect. When the Commons reconvened in Charleston on October 22, it immediately appointed a committee on grievances headed by Christopher Gadsden and composed of other leading members, including James Parsons, Thomas Lynch, John Rutledge, Rawlins Lowndes, Charles Pinckney, Thomas Bee, and Thomas Ferguson. The committee reported a week later that Montagu's actions justified the Commons in completely breaking off relations with him but that urgent business made such a course undesirable. It also recommended four resolutions declaring Montagu's calling the house to meet at Beaufort an act of "ill Will to the Body of the Free Men of this Province" and "a most unprecedented Oppression, and an Unwarrantable Abuse of a Royal Prerogative, which hath never been questioned by the People of this Colony." Charging that his not letting the Commons proceed to business at Beaufort was an "Evasion if not a direct Violation of the Election Law" by which no period of time greater than six months was to elapse between meetings of the legislature, the committee recommended that Garth be directed to petition the crown either to reprimand Montagu or to remove him from office.[58]

Montagu had anticipated such an action and prepared to meet it by perusing the Commons' journals each day. But when he asked the clerk for the journals the evening after the committee had presented its report, he found that Speaker Rawlins Lowndes had taken them home. Montagu then sent a note to Lowndes requesting the journals, but Lowndes, who was out for the evening, received the message late and did not send

[57] South Carolina Gazette, Sept. 17, 1772; Montagu to Hillsborough, Sept. 24, 1772, Transcripts of South Carolina Records, 33:173–80, S. C. Archives Department.

[58] Commons Journals, 39, pt. 1:4–6, 11–12, 20–24 (Oct. 10, 23, 29, 1772), S. C. Archives Department; South Carolina Gazette, Oct. 15, Nov. 2, 1772.

the journals to Montagu until the following morning. Montagu was greatly annoyed by Lowndes's delay, and when he discovered the committee's report in the journals, immediately sent for the house to prorogue it before it could adopt the report. But the Commons, after receiving the summons of the governor, finished debating the report and formally adopted it before attending him. Montagu was enraged by the Commons' actions, and when its committee of correspondence wrote a letter after the prorogation to Garth directing him to procure Montagu's removal, his rage turned to fury. As soon as he could get a quorum of the house together, on November 10, he dissolved it and issued writs for a new election.[59]

To protect himself against a possible attack from the agent, Montagu immediately wrote the earl of Dartmouth, who had replaced Hillsborough as colonial secretary in August 1772, complaining bitterly that the Commons had made, in addition to its earlier attempt to dispose of public money by its sole authority, two other innovations in the colony's constitution. It had, he reported, continued to engage in legislative business after being summoned to attend the governor, and its committee of correspondence had continued to act after the house had been prorogued. How "dangerous it is," Montagu declared, "to allow Houses of Assembly to proceed, as it were daily in altering the usage of Parliament, thereby taking the power of the King in the most alarming manner and changing the very Nature of the Constitution." In the *South Carolina Gazette*, William Henry Drayton, returned from England and now a member of the council, speculated whether such "unprecedented" innovations proceeded "from a *Malice propense*, designing to change, by Piece-Meal, the venerable Constitution of our Country." Montagu and Drayton had spotlighted the basic question in the long dispute: Could the Commons alter the constitution of the colony by its own action?[60]

---

[59]Commons Journals, 39, pt. 1:20–29 (Oct. 29, Nov. 10, 1772), S. C. Archives Department; Montagu to Dartmouth, Nov. 4, 1772, Transcripts of South Carolina Records, 33:188–92, ibid.; *South Carolina Gazette*, Nov. 12, 1772; Committee of Correspondence to Garth, Oct. 30, Nov. 20, 1772, "Garth Correspondence," *South Carolina Historical and Genealogical Magazine* 33 (1932): 262–64, 275–80.

[60]Montagu to Dartmouth, Nov. 4, 1772, Transcripts of South Carolina Records, 33: 188–92, S. C. Archives Department; *South Carolina Gazette*, Apr. 14, Nov. 5, 1772. Drayton's siding with Montagu evoked some spirited abuse from South Carolina patriots, one of whom in a veiled threat suggested that Drayton's epitaph might conclude with the lines "PREROGATIVE was my whole Aim, / Whilst I had spirits to declaim.— / Could I but sally forth anew, / With Life of Scraps, patch'd up with Glue; / That is the Theme I would insist on, / Shou'd I be feather'd, tar'd, or pis'd on" (ibid., Nov. 19, 1772).

That it could was the verdict of the electorate, which in mid-December 1772 returned all but nine of the innovating members of the previous house. No sooner had the Commons met the following January than it again disputed with Montagu, this time over his right to reject its choice as speaker. The Commons reelected Rawlins Lowndes speaker, but Montagu, recalling Lowndes's conduct the previous November, ordered the house to select another. When the Commons unanimously refused to make another choice, Montagu prorogued it. Apparently because of embarrassment at having committed the technical error of proroguing the Commons and not the council, he dissolved the house a few days later, for the fourth time since his return less than a year and a half earlier, and called for new elections. "By an unparalleled Succession of Prorogations and Dissolutions, the Inhabitants of this Province have been unrepresented in Assembly about three Years," complained the *South Carolina Gazette*, asking "*Whether this is a Grievance?* And, *if it is*, Whether it is one of *the least Magnitude?*"[61]

Montagu had disputed with the Commons for the last time. His failure to cope with it prompted him to abandon the struggle and return to England. The new house, composed mostly of the same men who had opposed Montagu through four different legislatures, was scheduled to meet on February 23, 1773, but the members carefully neglected to convene until March 11, the day after Montagu's departure. By this time the fiscal plight of the colony had become grave. No tax bill had been passed since 1769. Lieutenant Governor William Bull urged the new representatives to consider the state of the treasury, although he refrained from mentioning the additional instruction for fear it might "fix them more obstinately in their ill grounded opinion," as "is too much the spirit of popular Assemblies." But Bull's tact was of no avail. Montagu's behavior had goaded most Commons leaders to the point that they were willing to follow the suggestions of Christopher Gadsden, who was for letting "all *go to the Devil*" if Bull and the council would not agree with the Commons. Again the Commons defied the instruction by preparing a tax bill containing a clause to repay the Wilkes fund. When the council rejected it, Bull permitted the Commons to adjourn until summer. Before breaking up, the Commons wrote Garth asking him again to request withdrawal of the instruction and Montagu's permanent removal from the

---

[61] *South Carolina Gazette*, Nov. 26, 1772, Jan. 7, 14, Feb. 22, 1773; Montagu to Dartmouth, Jan. 21, 1773, Transcripts of South Carolina Records, 33:204–5, S. C. Archives Department.

governorship.[62] Garth did not have to seek the governor's dismissal. The ministry was so displeased with Montagu's conduct that he had already resigned his post. Even before the committee's letter reached England, metropolitan authorities were preparing to replace him with Nova Scotia governor Lord William Campbell.[63] But it was nearly two years before Campbell would arrive in South Carolina, and in the meantime Bull administered the colony.

Bull was no more successful than Montagu in dealing with the Commons over the additional instruction. After the prorogation in March, he optimistically wrote that, although some members were "as tenacious as ever," others had softened "their language" about the instruction. He suggested that the house might be persuaded to pass the declaratory act recommended by Hillsborough the previous year if it could be convinced that there was "not the least prospect or hope of the Royal Instruction's being revoked." Bull's optimism proved unjustified, however; a session in July failed to produce a tax bill. Bull reported to Dartmouth that the Commons seemed determined to adhere to its "right to be free from the influence" of the instruction, and Speaker Rawlins Lowndes wrote Peyton Randolph, speaker of the Virginia House of Burgesses, that the Commons would "never . . . Submit" to it.[64]

---

[62] *South Carolina Gazette*, Feb. 15, 1773; *South Carolina Gazette and Country Journal*, Mar. 30, 1773; Commons Journals, 39, pt. 2:4–6, 14, 17, 21–23 (Mar. 12, 19, 20, 27, 1773), S. C. Archives Department; Bull to Dartmouth, Mar. 30, 1773, Transcripts of South Carolina Records, 33:225–27, ibid.; Mark De Wolfe Howe, ed., "Journal of Josiah Quincy, Junior, 1773," Mar. 19, 1773, in Massachusetts Historical Society, *Proceedings* 49 (1915–16): 452; Committee of Correspondence to Garth, Mar. 27, 1773, "Garth Correspondence," *South Carolina Historical and Genealogical Magazine* 33 (1932): 273–74. On the growing resentment to Montagu, see Committee of Correspondence to Garth, Oct. 30, 1772, ibid., 262–64, and Diary of John Joachim Zubly, Mar. 24, 1772, Georgia Historical Society, Savannah. On Garth's proceedings against Montagu, see Garth to Committee of Correspondence, Feb. 2, 25, Apr. 3, 1773, and Garth's Petition to Crown, [Feb. 1773], Garth Letter Book, 1765–75, 141–47, 150, S. C. Archives Department.

[63] On Montagu's resignation, see Garth to Committee of Correspondence, May 4, 20, 1773, Committee of Correspondence to Garth, Apr. 1, 1773, and Laurens to James Laurens, Mar. 11, 1773, Laurens Letter Book, 1772–74, 54–55, 59–62, S. C. Historical Society; Montagu to Barnard Elliott, May 1, 1773, *South Carolina Historical and Genealogical Magazine* 33 (1932): 260–61; *South Carolina Gazette*, Mar. 8, 1773; and Dartmouth to Bull, June 10, 1773, Transcripts of South Carolina Records, 33:270–71, S. C. Archives Department.

[64] Bull to Dartmouth, Mar. 30, July 24, 1773, Transcripts of South Carolina Records, 33:225–27, 287–88, S. C. Archives Department; Rawlins Lowndes to Peyton Randolph,

At a session in August and September 1773, the Commons adopted a new expedient to replace the Wilkes fund. It directed Attorney General Sir Egerton Leigh to sue the executors of Motte's estate for the money owed the colony. Although the amount due was £61,474.16.5 Carolina currency, the Commons specified that Leigh sue for only £49,140. By this expedient, Bull later wrote, the Commons hoped to carry its "Points, in making the Public Treasury pay the £10500 equal to £1500 sterling without inserting that exceptionable sum in any Money Bill." Bull thwarted this ingenious contrivance by ordering Leigh to sue for the entire sum. The house again tried to assert its power to issue money from the treasury on its sole authority by ordering the treasurers to advance £1,500 currency to provide carriages for newly arrived Irish Protestants. The treasurers refused to comply with the order, and they probably would have been committed by the house had not its attention been diverted by a dispute over whether the council was actually an upper house of assembly.[65]

That dispute arose out of the council's attempt to force the Commons to accept the additional instruction. The council first tried to excite public opinion against the Commons by publishing a report purporting to show the alarming state of the treasury. The Commons denied that the fiscal situation was as desperate as the council had maintained, and it demonstrated its devotion to principle by replying that, although people might indeed lament that the failure to pass tax measures had seriously threatened the colony's public credit, its "Constituents would have had Reason for ever to lament the loss of their most valuable Privilege, the exclusive Right of Originating and Framing all Money Bills," had it passed a tax bill "in such a Manner as would have been agreeable to the Council." If the situation was not so grave as the council insisted, the prospects were still far from bright, particularly because the general duty law—which had been bringing substantial sums into the treasury since the passage of the last tax bill in 1769—expired at the end of the session. Bull maintained that the Commons wanted it to expire because it would not only "flatter the bulk of the People" by temporarily relieving them

---

July 9, 1773, Lowndes Papers, P-1756/328, South Caroliniana Library, University of South Carolina, Columbia.

[65] Commons Journals, 39, pt. 2: 39–40, 76, 92, 106–7, 115, 118 (Aug. 13, Sept. 3, 10, 1773, Mar. 3, 10–11, 1774), S. C. Archives Department; Bull to Dartmouth, Aug. 26, Sept. 18, 1773, Mar. 24, 1774, Transcripts of South Carolina Records, 33:292–94, 305–6; 34:21–22, ibid.

from taxes but also create a serious situation which would bring pressure on the crown to withdraw the additional instruction.[66]

But the council was determined to force the Commons to revive the duty law, and a majority of its members decided not to pass any other legislation until that was done. Two of the councillors, John Drayton and William Henry Drayton, refused to agree to "a Measure so fatal to the Freedom of our Country," arguing that it put an undue "force" on the Commons. At William Henry Drayton's request, Thomas Powell published their dissent on August 31, 1773, in the *South Carolina Gazette*. Upset by Powell's printing a portion of its journals without its consent, the council reprimanded Drayton, took Powell into custody, and, when he did not appear sufficiently contrite, sent him off to jail for "a high Breach of Privilege and a Contempt of this House."[67]

Powell's arrest provoked a formidable assault upon the council's legislative authority. When Powell applied for his release under a writ of habeas corpus, Edward Rutledge, brother of John and a rising young lawyer, represented him before justices of the peace Rawlins Lowndes and George Gabriel Powell—both members of the Commons. Rutledge denied the council's power to commit people for a breach of privilege of a legislative body on the grounds that the council was not an upper house of the legislature. Arguing that the council was in no way comparable to the House of Lords because it was composed not of independent men but of men "dependent on the Will of a King," Rutledge insisted that the council was "Nothing more than merely a Privy-Council, to assist the Governor with their Advice." Both Lowndes and George Gabriel Powell agreed with Rutledge and set the printer free. When the council asked the Commons to waive the usual exemption from arrest for Lowndes and Powell so it could proceed against them, the Commons reviewed the case, approved the conduct of the justices, and resolved that the council's committing the printer was "unprecedented, unconstitutional and Oppressive, and a Dangerous Violation of the Liberty of the Subject." The house then boldly requested Lieutenant Governor Bull to suspend those councillors responsible for the commitment and

---

[66] Bull to Dartmouth, Aug. 23, 1773, Transcripts of South Carolina Records, 33:292–300, ibid.; *South Carolina Gazette*, Aug. 16, 25, 1773; Commons Journals, 39, pt. 2:48–49, 51–53 (Aug. 18, 20, 1773), S. C. Archives Department; *Statutes at Large of South Carolina* 4:264–65.

[67] *South Carolina Gazette*, Aug. 30, Sept. 2, 13, 1773.

ordered the committee of correspondence to write Garth to ask their removal.[68]

Bull was alarmed at these proceedings. He had repeatedly warned London authorities about the declining position of the council. Now he added that the post of councillor had become "humiliating and obnoxious," that feeling against the council was "at a great heighth and seems approaching to a crisis."[69] Just how far South Carolina patriots were ready to go in their attack on the council was indicated immediately after the prorogation of the legislature in mid-September 1773. Adding insult to injury, Thomas Powell and Edward Rutledge brought suit against Attorney General Sir Egerton Leigh—the signer of the warrant to commit Powell—for damages. The suit failed, however, when Chief Justice Thomas Knox Gordon—one of Leigh's fellow councillors—ruled that the council was "an *Upper House of Assembly*" and did therefore have the power of commitment.[70]

Gordon's decision dampened the campaign against the council in South Carolina, although the controversy continued to receive some attention in London. Charles Garth dutifully, though pessimistically, presented the Commons' request for the removal of the offending councillors to Dartmouth. Reporting that Dartmouth had intimated that any application "denying the Council to be a Branch of the Legislature and an Upper House of Assembly" would be considered as an attempt "to subvert the Constitution" and that "no proceedings could be had upon it," Garth suggested in December 1773 that any charges should be limited to challenging the right of the council to imprison the subject for a breach of privilege.[71] To counter Garth's activities, Sir Egerton Leigh published in London in January 1774 a long pamphlet, *Considerations on Certain Political Transactions of the Province of South Carolina*, which reviewed

---

[68] Ibid., Sept. 2, 6, 13, 15, 1773; Commons Journals, 39, pt. 2:77–79, 82–90, 93–94 (Sept. 8, 11, 1773), S. C. Archives Department.

[69] For Bull's remarks on the declining position of the council, see Bull to Hillsborough, Oct. 20, Nov. 30, 1770, and to Dartmouth, Apr. 9, Sept. 18, 1773, Transcripts of South Carolina Records, 32:342–45, 371–75, 33:256, 303–10, S. C. Archives Department. For a contemporary newspaper comment to the same effect, see *South Carolina Gazette*, Oct. 18, 1770.

[70] Bull to Dartmouth, Oct. 20, 1773, and Leigh to Bull, Sept. 18, Oct. 16, 1773, Transcripts of South Carolina Records, 33:325–33, S. C. Archives Department.

[71] Committee of Correspondence to Garth, Sept. 16, 1773, Garth to Committee of Correspondence, Dec. 27, 1773, Jan. 9, Mar. 11, 1774, Garth's Petition to Crown, [Dec. 1773], Garth to Privy Council Committee on Plantation Affairs, [Jan. 1774], Garth Letter Book, 153–54, 158–65, ibid.

the Wilkes fund controversy and argued against the Commons' contention that the council was not an upper house. This pamphlet sent Leigh's old enemy, Henry Laurens, scurrying to the Board of Trade for materials with which to rebut Leigh's arguments. At Lauren's urging and with financial backing and editorial help both from him and from Ralph Izard, Jr., Arthur Lee of Virginia prepared the *Answer* to Leigh's pamphlet, which was published the following April.[72]

Perhaps better than any other surviving records, these pamphlets illustrate the wide gulf between the contending parties in the Wilkes fund controversy. In defending the additional instruction and the council's adherence to it, Leigh argued that "Our Constitution is *derivative,* and entirely flows from the Crown." The implications of this argument were that the constitutions of the colonies were, as Leigh remarked, "wholly *ex gratia,*" that colonial lower houses owed their existence not to any inherent right of the freeholders in the colonies to be represented but only to the king's pleasure, and that these houses had no rights or powers except those that were derived from the royal commissions and instructions or from the sanction of the crown. Although he recognized that the power of the South Carolina Commons had increased in practice to the point at which the "due equipoise" of the constitution had been upset, he denied that this development was permanent. Contending that precedents of "new Communities" and "*Infant Societies*" were "of very little weight," he declared that the Commons could not extend its power "beyond the original views and intention of those from whom they derive their whole authority" and denied that the Commons could by the practice of a few years change the constitution of the colony or acquire new powers. Thus the Commons' claim to the power to order money from the treasury by its sole authority was untenable, and the Wilkes vote was "an unconstitutional and unwarrantable stretch of Power." One of the functions of the crown was to check such "*novel Invention.*" Because legislative bodies were "equally liable with Individuals to be misled by passion, fancy, or caprice," they had to "have boundaries, restraints, and limitations." The additional instruction was, then, "only a *Remembrancer,*" a "*timely Correction*" to "*check*" a "departure from the Constitution" and to point out "the proper practice." Leigh argued that for simi-

---

[72] On the authorship of these pamphlets and the preparation and printing of the *Answer,* see Laurens to Gervais, Jan. 24, 1774, to James Laurens, Jan. 27, Feb. 17, Mar. 2, Apr. 13, 1774, to John Laurens, Jan. 28, Feb. 18, Apr. 8, 1774, to James Crokatt, Feb. 16, 1774, to Garden, Feb. 19, Apr. 13, 1774, Laurens Letter Book, 1772–74, 191–92, 194–96, 202, 211–21, 238–40, 261–62, 274–79, S. C. Historical Society; Ralph Izard, Jr., to Ed-

lar reasons the Commons' claim that the council was not an upper house was invalid. He conceded the Commons' point that the council did not stand upon the same independent footing as the House of Lords, but he insisted that the council derived its right to act as an upper house from the royal commission and instructions—the same instruments to which the Commons owed its legislative authority. That the crown should uphold the council's power to act in a legislative capacity was particularly important at such a critical juncture, when the "bands of our Society are now loosened, the plan of his Majesty's Government totally disordered, and the Commons are the *vortex* which swallows all the power."[73]

In his *Answer* Lee proceeded from entirely different assumptions and ended up with opposite conclusions. He dismissed Leigh's argument that the "Constitution and Liberties of the Provinces" were "merely *ex gratia*, flowing wholly from the Bounty of the Crown," as a doctrine which went "back somewhat more than a Century, into the Days of omnipotent Prerogative." Rather, he argued that rights were inherent, not permissive, and that South Carolinians were entitled to all of the traditional rights of Englishmen. He thus inferred that the existence of the Commons House depended not on the crown's pleasure as expressed in the original charter to the colony, or on the commissions and instructions, but upon the fundamental and unalterable right of the freeholders of South Carolina to be represented. "The Rights and Privileges of the Commons House," Lee wrote, "spring from the Rights and Privileges of *British* Subjects, and are coeval with the Constitution. They were neither created, nor can they be abolished by the Crown." Assuming that precedent and usage were just as important in shaping the constitution of South Carolina as they were in determining the British constitution, Lee argued in direct contrast to Leigh that "what has prevailed from the Beginning of the Colony, without Question or Controul, is Part of the Constitution." He thus implied that the South Carolina Commons, like the British House of Commons, could change the constitution by long usage unchallenged by the crown and that such change could not be undone by the unilateral action of the crown. Unlike Leigh, who argued from the premise that the constitution of the colony was static, Lee suggested that it was constantly changing. Thus, the vote of money to Wilkes was "not Novel"

---

ward Rutledge, May 25, 1775, *Correspondence of Mr. Ralph Izard of South Carolina*, ed. A. I. Deas (New York, 1844), 77.

[73] Sir Egerton Leigh, *Considerations on Certain Political Transactions of the Province of South Carolina* (London, 1774), 15, 18, 21–22, 25–26, 37, 42, 60.

but "*constitutional in its Mode, and laudable in its Intention*" because it "*was agreeable to the Usage and Practice, both antient and modern, of the Commons House of Assembly in the Province of South Carolina.*" Both because it attempted to curtail the "ancient and undoubted" power of the Commons to issue money from the treasury by its sole authority and because it violated the Commons' exclusive control over money matters by prescribing the form in which money bills should be framed, the additional instruction was "clearly unconstitutional" and "an arbitrary and dangerous Interposition of Prerogative." The issue was simply whether the Commons should bow to the "unconstitutional Mandate of a Minister" and "make a formal Surrender" of its "Privileges and the Rights of the People," or whether the crown should "retract from an Attempt . . . arbitrarily to interfere in the Exercise of that which is the peculiar and incommunicable Power of the Commons."[74]

Neither of these pamphlets had any noticeable impact in either London or South Carolina.[75] By the time of their publication, the storm over the Tea Act and the Coercive Acts had eclipsed both the Wilkes fund controversy and the dispute over the council's right to act as an upper house. Crown officials, Garth reported in April 1774, were so preoccupied with "all the Measures affecting Boston" that South Carolina matters had been pushed far down the agenda.[76] Still, the Commons never abandoned its intention of getting around the additional instruction. South Carolina patriots inevitably looked at broader metropolitan measures in terms of their particular problems, viewing the Coercive Acts as a precedent by which the ministry could justify a law to "Cram down the Instruction of the 14th April and every other Mandate which Ministers

---

[74] Arthur Lee, *Answer to Considerations on Certain Political Transactions of the Province of South Carolina* (London, 1774), 3, 12, 29–30, 43, 45–46, 48, 51–53, 59, 63, 101–4, 111, 120.

[75] Leigh's pamphlet was not noted in the Charleston newspapers until September, and the *Answer* was not mentioned at all (*South Carolina Gazette*, Sept. 19, 1774). Only forty-two copies of the *Answer* sold during the first month in London. See Laurens to James Laurens, May 12, 1774, and to Ralph Izard, Jr., Sept. 20, 1774, Laurens Letter Book, 1772–74, 305–8, 365–68, S. C. Historical Society; and Laurens to Izard, Feb. 10, 1775, "Izard-Laurens Correspondence," *South Carolina Historical and Genealogical Magazine* 22 (1921): 1–3.

[76] Garth to Committe of Correspondence, Apr. 21, 1774, Garth Letter Book, 171, S. C. Archives Department. See also Laurens's remark that "the Complexion of the Times" would prevent a hearing on the dispute with the Council. Laurens to James Laurens, Feb. 5, 1774, Laurens Letter Book, 1772–74, 198–201, S. C. Historical Society.

Shall think proper for keeping us in Subjection to the Task Master who Shall be put over us."[77]

The spring of 1774 marked the beginning of the fifth successive year of deadlock between metropolitan authorities and the Commons over the issues raised by the additional instruction, and there was little prospect of immediate solution. Bull reported in March 1774 that the Commons still demanded as its "sine quibus non" that the £1,500 sterling be replaced and that no money bills be passed in the form stipulated by the instruction. Despite Henry Laurens's confident prediction as early as the spring of 1773 that the instruction would be recalled, Dartmouth and his colleagues in the ministry remained insistent that the Commons either adhere to the instruction or pass a declaratory act.[78]

Events in the spring of 1774 finally led to the Commons' devising a means to ignore the additional instruction altogether. Unrest among the Indians on the southern frontier made the need for defensive measures urgent. To provide rangers to patrol the critical area, the Commons introduced a money bill without the clauses required by the additional instruction, hoping that public opinion would force the council to accept the measure and thereby admit the Commons' right to pass money bills without the objectionable clauses specified by the instructions. But the council preferred to assume the blame for not defending the frontier than to offend the ministry by passing a revenue measure which did not conform to the instruction. By rejecting the bill, the council gave the Commons an excuse for adopting a radical measure. Taking matters into its own hands, the house proceeded to audit accounts of all public creditors to January 1, 1773, and, without consulting either Bull or the council, ordered its clerk to issue certificates of indebtedness signed by him and five representatives to pay those accounts. The Commons promised to redeem the certificates the first time it succeeded in passing a tax bill, and its members, along with the Chamber of Commerce, pledged to accept the certificates as currency. The council vigorously protested this action, and Bull prorogued the legislature, but everyone in the colony except Bull—including even the councillors—accepted the certificates. The success of this measure made the passage of a tax bill less imperative

---

[77] Laurens to Gervais and to Thomas Savage, both Apr. 9, 1774, Laurens Letter Book, 1772–74, 266, 268–73, S. C. Historical Society.

[78] Dartmouth to Bull, Oct. 28, 1773, Jan. 8, May 4, 1774, and Bull to Dartmouth, Mar. 10, 1774, Transcripts of South Carolina Records, 33:335, 34:2–3, 15–19, 33–34, S. C. Archives Department; Laurens to James Laurens, Mar. 11, 1773, and to Garden, Apr. 8, 1773, Laurens Letter Book, 1772–74, 59–60, 96–97, S. C. Historical Society; Garth to

while at the same time permitting the Commons to sidestep the issue embodied in the additional instruction.[79]

Ironically, at the very time the Commons was acting unilaterally to ameliorate the colony's fiscal plight, metropolitan authorities were modifying the controversial instruction. As early as June 1773 Garth had urged Dartmouth to revoke the instruction because the bonds designed by Bull in 1770 to be signed by the treasurers prevented those officers from applying money except by ordinance or act of all three branches of the legislature. Garth had also persuaded South Carolina's new governor, Lord William Campbell, that withdrawal of the instruction was absolutely necessary. Upon Campbell's request colonial officials omitted the 1770 instruction from his instructions so that the South Carolina representatives would "have no longer any pretence to say that they are not left at liberty to frame their Money Bills as they think fit." At the same time, however, the ministry made it clear that it was neither recognizing the Commons' power to order money from the treasury without executive approval nor consenting to the repayment of the money sent to Wilkes, by inserting another instruction absolutely prohibiting Campbell to pass any bill to replace money ordered out of the treasury by the sole authority of the Commons.[80]

The South Carolina Commons, highly unlikely to have been satisfied by this arrangement, never had an opportunity to accept or to reject it. The ministry did not inform Bull of the precise changes in the royal instructions, and by the time Campbell arrived in the colony in June 1775 the Wilkes fund controversy had been pushed into the background

---

Committee of Correspondence, May 20, July 5, Nov. 13, 1773, Garth Letter Book, 152, 155, 157, S. C. Archives Department.

[79] Bull to Dartmouth, Mar. 24, May 3, 1774, Transcripts of South Carolina Records, 34:21–22, 36–40, S. C. Archives Department.

[80] Garth to Dartmouth, June 16, 1773, Dartmouth to Bull, May 4, 1774, Dartmouth et al. to Crown, June 20, 1774, ibid., 33:277–78, 34:33–34, 47–52; Labaree, *Royal Instructions* 1:210; Campbell to Dartmouth, Apr. 2, 1774, *The Manuscripts of the Earl of Dartmouth*, 3 vols. in 2 (London, 1887–96), 2:207; Garth to Lowndes, Feb. 1, 1773, and to Committee of Correspondence, Nov. 13, 1773, Mar. 11, Apr. 21, July 19, 1774, Garth Letter Book, 141, 157, 165, 171–72, 178–79, S. C. Archives Department; Laurens to John Laurens, Apr. 8, 1774, and to Gervais, Apr. 9, 16, 1774, Laurens Letter Book, 1772–74, 261–62, 268–73, 283–84, S. C. Historical Society; Laurens to John Laurens, Apr. 19, May 10, 1774, "Laurens Correspondence," *South Carolina Historical and Genealogical Magazine* 4 (1903): 101, 107. Two long official reports, one dated 1773 and the other without date, were prepared for Dartmouth and may be found in the Dartmouth Manuscripts, 777, William L. Salt Library, Stafford, Eng.

by questions of greater moment.[81] War had broken out in Massachusetts, and the Carolinians had turned their attention to broader questions of American rights.[82] The Wilkes fund dispute ended in stalemate, with neither the Commons nor crown officials ever having yielded on the issue of the right of the Commons House to issue money from the treasury by its single authority.

The Wilkes fund controversy brought a number of older political developments and issues to their culmination. The Commons' exclusive control over all financial matters had been the central issue in South Carolina politics from the introduction of royal government in 1721 until the mid-1750s. The antipathy of the Commons toward the royal instructions and the denial that they were binding derived from the 1720s and had acquired increasing currency in succeeding decades. The council had been declining in prestige and in political effectiveness since the 1740s, and the denial of its legislative authority was a reiteration of an earlier suggestion.

The controversy also produced a constitutional impasse, exposing a wide and evidently unbridgeable gulf between the notions of the ministry and those of the South Carolina Commons about the constitution of the colony. The ministry's shock at the Wilkes vote and its doctrinaire insistence upon adherence to the additional instruction left no doubt in American minds where British officials stood. On the one hand, British officialdom continued to insist that the colonies were subordinate political units whose constitutions had been set for all time by charters, commissions, and instructions—units with only a small measure of representative government, whose inferior legislative bodies were subject to both ministerial and parliamentary control. The Commons' sustained opposition, on the other hand, revealed its intense devotion to the principle of a dynamic constitution in which it, as the representative part, was a

---

[81] See Dartmouth to Bull, Dec. 10, 1774, and Alexander Innes to Dartmouth, May 1, 1775, Transcripts of South Carolina Records, 34:222, 35:92–99, S. C. Archives Department; Innes to Dartmouth, May 16, June 3, 1775, in B. D. Barger, ed., "Charles Town Loyalism in 1775: The Secret Reports of Alexander Innes," *South Carolina Historical Magazine* 43 (1962): 127–31; and Commons Journals, 39, pt. 2:180–81 (Jan. 25, 1775), S. C. Archives Department.

[82] Commons Journals, 39, pt. 2:293, 302–5 (July 11, 24, 29, 1775), S. C. Archives Department.

central and constructive force, just as the House of Commons in Britain was the dominant element in the British constitution.

Most important, the Wilkes fund controversy was instrumental in bringing South Carolina politicians to a full realization of the nature of the political challenge involved in Britain's new colonial policy. One of the central issues of the American Revolution was the threat to assembly rights, and no other single event was so important in bringing that fact home to South Carolina political leaders and in convincing them of the seriousness of the metropolitan challenge. Henry Laurens correctly interpreted the broader aims of British policy and the additional instruction as a "Scheme . . . to reduce us to the State of a Country Corporation." In attempting to curtail the Commons' authority to order money from the treasury without executive consent, the ministry was challenging a power which the Commons had exercised without contest for two decades; the additional instruction stood as a blatant symbol of the slight regard metropolitan authorities had for the rights of American lower houses. The South Carolina Commons shared Henry Laurens's belief that "the Representative Body of the People in Carolina, when regularly Assembled, have and ought to enjoy all the Rights and Privileges of a free People—or in other words—all the Rights and Privileges, as a Branch of the Legislature, which are held, enjoyed and exercised by the House of Commons in Great Britain."[83] Its stubborn resistance indicated how vital those rights were to American legislators and how far they would go to preserve the political structures they had built over the previous century.

For five crucial years beginning in December 1769 the Wilkes grant was the central issue in South Carolina politics, interrupting the normal process of government and contributing to the rise of an intense bitterness toward the ministry among South Carolina politicians. For them, the description in the *Gazette* of a statue of Lord Hillsborough inscribed with the motto "Massachusetts is my wash-pot and South Carolina my Footstool!" was no idle jest. "What Shall we Say," lamented Henry Laurens in April 1774 on the eve of the modification of the instruction, "of the Injury done to a province by a Ministerial Mandate held over that province and totally Stagnating public business for four Years[?]" In October 1774, after one of the frequent prorogations, the *South Carolina Gazette* complained that "we *still continue* in the Situation we have been for some Years past . . . with little more than a *nominal* Legislative Rep-

---

[83] Laurens to James Laurens, Dec. 12, 1771, Laurens Letter Book, 1771–72, 95–104, S. C. Historical Society.

resentation."[84] No annual tax bill was passed in South Carolina after 1769 and no legislation whatever after February 1771. For all practical purposes, royal government in South Carolina broke down four years earlier than it did in any of the other colonies. There was no "period of quiet" in that colony. After the repeal of most of the Townshend duties in 1770, while the flames of revolution cooled elsewhere in the colonies, the Wilkes fund controversy kept them burning brightly in South Carolina. Along with the contest over the location of the capital in Massachusetts, it stood as glaring testimony to the fact that, despite the repeal of most of the Townshend taxes, there was no relaxation in the broader objectives of the new colonial policy. With the exception of parliamentary taxation, no other issue was so important in persuading South Carolina politicians that their political fortunes would never be secure so long as they were subject to the whims of a group of politicians over whom they had no control and from whom they could expect no sympathetic hearing. In this sense, the Wilkes fund controversy was the bridge to Revolution in South Carolina.

Entitled "The Wilkes Fund Dispute in South Carolina," an early version of this chapter was presented as a paper at the Thirteenth Conference on Early American History held at the University of South Carolina, Columbia, March 23, 1962. It served as the core of the introduction to my *The Nature of Colony Constitutions: Two Pamphlets on the Wilkes Fund Controversy in South Carolina by Sir Egerton Leigh and Arthur Lee* (Columbia, S.C., 1970) and is reprinted here with permission from the *Journal of Southern History* 29 (1963):19–52.

[84] Laurens to Gervais, Apr. 16, 1774, ibid., 1772–74, 283–84; *South Carolina Gazette*, Sept. 6, 1773, Oct. 24, 1774.

Sixteen

The Currency Act of 1764 in Metropolitan-Colonial Relations, 1764–76

with Richard M. Jellison

Historians of the American Revolution have written much about the issues between Great Britain and its American colonies in the critical period between 1763 and 1776. Understandably, they have concentrated upon those areas where the conflict was most dramatic, upon the omnipresent questions of parliamentary taxation and the tightening of the mercantile system. Consequently, less dramatic issues have been pushed into the background, and their impact upon the Revolutionary crisis has never been adequately explored. Such is the case with the imperial prohibition by the Currency Act of April 19, 1764 (4 Geo. III, c. 34), of the emission of further legal tender paper money in the colonies south of New England. In many of those colonies that act was an underlying source of discontent for much of the last decade of the colonial period.[1]

Unlike other features of the general restrictive program adopted by metropolitan authorities after 1763, the Currency Act in no sense represented a sharp break with previous policy. Influenced by British mer-

---

[1] No previously published study has attempted to explore the impact of the Currency Act upon the Revolutionary movement, although Bernhard Knollenberg has briefly treated the initial reaction to it in his *Origin of the American Revolution, 1759–1766* (New York, 1960), 181, 204, 216. From every standpoint, Leslie Van Horn Brock, "The Currency of the American Colonies, 1700 to 1764," Ph.D. diss., University of Michigan, 1941, is the best treatment of the colonial experience with paper money before the pas-

chants who feared that colonial legislators would attempt to force payment of sterling debts in depreciated paper, metropolitan authorities had never been sympathetic to colonial paper money. In 1720 they had sent a circular instruction to the governors of ten colonies forbidding passage of laws to issue such currencies without a suspending clause, and they eventually gave a similar instruction to all governors.[2] Though told to adhere rigidly to this instruction, governors often ignored it in times of emergency, with the result that opponents of paper currencies began to demand parliamentary action. Parliament responded in 1741 by passing a statute aimed specifically at the Massachusetts land bank of 1740 to prohibit such organizations from issuing further legal tender paper bills, and the following year it contemplated placing strict regulations on the currencies of all the colonies. However, Parliament did not act again until 1751, when it forbade the emission of legal tender currencies in all of the New England colonies.[3] This prohibition did not apply to the colonies from New York to Georgia, and when, during the Seven Years' War, their legislatures found it necessary to issue large quantities of paper to pay for military operations and some depreciation followed, British merchants viewed the scene with increasing alarm.

The Virginia situation was particularly disturbing. The last of the colonial lower houses to have recourse to a paper currency, the Virginia House of Burgesses reluctantly turned to that expedient in 1755, when there was no other way to raise money for the war. Then, over the next seven years, the Burgesses issued about £440,000 in legal tender bills. Beginning in 1757, the issuing statutes all provided that the General Court should take depreciation into account when awarding judgments for sterling debts.[4] Nevertheless, British merchants trading to Virginia

---

sage of the Currency Act. An excellent published summary of scholarship on colonial paper currency experiments is E. James Ferguson, "Currency Finance: An Interpretation of Colonial Monetary Practices," *William and Mary Quarterly*, 3d ser., 10 (1953): 153–80. See also Ferguson's *The Power of the Purse: A History of American Public Finance, 1776–1790* (Chapel Hill, N.C., 1961), 3–24.

[2] Leonard W. Labaree, ed., *Royal Instructions to British Colonial Governors, 1670–1776*, 2 vols. (New York, 1935), 1:218–19.

[3] Heads of an Act to Regulate British American Currencies, [March 1742], Colonial Office Papers, 323/11, ff. 23–26, Public Record Office, London; Danby Pickering, ed., *The Statutes at Large from Magna Carta to the End of the Eleventh Parliament of Great Britain, Anno 1761, Continued to 1806*, 46 vols. (Cambridge, Eng., 1762–1807), 17:459–63, 20:306–9.

[4] Brock, "Currency of the American Colonies," table 28; Francis Fauquier to Board of Trade, Feb. 24, 1762, CO 5/130, ff. 219–22, PRO.

procured an additional instruction to Lieutenant Governor Francis Fauquier in January 1759 which required him to induce the Burgesses to amend the statutes to provide that sterling debts contracted before the acts became law were payable only in sterling money and that the paper bills were legal tender only for creditors willing to accept them.[5]

The Burgesses flatly refused to comply, and during the next three years it provided for four additional issues without the required limitations. An act of November 1761 for the retirement of all currency by October 20, 1769, did not satisfy the traders.[6] In 1762 merchants from London, Glasgow, and Liverpool, in a well-organized protest, presented memorials to the Board of Trade complaining of both the depreciation of the Virginia currency and the Burgesses' continued insistence that it pass as legal tender. The board sided with the merchants and declared "that the legislature of Virginia have been wanting, not only in a proper respect to the Crown, but also in justice to the . . . merchants in refusing to comply with what was recommended in his late majesty's additional instructions."[7] This stinging indictment only served to antagonize further the Burgesses, which firmly refused to remove the currency's legal tender requirements, resolving "that as the present Possessers of the Treasury Notes have received them under the Faith of a Law, making them a legal tender in all payments, . . . to alter that essential Quality of them now would be an Act of great Injustice."[8]

The Burgesses' continued defiance and the merchants' simultaneous alarm over the even more serious and rapid depreciation of North Caroli-

---

[5] Memorials of London and Bristol Merchants [1758], CO 5/1329, ff. 129, 131–32, PRO; W. L. Grant and J. Munro, eds., *Acts of the Privy Council of England, Colonial Series*, 6 vols. (London, 1908–12), 4:389–93 (July 28, 1758); Virginia Burgesses to William Pitt, [1758], Chatham Papers, Gifts and Deposits, 30/8, f. 96, PRO; Additional Instructions to Earl of Loudoun, Jan. 31, 1759, CO 5/1367, ff. 358–62, PRO.

[6] W. W. Hening, ed., *The Statutes at Large: Being a Collection of All the Laws of Virginia*, 13 vols. (Richmond, etc., 1809–23), 7:331–37, 347–53, 357–63, 465–66, 495–502; H. R. McIlwaine and John Pendleton Kennedy, eds., *Journals of the House of Burgesses of Virginia*, 13 vols. (Richmond, 1905–15), *1758–61*, 152, 167 (Nov. 21, 1759, Mar. 1, 1760).

[7] James Abercromby to Fauquier, Nov. 10, 1762, Robert A. Brock Collection, Henry E. Huntington Library, San Marino, Calif.; Memorials of London, Glasgow, and Liverpool Merchants, CO 5/1330, ff. 261–63, 277, 279, PRO; *Journal of the Commissioners for Trade and Plantations*, 14 vols. (London, 1920–38), *1759–63*, 330–34 (Feb. 1–7, 1763); Board of Trade to Fauquier, Feb. 7, 1763, CO 5/1368, 212–17, PRO.

[8] Virginia Committee to Edward Montagu, June 16, 1763, "Proceedings of the Virginia Committee of Correspondence," *Virginia Magazine of History and Biography* 11 (1903–4):

na's paper bills influenced colonial officials to move toward a total prohibition of legal tender currency in the colonies. In December 1763 the Board of Trade declared "that any further neglect of the Legislature of Virginia to give redress to the complaints of the merchants would be neither just or equitable" and threatened to "lay the matter before Parliament."[9] At the urging of Lord Hillsborough, then the first commissioner of trade and plantations, the board took steps to translate this threat into action, conducting a series of hearings early in 1764 during which six former governors agreed that it "would be highly expedient and proper" to extend to the other continental colonies Parliament's statute of 1751 restraining legal tender paper currencies in New England. The lone dissenters among representatives from the colonies were Thomas Penn and Richard Jackson, proprietor and agent, respectively, for Pennsylvania. They urged that action be postponed for a year to give the colonies an opportunity to present their sentiments upon it. Agents from the six royal colonies from New York to Georgia subsequently supported Penn and Jackson's suggestion, but the board was determined to act immediately. It noted that the New England colonies had not suffered greatly from the prohibition, having solved their currency problems by establishing crown-approved non–legal tender systems, and it contended that "inconveniencies" would "arise from any further delay." The agents again tried, without success, to persuade the board to postpone action, unanimously arguing that each colony should be permitted some stipulated amount of paper currency to pass as legal tender within the colonies, if not in payment of British debts. Equally unsuccessful was the suggested compromise by Charles Garth and William Knox, agents for South Carolina and Georgia, respectively, that the colonies be permitted to establish paper currencies if they obtained the crown's prior approval and did not make them legal tender in payment of British debts.[10] On February 9 the board submitted to the ministry a series of

---

345–49; Representation of Virginia Burgesses, May 1763, Stevens Transcripts, vol. 1, no. 1, Add. MSS. 42257, British Library, London.

[9] *Journal of the Commissioners for Trade and Plantations, 1759–63*, 418 (Dec. 8, 1763); Board of Trade to Fauquier, Dec. 9, 1763, CO 5/1368, ff. 245–46, PRO.

[10] *Journal of the Commissioners for Trade and Plantations, 1764–67*, 3–21 (Jan. 10–Feb. 13, 1764); Benjamin Franklin to Lord Kames, Jan. 1, 1769, *The Works of Benjamin Franklin*, ed. Jared Sparks, 10 vols. (Boston, 1836–40), 7:429; Richard Jackson to Franklin, Jan. 26 and [Feb.] 1764, in Carl Van Doren, ed., *Letters and Papers of Benjamin Franklin and Richard Jackson, 1753 to 1785* (Philadelphia, 1947), 116, 139. For an excellent account of the experience of the New England colonies, see Brock, "Currency of the American Colonies," 244–334.

proposals that formed the basis for the Currency Act, passed by Parliament in April 1764.

The Currency Act prohibited all of the continental colonies from issuing legal tender currency after September 1, 1764, and required that all such currency then circulating be punctually retired at the time appointed by the act of issue. The act threatened any governor who violated it with severe penalties, including a fine of £1,000 sterling, immediate dismissal, and lifetime exclusion from places of public trust.[11] Passed at a time when most of the colonies involved still had sufficient currency circulating from wartime issues[12] and when Americans were more alarmed by other more objectionable features of the Grenville program, the Currency Act encountered little immediate opposition, and for the first two years there were only sporadic protests.

Most of the initial objections emanated from the middle colonies, where many seemed to agree with Richard Jackson that it was "rather an Indecorum to make Laws respecting People so remote without their even knowing what we were about."[13] Israel Pemberton wrote from Pennsylvania that the act occasioned "a general clamour and uneasiness among the people." Benjamin Franklin offered a similar observation two weeks later, although he thought that the legal tender prohibition would not cause "much Inconvenience" if the colonies could "still make Money

---

[11] Board of Trade to Crown, Feb. 9, 1764, in William A. Whitehead et al., eds., *Archives of the State of New Jersey,* 1st ser., 80 vols. (Newark, N.J., 1880–1949), 9:405–14; Robert Charles to Cadwallader Colden, Apr. 14, 1764, *The Letters and Papers of Cadwallader Colden,* 9 vols., New-York Historical Society, *Collections* (New York, 1918–37), 7:300–301; *Statutes at Large of Great Britain* 26:103–5.

[12] With the exception of Maryland and possibly Georgia, the colonies appear to have issued enough paper to satisfy the demands of commerce for the moment. Of course, the amount of bills necessary for a trading medium depended upon a variety of factors including size of population, volume of trade, and the rate of exchange with sterling. For a summary of the currency situation in each colony in the early 1760s, see Brock, "Currency of the American Colonies," 345–46, 402–3, 436–37, 460–61, 464; Katherine L. Behrens, *Paper Money in Maryland* (Baltimore, 1923), 46–53; Richard S. Rodney, *Colonial Finances in Delaware* (Wilmington, Del., 1928), 30–37, 64–65; Clarence W. Loke, "The Currency Question in the Province of New York, 1764–1771," M.A. thesis, University of Wisconsin, 1941, 25–49.

[13] Jackson to Benjamin Franklin, [Feb.] 1764, in Van Doren, *Letters and Papers of Benjamin Franklin and Richard Jackson,* 116.

bearing Interest," a scheme he had already proposed to the Pennsylvania House of Representatives the previous December.[14] New York merchant John Watts was less optimistic. He thought the act both unwise and unjust and pointed out what almost every colonial man of affairs had long known, that the colonies had no other satisfactory medium of exchange. What little specie they acquired from the West Indies was quickly drained off to redress an unfavorable balance of trade with Great Britain, and Watts feared that "forbidding Paper Money to be a Legal Tender would . . . take away what little Energy it has." He pointed out that "the loss on Virginia Paper was honestly acquired, by the Government[']s exerting itself" during the war. "We have no resources upon an Emergency," he wrote Moses Frank in June 1764, "but in Paper Money." Parliament had rewarded the colonies for their exertions by the Currency Act. In fact, as Watts bitterly observed, those colonies that had contributed neither taxes nor men to the war had fared best. They had issued little or no paper money, saving both their money and their credit, and had suffered no reproaches from London.[15]

Maryland was one of those colonies to which Watts was referring, but both Governor Horatio Sharpe and lawyer Daniel Dulany from that colony echoed his sentiments. Lamenting the harsh terms of the Currency Act, Sharpe warned Cecelius Calvert in August 1764 that the trade of the colonies "must flag much from the Want of paper Currency."[16] A month later Dulany wrote Calvert in much the same vein, contending that America could not do without some sort of paper currency and predicting that if Parliament insisted upon preventing "our emitting Bills of Credit under one Denomination, we shall have a paper Circulation under another, if not under a publick Law . . . upon the Bottom of private Security." Dulany did not deny that some colonies, particularly Virginia, had emitted too much paper, but he thought it oppressive for the "Limb to be at once amputated before a milder Application is tried, be-

[14] Israel Pemberton to Samuel Fothergill, June 13, 1764, Pemberton Papers, 24:131, Historical Society of Pennsylvania, Philadelphia, as quoted by Payton W. Yoder, "Paper Currency in Colonial Pennsylvania," Ph.D. diss., Indiana University, 1941, 204; Franklin to Jackson, June 25, 1764, and Franklin's "Argument for Making Bills of Credit Draw Interest," Dec. 25, 1763, in Van Doren, *Letters and Papers of Benjamin Franklin and Richard Jackson*, 125–35, 169.

[15] John Watts to General Robert Monckton, Apr. 14, 1764, and to Moses Frank, June 9, 1764, *Letter Book of John Watts . . . [1762–65]*, New-York Historical Society, *Collections* 61 (1928): 242–43, 264.

[16] Sharpe to Calvert, Aug. 22, 1764, in William Hand Browne et al., eds., *Archives of Maryland*, 58 vols. (Baltimore, 1883–1959), 14:174.

cause a sore appears upon some part of it." Nor did Dulany stop there. He went on to question Parliament's competence to pass such legislation, bitterly asserting that the "wisest Legislators are often mistaken, the Parliament of England are often, very often, mistaken, even when the subject of their Deliberations is relative only to the internal Police of that Kingdom, which it may be presumed, they have understood, as well as the Affairs of America."[17]

Both the Pennsylvania and New York lower houses thought the matter serious enough to take official action in October 1764. The Pennsylvania House of Representatives instructed agent Richard Jackson to give particular attention to the currency question, warning that "under the present . . . Restraints, we shall, in a few Years, be without a necessary Medium of Trade."[18] At the same time, the New York assembly protested the inexpediency of the Currency Act in its petition to the House of Commons against the Sugar Act and the proposed stamp duties.[19]

As the paper money issued during the war was gradually paid into the colonial treasuries for taxes and retired according to law, colonials began to complain increasingly about the want of money with which to carry on trade. Virginia's Governor Francis Fauquier reported as early as June 1765 that "Circulating Currency" had "grown very scarce," so that people were "really distressed for Money of any kind to satisfy their Creditors." The situation would get worse, he said, as the number of bills decreased by "burning and sinking all that are received for Taxes."[20] Similar complaints came from John Watts in New York and Cortlandt Skinner in New Jersey.[21]

---

[17] Dulany to Calvert, Sept. 10, 1764, *The Calvert Papers* 2, Maryland Historical Society Fund Publications, no. 34 (1894): 245–46.

[18] "Votes and Proceedings of the House of Representatives of the Province of Pennsylvania," in Charles F. Hoban, ed., *Pennsylvania Archives*, 8th ser., 8 vols. (Harrisburg, Pa., 1931–35), 7:5680 (Oct. 20, 1764).

[19] *Journal of the Votes and Proceedings of the General Assembly of the Colony of New York . . . 1691 . . . [1765]*, 2 vols. (New York, 1764–66), 2:753–55, 769–80 (Sept. 19, Oct. 18, 1764).

[20] Fauquier to Earl of Halifax, June 14, 1765, CO 5/1345, PRO.

[21] John Watts to James Napier, Apr. 15, 1765, and to Moses Frank, Dec. 22, 1765, *Letter Book of John Watts*, 345, 406–7; David L. Cowen, "Revolutionary New Jersey, 1763–1787," New Jersey Historical Society, *Proceedings*, 71 (1953): 3.

Not until after the repeal of the Stamp Act did the colonies make a full-scale assault upon the Currency Act. Beginning in early 1766, one colony after another complained about the ill effects of the measure. These complaints culminated in the winter of 1766–67 in a concerted attempt by colonial agents to secure its repeal or alteration. Receiving strong backing from a number of London merchants and encouragement from key members of the ministry, they came very close to success.

The Pennsylvania House of Representatives initiated the attack. Like the other continental colonies, Pennsylvania suffered from a chronic shortage of specie. What gold and silver found its way into the colony was quickly drained off to pay debts to the British, and long experience had convinced the legislators that a legal tender paper currency was the only satisfactory medium of exchange. By the end of 1765 the Representatives had called in and retired over 20 percent of the £500,000 circulating in 1760, and the resulting shortage of money was compounded by the fact that a large part of the bills still current were being used in the neighboring colonies of New Jersey, Delaware, and Maryland. The Pennsylvania Representatives felt compelled in January 1766 to send a petition to the House of Commons requesting the repeal of the Currency Act.[22] Even before the arrival of this petition, Pennsylvania agent Benjamin Franklin, during his examination before the House of Commons in February 1766 on the American reaction to the Stamp Act, had singled out the Currency Act as one of the main causes of the Americans' dwindling respect for Parliament.[23]

Together with Richard Jackson, Franklin now succeeded in presenting the Pennsylvania petition to the House of Commons, and he happily reported to the Pennsylvania committee of correspondence in April 1766 that the Rockingham ministry was favorably disposed toward the colonies and, if it continued in power, "we may hope everything we can reasonably expect." Franklin's optimism rested on the assumption that the power of the opposition was diminishing and that a member of Parliament, probably Jackson, had requested him to draw up a bill to repeal the Currency Act. Franklin blamed the loss of value of the Virginia bills of credit for the legal tender restriction of the Currency Act and felt that any repeal bill would have to safeguard the merchants from such

---

[22] "Votes and Proceedings of the House of Representatives," *Pennsylvania Archives*, 8th ser., 7:5818, 5824–27 (Jan. 9, 14, 1766).

[23] The Examination of Franklin in the House of Commons, Feb. 1766, *The Complete Works of Benjamin Franklin*, ed. John Bigelow, 10 vols. (New York and London, 1887–88), 3:418.

depreciation. Therefore, he inserted a clause to make sterling debts to British merchants payable at the current rate of exchange. But the absence of complaints from other colonies at this time and the conviction that the whole question needed more extensive study decided the ministry against making any changes in the law at that session, although Franklin reported to the Pennsylvania committee in June that the act would certainly be repealed next year "if this Ministry continues, and no further Imprudencies appear in America to exasperate Government here against us."[24]

Meanwhile, both Maryland and New York were trying different lines of attack. In Maryland the situation was critical. The last of its paper bills were retired in the fall of 1765, and it was forced to rely upon Pennsylvania bills for a circulating medium.[25] Residents of Frederick County were particularly irate about the scarcity of money and petitioned the council for a new emission. In November 1765 the Maryland lower house prepared a bill to issue 140,000 Spanish dollars in paper, but a disagreement with the upper house over the journal of accounts prevented its passage. The lower house patterned this act after an earlier emission of 1732, proposing to issue the new bills on the security of the stock of the Bank of England and to put them in circulation by using them to pay the public debt. The bills were to remain current for ten years and then were to be sunk by bills of exchange drawn on trustees appointed in England to supervise the investment. To support these bills, the Maryland legislature provided in another bill at the same session to add £8,000 accumulated in gold and silver in the loan office to the £25,000 already invested by the colony in the Bank of England stock. The proposed notes, like those of the Bank of England and those of the 1732 issue, would accumulate interest and would thereby retain their value without a legal tender provision, thus obviating the prohibitions of the Currency Act. Both Governor Horatio Sharpe and Lord Baltimore approved the plan, and in December 1766 the Maryland legislature enacted it into law, providing for the issuance of £39,089 sterling in paper bills and expressly stipulating that the bills should not be legal tender "in discharge of any

---

[24] Franklin to Pennsylvania Committee of Correspondence, Apr. 12, June 10, 1766, "Original Letters and Documents," *Pennsylvania Magazine of History and Biography* 5 (1881): 353–54; Charles Garth to South Carolina Committee of Correspondence, July 9, 1766, Garth Letter Book, 1765–75, 8, South Carolina Archives Department, Columbia.

[25] Horatio Sharpe to Cecelius Calvert, Aug. 22, 1764, *Archives of Maryland* 14:174; "Votes and Proceedings of the House of Representatives," *Pennsylvania Archives*, 8th ser., 7:5824–27 (Jan. 14, 1766).

contract whatsoever . . . except such . . . as shall or may be made expressly and specifically for . . . the delivery of such bills of credit."[26]

This scheme proved entirely acceptable to metropolitan authorities, and despite the omission of a legal tender clause, the bills, as Governor Sharpe predicted, held their value and were readily accepted in payment of all debts. Maryland had found a successful formula for solving its currency problems within the context of the 1764 restriction. Thereafter, the Currency Act was not an issue of importance in the colony. Governor Sharpe reported in June 1767 that Marylanders no longer cared whether Parliament repealed the measure or not, although he noted that Maryland's neighbors were suffering for want of an adequate circulating medium.[27]

New York was less successful. Although there was still more than £300,000 in circulation in that colony, Governor Sir Henry Moore reported to the Board of Trade in March 1766 that New York was "greatly distressed for want of a proper currency" and that, to ensure the colony an adequate medium of exchange when current bills expired in November 1768, the assembly was determined to issue more. Moore asked the board to release him from the instruction forbidding him to assent to paper money bills.[28] Now under the presidency of Lord Dartmouth, who was inclined to treat American problems sympathetically, the board

---

[26] "Proceedings and Acts of the General Assembly," *Archives of Maryland* 59:195 (Nov. 30, 1765), 319–21, 61:264–75; Sharpe to Cecelius Calvert, Dec. 21, 1765, and to Lord Baltimore, Dec. 7, 1766, ibid., 14:251–52, 352; Behrens, *Paper Money in Maryland*, 51–52. A similar plan had been proposed but not adopted in South Carolina in 1736. See Richard M. Jellison, "Antecedents of the South Carolina Currency Acts of 1736 and 1746," *William and Mary Quarterly*, 3d ser., 16 (1959): 559–61.

[27] Sharpe to H. Hammersley, June 9, 1767, *Archives of Maryland* 14:391. During the remaining decade of the colonial period, the Maryland legislature followed the same formula in two additional emissions in 1769 and 1773. Sharpe suggested as early as 1767 that the colony needed an additional £30,000 in paper, and in December 1769 the legislature voted to add another £300,000 to remain current for twelve years. A dispute in the fall of 1771 over the right of the upper house to amend money bills prevented the passage of a bill to emit an additional £270,000 to establish a seminary of learning, but in 1773 the two houses agreed to add £346,667, the bulk of which was to be loaned to the counties for public improvements. Crown officials found both the 1769 and 1773 emissions acceptable. See "Proceedings and Acts of the General Assembly," ibid., 62:133–51 (Dec. 1769), 63:118–28, 176 (Oct. 22–25, Nov. 16, 1771), 64:242–53 (Dec. 1773); Behrens, *Paper Money in Maryland*, 52–56.

[28] Moore to Board of Trade, Mar. 28, 1766, in Edmund B. O'Callaghan and Berthold Fernow, eds., *Documents Relative to the Colonial History of the State of New York*, 15 vols. (Albany, 1853–87), 7:820–21.

acted favorably and promptly upon Moore's request. It secured an additional instruction revoking Moore's old instruction on currency bills and empowering him to pass a measure to emit an additional £260,000 for five years provided it included adequate provisions for retiring the bills and a clause suspending its execution until it had received the approval of crown officials. This instruction indicated that the Rockingham government was favorably disposed to the Americans' stand on legal tender currency. As it pointed out to Moore, the board insisted upon a suspending clause primarily because any law that provided for the issue of legal tender paper would violate the Currency Act and crown officials did not have the power to grant an exemption from an act of Parliament. However, if the measure included a suspending clause, crown officials could withhold their approval until the 1767 session of Parliament, when they might obtain "the further sense" of that body on the currency question. In the meantime, the board asked Moore to collect the arguments of the principal New York merchants in favor of a legal tender currency for Parliament's consideration.[29]

But these concessions did not satisfy the New York assembly. It thought £130,000 sufficient to satisfy the colony's currency needs and flatly refused to pass any measure with a suspending clause. Instead, it urged Moore to consider "the pressing Necessities" and assent to a bill to issue the smaller sum for eight years without such a clause. Moore, who could not grant the request without violating the board's instructions, submitted the assembly's proposal for the board's consideration in November 1766. As the year ended, New York had made no progress toward solving its currency difficulties.[30]

The Board of Trade's concessions to New York seemed a favorable omen, and throughout the fall of 1766 and the early months of 1767 colonial agents were confident that Parliament would repeal the Currency Act. Charles Garth was more cautious, writing the South Carolina committee of correspondence in September 1766 that Lord Hillsborough, who had been the chief force behind the passage of the measure in 1764 and who had just replaced Dartmouth at the head of the Board of Trade

---

[29] Board of Trade's Representation on the Circulation of Bills of Credit, May 16, 1766, and Board of Trade to Moore, July 11, 1766, ibid., 827–28, 844; Journal of the Votes and Proceedings of the General Assembly of the Colony of New York, Nov. 12, 1766, 6–8, Historical Society of Pennsylvania.

[30] Moore to Board of Trade, Nov. 15, 1766, *Documents Relative to the Colonial History of the State of New York* 7:878; Journal of the Votes and Proceedings of the General Assembly of New York, Nov. 1766, 6–8, Historical Society of Pennsylvania.

in August upon the formation of the Pitt ministry, might prove a "power-ful" obstacle. Still, Garth thought that a general protest from a number of colonies probably would succeed. Benjamin Franklin wrote in a similar vein to the Pennsylvania committee in early November, and Garth reported two weeks later that Chancellor of the Exchequer Charles Town-shend was "inclined to give us his Countenance."[31]

In South Carolina the Commons House of Assembly had already listed the Currency Act as a major grievance and—Garth's optimism having encouraged the Commons to petition the crown against the act—had directed Garth in June 1766 to attempt to secure its repeal. Indeed, with the sinking of the wartime public orders and tax certificates, South Carolina found itself without enough currency to satisfy the requirements of internal trade. Nor did it ease the situation that over a fourth of its regular £106,500 of legal tender notes were being used in North Carolina and Georgia. The Commons was not exaggerating when it complained in its petition that the colony was "not furnished with a sufficient Quantity of Gold and Silver to answer its Demand for Money" and asserted that it was "absolutely necessary to establish a Currency as a Medium of Trade." If the amount of money in the colony continued to decline, the Commons warned, South Carolina might find itself unable to continue importing goods from Britain and might be forced to set up its own manufacturing. To preclude such a development, the Commons requested the king to recommend a repeal of the legal tender prohibition and asked permission to issue an additional sum of legal tender paper equal to £50,000 sterling.[32]

With the South Carolina petition in hand, Garth joined Franklin, Jackson, New York agent Robert Charles, and Virginia agent Edward Montagu in a concerted attempt at repeal during the early months of 1767. Unexpected support came from Nova Scotia agent Joshua Mauger. Nova Scotia had not previously issued legal tender paper money, but as the colony's population expanded the need for a larger circulating medium became pressing, and in November 1766 its House of Assembly

---

[31] Garth to South Carolina Committee of Correspondence, June 6, July 9, Sept. 26, Nov. 24, 1766, Garth Letter Book, 3–5, 7–8, 14–15, 18, S. C. Archives Department; "Votes and Proceedings of the House of Representatives," *Pennsylvania Archives*, 8th ser., 7:5958 (Jan. 14, 1767).

[32] Journals of the Commons House of Assembly, June 24, 1766, 37:175–76, S. C. Archives Department; South Carolina Commons' Petition to the Crown, Nov. 28, 1766, Transcripts of Records Relating to South Carolina in the British Public Record Office, 31:300–308, ibid.

petitioned the crown for permission to issue a paper currency.[33] At first, prospects for repeal were excellent. When Garth presented the South Carolina petition to Lord Shelburne, then in charge of American affairs as secretary of state for the southern department, in January 1767, he found that Shelburne considered repeal "a very necessary Measure" and promised to "promote it to the utmost of his power." Meanwhile, Franklin and Garth had succeeded in interesting the Committee of North American Merchants, concerned in trading with the continental colonies, in the affair; and on January 28 that informal association agreed that repeal was "absolutely necessary" and that legal tender currency would not be prejudicial to the merchants if it were not extended to sterling debts. A short while later, the committee submitted to crown officials some minutes of its meetings recording its approval of the repeal of the Currency Act. With both the merchants and Lord Shelburne behind them, the agents' hopes ran high. In early February, Franklin prepared a repeal bill, which Jackson planned to introduce into the House of Commons and the duke of Grafton, first lord of the treasury, pledged to support in the House of Lords.[34]

But within a month the whole situation had altered. Chatham had replaced Hillsborough with Lord Clare as president of the Board of Trade the previous December, and Clare was almost as strong an opponent of legal tender currency as his predecessor. Hence, when the Privy Council referred the merchants' and agents' petitions to the Board of Trade, it tabled the whole question, sending its 1764 report against paper currency to the merchants to convince them of the folly of their heresy. At the merchants' request and probably with help from Garth, Charles, and Montagu, Franklin prepared a superb distillation of the American case for paper money as an answer to that report. He emphasized that the inability of the colonies to retain specie made paper currency absolutely necessary and offered evidence to refute the board's contention that colonial paper constantly depreciated to the detriment of British merchants. The exchange rate between sterling and the currency of most colonies had been remarkably stable for long periods, he said, and the

[33] See *A Journal of the Votes of the Lower House of Assembly, for the Province of Nova Scotia, May-June, 1765* (Halifax, 1765), June 7, 1765, Nov. 19–21, 1766. For the background to this request and Nova Scotia's early experiments in issuing interest-bearing notes, see John Bartlet Brebner, *The Neutral Yankees of Nova Scotia* (New York, 1937), 151–52.

[34] Garth to South Carolina Committee of Correspondence, Jan. 31, 1767, Garth Letter Book, 23–24, S. C. Archives Department; Shelburne to Board of Trade, Feb. 13, 1767, Shelburne Papers, 53:41–42, William L. Clements Library, Ann Arbor, Mich.; Franklin

provision made by most colonies for the payment of sterling debts according to current rates of exchange prevented the merchants from suffering any great loss from depreciation. In fact, Franklin argued, paper money had actually benefited the merchants by providing Americans with a medium to purchase greater quantities of British manufactures. This answer convinced the merchants, but the Board of Trade remained hostile. Lord Clare did give his tentative approval in April to legal tender money for the colonies if it was issued in limited amounts with land for security, but these terms would probably not have been satisfactory to all of the colonies. Furthermore, the continued refusal of the New York house to comply with the Quartering Act had made the ministry much less willing to grant any indulgence to the colonies. Garth wrote the South Carolina committee of correspondence on March 12 that the New York affair might well prove "fatal to our Scheme," although Franklin was more optimistic. Both agreed, however, that if repeal was to be accomplished, it would have to be asked as a favor to the merchants, not to the colonies.[35]

The affair dragged on into May 1767, when it became hopelessly entangled with Townshend's program of raising an American revenue. The ministry toyed with an old scheme, originally suggested by Franklin in 1764 or 1765 as a substitute for the Stamp Act, by which the colonies would be permitted to issue paper money through loan offices, with the money arising from the interest to be applied by Parliament for the service of the crown.[36] But this plan, which Franklin himself had long since abandoned, was even more objectionable than the Currency Act. Realizing that the ministry had taken it up primarily because it would enable them to extract a revenue from the colonies, Franklin and other colonial

to Jackson, Feb. 13, 1767, in Van Doren, *Letters and Papers of Benjamin Franklin and Richard Jackson*, 196–97.

[35] Shelburne to Board of Trade, Feb. 13, 1767, Shelburne Papers, 53:41–42, Clements Library; *Journal of the Commissioners for Trade and Plantations, 1764–67,* 367 (Feb. 17, 1767); Garth to South Carolina Committee of Correspondence, Mar. 12, 1767, Garth Letter Book, 30–31, S. C. Archives Department; Franklin to Lord Kames, Jan. 1, 1769, *Works of Benjamin Franklin* 7:429; Franklin's Answer to Board of Trade's Report on Currency, Mar. 11, 1767, and Franklin to Joseph Galloway, June 13, 1767, *The Writings of Benjamin Franklin*, ed. Albert Henry Smyth, 10 vols. (New York, 1905–7), 5:1–14, 25–28; Franklin to Galloway, Apr. 14, 1767, and *Pennsylvania Chronicle* (Philadelphia), May 25, 1767, *Benjamin Franklin's Letters to the Press, 1758–1775,* ed. Verner W. Crane (Chapel Hill, N.C., 1950), 80–81, 92–93.

[36] For an excellent discussion of the origins and history of this plan and an edition of it, see Crane, *Benjamin Franklin's Letters to the Press,* 25–30.

representatives also knew that Americans would correctly construe it as yet another attempt at parliamentary taxation. Clearly, as Franklin quickly pointed out, "no colony would make money on those terms." Along with Garth and others, he persuaded the ministry to drop the idea. At a meeting with the ministry on May 11, the agents reached a clear understanding that the colonies "should be indulged with an Act of Repeal only[,] without anything more, leaving it to the Crown as formerly to allow or withhold its Assent to Acts of this sort to be passed in any Legislature in America." Accordingly, the merchants drew up a petition asking for repeal, and Garth and Jackson prepared to present it to the House of Commons.

This difficult business finally seemed on the verge of success when events took a sudden turn for the worse. On May 13, just two days after the agents' meeting with the ministry, Townshend introduced to Parliament his proposals for levying duties upon the colonies. When he had finished, George Grenville rose, objected to the duties as mere trifles, and proposed a scheme which would "produce something valuable in America." What Grenville proposed was the emission by act of Parliament of a paper currency for the colonies through a general loan office, with Parliament to apply the interest. This plan differed only in detail from the one the ministry had just discarded, but when it became apparent that the House was reacting to it favorably, Townshend, not to be outdone by Grenville, interjected that it was a "proposition of his own" and that he had a bill ready to propose.[37] Townshend's abrupt about-face astonished the agents and put an end to any hope of repeal at that session of Parliament. Not wishing to open the way for the establishment of a system which would drain even more money from the colonies, the agents and merchants withdrew their support for repeal. By withholding their petition, the merchants prevented Townshend from introducing his plan, for he could not with propriety move for repeal without complaints from either the merchants or the agents.

After the failure of the general attempt, Franklin and Jackson considered introducing a bill to exempt Pennsylvania, which currently was in more favor than some of the other colonies, from the restrictions of the Currency Act. Franklin reasoned that such a measure could serve as a precedent for similar concessions to other colonies once the resentment

---

[37] William Strahan to David Hall, May 9, 1767, "Correspondence between William Strahan and David Hall, 1763–1777," *Pennsylvania Magazine of History and Biography* 10 (1886): 322–23; Franklin to Galloway, June 13, 1767, *Writings of Benjamin Franklin* 5:25–28; Garth to South Carolina Committee of Correspondence, May 17, June 6, 1767,

toward them had abated. At first the merchants trading to Pennsylvania favored the scheme, but they abandoned it when other merchants concerned in the American trade opposed the Pennsylvania group's proceeding alone. By mid-June the agents had given up all hope of obtaining any concession that year. Indeed, Garth despaired of ever obtaining repeal, and in July he suggested to the South Carolina committee that the colony follow the Maryland example and try to solve its money problems by establishing a non-legal tender currency.[38] Franklin shared Garth's pessimism and in May 1767 heartily approved the Pennsylvania Representatives' issue of a small amount of non–legal tender bills.[39]

Indeed, this was the last general assault upon the Currency Act, although individual colonies continued to press for repeal or a special exemption. American observers in London were optimistic as late as the fall of 1767, but metropolitan policy toward the colonies hardened in the wake of American protests against the Townshend measures and precluded any chance for success.

As long as Townshend remained on the scene there was little hope of repeal. The pessimism of Garth and Franklin in the summer of 1767 was due largely to Townshend's threat to introduce his plan to raise a revenue from an American currency at the next session with or without applications from the agents and merchants. Franklin saw in this threat a plan "to render Assemblies in America useless." But Townshend's death on

---

Garth Letter Book, 36–38, S. C. Archives Department; *Pennsylvania Chronicle*, July 27, 1767, in *Benjamin Franklin's Letters to the Press*, 99–100.

[38] Garth to South Carolina Committee of Correspondence, June 6, July 5, 1767, Garth Letter Book, 37–40, S. C. Archives Department; Franklin to Galloway, June 13, 1767, *Writings of Benjamin Franklin* 5:25–28; William Samuel Johnson to William Pitkin, May 16, 1767, in Massachusetts Historical Society, *Collections*, 5th ser., 9 (1885): 231.

[39] James T. Mitchell and Henry Flanders, eds., *The Statutes at Large of Pennsylvania from 1682 to 1801*, 17 vols. (Harrisburg, Pa., 1896–1915), 7:100–107; "Votes and Proceedings of the House of Representatives," *Pennsylvania Archives*, 8th ser., 7:5953, 6016 (Jan. 12, May 14, 1767); Stephen Sayre to Lord Dartmouth, Dec. 13, 1766, *The Manuscripts of the Earl of Dartmouth*, 3 vols. in 2 (London, 1887–96), 2:119; Franklin to Galloway, Aug. 8, 1767, *Writings of Benjamin Franklin* 5:43–44.

September 4 ended any real possibility that Parliament would adopt his plan, quite possibly, as Verner W. Crane has suggested, preventing a major crisis over this now-forgotten issue and giving the agents new hope for parliamentary action along lines favorable to the colonies.[40] From London, North Carolina councillor Henry Eustace McCulloh wrote home in September that currency would "certainly be an Object of parliamentary discussion" at the next session and was frankly optimistic about the outcome. Franklin was considerably less so. He dined with General Henry Seymour Conway, minister in the Commons, and Shelburne in mid-August and was delighted to find both of them in favor of repeal and to learn that Lord Clare had also come around to the American position. But there was still opposition among those members of the board who had signed the 1764 report and had helped prepare the Currency Act, and Franklin wisely suspected that there was much truth in what Soame Jenyns, one of those members, had once said in jest about another measure: that he had *"no kind of objection to it, provided we have heretofore signed nothing to the contrary."*[41]

Even had the board been more friendly to the American position, subsequent events would have prevented any concessions by Parliament. The colonies' adverse reaction to the Townshend measures in late 1767 and 1768 and, perhaps more important, the decision to remove American affairs from the jurisdiction of Shelburne and place them in a separate American department under the control of Hillsborough in January 1768 ended all hope of immediate repeal. Indeed, Hillsborough had never wavered in his support of the principles of the Currency Act, and his appointment represented a shift among colonial authorities from vacillation to a very rigid policy against legal tender paper money. Still, the merchants planned another attempt in early 1768, and in mid-February Franklin even managed to extract a pledge from Hillsborough not to oppose an application for the removal of the restraints from Pennsylvania, New York, and New Jersey. But Hillsborough's neutrality was not enough. The ministry was so indifferent about the matter that merchants and agents decided it would be useless to attempt to bring it be-

---

[40] Franklin to Galloway, Aug. 8, 1767, *Writings of Benjamin Franklin* 5:43–44; Garth to South Carolina Committee of Correspondence, July 5, 1767, Garth Letter Book, 39–40, S. C. Archives Department; *Benjamin Franklin's Letters to the Press*, 99–100.

[41] McCulloh to John Harvey, Sept. 13, 1767, in William L. Saunders, ed., *The Colonial Records of North Carolina*, 10 vols. (Raleigh, N.C., 1886–90), 7:517; Franklin to William Franklin, Aug. 28, 1767, *Writings of Benjamin Franklin* 5:45–47.

fore Parliament.[42] By April 1768 the ministry had adopted the doctrinaire position to which colonial officials were to adhere during the remainder of the colonial period. "But this Matter has already received so full a Discussion at the Board of Trade, at the Privy Council, and in each House of Parliament, and so strong and unanimous a Determination that Paper Currency with a legal Tender is big with Frauds, and full of Mischief to the Colonies, and to Commerce in general," Hillsborough declared to North Carolina governor William Tryon at that time, "that I apprehend no Consideration of a possible local Inconvenience will induce a Deviation from the sound Principles of the Act of Parliament relative thereto."[43]

Beginning in 1768 British politicians institutionalized the Currency Act and consistently refused to consider any proposals for the establishment of legal tender currencies. All of New York's old bills were scheduled for retirement by November 1768, and as that date approached, the currency situation grew more and more critical. In late 1767 and early 1768, money had been so scarce that farmers could not pay their debts, and some even lost their farms. Governor Moore warned crown officials that both commerce and the government service would languish if something was not done immediately. In response to this situation, the New York House of Assembly in December 1767 again tried to pass the bill it had first proposed in 1766 to issue £130,000 in legal tender bills. Although he approved the measure personally, Moore again had to reject it because it contained no suspending clause, and again he submitted the matter for the consideration of London authorities. Hillsborough did not share Moore's enthusiasm for the project, although he did offer to consider the measure in question if Moore would send him a copy. Moore promptly complied, but Hillsborough neglected to take any action. A year later New York was still awaiting an answer.[44]

Hillsborough treated similarly appeals from other colonies. In April 1768 he summarily dismissed a joint appeal from the North Carolina council and lower house for permission to issue paper money equal in

[42]Garth to South Carolina Committee of Correspondence, Jan. 17, 1768, Garth Letter Book, 57, S. C. Archives Department; Franklin to Galloway, Dec. 1, 1767, Jan. 9, Feb. 17, 1768, *Writings of Benjamin Franklin* 5:72, 90–91, 97–99.

[43]Hillsborough to William Tryon, Apr. 16, 1768, *Colonial Records of North Carolina* 7:709.

[44]Moore to Shelburne, Jan. 3, 1768, and to Hillsborough, May 14, Aug. 18, 1768, Hillsborough to Moore, Feb. 25, 1768, *Documents Relative to the Colonial History of the State of New York* 8:1, 13, 72, 96–97.

value to £75,000 sterling, expressing regret that the legislature still desired to introduce the "pernicious Medium of a Paper Currency with a
legal Tender."[45] The following June the Board of Trade flatly rejected a
proposal of the Virginia Burgesses, made in April 1767, to issue
£200,000, on the grounds that the Virginia council had opposed it.[46] The
ministry did not even bother to go through the customary formality of
submitting to the Board of Trade a Georgia request of April 1767 for
permission to emit £22,000,[47] and a petition from the Nova Scotia House
of Assembly in November 1768 received similar treatment.[48]

The same doctrinaire attitude induced crown officials to disallow a
South Carolina statute which added nothing to the colony's currency but
merely provided for the printing of new bills to replace £106,500 that
had been circulating in the colony for nearly forty years. The bills had
not been replaced since 1748, and many were lost, destroyed, or worn
out. The statute made the new bills, like the old ones, legal tender. Board
of Trade counsel Richard Jackson found the legal tender provision "repugnant" to the provisions of the Currency Act, and despite the objections of Garth, metropolitan authorities disallowed the law. This disallowance made the entire new issue illegal and might have left the colony

---

[45] North Carolina Legislature's Petition to Crown, Jan. 16, 1768, Hillsborough to Tryon,
Apr. 16, June 11, 1768, and Journal of the Upper House, Nov. 8, 1768, *Colonial Records
of North Carolina* 7:681–82, 709, 788–89, 892.

[46] The Burgesses had made this proposal despite its disclaimer at the time of Parliament's
passage of the Currency Act of any intention of issuing additional paper, contending that
it was imperative to increase the amount of currency in the colony. Virginia Committee
of Correspondence to Montagu, July 28, 1764, "Proceedings of the Virginia Committee
of Correspondence . . . ," *Virginia Magazine of History and Biography* 12 (1904–5): 11;
Journals of the House of Burgesses of Virginia, 1766–69, 115–16, 125–29 (Apr. 7, 11, 1767);
Journal of the Commissioners for Trade and Plantations, 1768–75, 29–31 (May 31, June 3,
7, 1768); Board of Trade to Crown, Jan. 10, 1768, CO 5/1346, PRO. For the background
to this petition, see Purdie and Dixon's *Virginia Gazette* (Williamsburg), July 11, 25, 1766,
and Robert Carter Nicholas to ——, July 16, 1773, *William and Mary College Quarterly*,
1st ser., 20 (1911–12): 234.

[47] This request arose out of a petition from the Savannah merchants and was supported
by both the council and Governor James Wright, although the latter thought £12,000
sterling sufficient. "Journal of the Commons House of Assembly," in Allen D. Candler,
ed., *The Colonial Records of the State of Georgia*, 21 vols. (Atlanta, 1904–16), 14:427–34,
469–74 (Feb. 4–11, Mar. 26, 1767); Wright to Shelburne, Apr. 6, 1767, in Unpublished
Georgia Colonial Records, 37:180–82, Georgia Department of Archives and History, Atlanta.

[48] *Journal and Votes of the House of Assembly for the Province of Nova Scotia* (Halifax,
1769), Nov. 10, 1768.

without legal paper money had not the members of the Commons personally agreed to receive those bills and had not the Commons resolved to redeem them. South Carolina merchant Henry Laurens thought the disallowance "a downright Robbery." "Those Tenders in Law have been our Property for Ages past," he wrote, "and cannot with any Colour of Justice be taken from us."[49]

In the face of these developments, few of the lower houses continued their attempts to secure the repeal or amendment of the Currency Act. The New Jersey House of Assembly directed agent Henry Wilmot to lobby against the act as late as May 1768, and the Pennsylvania House of Representatives, which had spearheaded the early opposition, continued to instruct its agents to seek repeal until October 1769.[50] But only the North Carolina lower house persisted in its efforts to emit a legal tender currency, making at least three such attempts between 1768 and 1774. In December 1768 the lower house directed agent Henry Eustace McCulloh to seek the repeal of the Currency Act, and Governor William Tryon supported the application. But Hillsborough informed Tryon even before he had heard from McCulloh that "no Petition that prays for Paper Currency as a Legal Tender can meet with . . . success," because crown officials could not accept any measure that was contrary to parliamentary restrictions. Nor did Hillsborough change his mind as a result of McCulloh's entreaties, and the agent found it necessary to report to the lower house in July 1769 that its application was unlikely to succeed because of Hillsborough's rigid opposition to legal tender currency.[51] A

[49] Thomas Cooper and David J. McCord, eds., *The Statutes at Large of South Carolina,* 10 vols. (Columbia, S.C., 1836–41), 4:312–24; Jackson to Board of Trade, Nov. 6, 1770, and Order in Council, Dec. 9, 1770, Transcripts of Records Relating to South Carolina, 32:351, 429–31, S. C. Archives Department; *Journal of the Commissioners for Trade and Plantations, 1768–75,* 211 (Nov. 14, 1770); Garth to South Carolina Committee of Correspondence, Nov. 24, 1770, Garth Letter Book, 110–11, S. C. Archives Department; Laurens to John Hopton, Jan. 29, 1771, Laurens Papers, South Carolina Historical Society, Charleston.

[50] *The Votes and Proceedings of the General Assembly of the Province of New Jersey,* [Apr.–May 1768] (Woodbridge, N.J., 1768), 33 (May 5, 1768); "Votes and Proceedings of the House of Representatives," *Pennsylvania Archives,* 8th ser., 7:6069–71, 6169, 6290, 6451 (Oct. 17, 1767, Feb. 20, Oct. 15, 1768, Oct. 17, 1769); Franklin to Pennsylvania Committee of Correspondence, Apr. 16, 1768, *Writings of Benjamin Franklin* 5:120.

[51] North Carolina Committee of Correspondence to McCulloh, Dec. 12, 1768, Tryon to Hillsborough, Feb. 25, 1769, Hillsborough to Tryon, Mar. 1, 1769, McCulloh to North Carolina Committee of Correspondence, July 14, 1769, and to John Harvey, July 24, 1769, *Colonial Records of North Carolina* 7:878–79, 8:11–12, 17–18, 56, 59; *North Carolina Gazette* (New Bern), Nov. 16, 1769.

similar attempt in 1771 with the backing of both Tryon and his successor, Josiah Martin, also failed because of the ministry's opposition, and a final effort in 1774 disappeared amid the excitement generated by the Intolerable Acts.[52]

Metropolitan refusal to repeal the Currency Act or to permit the establishment of legal tender currency forced American lower houses to look for other expedients to solve their money shortages. Most of them managed to work out some stopgap solution, none of which fully answered the needs of the situation. The problem of finding a more permanent arrangement was complicated by the inability of crown officials to decide whether laws requiring the acceptance of notes in payment to the government but not in private transactions violated the legal tender restriction of the Currency Act. This indecision caused still further irritation in the colonies.

The obvious solution was to devise some system of paper money that would not fall under metropolitan restrictions against legal tender. Of course, such notes could not be forced upon British merchants, but that condition was no longer an issue. At least as early as 1766, colonial agents had realized that the lower houses would never again be permitted to establish currencies that would be legal tender in payment of debts owed to British creditors and had offered to accept that limitation in return for the repeal of the Currency Act. The major problem was one of readjustment. Previously, Americans had thought the legal tender provision necessary to maintain the value of their notes. What was required was a general acceptance of the fact that paper notes could be adequately secured by other means. The Maryland legislature had already set an example, having worked out in 1766 a successful system of interest-bearing bills secured by stock invested in the Bank of England. But none of the other lower houses attempted to imitate it, largely because they lacked the surplus funds necessary for the original investment that would be required to establish it.

A second possibility, one for which most of the colonies did have adequate resources, was the land bank variation of the Maryland system.

---

[52] Journal of the Lower House, Jan. 26, 1771, Mar. 23–24, 1774, Martin to Hillsborough, Aug. 15, 1771, Hillsborough to Martin, Dec. 4, 1771, *Colonial Records of North Carolina* 8:471–72, 9:17–18, 65, 937.

Employed successfully by all the middle colonies through the middle years of the eighteenth century, the land bank system involved the establishment of a loan office which put the notes into circulation by loaning them to individuals for stipulated periods in return for mortgages on land. The promise to accept the bills in all payments to the government and the loan office assured their value, and the interest from them could be used to meet government expenses. This plan was the same as that proposed by Franklin as a substitute for the Stamp Act, although he had dropped it after Townshend had sought to use it in 1767 as a scheme to produce a colonial revenue. Still, the agents' failure to secure the repeal of the Currency Act in 1767 prompted Franklin and Thomas Pownall to publish the plan in the fourth edition of the latter's *The Administration of the Colonies* (London, 1768). They hoped that colonial legislatures would adopt the plan to satisfy their currency needs.[53]

For the moment, however, most lower houses preferred still a third solution, that of issuing notes to pay the public debt or some government expense, secured by a pledge to accept them at the treasury for taxes and by the assignment, in the act of emission, of tax revenues sufficient to retire the notes, usually at a set annual rate over a stipulated period of years. This formula was none other than the normal fiat currency or inconvertible money system employed by most American lower houses at one time or another during the eighteenth century. The only thing missing was the legal tender provision, and the South Carolina Commons had demonstrated, in its frequent issues of public orders and tax certificates during the previous thirty years, that the system could work without such a provision.[54] In fact, notes issued under either the land bank or the fiat currency system were readily accepted in payment of everything except British debts because of the provisions requiring colonial treasuries and loan offices to accept them. One by one in the late 1760s, the lower houses adopted either the land bank or the fiat currency system.

In the years after 1765, the legislatures of Georgia, South Carolina, Pennsylvania, North Carolina, and Virginia issued notes that were not legal tender, to meet extraordinary expenses and to ease their respective colonies' money problems. Between March 1765 and May 1770, the Georgia Commons provided for the emission of £8,120 to pay for several

[53]Crane reprints this plan in *Benjamin Franklin's Letters to the Press*, 25–30.

[54]Richard M. Jellison, "Paper Currency in South Carolina, 1703–1764," Ph.D. diss., Indiana University, 1952, 161–251.

important public works.[55] The South Carolina Commons voted to emit £60,000 in public orders in 1767 to build a new exchange, customhouse, and watchhouse in Charleston and £70,000 in 1769 to build courthouses and jails in newly created judicial districts.[56] Similarly, the Pennsylvania House of Representatives voted to issue £20,000 to pay current expenses in 1767; the experiment was so successful that it voted five additional issues before the Revolution, totaling £82,000.[57] The North Carolina lower house provided for the emission of £20,000 of debenture notes in 1768 to pay forces sent to suppress riots around Hillsboro and £60,000 in 1770 to pay the forces sent against the Regulators.[58] The Virginia House of Burgesses also found it necessary to make two issues, putting out £10,000 in 1769 to meet pressing contingent expenses and £30,000 in 1771 to relieve planters whose tobacco had been damaged in the flood of that year.[59]

These issues were not declared legal tender and therefore did not tech-

[55] The sum of £650 was issued in 1765 to build a fort and barracks in Augusta, £1,815 in 1766 to construct a courthouse in Savannah, £2,200 in 1768 to build a lighthouse on Tybee Island, and £3,455 in 1770 to enable the colony to pay its creditors and provide for a watch in Savannah. Apparently for reasons that had little to do with the paper money provision, crown officials disallowed the statute providing for the 1766 emission, although the notes issued upon the authority of the disallowed measure probably continued to circulate until the time originally appointed for their retirement. "Statutes Enacted by the Royal Legislature of Georgia," *Colonial Records of Georgia* 18:639–48, 743–48, 19, pt. 1: 83–89, 161–98, 147–51; Wright to Hillsborough, Dec. 26, 1768, in Unpublished Georgia Colonial Records, 28, pt. 2-B:683–84, Ga. Department of Archives and History; Georgia Committee of Correspondence to Franklin, May 19, 1768, *The Letters of the Hon. James Habersham, 1756–1775*, Georgia Historical Society, *Collections* 6 (1904): 72–73.

[56] *Statutes at Large of South Carolina* 4:257–61, 323–26.

[57] In 1769 the house authorized two emissions, £16,000 to meet government obligations and £14,000 to tide the managers of the poor in Philadelphia through the depression that followed the Townshend Acts. It emitted another £15,000 to put Philadelphia in a proper state of defense in 1771, £25,000 to pay current government expenses in 1772, and £12,000 to enable the wardens of the port of Philadelphia to erect piers and improve the harbor in 1773. "Votes and Proceedings of the House of Representatives," *Pennsylvania Archives*, 8th ser., 7:6016, 6369–70 (May 14, 1767, Feb. 18, 1769), 8:6848 (Mar. 21, 1772); *Statutes at Large of Pennsylvania* 7:100–107, 197–211, 8:15–22, 204–20, 264–84.

[58] "North Carolina Laws," in Walter L. Clark, ed., *The State Records of North Carolina, 1776–1790*, 16 vols. (Goldsboro, N.C., 1895–1907), 23:781–83, 850–51; Tryon to Hillsborough, Jan. 10, 1769, July 2, 1770, and Martin to Hillsborough, Dec. 12, 26, 1771, Apr. 12, 1772, *Colonial Records of North Carolina* 8:5–6, 212, 9:67–68, 75–77, 278.

[59] Hening, *Statutes* 8:342–48, 501; Robert Carter Nicholas to Lord Botetourt, Dec. 30, 1769, CO 5/1348, PRO; William Nelson to Hillsborough, July 15, 1771, and Hillsborough

nically violate the restrictions of the Currency Act. But metropolitan officials were unable to decide whether the clauses making such notes redeemable for taxes and public obligations did not, de facto, make them legal tender, and their policy toward these emissions was inconsistent. In June 1771 they disallowed the South Carolina measure of 1769 because it made the bills a tender in payment of taxes. Although they permitted the rest of the issuing statutes to stand, they warned Governor Dunmore in December 1771 that the Virginia emission of that year might also contravene the Currency Act and sharply censured James Habersham in February 1772 for having consented to one of the Georgia emissions when he was acting governor. Habersham found this censure difficult to accept, and in complaining to Governor James Wright, he pointed out the crux of the currency question and, incidentally, the weakness of much of Britain's new colonial policy. "It is easy for People in England to speculate and refine," he wrote, "but here we must act as *Necessity requires,* which is an infallible Rule." The ministry, he lamented, does "not truly understand our local Circumstances."[60]

There is little question that these issues of paper money helped to relieve the currency shortages in the four colonies, but in no case did they supply an adequate circulating medium. None of the five lower houses issued enough bills to replace the wartime issues as they were gradually retired. Of the four colonies Pennsylvania was probably best supplied, having issued just over £100,000 between 1767 and 1773. But the persistent demands of the House of Representatives and others for a loan office indicate that even that amount was insufficient and, perhaps more important, that they desired a more permanent solution to the problem.

South Carolina's issues were woefully inadequate, especially in view of its tremendous growth in population during the 1760s and 1770s. Merchant William Fyffe wrote from Georgetown in August 1767 that Carolinians were "in great Difficulties . . . by . . . not having a paper Cur-

---

to Lord Dunmore, Dec. 4, 1771, CO 5/1349, PRO; William Atkinson to Charles Steuert, Jan. 2, 1770, Steuert Papers, 5026, f. 2, National Library of Scotland, Edinburgh.

[60] Apparently the Board of Trade singled out this emission for censure because its legal counsel, Richard Jackson, suggested that making paper bills receivable for taxes might be a violation of the Currency Act. Jackson to Board of Trade, June 20, 1771, and Board of Trade to Habersham, Feb. 1, 1772, Unpublished Georgia Colonial Records, 28, pt. 2-B:762–64, 34:621–22, Ga. Department of Archives and History; Habersham to Wright, Dec. 4, 1772, *Letters of Habersham,* 217. For the Virginia and South Carolina cases, see Hillsborough to Dunmore, Dec. 4, 1771, CO 5/1349, PRO, and *Acts of the Privy Council, Colonial* 5:319–21 (June 27, 1771). See also "Votes and Proceedings of the House of Repre-

rency allowed them," and three years later Lieutenant Governor William Bull II reported that the scarcity of money made it necessary to carry on the colony's internal commerce by credit or barter. The Wilkes fund controversy, a prolonged contest over the Commons' right to order money from the treasury without the governor's consent, prevented any further emissions after 1769, and it is significant that, when the Commons gave up trying to solve that dispute within the context of the colonial constitution and began to act unilaterally in 1774, it issued paper certificates to pay the public debt that had accumulated during the five-year impasse.[61]

The situation in Virginia and North Carolina was little better. By 1767 only slightly more than £200,000 of the currency issued by Virginia during the war was still circulating. That amount fell to less than £100,000 by 1772, and specie was as scarce as ever. These conditions prompted the Burgesses to petition the crown for permission to issue a copper coinage in 1769, but the scheme was a long time in receiving the approval of the ministry and was not carried into execution until 1775, just two weeks before the beginning of the war. The issues of 1769 and 1771 helped ease the situation, but for the entire period after 1767 Virginia was without an adequate money supply.[62] Similarly, in North Carolina the total amount of old legal tender bills in circulation fell from just over £58,000 in 1770 to just under £43,000 in 1772. And, although the issues of 1768 and 1770 augmented these bills considerably, the lower house's persistent efforts to obtain permission to emit a legal tender currency and to prevent the retirement of the old bills strongly suggest that the colony's currency supply was insufficient.[63]

By the early 1770s Georgia's currency problem was probably the most

sentatives," *Pennsylvania Archives*, 8th ser., 7:6527 (May 15, 1770); *Journal of the Commissioners for Trade and Plantations, 1768–75*, 200 (July 18, 1770).

[61] William Fyffe to James Fyffe, Aug. 3, 1767, Fyffe Papers, Clements Library; Bull to Hillsborough, Nov. 30, 1770, and to Dartmouth, May 3, 1774, Transcripts of Records Relating to South Carolina, 32:402, 35:36–40, S. C. Archives Department.

[62] Purdie and Dixon's *Virginia Gazette*, Jan. 21, 1768; Richard Bland to Thomas Adams, Aug. 1, 1771, *William and Mary College Quarterly*, 1st ser., 5 (1896–97): 150–56; Robert Carter Nicholas to ——, July 16, 1773, ibid., 20 (1911–12): 234, and to Lord Botetourt, Dec. 30, 1769, CO 5/1348, PRO; *Journals of the House of Burgesses of Virginia, 1766–69*, 278–79 (Nov. 22, 1769), *1770–72*, 218 (Mar. 6, 1772); John Norton to John Pownall, Oct. 22, 1773, CO 5/1351, PRO; Dartmouth to Dunmore, Apr. 5, 1775, CO 5/1353, PRO.

[63] Tryon to Hillsborough, July 2, 1770, and Martin to Hillsborough, Jan. 30, 1772, *Colonial Records of North Carolina* 8:212, 9:231–33; *South Carolina Gazette* (Charleston), Mar. 14, 1768; *Georgia Gazette* (Savannah), Sept. 28, 1768.

serious on the continent. Its population and commerce were expanding at a phenomenal rate, but by 1773, when Governor Wright induced the Commons to exchange all the old bills for new ones, there was only £4,819 still circulating—considerably less than the £12,000 sterling Wright had recommended in 1767 as an adequate sum to meet the colony's currency requirements. Nor did the addition of £800 in March 1774 to pay for defending the colony's frontiers improve the situation. Georgia remained without a sufficient medium of exchange down to the Revolution.[64]

At best these non–legal tender issues provided only temporary relief, and the lower houses of New Jersey and New York, seeking a more permanent solution, proposed to establish new land banks. Initially, the Currency Act had caused little alarm in New Jersey. Its House of Assembly had emitted £347,500 during the French and Indian War, and in 1764 over £250,000 was still circulating. However, £12,500 was retired every year, and by 1767 various elements in the colony were beginning to demand a new emission. In June of that year, three counties petitioned the House of Assembly, complaining about the scarcity of money.[65] Five more petitions in April 1768 prompted the house to propose and the Council to accept a bill to establish a new land bank and to emit £100,000. Apparently, the house did not intend to make the bills legal tender, but it did include a clause stipulating that the bills "*by law* shall *pass current.*" Governor William Franklin was sympathetic to the measure but felt compelled to reject it because it was possible to interpret the clause as giving the bills a legal tender status and because the house refused to add a suspending clause as his instructions required. Nevertheless, Franklin strongly recommended the bill to Lord Hillsborough and in January 1769 sent him a copy. Franklin suggested that the house might even appropriate part of the interest arising from the bills to establish permanent salaries for the crown's officers in return for permission to pass the measure.[66] Metropolitan authorities disapproved the bill in

[64] "Statutes," *Colonial Records of Georgia* 19, pt. 1:418–26, pt. 2:3–8; Wright to Board of Trade, Dec. 30, 1773, Jan. 20, 1775, and Jackson to Board of Trade, May 25, 1775, Unpublished Georgia Colonial Records, 28, pt. 2-B:787–80, 895, 901, Ga. Department of Archives and History.

[65] Brock, "Currency of the American Colonies," 402–3; Donald L. Kemmerer, *Path to Freedom: The Struggle for Self-Government in Colonial New Jersey, 1703–1776* (Princeton, N.J., 1940), 303–5.

[66] *Votes and Proceedings of the General Assembly of New Jersey* [Apr.–May 1768], 14 (Apr. 21, 1768); Upper House Journals, May 5, 1768, *Archives of New Jersey*, 1st ser.,

May 1769 on the grounds that the clause implying that the bills should pass current was contrary to the Currency Act, but they did give Franklin permission to sign a similar measure if it omitted the objectionable clause and included a provision suspending its operation pending approval of the crown.[67]

The House of Assembly thought the crown's interpretation of the legal tender prohibition very strict, but in December 1769 it produced another measure designed to meet the crown's objections. This bill made the proposed emission of £100,000 a tender at the loan office but carefully specified that the notes "should not be a legal Tender for the Payment of Debts." Although he was disappointed that the house had refused to assign part of the interest on the bills to the payment of executive salaries, Franklin approved the bill and again recommended it strongly to Hillsborough. Both Franklin and the legislators were confident that the crown would now grant approval. Surprisingly, however, crown officials rejected the measure in June 1770 on the grounds that the notes were legal tender at the loan office that issued them.[68] The New Jersey house was understandably upset. Had it known "that so extensive a Construction would be put upon the Act of Parliament for restraining paper Currencies in America," Franklin wrote Hillsborough in September 1770, the house would not even have attempted to pass a paper money bill. In disgust he pointed out that it "would have been the Height of Absurdity to expect that any persons would mortgage their Estates to the Loan Office for Money which they could not afterwards oblige the Office to receive again in Discharge of their Mortgages." In fact, the disallowance seemed discriminatory in the extreme, because recent measures of both Pennsylvania and Maryland had been permitted to stand, despite the fact that they also required the acceptance of the bills at their respective treasuries. The legislature despaired of ever obtaining a currency bill which would satisfy the crown and, although it continued to receive peti-

17:488–89; Franklin to Hillsborough, June 14, Aug. 24, 1768, Jan. 10, 1769, and Hillsborough to Franklin, Nov. 10, 1768, Mar. 22, 1769, ibid., 10:32, 48–50, 60–61, 99–101, 103.

[67] Order in Council, May 26, 1769, and Henry Wilmot to New Jersey Committee of Correspondence, Dec. 12, 1769, *Archives of New Jersey*, 1st ser., 10:115–18, 142.

[68] Upper House Journals, Oct. 11, 17, Nov. 30, Dec. 1–6, 1769, ibid., 18:38, 43, 92, 94, 103; New Jersey Committee of Correspondence to Benjamin Franklin, Dec. 7, 1769, Franklin to Hillsborough, Feb. 12, 1770, and Order in Council, June 6, 1770, ibid., 10:136–37, 151–52, 196–97; *Acts of the General Assembly of the Province of New Jersey*, [Oct.–Dec. 1769] (Burlington, N.J., 1770), 25–54 (Dec. 6, 1769).

tions for additional paper money, waited for three years before making another attempt.[69]

Following some initial disappointments, New York was more success-ful in its attempt to establish a land bank. The currency shortage in that colony had been acute since early 1766, and in May 1769 the House of Assembly tried for the third time to push through a bill to establish a land bank and emit £120,000, this time without legal tender status. Gov-ernor Sir Henry Moore again rejected the measure because the house would not include a suspending clause, although he was equally con-vinced of the necessity for a new emission. Again Moore asked approval to pass the bill from Hillsborough, who had not yet handed down a rul-ing on a similar bill of December 1767.[70]

The wheels of administration in London moved slowly, and crown officials still had not reached a final decision by the end of 1769. In the meantime, Moore died. When the House of Assembly met again in No-vember 1769, it put considerable pressure upon his successor, Lieutenant Governor Cadwallader Colden, to approve a bill which was almost iden-tical to the one then under consideration in London. Both the house and the council had passed such a bill by early January. Again the bill con-tained no suspending clause, although a clause specifying that the law would not go into effect until the end of the following June amounted to the same thing. Colden hesitated briefly but approved the bill on January 5, on the unanimous advice of the council.[71]

In London, Hillsborough had already decided to reject the earlier bill because it violated the letter of the Currency Act by making the notes a legal tender at the loan office and at the colony's treasury. When he re-ceived on February 7 a copy of the bill passed by Colden, he immediately recommended its disallowance for the same reason. Acting with what must have been record dispatch, he managed to get the whole matter

---

[69] Upper House Journals, Aug. 21, Sept. 28, Oct. 18, 1770, *Archives of New Jersey*, 1st ser., 18:184, 192, 200; Franklin to Hillsborough, Sept. 29, 1770, ibid., 10:200–201.

[70] Moore to Hillsborough, May 14, Aug. 18, 1768, May 26, 29, 1769, *Documents Relative to the Colonial History of the State of New York* 8:72, 96–97, 168–70; *Journal of the Votes and Proceedings of the General Assembly of the Colony of New York*, [Apr.–May 1769] (New York, 1769), 85–86 (May 20, 1769); Hillsborough to Moore, July 15, 1769, *Letters and Papers of Cadwallader Colden* 7:159–60.

[71] Colden to Hillsborough, Oct. 4, 1769, Jan. 6, 1770, *Documents Relative to the Colonial History of the State of New York* 8:189, 200; *Journal of the Votes and Proceedings of the General Assembly of the Colony of New York*, [Nov. 1769–Jan. 1770] (New York, 1770), 67–70 (Jan. 4–5, 1770); Charles Z. Lincoln et al., eds., *The Colonial Laws of New York*, 5 vols. (Albany, 1894), 5:24–46.

before the Privy Council within three days, and on February 9 that body formally rejected the first bill and disallowed the January measure.[72] Highly displeased with Colden's behavior, Hillsborough censured him for his "impropriety." Colden defended himself by pointing out that the six-month delay between the passage of the measure and the emission of the currency amounted to a suspending clause and gave the crown plenty of time to reach a decision. This explanation convinced Hillsborough that Colden had "erred from real good intention," but the most important consequence of the affair was Parliament's enactment of a special statute permitting the New York legislature to pass the disallowed law.[73]

A variety of factors combined to induce Parliament to make this concession. Frederick, Lord North, became head of the ministry on January 31, 1770, and immediately inaugurated a program of conciliation toward the colonies. Upon his recommendation Parliament agreed in April to repeal most of the Townshend duties and to permit the Quartering Act to expire without renewal. The same placatory mood was undoubtedly in large part responsible for the favor to New York, although there were other considerations as well. The very boldness of the New York government in the affair served to drive home to the ministry the necessity for a new emission in the colony. Moreover, the ministry may well have calculated that the special concession would induce New York to abandon nonimportation and thus pave the way for the collapse of that movement in all the colonies. Whatever its motive, the ministry apparently decided upon the favor at the time of the rejection of the colony's paper money bills on February 9. A week later Hillsborough wrote Colden that Parliament would "be moved to pass an Act to enable the Legislature of New York to carry into execution the Bill they appear to be so desirous of." Upon a petition from New York agent Robert Charles, the ministry introduced such an act, and Parliament passed it in early May. The act empowered the New York legislature to set up a land bank and to issue £120,000 in bills, making them legal tender at the loan office and the colony's treasury. Charles Garth's attempt to add a clause extending the same concession to all the colonies failed when the ministry protested that there was nothing before Parliament to indicate that the other colo-

---

[72] Hillsborough to Colden, Dec. 9, 1769, and Board of Trade to Privy Council, Dec. 28, 1769, Feb. 8, 1770, *Documents Relative to the Colonial History of the State of New York* 8:193, 195–96, 202–3; *Acts of the Privy Council, Colonial* 5:215–16 (Feb. 9, 1770).

[73] Hillsborough to Colden, Feb. 17, June 12, 1770, and Colden to Hillsborough, Apr. 26, 1770, *Documents Relative to the Colonial History of the State of New York* 8:205–6, 212, 215.

nies wished such authority and suggested that it would be better to see how the exception worked out in a single colony before permitting a general departure from the Currency Act.[74]

New Yorkers were elated at this mark of Parliament's special favor, and it may well have been instrumental in deciding the colony to abandon nonimportation during the summer of 1770. Colden wrote Hillsborough in August that the House of Assembly would surely receive the measure with "the dutiful gratitude which may justly be expected." When the legislature reconvened in December 1770, the house immediately moved to take advantage of the concession, eventually passing in February 1771 a measure which was almost identical to the one disallowed the year before. For a time it appeared that the extensive jurisdiction provided by the act over criminal violations might cause crown officials to disallow it as well, but they eventually decided to let it stand. Thus, after five difficult years and a special act of Parliament, New York had finally solved its currency problems. Thereafter, the Currency Act was not an issue in New York.[75]

This concession was a harbinger of things to come. It served to emphasize the question raised by Garth at the time of its enactment: Should the same privilege be extended to all of the colonies? However salutary it may have been for New York, to other colonies seeking to emit money on the same terms it seemed both discriminatory and inconsistent. Most of them had issued non–legal tender bills and made them payable at their respective loan offices or treasuries without serious objection from the crown, but it will be recalled that in June 1770—just a month after Parliament's special favor to New York—the ministry turned down a similar scheme to establish a land bank in New Jersey because it made the issues a tender at the loan office. Similarly, in 1771 Hillsborough sharply censured the Virginia and Georgia governors for consenting to measures

[74] Hillsborough to Colden, Feb. 17, June 12, 1770, ibid., 8:205–6, 215; Garth to South Carolina Committee of Correspondence, May 14, 1770, Garth Letter Book, 107, S. C. Archives Department; *Statutes at Large of Great Britain* 28:306–10.

[75] Colden to Hillsborough, Aug. 18, 1770, *Documents Relative to the Colonial History of the State of New York* 8:245; *Colonial Laws of New York* 5:149–70; Edmund Burke to New York Committee of Correspondence, May 6, 1772, in Ross J. S. Hoffman, ed., *Edmund Burke, New York Agent* (Philadelphia, 1956), 205; Carl L. Becker, *The History of Political Parties in the Province of New York, 1760–1776* (Madison, Wis., 1909), 87–88.

that made new emissions receivable for taxes. This erratic policy was understandably galling to many American leaders, and such a rigid interpretation of the legal tender restriction was completely unrealistic. An increasing number of colonials were pointing out that it was unreasonable and impractical to expect paper money to retain its value if it was not a tender at the office that issued it.[76] But they would have to wait another three years before Parliament would grant a similar concession to the other colonies, thus belatedly paving the way for the eventual solution of the currency issue.

Metropolitan officials did nothing to clarify the situation until after Hillsborough had resigned as head of the American Department in August 1772. His successor, Lord Dartmouth, and the Board of Trade moved to relax the rigid interpretation of the Currency Act, and in May 1773 Parliament passed a statute empowering colonial legislatures to "create and issue Certificates, Notes, Bills or Debentures on the Security of any Taxes or Duties given and granted to his Majesty, and to make the same a legal Tender to the Public Treasurer in Discharge of any Taxes, Duties or other Debts due to or payable at or in the Public Treasury."[77] Now all of the colonies were to have the same privilege accorded to New York three years earlier. This statute did not alter the restriction on currency that was legal tender in payment of private debts, but it did represent a sensible modification of metropolitan policy, confirming the legality of the schemes worked out by the various colonies after their failure to obtain a repeal of the Currency Act. It might well have laid the foundation for a permanent paper money system which would have satisfied both the mother country and the colonies had the Revolution not intervened just two years later.

Two months before the passage of this statute, the Pennsylvania House of Representatives finally succeeded in pushing through a bill to establish a land bank similar to the one set up two years earlier in New York. Agitation for such a bank started as early as 1767 and reached flood stage in early 1769 when the Representatives received over fifty-

---

[76] See Joseph Galloway to Franklin, June 21, 1770, *Works of Benjamin Franklin* 7:481; Colden to Hillsborough, Feb. 21, 1770, *Documents Relative to the Colonial History of the State of New York* 8:206–7; William Franklin to Hillsborough, Sept. 29, 1770, *Archives of New Jersey*, 1st ser., 10:200–201; Habersham to James Wright, Dec. 4, 1772, *Letters of Habersham*, 217.

[77] Garth to South Carolina Committee of Correspondence, Apr. 3, May 4, 20, 1773, Garth Letter Book, 150–52, S. C. Archives Department; *Statutes at Large of Great Britain* 30:113–14.

five petitions demanding a general loan office. The Representatives had already issued a small amount of non–legal tender notes. But the desire for a more permanent solution to the currency problem, as well as public demand, prompted the Representatives to try on two different occasions during the next year to enact a bill to establish a loan office and to emit £120,000, only to fail when it could not reach an agreement with Governor Richard Penn over the disposition of the interest money and the patronage to the trusteeships of the loan office.[78] The ministry's treatment of New Jersey's land bank scheme in 1770 temporarily discouraged Pennsylvanians from making another attempt, but in July 1772 the Representatives tried again, this time to issue £200,000, and again failed because of Penn's objections to its scheme to establish separate loan offices in each county.[79] The following year the Representatives gave in on this point, and Penn accepted a bill to issue £150,000. Coming in the wake of the general parliamentary concession, this bill had every chance of passing. Benjamin Franklin reported in February 1774 that the Board of Trade had approved it, and the following July the Representatives learned that it had received the formal assent of the Privy Council. Pennsylvania became the second colony to establish a land bank in the 1770s.[80]

The parliamentary statute of 1773 also encouraged the New Jersey House of Assembly to renew its efforts to establish a land bank. In March 1774 it pushed through a measure to issue £100,000 which was strikingly similar to the bill disallowed by the Privy Council in 1770. Because of its previous experience, the house was careful not to specify that the bills should be a legal tender at the loan office, despite the concession granted by Parliament. That the bills would be acceptable both at the loan office and the New Jersey treasury was implicit in the measure, however.[81] Like the Pennsylvania law, this act encountered no op-

[78] *Pennsylvania Chronicle,* Dec. 2, 21, 1767, Jan. 7, 1768, as cited by Yoder, "Paper Currency in Colonial Pennsylvania," 312; "Votes and Proceedings of the House of Representatives," *Pennsylvania Archives,* 8th ser., 7:6293–95, 6320–22, 6377–78, 6391, 6473, 6483, 6506 (Jan. 4, 19, May 11, 13, 26, 1769, Jan. 17, 24, Feb. 12, 1770).

[79] *Pennsylvania Archives,* 8th ser., 8:6770, 6820–21, 6838–40 (Jan. 25, Mar. 3–18, 1772).

[80] Ibid., 6854–55, 6918–19, 6965, 7093 (Sept. 16, 1772, Jan. 20–21, 26, 1773, July 19, 1774); *The Acts of the Assembly of the Province of Pennsylvania* (Philadelphia, 1775), 474–82 (Feb. 26, 1773); Franklin to Galloway, Feb. 18, 1774, *Writings of Benjamin Franklin* 6:194.

[81] *Votes of Assembly* [Nov. 1773–Mar. 1774], 55–82 (Mar. 11, 1774); Upper House Journals, Mar. 10, 1774, *Archives of New Jersey,* 1st ser., 18:389; William Franklin to Dartmouth, June 13, 1774, ibid., 10:461–62.

position from metropolitan authorities, and it received their assent in February 1775. New Jersey thus became the third colony to establish a land bank, finally achieving the goal it had originally sought over seven years earlier.

The Board of Trade's attitude in recommending approval of this measure represented a distinct shift from its position at the time of the passage of the Currency Act eleven years before. Non–legal tender currency, the board admitted, had since 1764 had a "very salutary Effect, by enabling the planters to Extend their Improvements, to open new Channels of Commerce, to take off a greater Quantity of the Manufactures of Great Britain, and to pay for them with that Gold and Silver, which, was it not for the Advantage of this paper Medium must be retained in Order to answer the purposes of Circulation."[82] The passage might well have been taken from Benjamin Franklin's earlier arguments in favor of paper money. Except on the question of making colonial paper legal tender in private obligations, metropolitan authorities had come full circle to the American position. Americans probably would have decided eventually that defeat on this point was not very important anyway, but this concession was a little late, coming less than two months before the outbreak of hostilities at Lexington Green.

Compared to other issues in the debate between Britain and the American colonies, the Currency Act was not one of the more explosive ones. Still, with the single exception of Delaware, each of the colonies affected considered it a major grievance. Coming during a period when a growing population and an expanding trade were aggravating the chronic shortage of specie and creating a demand for even more paper money, it could scarcely have been more untimely, and it probably caused some economic hardship to the colonies. The failure of colonial agents and London merchants to secure repeal in 1767 and the subsequent institutionalizing of the policy against legal tender money under Hillsborough stymied later efforts and forced colonial legislatures to search for alternatives. In Pennsylvania, Virginia, North Carolina, South Carolina, and Georgia, the lower houses obtained temporary relief by issuing small sums of short-term non–legal tender bills secured by a pledge to accept them for taxes. But with the possible exception of Pennsylvania, none of these

---

[82] Dartmouth to William Franklin, Mar. 3, 1775, and Order in Council, Feb. 20, 1775, *Archives of New Jersey,* 1st ser., 10:549–51, 557–58.

colonies emitted enough to fulfill its money requirements. The New Jersey legislature tried to attain a more permanent solution by establishing a land bank but ran into opposition from metropolitan authorities. Only Maryland, where the legislature had worked out in 1766 an acceptable scheme to issue a non–legal tender currency secured by specie invested in the Bank of England, and New York, where the legislature had established a land bank after it had obtained a special favor from Parliament in 1770, achieved more permanent solutions and surmounted the problems presented by the Currency Act.

Throughout the late 1760s and early 1770s the Currency Act remained an important grievance in New Jersey and all of the colonies from Virginia south to Georgia. Several of them were guilty of permitting bills from old issues to remain current long after the dates fixed for retirement, in direct violation of the Currency Act, and the North Carolina lower house even took the desperate step of suspending taxes voted to retire its paper currency.[83] Following Parliament's belated general concession in 1773, both the Pennsylvania and New Jersey lower houses obtained permission to establish land banks similar to that of New York. But even after this relaxation of policy, none of the four southern colonies solved its financial problem, and they may have been responsible for the October 1774 citing of the Currency Act as a violation of colonial rights in the Declaration and Resolves of the First Continental Congress.[84] By then, however, the Currency Act was no longer a live issue: the four southern colonies would probably have worked out satisfactory arrangements of their own within the context of the statute of 1773 had not the war intervened.[85]

Still, the impact of the Currency Act upon the Revolutionary move-

---

[83] The action of the North Carolina lower house may be traced in the following letters: Tryon to Hillsborough, Feb. 10, 1769, Martin to Hillsborough, Jan. 30, 1772, and to Dartmouth, Jan. 13, Apr. 2, 1774, *Colonial Records of North Carolina* 8:10, 9:231–33, 817–18, 960–61.

[84] Worthington C. Ford, ed., *Journals of the Continental Congress, 1774–1789*, 34 vols. (Washington, D.C., 1904–37), 1:71 (Oct. 14, 1774).

[85] That crown officials probably would not have stood in the way is indicated by their subsequent attitude toward Nova Scotia. The demand for paper money in that colony culminated in July 1775 when the House of Assembly passed a bill to establish a loan office and to emit £40,000 only to have the council reject it. The house then appealed to London, and the Board of Trade ruled that the bill could be passed as long as it conformed with metropolitan currency regulations and if some obscurities were cleared up. However, provincial politics prevented the passage of the bill, and as late as January 1783 Governor John Parr reported that no paper money had ever been issued in the

ment should not be overlooked. Its psychological effects were especially important. At the very time when colonial legislatures were beginning to demand equality for the colonies within the empire, it served as a constant reminder that the economic well-being of the colonies was subordinate to the desires of the metropolitan government. Furthermore, the stubborn refusal of metropolitan authorities through the late sixties and early seventies to repeal the Currency Act or to relax their rigid interpretation of what constituted legal tender currency persuaded many Americans that British officials either did not understand or were utterly callous to colonial problems. It helped to convince American legislators that they could not count on the ministry for enlightened solutions to their problems—that, in fact, they were the only group capable of solving them.

Written in 1960 in coauthorship with Richard M. Jellison, this chapter is reprinted with his approval and minor verbal changes with permission from the *William and Mary Quarterly*, 3d ser., 18 (1961):485–518.

colony. *Journals and Votes of the House of Assembly for the Province of Nova Scotia,* [Oct.–Dec. 1774] (Halifax, Nova Scotia, 1774), Oct. 8, 1774; ibid., [June–July 1775], July 3, 11, 18, 1775; Petition of House of Assembly, July (?), 1775, in Nova Scotia MSS ser., 301, no. 7, Public Archives of Nova Scotia, Halifax; Francis Legge to Dartmouth, July 31, 1775, ibid., 44, no. 72; Board of Trade to Legge, June 3, 1776, ibid., 32, no. 34; Jackson to Board of Trade, Mar. 21, 1776, in Nova Scotia ser., A95, 207–8, Public Archives of Canada, Ottawa; Parr to Townshend, Mar. 21, 1776, ibid., A103, 2–5.

INDEX